THE DIARY OF
SAMUEL PEPYS

b

Edward Hyde, 1st Earl of Clarendon,
medal by Abraham and Thomas Simon (1662)

(Reproduced by permission of the Trustees of the British Museum)

THE DIARY
OF
SAMUEL PEPYS

A new and complete
transcription edited by

ROBERT LATHAM
AND
WILLIAM MATTHEWS

CONTRIBUTING EDITORS

WILLIAM A. ARMSTRONG · MACDONALD EMSLIE
SIR OLIVER MILLAR · the late T. F. REDDAWAY

VOLUME VIII · 1667

BELL & HYMAN
LONDON

Published by
BELL & HYMAN LIMITED
Denmark House
37–39 Queen Elizabeth Street
London SE1 2QB

First published in 1974 by
G. Bell & Sons Ltd
Reprinted 1975, 1978, 1983

© *Bell & Hyman Limited 1974*

ISBN 0 7135 1558 9

*Printed in Great Britain by Fletcher & Son Ltd, Norwich
and bound by Hunter & Foulis Ltd, Edinburgh*

CONTENTS

LIST OF ILLUSTRATIONS

READER'S GUIDE

This section is meant for quick reference. More detailed information about the editorial methods used in this edition will be found in the Introduction and in the section 'Methods of the Commentary' in vol. I, and also in the statement preceding the Select Glossary at the end of each text volume.

I. THE TEXT

The fact that the MS. is mostly in shorthand makes exact reproduction (e.g. of spelling, capitalisation and punctuation) impossible.

Spelling is in modern British style, except for those longhand words which Pepys spelt differently, and words for which the shorthand indicates a variant pronunciation which is also shown by Pepys's longhand elsewhere. These latter are given in spellings which reflect Pepys's pronunciations.

Pepys's capitalisation is indicated only in his longhand.

Punctuation is almost all editorial, except for certain full-stops, colons, dashes and parentheses. Punctuation is almost non-existent in the original since the marks could be confused with shorthand.

Italics are all editorial, but (in e.g. headings to entries) often follow indications given in the MS. (by e.g. the use of larger writing).

The **paragraphing** is that of the MS.

Abbreviations of surnames, titles, place names and ordinary words are expanded.

Single **hyphens** are editorial, and represent Pepys's habit of disjoining the elements of compound words (e.g. Wh. hall/White-hall). Double hyphens represent Pepys's hyphens.

Single **angle-brackets** mark additions made by Pepys in the body of the MS.; double angle-brackets those made in the margins.

Light **asterisks** are editorial (see below, Section II); heavy asterisks are Pepys's own.

Pepys's **alterations** are indicated by the word 'replacing' ('repl.') in the textual footnotes.

II. THE COMMENTARY

1. Footnotes deal mainly with events and transactions. They also identify MSS, books, plays, music and quotations, but give only occasional and minimal information about persons and places, words and phrases. The initials which follow certain notes indicate the work of the contributing editors. Light asterisks in the text direct the reader to the Select Glossary for the definition of words whose meanings have changed since the time of the diary. References to the diary are given by volume and page where the text is in page-proof at the time of going to press; in other cases, by entry-dates. In notes to the Introduction, since almost all the references there are to the text, a simpler form of reference (by entry-date only) is used.

2. The **Select List of Persons** is printed unchanged in each text volume. It covers the whole diary and identifies the principal persons, together with those who are described in the MS. by titles or in other ways that make for obscurity.

3. The **Select Glossary** is printed at the end of each text volume. It gives definitions of most recurrent English words and phrases, and identifications of certain recurrent places.

4. The **Companion** (vol. X) is a collection of reference material. It contains maps, genealogical tables, and a Large Glossary, but consists mainly of articles, printed for ease of reference in a single alphabetical series. These give information about matters which are dealt with briefly or not at all in the footnotes and the Select Glossary: i.e. persons, places, words and phrases, food, drink, clothes, the weather etc. They also treat systematically the principal subjects with which the diary is concerned: Pepys's work, interests, health etc. References to the *Companion* are given only rarely in the footnotes.

III. DATES

In Pepys's time two reckonings of the calendar year were in use in Western Europe. Most countries had adopted the New Style – the revised calendar of Gregory XIII (1582); Britain until 1752 retained the Old Style – the ancient Roman, or Julian, calendar, which meant that its dates were ten days behind those of the rest of Western Europe in the seventeenth century. 1 January in England was therefore 11 January by the New Style abroad. On the single occasion during the period of the diary when Pepys was abroad (in Holland in May 1660) he continued to use the Old Style, thus avoiding a break in the run of his dates. In the editorial material of the present work dates relating to countries which had adopted the new reckoning are given in both styles (e.g. '1/11 January') in order to prevent confusion.

For most legal purposes (from medieval times until 1752) the new year in England was held to begin on Lady Day, 25 March. But in accordance with the general custom, Pepys took it to begin on 1 January, as in the Julian calendar. He gives to all dates within the overlapping period between 1 January and 24 March a year-date which comprehends both styles – e.g. 'January 1 $16\frac{59}{60}$.' In the present commentary a single year-date, that of the New Style, has been used: e.g. '1 January 1660'.

THE DIARY
1667

JANUARY. 166$\frac{6}{7}$.

1. Lay long, being a bitter cold frosty day, the frost being now grown old and the Thames covered with Ice.[1] Up, and to the office, where all the morning busy. At noon to the Change a little, where Mr. James Houblon and I walked a good while, speaking of our ill condition in not being able to set out a fleet (we doubt) this year, and the certain ill effects that must bring – which is lamentable. Home to dinner, where the best powdered goose that ever I eat. Then to the office again, and to Sir W. Batten's to examine the commission going down to Portsmouth to examine witnesses about our prizes[2] – of which God give a good issue. And then to the office again, where late; and so home, my eyes sore. To supper and to bed.

2. Up I, and walked to White-hall to attend the Duke of York as usual. My wife up, and with Mrs. Pen to walk in the fields to frost-bite* themselfs. I find the Court full of great apprehensions of the French, who have certainly shipped landsmen, great numbers, at Brest; and most of our people here guess his design for Ireland.[3] We have orders to send all the ships we can possible to the Downes. God have mercy on us, for we can send forth no ships without men; nor will men go without money, every day bringing us news of new mutinies*a* among the seamen[4] – so that our condition is like to be very miserable. Thence to Westminster-hall and there met all the

a repl. same symbol badly formed

1. Cf. HMC, *Portland*, iii. 304. It thawed on the 6th: J. Goad, *Astro-Meteorologica* (1690), p. 306.
2. For the prize-ships, see above, vii. 418, 424 & nn. The commission was issued by the court of Admiralty.
3. According to a newsletter (5 January), fear of French intentions was 'the only discourse at Court and in town'; 20,000 men were being

embarked; 'Ireland, England, Barbados or Flanders – nobody knew which would be struck at': HMC, *Portland*, iii. 304. Cf. C. Bourel de la Roncière, *Hist. marine française*, v. 444–5.
4. Cf. Kempthorne to Navy Board, the Nore, 23 December 1666: *CSPD 1666–7*, pp. 367, 374. Want of pay and provisions was the main cause.

Houblons, who do laugh at this discourse of the French and say they are verily of opinion it is nothing but to send to their*ᵃ* plantations in the West Indys,[1] and that we at Court do blow up a design of invading us only to make the Parliament make more haste in the money matters – and perhaps it may be so, but I do not believe we have any such plots in our heads.   After them, I with several people; among others, Mr. George Mountagu,[2] whom I have not seen long.   He mighty kind. He tells me all is like to go ill, the King*ᵇ* displeasing the House of Commons by evading their Bill for examining accounts, and putting it into a commission, though thereon he hath left out Coventry and   , and named all the rest the Parliament named; and all country lords, not one Courtier.[3]   This doth not please them.   He tells me he finds the enmity almost over for my Lord Sandwich, and that now all is upon the Vice chamberlaine,[4] who bears up well and stands upon his vindication – which he seems to like well, and the others do construe well also.

Thence up to the Painted Chamber and there heard a conference between the House of Lords and Commons about the Wine=patent[5] – which I was exceeding glad to be at, because of my hearing exceeding good discourses, but especially from the Commons; among others, Mr Swinfin and a young man, one Sir Tho. Meres.   And do out-do the Lords infinitely.

a MS. 'this'   *b* preceded by blot

---

1. The French ships sailed to the W. Indies and were followed a few weeks later by an English squadron of five ships: *CSPCol., Am. and W. Indies, 1661–8*, p. 445. See below, p. 38, n. 1.

2. M.P. for Dover and cousin of Sandwich.

3. There were 11 others besides Coventry omitted from the House of Commons' list: *CJ*, viii. 661; *LJ*, xii. 57. For the bill, see above, vii. 400, 404 & nn. The 'country' (opposition) lords were the Earls of Bridgwater, Bolingbroke and Aylesbury, Viscount Conway, and Lords Lucas and Crew.

4. Carteret, whose work as Navy Treasurer was now under attack.

5. The Canary Company patent; for this dispute, see above, vii. 314, n. 2.   The *Journals* of the two houses record meetings of three conferences on this day (Swynfen and Meres, whom Pepys refers to later, being among the managers for the Commons), but none of the three was about the wine patent dispute: *LJ*, xii. 59; *CJ*, viii. 670. Pepys either misunderstood what he heard or made a mistake in his notes. Perhaps the drinking mentioned later in this entry has some responsibility for the confusion.

So down to the Hall and to the Rose tavern, while Doll Lane came to me and we did biber a good deal de vino, et jo did give ella 12 solidos para comprar ella some gans for a new ano's gift. I did tocar et no mas su cosa, but in fit time and place jo creo que je pouvais faire whatever I would con ella.

Thence to the Hall again and with Sir W Pen by coach to the Temple, and there light and eat a bit at an ordinary by; and then alone to the King's House and there saw *The Custome of the Country*, the second time of its being acted, wherein Knipp does the Widow well;[1] but of all the plays that ever I did see, the worst, having neither plot, language, nor anything in the earth that is acceptable. Only, Knipp sings a little song[2] admirably. But fully the worst play that ever I saw or I believe shall see. So away home, much displeased for the loss of so much time, and disobliging my wife by being there without her; and so by link walked home, it being mighty cold but dry; yet bad walking because very slippery with the frost and treading.

Home*a* and to my chamber to set down my journal; and then to thinking upon*b* establishing my Vows against the next year.[3] And so to supper and*c* to bed.

3. Up and to the office, where we sat all the morning. At noon by invitation to dinner to Sir W. Penn's – where my Lord Brouncker, Sir W. Batten and his lady – myself and wife – Sir J. Mennes, and Mr. Turner and his wife. Indifferent merry, to which I contributed the most. But a mean dinner, and in a mean manner. In the evening, I a little to the office and then to them, where I find them at Cards. Myself very ill with a cold (the frost continuing hard), so eat but little at supper; but very merry, and late home to bed – not much pleased with the manner of our entertainment, though to myself more civil then to any.

This day I hear hath been a conference between the two

---

a preceded by blot   *b* repl. 'did'   *c* blot above symbol

---

1. The play (now at the TR, Drury Lane) was a tragicomedy by Fletcher and Massinger; see above, v. 280, n. 1. The widow was Guiomar, mother of Duarte. (A).

2. Unidentified. (A).

3. For Pepys's vows, see above, ii. 242 & n. 1.

Houses about the bill for examining accounts, wherein the House of Lords their proceedings in petitioning the King for doing it by commission is in great heat voted by the Commons, after the conference, Unparliamentary[1] – the issue whereof, God knows.[a]

4. Up; and seeing things put in order for a dinner at my house today, I to the office awhile; and about noon home, and there saw all things in good order. Anon comes our company – my Lord Brouncker – Sir W. Penn, his Lady, and Peg and her servant, Mr. Lowder – my[b] Lady Batten – Sir W. Batten being forced to dine at Sir R Ford's, being invited – Mr. Turner and his wife. Here I had good room for ten, and no more would my table have held well had Sir J. Mennes (who was fallen lame) and his sister and niece and Sir W. Batten come, which was a great content to me to be without them. I did make them all gaze to see themselfs served so nobly in plate; and a neat dinner endeed, though but of seven dishes. Mighty merry I was and made them all – and they mightily pleased. My Lord Brouncker went away after dinner to the Ticket Office, the rest stayed; only my Lady Batten home, her ague-fit coming on her at table. The rest merry, and to cards and then to sing and talk; and at night to sup and then to cards; and last of all, to have a flagon of Ale and apples, drunk out of a wood[c] Cupp as a Christmas draught, made all merry; and they full of admiration at my plate, perticularly my flagons (which endeed are noble); and so late home, all with great mirth and satisfaction to them as I thought, and to myself to see all I have and do so much out-do, for neatness and plenty, anything done by any of them. They gone, I to bed much pleased. And do observe Mr. Lowder to be a pretty gentleman – and I think too good for Peg. And by the way, Peg Penn seems mightily to be kind to me, and I believe by her father's

a paragraph crowded into bottom of page   *b* repl. 'Sir'
                          c MS. 'wond'

---

1. The Commons' objection was that their own bill on the same subject was still pending when the Lords' petition (asking the King to institute an enquiry by royal commission) was presented on 21 December. See below, p. 10.

advice, who is also himself so – but I believe not a little troubled to see my plenty; and was much troubled to hear the song I sung – *The new Droll*[1] – it touching him home. So to bed.

5. At the office all the morning – thinking at noon to have been taken home, and my wife (according to appointment yesterday), by my Lord Brouncker to dinner and then to a play, but he had forgot it; at which I was glad, being glad of avoiding the occasion*a* of inviting him again and being forced to invite his doxy, Mrs.*b* Williams. So home and took a small snap of victuals, and away with my wife to the Duke's House and there saw *Mustapha*,[2] a most excellent play for words and design as ever I did see. I had seen it before but forgot it, so it was wholly new to me – which is the pleasure of my not committing these things to my memory. Home, and a little to the office and then to bed – where I lay with much pain in my head most of the night, and very unquiet, partly by my drinking before I went out too great a draught of sack, and partly my eyes being still very sore.

6. *Lords day.* Up pretty well in the morning; and then to church, where a dull doctor, a stranger, made a dull sermon. Then home, and Betty Michell and her husband came by invitation to dine with us; and she I find the same as ever (which I was afeared of the contrary) notwithstanding what yo haze ella hazer cum ego the last Sunday but one when we were abroad together. Here came also Mr. How to dine with me. And we had a good dinner – and good merry discourse, with much pleasure, I enjoying myself mightily to have friends at my table.

After dinner, young Michell and I, it being an excellent ⟨frosty⟩ day to walk, did walk out, he showing me the baker's house in pudding lane where the late great fire begun;[3] and

a repl. 'occ'-   *b* preceded by blot

---

1. Unidentified. (E).
2. A tragedy by Roger Boyle, Earl

of Orrery: see above, vi. 73 & n. 1. (A).
3. See above, vii. 268 & n. 1.

thence all along Thames-street, where I did view several places; and so up by London-Wall, by Blackfriars, to Ludgate, and thence to Bridewell, which I find to have been heretofore an extraordinary good house and a fine coming to it before the house by the bridge was built.[1] And so to look about St. Brides church and my father's house; and so walked home and there supped together, and then Michell and Betty home. And I to my closet, there to read and agree upon my vows for next year; and so to bed – and slept mighty well.

7. Lay long in bed. Then up and to the office, where busy all the morning. At noon (my[a] wife being gone to Westminster) I with my Lord Brouncker by coach as far as the Temple – in the way, he telling me that my Lady Denham is at last dead. Some suspect her poisoned, but it will be best known when her body is opened; which will be today, she dying yesterday morning.[2] The Duke of York is troubled for her; but hath declared he will never have another public mistress again – which I shall be glad of, and would the King would do the like. He tells me how the Parliament is grown so jealous of the King's being unfayre to them in the business of the Bill for examining accounts – Irish Bill, and the business of the papists,[3] that they[b] will not pass that business for money till they see themselfs secure that those Bills will pass, which they observe the Court to keep off till all the Bills come together, that the King may accept what he pleases and what he pleases to reject[4] – which will undo all our business, and the kingdom too.

He tells me how Mr. Henery Howard of Norfolke hath given our Royall Society all his grandfather's Library; which is a noble

a repl. 'home to dinner'   b repl. 'though'

---

1. The bridge was a footbridge built when Henry VIII acquired Bridewell. For the building, see above, i. 287, n. 2. (R).
2. The popular suspicion was that the Duchess of York had caused her death (see above vii. 365 & n. 2), but a post-mortem examination (made at her own wish) revealed no sign of

poison: below, p. 8; Orrery, *Coll. state letters* (1742), p. 219.
3. The two bills were passed later in the month; the resolutions against the Papists came to nothing: see above, vii. 343 & n. 4.
4. Cf. below, pp. 19, 22–3, 30, 31 & nn.

gift they value at 1000*l*.[1] And gives them accommodation to meet in at his house – Arundell-house, they being now disturbed at Gresham College.[2]

Thence, lighting at the Temple, to the ordinary hard by and eat a bit of meat; and then by coach to fetch my wife from her b[r]other's, and thence to the Duke's house and saw *Macbeth*; which though I saw it lately,[3] yet appears a most excellent play in all respects, but especially in divertisement, though it be a deep tragedy; which is a strange perfection in a tragedy, it being most proper here and suitable.

So home, it being the last play now I am to see till a fortnight hence, I being from the last night entered into my vows for the year coming on.[4]

Here I met with the good news of Hoggs bringing in two prizes more to Plymouth; which if they prove but any part of them,[5] I hope at least we shall be no losers by them.

So home from the office to write over fair my vows for this year, and then to supper and to bed – in great peace of mind, having now done it and brought myself into order again and a resolution of keeping it – and having entered my Journall to this night. So to bed, my eyes failing me with writing.

---

1. This gift of c. 4,000 books and 500 volumes of MSS was made at Evelyn's instigation, and included the whole library apart from certain volumes on heraldry, which went to the College of Arms. The presentation took place on 2 January. The greater part had been bought by Howard's grandfather, the 2nd Earl of Arundel – collector of the Arundel marbles – during his embassy to Vienna in 1636. It was transferred to Gresham College in 1678, and catalogued in 1681. Most of the MSS were disposed of to the British Museum in 1830; some 400 of the printed books were sold in 1925. Evelyn, iii. 472 & n. 3 and authorities there cited; A. R. Wagner, *Hist. heraldry of Brit.*, p. 32.

2. Since the Fire, the Society had met in Dr Walter Pope's lodgings at Gresham College, and had made several attempts to find other accommodation. It seems probable that these rooms were now commandeered by the city corporation, which had been meeting elsewhere in the college after being driven out of Guildhall by the Fire: Birch, ii. 113, 114, 128, 132, 138; C. R. Weld, *Hist. Royal Soc.* (1848), i. 194 n.

3. On 28 December 1666. This was Davenant's adaptation. (A).

4. One was a vow not to visit theatres more often than once a week: see above, p. 3 & n. 3. (A).

5. I.e. if any of the cargo is proved to be legitimate prize.

8. Up, and to the office, where we sat all the morning. At noon*ᵃ* home to dinner, where my Uncle Thomas with me – to receive his quarterage.¹ He tells me his son Thomas is set up in Smithfield, where he hath a shop, I suppose a booth.² Presently after dinner to the office and there set close to my business and did a great deal before night; and am resolved to stand to it, having been a truant too long. At night to Sir W. Batten's to consider some things about our prizes, and then to other talk; and among other things, he tells me that he hears for certain that Sir W Coventry hath resigned to the King his place of Commissioner of the Navy – the thing he hath often told me he had a mind to do; but I am surprized to think that he hath done it, and am full of thoughts all this evening after I heard it, what may be the consequences of it to me.³ So home and to supper, and then saw the Catalogue of my books which my brother hath wrote out, now perfectly Alphabeticall;⁴ and so to bed. ⟨Sir Rd. Ford did this evening at Sir W. Batten's tell us that upon opening the body of my Lady Denham, it is said that they found a vessel about her matrix, which had never been broke by her husband, that caused all pains in her body – which, if true, is excellent invention to clear both the Duchesse from poison and the Duke from lying with her.⟩*ᵇ*

a repl. 'home'
b entry crowded into bottom quarter of page; addition inserted in even smaller hand

---

1. The legacy under the will of Robert Pepys of Brampton, of which Pepys was an executor.
2. Pepys supposed that it was one of the temporary buildings replacing those burnt-out in the Great Fire. But it appears to have been a building with four hearths: PRO, E 179/147/627, p. 88. The son was a turner. (R).
3. An order was this day issued for the preparation of a warrant of sur-

render: *CSPD 1666–7*, p. 444. On the 10th Pepys wrote to Coventry: 'What little temptation you had to continue with us, I am too well acquainted, nevertheless you will give him who so well also knows the effects of your coming hither, leave to be apprehensive of what may follow your leaving us . . .' (*Further Corr.*, p. 155).
4. Cf. above, vii. 412 & n. 2.

9. Up, and with Sir W. Batten and W. Penn in a hackney-coach to White-hall, the way being most horribly bad upon the breaking up of the frost, so as not to be passed almost. There did our usual with the Duke of York; and here I do hear by my Lord Brouncker that for certain Sir W. Coventry hath resigned his place of Commissioner up; which I believe he hath done upon good grounds of security to himself, from all the blame which must attend our office this next year. But I fear the King will suffer by it. Thence to Westminster hall and there to the conference of the House[s] about the word "Nusance", which the Commons would have, and the Lords will not, in the Irish Bill.[1] The Commons do it professedly to prevent the King's dispensing with it; which Sir Rob. Howard and others did expressly repeat often: "The King nor any King ever could do anything which was hurtful to their people." Now the Lords did argue that it was an ill precedent and that which will ever hereafter be used as a way of preventing the King's dispensation with acts; and therefore rather*a* advise to pass the Bill without that word, and let it go, accompanied with a petition to the King that he will not dispense with it; this being a more civil way to the King. They answered well, that this doth*b* imply that the King should pass their Bill, and yet with design to dispense with it; which is to suppose the King guilty of abusing them. And more, they produce precedents for it; namely, that against new buildings and about Leather,[2] wherein the word "nusance" is used to that

a repl. 'have'   *b* repl. 'is'

1. For the bill, see above, vii. 314 & n. 1; below, p. 14. A free conference between the two houses was held at 10 a.m. in the Painted Chamber, Howard being the principal manager for the Commons: *LJ*, xii. 68; *CJ*, viii. 673; Milward, pp. 14, 15, 47, 66. It was one of the accepted limitations of the King's power of dispensation – his right to authorise certain individuals to disregard a statute – that he could not, by so doing, deprive other individuals of their rights at common law. This rule would apply if, as the Commons urged, the importation of Irish cattle were declared a 'common nuisance', but would not apply if the Lords succeeded in substituting the words 'detriment and mischief'. The Commons eventually won their point. Pepys's statement of the Lords' argument, which follows, appears to be incomplete: see the fuller summary in Clarendon, *Life*, iii. 156–7, 159–65.

2. The act for rebuilding London after the Fire (18–19 Car. II c. 8, 1666), sect. i; and the act prohibiting the export of leather (14 Car. II. c. 7, 1662), sect. x.

purpose; and further, that they do not rob the King of any right he ever had, for he never had a power to do hurt to his people,*a* and would exercise it; and therefore there is no danger, in the passing*b* this Bill, of imposing on his prerogative. And concluded that they think they ought to do this, so as the people may really have the benefit of it when it is passed, for never any people could expect so reasonably to be indulged something from a king, they having already given him so much money, and are likely to give more. Thus they broke up, both adhering to their opinions. But the Commons seemed much more full of judgment and reason then the Lords.

Then the Commons made their report to the Lords of their vote: that their Lordships' proceedings in the Bill for examining accounts were unparliamentary,[1] they having, while a Bill was sent up to them from the Commons about that business, petitioned his Majesty that he would do the same thing by his commission. They did give their reasons: *viz.*, that it had no precedent – that the King ought not to be informed [of] anything passing in the Houses till it comes to a Bill – that it will wholly break off all correspondence between the two Houses, and in the issue wholly infringe the very use and being of parliaments. Having left these arguments with the Lords, they all broke up; and I by coach to the ordinary by the Temple and there dined alone on a rabbit, and read a book I brought home today from Mrs. Michells, of the proceedings of the Parliament in the 3 and 4th year of the late King, a very good book for good speeches and arguments of law.[2]

Thence to Faythorne and bought a head or two; one of them my Lord of Ormonds, the best I ever saw.[3] And then to

---

a repl. 'p'-   *b* repl. two incomplete words

---

1. *CJ*, viii. 672–3. See above, p. 4, n. 1.

2. *Ephemeris Parliamentaria; or A faithfull register of the transactions in Parliament, in the third and fourth years of the reign of our late Sovereign Lord King Charles: containing the severall speeches, cases, and arguments of law transacted* (1654); PL 2115. The proceedings of 1627–8 on the Petition of Right reported there are a *locus classicus* for the study of the clash between government and the individual.

3. Possibly the engraving by David Loggan (d. 1692), who had been working in London since the Interregnum: F. O'Donoghue, *Cat. engraved Brit. portraits in BM*, iv. 380. (OM).

Arundell-house, where first the Royall Society met by the favour of Mr. Harry Howard, who was there and hath given us his grandfather's Library, a noble gift; and a noble favour and undertaking it is for him to make his house the seat for this College. Here was an experiment shown, about improving the use of powder for *a* Creating of Force in winding up of Springs, and other uses of great worth.[1] And here was a great meeting of worthy noble persons; but my Lord Bruncker, who pretended to make a congratulatory speech upon their coming hither and in thanks to Mr. Howard, doth it in the worst manner in the world, being the worst speaker; so as I do wonder at his parts and the unhappiness of his speaking.

Thence home by coach and to the office; and then home to supper, Mercer and her sister there, and to Cards; and then to bed.

Mr. Cowling did this day in the House lobby tell me of the many complaints among people against Mr. Townesend in the Wardrobe, and advises me to think of my Lord Sandwiches concernment there under his care.[2] He did also tell me, upon my demanding it, that he doth believe there are some things on foot for a peace between France and us – but that we shall be fooled *b* in it.[3]

10. Up, and at the office all the morning. At noon home; and there being business to do in the afternoon, took my Lord Brouncker home with me, who dined with me – his discourse

---

a repl. 'they'   *b* ? 'foiled'

---

1. The official minutes record no such experiment on this day, mentioning only a resolution to arrange one for the next meeting: Birch, ii. 139. Cf. also ib., pp. 137, 142. Cf. Hooke's machine (c. 1663) for determining the strength of gunpowder by weight: Gunther, vi. 153.

2. Richard Cooling ('Cowling') was secretary to Manchester (Sandwich's cousin), the Lord Chamberlain. For further complaints, by him and others, of Townshend's inefficiency, see below, p. 597; 5 February 1668;

Sandwich MSS, Letters from Ministers, i, f. 115r. The Wardrobe was reorganised at the end of the year: below, p. 597 & n. 2.

3. The country party in the Commons strongly suspected the pro-French faction at court. But there was at the moment no question of a separate peace with France – neither Charles nor Louis wanted it. St Albans was sent to Paris on 28 January to sound out the prospects for a general peace. For Clarendon's account, see *Life*, iii. 203–7.

and mine about the bad performances of the Controller's and Surveyor's places by the hands they are now in, and the shame to the service, and loss the King suffers by it. Then after dinner to the office, where we and some of the chief of Trinity-house met to examine the occasion of the loss of the *Prince Royall*, the maister and Mates being examined – which*a* I took and keep.[1] And so broke up, and*b* I to my letters by the post; and so home and to supper with my mind at pretty good ease, being entered upon minding my business; and so to bed. ⟨This noon Mrs. Burroughs came to me about busi[ness], whom I did besar and haza ella tocar mi chose.⟩*c*

11. Up, being troubled at my being found abed a-days by all sorts of people – I having got a trick of sitting up later then I need, never supping, or very seldom, before 12 at night. Then to the office; there busy all the morning; and among other things, comes Sir W. Warren and talked*d* with me a good while; whose discourse I love, he being a very wise man and full of good counsel, and his own practices for wisdom much to be observed. And among other things, he tells me how he is fallen in with my Lord Brouncker, who hath promised him most perticular inward friendship, and yet not to appear at the board to do so. And he told me*e* how my Lord Brouncker should take notice of the two flagons he saw at my house at dinner at my late feast, and merrily (yet I know enviously) said I could not come honestly by them.[2] This I am glad to hear, though vexed to see his ignoble soul. But I shall beware of him; and yet it is fit he should see I am no mean fellow but can live in the world and have something. At noon home to dinner; and then to the

a repl. 'this'   *b* preceded by blot
c addition crowded into bottom of page   *d* MS. 'walked'
e repl. 'him'

---

1. 'Examinacions touching the Losse of the Prince': Rawl. A 195a, ff. 51+ (copy of report in unidentified clerical hand). Cf. *CSPD 1666–7*, p. 445. All witnesses except one agreed that the surrender (during the Four Days Battle, June 1666) was made without the knowledge of the squadron commander, Ayscue.

2. These silver and gilt flagons (used at the dinner-party on the 4th) had been a present from Denis Gauden, the navy victualler: above, v. 225.

office with my people and very busy, and did despatch to my
great satisfaction abundance of business, and do resolve by the
grace of God to stick to it till I have cleared my hand*a* of most
things wherein I am in arrear in public and private matters. At
night home to supper and to bed. ⟨This day, ill news of my
father's being very ill of his old grief,*b* the Rupture, which
troubles me.⟩*c*

12. Up, still lying long in bed. Then to the office, where sat
very long. Then home to dinner; and so to the office again,
mighty busy, and did to the joy of my soul despatch much
business – which doth make my heart light and will enable me
to recover all the ground I have lost (if I have by my late minding
my pleasures lost any) and support myself. So home to supper,
and then to read a little in Moore's *Antidote against Atheisme*,[1]
a pretty book; and so to bed.

13. *Lords day.* Up, and to church, where young Lowder
came to church with Sir W. Penn and his Lady and daughter;
and my wife tells me that either they are married or the match is
quite perfected; which I am apt to believe, because all the peoples
eyes in the church were much fixed upon them.[2] At noon sent
for Mercer, who dined with us, and very merry; and so I after*d*
dinner walked to the old Swan, thinking to have got a boat to
White-hall; but could not, nor was there anybody at home at
Michells, where I thought to have sat with her – et peut être
obtain algo de her – which I did intend para essayer. So home
to church, a dull sermon; and then home at my chamber all the
evening. So to supper and to bed.

14. Up, and to the office, where busy, getting beforehand
with my business as fast as I can. At noon home to dinner, and

---

  a MS. 'hearts'   *b* repl. 'dis'-
  c addition inserted in small hand   *d* repl. 'home'

---

1. Henry More, *An antidote against
atheism, or, An appeal to the naturall
faculties of the minde of man, whether
there be not a God;* first pub. 1653; a
famous defence of faith; perhaps the
most influential of all the works of the

Cambridge Platonist School; PL 867
(1655, 2nd ed.).
2. Their marriage licence was issued
on 12 February, and they were married on 15 February.

presently afterward to my office again. I understand my father is pretty well again, blessed be God – and would have my Brother John come down to him for a little while. Busy till night, pleasing myself mightily to see what a deal of business goes off of a man's hand when he stays by it. And then at night, before it was late (yet much business done), home to supper, discourse with my wife, and to bed. Sir W. Batten tells me the Lords do agree at last with the Commons about the word "Nusance" in the Irish Bill¹ and do desire a good correspondence between the two Houses. And that the King doth intend to prorogue them the last of this month.

15. Up, and to the office, where busy all the morning. Here my Lord Brouncker would have made me promise to go with him to a play this afternoon, where Knipp acts Mrs. Weaver's great part in *The Indian Emperour*² – and he says is coming on to be a great actor. But I am so fell to my business, that I, though against my inclination, will not go. At noon dined with my wife – and were pleasant; and then to the office, where I got Mrs. Burroughs sola cum ego – and did tocar su mamelles so as to hazer me hazer. She gone, I to my business and did much; and among other things tonight, we were all mightily troubled how to prevent the sale of a great deal of hemp and timber-deals and other good goods tomorrow at the candle³ by the Prize-Office, where it will be sold for little.⁴ And we shall be found to want the same goods and buy at extraordinary prices, and perhaps the very same goods now sold; which is a most horrid evil and a shame. At night home to supper and to

---

1. *LJ*, xii. 74. See above, pp. 9–10 & n.

2. This was the role of Alibech. The play was a heroic tragedy by Dryden, designed as a sequel to *The Indian Queen*; first acted in 1665, and published in 1667. According to Downes (p. 9) the leading feminine roles, Cyderia and Almeria, were played by Nell Gwyn and Mrs Marshall respectively; Mohun played the Emperor; Hart, Cortez; Burt, Vacquez. (A).

3. For auction sales by candle, see above, i. 284, n. 2.

4. See Pepys's note in NWB, p. 106. After his angry reception by Ashley on the 16th, Pepys persuaded Batten to go to see him on the 18th. Despite their efforts and an order from the King himself, the goods were sold, and this at a time when the Navy Office had neither money nor credit to buy them. The interviews are described briefly in both the diary and the NWB.

bed – with my mind mighty light to see the fruits of my diligence in having my business go off my hand so merrily.

16. Up, and by coach to White-hall – and there to the Duke of York as usual. Here Sir W. Coventry came to me aside in the Duke's chamber, to tell that he had not answered part of a late letter of mine, because *littera Scripta manet* – about his leaving the office – he tells me because he finds that his business at Court will not permit him to attend it; and then he confesses that he seldom of late could come from it with satisfaction, and there-[fore] would not take the King's money for nothing.[1] I professed my sorrow for it, and prayed the continuance of his favour; which he promised. I do believe he hath done like a very wise man in reference to himself; but I doubt it will prove ill for the King and for the office. Prince Rupert, I hear today, is very ill[2] – yesterday given over, but better*a* today. This day before the Duke of York, the business of the Mustermaisters was reported, and Balty found the best of the whole number, so as the Duke enquired who he was and whether he was a stranger by his two names, both strange. And offered that he and one more, who hath done the next best,[3] should have not only their own, but part of the others' salary; but that, I having said he was my brother-in-law, did stop; but they two are ordered their pay, which I am glad of, and some of the rest will lose their pay and others be laid by the heels. I was very glad of this being ended so well. I did also this morning move in a business wherein Mr. Hater hath concerned me, about getting a ship, laden with salt from France, permitted to unload, coming in after the King's declaration was out; which I have hopes by some dexterity to get done.[4] Then with the Duke of York

a repl. 'pr'-

1. Coventry's salary came to an end on the following 25 March. His court business was his work as a Privy Councillor. For Pepys's letter, see above, p. 8 & n. 3.

2. Of a head wound: see below, p. 41 & n. 1; above, vi. 12, n. 2.

3. Richard Ward: below, p. 19 & n. 1.

4. The *Falcon* of Hamburg (re-cently arrived at Plymouth) had been loaded with bay salt at La Rochelle before news had reached her of the proclamation of 10 November 1666 prohibiting trade with France. The council later this day made an order allowing her to discharge cargo, provided that the navy victuallers had first refusal of it at the market price: PRO, PC 2/59, p. 270.

to the King to receive his commands for stopping the sale this
day of some prize-goods at the Prize-Office, goods fit for the
Navy, and received the King's commands and carried them to
the Lords' House to my Lord Ashly,[1] who was angry much thereat; and I am sorry it fell to me to carry that order, but I cannot
help it; so against his will, he signed a note I writ to the Commissioners of Prizes, which I carried and delivered to Kingdom[2]
at*a* their new office in Aldergate Streete.   Thence a little to the
Exchange, where it was hot that the Prince was dead, but I did
rectify it.   So home to dinner and found Balty, told him the
good news, and then after dinner away; I presently to White-
hall and did give the Duke of York a memorial of the salt business
against the Council.   And did wait all the Council for answer –
walking a good while with Sir St. Fox; who, among other
things, told me his whole mystery in the business of the interest
he pays as Treasurer for the Army.   They give him 12*d* per cent
quite*b* through the Army, ⟨with condition⟩ to be paid weekly.
This he undertakes upon his own private credit,[3] and to be paid
by the King at the end of every four months.   If the King pay
him not at the end of the four months, then for all the time he
stays longer, my Lord Treasurer by agreement allows him
8 per cent per annum for the forbearance – so that in fine, he hath
about twelve per cent from the King and the Army for fifteen or
sixteen months' interest – out of which he gains soundly, his
expense being about 130000*l* per annum – and hath no trouble in
it compared (as I told him) to the trouble I must have to bring
in an account of interest.   I was, however, glad of being thus
enlightened.   And so away to the other council door, and there
got in and hear a piece of a cause heard before the King, about a
ship*c* deserted by her fellows (who were bound mutually to
defend each other) in their way to Virginy and taken by the
enemy[4] – but it was but meanly pleaded.

a   repl. 'in'   *b*   s.h. repl. l.h. 'nom'-   *c*   repl. 'shop'

1. Treasurer of the Prize Commission.   The goods in dispute
consisted mostly of hemp.   Pepys
had written to Coventry on the 10th
to stop the sale: NMM, LBK/8,
p. 441.   Cf. his note in NWB,
p. 106.

2. Richard Kingdon, a Prize Commissioner.

3. Similarly Carteret, as Navy
Treasurer, used his private credit.

4. This concerned the *Alexander* of
Bristol, which had straggled from the
convoy: PRO, PC 2/59, p. 269.

Then all withdrew; and by and by the Council rose and I spoke with the Duke of York and he told me my business was done, which I found accordingly in Sir Edw. Walker's[1] books; and so away, mightily satisfied, to Arundell-house and there heard a little good discourse;[2] and so home and there to Sir W. Batten, where I heard the examinations in two of our prizes, which do make but little for us, so that I do begin to doubt their proving prize, which troubled me. So home to supper with my wife; and after supper my wife told me how she had moved to W Hewer the business of my sister for a wife to him, which he receive[d] with mighty*a* acknowledgement as she says, above anything. But says he hath no intention to alter his condition, so that I am in some measure sorry she ever moved it; but I hope he will think it only came from her.

So after supper, a little to the office to enter my Journall, and then home to bed. Talk there is of a letter to come from Holland, desiring a place of treaty; but I do doubt it.[3] This day I observe still in many places the smoking remains of the late fire.[4] The ways mighty bad and dirty. This night Sir R. Ford told me how this day at Christ Church Hospital they have given a living of 200*l* per annum to Mr. Sanchy, my old acquaintance; which I wonder at, he commending him mightily; but am glad of it.[5] He tells me too, how the famous Stillingfleete was a Bluecoat boy.[6] The children*b* at this day are provided for in the country by the House, which I am glad also to hear.[7]

a MS. 'my'   *b* MS. 'church'

---

1. Clerk of the Council.
2. The subjects now discussed at the Royal Society were (principally) birds called *coccothrostes*, Col. Blount's chariot, and 'a preparation of mercury fit to take off any impression of a seal or medal': Birch, ii. 139–40.
3. The Dutch had sent a letter on 3/13 January asking that the place chosen should be on neutral territory: D'Estrades, *Lettres* (1709), iv. 8–9. Cf. below, p. 61 & n. 3.
4. Cf. above, vii. 393, n. 1.
5. Clement Sankey was a Fellow of Magdalene who was now appointed

to St Clement Eastcheap. He soon made his name in London (see below, p. 151), and became a Canon of York in 1669.
6. A mistake: Edward Stillingfleet, the divine, was educated at Cranborne, Dorset, and at Ringwood, Hants., not at Christ's Hospital.
7. Most of the boys were boarded out at Ware and Hertford after the Fire, in which the school buildings in Newgate St had suffered badly. They returned to London in November 1667: E. H. Pearce, *Annals Christ's Hosp.*, pp. 209–10.

17. Up, and to the office, where all the morning sitting. At noon home to dinner and then to the office, busy also till very late, my heart joyed with the effects of my fallowing my business, by easing my head of cares; and so home to supper and to bed.

18. Up, and most of the morning finishing my entry of my Journall during the late fire out of loose papers into this*a* book, which did please me mightily when done, I writing till my*b* eyes were almost blind therewith to make end of it.¹ Then all the rest of the morning, and after a mouthful of dinner, all the afternoon in my closet till night, sorting all my papers which have lain unsorted for all the time we were at Greenwich during the plague. Which did please me also – I drawing on to put my office into a good posture, though much is behind.

This morning came Captain Cocke to me, and tells me that the King comes to the House this day to pass the pole bill and the Irish bill. He tells me too, that though the faction* is very froward in the House, yet ⟨all⟩ will end well there. But he says that one had got a Bill ready to present in the House against Sir W. Coventry for selling of places; and says he is certain of it, and how he was withhelde*c* from the doing it.² He says that the Vicechamberlaine is now one of the greatest men in England again, and was he that did prevail with the King to let the Irish Bill go with the word "Nusance".³ He told me that Sir G. Carteret's declaration of giving double to any man that will proof that any of his people have demanded or taken anything for*d* forwarding the payment of the wages of any man (of which he sent us a copy yesterday, which we approved of) is set up, among other places, upon the House of Lords' door.⁴ I do not know how wisely this is done.

This morning also, there come to the*e* office a letter from the

---

a MS. 'to this'   *b* repl. 'might'
c repl. 'prove'   *d* repl. 'to'   *e* repl. 'me a'

---

1. Cf. above, vol. i, pp. cii–ciii.
2. A similar bill in 1663 had got as far as report stage, but no further: see above, iv. 156, 169 & nn.

3. See above, pp. 9–10.
4. See *CSPD 1666–7*, pp. 457–8. It was also displayed at the Navy Office.

Duke of York, commanding our payment of no wages to any of the muster-maisters of the fleet the last year, but only to my brother Balty (taking notice that he had taken pains therein) and one Ward; who, though he had not taken so much as the other, yet had done more then the rest.[1] This I was exceeding glad [of] for my own sake and his. At night, I by appointment home, where W. Batelier and his sister Mary, and the two Mercers, to play at cards and sup; and did cut our great cake lately given us by Russell[2] – a very good one. Here very merry, late.

Sir W Pen told me this night how the King did make them a very sharp speech in the House of Lords today, saying that he did expect to have had more Bills. That he purposes to prorogue them on Monday come sennit. That whereas they have unjustly*a* conceived some jealou[s]ys* of his making a peace, he declares he knows of no such thing or treaty.[3] And so left them – but with so little effect, that as soon as come into the House, Sir W Coventry moving that now the King hath declared his intention of proroguing them, it would be loss of time to go on with the thing they were upon when they were called to the King, which was the calling over the Defaults of members appearing in the House;[4] for that before any person could now come or be brought to town, the House would be up. Yet the faction did desire to delay time, and contend*b* so as to come to a division of the House; where, however, it was carried by a few voices[5]

---

a preceded by blot   *b* repl. 'conc'—

---

1. Dated this day; copy (in Hewer's hand) in PRO, Adm. 2/1745, f. 153r; abstract in BM, Add. 9314, f. 9r. Cf. above, p. 15.

2. John Russell, master ropemaker, Woolwich yard.

3. 'I have now passed your Bills; and I was in good Hope to have had other Bills ready to pass too. . . . This is the First Day I have heard of any Money towards a Supply . . . and what that will amount to, God knows; and what Time I have to make . . . Preparations . . . to meet Three such Enemies as I have . . .; and I must tell you, what Discourses

soever are abroad, I am not in any Treaty': *LJ*, xii. 81. It was true that no formal negotiations had yet started, but soundings had been made with both Holland and France over the past four months: Feiling, pp. 209+. The King was angry at being forced to accept the Irish Cattle bill, to which he gave assent only under pressure and as a means of getting his Poll Bill; see Arlington to Ormond, 19 January: Carte 46, ff. 440–1.

4. I.e. members failing to attend without authorised excuse: *CJ*, viii. 678.

5. By 118 to 108: ib., p. 679.

that the debate should be laid by.   But this shows that they are
not pleased, or that they have any awe over them from the
King's displeasure.

The company being gone, to bed.

19.   Up, and at the office all the morning.   Sir W. Batten
tells me, to my wonder, that at his coming to my Lord Ashly
yesterday morning, to tell him what prize-goods he would have
saved for the Navy and not sold, according to the King's order
on the 17th – he fell quite out with him in high terms; and he
says too, that they did go on to the sale yesterday, even of the
very hemp and other things.   At which I am astonished – and
will never wonder at the ruine of the King's affairs, if this be
suffered.   At noon dined, and Mr. Pierce came to see me, he
newly come from keeping his Christmas in the country.

So to the office, where very busy, but with great pleasure, till
late at night; and then home to supper and to bed.

20.   *Lords day.*   Up betimes and down to the Old Swan;
there called on Michell and his wife, which in her night linen
appeared as pretty almost as ever to my thinking I saw woman.
Here I drank some burned brandy.   And they showed me their
house which, poor people, they have built,[1] and it is very pretty.
I invited them to dine with me; and so away to White-hall to
Sir W. Coventry, with whom I have not been alone a good while.
And very kind he is.   And tells me how the business is now
ordered, by order of[a] council, for my Lord Brouncker to assist
Sir J. Mennes in all matters of accounts relating to the Treasurer
and Sir W. Penn in all matters relating to the victuallers' and
pursers' accounts[2] – which I am very glad of, and the more for
that I think it will not do me any hurt at all.   Other discourse;
much especially about the heat the House was in yesterday about

a repl. 'c'-

1. The old one having been destroyed in the Fire.
2. The order was issued on 16
January: PRO, Adm. 106/14, ff. 236–7
(printed Penn, *Memorials*, ii. 435–6).

For the regulations which the Board
and Admiral then made (1 February),
see PRO, Adm. 106/3520, ff. 34*v*–35*v*;
Duke of York, *Mem.* (*naval*), pp. 56–7.
Cf. above, iv. 61; *Cat.*, i. 17.

the ill management of the Navy; which I was sorry to hear, though I think they were well answered both by Sir G. Carteret and W. Coventry, as he informs me the substance of their speeches. Having done with him, I home, mightily satisfied with my being with him; and coming home, I to church, and there beyond expectation find our seat and all the church crammed by twice as many people as used to be; and to my great joy find Mr. Frampton[1] in the pulpit. So to my great joy I hear him preach, and I think the best sermon, for goodness – oratory – without affectation or study – that ever I heard in my life. The truth is, he preaches the most like an Apostle that ever I heard man. And was much the best time that ever I spent in my life at church. His text, *Ecclesiastes* 11, verse 8th – the words –[2] "But if a man live many years and rejoice in them all, yet let him remember the days of darkness, which shall be many. All that cometh is vanity."

He done, I home; and there Michell and his wife and we dined, and mighty merry; I mightily taken, more and more, with her. After dinner, I with my brother away by water to White-hall and there walked in the park. And a little to my Lord Chancellors, where the King and Cabinet*a* met, and there met Mr. Brisband, with whom good discourse; to White-hall towards night, and there he did lend me the *Third Advice to a paynter*,[3] a bitter Satyr upon the service of the Duke of Albemarle the last year. I took it home with me and will copy it, having the former – being also mightily pleased with it.

So after reading it, I to Sir W. Penn to discourse a little with him about the business of our prizes; and so home to supper and to bed.

21. Up betimes, and with Sir W. Batten, W. Penn, R. Ford, by coach to the Swedes Resident's in the piattza to discourse

a repl. 'cab'-

---

1. Robert Frampton, recently chaplain to the Levant Company; later Dean (1673) and Bishop (1680) of Gloucester. On 16 September 1666 he had preached before the King 'so excellently and rhetorically that not only the King but [the] whole court wept': T. Flatman to Gilbert Sheldon (Tanner 45, f. 108r).

2. A loose recollection.

3. See above, vii. 407 & n. 4; this was a MS. copy.

with him about two of our prizes, wherein he puts in his concernment as for his countrymen.[1]   We had no satisfaction, nor did
give him any; but I find him a cunning fellow.   He[a] lives in
one of the great houses there, but ill-furnished, and came to us
out of bed in his Furred mittins and furred cap.   Thence to
Exeter-house to the Doctors Commons, and there with our
proctors to Dr. Walker, who was not very well; but however,
did hear our matters, and after a dull-seeming hearing of them
read, did discourse most understandingly of them, as well as
ever I heard man – telling us all our grounds of pretence to the
prize would do no good, and made it appear but thus and thus it
may be.   But yet did give us but little reason to expect it[b] would
prove[2] – which troubled us, but I was mightily taken to hear his
manner of discourse.   Thence with them to Westminster hall,
they setting me down at White-hall, where I missed of finding
Sir G. Carteret.   Up to the Lords' House, and there came
mighty seasonably to hear the Solicitor about my Lord Buckinghams pretence to the Title of Lord Rosse.[3]   Mr. Atturny
Mountagu is also a good man, and so is old Sir P. Ball.   But the
Sollicitor, and Scruggs after him, are excellent men.[4]   Here
spoke with my Lord Bellasses about getting some money for
Tanger; which he doubts we shall not be able to do out of the

---

a   repl. 'Thence we away'   b   symbol blotted

---

1. See above, p. 7; vii. 424 &
n. 2.   The Swedish resident (living
in the Piazza, Covent Garden) was
Leijonbergh, who later married Batten's widow.   Pepys almost fought
a duel with him in 1670 over what
appears to have been a dispute about
Lady Batten's share of the prize-
money: Rawl. A 174, f. 249r.
   2. Sc. would prove to be prize.
Dr Walter Walker was an advocate
practising in admiralty causes.
   3. The Duke of Buckingham
claimed the barony of de Ros (de
Roos) (the premier barony of England; cr. 1264) by descent through his
mother.   In a petition of 12 Decem-

ber 1666 he had protested against the
claims of the Viscount Manners, eldest
son of the Earl of Rutland.   In February Buckingham was granted it (and
held it until it fell into abeyance on his
death in 1687), but the Manners
family were allowed to use it as a
courtesy title.   *LJ*, xii. 83, 96; GEC,
iv. 733–4; ib., xi. 111–12; HMC,
Rep., 8/1/105.
   4. The Solicitor-General was Sir
Heneage Finch, whose oratory Pepys
often admired: cf. above, v. 140 &
n. 2.   Sir William Scroggs (later a
judge, 1676, and Lord Chief Justice,
1678) was now a rising barrister of
Gray's Inn.

Poll bill, it being so strictly tied for the Navy.[1] He tells me the Lords have passed the Bill for the accounts with some little amendments.[2] So down to the hall; and thence with our company to Exeter-house and then did the business I have said before, we doing nothing the first time of going, it being too early.

At home find Lovett, to whom I did give my Lady Castlemaine's head to do.[3] He is talking of going into Spain to get money by his art;[a] but I doubt he will do no good, he being a man of an unsettled head.

Thence by water down to Deptford, the first time I have been by water a great while, and there did some little business – and walked home; and there came into my company three drunken Seamen, but one especially – who told me such stories, calling me Captaine, as made me mighty merry; and they would leap and skip, and kiss what maids they met all the way. I did at first give them money to drink, lest they should know who I was and so become troublesome to me. Parted at Redriffe; and there home and to the office, where did much business; and then to Sir W. Batten, where W. Penn and R. Ford and I – to hear a proposition R. Ford was to acquaint us with from the Swedes Embassador, in manner of saying that for money he might be got to our side and relinquish the trouble he may give us. Sir W. Penn did make a long simple declaration of his resolution to give nothing to deceive any poor man of what was his right by law, but ended in doing whatever anybody else would; and we did commission R. Ford to give promise of not beyond 350*l* to him and his secretary, in case they did not oppose us in the *Phœnix* (the net profits of which, as R. Ford cast up before us, the Admiralls tenths and ship's thirds[4] and other charges all

a l.h. repl. s.h. 'heart'

1. Cf. 18–19 Car. II c. 1, sect. xxxiv. The money was later obtained from the Eleven Months Tax: below, p. 344 & n. 3.
2. This was in committee stage: *LJ*, xii. 82. For the bill, see above, vii. 399–400 & n.
3. See above, vii. 359, n. 3. (OM).
4. By the current rules (of 1666)

prize-goods were shared between the Lord High Admiral (one-tenth), the ship's officers (one-tenth) and the crew (one-third): *CSPD Add. 1660–85*, pp. 159–60; cf. Ehrman, p. 130. The prize was the *Phoenix* of Riga. For the outcome of the dispute, see below, p. 123 & n. 1.

cleared, will amount to 3000*l*) and that we did gain her.   R. Ford did pray for a curse upon his family if he was privy to anything more then he told us (which I believe he is a knave in); yet we all concluded him the*a* most fit man for it and very honest, and so left it wholly to him to manage as he pleased.

Thence to the office a little while longer; and so home, where*b* W Hewers's mother was, and Mrs. Turner our neighbour, and supped with us.   His mother a well-favoured old little woman, and a good woman I believe.   After we had supped, and merry, we parted late – Mrs. Turner having stayed behind to talk a little about her lodgings; which now my Lord Brouncker, upon Sir W. Coventry's surrendering, doth claim.   But I cannot think he will come to live in them, so as to need to put them out.   She gone, we to bed all.

This night at supper, comes from Sir W. Coventry the Order of Councell for my Lord Brouncker to do all the Controllers part relating to the Treasurer's accounts, and Sir W. Penn all relating to the Victuallers, and Sir J. Mennes to do the rest. This I hope will do much better for the King then now, and I think will give neither of them ground to overtop me, as I feared they would – which pleases me mightily.

This evening*c* Mr. Wren and Captain Cocke called upon me at the office;[1] and there told me how the House was in better temper* today and hath passed the Bill for the remainder of the money; but not to be passed finally till they have done some other things which they will have pass with it;[2] wherein they are very open what their meaning is, which was but doubted before, for they do in all respects doubt the King's pleasing them.

22.   Up, and there came to me Darnell the Fidler, one of the Duke's house, and brought me a set of lessons, all three parts. I heard them play[ed] to the Duke of York this Christmas at his

---

a repl. 'a'   *b* MS. 'Mr.'   *c* repl. 'after'

---

1. Cocke and Matthew Wren (secretary now to Clarendon, later to Coventry) were close friends: their association can be traced in the diary. Wren was godfather to Cocke's son, Matthew, and left legacies at his death to him and to his mother and to Cocke's servants.

2. They would grant supply only if allowed to conduct their own enquiry into the government's financial administration.   Cf. above, p. 2 & n. 3.

lodgings, and bid him get me them. I did give him a Crowne for them – and did enquire after the music of *The Siege of Rhodes*,[1] which he tells me he can get me, which I am mighty glad of. So to the office, where among other things I read the Council's order about my Lord Brouncker and W. Penn to be assistants to the Controller – which quietly went down, with Sir J. Mennes, poor man, seeming a little as if he would be thought to have desired it, but yet apparently to his discontent. And I fear, as the order runs, it will hardly do much good. At noon[a] to dinner; and there comes a letter from Mrs. Pierce, telling me she will come and dine with us on Thursday next with some of the players, Knipp, &c., which I was glad of but my wife vexed, which vexed me but I seemed merry, but know not how to order the matter whether they shall come or no. After dinner to the office and there late, doing much business; and so home to supper and to bed.

23. Up, and with Sir W. Batten and W. Penn to White-hall, and there to the Duke of York and did our usual business. Having done there, I to St. James's to see the Organ Mrs. Turner told me of the other night, of my late Lord Aubigny's;[2] and I took my Lord Brouncker with me, he being acquainted with my present Lord Almoner, Mr. Howard,[3] brother to the Duke of Norfolke. So he and I thither and did see the Organ; but I do not like it, it being but a bawble, with a virginall joining to it – so I shall not meddle with it.[4] Here we sat and talked with him a good while, and he seems a good-natured gentleman. Here I observed the Deske which he hath to remove, and is fastened to one of the armes of his Chayre. I do also observe the counterfeit windows there was in the form of Doores, with Looking glasses instead of windows, which makes the room seem both bigger and

---

a repl. 'home'

---

1. For the opera, see above, ii. 130 & n. 2. The vocal music was by Henry Lawes, Capt. Cooke, and Matthew Locke; the instrumental by Charles Coleman and George Hudson: William Davenant, *The siege of Rhodes* (1656), p. 41. The music has not been traced. (E).

2. Late Almoner to the Queen Mother; he had died in November 1665.

3. Philip Howard, Lord Almoner to the Queen; later (1675) a cardinal.

4. The claviorganum, known since the 15th century. It never achieved success or popularity. (E).

lighter I think; and I have some thoughts to have the like in one of my rooms. He discoursed much of the goodness of the Musique in Rome, but could not tell me how long Musique had been in any perfection in that Church – which I would be glad to know. He speaks much of the great buildings that this Pope (whom in mirth to us he calls Antichrist) hath done in his time.[1] Having done with this discourse, we away; and my Lord and I walking into the parke*a* back again, I did observe the new buildings;[2] and my Lord seeing I had a desire to see them, they being the place for the priests and Friers, he took*b* me back to my Lord Almner and he took us quite through the whole house and chapel and the new Monastery, showing me most excellent pieces in Wax=worke – a crucifix given by a Pope to Mary Queene of Scotts, where a piece of the*c* Cross is – two bits set in the manner of a cross in the foot of the crucifix.[3] Several fine pictures, but especially very good prints of holy pictures. I saw the Dortoire and the Cells of the priests, and we went into one – a very pretty little room, very clean, hung with pictures – set with books. The*d* priest was in his Cell – with his hair-cloths to his skin, bare-legged, with a Sandall only on, and his little bed without sheets, and no feather bed; but yet I thought saft enough. His Cord about his middle. But in so good company, living with care, I thought it a very good life. A pretty Library they have, and I was in the Refectoire, where every man his napkin – knife – cup of earth – and basin of the same – and a place for one to sit and read while the rest are at meals. And into the Kitchin I went, where a good neck of Mutton at the fire – and other vic-

---

a l.h. repl. s.h. 'park'   *b* MS. 'take'   *c* repl. 'our'
d repl. 'He hath'

---

1. Under Alexander VII (Pope, 1655–67), who with his two immediate predecessors transformed much of Rome, some of Bernini's greatest work was done – e.g. the colonnade in the Piazza of St Peter's. See R. Wittkower, *Art and architecture in Italy 1600–1750* (1965), pt 2.

2. These lay to the east of St James's Palace; they were begun in October 1664 and finished in May 1666: PRO, Works 5/9, n.p. Cf. also *CTB*, iii. 897, 916. Descriptions in Magalotti, p. 170; W. M. Brady, *The episc. succession*, iii. 113.

3. Untraced; not in the official inventory taken of Mary's jewels (20 February 1587) in BM, Stowe 560, ff. 27+.

tuals boiling – I do not think they feed very hard. Their windows looking all into a fine garden and the park. And mighty pretty rooms all. I wished myself one of the Capuchins[1] – having seen what we could here, and all with*a* mighty pleasure. So away with the Almoner in his coach, talking merrily about the difference in our religions, to White-hall and there we left him; and in my Lord Brouncker's coach, he carried me to the Savoy, and there we parted. I to the Castle Taverne, where was and did come all our company – Sir W. Batten, W. Penn, R. Ford, and our counsel Sir Ell. Layton, Walt. Walker, Dr. Budd, Mr. Holder, and several others; and here we had a bad dinner of our preparing and did discourse something of our business of our prizes, which was the work of the day. I stayed till dinner was over; and there being no use of me, I away after dinner without taking leave; and to the New Exchange, there to take up my wife and Mercer, and to Temple Barr to my ordinary and had a dish of meat for them, they having not dined; and thence to the King's House and there saw *The Humerous Lieutenant*[2] – a silly play, I think – only the spirit in it, that grows very Tall and then sinks again to nothing, having two heads treading upon one, and then Knipps singing, did please us. Here, in a box above, we spied Mrs. Pierce; and going out, they called us, and so we stayed for them and Knipp took us all in and brought to us Nelly,[3] a most pretty woman, who acted the great part, Cœlia, today very fine, and did it pretty well; I kissed her and so did my wife, and a mighty pretty soul she is. We also saw Mrs. Hall*b*, which is my little Roman-nose black girl that is mighty pretty: she is usually called Betty. Knipp made us stay in a box and see the dancing preparatory to tomorrow for *The Goblins*, a play of Suckelings[4] not acted these 25 years, which was pretty; and so away thence, pleased with this sight also, and especially kissing of

a repl. 'without'   *b* MS. 'Ball'

1. Observant Franciscans; in this case Portuguese.

2. A tragicomedy by John Fletcher; see above, ii. 80 & n. 3. Song and spectacle appear to have been added to the play on this occasion. (A).

3. Nell Gwyn; according to Downes (p. 3), Mrs Marshall played Celia in earlier productions of this play by the King's company. (A).

4. A comedy by Sir John Suckling, written about 1637 and published in 1647. (A).

Nell; we away, Mr. Pierce and I on foot to his house, the women by coach. In our way we find the Guards of Horse in the street, and hear the occasion to be news that the Seamen are in a mutiny,[1] which put me into a great fright; so away with my wife and Mercer home, preparing against tomorrow night to have Mrs. Pierce and Knipp and a great deal more company to dance. And when I came home, hear of no disturbance there of the seamen, but that one of them[a] being arrested today, others do go and rescue him. So to the office a little, and then home to supper and to my chamber a while, and then to bed.

24. Up, and to the office, full of thoughts how to order the business of our merry meeting tonight. So to the office, where busy all the morning. 《While we were sitting in the morning at the office, we were frighted with news of fire at Sir W. Batten's, by [a] chimney taking fire; and it put me into much fear and trouble, but with a great many hands and pains it was soon stopped.》 At noon home to dinner and presently to the office to despatch my business betimes; and also we sat all[b] the afternoon to examine the loss of the *Bredagh*, which was done by as plain negligence as ever[c] ship was.[2] We being rose and I ending my letters and getting the office swept and a good fire made and abundance of candles lighted, I home, where most of my company come of this end of the town – Mercer and her sister – Mr. Batelier and Pendleton – (my Ladies Pen and Pegg and Mr. Lowder; but they did not stay long, and I believe it was by Sir W. Penn's order, for they had a great mind to have stayed) and also Captain Rolt; and anon, at about 7 or 8 a-clock comes Mr. Harris of the Duke's playhouse and brings Mrs. Pierce with him, and also one dressed like a country-maid, with a straw hatt on,[3] which at first I could not tell who it was, though I expected Knipp – but it was she, coming off the stage just as she[d]

a preceded by blot   b repl. 'after'   c MS. 'if'
                   d MS. 'we'

---

1. Possibly the mutiny of the men of the *York* and *Eagle*: see *CSPD 1666-7*, p. 468.

2. She was lost off the Texel on 15 August 1666; Pepys preserved a clerk's notes of this examination: Rawl. A 195a, ff. 55-7. Cf. *CSPD 1666-7*, p. 469.

3. Impersonations in stage costume were not uncommon. (A).

acted this day in *The Goblins* – a merry jade. Now my house is full, and four fiddlers that play well. Harris I first took to my closet; and I find him a very curious and understanding person in all, pictures and other things – and a man of fine conversation. And so is Rolt. So away with all my company down to the office, and there fell to dancing and continued at [it] an hour or two – there coming Mrs. Anne Jones, a merchant's daughter hard by, who dances well. And all in mighty good humour; and danced with great pleasure, and then sung, and then danced, and then sung many things of three voices, both Harris and Rolt singing their parts excellently. Among other things, Harris sung his Irish song,[1] the strangest in itself and the prettiest sung by him that ever I heard. Then to supper in the office, a cold good supper and wondrous merry. Here was Mrs. Turner also; but poor woman, sad about her lodgings[2] – and also Mrs. Markeham. After supper to dancing again and singing, and so continued till almost 3 in the morning and then with extraordinary pleasure broke up; only, towards morning Knipp fell a little ill, and so my wife home with her to put her to bed, and we continued dancing – and singing;[a] and among other things, our Mercer unexpectedly did happen to sing an Italian song I knew not, of which they two sung the other two parts too, that did almost ravish me and made me in love with her more then ever with her singing. As late as it was, yet Rolt and Harris would go home tonight, and walked it, though I had a bed for them; and it[b] proved dark, and a misly night – and very windy. The company being all gone to their homes, I up with Mrs. Pierce to Knipp, who was in bed; and we waked her and there I handled her breasts and did baiser la and sing a song, lying by her on the bed; and then left my wife to see Mrs. Pierce in bed with[c] her in our best chamber, and so to bed myself – my mind mightily satisfied with all this evening's work, and thinking it to be one of the merriest enjoyments I must look for in the world, and did content myself therefore with the thoughts of it, and so to bed. Only, the Musique did not please me, they not being contented with less then 30s.

a repl. 'among other'   *b* repl. symbol rendered illegible   *c* MS. 'to'

---

1. Unidentified. (A).   2. See below, pp. 38, 63.

25. Lay pretty long; then to the office, where Lord Brouncker and Sir J. Mennes and I did meet, and sat private all the morning about dividing*ᵃ* the Controller's work, according to the late order of Council, between them two and Sir W. Penn. And it troubled me to see the poor honest man, Sir J. Mennes, troubled at it; and yet the King's work cannot be done without it. It was at last friendlily ended, and so up and home to dinner with my wife. This noon I saw the Poll Bill, now printed; wherein I do fear I shall be very deeply concerned, being to be taxed for all my offices and then for my money that I have, and my title as well as my head.¹ It is a very great tax; but yet I do think it is so perplexed it will hardly ever be collected duly. The late invention of Sir G Downing's is continued, of bringing all the money into the Exchequer.² And Sir G. Carteret's 3*d* is turned for all the money of this Act into but a penny per cent, which I am sorry for.³ After dinner to the office again, where Lord Brouncker, W. Batten, and W. Penn and I met to talk again about the Controller's office; and there W. Penn would have a piece of the great office cut out to make an office for him, which I opposed, to the making him very angry;⁴ but I think I shall carry it against him, and then I care not. So, a little troubled at this Fray, I away by coach with my wife, and left her at the New Exchange and I to my Lord Chancellors; and then back, taking up my wife, to my Lord Bellasses and there spoke with Mr. Moone; who tells me that the peace between us and Spayne is, as he hears, concluded on;⁵ which I should be glad of. And so home; and after a little at my office, home to finish my Journall for yesterday and today; and then a little supper and to bed.

a repl. 'diving'

---

1. The act (18–19 Car. II c. 1), passed on 18 January, was now printed as *The poll-bill as to be given in charge* (1666/7). Pepys would in theory be taxed in respect of his offices as Clerk of the Acts, Treasurer for Tangier and Surveyor of Victualling, and also in respect of his title as an 'esquire'. For his assessment, see below, p. 152.

2. See above, vi. 292, n. 3.

3. Sect. xxv of the Poll Act reduced the Treasurer's poundage on all purchases.

4. Cf. above, iii. 41 & n. 3.

5. It was not concluded until 3/13 May.

⟨This day the House hath passed the Bill for the Assessement, which I am glad of[1] – and also our little Bill for giving*a* any one of us in the office the power of Justice of Peace is done as I would have it.⟩[2]

26. Up, and at the office sat all the morning – where among other things, I did the first unkind [thing] that ever I did design to Sir W. Warren. But I did it now to some purpose, to make him sensible how little any friendship shall avail him if he wants mine. I perceive he doth nowadays court much my Lord Brouncker's favour, who never did any man much courtesy at the Board, nor ever will be able – at least, so much as myself. Besides, my Lord would do him a kindness in concurrence with me; but he would have the danger of the thing to be done lie upon me, if there be any danger in it (in drawing up a letter to Sir W. Warren's advantage); which I do not like, nor*b* will endure. I was, I confess, very angry, and will venture the loss of Sir W. Warren's kindnesses rather then he shall have any man's friendship in greater esteem then mine.[3]

At noon home to dinner; and after dinner to the office again and there all the afternoon. And at night poor Mrs. Turner came and walked in the garden for my advice about her husband and her, relating to my Lord Brouncker's late proceedings with them;[4] and I do give her the best I can, but yet can lay asides some ends of my own in what advice I do give her. So she being gone, I to make an end of my letters; and so home to supper and to bed – Balty lodging here with my brother, he being newly returned from mustering in the River.

a repl. 'mak'-   *b* repl. 'will'

---

1. *CJ*, viii. 683; an Eleven Months Assessment on land, to produce £1¼m., which became law on 8 February. There had been 'hot disputes' on 19 January about the clause which reserved £38,000 of its proceeds for the payment of seamen: Carte 46, f. 440*v*.

2. This was 18–19 Car. II c. 12, amending the previous act of 1664 (16 Car. II c. 5) which had similarly empowered any two members of the Board. Cf. above, iv. 82 & n. 1.

3. Warren and the Board were now negotiating about masts: see Tanner 45, ff. 68, 133, 135, etc. For his newly-sprung friendship with Brouncker, see above, p. 12. His estrangement from Pepys lasted until December.

4. Brouncker had taken over the Turners' house: below, pp. 38, 63.

27. *Lords day.* Up betimes; and leaving my wife to go by coach to hear Mr. Frampton preach, which I have a mighty desire she should – I down to the Old Swan, and there to Michell and stayed while he and she dressed themselfs; and here had a baiser or two of her, whom I love mightily. And then took them in a Sculler (being by some means or other disappointed of my own boat)[1] to White-hall; and so sent them to Westminster. Sir W. Coventry, Brouncker, and I all the morning together, discoursing of the office businesses, and glad of the Controller's business being likely to be put into better order then formerly. And did discourse of many good things, but especially of having something done to bringing the Surveyors matters into order also. Thence I up to the King's closet[2] and there heard a good Anthemne and discoursed with several people here about business; among others, with Lord Bellasses; and so from one to another after sermon till the King had almost dined; and then home with Sir G Carteret and dined with him, being mightily ashamed of my not having seen my Lady Jemimah so long, and my wife not at all yet since she come – but she shall soon do it. I thence to Sir Ph. Warwicke by appointment, to meet Lord Bellasses;[3] and up to his chamber, but find him unwilling to discourse of business on Sundays; so did not enlarge, but took leave and went down and sat in a low room reading Erasmus *de scribendis Epistolis,* a very good book; especially, one letter of advice to a Courtier most true and good – which made me once resolve to tear out the two leaves that it was writ in – but I forebore it.[4] By and by comes Lord Bellasses; and then he and I up*a* again to Sir Ph. Warwick and had much discourse of our Tanger business, but no hopes of getting any money. Thence I through the garden into the parke, and there met with Roger Pepys and he and I to

a repl. 'home'

---

1. The office boat, which could be used on Sundays, when other boats were hard to come by.

2. Cf. above, i. 276 & n. 5.

3. Governor of Tangier.

4. Pepys kept a copy of *De conscribendis epistolis* (Leyden, 1645; PL 27) in which this letter ('Scribis te nolen-

tem . . .') under the title *Aliud exemplum de vita aulica* begins at p. 480. The mutilation of books and MSS was not uncommon: Pepys made up the medieval section of his 'Calligraphical Collection' (PL 2981) largely from snippets cut from MSS.

walk in the Pell Mell. I find by him that the House of Parliament continues full of ill humours; and he seems to dislike those that are troublesome more then needs. And doth say how in their late Poll Bill, which cost so much time – the Yeamonry, and endeed two-thirds of the nation, are left out to be taxed.[1] That there is not effectual provision*a* enough made for collecting of the money. And then, that after a man his goods are distrained and sold, and the over-plus returned, I am to have ten days to make my complaint of being over-rated if there be cause when my goods are sold, and that is too late. These things they are resolved to look into again, and mend them before they rise; which they expect at furthest on Thursdy next. Here we met with Mr. May,[2] and he and we to talk of several things, of building and such like matters; and so walked to White-hall and there I showed my Cosen Roger the Duchesse of York sitting*b* in state while her own mother stands by her.[3] He had a desire and I showed*c* him my Lady Castlemayne, which he approves to be very handsome, and wonders that she cannot be as good within as she is fair without. Her little black* boy came by him; and a dog being in his way, the little boy called to the dog: "Pox of this dog!" "Now," says he, blessing himself, "would I whip this child till the blood came if it were my child!" – and I believe he would. But he doth by no means like the liberty of the Court, and did come with expectation to find*d* them playing at Cards tonight, though Sunday; for such stories he is told, but*e* how true I know not.[4]

a repl. 'por'-   b repl. 'set'-   c preceded by blot
    d preceded by blot   e repl. 'by'

1. The poll bill (q.v. above, p. 30 & n. 1) had provoked lengthy debates as to who should be included. An explanatory act (18–19 Car. II c. 6) was passed on 8 February a few days before the act was to come into effect, but did not cover all the criticisms (especially of sect. xix) which Pepys here reports. Roger Pepys had been appointed one of the poll-tax commissioners for Cambridgeshire.

2. Hugh May, Deputy-Surveyor of the King's Works.

3. The rules governing the rare situation resulting from the marriage of a commoner into the royal family were strictly enforced. Ailesbury later wrote that the Duchess never called Clarendon father, and that the Earl himself was guilty of a solecism in addressing her in letters as daughter: *Memoirs* (ed. Buckley), i. 346.

4. On Sunday 17 February Pepys himself saw gaming at court.

After walking up and down the Court with him, it being now dark and past 6 at night, I walked to the Swan in the Palace yard and there with much ado did get a waterman; and so I sent for the Michells and they came, and their father Howlett and his wife with them, and there we drank; and so into the boat – poor Betty's head akeing. We home by water, a fine moonshine and warm night, it having been also a very summers day for warmth. I did get her hand to me under my cloak and did oter sa gans, but ella ne voudroit tocar mi cosa today, whatever the matter was, and I was loath to contrendre her to faire, de*ª* peur qu'elle faisait son mari prendre notice thereof. So there we parted at their house, and he walked almost home with me; and then I home and to supper, and to read a little and to bed. My wife tells me Mr. Frampton is gone to sea,[1] and so she lost her labour today in thinking to hear him preach – which I am sorry for.

28. Up, and down to the Old Swan and there drank at Michells and saw Betty, and so took boat and to the Temple; and thence to my tailor's and other places about business in my way to Westminster,*ᵇ* where I spent the morning at the Lords' House door, to hear the conference between the two Houses about my Lord Mordant, of which there was great expectations – many hundreds of people coming to hear it.[2] But when they came, the Lords did insist upon my Lord Mordant's having leave to sit upon a stool uncovered within their Barr and that he should have counsel; which the Commons would not suffer, but desired*ᶜ* leave to report their Lordshipps resolution to the House of Commons, and so parted for this day; which troubled me, I having by this means lost the whole day. Here I hear from Mr. Hayes that Prince Rupert is very bad still; and so bad,

a repl. same symbol   *b* repl. 'Wh'-
c MS. 'discerned'

---

1. Robert Frampton was on his way to Aleppo, where he served as chaplain to the Levant Company (with intervals at home), 1665–70. He had just been married in England, but now chose to return to Aleppo on hearing that the plague had broken out there: *DNB*.

2. *LJ*, xii. 93–4; for the case, see above, vii. 386 & n. 2. The public were admitted to conferences but not to debates.

that he doth now yield to be trapan'd. It seems, as Dr. Clerke also tells me, it is a clap of the pox which he got about twelve year ago – and hath eaten to his head and come through his Scull; so his Scull must be opened and there is great fear of him.[1]

Much work I find there is to do in the two Houses in a little time, and much difference there is between the two Houses in many things to be reconciled; as, in the Bill for examining our accounts – Lord Mordants [business] – Bill for building the City – and several others. A little before noon I went to the Swan and eat a bit of meat, thinking I should have had occasion to [have] stayed*a* long at the House, but I did not; but so home by coach, calling at Broadstreete and taking the goldsmith home with me, and paid him 15*l* 15*s*. 00*d*. for my silver standish. He tells me gold holds up its price still, and did desire me to let him have what old 20*s* pieces I have, and he would give me 3*s*–2*d* change for each. He gone, I to the office, where business all the afternoon. And at night comes Mr. Gawden at my desire to me, and tomorrow I shall pay him some money and shall see what present he will make me, the hopes of which do make me to part with my money out of [my] Chest; which I should not otherwise do, but lest this alteration in the Controller's office should occasion my losing my concernment in the victualling and so he have no more need of me. He gone, I to the office again, having come thence home with him to talk; and so after a little more business, I to supper; and then sent for Mercer and begun to teach her *It is decreed*,[2] which will please me well; and so after supper and reading a little, and my wife's cutting*b* off my hair short, which is grown too long upon my crown of my head, I to bed.

I met this day in Westminster hall Sir W. Batten and W. Penn; and the latter, since our falling out the other day, doth look mighty reservedly upon me; and still he shall do so for me, for I will be hanged before I seek to him, unless I see I need it.

29. Up, and to the office all the morning, where Sir W. Penn and I look much askewe one upon another, though afterward

---

a repl. symbol rendered illegible   *b* repl. 'cut'-

---

1. See above, vi. 12 & n. 2; below,   2. See above, vii. 91 & n. 4.   (E). p. 41 & nn.

business made us speak friendly enough; but yet we hate one another. At noon home to dinner and then to the office, where all the afternoon expecting Mr. Gawden to come for some money I am to pay him; but he comes not, which makes me think he is considering whether it be necessary to make the present he hath promised[1] – it being possible this alteration in the Controllers duty may make my[a] place in the victualling unnecessary – so that I am a little troubled at it. Busy till late at night at the office; and Sir W. Batten came to me and tells me that there is news upon the Exchange today that my Lord Sandwiches Coach and the French Embassador's at Madrid meeting and contending for the way, they shot my Lord's Postillion, and another man dead and we have killed 25 of theirs, and that my Lord is well. How true this is I cannot tell, there being no news of it at all at Court, as I am told late by one come thence; so that I hope it is not so.[2]

By and by comes Mrs. Turner to me to make her complaint of her sad usage she receives from my Lord Brouncker; that he thinks much she hath not already got another house, though he himself hath imployed her night and day, ever since his first mention of the matter, to make part of her house ready for him as he ordered, and promised she should stay till she had fitted herself – by which, and what discourse I remember he had of the business before Sir W. Coventry on Sunday last, I perceive he is a rotten-hearted false man as any else I know, even as Sir W. Penn himself; and therefore I must beware of him accordingly – and I hope I shall. I did pity the woman with all my heart, and gave her the best counsel I could; and so falling to other discourse, I made her laugh and merry, as sad as she came to me; so that I perceive no passion in a woman can be lasting long. And so parted, and I home and there teaching my girl Barker part of my song *It is decreed*, which she will sing prettily; and so after supper[b] to[c] bed.

a repl. 'it'   *b* repl. 'then'   *c* repl. 'then'

---

1. See above, vii. 402.
2. It was untrue: see below, pp. 37, 42. Relations with the French in Madrid were bad, since the English aims in the peninsula (a trade treaty with Spain and a peace between Spain and Portugal) were inimical to French interests.

30. *Fast day for the King's death.*[1] I all the morning at my chamber, making up my month's accounts; which I did before dinner to my thorough content, and find myself but a small gainer this month, having no manner of profits but just my salary. But blessed be God that I am*ᵃ* able to save out of that, living as I do. So to dinner. Then to my chamber all the afternoon; and in the evening my wife and I and Mercer and Barker to little Michells, walked, with some neats' tongues and cake and wine; and there sat with the little Couple with great pleasure, and talked and eat and drank and saw their little house, which is very pretty – and I much pleased therewith; and so walked home about 8 at night, it being a little Mooneshine and fair weather; and so into the garden and with Mercer sang till my wife put me in mind of its being a fast-day, and so I was sorry for it and stopped; and home to Cards a while, and had opportunity para besar Mercer several times, and so to bed.

31. Up, and to the office, where we met and sat all the morning. At noon home to dinner; and by and by Mr. Osborne comes from Mr. Gawden and takes money and notes for 4000*l* and leaves me acknowledgment for 4800*l* and odd pounds; implying as if D. Gawden would give the 800*l* between Povy and myself; but how he will divide it I know not till I speak with him, so that my content is not yet full in that business. In the evening stepped out to Sir Rob. Viners to get the money ready upon my notes to D. Gawden, and there hear that Mr. Temple[2] is very ill. I met on the Change with Captain Cocke, who tells me he hears no certainty of the business of Madrid, how our Embassador and the French met, and says that two or three of my Lord's men and twenty-one of the Frenchman's are killed, but nothing at Court of it. He fears the next year's service through the badness of our counsels at White-hall; but that if they were wise and the King would mind his business, he might do what he would yet. The Parliament is not yet up, being finishing some Bills. So home and to the office, and late home to supper and to talk with my wife, with pleasure, and to bed. I met this

a repl. 'have'

1. See above, ii. 26, n. 1.   2. James Temple, Vyner's clerk.

evening at Sir R Viners our Mr. Turner, who I find in a melancholy condition about his being removed*a* out of his house; but I
find him so silly and so false, that I dare not tell how to trust any
advice to him, and therefore did speak only generals to him.
But I doubt his condition is very miserable, and do pity his family.
Thus the month ends. Myself in very good health, and content
of mind in my family.* All our heads full in the office at this
dividing of the Controller's duty, so that I am in some doubt
how it may prove to intrench upon my benefits; but it cannot be
much. The Parliament upon breaking up – having given the
King money with much ado and great heats, and neither side
pleased, neither King nor them. The imperfection of the Pole
Bill, which must be mended before they rise, there being several
horrible oversights to the prejudice of the King, is a certain sign
of the care anybody hath of the King's business. Prince Rupert
very ill, and to be trepan'd on Saturday next. Nobody knows
who commands the fleet next year, or endeed whether we shall
have a fleet or no. Great preparations in Holland and France.
And the French have lately taken Antego[1] from us, which vexes
us. I am in a little care, through my at last putting a great deal
of money out of my hands again into the King's, upon tallies for
Tanger; but the interest which I wholly lost while in my trunk
is a temptation while things look safe, as they do in some measure
for six months I think, and I would venture but little longer.

a   repl. 'rev'-

---

1. Antigua (Leeward Is.); taken in
November 1666 by the French; re-
occupied by the English in the early
spring of 1667, and restored to them
by the Treaty of Breda in July 1667.

FEBRUARY

1. Up, and to the office, where I was all the morning doing business. At noon home to dinner; and after dinner down by water, though it was a thick misty^a and raining day, and walked to Deptford from Redriffe and there to Bagwells by appointment – where the moher erat within expecting mi venida. And did sensa alguna difficulty monter los degres and lie, comme jo desired it, upon lo lectum;^b and there I did la cosa con much voluptas. Je^c besa also her venter and cons and saw the poyle thereof. She would seem alguns veces very religious, but yet did permit me to hazer todo esto et quicquid amplius volebam. By and by su marido came in, and there, without any notice taken by him, we discoursed of our business of getting him the new ship building by Mr. Deane,[1] which I shall do for him. Thence by and by, after little talk, I to the yard and spoke with some of the officers, but stayed but little; and the new Clerk of the Cheque, Fownes, did walk to Redriffe back with me. I perceive he is a very child, and is led by the nose by Cowly[2] and his kinsman that was his clerk; but I did make him understand his duty and put both understanding and spirit into him, so that I hope he will do well. 《Much surprised to hear this day at Deptford that Mrs. Batters is going already to be married to him that is now the Captain of her husband's ship[3] – she seemed the most passionate mourner in the world. But I believe it cannot be true.》 Thence by water to Billinsgate and thence to the Old Swan and there took boat, it being now night, to Westminster; there to the Hall and find Doll Lane, and con ella I went to the Bell tavern, and ibi^d jo did do what I would con ella as well as I could, she sedento sobra una^e chair and

---

a MS. 'masty' b repl. 'c'- c repl. 'je'
d repl. 'ibi' e repl. 'the'

---

1. The *Rupert*; William Bagwell (now master-carpenter of the *Providence*) was as a result sent away to Harwich as ship's carpenter. The warrant passed on 12 February: PRO, Adm. 106/14, f. 370r.

2. Thomas Cowley, his predecessor.
3. The *Joseph* fireship; her husband's death had occurred on the previous 17 December.

making some little resistance – but all with much content, and jo tena much plazer cum ista.   There parted, and I by coach home and to the office, where pretty late doing business; and then home and merry with my wife, and to supper.   My brother and I did play, he the bass and I upon my viallin, which I have not seen out of the case now I think these three years or more, having lost the key and now forced to find an expedient to open it. Then to bed.

2.   Up, and to the office.   This day I hear that Prince Rupert is to be trepanned – God give good issue to it.   Sir W. Penn looks upon me and I on him, and speak about business together at the table well enough, but no friendship or intimacy since our late difference about his closet,¹ nor do I desire to have any.   At noon dined well, and my brother and I to write over once more with my own hand my Catalogue of books,² while he reads to me.   After something of that done, and dined, I to the office, where all the afternoon till night busy.   At night, having done all my office matters, I home, and my brother and I to go on with my Catalogue, and so to supper.   Mrs. Turner came to me this night again to condole her condition and the ill usage*a* she receives from my Lord Brouncker;   which I could never have expected from him – and shall be a good caution to me while I live.   She gone, I to supper;   and then to read a little and to bed.   This night comes home my new Silver Snuffe=dish which I do give myself for my closet;   which is all I purpose to bestow in plate of myself or shall need many a day, if I can keep what I have. So to bed.   I am very well pleased this night with reading a poem I brought home with me last night from Westminster hall, of Driden's upon the present war – a very good poem.³

3.   *Lords day.*   Up, and with Sir W. Batten and W. Penn by coach to White-hall;   and there to Sir W. Coventry's*b* chamber

a repl. 'usual'   *b* repl. 'Penn's'

---

1. See above, p. 30 & n. 4.
2. See above, vii. 412, n. 2.
3. *Annus Mirabilis: the year of won-ders, 1666; an historical poem* (1667);

licensed for publication 21 January (*Trans. Stat. Reg.*, ii. 373);   not in the PL.

and there stayed till he was ready – talking; and among other things, of the Princes being trepanned,[1] which was in doing just as we passed through the Stone Gallery, we asking at the door of his lodgings and were told so. We are all full of wishes for the good success – though I dare say but few do really concern ourselfs for him in our hearts. Up to the Duke of York, and with him did our business we come about; and among other things, resolve upon a meeting at the office tomorrow morning, Sir W. Coventry to be there to determine of all things necessary for the setting of Sir W. Penn to work in his victualling business. This did awake in me some thoughts of what might in discourse fall out touching my imployment – and did give me some apprehension of trouble. Having done here, and after our laying our necessities for money open to the Duke of York, but nothing obtained concerning it – we parted; and I with others into the House and there hear that the work is done to the Prince in a few minutes, without any pain at all to him, he not knowing when it was done. It was performed by Moulins.[2] Having cut the outward table,[3] as they call[a] it, they find the inner all corrupted, so as it came out without any force; and their fear is that the whole inside[b] of his head[c] is corrupted like that – which doth yet make them afeared of him; but no ill accident appeared in the doing of the thing, but all with all imaginable success; as[d] Sir Alexander Frazier[4] did tell me himself, I asking him, who is very kind to me. I to the Chapel a little; but hearing nothing, did take a turn into the park, and then back to Chapel and heard a very good Anthemne to my heart's delight; and then[e] to Sir G. Carteret's to dinner, and before dinner did walk with him alone a good while and from him hear our case likely, for all these acts, to be bad for money; which troubles me, the year spending so fast. And he tells me that he believes the Duke of York will go to sea

a repl. 'n'-   *b* repl. 'in'-   *c* repl. 'b'-
d repl. 'which my'   *e* preceded by blot

---

1. He was being operated on for a head wound: see above, vi. 12, n. 2.
2. James Molins (Mullins), Surgeon to St Thomas's and St Bartholomew's hospitals.
3. The tables are two dense bony layers of the skull.

4. Physician to the King. But a second trepanning was necessary shortly afterwards. In convalescence Rupert amused himself by making instruments for his surgeons to use in dressing his wounds: *CSPD 1666–7*, p. 523.

with the fleet – which I am sorry for in respect to his person, but yet there is no person in condition to command the fleet, now the captains are grown so great, but him – it being impossible for anybody else but him to command any order or discipline among them.[1] He tells me there is nothing at all in the late discourse about my Lord Sandwich and the French Embassadors meeting and contending for the way; which I wonder at, to see the confidence of report without any ground. By and by to dinner, where very good company. Among other discourse, we talked much of Nostradamus his prophecy of these times and the burning of the City of London, some of whose verses are put into Bookers Almanac this year.[a2] And Sir G. Carteret did tell a story, how at his death he did make the town swear that he should never be dug up, or his tomb opened, after he was buried; but they did after 60 years do it, and upon his breast they found a plate of brasse, saying what a wicked and unfaithful people the people of that place were, who after so many vows should disturb and open him such a day and year and hour – which if true, is very strange.[3] Then we fell to talk of the burning of the City; and my Lady Carteret herself did tell us how abundance of pieces of burnt papers were cast by the wind as far as Cranborne;[4] and among others, she took up one, or had one brought her to see, which was a little bit of paper that had been printed, wherein there remained no more nor less then these

a repl. same symbol badly formed

---

1. Cf. above, vii. 409–10.

2. John Booker in his *Telescopium Uranicum for MDCLXVII* [1666, n.p.] quoted Quatrain 51 from no. 2 of Nostradamus's *Centuries*: 'Le sang du Juste a Londres fera faute / Bruslez par foudres, de Vingt Trois les Six / Le Dame Antique, cherra de place haute / De mesme secte plusieurs seront occis'. Booker added that this was of all prophecies 'the most remarkable, and of it self able to stop the mouth of all Astrologomastiges. I shall forbear the translation and exposition of the same, I shall leave it to

posterity to be admired at'. Nostradamus (Michel de Notredame) was the most eminent of 16th-century astrologers. Pepys kept a copy of the work from which this extract came: *Les vrayes centuries et propheties*, Amsterdam, 1668 (PL 134), but not Booker's work.

3. He had died at Salon (nr Aix-en-Provence) in 1566, and had at his own wish been immured in the masonry of the church of the Cordeliers there. I have not traced this story elsewhere.

4. Her house in Windsor Forest.

words: *Time is; it^a is done.* After dinner I went and took a turn into the park, and then took boat and away home; and there to my chamber and to read, but did receive some letters from Sir W. Coventry touching the want of victuals to Kempthornes fleet, going to the Streights and now in the Downes which did trouble me, he saying that this disappointment might prove fatal[1] – and the more because Sir W. Coventry doth intend to come to the office upon business tomorrow morning, and I shall not know what answer to give him. This did mightily trouble my mind; how[ever], I fell to read a little in Hakewills *apology*, and did satisfy myself mighty fair in the truth of the saying that the world doth not grow old at all, but is in as good condition in all respects as ever it was as to Nature.[2] I continued reading this book with great pleasure till supper; and then ⟨to⟩ bed but sooner then ordinary, for rising betimes in the morning tomorrow. So after reading my usual vows, to bed – my mind full of trouble against tomorrow; and did not sleep any good time of the night for thoughts of tomorrow morning's trouble.

4. I up, with my head troubled to think of the issue of this morning; so made ready and to the office, where Mr. Gawden comes and he and I discourse the business well; and thinks I shall get off well[b] enough, but I do by Sir W. Coventry's silence conclude that he is not satisfied in my management of my place[3] and the charge it puts the King to – which I confess I am not in present[c] condition, through my late laziness, to give any good

---

a l.h. repl. s.h. 'is, it'   *b* repl. 'with'   *c* repl. same symbol

---

1. Some supplies had already been sent to him at the Nore; he had to wait at Plymouth for others: *CSPD 1666-7*, pp. 478, 503.

2. Dr George Hakewill's *An apologie or declaration of the power and providence of God in the gouernment of the world* was first published in 1627; Pepys retained the 1635 edition (PL 2016). It was an important contribution to the early 17th-century controversy about the 'decay of nature'. Hakewill argued that 'although the

Creator and Disposer of all things hath left all Particulars and Individuals, under the circle of the Moone, to the stroake of *Time* and *Death*; yet by His powerfull Hand He holdeth backe the Sythe of *Time* from destroying or impayring the Universe: Though the same Hand shall at last destroy the Whole by *Fire*'.

3. That of Surveyor-General of the Victualling, which Pepys did not resign until 28 July 1667, at the end of the war.

answer to.   But here doth D. Gawden give me a good cordiall this morning, by telling me that he doth give me 5 of the 800*l* on his account remaining in my hands*ᵃ* to myself, for the service I do him in my victualling business, and 100*l* for*ᵇ* my perticular share of the profits of my Tanger imployment as*ᶜ* Treasurer. This doth begin to make my heart glad, and I did dissemble it the better; for when Sir W. Coventry did come and the rest met, I did appear unconcerned*ᵈ* and did give him answer pretty satisfactory which he asked me.   So that I did get off this meeting without any ground lost, but rather a great deal gained, by interposing that which did belong to my duty to do; and neither W. Coventry nor W. Penn did oppose anything thereunto, which did make my heart very glad.   All*ᵉ* the morning at this work, Sir W. Penn making a great deal of do for the fitting him in his setting ⟨out⟩ in his imployment;[1] and I do yield to every trouble that he gives me without any contradiction.   Sir W. Coventry being gone, we at noon to dinner to Sir W. Penn, he inviting me and my wife; and there a pretty good dinner, intended endeed for Sir W. Coventry, but he would not stay.   So here I was mighty merry and all our differences*ᶠ* seemingly blown over; though he knows, if he be not a fool, that I love not him; and I*ᵍ* do the like, that he hates me.   As soon as dined, my wife and I out to the Dukes playhouse and there saw *Heraclius*,[2] an excellent play, to my extraordinary content; and the more from the house being very full, and great company; among others, Mrs. Steward, very fine, with her locks done up with puffes,[3] as my wife calls them; and several other*ʰ* great ladies had their hair so, though I do not like it; but my wife doth mightily – but it is only because she sees it the fashion.   Here I saw my Lord Rochester and his lady, Mrs. Mallett, who hath after all this ado married him;[4] and, as I hear some say in the pit, it is a great act of charity, for he hath no estate.   But it was pleasant to see how

a repl. 'minds'   *b* repl. 'in my'   *c* repl. full stop
    d repl. 'uncern'-   *e* repl. 'at'   *f* repl. 's'-
        g repl. 'he do'   *h* preceded by blot

1. As Mennes's assistant in the Comptroller's business.
2. A translation of Pierre Corneille's *Heraclius*: see above, v. 78 & n. 1. (A).
3. Artificial rolls of hair.
4. He had married her on 29 January 1667; in 1665 he had tried to abduct her (see above, vi. 110 & n. 2).

everybody rose up when my Lord Jo. Butler, the Duke of Ormonds son, came into the pit toward the end of the play, who was a servant to Mrs. Mallet, and now smiled upon her and she on him. I had sitting next*a* to me a woman the likest my Lady Castlemayne that ever I saw anybody like another; but she is a whore I believe, for she is acquainted with every fine fellow and called them by their name, Jacke and Tom – and before the end of the play fished to another place. Mightily pleased with the play, we home by coach; and there a little to the office and then to my chamber and there finished my Catalogue of my books with my own hand; and so to supper and to bed, and had a good night's rest,*b* the last night's being troublesome; but now my heart light and I full of resolution of standing close to my business.

5. Up, and to the office, where all the morning doing business, and then home to dinner. Heard this morning that the Prince is much better and hath good rest. All the talk is that my Lord Sandwich hath perfected the peace with*c* Spain; which is very good, if true.[1] Sir H. Cholmly was with me this morning, and told me of my Lord Bellasses base dealings with him, by getting him to give him great gratuities, to near 2000*l*, for his friendship in the business of the Molle; and hath been lately underhand endeavouring to bring another man into his place as Governor, so as to receive his money of Sir H. Cholmly for nothing.[2] Dined at home; and after dinner came Mrs. Daniel and her sister and stayed and talked a little, and then I to the office; and after setting my things in order at the office, I abroad with my wife and little Betty Michell and took them, against my vows but I will make good my forfeit, to the King's house to show them a play, *The Chances*:[3] a good play I find it – and the actors most

a repl. 'm'- *b* repl. 'lodging' *c* repl. 'of'-

---

1. The news was premature: see below, pp. 190 & n. 1, 453 & n. 2.
2. Cholmley had hoped to become Governor. Belasyse was in 1668 succeeded by the Earl of Middleton.
3. A comedy by John Fletcher, written about 1617 and published in 1647. The production which Pepys saw probably used the revision of the play made by the 2nd Duke of Buckingham, and published in 1682. It is generally agreed that Buckingham improved both the structure and the characterisation of the play. (A).

good in it.[1]   And pretty to hear Knipp sing in the play very properly, *All night I Weepe*[2] – and sung it admirably.   The whole play pleases me well – and most of all, the sight of many fine ladies; among other, my Lady Castlemaine and Mrs. Middleton; the latter of the two hath also a very excellent face and body I think.   Thence by coach to the New Exchange and there laid out money, and I did give Betty Michell[a] two pair of gloves and a dressing-box.   And so home in the dark over the ruins with a link.   I was troubled with my pain, having got a bruise on my right testicle, I know not how.   But this I did make good use of to make my wife shift sides with me, and I did come to sit avec Betty Michell[b] and there had her mano, which ella did give me very frankly now, and did hazer whatever I voudrais avec la – which did plazer me grandement.   And so set her at home, with my mind mighty glad of what I have prevailed for so far; and so home and to the office and did my business there, and then home to supper; and after to set some things right in my chamber and so to bed.   This morning, before I went to the office, there came to me Mr. Young and Whistler, Flaggmakers, and with mighty earnestness did present me with and press me to take a box, wherein I could not guess there was less then 100*l* in gold.   But I do wholly refuse it, and did not at last take it – the truth is, not thinking them safe men to receive such a gratuity from nor knowing any considerable courtesy that ever I did do them – but desirous to keep myself free from their reports and to have it in my power to say I had refused their offer.

6.   Up, lying a little long in bed, and by water to White-hall; and there find the Duke of York gone out, he being in haste to go to the Parliament, and so all my Brethren were gone to the House too.   So I to Sir Ph. Warwicke's about my Tanger business and then to Westminster hall; and walked up and down and hear that the Prince doth still rest well by day and night, and

a   name in s.h.   *b*   name in s.h.

---

1. According to Downes (p. 16), the part of Don John in this play was one of Charles Hart's best performances. (A).

2. The song was probably inserted for Constancia's off-stage singing in II, 2 or IV, 3.   It is not in the text of the play or in that of the Duke of Buckingham's alteration. (E).

out of pain, so as great hopes is conceived of him; though I did
meet Dr. Clerke and Mr. Pierce and they do say they believe
he will not recover it, they*a* supposing that his whole head
within is eaten by this corruption which appeared in this piece
of the inner table.[1] Up to the Parliament doore and there discoursed with Roger Pepys, who goes out of town this week, the
Parliament rising this week also. So down to the hall and there
spied Betty Michell; and so I sent for ⟨burnt⟩ wine to Mrs.
Michells and there did drink with the two mothers,[2] and by that
means with Betty, poor girl, whom I love with all my heart.
And God forgive me, it did make me stay longer and hover all
the morning up and down the Hall to buscar occasions para
hablar con ella – but yo no podra. So home by water and to
dinner, and then to the office, where we sat upon Denis Gawden's
accounts; and before night I rose and by water to White-hall
to attend the Council, but they sat not today; so to Sir W.
Coventry's chamber and find him within and with a letter from
the Downes in his hands,[3] telling the loss of the *St. Patricke*,
coming from Harwich in her way to Portsmouth and would
needs chase two ships (she having the Malago fireship in company) which from English colours put up Dutch, and he would
clap*b* on board the Viceadmirall; and after long dispute, the
Admirall came on the other side of him, and both together took
him – our fireship (Seely) not coming in to fire all three, but
came away leaving her in their possession, and carried away by
them – a ship built at Bristoll the last year, of fifty guns and
upward – and most excellent good ship.[4] This made him very
melancholy. I to talk of our wants of money, but I do find
he is not pleased with that discourse but grieves to hear it, and
doth seem to think that Sir G. Carteret doth not mind the getting
of money with the same good cheer that he did heretofore. Nor
do I think he hath the same reason.[5] Thence to Westminster-

---

a repl. 'supposing'   *b* repl. 'fall'

1. See above, p. 41 & nn.
2. Mrs Howlett and Mrs Mitchell, mothers of Betty Mitchell and of her husband.
3. Cf. M. Lodge to Williamson, Deal, 5 February: PRO, SP 29/190, no. 108; summary in *CSPD 1666–7*,

p. 496. For details of the action, see ib., p. 499.
4. Capt. William Seeley was con-demned at the end of the month to be shot for cowardice: ib., p. 537.
5. See above, p. 30 & n. 3.

hall, thinking to see Betty Michell, she staying there all night;
and had hopes to get her out al[one], but missed; and so away by
coach home and to Sir W. Batten's to tell my bad news; and
then to the office and home to supper, where Mrs. Hewers
was; and after supper and she gone, W. Hewer with me, talking
very late of the ill manner of Sir G. Carteret's accounts being
kept, and in what a sad condition he would be if either Fenn or
Wayth should break or die.[1]   And I am resolved to take some
time to tell Sir G. Carteret or my Lady of it, I do love them so
well and their family.   So to bed – my pain pretty well gone.

7.   Lay long with pleasure with my wife; and then up and to
the office, where all the morning; then home to dinner, and
before dinner I went into my green dining room; and there
talking with my brother upon matters relating to his Journy to
Brampton tomorrow and giving him good counsel about spending that time which he shall stay in the country with my father,
I looking another way, I heard him fall down, and turned my
head and he was fallen down all along upon the ground, dead –
which did put me into a great fright; and to see my brotherly
love, I did presently lift him up from [the] ground, he being as
pale as death.   And being upon his legs, he did presently come
to himself, and said he had something[a] come into his stomach,
very hot; he knew not what it was, nor ever had such a fit
before.[2]   I never was so frighted but once, when my wife was ill
at Ware upon the road.[3]   And I did continue trembling a good
while, and ready to weep to see him, he continuing mighty pale

a repl. 'a'

1. Carteret used the credit of his
principal assistants (Fenn and Waith)
as well as his own.   The disorderli-
ness of his accounts was later criticised
by the Brooke House Committee
appointed in December 1667 to enquire into the war finances: Grey, i.
170.
   2. Dr C. E. Newman writes: 'The
faint was almost certainly one of the
kind (alarming but harmless) now
called "vaso-vagal attacks", and

caused by a temporary failure of the
blood supply to the brain.   Raising
the patient to his feet was probably the
worst way of dealing with him.   The
hot sensation may, just possibly, have
been the sign of a minor anginal
attack; more probably it was caused
by gastric juice running back up the
oesophagus.'
   3. On 14 September 1663: 'a great
trial of my true love and passion for
her' (above, iv. 307).

all dinner, and melancholy, that I was loath to let him take his journey tomorrow. But begun to be pretty well; and after dinner my wife and Barker fell to singing, which pleased me pretty well, my wife taking mighty pains and pride that she shall come to trill;* and endeed, I think she will. So to the office and there all the afternoon late doing business; and then home and find my brother pretty well. So to write a letter to my Lady Sandwich for him to carry, I having not writ to her a great while.[1] Then to supper and so to bed. I did this night give him 20*s* for books and as much for his pocket, and 15*s* to carry him down. And so to bed. Poor fellow, he is so melancholy and withal, my wife says, harmless, that I begin to love him, and would be loath he should not do well.

8. This morning my brother John came up to my*ᵃ* bedside and took his leave of us, going this day*ᵇ* to Brampton. My wife loves him mightily, as one that is pretty harmless; and I do begin to fancy him from yesterday's accident, it troubling me to think I should be left without a*ᶜ* brother or son, which is the first time that ever I had thoughts of that kind in my life. He gone, I up and to the office, where we sat upon the Victualler's accounts all the morning. At noon Lord Brouncker, W. Batten, W. Penn and myself to the Sun in Leadenhall-street to dinner, where an exceeding*ᵈ* good dinner and good discourse. Sir W. Batten comes this morning from the House, where the King hath prorogued this Parliament to October*ᵉ* next – I am glad they are up. The Bill for Accounts was not offered, the party being willing to let it fall – but the King did tell them he expected it.[2] They are parted with great heart-burnings, one party against the other.

a MS. 'his'   *b* repl. 'to'   *c* repl. 'my'
d preceded by blot   *e* repl. 'the'

1. Pepys's s.h. copy is in Rawl. A 195a, f. 167r; translated and printed in Smith, i. 115+. 'As for court matters . . . they seem to me just that they have always been – that ladies lie longest in bed, and govern all when they are up.'
2. *LJ*, xii. 111. The bill providing for examination of accounts (q.v. above, vii. 400 & n. 1) was now abandoned, the Commons alleging that the Lords' amendments made it unworkable: see the debates of 7, 8 February in Milward, pp. 81, 82. The scheme was revived in another form (as the Brooke House Committee) at the end of the year: see below, p. 559 & n. 2.

Pray God bring them hereafter together in better temper. It is said that the King doth entend himself in this interval to take away my Lord Mordants' government, so as to do something[a] to appease the House against they come together, and let them see he will do that of his own accord which is fit, without their forcing him.[1]   And that he will have his Commission for Accounts go on[2] – which will be good things.

At dinner we talked much of Cromwell, all saying he was a brave fellow and did owe his Crowne he got to himself as much as any man that ever got one.[3]

Thence to the office and there begun the accounts which Sir W. Penn by his late imployment hath examined;[b] but beginning to examine it in the old manner, a clerk to read the petty-warrants, my Lord Brouncker upon very good ground did except against it and would not suffer him to go on.   This being W. Penn's clerk, he took it in snuff, and so hot they grew upon it that my Lord Brouncker left the office.   He gone, W. Penn ranted like a devil, saying that nothing but ignorance could do this.   I was pleased at heart all this while.   At last moved to have my Lord Brouncker desired to return, which he did, and I read[c] the petty-warrants all the day till late at night, that I was very weary, and troubled to have my private business of my office stopped to attend this – but mightily pleased at this falling-out; and the truth is, W. Penn doth make so much noise in this business of his, and doth it so little and ill, that I think the King will be little the better by changing the hand.

So up and to my office a little; but being at it all day, I could not do much there; so home and to supper, and teach Barker to sing another piece of my song;[4] and then to bed.

9.   To the office, where we sat all the morning, busy.   At noon home to dinner and then to my office again, where also

---

a repl. incomplete symbol   *b* repl. 'm'-   *c* repl. 'ready'

---

1. See above, vii. 386 & n. 2. Mordaunt resigned as Governor and Constable of Windsor Castle in September 1668: *CSPD 1667–8*, p. 608.
2. See above, p. 2, n. 3.
3. For Cromwell's high reputation at this time (even among royalists), see below, p. 332 & n. 2; p. 382 & n. 2.
4. *It is decreed*: see above, vii. 91, n. 4.

busy, very busy, late; and then went home and read*a* a piece of a play (*Every Man in his Humour*,[1] wherein is the greatest propriety of speech that ever I read in my life); and so to bed. This noon came my wife's Wachmaker and received 12*l* of me for her watch; but Captain Rolt coming to speak with me about a little business, he did judge of the work to be very good work, and so I am well contented; and he hath made very good, that I know, to Sir W. Penn and Lady Batten.

10. *Lords day.* Up and with my wife to church, where Mr. Mills made an unnecessary sermon upon Originall Sin, neither understood by himself nor the people. Home, where Michell and his wife, and also there came Mr. Carter, my old acquaintance of Magdalen College, who hath not been here of many years. He hath spent his time in the North with the Bishop of Carlisle much.[2] He is grown a very comely person and of good discourse, and one that I like very much. We had much talk of all our old*b* acquaintance of the College, concerning their various fortunes; wherein, to my joy, I met not with any that have sped better then myself. After dinner he went away; and awhile after him,*c* Michell and his wife, whom I love mightily; and then I to my chamber, there to my Tanger accounts, which I had let run a little behind-hand, but did settle them very well to my satisfaction; but it cost me sitting up till 2 in the morning, and the longer by reason that our neighbour Mrs. Turner, poor woman, did come to take her leave of us, she being to quit her house tomorrow to my Lord Brouncker, who hath used her very unhandsomely. She is going to lodgings, and doth tell me very odde*d* stories how Mrs. Williams[3] doth receive the applications of

a repl. 'ready' *b* repl. 'old' *c* MS. 'them'
d MS. 'odde' (l.h.) followed by same word in s.h.

---

1. Ben Jonson's comedy, first acted in 1598, and published in 1601; PL 2645 (*Works*, 1692). Pepys never saw it acted during the diary period, though it was occasionally performed by the King's Company between 1663 and 1669. (A).

2. Charles Carter had been at Magdalene from 1648 to 1651. (Pepys was there from 1651 to 1654.) He was now Rector of Irthlingborough, Northants, and had presumably been chaplain to the Bishop of Carlisle (Edward Rainbowe), who had been Master of Magdalene, 1642–50.

3. Brouncker's mistress.

people and hath presents, and she is the hand that receives all, while my Lord doth the business – which will shortly come to be loud talk if she continues here I do foresee, and bring my Lord no great credit.   So having done all my business, to bed.

11.   Up, and by water to the*a* Temple; and thence to Sir Ph. Warwickes about my Tanger warrant for tallies, and there met my Lord Bellasses and Creed and discoursed about our business of money; but we are defeated as to any hopes of getting any-thing upon the Pole=bill[1] – which I seem* but [am] not much troubled at,*b* it not concerning me much.   Thence with Creed to Westminster-hall, and there up and down and hear that Prince Rupert is still better and better – and that he did tell Dr Trout-becke expressly that my Lord Sandwich is ordered home.[2]   I hear too that Prince Rupert hath begged the having of all the stolen prize-goods which he can find, and that he is looking out anew after them[3]; which at first troubled me but I do see it cannot come to anything – but is done by Hayes[4] or some of his little people about him.   Here, among other news, I bought the King's speech at proroguing the House the other day, wherein are some words which cannot but import some prospect of a peace; which God send us.[5]   After walking a good while in the Hall, it being term-time, I home*c* by water, calling at Michell's and giving him a fair occasion to send his wife to the New Exchange to meet my wife and me this afternoon.   So home to dinner; and after dinner, by coach to Lord Bellasses and with him to Povy's house, whom we find with Auditor Beale and Vernatty*d* about their accounts still – which is never likely to have end.[6]   Our

a   repl. 'Westminster and'   b   repl. 'it'
c   repl. 'to'   d   repl. 'others'

---

1. Pepys obtained assignments for this purpose from the Eleven Months Tax in the following June and July: below, pp. 295, 344. For the poll-bill, see above, p. 30 & n. 1.

2. A canard.

3. He had been licensed to search for prize-goods: *CSPD 1667*, p. 228.

4. James Hayes, Rupert's secretary.

5. 'And yet I must tell you, that if any good Overtures be made for an Honourable Peace, I will not reject them': *His Majestie's . . . speech to both Houses of Parliament on Friday the 8th of February . . . at their prorogation*, p. 4.

6. For the accounts of Vernatty, paymaster at Tangier, see above, vii. 264, 342 & nn.

business was to speak with Vernatty, who is certainly a most cunning knave as ever was born. Having done what we had to do there, my Lord carried me and set me down at the New Exchange, where I stayed at Pottle's shop till B. Michell*a* came, which she did about 5 a-clock and was surprised not to trover mi moher there. But I did make an excuse good enough, and so I took ella down and over the way to the cabinet-makers, and there bought a dressing-box for her of 20*s*, but would require an hour's time to make fit. This I was glad of, thinking to have got ella to andar to a casa de biber; but ella would not, so I did not much press it but suffered ella to andar a la casa de uno de sos hermanos, and I passed my time walking up and*b* down; and among other places, to one Drumbelby, a maker of flagelettes, the best in town. He not within. My design to bespeak a pair of flagelettes of the same tune.* Ordered him to come to me in a day or two, and so I back to the Cabinet-makers and there stayed; and by and by Betty*c* comes, and here we stayed in the shop and above, seeing the workmen*d* work; which was pretty, and some exceeding good work and very pleasant to see them do it – till it was late, quite dark. And the mistress of the shop took us into the kitchen and there talked and used us very prettily; and took her for my wife, which I owned and her big belly; and there very merry till my thing done, and then took coach and home, in the way tomando su mano and putting it where I used to do; which ella did suffer, but not avec tant de freedom as heretofore, I perceiving plainly she had alguns apprehensions de me, but I did offer natha more then what I had often done. But now comes our trouble; I did begin to fear that su marido might go to my house to enquire por ella, and there trovando mi moher at home, would not only think himself, but give my femme occasion to think strange things. This did trouble me mightily; so though ella would not seem to have me trouble myself about it, yet did agree to the stopping the coach at the street's end; and yo allais con ella home and there presently*e* hear by him that he had newly sent su maid to my house to see for her mistress. This doth much perplex* me, and I did go presently home (Betty*f* whispering me, behind the tergo de her mari, that*g* if I would say

---

a   name in s.h.   *b*   MS. 'an'   *c*   name in s.h.   *d*   repl. 'working'
    e   repl. 'th'-   *f*   name in s.h.   *g*   repl. bracket

that we did come home by water, ella could make up la cosa well satis). And there in a sweat did walk in the entry antes my door, thinking what I should say a my femme; and as God would have it, while I was in this case (the worst in reference a my femme that ever I was in in my life), a little woman comes stumbling to the entry-steps in the dark; whom asking whom she was, she enquired for*a* my house; so knowing her voice and telling her su dona is come home, she went away. But Lord, in what a trouble was I when she was gone, to recollect whether this was not the second time of her coming; but at last concluding that she had not been here before, I did bless myself in my good fortune in getting home before her, and do verily believe she had loitered some time by the way, which was my great good fortune; and so I in a-door and there find all well. So,*b* my heart full of joy, I to the office a little and then home; and after supper and doing a little business in my chamber, I to bed – after teaching Barker a little of my song.[1]

12.   Up, and to the office, where we sat all the morning – with several things (among others) discoursed relating to our two new Assistant=Controllers; but especially Sir W. Penn, who is mighty troublesome in it. At noon home to dinner, and then to the office again and there did much business; and by and by comes Mr. Moore, who in discourse did almost convince me that it is necessary for my Lord Sandwich to come home and take his command at Sea this year, for that a peace is like to be. Many considerations he did give me hereupon which were very good, both in reference to the public and his private condition. By and by with my Lord Brouncker by coach to his house, there to hear some Italian Musique; and here we met Tom Killigrew,[2] Sir Rob. Murray,[3] and the Italian Seignor Baptista – who hath composed a play in Italian for the Opera which T. Killigrew doth intend to have up; and here he did sing one of the acts.[4] Himself

a repl. 'how'   *b* repl. 'and none'

---

1. See above, vii. 91 & n. 4. (E).
2. Manager of the Theatre Royal in Bridges St, Drury Lane. (A).
3. Courtier and virtuoso.

4. The composer was probably Giovanni Battista Draghi: J. Pulver, *Biog. Dict.*, p. 149. The play has not been traced. (E).

is the poet as well as the Musician, which is very much; and did sing the whole from the words without any Musique pricked, and played all along upon a Harpsicon most admirably; and the composition most excellent. The words I did not understand, and so know not how they are fitted; but believe very well, and all in the Recitativo* very fine. But I perceive there is a proper accent* in every country's discourse; and that doth reach in their setting of notes to words, which therefore cannot be natural to anybody else but them; so that I am not so much smitten*a* with it as it may be I should be if I were acquainted with their accent. But the whole composition* is certainly most excellent; and the poetry, T. Killigrew and Sir R. Murray, who understood the words, did say was excellent. I confess I was mightily pleased with the music. He pretends not to voice, though it be good but not excellent. This done, T. Killigrew and I to talk; and he tells me how the Audience at his House is not above half so much as it used to be before the late fire. That Knipp is like to make the best actor that ever came upon the stage, she understanding so well. That they are going to give her 30*l* a year more. That the stage is now by his pains a thousand times better and more glorious then ever heretofore. Now, wax-candles, and many of them; then, not above 3*lb*. of tallow.[1] Now, all things civil, no rudeness anywhere;[2] then, as in a bear-garden. Then, two or three fiddlers; now, nine or ten of the best.[3] Then, nothing but rushes upon the*b* ground and everything else mean; and now, all otherwise.[4] Then, the Queen seldom

a repl. 'smited'   *b* preceded by blot

---

1. Wax candles were used to illuminate the stage and auditorium of the Restoration theatre. Tallow candles had been used for the same purpose in the roofed 'private' theatres of the Elizabethan period. (A).

2. An exaggeration; Restoration audiences were often noisy and sometimes riotous: see, e.g. below, p. 348; M. Summers, *Restoration Theatre*, pp. 78–82. (A).

3. Another exaggeration: the musi-

cal effects in the early 17th-century theatres were often very elaborate. (A).

4. In Restoration theatres a green cloth was spread on the stage to protect the actors' costumes (see Summers, op. cit., pp. 269–70), whereas rushes had been used for this purpose on Elizabethan stages. The costumes of the Elizabethan actors, far from being 'mean', were often very expensive garments. (A).

and the King never would come;[1] now, not the King only for state, but all civil people do think they may come as well as any. He tells me that he hath gone several times, eight or ten times he tells me, hence to Rome to hear good music; so much he loves it, though he never did sing or play a note. That he hath ever endeavoured, in the last King's time and in this, to introduce good Musique; but he never could do it, there never having been any music here better then ballads. "No", [he] says "*Hermitt poore*[2] and *Chivy chase*[3] was all the music we had – and yet no ordinary Fidlers get so much money as ours do here, which speaks our rudenesse still." That he hath gathered nine Italians from several Courts in Christendome to come to make a consort for the King, which he doth give 200*l* a year apiece to, but badly paid, and do come in the room of keeping four ridiculous Gundilows – he having got the King to put them away and lay out the money this way. And endeed, I do commend him for it, for I think it is a very noble undertaking. He doth entend to have some times of the year these Operas to be performed at the two present Theatres, since he is defeated in what he intended in Moore Fields on purpose for it.[4] And he tells me plainly that the Citty Audience was as good as the Court – but now they are most gone. Baptista tells me that Jiacomo Charissimi[5] is still alive at Rome, who was maister to Vincentio,[6] who is one of the Italians the King hath here, and the chief composer of them. My great wonder is how

1. Henrietta-Maria attended four performances of plays at the Blackfriars Theatre between 1634 and 1639, but all were almost certainly special evening productions for the court: G. E. Bentley, *Jacobean and Caroline stage*, iv. 35. There is no record of Charles I's having attended a performance at a professional theatre. (A).

2. Probably Nicholas Lanier's setting of the Elizabethan lyric: cf. Playford's *Select ayres* etc. (1659), p. 1. (E).

3. *Chevy Chase*; the tune to the famous 16th-century Border ballad of that name; used as a tune to a score or so of ballads: see C. M. Simpson, *Brit. broadside ballad and its music*, pp. 96+. (E).

4. In addition to the two public theatres (the TR, Drury Lane and the LIF), Killigrew had hoped to set up a 'nursery' – a minor theatre for the training of young actors – in Moorfields: above, v. 230 & n. 3. (A).

5. Giacomo Carissimi (d. 1674), famous for his declamatory vocal compositions. 'Baptista' was Draghi: see above, p. 54, n. 4. (E).

6. Vicenzo Albrici.

this man[1] doth do to keep in memory so perfectly the music of that whole Act, both for the voice and for the instrument too – I confess I do admire it. But in Recitativo the sense much helps him, for there is but one proper way of discoursing and giving the accent. Having done our discourse, we all took coaches (my Lord's and T. Killigrew's) and to Mrs. Knepp's chamber, where this Italian is to teach her to sing*a* her part. And so we all thither, and there she did sing an Italian song or two very fine, while he played the bass upon a Harpsicon there; and exceedingly taken I am with her singing, and believe she will do miracles at that and acting. Her little girl is mighty pretty and witty. After being*b* there an hour, and I mightily pleased with this evening's work, we all parted; and I took coach and home, where late at my office and then home to enter my last three days' Journal; and so to supper and to bed – troubled at nothing but that these pleasures do hinder me in my business, and the more by reason of our being to dine abroad tomorrow, and then Saturdy next is appointed to meet again*c* at my Lord Brouncker's lodgings and there to have the whole Quire of Italians.*d* But then I do consider that this is all the pleasure I live for in the world, and the greatest I can ever expect in the best of my life; and one thing more, that by hearing this man tonight, and I think Captain Cooke tomorrow and the Quire of Italians on Saturday, I shall be truly able to distinguish which of them pleases me truly best, which I do much desire to know and have good reason and fresh occasion of judging.

13.*e* Up, and by water to White-hall, where to the Duke of York and there did our usual business; but troubled to see that at this time, after our declaring a debt to the Parliament of 900000*l* and nothing paid since, but the debt encreased and now the fleet to set out, to hear that the King hath ordered but 35000*l* for the setting out of the fleet out of the Pole bill to buy all

---

a MS. 'since'   *b* repl. 'an'
c repl. 'at'   *d* repl. 'mus'- 'mus'-
e The entries from here until 28 February are in a much smaller hand so that the month is completed in the fourteen remaining pages of the volume.

---

1. Draghi: see above, p. 54, n. 4. (E).

provisions, when five times as much had been little enough to have done anything to purpose.[1] They have endeed ordered more for paying off of seamen and the yards to some time, but not enough for that neither.[2] Another thing is the acquainting the Duke of York with the case of Mr. Lanyon, our Agent at Plymouth, who hath trusted us to 8000*l* out of purse; we are not in condition, after so many promises, to obtain him a farding; nor, though a message was carried by Sir G. Carteret and W. Coventry to the Comissioners for Prizes that he might have 3000*l* out of 20000*l* worth of prizes to be shortly sold there, that he might buy at the candle and pay for the goods out of bills and all would [not] do[a] anything, but that money must go all another way, while the King's service is undone and those that trust him perish.[3] These things grieve me to the heart. The Prince, I hear, is every day better and better. So away by water home, stopping at Michells, where Mrs. Martin was; and there drank with them and whispered with Betty,[b] who tells me all is well but was prevented in something she would have said, her marido venando just then a nous, which did trouble me; and so drank and parted and home; and there took up my wife by coach and to Mrs. Pierces, there to take her up, and with them to Dr. Clerke's[4] by invitation, where we have not been a great while; nor had any mind to go now but that the Doctor, whom I love, would have us choose a day. Here was his wife, painted, and her sister Worshipp, a widow now and mighty pretty in her mourning. Here was also Mr. Pierce and Mr. Floyd, secretary to the Lords Comissioners of Prizes, and Captain Cooke to dinner, an ill and little mean one, with foul

---

a repl. 'not be done'   *b* name in s.h.

---

1. In fact on 16 February a warrant for £426,000 was issued for this purpose: *CSPD 1666–7*, p. 519 (35,000 was the number of the seamen to be provided for). For the debt of £900,000, see above, vii. 294 & n. 1.

2. An order was made this day for the payment of over £1¼m. to cover wages, etc., for the past five years: *CSPD 1666–7*, p. 512.

3. Pepys, writing to Lanyon on 19 January, had promised to do his best for him: *Shorthand Letters*, pp. 88–9. For the sale of the prize goods, see below, p. 144; *CSPD 1666–7*, p. 509.

4. Timothy Clerke, physician to the King's Household.

cloth and dishes and everything poor. Discourse most about plays and the opera; where among other vanities, Captain Cooke had the arrogance to say that he was fain to direct Sir W Davenant in the breaking of his verses into such and such lengths, according as would be fit for music,[1] and how he used to swear at Davenant and command him that way when W. Davenant would be angry, and find fault with this or that note; but a vain coxcomb I perceive he is, though he sings and composes so well. But what I wondered at, Dr. Clerke did say that Sir W. Davenant is no good judge of a dramatic poem, finding fault with his choice of *Henery the 5th*[2] and others for the stage, when I do think and he confesses the *Siege of Rhodes*[3] as good as ever was writ. After dinner, Captain Cooke and two of his boys to sing; but it was endeed, both in performance and composition, most plainly below what I heard last night, which I could not have believed. Besides, overlooking the words when he sung, I find them not at all humourd* as they ought to be, and as I believed he had done all he had set – though he himself doth endeed sing in a manner, as to voice and manner, the best I ever heard yet; and a strange mastery he hath in making of extraordinary surprizing closes, that are mighty pretty; but his bragging that he doth understand tones and sounds as well as any man in the world, and better then Sir W. Davenant or anybody else, I do not like by no means; but was sick of it and him for it. He gone, Dr. Clerke fell to reading a new play, newly writ, of a friend's of his; but by his discourse and confession afterward, it was his own.[4] Some things, but very few, moderately good; but infinitely far from the conceit, wit, design, and language of very many plays that I know – so that but for compliment, I was quite tired with hearing it. It being done, and commending the play, but against my judgment, only the prologue magnifying the happiness of our former poets when such sorry things did please the world as was

---

1. Cooke was probably referring to *The siege of Rhodes*: q.v. above, ii. 130, n. 2. Davenant had to convert it into an opera in 1656 in order to evade the official prohibition of the performance of plays, and in so doing made 'frequent alterations of measure [since they] are necessary to *Recitative*

Musick for variation of *Ayres*': 1656 ed., sig. A 2*v*. (E).

2. By Roger Boyle, Earl of Orrery; a play which Davenant had produced: see above, v. 240 & n. 2. (A).

3. See above, ii. 130 & n. 2. (A).

4. There is no record of his having published a play. (A).

then acted was very good – so set Mrs. Pierce at home and away ourselves home; and there to my office and then my chamber till my eyes were sore at writing and making ready my letter*a* and accounts for the Commissioners of Tanger tomorrow – which being done, to bed – hearing that there was a very great disorder this day at the Ticket office, to the beating and bruising of the face of Carcasse very much.[1]   A foul evening this was tonight, and mightily troubled to get a coach home; and, which is now my common practice, going over the ruins in the night, I rid*b* with my sword drawn in the Coach.[2]

14.   Up and to the office, where Carcasse comes with his plastered face and called himself Sir W. Batten's martyr; which made W. Batten mad almost, and mighty quarrelling there was. We spent the morning almost wholly upon considering some way of keeping the peace at the Ticket Office; but it is plain that the care of that office is nobody's work, and that is it that makes it stand in the ill condition it doth.[3]   At noon home to dinner; and after dinner by coach to my Lord Chancellor's, and there a meeting – the Duke of York – the Duke of Albemarle – and several other Lords of the Commission of Tanger; and there I did present a state of my accounts, and managed them well; and my Lord Chancellor did say, though he was in other things in an ill humour, that no man in England was of more method nor made himself better understood then myself.   But going,

a repl. 'Tanger'   *b* MS. 'rit'

---

1. This incident has not been traced elsewhere.   There had been another riot on 29 January when rioting seamen advanced down the Strand on Whitehall: see HMC, *Le Fleming*, p. 44.   For Carkesse, see below, p. 64 & n. 1.

2. Cf. James Hickes to Joseph Williamson, 12 December 1666: 'For want of good watches, no one dares to go in the ruins after the close of the evening' (*CSPD 1666–7*, p. 340).

The police system of the parishes and wards had broken down from lack of men and organisation.   In the summer of 1668 things improved, and the city ordered the watches to be re-established, and to be paid for by the owners of new buildings: T. F. Reddaway, *Rebuilding of London*, p. 144, n. 3.

3. On 8 December 1668 it was put under Brouncker's supervision: BM, Add. 36782, f. 79*v*.

after the business of money was over, to other businesses of settling the garrison, he did fling out, and so did the Duke of York, two or three severe words touching my Lord Bellasses – that he would have no Governor come away from thence in less then three years; no, though his lady were with child. "Nay," says the Duke of York, "there should be no Gove[r]nor continue so*a* longer then three years." "Nor," says Lord Arlington, "when our rules are once set and upon good judgment declared, no Governor should offer to alter them." "We must correct the many things that are amiss there; for" (says [the] Lord Chancellor) "you must think we do hear of more things amisse then we are willing to speak before our friends faces."*b* My Lord Bellasses would not take notice of their reflecting on him, and did wisely; but they were all so many reflections on him. Thence away by coach with Sir H. Cholmly and Fitzgerald and Creed, setting down the two latter at the New Exchange; and H. Cholmly and I to the Temple and there walked in the dark in the walks, talking of news; and he surprizes me with the certain news that the King did last night in council declare his being in Treaty with the Dutch.[1] That they had sent him a very civil letter, declaring that if nobody but themselfs were concerned, they would not dispute the place of treaty but leave it to his choice; but that being obliged to satisfy therein a prince of equal quality with himself,[2] they must except any place in England or Spain. And so the King hath chosen The Hague, and thither hath chose my Lord Hollis and Harry Coventry to go Embassadors to treat;[3] which is so mean a thing as all the world will believe that we do go to beg a peace of them, what-

a repl. 'there'   *b* repl. 's'–

---

1. The official report of the King's speech (PRO, PC 2/59, f. 160r) is in much the same words as those which follow.

2. Louis XIV. For the significance of this argument about the venue, see above, vii. 361, n. 3.

3. Charles had proposed The Hague in a letter of 30 January, and appoin-

ted Lord Holles and Henry Coventry (brother of Sir William) soon afterwards. Breda was later substituted for The Hague: see below, p. 124 & n. 2. Negotiations for a peace treaty between all the belligerents opened there in mid-May and were concluded in August.

ever we pretend; and it seems all our Court are mightily for a peace, taking this [to] be the time to make one, while the King hath money, that he may save something of what the Parliament hath given him to put him out of debt, so as he may need the help of no more Parliaments as to the point of money. But our debt is so great, and expense daily so encreased, that I believe little of the money will be saved between this and the making of the peace up. But that which troubles me most is that we have chosen a son of Secretary Morris, a boy never used to any business, to go Secretary*ᵃ* to the Embassy;¹ which shows how little we are sensible of the weight of the business upon us. God therefore give a good end to it, for I doubt it; and yet do much more doubt the issue of our continuing the war, for we are in no wise fit for it. And yet it troubles me to think what Sir H. Cholmly says, that he believes they will not give us any reparation for what we have suffered by the warr, nor put us into any better condition then what we were in before the war, for that*ᵇ* will be shameful for us. Thence parted with him and home through the dark over the ruins by coach, with my sword drawn, to my office, where despatched some business; and so home to my chamber and to supper and to bed.

This morning came up to my wife's bedside, I being up dressing myself, little Will Mercer to be her Valentine; and brought her name writ upon blue paper in gold letters, done by himself, very pretty² – and we were both well pleased with it. But I am also this year my wife's Valentine, and it will cost me 5*l* – but that I must have laid out if we had not been Valentines. So to bed.

15. Up, and with W. Batten and J. Mennes by coach to White-hall, where attended upon the Duke of York to complain of the disorders*ᶜ* the other day among the seamen at the pay at

---

a　MS. 'Embassador'　　　*b*　repl. 'that' misplaced
c　repl. 'rudeness'

---

1. Nicholas, youngest son of Sir William Morice, was now appointed to this post. He was elected to parliament (for Newport, Cornwall) in March.

2. Possibly it had been drawn by lot: cf. below, p. 65. Will Mercer was 16.

the Ticket Office; and that it arises from lack of money, and that we desire, unless better provided for with money, to have nothing more to do with the payment of tickets, it being not our duty; and the Duke of York and W. Coventry did agree to it, so that I hope we shall be rid of that trouble. This done, I moved for allowance for a house for Mr. Turner, and got it granted.[1] Then away to Westminster-hall and there to the Exchequer about my tallies; and so back to White-hall and so with Lord Bellasses to the Excise Office, where met by Sir H Cholmly to consider about our business of money there; and that done, home and to dinner, where I hear Pegg Pen is married this day privately;[2] no friends but two or three relations on his side and hers – borrowed many things of my kitchen for dressing*a* their dinner. So after dinner I to the office and there busy and did much business, and late at it. Mrs. Turner came to me to hear how matters went; I told her of our getting rent for a house for her. She did give me account of this wedding today, its being private being imputed to its being just before Lent, and so in vain to make new clothes till Easter, that they might see the fashions as they are like to be this summer – which is reason good enough. She tells me she hears he[3] gives 4500*l* or 4000*l* with her. They are gone to bed – so I wish them much sport, and home to supper and to bed. They own the treaty for a peace publicly at Court, and the Commissioners providing themselfs to go over as soon as a passe comes for them.

16. Up and to the office, where all the morning. Among other things, great heat we were all in on one side or other in the examining witnesses against Mr. Carcasse about his buying of

---

a repl. 'their'

---

1. On 10 June 1667 the Treasurer paid a fine of £108 to Joseph Batelier, owner of a house in Crutched Friars, for this purpose. The Admiral's order referred to Thomas Turner's long service as a clerk in the Navy Office, and to his having lived in an official house for 20 years. PRO, Adm. 20/7/1, p. 434. Brouncker now occupied the Turners' old lodging in the Navy Office building.

2. She married Anthony Lowther: the licence (12 February) gives his age as 24 and hers as 15.

3. Sir William Penn.

tickets, and a cunning knave I do believe he is and will appear, though I have thought otherwise heretofore.[1]   At noon home to dinner and there find Mr. Andrews and Pierce and Hollyard, and they dined with us and merry; but we did rise soon for saving of my wife's seeing a new play this afternoon, and so away by coach and left her at Mrs. Pierces; myself to the Excise Office about business, and thence to the Temple to walk a little only, and then to Westminster to pass away time till anon.   And here I went to Mrs. Martin's to thank her for her oysters and there yo did hazer tout ce que je would con her, and she grown la plus bold moher of the orbis – so that I was almost defessus of the pleasure que ego was used para tener with ella.

Thence away to my Lord Bruncker's, and there was[a] Sir Rob. Murray, whom I never understood so well as now by this opportunity of discourse; he is a most excellent man of reason and[b] learning, and understands the doctrine of Musique and everything else I could discourse of very finely.[2]   Here came Mr. Hooke, Sir George Ent, Dr. Wren, and many others; and by and by the music, that is to say, Seignor Vincentio,[3] who is the

----

a repl. 'when'   *b* repl. 'of l'-

----

1. Cf. above, vi. 193. James Carkesse was also accused of receiving bribes, and his clerkship in the Ticket Office was now in jeopardy. Many references follow in which Pepys's hostility is evident. Dismissed in March, Carkesse petitioned the King, who ordered an enquiry by the committee of council dealing with seamen's complaints. Their report was in his favour, and in March 1668 he was re-employed in his old position as Brouncker's clerk. There had been irregularities, but the evidence against Carkesse was disputable. (PRO, PC2/59, pp. 555–12; ib., 60, p. 110; Adm. 106/3520, f. 40*v*; BM, Add. 9311, f. 164*r*.) He was dismissed some time later, and in 1679 was confined to a madhouse. From there he published in 1679 a book of verse (*Lucida Intervalla*) in which it would seem that he was suffering from persecution mania, and showed particular hostility to Pepys. He wrote that he had been Pepys's rival for the esteem of the Duke of York for 'more than years *thirteen*'.

2. Moray was, with Brouncker, one of the founders of the Royal Society.   In a letter to Christian Huygens of August 1661 he confessed that his passion for music ('tant la theorie que la pratique') had suffered much from the distractions of the last twenty years: Huygens, *Oeuvres Complètes*, iii. 312. He does not appear to have published on the subject.

3. See above, p. 56, n. 6.   (E).

maister Composer, and six*a* more, where of two Eunuches (so tall, that Sir T. Harvy said well that he believes they did grow large by being gelt, as our Oxen do) and one woman, very well dressed and handsome enough but would not be kissed, as Mr. Killigrew, who brought the company in, did acquaint us. They sent two Harpsicons before; and by and by, after tuning them, they begun; and I confess, very good music they made; that is, the composition* exceeding good, but yet not at all more pleasing to me then what I have heard in English by Mrs. Knipp, Captain Cooke and others. Nor do I dote of the Eunuchs; they sing endeed pretty high and have a mellow kind of sound, but yet I have been as well satisfied with several women's voices, and men also, as Crispe of the Wardrobe. The woman sung well, but that which distinguishes all is this: that in singing, the words are to be considered and how they are fitted with notes, and then the common accent* of the country is to be known and understood by the hearer, or he will never be a good judge of the vocall music of another country. So that I was not taken with this at all, neither understanding the first nor by practice reconciled to the latter, so that their motions and risings and fallings, though it may be pleasing to an Italian or one that understands that tongue, yet to me it did not; but do from my heart believe that I could set*b* words in English, and make music of them, more agreeable to any Englishman's eare (the most judicious) then any Italian music set for the voice and performed before the same man, unless he be acquainted with the Italian accent of speech. The composition as to the Musique part was excceding good, and their justness in keeping time by practice much before any that we have, unless it be a good band of practised fiddlers. So away; here being Captain Cocke, with him stole away, leaving them at it, in his coach; and to Mrs. Pierces, where I took up my wife and there find that Mrs. Pierce's little girl is my Valentine, she having drawn me – which I was not sorry for, it easing me of something more that I must have given to others. But here I do first observe the fashion of drawing of Motto's as well as names; so that Pierce, who drew my wife, did draw also a motto, and this girl drew another for me. What mine was I have forgot; but my wife's was (*Most virtuous and most fair*); which, as it

a   repl. 'the'   *b*   repl. 'make'

may be used, or an Anagram made*a* upon each name, might be very pretty. Thence with Cocke and my wife; set him at home, and then we home. To the office and there did a little business, troubled that I have so much been hindered by matters of pleasure from my business; but I shall recover it I*b* hope in a little time. So home and to supper, not at all smitten with the music tonight, which I did expect should have been so extraordinary, Tom Killigrew crying it up, and so all the world, above all things in the world; and so to bed. One wonder I observed today: that there was no Musique in the morning to call up our new-married people; which is very mean methinks, and is as if they had married like dog and bitch.

17. *Lords day.* Up, and called at Michell's and took him and his wife and carried them to Westminster, I landing at White-hall and having no pleasure in the way con ella; and so to the Duke's, where we all met and had a hot encounter before the Duke of York about the business of our payments at the Ticket Office; where we urged that we had nothing to do to be troubled with the pay, having examined the tickets. Besides, we are*c* neglected, having not money sent us in time. But to see the baseness of my brethren, not a man almost put in a word but Sir W. Coventry, though at the office like very devils in this point. But I did plainly declare that without money no fleet could be expected, and desired the Duke of York to take notice of [it] and notice was taken of it – but I doubt will do no good. But I desire to remember it as a most prodigious thing*d* that to this day my Lord Treasurer hath not consulted counsel (which Sir W. Coventry and I and others do think is necessary)*e* about the late Pole act, enough to put the same into such order as that anybody dare lend money upon it, though we have from this office under our hands related the necessity thereof to the Duke of York.[1] Nor was*f* like to be determined in, for aught I see, a good while, had not Sir W. Coventry plainly said that he did believe it would

---

a repl. symbol rendered illegible　　　*b* repl. symbol rendered illegible
c MS. 'a'　　*d* repl. 'thing'　　*e* MS. 'not necessary'　　*f* repl. 'is'

---

1. For the poll act, see above, p. 30 & n. 1. For Southampton's laziness, see above, vi. 218, n. 1.

be a better work for the King then going to church this morning, to send for the Atturny Generall to meet at the Lord Treasurer's this afternoon and to bring the thing to an issue, saying that himself, were he going to the Sacrament, would not think he should offend God to leave it and go to the ending this work, so much it is of moment to the King and Kingdom. Hereupon the Duke of York said he would presently speak to the King, and cause it to be done this afternoon. Having done here, we broke up, having done nothing almost though, for all this; and by and by I met Sir G. Carteret, and he is stark mad at what hath passed this morning, and I believe is heartily vexed with me. I said little, but I am sure the King will suffer if some better care be not taken then he takes to look after this business of money. So parted, and I by water home and to dinner, W. Hewer with us; a good dinner and very merry, my wife and I; and after dinner, to my chamber to fit something against the Council anon; and that being done, away to White-hall by water and thence to my Lord Chancellors, where I met with and had much pretty discourse with one of the Progers's that knows me.[1] And it was pretty to hear him tell me of his own accord, as a matter of no shame,[a] that in Spain he had a pretty woman his mistress; whom, when money grew scarce with him, he was forced to leave, and afterward heard how she and her husband lived well, she being kept by an old Fryer who used her as his whore; but this, says he, is better then as our Ministers do, who have wifes that lay up their estates and do no good nor relieve any poor; no, not our greatest prelates – and I think he is in the right for my part. Stayed[b] till the Council was up, and attended the King and Duke of York round the park and was asked several Questions by both; but I was in pain lest they should ask me what I could not answer; as the Duke of York did the value of the hull of the *St. Patricke*, lately lost;[2] which I told him I could not presently answer – though I might have easily furnished myself to answer all those

a repl. 's'- *b* MS. 'state'

---

1. There were several of this name serving in court office at this time. This may have been Harry Progers, who was in Spain during the Inter-regnum as secretary to the royalist embassy: Clarendon, *Hist.*, v. 139.
2. See above, p. 47 & n. 4.

Questions. They stood a good while to see the ganders[a] and geese tread one another in the water, the goose being all the while kept for a great while quite under water, which was new to me; but they did make mighty sport at it, saying (as the King did often), "Now you shall see a marriage between this and that" – which did not please me. They gone, by coach[b] to my Lord Treasurer's, as the Duke of York told me, to settle the business of money for the Navy; I walked into the Court to and again till night, and then met Collonell Reames[1] and he and I walked together a great while, complaining of the ill-management of things, whereof he is as full as I am. We run over many persons and things, and see nothing done like men like to do well while the King minds his pleasures so much. We did bemoan it that nobody would or had authority enough with the King to tell him how all things go to wrack and will be lost. Then he and I parted, and I to Westminster to the Swan, and there stayed till Michell and his wife came. Old Michell and his wife came to see me, and there we drank and laughed a little; and then the young ones and I took boat, it being fine moonshine. I did to my trouble see all the way that ella did get as close a su marido as ella could, and turn her manos away quando yo did endeavour to take one de los – so that I had no pleasure at all con ella ce night. When we landed, I did take occasion to send him back a the bateau while I did get un baiser or two, and would have taken la by la hand; but ella did turn away, and quando I said "Shall I not tocar te?" answered "Yo no love touching", in a slight modo. I seemed* not to take notice of it, but parted kindly et su marido did andar with me almost a mi casa, and there parted; and so I home, troubled at this; but I think I shall make good use of it and mind my business more. At home by appointment comes Captain Cocke to me to talk of State matters and about the peace; who told me that the whole business is managed between Kevet, Burgomaister of Amsterdam, and my Lord Arlington, who hath, by the interest of his wife there, some

a repl. 'geese and'   *b* repl. 'into'

---

1. Bullen Reymes, M.P.; Commissioner for the Sick and Wounded; member of the Fishery Committee; Deputy-Treasurer for prize goods, Portsmouth.

interest.[1] We have proposed The Hague, but know not yet whether the Dutch will like it; or if they do, whether the French will. We think we shall have the help of the information of their affairs and state, and the helps of the Prince of Orange his faction; but above all, that De Witt, who hath all this while said he cannot get peace, his mouth will now[a] be stopped, so that he will be forced to offer fit terms for fear of the people; and lastly, if France or Spayne do not please us, we are in a way presently to clap up a peace with the Dutch, and secure them. But we are also in treaty with France, as he says; but it must be to the excluding our alliance with the King of Spain or House of Austria – which we do not know presently what will be determined in.[2] He tells me the Vicechamberlaine is so great with the King, that let the Duke of York and Sir W. Coventry and this office do or say what they will, while the King lives, G. Carteret will do what he will; and advises me to be often with him, and eat and drink with him. And tells me that he doubts he is jealous* of me, and was mighty mad today at our discourse to him before the Duke of York. But I did give him my reasons, that the office is concerned to declare that without money the King's work cannot go on. From that discourse we run to others; and among the rest, he assures me that Henr. Brunker is one of the shrewdest fellows for parts in England, and a dangerous man.[3] That if ever the[b] Parliament comes again, Sir W. Coventry

a MS. 'not' *b* repl. 'another'

1. Both were representatives of the Orange interest, which was now reviving. Arlington's wife (Isabella van Beverweerd) was a member of the Orange family. Johan Kievit, once Burgomaster of Rotterdam (not Amsterdam), had since 1666 been an exile in England: for his part in the negotiations, see Feiling, pp. 199+.

2. The government was divided between the Arlington group, which put a Dutch treaty first, and the Clarendon group, which staked everything on an understanding with France. Since everyone knew of Louis' preparations against the Spanish Netherlands, the choice between methods of peace-making was really a choice of side in the war which would follow. On 11 February Charles II agreed to St Albans's proposal for a peace on French terms, and assured Louis that Sandwich's negotiations in Madrid were concerned only with commerce. See below, p. 176 & n. 1.

3. He was a brother of Lord Brouncker, Pepys's colleague, and a Groom of the Bedchamber to the Duke of York. 'Hard, covetous, vicious' (according to Evelyn, 24 March 1688), he was almost universally disliked. Cf. Burnet, i. 391, n. 3.

cannot stand; but in this I believe him not. That while we want money so much in the Navy, the officers of the Ordinance have at this day 300000*l* good in tallies which they can command money upon – got by over-estimateing their charge, in getting it reckoned as a fifth part of the expense of the Navy. That Harry Coventry, who is to go upon this treaty with Lord Hollis (who he confesses to be a very wise man) into Holland, is a mighty quick, ready man, but not so weighty as he should be, he knowing him so well in his drink as he doth.[1] That unless the King doth do something against my Lord Mordant and the patent for the Canary Company[2] before the Parliament next meets, he doth believe there will be a civil war before there will be any more money given, unless it may be at their perfect disposal. And that all things are now ordered to the provoking of the Parliament against they come next and the spending the King's money, so as to put him into a necessity of having it at the time it is prorogued for, or sooner. Having discoursed all this and much more, he away. And I to supper and then to read[a] my vows, and to bed – my mind troubled about Betty Michell[b] pour sa carriage this night envers moy, but do hope it will put me upon doing mi mismo some bonum. This evening, going to[c] the Queen's side[3] to see the ladies, I did find the Queene, the Duchess of Yorke, and another or two at Cards, with the room full of great ladies and men – which I was amazed at to see on a Sunday, having not believed it; but contrarily, flatly denied the same a little while since to my Cosen Roger Pepys.[4] I did this day, going by water, read the Answer to the *Apology for Papists*,[5] which did like me mightily, it being a thing as well writ as I think most things that ever I read in my life, and glad I am that I read it.

---

a repl. 'ready'　　　*b* name in s.h.　　　*c* repl. 'through the'

---

1. Cf. Burnet (i. 548): 'A man of wit and heat, of spirit and candour'. To Marvell (*Last Instructions*, l. 228) he was 'Hector Harry'.
2. See above, vii. 314 & n. 2.
3. Of Whitehall Palace.
4. See above, p. 33.
5. *The late apology in behalf of the papists, reprinted and answered in behalf of the royallists* (1667); usually attributed to William Lloyd, chaplain to the King (d. 1717); not in the PL. For the original *Apology* (by Lord Castlemaine), see above, vii. 393 & n. 4.

18. Up, and to my bookbinders and there mightily pleased to see some papers of the account we did give the Parliament of the expense of the Navy, sewed together; which I could not have conceived before how prettily it was done.[1] Then by coach to the Exchequer about some tallies; and thence back again home, by the way meeting Mr. Weaver of Huntington, and did discourse our business of law together;[2] which did ease my mind, for I was afeared I have omitted the doing what I in prudence ought to have*a* done. So home and to dinner; and after dinner to the office, where yo had Mrs. Burrows all sola a my closet, and did there besar*b* and tocar su mamelles as much as yo quisere hasta a hazer me hazer, but ella would not suffer that yo should poner mi mano abaxo*c* ses jupes, which yo endeavoured. Thence away, and with my wife by coach to the Duke of York's playhouse, expecting a new play; so stayed not no more then other people, but to the King's to *The Mayds Tragedy*;[3] but vexed all the while with two talking ladies and Sir Ch. Sidly, yet pleased to hear their discourse, he being a stranger;[4] and one of the ladies would, and did, sit with her mask on all the play;[5] and being exceeding witty as ever I heard woman, did talk most pleasantly with him; but was, I believe, a virtuous woman and of quality. He would fain know who she was, but she would not tell. Yet did give him many pleasant hints of her knowledge of him, by that means setting his brains at work to find out who

---

a repl. 'of'   *b* repl. 'tocar'   *c* repl. 'under'

---

1. 'Collections towards the Stateing the Expence of his Ma(ts) Navy from the beginning of the present warr, and more especially for the justifieing the accompt thereof presented to the Parliament at theire Session begun 18 September 1666'; 159 pp.; written partly by Pepys but mostly in Gibson's hand; bound in black morocco, gold-tooled: PL 2589.

2. This business appears to have concerned the Pepys property at Brampton: cf. below, 17 February 1669. Richard Weaver was a Huntingdon attorney.

3. A tragicomedy by Beaumont and Fletcher; see above, ii. 100 & n. 4. (A).

4. Sedley was a well-known wit and man-about-town. Contemporary plays and pamphlets contain many references to the noisy chatter of spectators in the pit; see M. Summers, *Restoration Theatre*, pp. 68–75. (A).

5. Women playgoers frequently wore masks: cf. above, iv. 181 & n. 3. (A).

she was; and did give him leave to use*ᵃ* all means to find out
who she was but pulling off her mask. He was mighty witty;
and she also making sport with him very inoffensively, that a
more pleasant rencontre I never heard. But by that means lost
the pleasure of the play wholly, to which now and then Sir Ch.
Sidlys exceptions against both words and pronouncing was very
pretty.[1] So home and to the office; did much business; then
home to supper and to bed.

19. Up, and to the office, where all the morning doing little
business, our want of money being so infinite great. At noon
home, and there find old Mr. Michell and Howlett come to desire
mine and my wife's company to dinner to their son's; and so
away by coach with them, it being Betty's wedding-day a year –
as also Shrove tuseday. Here I made myself mighty merry, the
two old women being there also; and a mighty pretty dinner we
had in this little house, to my exceeding great content and my
wife's, and my heart pleased to see Betty. But I have not been
so merry a very great while as with them, everything pleasing me
there as much as among so mean company I could be pleased.
After dinner I fell to read the Acts about the building of the City
again;[2] and endeed, the laws seem to be very good, and I pray
God I may live to see it built in that manner. Anon, with much
content home, walking with my wife and her woman; and there
to my office, where late doing much business; and then home to
supper and to bed. This morning I hear that our discourse of
peace is all in the dirt, for the Dutch do not like of the place;[3]
or at least, the French will not agree to it; so that I do wonder

a repl. 'find'

---

1. Sedley had also been critical of
the performance at which Pepys saw
him on 4 October 1664. (A).
2. 18–19 Car. II, cc. 7 and 8;
passed on 8 February. The first
established a Court of Claims,
manned by the Common Law judges,
which speedily settled disputes between landlords and lessees which
would otherwise have delayed rebuilding for years: see T. F. Reddaway, *Rebuilding of London*, pp. 91+ ;
Philip E. Jones (ed.), *Fire Court*.
The second laid down (*inter alia*) strict
building regulations, opened the
labour market and prevented profit-
eering, but left much to be decided by
the King and the civic authorities.
(R).
3. The Hague, which the English
had proposed: see above, p. 61 &
n. 3.

what we shall do, for carry on the war we cannot. I long to hear the truth of it tomorrow at Court.

20. Up, and with Sir W. Batten and W. Penn by coach to White-hall, by the way observing Sir*ᵃ* W. Penn's carrying a favour to Sir W. Coventry for his daughter's wedding,[1] and saying that there was others for us when we will fetch them; which vexed me, and I am resolved not to wear it when he gives me one. His wedding hath been so poorly kept, that I am ashamed of it for a fellow that makes such a flutter as he doth. When we came to the Duke of York here, I heard discourse how Harris of his playhouse is sick; and everybody commends him, and above all things, for acting the Cardinall.[2] Here they talk also how the King's viallin,*ᵇ* Bannister, is mad that the King hath a Frenchman come to be chief of some part of the King's music[3] – at which the Duke of York made great mirth. Then withdrew to his closet, all our business lack of money and prospect of the effects of it, such as made Sir W. Coventry say publicly before us all, that he doth heartily wish that his Royal Highness had nothing to do in the Navy, whatever became of him; so much dishonour, he says, is likely to fall under the management of it. The Duke of York was angry, as much as he could be or ever I saw him, with Sir G. Carteret for not paying the masters of some ships on Monday last according to his promise: and I do think Sir G. Carteret will make himself unhappy by not taking some course, either to borrow more money or wholly lay aside his pretence to the charge of raising money, which he hath nothing to do to trouble himself with. Thence to the Exchequer and there find the people in readiness to despatch my tallies today, though Ashwednesdy;[4] so I back by

a repl. 'his'   *b* MS. 'viallins'

1. See above, p. 63 & n. 2.
2. Probably the role of Cardinal Wolsey, which Henry Harris played when Shakespeare's *Henry VIII* was presented at the LIF. (A).
3. Louis Grabu, a court musician after the Restoration, was appointed 'composer to his Majesty's musique' in 1665. At Nicholas Lanier's death in February 1666 he was admitted

'Master of the English Chamber musick in ordinary', took over the directorship of the '24 violins' from John Banister later that year, and was given full charge of them on 4 August 1667. (E).
4. The Exchequer was notorious for its punctilious observance of all possible holidays: cf. above, i. 320 & n. 1.

coach to London to Sir R. Viners, and there got 100*l* and come
away with it and pay my fees round; and so away with the
Chequer-men to the Leg in King-street, and there had*ᵃ* wine for
them; and here was one in company with them that was the
man that got the vessel to carry over the King from Bredhemson;
who hath a pension of 200*l* per annum, but ill paid and the man is
looking after getting of a prize-ship to live by;[1] but the trouble
is that this poor man, who hath received no part of his money
these four years and is ready to starve almost, must yet pay to the
Poll Bill for this pension.   He told me several perticulars of the
King's coming thither; which was mighty pleasant and shows
how mean a thing a king is, how subject to fall, and how like
other men he is in his afflictions.   Thence with my tallies home;
and a little dinner and then with my wife by coach to Lincoln's
Inn Fields; sent her to her brother's, and I with Lord Bellassis
to Lord Chancellors.   Lord Bellasses tells me how the King of
France hath caused the stop to be made to our proposition of
treating in The Hague – that he being greater then*ᵇ* they, we
may better come and treat at Paris; so that God knows what will
become of the peace.   He tells me too, as a grand secret, that he
doth believe the peace, offensive and defensive, between Spayne
and us is quite finished; but must not be known, to prevent the
King of France's present falling upon Flanders.[2]   He doth believe

---

a repl. 'take'   *b* repl. same symbol badly formed

---

1. Francis Mansell, merchant, had
provided the ship which had carried
the King from Shoreham, near
Brighton ('Bredhemson'), where
Charles had embarked for France in
1651 after his flight from the battle of
Worcester.   Mansell had recently appealed to the King about his pension
(£200 p.a. granted in 1661, but
'stayed four years ago'), and on 22
February a warrant was issued for its
continuation: *CSPD 1666–7*, p. 525.
His plea for a prize ship at Plymouth
worth £180 (ib., *1667–8*, p. 131) presumably fell to the ground in consequence.

2. The Anglo-Spanish treaty was
not concluded until 3 May.   It was
not in fact an 'offensive and defensive'
alliance; it was mainly commercial,
but included a secret clause by which
each country agreed not to support
the enemies of the other: Feiling,
pp. 214–16.   Charles had entered into
an understanding with the French on
12 February, and it was not until
18 March that serious negotiations
with the Dutch were resumed.
Louis wanted to concentrate the peace
parleys in French hands, but not
necessarily in Paris. (He preferred
Dover.)   He invaded the Spanish
Netherlands in May 1667.

the Duke of York will be made General of the Spanish armies there and Governor of Flanders if the French should come against it and we assist the Spanyard. That we have done the Spanyard abundance of mischief in the West Indys by our privateers at Jamaica; which they lament mightily, and I am sorry for it to have it done at this time.[1] By and by came to my Lord Chancellor, who*a* heard mighty quietly my complaint for lack of money and spoke mighty kind to me; but little hopes of help therein – only his good words. He doth prettily call upon Povys account, with sometimes seeming friendship and pity, and this day quite the contrary. He doth confess our straits here and everywhere else arises from our out-spending our revenue; I mean, that the King doth do so. Thence away; took up my wife, who*b* tells me her brother hath laid out much money upon himself and wife for clothes, which I am sorry to hear, it requiring great expense. So home and to the office a little; and then home to supper, where Mrs. Turner came to us and sat and talked. Poor woman, I pity her, but she is very cunning. She concurs with me in the falseness of Sir W. Penn's friendship. And she tells pretty stories of my Lord Brunckert since he came to our end of the town, of people's applications to Mrs. Williams.[2] So she gone, I back to my accounts of Tanger, which I am settling, having my new tallies from the Exchequer this day; and having set all right as I could wish, then to bed.

21. Up, and to the office, where sat all the morning; and there a most furious conflict between Sir W. Penn and I, in few words and on a sudden occasion of no great moment, but very

---

a MS. 'how'   *b* MS. 'with'

---

1. The privateers and buccaneers of Jamaica in the 1660s (some, like the famous Morgan, acting under commissions issued by the governors) conducted an almost continuous campaign against Spanish trading fleets and even ports. Under Edward Mansfield, and commissioned by Governor Sir Thomas Modyford, their attacks reached a climax in 1665–6 in raids on Cuba, Providence and Nicaragua. (See C. H. Haring, *Buccaneers in W. Indies in 17th cent.*, esp. ch. v.) Pepys's disapproval arose not only from the national danger of annoying Spain, but also from his personal interest in the success of Sandwich's Spanish mission. The negotiations for a trade treaty were delayed by these exploits.

2. Cf. above, pp. 51–2.

bitter and stared one on another; and so broke off and to our business, my heart as full of spite as it could hold, for which God forgive me and him.   At the end of the day came witnesses on behalf of Mr. Carcasse;[1] but instead[a] of clearing him, I find they were brought to recriminate Sir W Batten; and did it by oath very highly, that made the old man mad and, I confess, me ashamed, so that I caused all but ourselfs to withdraw, being sorry to have such things declared in the open office before a hundred people.   But it was done home, and I do believe true, though W. Batten denies all; but is cruel mad and swore one of them, he or Carcasse, should not continue in the Office; which is said like a fool.   He gone (for he would not stay) and W. Penn gone a good while before – Lord Brouncker, Sir T. Harvy and I stayed and examined the witnesses, though amounting to little more then a reproaching of Sir W. Batten: I home, my head and mind vexed about the conflict between Sir W. Penn and I, though I have got, not lost, any ground by it.   At home was Mr. Daniel and wife and sister, and dined with us.   And I disturbed at dinner, Collonell Fitzgerald coming to me about tallies, which I did go and give him; and then to the office, where did much business and walked an hour or two with Lord Brouncker, who is mightily concerned in this business, for Carcasse and against Sir W. Batten;[2] and I do hope it will come to a good heighth, for I think it will be good, for the King as well as for me, that they two do not agree – though I do, for aught I see yet, think that my Lord is for the most part in the right.   He gone, I to my office again to despatch business; and late at night comes in Sir W. Batten, W. Penn and J. Mennes to the office, and what was it but to examine one Jones, a young Merchant, who was said to have spoke the worst against Sir[b] W. Batten, but he doth deny it wholly; yet I do believe Carcasse will go near to prove all that was sworn in the morning, and so it be true I wish it may.   That done, I to end

---

a repl. 'to'   *b* repl. 'but'

1. For this case, see above, p. 64, n. 1.

2. Brouncker supported Carkesse throughout the dispute, and may well have been the means of restoring him to office after his dismissal.   On 14 March 1667, six days after Carkesse's removal, Brouncker and his mistress, Abigail Williams, were godparents at the christening of his son: *Harl. Soc. Reg.*, 46/74.

my letters; and then home to supper and set right some accounts of Tanger; and then to bed.

22. Up, and to the office, where I a while; and then home with Sir H Cholmly to give him some tallies upon the business of the Molle at Tanger; and then out with him by coach to the Excise Office, there to enter them, and so back again with him to the Exchange; and there I took another coach and home to the office and to my business till dinner – the rest of our officers having been this morning upon the Victuallers' accounts. At dinner all of*ᵃ* us, that is to say, Lord Brouncker, J. Mennes, W. Batten, T. Harvy and myself, to Sir W. Penn's house to dinner, where some other company; it is instead of a wedding dinner for his daughter, whom I saw in palterly clothes, nothing new*ᵇ* but a bracelet that her servant* hath given her, and ugly she is as heart can wish. A sorry dinner, not anything handsome nor clean but some silver plates they borrowed of me. My wife was here too. So a great deal of talk, and I seemingly merry – but took no pleasure at all. We had favours given us all and we put them in our hats*ᶜ* – I against my will but that my Lord and the rest did – I being displeased that he did carry Sir W. Coventry's himself several days ago, and the people up and down the town long since, and we must have them but today. After dinner, to talk a little; and then I away to my office to draw up a letter of the state of the Office and Navy for the Duke of York against Sunday next, and at it late; and then home to supper and to bed – talking with my wife of the poorness and meanness of all that Sir W. Penn and the people about us do, compared with what we do.

23. This day I am by the blessing of God 34 years old – in very good health and mind's content, and in condition of estate much beyond whatever my friends* could expect of a child of theirs this day 34 year. The Lord's name be praised and may I be ever thankful for it. Up betimes to the office, in order to my letter to the Duke of York tomorrow. And then the office met and spent the greatest part about this letter. At noon home to dinner and then to the office again, very close at it all the day till midnight, making an end and writing fair this great letter and

a repl. 'so'   *b* repl. 'do'   *c* MS. 'hearts'

other things, to my full content – it abundantly providing for the
vindication of this office, whatever the success be of our wants of
money.[1]   This evening Sir W. Batten came to me to the office
on purpose, out of spleen (of which he is full) to Carcasse, to tell
me that he is now informed of many double-tickets[2] now found
of Carcasse's making which quite overthrew him.   It is strange
to see how, though I do believe this fellow to be a rogue and
could be contented to have him removed, yet to see him perse-
cuted by Sir W. Batten, who is as bad himself, and that with so
much rancour, I am almost the fellow's friend.   But[a] this good
I shall have from it: that the differences between W. Batten and
my Lord Brouncker will do me no hurt.

24.   *Lords day.*   Up, and with W. Batten by coach; he set
me down at my Lord Brouncker's (his fewd there not suffering
him to light himself);   and I with my Lord, by and by when
ready, to White-hall.   And by[b] and by up to the Duke of York
and there presented our great letter and other papers;   and among
the rest, my report of the victualling,[3] which is good I think,
and will continue my pretence to the place, which I am still
afeared Sir W. Coventry's imployment may extinguish.[c4]   We
have discharged ourselfs in this letter fully from blame[d] in the bad
success of the Navy if money do not come soon to us – and so
my heart is at pretty good rest in this point.   Having done here,

---

a MS. 'by'   b repl. 'after'   c repl. 'sp'-   d repl. 'fear'

---

1. Dated this day; copies (in
Pepys's hand) in NMM, LBK/8, ff.
458–60 (printed in *Further Corr.*, pp.
158+).   It asked for a minimum of
£526,135 to be paid in weekly instalments of £40,000 in order to set out a
summer fleet. At 14 March Pepys
reports that the sum has been granted,
though not in ready money.
2. Two tickets made out for the
same service. Pepys has a note in
NWB, p. 105 about the payment of
two soldiers in December 1666, adding that Carkesse did not keep a
register of all tickets issued.

3. Copy (23 February) in NMM,
LBK/8, pp. 467–8.   Pepys there mentions (p. 466) that another copy 'is
entred in my Victualling booke'.   A
third (in his own hand) is in Longleat,
Coventry MSS 97, f. 59.
4. Coventry had ceased to be a
Navy Commissioner in January;
Pepys now feared – needlessly as it
turned out – that he would take over
the control of victualling. He became a Treasury Commissioner in
May.

Sir W. Batten and I home by coach; and though the sermon[a] at our church was begun, yet he would light and go home and eat a slice of roast beef off of the spit, and did; and then he and I to church in the middle of the sermon. My Lady Pen there saluted me with great content, to tell me that her daughter and husband are still in bed, as if the silly woman thought it a great matter of honour – and did, going out of the church, ask me whether we did not make a great show at Court today with all our favours in our hats. After sermon home and alone with my wife dined. Among other things, my wife told me how ill a report our Mercer hath got by her keeping of company, so that she will not send for her to dine with us or be with us as heretofore – and which is more strange, tells me that little Mis Tooker[1] hath got a clap, as young as she is; being brought up loosely by her mother – having been in bed with her mother when her mother hath had a man come into bed and lay with her. In the afternoon away to White-hall by water, and took a turn or two in the park and then back to White-hall; and there meeting my Lord Arlington, he, by I know not what kindness, offered to carry me along with him to my Lord Treasurer's, whither I told him I was going. I believe he had a mind to discourse of some Navy businesses; but Sir Tho. Clifford coming into the coach to us, we were prevented; which I was sorry for, for I had a mind to begin an acquaintance with him. He speaks well and hath pretty slight superficial parts, I believe.[2] He in our going talked much of the plain habit of the Spaniards; how the King and lords themselfs wear but a cloak of Colchester bayze,[3] and the ladies mantles, in cold weather, of white flannel. And that the endeavours frequently of setting up the manufacture of making these stuffs there have only been prevented by the

---

a repl. 'church'

---

1. Frances Tooker of Greenwich, a neighbour of Pepys during his stay there during the Plague in 1665.

2. His talents were to some extent concealed by the courtliness of his manners. He had, for instance, a fluent command of Latin, French and Spanish – hence his value as a diplo-

matist. Cf. Evelyn, iv. 118. But Clarendon took a low view of his knowledge of the law and the constitution: *Life*, ii. 204.

3. Spain (where Arlington had served as King's Resident in 1658–60) was one of the principal markets for English cloth.

Inquisition – the English and Duchmen that have been sent for to work being taken with a Psalm-book or Testament, and so clapped up and the house pulled down by the Inquisitors, and the greatest lord in Spain dare not say a word against it – if the ⟨word*a*⟩ "Inquisition" be but mentioned.[1]   At my Lord Treasurers light and parted with them, they going into Council, and I walked with Captain Cocke, who takes mighty notice of the differences growing in our office between Lord Brouncker and W. Batten, and among others also; and I fear it may do us hurt, but I will keep out of them.   By and by comes Sir St. Fox,[2] and he and I walked and talked together on many things, but chiefly want of money and the straits the King brings himself and affairs into for want of it.   Captain Cocke did tell me, which I must not forget, that the answer of the Dutch, refusing The Hague for a place of treaty and proposing The Boysse,[3] Bredah, Bergen-op-Soome, or Mastricht, was seemingly stopped*b* by the Swedes Imbassador (though he did show it to the King, but the King would take no notice of it, nor does not) from being delivered to the King; and he hath wrote to desire them to consider better of it. So that though we know their refusal of the place, yet they know not that we know it, nor the King obliged to show his sense of the affront.[4]   That the Duch are in very great straits, so as to be said

a l.h. repl. s.h. 'word'   *b* repl. 'sent'

---

1. Many foreigners, including Protestants from England and Holland, worked in Spain without taking up permanent residence, since the country was chronically short of labourers and technicians.   But it was only the Catholic Italians and French who found life under the Inquisition comfortable.

2. Paymaster of the Army.

3. Bois-le-duc ('s Hertogenbosch). This and the other towns here mentioned were all in the United Provinces.

4. For the considerations involved in the choice of a place of meeting, see above, vii. 361, n. 3.   For this phase of the negotiations, see D'Estrades, *Lettres* etc. (1709), iv. 56–8, 96–7; Arlington, *Letters to Temple*, i. 130; *CSPVen. 1666–8*, pp. 144, 146. The Dutch had (on 14/24 February) declined the English proposal (31 January/10 February) of The Hague, on the gound that it was 'an open place'.   (They feared the influence of the Orangists there.)   Breda was ultimately chosen: see below, p. 124 & n. 2.   The Swedes acted as mediators; their London ambassador, Coyet, had been a fellow-student of Jan de Witt at Leyden: A. L. Pontalis, *De Witt* (trans.), i. 280.

to be not able to set out*a* their fleet this year.[1]   By and by comes Sir Robt. Viner and Lord Mayor to ask the King's direction about measuring*b* out the streets according to the new Act for building of the City, wherein the King is to be pleased.[2]   But he says that the way proposed in Parliament by Collonell Birch would have been the best, to have chosen some persons in trust and sold the whole ground, and let it be sold again by them with preference to the old owner;[3] which would have certainly caused the City to be built where these trustees pleased; whereas now, great differences will be and the streets built by fits, and not*c* entire till all differences be decided.   This, as he tells it, I think would have been the best way.   I enquired about the Frenchman that was said to fire the City, and was hanged for it by his own confession that he was hired for it by a Frenchman of Roane, and that he did with a stick reach in a Fireball in at a window of the house – whereas the maister of the house, who is the King's Baker, and his son and daughter do all swear there was no such window – and that the fire did not begin thereabouts.[4]   Yet the fellow,*d* who though a mopish besotted fellow did not speak like a madman, did swear that he did fire it;   and did not this like a madman, for being tried on purpose and landed with his keeper[5] at the Tower Wharf, he could carry the keeper to the very house.

----

a   repl. same symbol badly formed   *b*   repl. 'metion'-
       c   repl. 'great'   *d*   repl. 'fanlow'

----

1. This rumour was exaggerated, but they were having difficulties with equipment and recruitment: *CSPVen. 1666–8*, p. 144.

2. Cf. above, p. 72, n. 2.

3. I have not traced this proposal.

4. Robert Hubert, a London watchmaker and native of Rouen, had been tried at the Middlesex Michaelmas sessions of 1666 and executed on 27 October. The only evidence against him was his own confession, which he later recanted. It does not appear to be true that he was a Catholic, as he alleged. The fact that he was able to identify the site of the baker's house proved nothing, since for a long time it had been on public show. He was in fact mentally disordered and had landed in London from Sweden two days after the fire had started. BM, Add. 27962 R, ff. 480*v*–482*r*; HMC, *Portland*, iii. 301–2; *State Trials* (ed. Howell), vi. 807+; Bell, *Fire*, pp. 192–4. Pepys kept a print of the inscription put up at the spot in 1681 which recorded the story about Hubert: PL 2972, pp. 74–5. The King's baker was Thomas Farryner.

5. The keeper of the prison in which he was lodged (the White Lion Gaol), John Lowman: Bell, *Fire*, pp. 193–4.

Asking Sir R. Viner what he thought was the cause of the fire, he tells me that the Baker, son, and his daughter did all swear again and again that their*ᵃ* Oven was drawn by 10 a-clock at night. That having occasion to light a candle about 12, there was not so much fire in the bakehouse as to light a match for a candle, so as they were fain to go into another place to light it. That about 2 in the morning they felt themselfs almost choked with smoke; and rising, did find the fire coming upstairs – so they rose to save themselfs; but that at that time the bavins were not on fire in the yard. So that they are, as they swear, in absolute ignorance how this fire should come – which is a strange thing, that so horrid an*ᵇ* effect should have so mean and uncertain a beginning. By and by called in to the King and Cabinet and there had a few insipid words about money for Tanger, but to no purpose. Thence away, walked to my boat at White-hall, and so home and to supper; and then to talk with W Hewer about business of the differences at present among the people of our office; and so to my Journall and to bed. This night, going through bridge by water, my waterman told me how the mistress of the Beare tavern at the bridge-foot did lately fling herself into the Thames and drownded herself; which did trouble me the more when they tell me it was she that did live at the White Horse tavern in Lumbard-street; which was a most beautiful woman, as most I have seen.[1] It seems hath had long melancholy upon her, and hath endeavoured to make away with herself often.

25. Lay long in bed, talking with pleasure with my poor wife how she used to make coal fires and wash my foul clothes with her own hand for me, poor wretch, in our little room at my Lord Sandwiches;[2] for which I ought for ever to love and admire her, and do, and persuade myself she would do the same thing

a repl. 'the'   *b* repl. 'a'

---

1. Cf. above, vii. 68 & n. 3. She was said to have committed suicide because of the destruction of the White Horse tavern in the Fire.

2. In Sandwich's lodgings in White-hall Palace. It was possibly the room which Pepys kept, after moving to Axe Yard, until February 1660: cf. above, i. 186 & n. 1.

again if God should reduce us to it. So up, and by coach abroad to the Duke of Albemarle's about sending soldiers down to some ships; and so home, calling at a belt-makers to mend my belt, and so home and to dinner, where pleasant with my wife; and then to the office, where mighty busy all the day, saving going forth to the Change to pay for some things and on other occasions; and at my goldsmith's did observe the King's new Medall, where in little there is Mrs. Stewards face, as well done as ever I saw anything in my whole life I think – and a pretty thing it is that he should choose her face*a* to represent Britannia by.[1] So at the office late very busy, and much business with great joy despatched; and so home to supper and to bed.

26. Up, and to the office, where all the morning. And here did receive another reference from Sir W. Coventry about the business of some of the Muster-maisters, concerning whom I had returned their*b* small performances; which doth give me a little more trouble, for fear W. Coventry should think that I had a design to favour my brother Balty, and to that end to disparage all [the] rest – but I shall clear all very well; only, it doth exercise my thoughts more then I am at leisure for. At home find Balty and his wife, very fine; which I did not like, for fear he doth spend too much of his money that way and [not] lay up anything. After dinner to the office again, where by and by Lord Brouncker, W. Batten, J. Mennes and I met about receiving Carcasses answers to the depositions against him[2] – wherein I did see so much favour from my Lord to him that I do again begin to see that my Lord is not right at the bottom, and did make me the more earnest against him, though said little. But [my] Lord rising, declaring his judgment in his behalf and going away, I did hinder our arguing it by ourselfs and so*c* broke up the meeting; and myself went full of trouble to my office, there to write over the deposi-

---

a repl. 'place'   *b* repl. 's'–   *c* repl. 'up'

1. The medal is usually known as the Breda medal. Engraved by Jan Roettier, it was issued in copper, silver and gold, but not dated. The portrait of Frances Stewart as Britannia is on the reverse and is closely connected with Roettier's portrait medal of her: BM, *Medallic Illust.*, i (1885), pp. 535–6, no. 186; G. Wilson Peck, *Engl. copper coins*, p. 110. (OM).

2. See above, p. 64, n. 1.

tion and his answers side by[a] side; and then home to supper and to bed, with some trouble of mind to think of the issue of this, how it will breed ill blood among us here.

27. Up by candle-light about 6 a-clock, it being bitter cold weather again after all our warm weather, and by water down to Woolwich ropeyard (I being this day at a leisure, the King and Duke of York being gone down to Sherenesse this morning to lay out the design for a fortification there to the River Medway,[1] and so we do not attend the Duke of York as we should otherwise have done); and then to the Dockyard to enquire of the state of things; and went into Mr. Pett's and there, beyond expectation, he did present me with a Japan cane with a silver head, and his wife sent me by him a ring with a Woolwich stone,[2] now much in request; which I accepted, the value not being great and knowing that I had done them courtesies, which he did own in very high terms; and then, at my asking, did give me an old draft of an ancient-built ship, given him by his father, of the *Beare* in Queen Elizabeths time.[3] This did much please me, it being a thing I much desired to have, to show the difference in the built of ships now and heretofore. Being much taken[b] with this kindness – away to Blackwall and Deptford to satisfy myself there about the King's business; and then walked to Redriffe and so home about noon; there find Mr. Hunt, newly come out of the country, who tells me the country is much impoverished by the greatness of taxes. The Farmers do break every day almost, and 1000*l* a year become not worth 500*l*.[4]

a repl. 'then'　　　*b* repl. 'taking'

---

1. See below, p. 98 & n. 2, p. 127 & n. 1.
2. A variety of chalcedony found in the local flint-beds. Braybrooke (1858, iii. 335) states that Woolwich stones were still known by that name in his day.
3. The *White Bear* (usually called the *Bear*), built c. 1563, 1000 tons; one of the most famous Elizabethan ships, and one of the two largest of the fleet which defeated the Armada.

The engraving was probably that said to be of the *Bear*, by one of the Visschers, reproduced in e.g. M. Lewis, *Spanish Armada*, illust. 11. There is no copy in the PL. Pett's father, Phineas, had been master-shipwright at Chatham, 1605–29.
4. John Hunt was an excise officer for Cambridgeshire. For the agricultural depression, see below, p. 158, n. 1.

He dined with us, and we had good discourse of the general ill state of things; and by the way he told me some ridiculous pieces of thrift of Sir G Downing's, who is their*ᵃ* countryman – in inviting some poor people at Christmas last, to charm the country people's mouths; but did give them nothing but beef, porridge, pudding, and pork, and nothing said all dinner, but only his mother would say, "It's good broth, son." He would answer, "Yes, it is good broth." Then*ᵇ* his lady confirm all and say, "Yes, very good broth." By and by she would begin and say, "Good pork;" "Yes," says the mother, "good pork." Then he cries, "Yes, very good pork." And so they said of all things; to which nobody made any answer, they going there not out of love or esteem of them, but to eat his victuals, knowing him to be a niggardly fellow – and with this he is jeered now all over the country.[1] This day, just before dinner, comes Captain Story of Cambrige to me to the office about a bill for prest money for men sent out of the country and the countries about him to the fleet the last year.[2] But Lord, to see the natures of men. How this man, hearing*ᶜ* my name, did ask me of my country, and told me of my Cosen Roger that he was not so wise a man as his father, for that he doth not agree in Parliament with his fellow-burgesses and knights of the shire, whereas I know very well the reason – for he is not so high a flyer as Mr. Chichly[3]

---

a MS. 'the'   *b* MS. 'Then says'   *c* repl. 'knowing'

---

1. Downing had bought East Hatley, Cambs., in January 1661, and his mother lived with him there for the next ten years, on an allowance of £23 p.a. Both were equally mean. She was Lucy Winthrop, of Groton, Suff., sister of John Winthrop, first Governor of Massachusetts. See J. Beresford, *Godfather of Downing St*, esp. pp. 125, 129–30.

2. Thomas Story's bill for £200 5s. had been entered in the Navy Treasurer's ledger on 26 February and he had written to Pepys about it on the same day. It was for pressing 400 men from Cambridgeshire and neighbouring counties and carrying them to Harwich. PRO, Adm. 20/7/2, p. 609; *CSPD 1666–7*, p. 533.

3. Thomas Chicheley, of Wimpole, Cambs.; M.P. for the county; a wealthy landowner; now an Ordnance Commissioner; later (1670–4) Master-General of the Ordnance. His strong views on the Church are referred to below, 11 March 1668. In 1679 he displaced Roger Pepys as member for Cambridge borough in the elections to the first Exclusion Parliament.

and others, but loves the King better then any of them and to
better purpose. But yet he says that he is a very honest gentleman; and thence run into a hundred stories of his own services to
the King, and how he at this day brings in the taxes before anybody here thinks they are collected – discourse very absurd to
entertain a stranger with.[1] He being gone, and I glad of it, I
home then to dinner. After dinner with my wife by coach
abroad, and set Mr. Hunt down at the Temple and her at her
brother's. And I to White-hall to meet W. Coventry, but found
him not. But met Mr. Cooling,[2] who tells me of my Lord Duke
of Buckingham's being sent for last night by a Serjeant-at-armes
to the Tower for treasonable practices; and that the King is
infinitely angry with him and declared him no longer one of his
Council – I know not the reason of it, or occasion.[3] To Westminster-hall and there paid what I owed for books; and so by
coach took up my wife to the Exchange and there bought things
for Mr. Pierces little daughter, my Valentine; and so to their
house, where we find Knipp,*a* who also challengeth me for her
valentine. She looks well, sang well, and very merry we were
for half an hour. Tells me Harris[4] is well again, having been very
ill. And so we home and I to the office; then at night to Sir W.
Penn and sat with my Lady and the young couple[5] (the husband
⟨Sir William⟩ out of town) talking merrily; but they make a very
sorry couple methinks, though rich. So late home and to
bed.

a repl. 'him there'

---

1. Story was collector of assess-
ments and a farmer of the excise for
Cambridgeshire. In June 1667 he
was given command of a troop of
horse in the county: *CSPD Add.
1660–70*, p. 725.

2. Secretary to Manchester, the
Lord Chamberlain.

3. Since the autumn of 1666 Buckingham had led a fierce parliamentary
attack on the government, charging
them with inefficiency and corruption
in the conduct of the war. Cf. above,
vii. 309 & n. 1. Temporarily therefore out of royal favour (and Lady
Castlemaine's), he had been dismissed

from office on 25 February and a
warrant had been issued for his arrest:
CSPD 1666–7, p. 532. For the
charges of treason trumped up against
him, see below, pp. 93–4 & n. After
evading arrest and going into hiding,
he gave himself up at the end of June
and was committed to the Tower.
But he was never tried, and was
restored to office and favour in September. See Clarendon, *Life*, iii.
273+; A. Browning, *Danby*, i. 42+.

4. Henry Harris, the actor. (A).

5. Anthony Lowther and his newly-
wed wife Margaret (Penn).

28. Up, and there comes to me Drumbleby with a flagelette made to suit with my former,[1] and brings me one Greeting, a master to teach my wife. I agree by the whole with him, to teach her to take out any lesson of herself for 4*l.* She was not ready to begin today, but doth tomorrow.[2] So I to the office, where my Lord Brouncker and I only, all the morning, and did business. At noon to the Exchange and to Sir Rob. Viner's about settling my accounts there. So back home and to dinner, where Mr. Holliard[3] dined with us – and pleasant company he is. I love his company and he secures me against ever having the stone again. He gives it me as his opinion that the City will never be built again together as is expected while any restraint is laid upon them. He hath been a great loser, and would be a builder again; but he says he knows not what restrictions there will be, so as it is unsafe for him to begin.[4] He gone, I to the office and there busy till night, doing much business; then home and to my accounts; wherein, beyond expectation, I succeeded so well as to settle them very clear and plain, though by borrowing of monies this month to pay D Gawden and chopping and changing with my Tanger money, they were become somewhat intricate. And blessed be God, upon the evening my accounts, I do appear 6800*l* creditor. This done, I to supper about 12 at night, and so to bed – the weather for three or four days being come to be exceeding cold again, as any time this year.

I did within these six days see smoke still remaining of the late fire in the City;[5] and it is strange to think how to this very day I cannot sleep a-night without great terrors of fire; and this very night could not sleep till almost 2 in the morning through thoughts of fire.

Thus this month is ended with great content of mind to me –

1. See above, p. 53; below, p. 396. (E).
2. The lessons continued until 20 May 1667 and were resumed on 13 August 1668. Thomas Greeting was a court musician. (E).
3. Thomas Hollier, surgeon.
4. The widths of streets and the lines of frontages had been left by the recent rebuilding act for decision by the King and city: see above, p. 72,

n. 2. Rebuilding could not be undertaken in advance of their decisions. Hollier had property on the w. side of Warwick Lane. In 1669 the Royal College of Physicians bought a site from him there for £1200 on which they built the college which they occupied until 1825: Sir G. Clark, *Hist. R. Coll. Physicians,* i. 186, 329.
5. Cf. above, vii. 393, n. 1.

thriving in my estate, and my matters in my offices going pretty well as to myself. This afternoon Mr. Gawden was with me, and tells me more then I knew before: that he hath orders to get all the victuals he can to Plymouth and the Western ports and other outports, and some to Scotland; so that we do entend to keep but a flying fleet[1] this year; which it may be may preserve us a year longer, but the end of it must be ruin.

Sir J. Mennes this night tells me that he hears for certain that ballads are made of us in Holland*a* for begging of a peace; which I expected, but am vexed at.[2] So ends this month, with nothing of weight upon my mind but for my father and mother, who are both ill and have been so for some weeks – whom God help, but I do fear my poor father will hardly be ever thoroughly well again.*b*

a repl. 'Hold
b Here end the entries in the fourth volume of the MS. Two blank pages follow.

---

1. See below, p. 98 & n. 1.
2. These do not appear in W. P. C.
Knuttel's *Catalogus* (1889–1920) of Dutch pamphlets.

1. Up, it being very cold weather again after a good deal of warm summer weather – and to the office, where I settled to do much business today. By and by sent for to Sir G Carteret to discourse of the business of the Navy and our wants, and the best way of bestowing the little money we have, which is about 30000*l*, but God knows we have need of ten times as much – which doth make my life uncomfortable,[a] I confess, on the King's behalf, though it is well enough as to my own perticular; but the King's service is undone by[b] it. Having done with him, back again to the office; and in the street in Mark-lane do observe (it being St. Davids' day) the picture of a man dressed like a Welchman, hanging by the neck upon one of the poles that stand out at the top of one of the merchants' houses, in full proportion and very handsomely done[1] – which is one of the oddest sights I have seen a good while, for it was so like a man that one would have thought it was endeed a man.

Being returned home, I find Greeting the flagelette-master come and teaching my wife; and I do think my wife will take pleasure in it, and it will be easy for her and pleasant – so I, as I am well contented with the charge it will occasion me.

So to the office till dinner, busy; and then home to dinner, and before dinner making my wife to sing; poor wretch, her ear[c] is so bad that it made me angry, till the poor wretch cried to see me so vexed at her, that I think I shall not discourage her so much again but will endeavour to make her understand sounds and do her good that way, for she hath a great mind to learn, only to please me; and therefore I am mighty unjust to her in discouraging her so much. But we were good friends, and to

a repl. 'uncomp'–   *b* repl. 'that'
c MS. 'hear', repl. 'is' or 'h'–

---

1. This and similar customs were common: cf. J. Brand, *Pop. Antiq.* (ed. Hazlitt), i. 58–61; A. R. Wright, *Brit. cal. customs* (*Engl.* ed. Lones), ii. 158+.

dinner; and had she not been ill with those and that it were not Friday (on which in Lent there are no plays), I had carried her to a play. But she not being fit to go abroad, I to the office; where all the afternoon close, examining the collection of my papers of the accounts of the Navy since this war[1] to my great content; and so at night home to talk and sing with my wife; and then to supper and so to bed with great pleasure. But I cannot but remember that just before dinner one[a] of my people came up to me and told me a man come from Huntington would speak with me, how[b] my heart came into my mouth, doubting that my father (who hath been long sick) was dead. It put me into a trembling; but blessed be, it was no such thing, but a countryman come about ordinary business to me, to receive 50*l* paid to my father in the country for the Perkins's for their legacy, upon the death of their mother, by my Uncle's Will.[2] So though I get nothing at present, at least by that estate, I am fain to pay this money rather then rob my father. And much good may it do them, that I may have no further trouble from them.

I hear today that Tom Woodall, the known Chyrurgeon, is killed at Somerset-house by a Frenchman, but the occasion Sir W. Batten could not tell me.[3]

2. Up, and to the office, where sitting all the morning; and among other things, did agree upon a distribution of 30000*l* and odd, which is the only sum we hear of like to come out of all the Poll Bill for the use of this office for buying of goods. I did herein some few courtesies for perticular friends I wished well to, and for the King's services also – and was therefore well pleased with what was done. Sir W Pen this day did bring an order[c] from the Duke of York for our receiving from him[4] a small vessel

---

a repl. 'a'   *b* repl. 'my'   *c* repl. 'great order for better'

---

1. See above, p. 71 & n. 1.

2. Robert Pepys of Brampton (d. 1661) had left to his sister Jane Perkins £5 p.a. during her life, and after her death £50 to be divided between her son Francis and her daughters Elizabeth and Mary.

3. Woodall, a surgeon-in-ordinary to the King, had been killed in a drunken quarrel: below, p. 92.

4. Penn.

for a fireship and taking away a better of the King's for it, it being expressed for his great service to the King. This I am glad of; not for his sake, but that it will give me a better ground, I believe, to ask something for myself of this kind; which I was fearful to begin.[1] This doth make Sir W. Penn the most fond to me that can be. I suppose it is this: lest it should find any opposition from me; but I will not oppose, but promote it.

After dinner with my wife to the King's house, to see *The Mayden Queene*, a new play of Dryden's mightily commended for the regularity of it and the strain and wit; and the truth is, there is a comical part done by Nell, which is Florimell, that I never can hope ever to see the like done again by man or woman.[2] The King and Duke of York was at the play; but so great performance of a comical part was never, I believe, in the world before as Nell doth this, both as a mad girle and then, most and best of all, when she comes in like a young gallant; and hath the motions and carriage of a spark the most that ever I saw any man have. It makes me, I confess, admire her. Thence home and to the office, where busy a while; and then home to read the lives of Henry the 5th and 6th, very fine, in Speede;[3] and so to bed. This day I did pay a bill of 50*l* from my father, it being so much out of my own purse given to pay my Uncle Robert's legacy to my aunt Perkins's child.

3. Lay long, merrily talking with my wife; and then up and to church, where a dull sermon of Mr. Mills touching Originall Sin; and then home and there find little Michell and his wife, whom I love mightily. Mightily contented I was in their company, for I love her much; and so after dinner I left them and by water from the Old Swan to White-hall; where walking in the galleries, I in the first place met Mr. Pierce, who tells me the

---

1. See below, p. 441. The *Flying Greyhound* hired to Pepys and his colleagues in 1666 was due to be returned in the spring of 1667 for use as a fireship: above, vii. 301, n. 1.

2. The play was *Secret Love, or The maiden Queen*, a tragicomedy, first acted in this year, and published in 1668. The cast listed by Downes (p. 7) includes Nell Gwyn as Florimel, Mrs Knepp as Asteria, Mrs Corey as Melissa, Hart as Celadon, Mohun as Philicles and Burt as Lysimantes. (A).

3. John Speed, *The history of Great Britaine* (1650), pp. 635-85; PL 2906.

story of the death of Tom Woodall the surgeon, killed in a drunken quarrel, and how the Duke of York hath a mind to get him one of his places in St. Tho. Hospitall.[1]   Then comes Mr. Hayward the Duke of York's servant to us and tells us that the Swedes Imbassador hath been here today with news, and that it is believed that the Dutch will yield to have the treaty at London or Dover; neither of which will get our King any credit, we having already consented to have it at The Hague – which it seems De Witt opposed as a thing wherein the King of England must needs have some profound design, which in my conscience he hath not.[2]   They do also tell me that news is this day come to the King that the King of France is come with his army to the frontiers of Flanders, demanding leave to pass through their country towards Poland, but is denied; and thereupon, that he is gone into the country: how true this is, I dare not believe till I hear more.[3]

From them I walked into the park, it being a fine but very cold day, and there took two or three turns the length of the Pell Mell.   And there I met Serjeant Barcroft, who was sent for the Duke of Buckingham to have brought him prisoner to the

---

1. Pearse was already Surgeon-in-Ordinary to the Duke. If peace were to be made he might lose his post of Surgeon-General to the fleet. He does not appear to have been given a hospital post, but his naval pay was continued after the peace: see below, p. 198 & n. 1.

2. The Hague was the centre of the Orangist faction, whose members were enemies of de Witt's republican party. (The de Witt brothers were in 1672 to meet their deaths at the hands of a mob there.) There was no truth in the news about London and Dover.

3. Another canard. Louis' diplomatic and military preparations for the invasion of Flanders (which took place, without any declaration of war,

on 14/24 May) were not completed until the end of April, though there were said to be 50,000 horse and foot on the frontier by the end of March: Bodl., Clar. 85, ff. 133+.   There was civil war in Poland at this time, in which Louis was promoting the election of a French candidate to the Polish throne. During the winter he had allowed his ambitions in the Low Countries to take precedence of his Polish interests, but as late as April he was thinking of sending a small expeditionary force to Poland. F. A. M. Mignet, *Négociations relatives à la succession d'Espagne* (1835+), ii. 508–10;   A.-M. Gasztowtt, *Une mission diplom. en Pologne . . . 1665–8*, p. 52.

Towre.[1] He came to town this day; and brings word that being overtaken and outridd by the Duchess of Buckingham, within a few miles of the Duke's house of Westthorp[2] he believes, she got thither about a quarter of an hour before him and so had time to consider – so that when he came, the doors were kept[a] shut against him. The next day, coming with officers of the neighbour market-town[3] to force open the doors, they were open for him, but the Duke of Buckingham[b] gone; so he took horse presently, and heard upon the road that the Duke of Buckingham was gone before him for London; so that he believes he is this day also come to town before him – but no news is yet heard of him.[4] This is all he brings. Thence to my Lord Chancellor; and there meeting Sir H. Cholmly, he and I walked in my Lord's garden and talked, among other things, of the treaty; and he says there will certainly be a peace, but I cannot believe it. He tells me that the Duke of Buckingham his crimes, as far as he knows, is his being of a Caball with some discontented persons of the late House of Commons,[5] and opposing the desires of[c] the King in all his matters in the House – and endeavouring to become popular – and advising how the Commons' House should proceed, and how he would order the House of Lords – and that he hath been endeavouring to have the King's nativity calculated; which was done, and the fellow now in the Tower about it – which itself hath heretofore, as he says, been held treason,[d] and people died for it – but by the

a	repl. 'op'-	*b*	MS. 'York'
c	repl. 'in'	*d*	repl. 'treasure'

---

1. For Buckingham's alleged offences, see above, p. 86 & n. 3; below, pp. 93–4. John Barcroft was one of the sergeants-at-arms to the King. (It was a sergeant-at-arms rather than a Council messenger who would be employed to arrest so exalted a malefactor.) Barcroft's (undated) narrative of his misadventure is in Bodl., Clar. 85, ff. 96–7; cf. also HMC, *Le Fleming*, pp. 45–6.

2. *Recte* Wothorpe Lodge, Northants.

3. Stamford, Lincs.

4. Buckingham was said to have gone into hiding in the house of Sir Henry Belasyse: Sir John Reresby, *Memoirs* (ed. Browning), p. 66.

5. During the late session Buckingham had built up a connection in the Commons which included the ablest critics of the government – Temple, Garroway, Seymour and Howard. A. Browning, *Danby*, i. 42.

Statute of Treasons, in Queen Mary's times and since, it hath been left out.[1] He tells me that this silly Lord hath provoked, by his ill-carriage, the Duke of York, my Lord Chancellor, and all the great persons, and therefore most likely will die. He tells me too, many practices of treachery against this King; as betraying him in Scotland and giving Oliver an account of the King's private councils; which the King knows very well and yet hath pardoned him.[2]

Here I passed away a little time more, talking with him and Creed, whom I met there; and so away, Creed walking with me to White-hall; and there I took water, and staying at Michells to drink, I home and there to read very good things in Fullers *Church History* and *Worthies*,[3] and so to supper; and after supper had much good discourse with W. Hewers, who supped with us, about[a] the Ticket Office and the knaveries and extortions every day used there; and perticularly of the business of Mr. Carcasse,[4] whom I fear I shall find a very rogue. So parted with him, and then to bed.

a MS. 'by'

---

1. John Heydon, astrologer and Rosicrucian, an associate of Buckingham, had been arrested in January, and among his papers was found an unsigned letter ordering him to cast the King's nativity. He was examined by several members of the government, and also (according to his letter of 13 March) tortured. Another charge was that Buckingham had used him to incite seamen to mutiny. H. Slingsby, *Diary* (ed. Parsons), p. 368; HMC, *Le Fleming*, pp. 44–6; *CSPD 1666–7*, pp. 428, 431; T. Carte, *Hist. Ormonde* (1735–6), ii. 347, iv. 293–4. In 1655–7 he had been imprisoned for forecasting that Cromwell would be hanged: Carte, ii. 347. The casting of the ruler's horoscope had never, in Mary's time or at any other time, been made treasonable *per se*, though it might

come within the terms of 'compassing or imagining' the death of the King, Queen or heir, which had been one of the basic treasons since 1353. An act of 23 Eliz. c. 2 (valid only during Elizabeth's reign) had made it a felony to calculate the royal nativity. See Sir Matthew Hale, *Historia placitorum coronae* (1800 ed.), i. 107–8, 332. All these matters were pretexts used by Buckingham's political enemies for their own purposes.

2. The King had reason to distrust Buckingham in Scotland in 1650–1, but his intrigues were with Argyll (leader of a rival royalist faction), not with Cromwell: Clarendon, *Hist.*, v. 171; *Nicholas Papers* (ed. G. F. Warner), i. 201.

3. See above, i. 56, n. 6; ii. 21, n. 1.

4. See above, p. 64 & n. 1.

4. Up, and with Sir J. Mennes and W. Batten by barge to Deptford by 8 in the morning, where to the King's yard a little to look after business there, and then to a private storehouse to look upon some cordage of Sir W. Batten's; and there being a hole formerly made for a drain for Tarr to run into, wherein the barrel stood still full of stinking water, Sir W. Batten did fall with one leg into it; which might have been very bad to him, by breaking a leg or other hurt, but thanks be to God he only sprained his foot a little. So after his shifting his stocking at a strong-water shop close by, we took barge again and so to Woolwich, where our business was chiefly to look upon the ballast-wharf there, which is offered us for the King's use to hire. But we do not think it worth the laying out*a* much money upon, unless we could buy the fee-simple of it; which cannot be sold us, so we wholly flung it off.[1] So to the Dockyard and there stayed a while, talking about business of the yard, and thence to the Ropeyard; and so to the White Hart and there dined, and Captain Cocke with us, who we find at the Ropeyard; and very merry at dinner, and many pretty tales*b* of Sir J. Mennes, which I have entered in my tale book.[2] But by this time Sir W. Batten was come to be in much pain in his foot, so as he was forced to be carried down in a chair to the barge again; and so away to Deptford, and there I a little in the yard; and then to Bagwells, where I find his wife washing, and I*c* did hazer todo que jo voudrais con her; and then sent for her husband and discoursed of his going to Harwich this week to his charge of the new ship building there which I have got him[3] – and so away, walked to Redriffe and there took boat and away home, upon Tower-hill, near the Ticket Office, meeting with my old acquaintance Mr. Chaplin the cheesemonger; and there fell to talk of news and he tells me that for certain the King of France is denied passage with his army*d* through Flanders[4] – and that he hears that the Dutch

---

a repl. 'up'   *b* repl. 'tallies'   *c* MS. 'all I'   *d* repl. 'tr'-

1. I have found nothing more about this proposal.

2. Not extant, alas; possibly the 'Anecdotes' referred to by Pepys in a memorandum of c. 1698: *Priv. Corr.*, i. 165.

3. The *Rupert*, a 3rd-rate: see above, p. 39 & n. 1. Mrs Bagwell, as a result, was in Harwich with her husband until 6 January 1668.

4. See above, p. 92 & n. 3.

do stand upon high terms with us, and will have a promise of not
being obliged to strike the flag to us before they will treat with
us, and other high things which I am ashamed of and do hope
will never be yielded to.[1] That they do make all imaginable
preparations, but that he believes they will be in mighty want
of men. That the King of France doth court us mightily. He
tells me too, that our Lord Treasurer is going to lay down, and
that my Lord Arlington is to[a] be Lord Treasurer; but I believe
nothing of it – for he is not yet of an estate visible enough to
have that charge I suppose upon him.[2] So[b] being parted from
him, I home to the office; and after having done business there,
I home to supper; and there mightily pleased with my wife's
beginning on the Flagelette, believing that she will come to [play]
very well thereon. So to bed. This day in the barge I took
Berchensha's translation of Alsted his *Templum*;[3] but the most
ridiculous book, as he hath translated it, that ever I saw in my life;
I declaring that I understood not three lines together, from one
end of the book to the other.

5. Up, and to the office, where met and sat all the morning,
doing little for want of money – but only bear the countenance

repl. 'the'   b repl. 'thence'

---

1. In a treaty of September 1662
the Dutch had agreed that their ships
(both merchantmen and men-of-war)
should strike flag and lower top-
sails on meeting a British man-of-war
in British seas. This agreement was
in fact repeated in the peace of
August 1667. The Dutch also insisted, in these preliminaries, on the
retention of the island of Pulo Run (in
the E. Indies) which England claimed
under the 1662 treaty: cf. Bodl.,
Clar. 85, ff. 84*r*, 86*r*.

2. Arlington was a younger son
and his elder brother now owned the
family house at Harlington, Middlesex. It was stated in his marriage

contract (1666) that in five years he
would have £4000 p.a. clear in land:
V. H. Barbour, *Arlington*, pp. 100–01.
It had been common knowledge for
months that he aimed at the Lord
Treasurership: cf. below, pp. 118–19;
CSPD 1667–8, p. 259. But Southampton, despite illness, hung on to the
office until his death in May 1667, and
was succeeded by a commission of
which Arlington was not a member.
In 1672 and 1673 he was again twice
disappointed of his hopes.

3. John Birchensha, *Templum Mu-
sicum* (1664); a translation of bk xiv
of J. H. Alstedt, *Encyclopaedia* (1630;
PL 2523–4). (E).

of an office. At noon home to dinner and then to the office again; and there comes Martin my purser and I walked with him awhile in the garden, I giving him good advice to beware of coming any more with high demands for supernumeraries or other things; for now Sir W Pen is come to mind that business, the passing of his accounts will not be so easy as the last. He tells me he will never need it again, it being as easy and to as much purpose to do the same thing otherwise; and how he doth keep his Captain's table, and by that means hath the command of his Captains; and doth not fear, in a 5th-rate ship constantly imployed, to get 1000*l* in five years time. And this year, besides all his spendings, which are I fear high, he hath got at this day clear above 150*l* in a voyage*a* of about five or six months – which is a brave trade.[1]

He gone, I to the office and there all the afternoon late, doing much business; and then to see Sir W. Batten, whose leg is ill, but better*b* then it was and like to do well. I by discourse do perceive he and his Lady are to their hearts out with my Lord Brouncker and Mrs. Williams, to which I added something; but I think did not venture too far with them. But Lord, to see to what a poor content any acquaintance among these people, or the people of the world as they nowadays go, is worth; for my part, I and my wife will keep to one another and let the world go hang – for there is nothing but falseness in it. So home to supper; and hear my wife and girl sing a little and then to bed with much content of mind.

6. Up, and with W. Penn*c* to White*d*-hall by coach; and by the way agreed to acquaint W. Coventry with the business of Mr. Carcasse, and he and I spoke to W. Coventry that we might move it to the Duke of York; which I did in a very indifferent, that is, impartial manner, but vexed I believe Lord Brouncker. Here the Duke of York did acquaint us (and the King did the like also, afterward coming in) with his resolution of altering the manner of the war*e* this year; that is, that we shall keep what fleet we

a repl. 'v'-   *b* repl. symbol rendered illegible   *c* repl. 'Batten'
     d repl. 'Westminster'-   *e* repl. 'water'

1. For pursers' profits, see above, vi. 306 & n. 1.

have abroad in several squadrons; so that now all is come out, but we are to keep it as close as we can, without hindering the work that is to be done in preparation to this.¹ Great preparations there are to fortify Sheernesse² and the yard at Portsmouth,³ and forces are drawing down to both those places, and elsewhere by the seaside; so that we have some fear of an invasion, and the Duke of York himself did declare his expectation of the enemy's blocking us up here in the River, and therefore directed that we should send away all the ships that we have to fit out hence. Sir W. Penn told me, going with me this morning to White-hall, that for certain the Duke of Buckingham is brought into the Tower, and that he hath had an hour's private conference with the King before he was sent thither.⁴

To Westminster-hall; there bought some newsbooks and, as everywhere else, hear everybody complain of the dearness of coals, being at 4l per chaldron;⁵ the weather too being become most bitter cold, the King saying today that it was the coldest day he ever knew in England.⁶ Thence by coach to my Lord

1. The decision to lay up the big ships and abandon all hope of setting out a battle fleet was made by the Cabinet by February, the Duke of York dissenting: Feiling, p. 206.

2. An agreement was signed this day with Sir Bernard de Gomme, joint engineer-in-chief of royal castles and forts, for the construction of works at Sheerness: BM, Sloane 2448, f. 44r. Cf. below, p. 127 & n. 1. The work, although vital to the defence of Chatham, proceeded slowly and was not completed when the Dutch sailed into the Medway in June. They were able to take it on the afternoon of the 10th without loss of life. See below, pp. 258 + .

3. Commissions for the fortification of Portsmouth dockyard had been set up in 1665 and 1666, and the work was now within a few weeks of completion: CSPD 1664–5, p. 510; ib. Add. 1660–85, p. 160; ib. 1666–7, p. 599.

4. For Buckingham's movements, see above, p. 86 & n. 3.

5. In the previous December the price had been 63s. a chaldron: above, vii. 401 & n. 5. Because of the war the price now continued to rise during the summer, when normally a fall would have been expected. At 26 June Pepys records the highest known price of the century for London – 110s. a chaldron (c. 82s. 6d. a ton). By September it had dropped to 28s.–29s. See below, pp. 187, 295–6, 435; J. U. Nef, Rise Brit. coal industry, ii. 81, 403–4.

6. Similarly, Anthony à Wood (at Oxford) remarked that such weather 'hath not bin remembered by man': see L. & T., ii. 103. The Thames at Oxford, though not at London, was frozen over so that carts could be driven across it. Cf. also Evelyn, 10 March; R. Boyle, Gen. hist. of the air (1692), pp. 114–15.

Crews, where very welcome. Here I find they are in doubt where*a* the Duke of Buckingham is; which makes me mightily reflect on the uncertainty of all history, when in a business of this moment and of this day's growth we cannot tell the truth. Here dined my old acquaintance Mr. Burfett, that was my Lord Sandwiches chaplain, and my Lady Wright and Dr. Boreman, who is preacher at St. Gyles in the Fields; who after dinner did give my Lord an account of two papists, women, lately converted; whereof one wrote her recantation, which he showed under her own hand, mighty well drawn, so as my Lord desired a copy of it after he had satisfied himself from the Doctor that to his knowledge she was not a woman under*b* any necessity.[1] Thence by coach home and stayed a very little; and then down by water to Redriffe and walked to Bagwells; where la moher was dentro sed would not have me demorer there parceque Mrs. Batters and one of my ancillas, I believe Jane (for she was gone abroad today), was in the town and coming thither; so I away presently, esteeming it a great escape. So to the yard and spoke a word or two; and then by water home, wondrous cold and reading a ridiculous ballad made in praise of the Duke of Albemarle to the tune of *St. George*, the tune being printed too.[2] And I observe that people have some great encouragement to make ballads of him of this kind; there are so many, that hereafter will sound like *Guy of Warwicke*.[3] Then abroad with my wife, leaving her at the Change; while I to Sir H. Cholmly's, a pretty house,[4]

a repl. 'where'   *b* repl. 'any'

1. There appears to be no account of these conversions in Robert Boreman's published writings.

2. *A heroical song on . . . George Duke of Albemarle . . . made in August 1666.* The refrain runs: 'Lord George was born in England, restor'd his Countryes Joy,/Come let us sing Vive le Roy'. See C. M. Simpson, *Brit. broadside ballad and its music*, pp. 628–30. (E).

3. References to a ballad on Guy of Warwick (one of the best-known heroes of English folklore) abound

from the 1580s onwards. His exploits (celebrated in several late-medieval verse romances) had been set in the period of the Crusades, and the Earls of Warwick claimed descent from him. Cf. Simpson, op. cit., pp. 283–5.

4. A large establishment in the fashionable new Pall Mall, taxed on 23 hearths in 1666, and described in the hearth-tax returns of 1666 as 'empty, new built': PRO, E 179/252/32, St Martin's, f. 3r. (R).

and a fine worthy well-disposed gentleman he is.   He and I to Sir
Ph. Warwicke's about money for Tanger, but to little purpose.
H. Cholmly tells me, among other things, that he hears of little
hopes of a peace, their demands being so high as we shall never
grant; and could tell me that we shall keep no fleet abroad this
year, but only squadrons; and among other things, that my Lord
Bellasses, he believes, will lose his command of Tanger by his
corrupt covetous ways of endeavouring to sell his command[1] –
which I am glad, for he is a man of no worth in the world but
compliment.   So to the Change and there bought 32s worth of
things for Mrs. Knipp, my valentine – which is pretty, to see
how my wife is come to condition with me, that whatever I do
give to anybody else, I shall give her as much; which I am not
much displeased with.   So home and to the office and Sir W.
Batten, to tell him what I had done today about Carcasse's
business;[2] and God forgive me, I am not without design to give
a blow to Sir W. Batten by it.   So home, where Mr. Batelier
supped with us and talked away the evening pretty late; and so
he gone and we to bed.

7.   Up, and to the office, my head full of Carcasse's business.
Then hearing that Knipp is at my house, I home, and it was
about a ticket for a friend of hers.   I do love the humour of the
Jade very well.   So to the office again, not being able to stay,
and there about noon my Lord Brouncker did begin to talk of
Carcasse's business.   Only Commissioner Pett, my Lord, and I
there; and it was pretty to see how Pett hugged the occasion of
having*a* anything against Sir W. Batten;   which I am not much
troubled at I confess, for I love him not neither – though I did
really endeavour to quash it all I could, because I would prevent
their malice taking effect.   My Lord I see is fully resolved to
vindicate Carcasse, though to the undoing W. Batten; but I
believe he will find himself in a mistake and do himself no good,
and that I shall be glad of, for though I love the treason I hate the

a repl. 'an'-

---

1. E.g.   to   Cholmley   himself: practices in the Ticket Office: see
above, p. 45.   above, p. 64 & n. 1.
2. Carkesse was accused of corrupt

traitor[1] – but he is vexed at my moving it to the Duke of York yesterday; which I answered well, so as I think he could not answer; but Lord, it is pretty to see how Pett hugs this business – and how he favours my Lord Brouncker, who to my knowledge hates him – and hath said more to his disadvantage, in my presence, to the King and Duke of York, then any man in England. And so let them thrive one with another by cheating one another, for that is all I observe among them. Thence home late and find my wife hath dined, and she and Mrs. Hewers going to a play. Here was Creed; and he and I to Devonshire-house to a burial of a kinsman[a] of Sir R. Viners and there I received a ring,[2] and so away presently to Creed, who stayed for me at an alehouse hard by, and thence to Dukes playhouse, where he parted; and I in and find my wife and Mrs. Hewers, and sat by them and saw *The English Princesse or Richard the Third*;[3] a most sad, melancholy play, and pretty good, but nothing eminent in it as some Tragedys are. Only, little Mis Davis did dance a Jigg after the end of the play,[4] and there telling the next day's play;[5] so that it came in by force only to please the company to see her dance in boy's clothes; and the truth is, there is no comparison between Nell's[b] dancing the other day at the King's house in boy's clothes[6] and this, this being infinitely beyond the other. Here was Mrs. Clerke and Pierce, to whom one word only of "How do you?", and so away home, Mrs. Hewers with us; and I to the office, and so to W. Batten's and there talked privately with him and W. Penn about business of Carcasse against tomorrow; wherein I think I did give them proof enough of my ability as well as friendship

a repl. 'ns'- *b* repl. 'her'

1. A proverbial saying, implying here that Pepys was divided in mind, since although he approved of any attack on Batten, he disapproved in this case of the attacker (Brouncker).

2. The burial has not been traced. For funeral rings, see above, ii. 74, n.2.

3. *The English Princesse or The death of Richard the III*: a tragedy by John Caryl, published in this year; this is the first definite record of a performance. According to Downes (p. 27), Betterton played King Richard; Harris, the Duke of Richmond; Smith, Sir William Stanley. (A).

4. This was an Elizabethan practice which continued in Restoration theatres. A jig was a song and dance elaborating a dramatic action, or sometimes just a dance in character. (A).

5. This form of theatrical publicity was used in England until the mid-19th century. (A).

6. See above, p. 91. (A).

to W. Batten and the honour of the office, in my sense of this rogue's business. So back to finish my office business, and then home to supper and to bed.

This day Commissioner Taylor came to me for advice, and would force me to take ten pieces in gold of him; which I had no mind to, he being become one of our number at the Board.[1]

This day was reckoned by all people the coldest day that ever was remembered in England – and God knows, coles at a very great price.[2]

8. Up, and to the Old Swan, where drink at Michells; but not seeing her whom I love, I by water to White-hall and there acquainted Sir G. Carteret betimes what I had to say this day before the Duke of York in the business of Carcasse; which he likes well of, being a great enemy to him; and then I being too early here to go to Sir W. Coventry's chamber, having nothing to say to him and being able to give him but a bad account of the business of the office (which is a shame to me, and that which I shall rue if I do not recover), to the Exchequer about getting a Certificate of Mr. Lanyon's entered at Sir R. Long's office;[3] and strange it is to see what horrid delays there are at this day in the business of money, there being nothing yet come from my Lord Treasurer to set that business of money in action since the Parliament broke off, notwithstanding the greatness and number of the King's occasions for it. So to the Swan, and there have three or four besados of the little ancilla there; and so to Westminster hall, where I saw Mr. Martin the purser come through with a picture in his hand which he had bought, and observed how all the people of the Hall did fleer and laugh[a] upon him,

a repl. 'there'

---

1. John Taylor, now Navy Commissioner at Harwich, had, when he was a timber merchant in Wapping, given several presents to Pepys: above, vi. 274, 280. His accounts for the building of a ship were now under examination.

2. For the weather, see above, p. 98 & n. 6; for the price of coal, see loc. cit., n. 5.

3. The certificate acknowledging receipt of Lanyon's supplies (for Tangier) would be carried to Long, Auditor of the Receipt, who would draw up an order authorising payment requiring the signature of the Lord Treasurer. Lanyon's order was for close on £3000: PRO, E 403/2430.

crying, "There is plenty grown up on a sudden!" and the truth is, I was a little troubled that my favour should fall on so vain a fellow as he; and the more because methought the people do gaze upon me as the man that had raised him, and as if they guessed whence*a* my kindness*b* to him springs.

So thence to White-hall, where I find all met at the Duke of York's chamber; and by and by the Duke of York comes and Carcasse is called in, and I read the depositions and his answers, and he added with great confidence and good words, even almost to persuasion, what to say; and my Lord Brouncker, like a very silly solicitor, argued against me and us all for him; and being asked first by the Duke of York his opinion, did give it for his being excused. I next did answer the contrary very plainly; and had in this dispute (which vexed and will never be forgot by my Lord) many occasions of speaking severely, and did, against his bad practices. Commissioner Pett, like a fawning rogue, sided with my Lord Brouncker, but to no purpose; and W. Penn, like a cunning rogue, spoke mighty indifferently and said nothing in all the fray, like a knave as he is. But W. Batten spoke home, and did come off himself by the Duke's kindness very well; and then Sir G. Carteret and Sir W. Coventry, and the Duke of York himself, flatly as I said; and so he was declared unfit to continue in, and therefore to be presently discharged the office; which among other good effects, I hope will make my Lord Brouncker not altogether so high – when he shall consider he hath had such a public foyle as this is. So home with W. Batten, W. Penn by coach and there met at the office; and my Lord Brouncker presently after us and there did give order to Mr. Stevens for securing the tickets in Carcasse's hands, which my Lord against his will could not refuse to sign; and then home to dinner, and so away with my wife by coach, she to Mrs. Pierces and I to my Lord Bellasses; and with him to Lord Treasurers, where by agreement we met with Sir H. Cholmly and there sat and talked all the afternoon almost about one thing or other, expecting Sir Ph. Warwicks coming; but he came not, so we away towards night, Sir H. Cholmly and I to the Temple and there parted, telling me of my Lord Bellasses want*c* of generosity, and that he will certainly be turned out of his government, and he

a MS. 'when'   *b* repl. 'kins'-
c repl. same symbol badly formed

thinks himself stands fair for it.[1] So home and there find, as I expected, Mrs. Pierce and Mr. Batelier. He went for Mrs. Jones – but no Mrs. Knipp came, which vexed me, nor any other company. So with one fidler we danced away the evening; but I was not well contented with*a* the littleness of the room and my wife's want of preparing things ready as they should be for supper and bed – so not very merry, though very ⟨well⟩ pleased. So after supper to bed – my wife and Mrs. Pierce, and her boy James and I. Yesterday I begun to make this mark (✓) stand instead of three pricks, thus (.·.); which therefore I must observe everywhere, it being a mark more easy to make.*b*

9. Up, and to the office, where sat all the morning busy. At noon home to dinner, where*c* Mrs. Pierce did continue with us, and her boy (who I still find every day more and more witty beyond his age) and did dine with us; and by and by comes in her husband and a brother-in-law of his, a parson, one of the tallest biggest men that ever I saw in my life. So to the office, where a meeting extraordinary about settling the number and wages of my Lord Brouncker's clerks for his new work upon the Treasurer's accounts;[2] but this did put us upon running into the business of yesterday about Carcasse, wherein I perceive he is most dissatisfied with me; and I am not sorry for it, having all the world but him of my side therein, for it will let him know another time that he is not to expect our submitting to him in everything, as I think he did heretofore expect. He did speak many severe words to me and I returned as many to him, so that I do think there cannot for a great while be any right peace between us – and I care not a fart for it; but however, I must look about me and mind my business, for I perceive by his threats and inquiries he is and will endeavour to find out something against me or mine. Breaking up here somewhat brokenly, I home and carried Mrs. Pierce and wife to the New Exchange,

a repl. 'there'
b These marks represent major pauses (full stops or dashes). Pepys had tentatively begun to use the new mark on 7 March and he frequently used the old one until 17 March.
c repl. 'and then'

1. See above, p. 45 & n. 2.   2. See above, p. 20.

and there did give her and myself a pair of gloves and then set her down at home; and so back again straight home and there to do business; and then to Sir W. Batten, where W. Penn and others, and mighty merry; only, I have got a great cold, and the scolding this day at the office with my Lord Brouncker hath made it worse, that I am not able to speak. But Lord, to see how kind Sir W. Batten and his Lady are to me upon this business of my standing by W. Batten against Carcasse; and I am glad of it. Captain Cocke,[a] who was here tonight, did tell us that he is certain that yesterday a proclamation was voted at the Council touching the proclaiming of my Lord Duke of Buckingham a Traytor, and that it will be out on Monday.[1] So home late and drank some buttered ale, and so to bed and to sleep. This cold did most certainly come by my staying a little too long[b] bare-legged yesterday morning when I rose while I looked out fresh socks and thread stockings, yesterday's having in the night, lying near the window, been covered with Snow within the window, which made me I durst not put them on.

10. *Lords day.* Having my cold still grown more upon me, so as I am not able to speak, I lay in bed till noon; and then up and to my chamber with a good fire and there spent an hour on Morly's *Introduction to Music*, a very good but inmethodical book.[2] Then to dinner, my wife and I; and then I all the afternoon alone in my chamber, preparing a letter for Comissioner Taylor to the City about getting his accounts for the *Loyall London*, by him built for them, stated and discharged, they owing him still above 4000*l*.[3] Towards the evening comes Mr. Spong[4]

---

a repl. 'Sir W. Batten'   *b* repl. symbol rendered illegible

---

1. The proclamation was dated 8 March: Steele, no. 3486. Buckingham was accused of trying to raise mutiny and sedition, and of resisting arrest.

2. Thomas Morley, *A plaine and easie introduction to practicall musicke* (1597); PL 2031. Modern ed. (1952) by R. A. Harman. (E).

3. This was the ship given to the King by the city in 1666 to replace the *London* which was lost in an explosion

in 1665: see above, vi. 52, n. 1. For the accounts, see LRO, MS. 'Ship London 1664–6'; ib., MS. 289, ff. 21+. Taylor was paid £1400 on account on 19 March: MS. 289, f. 28r. In all he received c. £14,000 by January 1669 for the building and fitting-out of the ship, the money being raised mostly by voluntary subscription from individuals and by a levy on the city companies.

4. Mathematical instrument maker.

to see me, whose discourse about several things I proposed to him was very good, better then I have had with anybody a good while. He gone, I to my business again; and anon comes my Lady Pen and her son-in-law and daughter and there we talked all the evening away, and then to supper; and after supper comes Sir W. Penn, and there we talked together and then broke up, and so to bed. He tells me that our Mr. Turner hath seen the proclamation against the Duke of Buckingham, and that therefore it is true what we heard last night. ⟨Yesterday and today I have been troubled with a hoarseness through cold, that [I] could not almost speak.⟩

11. Up, with my cold still upon me and hoarseness; but I was forced to rise and to the office, where all the morning busy; and among other things, Sir W. Warren came to me, to whom of late I have been very strange, partly from my indifference now, more then heretofore, to get money, but most from my finding that he is become great with my Lord Brouncker and so I dare not trust him as I used to do, for I will not be inward with him that is open to another. By and by comes Sir H. Cholmly to me about Tanger business; and then talking of news, he tells me how yesterday the King did publicly talk of the King of France's dealing with all the princes of Christendome. To the States of Holland, he hath advised them on good grounds to refuse to treat with us at The Hague, because of having opportunity of spies by reason of our interest in the House of Orange;[1] and then, it being a town in one particular province, it would*a* not be fit to have it but in a town wherein the provinces have equal interest, as at Mastricht and other*b* places named.[2] That he advises them to offer no terms, nor accept of any, without his

a repl. 'will'   *b* repl. 's'-

---

1. For the Orangists, see above, p. 92, n. 2. Louis' letter is referred to in D'Estrades, *Lettres*, etc. (1709), iv. 73, 58–9; F. A. M. Mignet, *Négociations relatives à la succession d'Espagne* (1835–41), i. 522.

2. Maastricht and the other towns canvassed in this connection were in the frontier area near to the Spanish Netherlands held in common ownership by the seven united provinces and known as the 'Lands of the Generality'.

privity and consent, according to agreement; and tells them, if not so, he hath in his power to be even with them, the King of England being come to offer him any terms he pleases and that my Lord St. Albans is now at Paris, Plenipotentiary, to make what peace he pleases; and so he can make it and exclude them, the Dutch, if he sees fit.[1] A copy of this letter of the King of France's the Spanish Embassador here gets, and comes and tells all to our King; which our King denies, and says the King of France only uses his power of saying anything. At the same time, the King of France writes to the Emperor that he is resolved to do all things to express affection to the Emperor, having it now in his power to make what peace he pleases between the King of England and him and the States of the United Provinces; and therefore, that he would not have him to concern himself in a friendship with us, and assures him that on that regard he will not offer anything to his disturbance in his interest in Flanders or elsewhere.[2] He writes at the same time to Spain to tell him that he wonders to hear of a league almost ended between the Crown of Spain and England by my Lord Sandwich, and all without his privity, while he[3] was making a peace upon [what] terms he pleased with England.[4] That he is a great lover of the Crown of Spain, and would take the King and his affairs, during his minority, into his protection; nor would offer to set his foot in Flanders, or anywhere else, to disturb him, and therefore would not have him to trouble himself to make peace with anybody; only, he hath a desire to offer an exchange, which he thinks may be of moment to both sides; that is, that he will enstate the King of Spain in the kingdom of Portugall, and he and the Dutch will put him into possession of Lisbon; and that being done, he[5] may have Flanders: and this, they say, doth mightily take in

---

1. This story about St Albans's powers was untrue, but was widely believed in many parts of Europe (as it was intended to be): Feiling, pp. 213–16. Sent as envoy to Paris on 28 January, St Albans was not empowered even to sign preliminaries: *CSPD 1666–7*, p. 475. For his instructions, see Lister, iii. 443–4.

2. The Emperor had been attempt-

ing to delay the conclusion of the peace in order to stave off the French attack on the Spanish Netherlands: *CSP Ven. 1666–8*, p. 144. Louis' letter has not been traced.

3. The King of Spain.

4. For the Anglo-Spanish treaty, see below, p. 453, n. 2.

5. Louis XIV.

Spain, which is sensible of the fruitless expense Flanders, so far off, gives them and how much better it would be for them to be masters of Portugall; and the King of France offers for security herein, that the King of England shall be bond for him and that he will counter-secure the King of England with Amsterdam; and it seems hath assured our King that if he will make a league with him, he will make a peace exclusive to the Hollander.[1] These things are almost Romantique,* but yet true, as Sir H. Cholmly tells me the King himself did relate it all yesterday; and it seems as if the King of France did think other princes fit for nothing but to make sport for him – but simple princes they are, that are forced to suffer this from him. So at noon with Sir W. Penn by coach to the Sun in Leadenhall-street, where Sir R Ford, Sir W. Batten, and Commissioner Taylor (whose feast it was) was; and we dined and had a very good dinner. Among other discourses, Sir R Ford did tell me that he doth verily believe[a] that the City will in few years be built again in all the greatest streets, and answered the objections I did give to it. Here we had the proclamation this day come out against the Duke of Buckingham, commanding him to come in to one of the Secretaries, or to the Lieutenant of the Tower[2] – a silly, vain man to bring himself to this; and there be many hard circumstances in the proclamation of the causes of this proceeding of the King's, which speak great displeasure of the King's and crimes of his.

Then to discourse of the business of the day; that is to say, Commissioner Taylors accounts for his ship he built, the *Loyall London*; and it is pretty to see how dully this old fellow makes his demands, and yet plaguy wise sayings will come from the man sometimes; and also how Sir R. Ford and W. Batten did with seeming violence advise him what to do and how to come prepared to answer objections to the Common Council.[3]

Thence away to the office, where late busy;[b] and then home to supper, mightily pleased with my wife's Trill;* and so to bed.

---

a repl. symbol rendered illegible   *b* repl. 'business'

---

1. Cf. the similar report (5/15 March) in *CSPVen. 1666–8*, p. 142.

2. See above, p. 105, n. 1.
3. See above, loc. cit., n. 3.

This night Mr. Carcasse did come to me again to desire favour and that I would mediate that he might be restored; but I did give him no kind answer at all, but was very angry; and I confess, a good deal of it from my Lord Brouncker's simplicity and passion.

12. Up, and to the office, where all the morning; and my Lord Brouncker mighty quiet and no words all day; which I wonder at, expecting that he would have fallen again upon the business of Carcasse, and*ᵃ* the more for that here happened that Perkins, who was the greatest witness of all against him, was brought in by Sir W. Batten to prove that he did really belong to the *Prince*; but being examined, was found rather a fool then anything, as not being able to give any account when he came in nor when he came out of her, more than that he was taken by the Dutch in her – but*ᵇ* did agree in earnest to Sir W. Penn's saying that she lay up all the winter before at Lambeth. This I confess did make me begin to doubt the truth of his evidence;[1] but not to doubt the faults of Carcasse, for he was condemned by many other better evidences then his, besides the whole world's report. At noon home and there find Mr. Goodgroome, whose teaching of my wife, only by singing over and over again to her and letting her sing with him, not by herself, to correct her faults, I do not like at all but was angry at it; but have this content, that I do think she will come to sing pretty well and to trill* in time, which pleases me well. He dined with us; and then to the office, where we had a silly meeting to little purpose and then broke up; and I to my office and busy late to good purpose; and so home to supper and to bed. ⟨This day a poor seaman, almost starved for want of food, lay in our yard a-dying; I sent him half-a-crown – and we ordered his ticket to be paid.⟩*ᶜ*

13. Up, and with W. Batten to the Duke of York to our usual attendance, where I did fear my*ᵈ* Lord Brouncker might

---

a repl. 'but here'   *b* repl. 'but was made believe'
   c insertion added in small hand   *d* repl. 'Sir'

---

1. Perkins's evidence was discounted by the Privy Council later: PRO, PC 2/60, p. 110.

move something in revenge that might trouble me, but he did not; but contrarily, had the content to hear Sir G. Carteret fall foul on ⟨him⟩ in the Duke of York's bedchamber for his directing people with tickets and petitions to him, bidding[a] him mind his Controller's place and not his, for if[b] he did he should be too hard for him; and other high words, which I was glad of. Having done our usual business with the Duke of York, I away; and meeting Mr. D. Gawden in the presence-chamber, he and I to talk; and among other things, he tells me, and I do find everywhere else also, that our maisters do begin not to like of their counsels[c] in fitting out no fleet, but only squadrons, and are finding out excuses for it; and among others, he tells me a Privy-Councillor did tell him that it was said in Council that a fleet could not be set out this year for want of victuals; which gives him and me a great alarme, but me especially, for had it been so, I ought to have represented it; and therefore it puts me in policy presently to prepare myself to answer this objection if ever it should come about, by drawing up a state of the Victualler's stores; which I will presently do. So to Westminster-hall and there stayed and talked; and then to Sir G. Carteret's to dinner, where I dined with the ladies, he not at home; and very well used I am among them, so that I am heartily ashamed that my wife hath not been there to see them; but she shall very speedily. So home by water, and stepped into Michells and there did besar my Betty,[d] que egrotat a little. At home find Mr. Holliard and made him eat a bit of victuals. Here I find Mr. Greeten, who teaches my wife on the flagelette; and I think she will come to something on it. Mr. Holliard advises me to have my father come up to town, for he doubts else in the country he will never find ease, for, poor man, his grief[1] is now grown so great upon him that he is never at ease. So I will have him up at Easter.

By[e] and by, by coach; set down Mr. Holliard near his house in Hatton-garden and myself to Lord Treasurer's, and sent my wife to the New Exchange. I stayed not here, but to Westminster-hall and thence to Martin's, where he and she both

a repl. 'telling'   *b* repl. 'he'   *c* repl. 'intention'
d name in s.h.   *e* repl. 'then'

---

1. Pain from a rupture: above, p. 13.

within, and with them the little widow that was once there with her when I was there,[1] that dissembled so well to be grieved at hearing a tune that her late husband liked; but there being so much company, I had no pleasure here; and so away to the Hall again, and there met Doll Lane*a* coming out, and per contract did hazer bargain para andar to the cabaretto de vin called the Rose; and ibi I stayed two hours, sed she did non venir, lequel troubled me; and so away by coach and took up my wife, and away home; and so to Sir W. Batten's, where I am told that it is entended by Mr. Carcasse to pray me to be godfather with Lord Brouncker tomorrow to his child; which I supposed they tell me in mirth, but if he should ask me, I know not whether I should refuse it or no.

Late at my office, preparing *b* a speech against tomorrow morning before the King at my Lord Treasurer's; and the truth is, it run in my head all night.

So home to supper and to bed. The Duke of Buckingham is concluded gone over sea, and it is thought to France.[2]

14. Up, and with W. Batten and W. Penn to my Lord Treasurer's, where we met with my Lord Brouncker an hour before the King came, and had time to talk a little of our business. Then came much company; among others, Sir H. Cholmly, who tells me that undoubtedly my Lord Bellasses will go no more as Governor to Tanger, and that he doth put in fair for it and believes he shall have it; and proposes how it may conduce to his account and mine in the business of money. Here we fell into talk with Sir St. Fox; and among other things, of the Spanish manner of walking when three*c* are together; and showed me how, which was pretty, to prevent differences.[3] By and by comes the King and Duke of York, and presently the officers

a name in s.h.   *b* repl. 'making'   *c* repl. 'two'

1. Widow Burroughs: above, vii. 345.
2. He was in fact hiding in London: see above, p. 86 & n. 3; p. 93 & n. 4.

3. This is not among the oddities Pepys noticed in his own visit to Spain in 1684: *Tangier Papers*, pp. 251+.

of the Ordinance were called – my Lord Barkely, Sir Jo. Duncomb, and Mr. Chichly – then we, my Lord Brouncker, W.
Batten, W. Penn, and myself, where we find only the King
and Duke of York and my Lord Treasurer and Sir G. Carteret;
where I only did speak, laying down the state of our wants;[1]
which the King and Duke of York seemed very*a* well pleased
with, and we did get what we asked, 500000*l*, assigned upon the
Eleven Months Tax:[2] but that is not so much ready money,
or what will raise 40000*l* per week, which we desired and the
business will want. Yet are we fain to come away answered;
when God knows it will undo the King's business to have matters
of this moment put off in this manner. The King did prevent
my offering anything by and by as Treasurer for Tanger, telling
me that he had ordered us 30000*l* on the same tax; but that is not
what we would have to bring our payments to come within a
year. So we gone out, in went others – *viz.*, one after another,
Sir St. Fox for the army – Captain Cocke for sick and wounded –
Mr. Ashburnham for the household. Thence W. Batten,
W. Penn and I back again, I mightily pleased with what I had
said and done and the success thereof. But it being a fine*b*
clear day, I did *en gayeté de Cœur* propose going to Bow for ayre
sake and dine there; which they imbraced, and so W. Batten
and I (setting W. Penn down at Mark-lane end) straight to Bow
to the Queen's Head and there bespoke our dinner, carrying
meat with us from London; and anon*c* comes W. Penn with
my wife and Lady Batten, and then Mr. Lowder with his mother
and wife. While W. Batten and I were alone, we had much
friendly discourse, though I will never trust him far. But we
do propose the getting the *Flying greyhound*, our privateer, to us
and W. Penn at the end of the year when we call her home – by
begging her of the King; and I do not think we shall be denied
her.[3] They being come, we to Oysters and so to talk; very

a repl. 'mighty'   *b* MS. 'find'   *c* MS. 'another'

1. For Pepys's notes of his speech,
see below, p. 114 & n. 3. This was a
meeting of the cabinet: S. B. Baxter,
Devel. Treasury 1660–1702, pp. 50–
1.
2. £380,000 had been assigned to

the navy by the statute imposing the
tax: 18–19 Car. II c. 13, sect. x.
3. See below, p. 441. The *Flying
Greyhound* served as their privateer
from September 1666 until the end of
the war.

pleasant I was all day; and anon*a* to dinner, and I made very good company. Here till the evening, so as it was dark almost before we got home (back again in the same method ⟨I think⟩ we went); and spent the night talking at Sir W. Batten's; only, a little at my office to look over*b* the Victualler's contract and draw up some arguments for him to plead for his charges in transportation of goods beyond the ports which the letter of one*c* article in his contract doth*d* lay upon him. This done, I home to supper and to bed – troubled a*e* little at my fear that my Lord Brouncker should tell Sir W. Coventry of our neglecting the office this afternoon (which was intended) to look after our pleasures; but nothing will fall upon me alone about this.

15. Up, and pleased at Tom's teaching of Barker something to sing a third part to a song, which will please me mightily. So I to the office all the morning, and at noon to the Change, where I do hear that letters this day come to Court do tell us that we are likely not to agree, the Dutch demanding high terms and the King of France the like, in a most braveing manner.[1] The*f* merchants do give themselfs over for lost, no man knowing what to do, whether to sell or buy, not knowing whether peace or war to expect; and I am told that could that be now known, a man might get 20000*l* in a week's time – by buying up of goods in case there should be war. Thence home and dined well; and then with my wife, set her at Unthankes and I to Sir G. Carteret, where talked with the ladies a while; and my Lady Carteret talks nothing but sorrow and afflictions*g* coming on us; and endeed, I do fear the same. So away, and met Dr. Fuller, Bishop of Limricke, and walked an hour with him in the Court, talking of news only; and he doth think that matters will be bad with us. Then to Westminster-hall and then spent an hour or two walking up and down, thinking para aver got out Doll Lane,*h* sed yo no

a MS. 'another'   *b* repl. 'vit'-   *c* repl. 'his'   *d* MS. 'to'
e l.h. repl. s.h. 'at'   *f* repl. 'people'   *g* repl. 'tr'-
h name in s.h.

1. Cf. St Albans to Clarendon, Paris, 13/23 March: Bodl., Clar. 85, ff. 133+. For the negotiations, see above, p. 96, n. 1; Feiling, pp. 215-16.

could do it, having no opportunity de hazer le, ainsi lost the todo afternoon; and so away and called my wife and home, where a little at the office and then home to my closet to enter my Journalls, and so to supper and to bed.

This noon came little Mis Tooker, who is grown a little woman; ego had l'opportunity para besar her and tocar la abaxo con my hand. She is pretty still, but had no mind to be vido, being not habilado as ella would be. My wife did tell me the other day that she heard she had had the gran pecho,[1] but I hope no such thing. I sum certain that I should have been glad para aver tempo and lugar to have hecho algo con her.

This morning I was called up by Sir Jo. Winter, poor man, come in his sedan from the other end of the town before I was up, and merely about the King's business; which is a worthy thing of him, and I believe him to be a worthy good man, and I will do him the right to tell the Duke of York of it, who did speak well of him the other day. It is about helping the King in the business of bringing down his timber to the sea-side in the Forest of Deane.[2]

16. Up, and to the office, where all the morning. At noon home to dinner; and then to the office again in the afternoon and there all day, very busy till night; and then having done much business, home to supper, and so to bed. This afternoon came home Sir J. Mennes, who hath been down, but to little purpose, to pay the ships below at the Nore. This evening, having done my letters, I did write out the heads of what I had prepared to speak to the King the other day at my Lord Treasurer's, which I do think convenient to keep by me for future use.[3] The weather is now grown warm again, after much cold weather; and it is observable that within these eight days I did see smoke remaining, coming out of some cellars, from the late great Fire, now above six months since.[4] There was this day at the office (as he is most days) Sir W. Warren; against whom I did manifestly plead, and heartily too, God forgive me – but the reason is because I do

1. The pox: see above, p. 79 & n. 1.
2. See below, p. 191 & n. 4.
3. 'The heads of what I delivered in discourse to his Ma^ty March 14th

1666 . . .': copy (in Gibson's hand) in NMM, LBK/8, pp. 475–9; printed in *Further Corr.*, pp. 162–7.
4. Cf. above, vii. 393, n. 1.

find that he doth now wholly rely almost upon my Lord
Brouncker, though I confess I have no greater ground of*ᵃ* my
leaving him then the confidence which I perceive he hath got in
my Lord Brouncker, whose seeming favours only do obtain of
him as much compensation, I believe (for he doth*ᵇ* know well
the way of using his bounties), as mine more real. Besides, my
Lord and I being become antagonists, I do not think it safe for me
to trust myself in the hands of one whom I know to be a knave
and using all means to become gracious there.

17. *Lords day.* Up betimes with my wife, and by coach with
Sir W. Penn and Sir Tho. Allen to White-hall; there my wife
and I the first time that ever we went to my Lady Jemimah's
chamber at Sir Edw. Carteret's¹ lodgings. I confess I have been
much to blame and much ashamed of our not visiting her sooner,
but better now then never. Here we took her before she was up,
which I was sorry for, so only saw her and away to chapel,
leaving further visit till after sermon. I put my wife into the
pew below in the chapel; but it was pretty to see (myself being
but in a plain band, and every way else ordinary) how the verger
took me for her man I think; and I was fain to tell him she was a
kinswoman of my Lord Sandwiches, he saying that none under
Knight Baronets ladies are to go into that pew. So she being
there, I to the Duke of York's lodging, where in his dressing-
chamber he talking of his Journy tomorrow or next day to
Harwich – to prepare some fortifications there;*ᶜ*² so that we
are wholly upon the defensive part this year; only, we have
some expectations that we may by*ᵈ* our squadrons annoy them
in their trade by the North of Scotland and to the Westward.
Here Sir W. Penn did show the Duke of York a letter of Hogg's
about a prize he drove in within the Sound at Plymouth, where

a repl. 'of his desiring to make use of me'   *b* repl. 'did'
     c MS. 'some there'   *d* MS. 'be'

1. Gentleman-usher to the King
and great-uncle of Sir George
Carteret, Pepys's colleague. Lady
Jemimah Mountagu had married
Philip, Sir George's son, in July 1665.
2. On 20–1 March the Duke, with

de Gomme the engineer, was busy at
Harwich preparing plans for the construction of a second fort to secure the
harbour: *CSPD 1666–7,* p. 577;
BM, Egerton 2539, f. 91r.

the Vice-Admirall claims her.[1]   Sir W. Penn would have me to
speak to the letter; which I did, and I think without any offence;
but afterwards I was sorry for it, and Sir W. Penn did plainly say
that he had no mind to speak to the Duke of York about it, so
that he put me upon it; but it shall be the last time I will do such
another thing – though I think no manner of hurt done by[a] it to
me at all.

That done, I to walk in the parke, where to the Queenes chapel[2]
and there heard a Fryer preach, with his Cord about his middle,
in Portuguez – something I could understand, showing that God
did respect the meek and humble as well as the high and rich.
He was full of action; but very decent and good I thought, and
his manner of delivery very good.   I went back to White-hall,
and there up to the closet and spoke with several people till
sermon was ended, which was preached by the Bishop of Hereford, an old good man, that they say made an excellent sermon.[3]
He was by birth a Catholique and a great gallant, having 1500*l* per
annum patrimony, and is a Knight-Barronet – was turned from his
persuasion by the late Archbishop Laud.[4]   He and the Bishop of
Exeter, Dr. Ward, are the two Bishops that the King doth say he
cannot have bad sermons from.[5]   Here I met with Sir H Cholmly,

a repl. 'in it'

1. Edward Hogg commanded the
privateer *Flying Greyhound* which had
been hired to Pepys, Penn and Batten.
The prize may possibly have been the
Stralsund: cf. *CSPD 1666-7*, pp. 583,
595. The Vice-Admiral was John
Fowell: PRO, HCA 50/3, f. 185*r*.

2. In St James's Palace.

3. Dr Herbert Croft, the Bishop,
was 64. 'A most moving patheticall
Sermon . . . wherein he hitt right
upon the great Sin of this Nation viz
Ingratitude to Almighty God for the
great Mercies we have received from
him, he preached it so passionately
that I hope his Sermon wilbe attended
with good Effects': Sir J. Nicholas
to Sir E. Nicholas, 20 March (BM,
Egerton 2539, f. 90*v*).

4. He was the third son of Sir
Henry Croft, of Croft Castle, Here-

ford, a convert to Catholicism, and
had become heir to the family estates
on the death of his brothers.   He was
not a baronet, but his father, grandfather and great-grandfather had all
been knights.   Laud persuaded him
to go to Oxford and take orders, but
his conversion from Catholicism is
usually attributed to Morton, Bishop
of Durham: Wood, *Ath. Oxon.* (ed.
Bliss), iv. 310.

5. Croft (whom the King made
Dean of the Chapel Royal in February 1668) was an advocate of the
new plain style of preaching. (Cf.
his *Naked Truth*, 1675, in *Somers
Tracts*, ed. Scott, vi. 290+.) Seth
Ward of Salisbury was one of the
ablest of Caroline bishops, and a
founder of the Royal Society.

who tells me that undoubtedly my Lord Bellasses*a* doth go no more to Tanger, and that he doth believe he doth stand in a likely way to go Governor – though he says, and showed me, a young silly Lord (one Lord Allington) who hath offered a great sum of money to go; and will put hard for it, he having a fine lady and a great man would be glad to have him out of the way.[1]

After Chapel, I down and took out my wife from the pew, where she was talking with a lady whom I knew not till I was gone; it was Mrs. Ashfield of Brampton,[2] who had with much civility been, it seems, at our house to see her; I am sorry I did not show her any ⟨more⟩ respect.

With my wife to Sir George*b* Carteret's, where we dined; and mightily made of, and most extraordinary people they are to continue friendship with – for goodness, virtue, and nobleness and interest. After dinner, he and I alone a while and did joy ourselfs in my Lord Sandwiches being out of the way all this time. He concurs that we are in a way of ruin by this being forced to keep only small squadrons out; but doth tell me that it was not choice, but only force; that we could not keep out the whole fleet. He tells me that the King is very kind to my Lord Sandwich, and did himself observe to him (Sir G. Carteret) how those very people, meaning the Prince and Duke of Albemarle, are punished in the same kind as they did seek to abuse my Lord Sandwich. Thence away, and got a hackney-coach and carried my wife home, and there only drank and myself back again to my Lord Treasurer's, where the King, Duke of York, and Sir G. Carteret and Lord Arlington was and none else; so I stayed not, but to White-hall; and there, meeting with nobody I would speak with, walked into the park and took two or three turns all

a repl. 'Brouncker'   *b* repl. 'my Lady'

---

1. Neither Cholmley nor Allington was appointed; in May 1668 the 1st Earl of Middleton succeeded Belasyse as Governor of Tangier. Allington was a young army officer; his wife (whose association with this anonymous 'great man' has not been traced elsewhere) was Juliana, daughter of the 3rd Viscount Campden. Allington's interest was said to depend on the influence of his mother-in-law, the Countess of Chesterfield: see Sir John Nicholas's letter, 20 March, in BM, Egerton 2539, f. 91*r*.

2. Lucy, wife of Sutton Ashfield, a man of substance in the parish.

alone; and then took coach and home, where I find Mercer, who I was glad to see but durst [not] show so, my wife being displeased with her; and endeed, I fear she is grown a very gossip. I to my chamber and there fitted my arguments which I have promised Mr. Gawden in his behalf in some pretences to allowance of the King;[1] and then to supper, and so to my chamber a little again and then to bed. Duke of Buckingham not heard of yet.

18. Up betimes, and to the office to write fair my paper for D. Gawden against anon; and then to other business, where all the morning. D. Gawden by and by comes, and I did read over and give him the paper, which I think I have much obliged him in. A little before noon comes my old good friend Mr. Rd. Cumberland[2] to see me, being newly come to town, whom I have not seen almost, if not quite, these seven years – in his plain country-parson dress. I could not spend much time with him, but prayed him come with his brother, who was with him, to dine with me today; which he did do and I had a great deal of his good company; and a most excellent person he is as any I know, and one that I am sorry should be lost and buried in a little country town, and would be glad to remove him thence; and the truth is, if he would accept of my sister's fortune, I should give 100*l* more with him then to a man able to settle her four times as much as I fear he is able to do. And I will think of it, and a way how to move it, he having in discourse said he was not against marrying, nor yet engaged.[3] I showed him my closet, and did give him some very good music, Mr. Cæsar being here upon his Lute. They gone, I to the office, where all the afternoon very busy; and among other things, comes Captain Jenifer to me, a great servant of my Lord Sandwiches, who tells me that he doth hear for certain, though I do not yet believe it, that Sir W. Coventry is to [be] Secretary of State and my Lord

---

1. On 10 May imprests totalling £62,000 were issued to him: PRO, Adm. 20/9, p. 850.

2. Now Rector of Brampton, Northants.; later (1691) Bishop of Peterborough. He had been at school and college with Pepys. Their fathers had been neighbours and fellow tailors.

3. Pepys still entertained these (false) hopes almost a year later: below, 9 January 1668. Cumberland married Anne Quinsey, a Lincolnshire spinster, in 1670.

Arlington Lord Treasurer.[1] I only wish that the latter were as fit*a* for the latter office as the former is for the former – and more fit then my Lord Arlington. Anon Sir W. Penn came and talked with me in the garden; and tells me that for certain the Duke of Richmond is to marry Mrs. Stewart, he having this day brought in an account of his estate and debts to the King on that account.[2] At night home to supper and so to bed. My father's letter this day doth tell me of his own continued illness, and that my mother grows so much worse that he fears she cannot long continue – which troubles me very much. ⟨This day Mr. Cæsar told me a pretty experiment of his, of Angling with a Minikin, a gut-string varnished over, which keeps it from swelling and is beyond any hair for strength and smallness – the secret I like mightily.⟩

19. Up and to the office, where we sat all the morning. At noon dined at home very pleasantly with my wife; and after dinner with a great deal of pleasure had her sing, which she begins to do with some pleasure to me, more then I expected. Then to the office again, where all the afternoon close; and at night home to supper and to bed. It comes in my mind this night to set down how a house was the other day in Bishopsgate-street blowed up with powder; a house that was untenanted and between a flax shop and a   , both bad for fire; but thanks be to God, it did no more hurt, and all do conclude it a plot.[3] I would also remember to my shame how I was pleased

a MS. 'fat'

---

1. The illness of the Lord Treasurer Southampton – he died in May – was encouraging the speculation that the government would soon be reconstructed. Secretary Arlington and Coventry were its leading critics. Cf. above, p. 96 & n. 2.

2. His previous (second) wife having died on or shortly before 6 January, Richmond married Frances Stewart privately some time during this month. The King was his nearest collateral heir male and was said to

have given him a portion on his marriage: H. Isham to Sandwich, 26 March (Carte 75, f. 512r).

3. A newsletter of 16 March (PRO, SP 29/194, no. 23) reported that the fire had occurred at about 4 a.m. on the 14th, and that the house was near Bishopsgate St. The writer (Henry Muddiman) added that 'it being seated advantageously to promote a second fire [it] doth confirm the Jealousy of such who believe the former was began by designe'.

yesterday to find the vetus maid of Magister Griffin*a* sweeping of nostra office, ella con the Roman nariz and bon body which I did heretofore like, and doth still refresh me to think que ella is come otra vez to us, that I may ver her a lo cuando.   This afternoon I am told again that the town doth talk of my Lord Arlington's being to be Lord Treasurer and Sir W. Coventry to be Secretary of State.   And that for certain the match is concluded between the Duke of Richmond and Mrs. Stewart – which I am well enough pleased with; and it is pretty to consider how his quality will allay people's talk, whereas had a meaner person married her, he would for certain have been reckoned a cuckold[1] at first dash.

20.   Up pretty betimes, and to the Old Swan and there drank at Michell's; but his wife is not there, but gone to her mother's who is ill, and so hath stayed there since Sunday.   Thence to Westminster-hall and drank at the Swan and besado the petite moza; and so to Mrs. Martins who I find in opposante and su hermana rising.   So here I had opportunity para tocar tout sobra su body as I would, and did traher sus pernos out of the lecto and do hazer myself hazer.   I sent for some burnt wine and drank; and then away, not pleased with my folly; and so to the Hall again and there stayed a little, and so home by water again – where after speaking with my wife, I with Sir W. Batten and J. Mennes to our church to the vestry to be assessed by the late Pole=bill, where I am rated at an Esquire; and for my office, all will come to about 50*l* – but not more then I expected, nor so much by a great deal as I ought to be for all my offices – so shall be glad to escape so.[2]   Thence by water again to White-hall, and there up into the House and do hear that news is come now that the enemy doth incline again to a peace; but could hear no perticulars, so do not believe it.   I had a great mind to

a   name in s.h.

---

1. Because of her association with the King.

2. He had been rated at £5 as an esquire, and at £52 10*s*. for his salary as Clerk of the Acts (£350 p.a. at 3*s*.

in the pound).   His salaries from his Tangier and victualling posts had not been taxed, nor were any of his 'profits'.

have spoke with the King about a business proper enough for me, about the French Prize man-of-war*ᵃ* 1 how he would have her altered,*ᵇ* only out of a desire to show myself mindful of business; but my linen was so dirty and my clothes mean, that I neither thought it fit for me to do that, nor go to other persons at the Court with whom I had business; which did vex me and I must remedy. Here I hear that the Duke of Richmond and Mrs. Stewart were betrothed last night. Thence to West-minster-hall again, and there saw Betty Michell and bought a pair of gloves of her, she being fain to keep shop there, her mother being sick and father gathering of the tax. I aime her de todo mi corazon. Thence, my mind wandering all this day upon mauvais amours which yo be merry for. So home by water again, where I find my wife gone abroad; so I to Sir W. Batten to dinner, and had*ᶜ* a good dinner of Ling and herring pie, very good meat – best of that kind that ever I had – thus having dined, I by coach to the Temple and there did buy a little book or two; and it is strange how Rycaut's discourse of Turky, which before the fire I was asked but 8*s* for, there being all but 22 or there-abouts burnt, I did now offer 20*s*, and he demands 50*s*; and I think I shall give it him, though it be only as a monument of the Fire.² So to the ⟨New⟩ Exchange, where I find my wife; and so took her to Unthankes and left her there, and I to White-hall and thence to Westminster, only out of idleness and to get some little pleasure to my mauvaises*ᵈ* flammes; but sped not, so back and took up my wife and to *Polichenelli* at Charing-cross,³ which is prettier and prettier, and so full of variety that it is extra-ordinary good entertainment. Thence by coach home – that is, my wife home; and I to the Exchange and there met with Fenn,

---

a MS. 'water'   *b* repl. 'alt'-
c repl. 'to'   *d* repl. same symbol badly formed

---

1. The *Rubis*: see above, vii. 350 & n. 1.
2. For the book and its purchase, see below, p. 156 & n. 2. In November 1666 Lord Herbert gave 20*s*. for a copy, and reported that the author himself had none left: HMC,

Beaufort, p. 55. The third edition of 1670 cost only 10*s*. bound: E. Arber, *Term Cat.*, i. 22.
3. A popular puppet-play of Italian origin; the puppeteer was Antonio Devoto: see above, vii. 257 & n. 2; iii. 254, n. 5. (A).

who tells me they have yet no orders out of the Exchequer for money upon the Acts, which is a thing not to be borne by any prince of understanding or care – for no money can be got advanced upon the acts, only from the weight of orders in form out of the Exchequer, so long time after the passing of the acts.[1] So home to the office a little, where I met with a sad letter from my brother, who tells me my mother is declared by the Doctors to be past recovery and that my father is also very ill every hour; so that I fear we shall see a sudden change there – God fit them and us for it. So to Sir W. Penn's, where my wife was, and supped with a little, but yet little, mirth and a bad nasty supper; which makes me not love that family, they do all things so meanly, to make a little bad show upon their backs. Thence home and to bed, very much troubled about my father's and my mother's illness.

21. Up and to the office, where sat all the morning. At noon home to dinner and had some melancholy discourse with my wife about my mother's being so ill and my father. And after dinner, to cheer myself and having the opportunity of Sir W. Coventry and the Duke of York's being out of town, I alone out and to the Duke of York's play-house, where unexpectedly I came to see only the young men and women of the house Act – they having liberty to act for their own profit on Wednesdays and Fridays this Lent;[2] and the play they did yesterday, being Wednesdy, was so well taken, that they thought fit to venture it publicly today – a play of my Lord Falklands called *The Wedding night*,[3] a kind of a Tragœdy; and some things very good in it, but the whole together, I thought, not so. I confess I was well enough pleased with my seeing it; and the people did

1. Fenn (Paymaster to the Navy Treasurer) thought that the Lord Treasurer ought to have issued orders immediately after the passage of the two acts (for the Eleven Months Tax and the Poll Tax) had authorised them. He now feared that the money market would be congested and discount rates raised by a sudden rush of orders.

2. 'The young men and women of the house' were the players who were not shareholders in the theatre; they had been allowed to set aside the prohibition of plays on Fridays during Lent: see above, p. 90. (A).

3. *The marriage night*, a tragi-comedy by Henry Cary, Viscount Falkland, first acted in 1663, and published in 1664. (A).

do better (without the great Actors) then I did expect, but yet far short of what they do when they are there; which I was glad to find the difference of. Thence to rights home, and there to the office to my business hard – being sorry to have made this scape without my wife, but I have a good salvo to my oath in doing it. By and by in the evening comes Sir W. Batten's Mingo to me to pray me to come to his maister and Sir Rd. Ford, who have very ill news to tell me. I knew what it was: it was about our trial for a good prize today, the *Phœnix*, worth 2 or 3000*l*.[1] I went to them, where they told me with much trouble how they had sped; being cast and sentenced to make great reparation for what we had imbezzled; and they did it so well that I was much troubled at it – when by and by Sir W. Batten asked me whether I was mortified enough, and then told me we had got the day; which was mighty welcome news to me and us all – but it is pretty to see what money will do. Yesterday, Walker[2] was mighty cold on our behalf, till Sir W. Batten promised*a* him, if we sped in this business of the goods, a coach; and if at the next trial we sped for the ship, we would give him a pair of horses – and he hath strove for us today like a prince. Though the Swedes Agent was there with all the vehemence he could to save the goods, but yet we carried it against him. This put me into mighty good heart. And then we go to Sir W. Penn, who is come back tonight from Chatham; and did put him into the same condition, and then comforted him. So back*b* to my office and wrote an affectionate and sad letter[3] to my father about his and my mother's illness. And so home to supper, and to bed late.

22. Up and by coach to Sir Ph. Warwicke about business for Tanger, about money. And then to Sir St. Fox to give him

---

a repl. 'pro'-   *b* repl. 'home'

---

1. A ship of Riga recently brought into Dover. The Prize Commissioners on 8 March had referred the issue to Dr Leoline Jenkins, Judge of the High Court of Admiralty, who now upheld the claim of the Swedish Resident (Leijonbergh) that the ships and goods were Swedish. The ship was discharged on 28 March. PRO, HCA, 3/252, *sub* 22 March; BM, Harl. 1510, ff. 31*v*, 40*v*.

2. Sir Walter Walker, advocate in the Court of Admiralty.

3. Untraced.

account of a little^a service I have done him about money coming
to him from our office; and then to Lovetts and saw a few
baubling things of their doing, which are very pretty; but the
quality of the people, living only by shifts, doth not please me,
that it makes me I do no more care for them, nor shall have more
acquaintance with them after I have got my Lady Castlemaine's
picture home.¹ So to White-hall, where the King at chapel;
and I would not stay, but to Westminster to Herbert's and there,
he being not well, I sent for a quart of claret and burnt it and
drank, and had a besado or three or four of Sarah,^b whom yo
trouvais aqui; and so by coach to Sir Rob. Viner's about my
accounts with him; and so to the Change, where I hear for
certain that we are going on with our treaty of peace, and that
we are to treat at Bredah.² But this our condescension people do
think will undo us – and I do much fear it. So home to dinner,
where my wife having dressed herself in a silly dress, of a blue
petticoat uppermost and a white satin waistcoat^c and white hood
(though I think she did it because her gown is gone to the tailor's)
did, together with my being hungry (which always makes me
peevish), make me angry. But when my belly was full, was
friends again, and dined and then by water down to Greenwich
and thence walked to Woolwich, all the way reading Playfords
Introduction to Musique,³ wherein are some things very pretty.
At Woolwich I did much business, taking an account of the
state of the ships there under hand; thence to Blackewall and did
the like for two ships we have repairing there; and then to
Deptford and did the like there; and so home, Captain Perriman
with me from Deptford, telling me many perticulars how the
King's business is ill ordered; and indeed so they are, God knows.⁴

a repl. 'serv'-   *b* name in s.h.   *c* MS. 'coach'

1. See above, p. 23 & n. 3.
2. By a decision of 20 March:
PRO, PC 2/59, f. 178r; (wrongly
dated the 18th in Feiling, p. 216).
3. John Playford, *A brief introduction to the skill of musick*, an octavo, of
which editions were published in
1664, 1666 and 1667; possibly one of
the books bought on 20 March. Not
in the PL. (E).

4. John Perryman was a Navy
Board agent for river business. On
18 March he had reported a shortage
of river pilots because the pay was too
small and often not forthcoming.
Trumpeters were employed as able
seamen on board ship. See NWB,
p. 108.

So home and to the office, where did business; and so home to
my chamber, and then to supper and to bed. Landing at the
Tower tonight, I met on Tower hill with Captain Cocke and
spent half an hour walking in the dusk of the evening with him,
talking of the sorrowful condition we are in. That we must be
ruined if the Parliament do not come and chastize us. That
we are resolved to make a peace whatever it cost. That the
King is disobliging the Parliament in this interval[1] all that may
be, yet his money is gone and he must have more; and they
likely not to give it without a great deal of do. God knows
what the issue of it will be. But the considering that the Duke
of York, instead of being at sea as Admirall, is now going from
port to port, as he is at this day at Harwich and was the other
day with the King at Sheernesse and hath ordered at Portsmouth
how Fortificacions shall be made to oppose the enemy in case of
invasion, is to us a sad consideration and a shameful to the nation,
especially after so many proud vaunts as we have made against
the Dutch; and all from the folly of the Duke of Albemarle, who
made nothing of beating them; and Sir John Lawson, he always
declared that we never did fail to beat them with lesser numbers
then theirs – which did so prevail with the King as to throw us
into this war.

23. At the office all the morning, where Sir W. Penn came,
being returned from Chatham from considering the means of
fortifying the River Medway, by a chain at the stakes and ships
laid there, with guns to keep the enemy from coming up to burn
our ships[2] – all our care now being [to] fortify ourselfs against
their invading us. At noon home to dinner, and then to the
office all the afternoon again – where Mr. Moore came, who
tells me that there is now no doubt made of a peace being agreed
on, the King having declared this week in council that they would

---

1. On 8 February Parliament had
been prorogued to 10 October. (It
re-assembled briefly on 25 and 29
July, only to be prorogued again until
10 October.)
2. The Duke of York gave orders
on the 25th for the disposition of the

ships laid up in the Medway, and for
the completion of the chain: see
Mem. (naval), pp. 57–8. The work
was so bungled that the Dutch were
not prevented from making their
remarkable raid up the Medway in
June: see below, pp. 256+.

treat at Bredagh. He gone, I to my office, where busy late; and so to supper and to bed – vexed with our maid Luce, our cook-maid, who is a good drudging servant in everything else and pleases us, but that she will be drunk, and hath been so last night and all this day, that she could not make clean the house – my fear is only fire.

24. *Lords day.* With Sir W. Batten to White-hall; and there I to Sir G. Carteret, who is mighty cheerful, which makes me think and by some discourse that there is expectations of a peace – but I did not ask him. Here was Sir J. Mennes also; and they did talk of my Lord Brouncker, whose father it seems did give Mr. Ashburnham and the*ᵃ* present Lord Digby 1200*l* to be made an Irish lord, and swore the same day that he had not 12*d* left to pay for his dinner.[1] They made great mirth at this, my Lord Brouncker having lately given great matter [of] offence both to them and us all, that we are at present*ᵇ* mightily displeased with him. By and by to the Duke of York, where we all met, and there was the King also; and all our discourse was about fortifying of Medway and Harwich, which is to [be] entrenched quite round, and Portsmouth; and here they advised with Sir Godfry Lloyd and Sir Bernd. De Gum, the two great engineers, and had the plats drawn before them;[2] and endeed, all their care they now take is to fortify themselfs, and are not ashamed of it; for when by and by my Lord Arlington came in with letters, and seeing the King*ᶜ* and Duke of York give us and the officers of the Ordinance directions in this matter, he did move that we might do it as privately as we could, that it might not come into the Dutch gazette presently, as the King's and Duke of York's going down the other day to Sherenesse was

a repl. 'somebody else'   *b* repl. 'promise'   *c* repl. 'G'-

———————

1. The title dated from September 1645. John Ashburnham was then Paymaster of the Army and Digby (Earl of Bristol) a Secretary of State.
2. Lloyd and de Gomme had been joint engineers-in-chief since 1661 of all royal castles and fortifications in England and Wales. De Gomme had accompanied the Duke to Harwich on 20–1 March: *CSPD 1666–7*, p. 577. Some of his plans and charts of the Medway (possibly those referred to here) are in BM, Add. 16370, ff. 35–8, and in the NMM, Greenwich. Cf. also above, p. 98, n. 2.

the week after in the Harlem gazette:[1] the King and Duke of York both laughed at it and made no matter, but said, "Let us be safe, and let them talk, for there is nothing will trouble them more, nor will prevent their coming more, then to hear that we are fortifying ourselfs." And the Duke of York said further: says "What said Marshal Turin,[2] when some in vanity said that the enemies were afeared, for they entrenched themselfs? 'Well,' says he, 'I would they were not afeared, for then they would not entrench themselfs, and so we could deal with them the better.' "

Away thence and met with Sir H. Cholmly, who tells me that he doth believe the government * of Tanger is bought by my Lord Allington, for a sum of money to my Lord Arlington and something to Lord Bellasses, who (he did tell me perticularly how) is as very a false villain as ever was born, having received money of him[3] here upon promise and confidence of his return, forcing him to pay it by advance here and promising to ask no[a] more there, when at the same time he was treating with my Lord Allington to sell his command to him; and yet told Sir H. Cholmly nothing of it, but when Sir H. Cholmly told him what he had heard, he confessed that my Lord Allington had spoken to him of it, but that he was a vain man to look after it, for he was nothing fit for it; and then goes presently to my Lord Allington and drives on the bargain, yet tells Lord Allington what he himself had said of him, as Sir H. Cholmly had said them. I am glad I am informed hereof, and shall know him for a l[iar] &c. Sir H. Cholmly tells me further that he is confident there

---

a repl. 'more'

---

1. The visit to Sheerness on 27 February had been mentioned in the *Oprechte Haerlemse Saterdaegse Courant* of 9/19 March. It is interesting that Arlington should have expressed surprise, for he cannot have been ignorant of the fact that he himself was in a sense responsible for the 'leak'. His own intelligence from Holland came in part from Abraham Casteleyn, publisher of the Haarlem *Courant*, and was supplied to Williamson, Arlington's secretary, in exchange for

similar news from England: see P. Fraser, *Intelligence of Secretaries of State*, pp. 73. 90. The Haarlem gazette was the best of the continental news sheets, and the two issues published every week arrived regularly in Williamson's office throughout the war.

2. Turenne, under whom the Duke of York had served in France and the Netherlands, 1652–5.

3. Cholmley. See above, p. 117 & n. 1.

will be a peace, and that a great man did tell him that my Lord
Albemarle did tell him the other day at White-hall, as a secret,
that we should have a peace, if anything that the King of France
can ask and our King can give will gain it – which he is it seems
mad at.

Thence back with Sir W. Batten and W. Penn home by coach
and heard a piece of sermon; and so home to dinner, where
Balty come very fine and dined with us – and after dinner with
me by water to White-hall; and there he and I did walk round
the park, I giving him my thoughts about the difficulty of getting
imployment for him this year – but advised him how to imploy
himself, and I would do what I could. So he and I parted, and
I to Martin's, where I find her within, and su hermano and la
veuve Burroughs. Here I did demorar toda the afternoon
bezando las and drank; and among other things, did by a trick*a*
arrive at tocando el poil de la thing de the veuve abovesaid.
By and by came up the mistress of the house, Cragg, a pleasant
jolly woman. I stayed then but a little, and away home by
water through bridge, a brave evening; and so home to read, and
anon to supper, W. Hewer with us, and then to read myself
asleep again; and then to bed.*b* And mightily troubled the most
of the night with fears of Fire, which I cannot get out of my
head to this day since the last great fire. I did this night give the
waterman who uses to carry me 10s, at his request, for the painting
of his new boat, on which shall be my arms.[1]

25. *Lady day.* Up, and with Sir W. Batten and W. Penn by
coach to Exeter-house to our lawyers to have consulted about our
trial tomorrow, but missed them; so parted and W. Penn and I
to Mr. Povy's about a little business of*c* W. Penn's; where we
went over Mr. Povy's house,[2] which lies in the same good
condition as*d* ever, which is most extraordinary fine; and he was

---

a	repl. 'wile'	*b*	repl. 'the'
c	repl. 'where'	*d*	MS. 'that'

---

1. Boats in public use often bore
the arms of important individuals:
Monconys, ii. 12. For Pepys's arms,
see above, iii. 50, n. 3.

2. In Lincoln's Inn Fields; see
above, v. 161-2 & nn.

now at work with a cabinet-maker, making of a new inlaid table. Having seen his house, we away (having in our way thither called at Mr. Lilly's,[1] who was working; and endeed, his pictures are without doubt much beyond Mr. Hales's, I think I may say I am convinced); but a mighty proud man he is, and full of state. So home and to the office; and by and by to dinner, a poor dinner, my wife and I, at Sir W. Penn's; and then he and I before to Exeter-house, where did not stay; but to the King's playhouse, and by and by comes Mr. Lowder and his wife and mine and into a box forsooth, neither of them being dressed, which I was almost ashamed of – Sir W. Penn and I in the pit; and here saw *The Mayden Queene* again; which endeed, the more I see the more I like, and is an excellent play, and so done by Nell her merry part, as cannot be better done in Nature I think.[2] Thence home, and there I find letters from my brother which tell me that yesterday, when he wrote, my mother did rattle in the throat, so as they did expect every moment her*ª* death, which though I have a good while expected, did much surprize me; yet was obliged to sup at Sir W. Penn's, and my wife; and there counterfeited some little mirth, but my heart was sad; and so home after supper and to bed, and much troubled in my sleep with dreams of my being crying by my mother's bedside, laying*ᵇ* my head over hers and crying, she almost dead and dying, and so waked; but which is strange, methought she had hair on*ᶜ* her face, and not the same kind of face as my mother really has; but yet did not consider that, but did weep over her as my mother – whose soul God have mercy of.

26. Up, with a sad heart in reference to my mother, of whose death I do undoubtedly expect to hear the next post, if not of my father's also, who, by his pain as well as his grief for her, is very ill. But on my own behalf, I have cause to be joyful this day, as being my usual feast-day for my being cut of the stone this day nine years;[3] and through God's blessing am at this day and

a repl. 'her dead'   *b* repl. 'lying'   *c* MS. 'off'

---

1. Peter Lely lived in the Piazza, Covent Garden. (OM).
2. For the play (by Dryden), see above, p. 91 & n. 2 Nell Gwyn played Florimel. (A).
3. Cf. above, i. 97 & n. 3.

have long been in as good condition of health as ever I was in my life, or any man in England is, God make me thankful for it. But the condition I am in in reference to my mother makes it unfit for me to keep my usual feast, unless it should please God to send her well (which I despair wholly of); and then I will make amends for it by observing another day in its room. So to the office, and*a* at the office all the morning, where I had an opportunity to speak to Sir Jo. Harman about my desire to have my brother Balty go again with him to sea as he did the last year; which he doth seem not only contented, but pleased with – which I was glad of. So at noon home to dinner, where I find Creede, who dined with us;*b* but I had not any time to talk with him, my head being busy; and before I had dined, was called away by Sir W. Batten, and both of us in his coach (which I observe his coachman doth always go now from hence towards White-hall through Tower-street, and it is the best way) to Exeter-house, where the Judge was sitting;[1] and after several little causes, comes on ours;[2] and while the several depositions and papers were at large reading (which they call the Preparatory), and being cold by being forced to sit with my hat off, close to a window in the Hall, Sir W. Penn and I to the Castle tavern hard by and got a lobster, and he and I stayed and eat it and drank good wine; I, only burned wine – as my whole custom of late hath been,*c* as an evasion, God knows, for my drinking of wine (but it is an evasion which will not serve me now hot weather is coming, that I cannot pretend, as endeed I really have done, that I drink it for cold), but I will leave it off; and it is but seldom, as*d* when I am in women's company, that I must call for wine, for I must be

---

a repl. '27. Up'   *b* repl. 'bus'-   *c* repl. full stop or dash
                 d repl. full stop or dash

---

1. At the court of Admiralty: prize-cases seem mostly to have been tried at Exeter House. The judge was Sir Leoline Jenkins.

2. This concerned the *Lindenbaum* (Capt. Jean-François Vlaming), a Swedish ship which had been captured in mid-January by the privateer the *Flying Greyhound* (Capt. Edward Hogg; hired by Pepys, Penn and Batten). She had been on her way from Bordeaux to Ostend with a cargo mostly of wine. The Swedes claimed that the cargo, being carried in a neutral ship and owned by a Stockholm merchant, could not be adjudged prize. The case went to appeal. See PRO, HCA 3/252; ib., 14/54, nos 302, 218; ib., 30/181; below, pp. 135, 135–6, 159, 231 & nn.

forced to drink to them. Having done here, then we back again to the Court and there heard our cause pleaded, Sir   Turner,[1] Sir W. Walker, and Sir Ellis Layton being our counsel against only Sir Robt. Wiseman on the other. The second of our three counsel was the best; and endeed, did speak admirably, and is a very shrowd man. Nevertheless, as good as he did make our case and the rest, yet when Wiseman came to argue (nay, and though he did begin so sillily that we laughed in scorn in our sleeves at him), yet he did so state the case, that the Judge did not think fit to decide the cause tonight, but took to tomorrow and did stagger us in our hopes, so as to make us despair of the success.* I am mightily pleased with the judge, who seems a very rational, learned, and uncorrupt man; and much good reading and reason there is heard in hearing of this law argued, so that the thing pleased me, though our success doth shake me. Thence Sir W. Penn and I home and to write letters; among others, a sad one to my father upon fear of my mother's death; and so home to supper and to bed.

27.ᵃ W. Penn and I to White-hall; and in the coach did begin our discourse again about Balty, and he promises me to move it this very day. He and I met my Lord Brouncker at Sir G. Carteret's by appointment, there to discourse a little business, all being likely to go to wrack for lack of money still. Thence to the Duke of York's lodgings and did our usual business; and Sir W. Penn telling me that he had this morning spoke of Balty to Sir W. Coventry, and that the thing was done, I did take notice of it also to W. Coventry, who told me that he had both the thing and the person in his head before to have done it – which is a double pleasure to me. Our business with the Duke of York being done, W. Penn and I towards the Exchequer, and in our way met Sir G Downing going to chapel; but we stopped, and he would go with us back to the Exchequer and showed us in his office his chests full, and ground and shelves full of money, and says that there is 50000*l* at this day in his office of people's

a repl. '26'

_____

1. Sir William Turner, civil lawyer.

money; who may demand it this day and might have had it away several weeks ago upon[a] the late Act, but do rather choose to have it continue there then to put it into the Banquier's hands; and I must confess it is more then I should have believed[b] had I not seen it, and more then ever I could have expected would have arisen for this new act in so short a time; and if it do so now already, what would it do if the money was collected upon the Act and returned into the Exchequer so timelily as it ought to be.[1]   But it comes into my mind here to observe what I have heard from Sir Jo. Bankes (though I cannot fully conceive the reason of it): that it will be impossible to make the Exchequer ever a true bank to all intents, unless the Exchequer stood nearer the Exchange, where merchants might with ease, while they are going about their business, at all hours and without trouble or loss of time, have their satisfaction; which they cannot have now with[out] much trouble and loss of half a day, and no certainty of having the offices open.[2]   By this, he means a bank for common practice and use of merchants, and therein I do agree with him.   Being parted from Sir W. Penn and G. Downing, I to Westminster-hall and there met Balty, whom I had sent for; and there did break the business of my getting him the[c] place of going again as Muster-maister with Harman this voyage to the West Indys;[3] which endeed I do owe to Sir W. Penn. He is mighty glad of it and earnest to fit himself for it; but I do find, poor man, that he is troubled how to dispose of his wife, and apparently it is out of fear of her and his honour, and I believe he hath received some cause of this his jealousy[d] and care.   And I

---

a   repl. 'but'   b   repl. 'obliged'   c   repl. 'a'   d   repl. 'jealous'

---

1. The number of creditors who lent money on both the Additional Aid and the Eleven Months Tax was not large, and in any case their loans did not bear interest after the date on which repayment fell due.   Downing may well have exaggerated.

2. The Exchequer was apt to have many holidays: cf. above p. 73 & n. 4. The Bank of England (founded in

1694) was situated close by the Exchange.

3. Sir John Harman sailed on 28 April from Plymouth with the only squadron of men-of-war sent out into those waters in the whole of the reign: *CSPD 1667*, pp. 10, 54, 67. He returned a year later: ib., *1667–8*, p. 368.

do pity him in it, and will endeavour to find out some way to do it for him. Having put him in a way of preparing himself for the voyage, I did go to the Swan; and there sent for Jervas my old periwig-maker and he did bring me a periwig; but it was full of nits, so as I was troubled to see it (it being his old fault) and did send him to make it clean; and in the meantime, having stayed for him a good while, did go away*a* by water and to the Castle Taverne by Exeter-house and there met W. Batten, W. Penn and several others; among the rest, Sir Ellis Layton, who doth apply himself to discourse with me; and I think by his discourse, out of his opinion of my interest in Sir W. Coventry. The man I find a wonderful witty, ready man for sudden answers and little tales and sayings very extraordinary witty; but in the bottom, I doubt he is not so.[1] Yet he pretends to have studied men; and the truth is, in several that I do know he did give me a very inward account of them. But above all things, he did give me a full account, upon my demand, of this Judge of the Admirallty, Judge Jenkins; who he says is a man never practised in this Court, but taken merely for his merit and ability's sake from Trinity-hall,[2] where he had alway lived; only, by accident the business of the want of a judge being proposed to the Archbishop of Canterbury that now is, he did think of this man and sent for him up.[3] And here he is, against the gré and content of the old Doctors, made judge; but is a very excellent man both for judgment, temper (yet Majesty enough), and by all men's report – not to be corrupted. After dinner to the Court, where Sir Ellis Layton did make a very silly motion in our behalf that did neither hurt nor good. After him, Walker and Wiseman; and

a repl. 'home'

---

1. Cf. above, v. 300 & n. 5. Leighton practised in the court of Admiralty and served in the Prize Office, as well as being secretary to the Royal African Company and principal man of business to the Duke of Buckingham. Like Buckingham, he had a reputation for brilliance and instability.

2. *Recte* Jesus College, Oxford, of which he was Principal, 1661–73. He had in fact served on a committee on prize-law in 1665, and since February 1665 had been an assistant to Exton, a judge of the Admiralty Court, on whose death he had now succeeded to the bench.

3. Jenkins became at this time a deputy-judge of the Prerogative Court of the Archbishop, succeeding to a judge's place in 1669.

then the Judge did pronounce his sentence; for some, a part of
the goods and ship and the freight of the whole to be free, and
returned and paid by us; and the remaining (which was the
greater part) to be ours. The loss of so much troubles us, but
we have got a pretty good part, thanks be to God; so we are not
displeased, nor yet have cause to triumph, as we did once expect.
Having seen the end of this, I being desirous to be at home to see
the issue of my country letters about my mother, which I expect
shall give me tidings of her death, I directly home and there to the
office, where find no letter from my father or brother; but by
and by the boy tells me that his mistress sends me word that she
hath opened my letter, and that she is loath to send me any more
news. So I home, and there up to my wife in our chamber;
and there received from my brother the news of my mother's
dying on Monday, about 5 or 6 a-clock in the afternoon, and
that the last time she spoke of her children was on Friday last,
and her last words was, "God bless my poor Sam!"[1] The
reading hereof did set me a-weeping heartily; and so, weeping
to myself a while and my wife also to herself – I then spoke to
my wife, recollecting myself, and endeed having some thoughts
how much better, both for her and us, it is then it might have
been had she outlived my father and me or my happy present
condition in the world, she being helpless,[a] I was the sooner at
ease in my mind; and then found it necessary to go abroad with
my wife to look after the providing mourning to send into the
country, some tomorrow and more against Sundy, for my family,
being resolved to put myself and wife, and Barker and Jane,
W Hewers and Tom, in mourning; and my two under-maids,
to give them hoods and scarfs and gloves. So to my tailor's and
up and down; and then home and to my office a little; and then
to supper and to bed – my heart sad and afflicted, though my
judgment at ease.

28. My tailor came to me betimes this morning; and having
given him directions, I to the office and there all the morning.
At noon dined well. Balty, who is mighty thoughtful how to

a repl. 'hope'

---

1. She was buried on the 27th at St Mary's, Brampton, Hunts.

dispose of his wife and would fain have us provide a place for her, which the thoughts of what I should do with her if he should miscarry at sea makes me avoid the offering him that she should be at my house – I find he is plainly jealous* of her being in any place where she may have ill company; and I do pity him for it and would be glad to help him, and will if I can. Having dined, I down by water with Sir W. Batten, W. Penn and Sir R. Ford to our prize, part of whose goods were condemned yesterday, the *Lindeboome*; and there we did drink some of her wine, very good.[1] But it did grate my heart to see the poor maister come on board, and look about into every corner and find fault that she was not so clean as she used to be, though methought she was very clean. And to see his new maisters come in, that had nothing to do with her, did trouble me to see him. Thence to Blackewall; and there to Mr. Johnson's to see how some works upon some of our repaired ships goes on; and at his house eat and drank and mighty extraordinary merry (too merry for me, whose mother died so lately; but they know it not, so cannot reproach me thereon, though[a] I do reproach myself); and in going home had many good stories of Sir W. Batten, and one of W. Penn, the most tedious and silly and troublesome (he forcing us to hear him) that ever I heard in my life. So to the office a while, troubled with Sir W. Penn's impertinencies, he being half foxed at Johnson's; and so to bed.

29. Lay long, talking with my wife about Balty, whom I do wish very well to and would be glad to advance him – for he is very sober and willing to take all pains. Up, and to Sir W. Batten, who I find hath had some words with Sir W. Penn about the imploying of a Cooper about our prize wines, W. Batten standing and endeed imposing upon us Mr. Morrice; which I like not, nor doth W. Penn, and I confess the very thoughts of what our goods will come to when we have them doth discourage me in going any further in the adventure. Then to the office till noon, doing business; and then to the Exchange and thence to the Sun tavern and dined with W. Batten, R. Ford and the Swedes Agent, to discourse of a composition about our prizes

---

a repl. closing bracket

1. See above, p. 130 & n. 2.

that are condemned; but did do little, he standing upon high
terms and we doing the like.[1]   I home and there find Balty and
his wife, got thither both by my wife for me to give them good
advice, for her to be with his father and mother all this time of
absence for saving of money; and did plainly and like a friend tell
them my mind of the necessity of saving money, and that if I did
not find they did endeavour it, I should not think fit to trouble
myself for them.   But I see she is utterly against being with his
father and mother, and he is fond of her; and I perceive the
differences between the old people and them are too great to be
presently forgot, and so he doth propose that it will be cheaper[a]
for him to put her to board at a place he is offered at Lee; and I,
seeing that I am not like to be troubled with the finding a place
for her, and having given him so much good advice, do leave them
to stand and fall as they please, having discharged myself as a
friend,* and not likely to be accountable for her nor be troubled
with her, if he should miscarry I mean, as to her lodging.   And
so broke up.   Then he and I to make a visit to W. Penn, who
hath thought fit to show kindness to Balty in this business
endeed, though he be a false rogue; but it was, he knew, a thing
easy to do.   Thence together to my shoemaker's, cutler's,
tailor's, and up and down about my mourning; and in my going
do observe the great streets in the City are marked out with piles
drove into the ground; and if ever it be built in that form, with
so fair streets, it will be a noble sight.[2]   So to the Council
chamber, but stayed not there; but to a periwig-maker's of his
acquaintance and there bought two periwigs, mighty fine; endeed,
too fine I thought for me; but he persuaded me, and I did
buy them, 4*l.* 10*s.* the two.   Then to the Exchange and bought
gloves, and so to the Bull-head taverne, whither he brought my

a   repl. same symbol badly formed

---

1. One of the cases – that of the
Lindenbaum – went to appeal: above,
loc. cit. The Swedish agent was
probably the Resident, Leijonbergh.
    2. The lines of the streets were
staked out with all speed after the
King, on 22 March, had approved
revised proposals made by the city.
The widenings were set out and the
rules for rebuilding embodied in an
act of Common Council of 29 April.
T. F. Reddaway, *Rebuilding of London*,
pp. 109–10.   (R).

French Gun and one True Locke the famous gunsmith,[1] that is a mighty ingenious man, and he did take my gun in pieces and made me understand the secrets thereof; and upon the whole, doth find it a very good piece of work and truly wrought, but for certain not a thing to be used much with safety; and he doth find that this very gun was never yet shot off. I was mightily satisfied with it and him and the sight of so much curiosity of this kind. Here he brought also a haberdasher at my desire, and I bought a hat of him. And so away and called my wife from his house; and so home and to read, and then to supper and to bed, my head full in behalf of Balty, who tells me strange stories of his mother; among others, how she in his[2] absence in Ireland did pawne all his things that he had got in his service under Oliver, and run of her own accord, without her husband's leave, into Flanders. And that his ⟨purse⟩ and 4s a week which his father receives of the French church is all the subsistence his father and mother have. And that about 20*l* a year maintains them; which, if it please God, I will find one way or other to provide for them, to remove that scandal away.[3]

30. Up; and the French[a] periwig-maker of whom I bought two yesterday comes with them, and I am very well pleased with them. So to the office, where all the morning. At noon home to dinner; and thence, with my wife's knowledge and leave, did by coach go see the silly play of my Lady Newcastle's called *The Humorous Lovers*, the most silly thing that ever came upon a stage;[4] I was sick to see it, but yet would not but have seen it, that I might the better understand her. Here I spied Knipp and

a repl. 'periwig'

---

1. Either Edmund or George Tru-locke. Balty had perhaps borrowed the gun during his service in the army: cf. above, vi. 271 & n. 1.

2. Possibly this refers to her husband. Nothing more is known of this story.

3. Alexandre St Michel and his

wife went to Paris a few months later, and Balty was made Deputy-Treasurer of the fleet: below, pp. 148–9, 281.

4. This comedy was in fact by her husband the Duke: it was first acted in this year and published in 1677. Pepys saw it at the LIF. (A).

Betty[1] of the King's House, and sent Knipp Oranges; but having little money about me, did not offer to carry them abroad, which otherwise I had I fear been tempted to. So with W. Penn home (he being at the play also), a most summer evening. And to my office; where among other things, a most extraordinary letter to the Duke of Yorke touching the want of money and the sad state of the King's service thereby;[2] and so to supper and to bed.

31. *Lords day.* Up; and my tailor's boy brings my mourning*a* clothes home, and my wife's, hers and Barker's; but they go not to church this morning. I to church, and with my mourning, very handsome, and new periwig make a great show. After church, home to dinner, and there came Betty Michell and her husband; I do and shall love her; but, poor wretch, she is now almost ready to lie down. After dinner, Balty (who dined also with us) and I with Sir J. Menues in his coach to White-hall, but did nothing; but by water to Strand bridge[3] and thence walked to my Lord Treasurer's, where the King, Duke of York, and the Caball,* and much company without; and a fine day. Anon comes out from the Caball my Lord Hollis and Mr. H. Coventry, who it is conceived have received their instructions from the King this day; they being to begin their journey towards their treaty at Bredagh speedily, their passes being come.[4] Here I saw the Lady Northumberland and her daughter-in-law

a repl. 'cloth'

1. Betty Ball: above, p. 27. (A).
2. Navy Board to Duke of York, 31 March (in Pepys's hand), Longleat, Coventry MSS, 97, ff. 67–8; copy (in Gibson's hand) NMM, LBK/8, pp. 471–2; printed in *Further Corr.*, pp. 165–7. The Board stated that it needed £40,000 per week, and complained that not a penny had yet arrived of the £30,000 or so which had supposedly been made available five weeks before.
3. Landing-stairs near Somerset House.

4. They did not set out until 29 April, arriving at Breda on the 4/14th. The treaty with the Dutch was signed there on 21/31 July. Holles was ambassador to France, and Coventry had recently completed a successful mission to Sweden. Copies of their instructions (18 April) are in Bodl., Clar. 85, f. 441r; PRO, SP 84/182, f. 95r; partially printed in *Cal. court mins. E. India Co., 1664–7* (ed. E. B. Sainsbury), pp. 314–15. Cf. below, p. 189; Feiling, pp. 219+.

(my Lord Treasurer's daughter), my Lady Piercy, a beautiful lady endeed.[1] So away back by water; and left Balty at White-hall, and I to Mrs. Martin and there haze todo which yo would hazer con her; and so by coach home and there to my chamber; and then to supper and bed – having not had time to make up my accounts of this month at this very day, but will in a day or two and pay my forfeit for not doing it, though business hath most hindered me.

The month shuts up, only with great desires of peace in*a* all of us, and a belief that we shall have a peace in most people, if a peace can be had on any terms, for there is a necessity of it; for we cannot go on with the war, and our maisters are afeared to come to depend upon the good will of the Parliament any more as I do hear.

a repl. 'on'

---

1. The Countess of Northumberland was the wife of the 10th Earl. Her daughter-in-law, one of the greatest beauties of her time (and a co-heiress) had married Lord Joscelin Percy (later the 11th Earl) in 1662. In 1671, when she was a widow, the 3rd Duke of Somerset is said to have died for love of her. For portraits of her, see *Pub. Walpole Soc.*, viii. 89+ .

APRILL.

1. Up, and with Sir J. Mennes in his coach; set him down at the Treasurer's Office in Broad-street, and I in his coach to White-hall; and there had the good fortune to walk with Sir W. Coventry into the garden, and there read our melancholy letter to the Duke of York, which he likes; and so to talk, and he flatly owns that we must have a peace, for we cannot set out a fleet; and (to use his own words) he fears we shall soon have enough of fighting in this new way that we have thought on for this year.[1] He bemoans the want of money, and discovers himself jealous that Sir G. Carteret doth not look after or concern himself for getting money as he used to do; and did say it is true, if Sir G. Carteret would only do his work and my Lord Treasurer would do his owne, Sir G. Carteret hath nothing to do to look after money; but if he will undertake my Lord Treasurer's work, to raise money of the banquiers, then people must expect that he will do it;[2] and did further say that he[3] and my Lord Chancellor do at this very day labour all they can to villify this new way of raising money and making it payable, as it now is, into the Exchequer; and expressly said that in pursuance hereof my Lord Chancellor hath prevailed with the King, in the close of his last speech to the House, to say that he did hope to see them come to give money as it used to be given, without so many Provisos; meaning (as Sir W. Coventry says) this new method of the Act.[4] While we were talking, there come Sir Tho. Allen with two ladies, one of which was Mrs. Rebecca Allen that I knew heretofore, the clerk of the ropeyard's daughter at Chatham; who, poor heart, came to desire favour for her

---

1. By small squadrons at sea, and fortifications on land: see above, pp. 97–8 & n.

2. For Carteret's methods, see above, p. 48 & n. 1; below, p. 290 and n. 2.

3. Carteret.

4. 'I hope we shall live to see Bills of this Nature in the old Stile, with fewer Provisos': King's speech, 8 February (*LJ*, xii. 111). He was referring to the Eleven Months Tax which had appropriated supplies to the navy: see above, p. 31, n. 1.

husband,[1] who is clapped up, being a Lieutenant, for sending a challenge to his Captain in the most saucy base language that could be writ. I perceive Sir W. Coventry is wholly resolved to bring him to punishment – "for bear with this," says he, "and no discipline shall ever be expected." She in this sad condition took no notice of me, nor I of her. So away we to the Duke of York; and there in his closet W. Coventry and I delivered the letter, which the Duke of York made not much of I thought, as to laying it to heart as the matter deserved; but did promise to look after the getting of money for us, and I believe Sir W. Coventry will add what force he can to it. I did speak to W. Coventry about Balty's warrant which is ready, and about being Deputy-Treasurer,[2] which*a* he very readily and friendlily agreed to, at which I was glad; and so away and by coach back to Broadstreete to Sir G. Carteret's and there find my Brethren passing his accounts, which I helped till dinner; and dined there, and many good stories at dinner; among others, about discoveries of murder; and Sir J. Mennes did tell one of the discovery of his own great-grandfather, fifteen years after he was murdered.[3] Thence after dinner home, and by water to Redriffe, and walked (fine weather) to Deptford and there did business and so back again; walked, and pleased with a jolie femme that I saw going and coming in the way, which yo could aver sido contented para aver stayed with if yo could have*b* ganar acquaintance con ella; but at such times as those I am at a great loss, having not confidence, ni alguno ready wit. So home and to the office, where late; and then home to supper and bed. This evening Mrs. Turner came to my office and did walk an hour with me in the garden, telling me stories how Sir Edwd Spragge hath lately made love to our neighbour, a widow, Mrs. Hollworthy, who is a woman of state and wit and spirit, and doth contemn him the most and sent him away with the greatest scorn in*c* the world. She tells me also odd stories how the parish talks

   a Here begin two pages headed 'March'   *b* repl. full stop
               c repl. 'and'

---

1. Henry Jowles.   3. This affair has not been traced.
2. See below, p. 142.

of Sir W. Penn's family, how poorly they clothe their daughter so soon after marriage – and do say that Mr. Lowder was married once before;[1] and some such thing there hath been, whatever the bottom of it is. But to think of the clutter they make with his coach and his own fine clothes, and yet how meanly they live within doors and nastily, and borrowing everything of neighbours, is a most shitten thing.

2. Up and to the office, where all the morning sitting; and much trouble, but little business done for want of money, which makes me mighty melancholy. At noon home to dinner, and Mr. Deane with me; who hath promised me a very fine draught of the *Rupert*, which he will make purposely for me with great perfection; which he[a] will make one of the beautifullest things that ever was seen of that kind in the world – she being a ship that will deserve it.[2] Then to the office, where all the afternoon very busy; and in the evening, weary home; and there to sing, but vexed with the unreadiness of the girl's voice to learn ⟨the latter⟩ part of my song,[3] though I confess it is very hard half-notes. So to supper and to bed.

3. Up and with Sir W. Batten[b] to White-hall to Sir W. Coventry's chamber, and there did receive the Duke's order for Balty's receiving of the contingent money to be paymaister of it; and it pleases me the more for that it is but 1500*l*, which will be but a little sum for to try his ability and honesty in the disposing of – and so I am the willinger to trust him and pass my word for him therein. By and by up to the Duke of York, where our usual business; and among other things, I read two most dismal letters of the straits we are in (from Collonell Middleton and

a MS. 'I'   *b* repl. 'Coventry'

---

1. His marriage licence described him as a bachelor.
2. I have not traced the drawing. The *Rupert* was a 3rd-rate built by Deane at Harwich in 1666 and much admired by the King and the Duke of York: above, vii. 119, 127.

3. The song was *It is decreed* (q.v. above, vii. 91 & n. 4) which towards the end has many quavers. The girl was Barker. (E).

Comissioner Taylor) that ever were writ in the world,[1] so as the Duke of York would have them to show the King. And to every demand of money, whereof we proposed many and very pressing ones, Sir G. Carteret could make no answer but "No money", which I confess made me almost ready to cry for sorrow and vexation; but that which was the most considerable was when Sir G. Carteret did say that he had no fond to raise money on; and being asked by Sir W. Coventry whether the Eleven Months Tax was not a fond, and he answered no – that the banquiers would not lend money upon it.[2] Then Sir W. Coventry burst[a] out and said he did supplicate his Royal Highness, and would do the same to the King, that he would remember who they were that did persuade the King from parting with the Chimney-money to the Parliament,[3] and taking that in the lieu which they would certainly have given and which would have raised infallibly ready money – meaning the banquiers and the[b] farmers of the Chimney-money (where Sir G. Carteret I think is one[4]); saying plainly that whoever did advise the King to that, did as much as in them lay cut the King's throat and did wholly

a repl. 'fl'-   *b* repl. 'I believe'

---

1. Taylor's letter (Harwich, 30 March) is in PRO, SP 46/136, no. 443: summary in *CSPD Add. 1660–85*, pp. 172–3. He reported that carpenters were dying of hunger, and that only with difficulty were some of them restrained from marching to London. The original of Middleton's letter (Portsmouth, 31 March) has not been traced, but (as with Taylor's) much of it was incorporated in an undated memorandum by Pepys (in Gibson's hand) of which a copy is in NMM, LBK/8, pp. 475+. He wrote: 'Just now is with me a poore Oare-maker crying and wringing his hands for Money, and desires to bee a labourer in the Yard ... hee dareth not goe home to his wife any more for hee shalbee carryed to Jayle by his

Timber Merchant ...'. Middleton had pawned his own plate to pay for whale-oil – 'I had rather drinke in a horneing Cupp then that the Kings shipps should stay heere.' Several similar letters from Middleton at this time are summarised by Pepys in NWB, pp. 108–9.
2. This tax for £1¼m., voted in February, had been specifically designed to attract credit, loans being secured on its revenue. The bankers did in fact lend money on it: see e.g. below, p. 529 & n. 1.
3. In October 1666 a proposal to compound the hearth-tax for a lump sum of £1,600,000 had been voted, but lapsed: see above, vii. 326, 330.
4. He was not.

betray him – to which the Duke of York did assent, and remembered that the King did say again and again at that time that
he was assured, and did fully believe, the money would be raised
presently upon a land-tax.   This put us all into a stound.   And
Sir W. Coventry went on to declare that he was glad he was
come to have so little*a* concern in the Navy as he hath,[1] for he
cannot now give any good account of the Navy business – and
that all his work now was to be able to provide such orders as
would justify his Royal Highness in business when it shall be
called to account; and that he doth do, not concerning himself
whether they are or can be performed or no; and that when it
comes to be examined and falls on my Lord Treasurer, he cannot
help it, whatever the issue of it shall be.   Hereupon, Sir W. Batten*b* did pray him to keep also by him all our letters that come from
the office that may justify us; which he says he doth do.   And
God knows it is an ill sign when we are once to come to study
how to excuse ourselfs*c* – it is a sad consideration; and therewith
we broke up, all in a sad posture, the most that ever I saw in my
life.   One thing more Sir W. Coventry did say to the Duke of
York, when I moved again that of about 9000*l* debt to Lanyon at
Plymouth, he might pay 3700*l* worth of prize-goods that he
bought lately at*d* the candle,[2] out of this debt due to him from the
King.   And*e* the Duke of York and Sir G. Carteret and Lord
Berkely saying, all*f* of them, that my Lord Ashly would not be
got to yield to it, who is Treasurer of the Prizes – Sir*g* W. Coventry
did plainly desire that it might be declared whether the proceed
of the prizes were to go to the helping on of the war, or no;
and if it were, how then this could be denied.   Which put them
all into another stound; and it is true, God forgive us.[3]
   Thence to the chapel, and there by chance hear that Dr. Crew[4]

---

a MS. 'lately'   *b* repl. 'Coventry'   *c* MS. 'herselfs'
       d repl. symbol rendered illegible   *e* repl. 'but'
              f MS. 'that all'   *g* repl. 'that'

---

1. Since January he had no longer
been a Navy Commissioner.   He was
still (until September) secretary to the
Lord High Admiral.
   2. For auction-sales by candle, see
above, i. 284, n. 2.

3. For the difficulty of securing
prize-goods for the use of the navy,
see above, p. 14, n. 4.
   4. Nathaniel Crew (son of Lord
Crew), chaplain to the King, and
later (1674) Bishop of Durham.

is to preach; and so into the Organ-loft, where I met Mr. Carteret and my Lady Jemimah and Sir Tho. Crew's two daughters, and Dr. Childe played – and Dr. Crew did make a very pretty, neat, sober, honest sermon; and delivered it very readily, decently, and gravely, beyond his years¹ – so as I was exceedingly taken with it, and I believe the whole chapel – he being but young; but his manner of his delivery I do like exceedingly. His text was, "But first seeke the kingdom of God and all these things shall be added unto you."²   Thence with my Lady to Sir G. Carteret's lodgings, and so up into the house and there do hear that the Dutch letters are come and say that the Dutch have ordered a passe*ᵃ* to be sent for our Commissioners; and that it is now upon the way, coming with a Trumpeter, blinded as is usual.³ But I perceive everybody begins to doubt the success of the treaty, all their hopes being only that if it can be had on any terms, the Chancellor will have it; for he dare not come before a Parliament, nor a great many more of the Courtiers, and the King himself doth declare he doth not desire it, nor entend it but on a strait – which God*ᵇ* defend him from.   Here*ᶜ* I hear how the King is not so well pleased of this marriage between the Duke of Richmond and Mrs. Stewart as is talked; and that he by a wilde∗ did fetch her to the Beare at the Bridge-foot, where a coach was ready, and they are stole away into Kent without the King's leave;⁴ and that the King hath said he will never see her more, but people do think that it is only a trick.   This day I saw Prince Rupert abroad in the Vane Roome, pretty well as he used to be,

---

a l.h. repl. s.h.   *b* MS. 'great'   *c* repl. 'thence hear how'

---

1. He was 34; the same age as Pepys.

2. A loose recollection of Luke, xii. 31.

3. The passports were issued ('in the most ample style') on 26 March/ 7 April: D'Estrades, *Lettres* &c (1709), iv. 128–30. For the departure of the commissioners, see above, p. 138, n. 4.

4. To Cobham Hall, the Duke's house near Gravesend. They had been married on 30 March: C. H. Hartmann, *La Belle Stuart*, p. 113 n. The King never forgave Richmond and later refused him several diplomatic appointments: cf. Burnet, i. 452–3; HMC, *Le Fleming*, pp. 46–7. Charles was said to have suspected Clarendon of arranging the match to scotch his own plans for a divorce: Burnet, loc. cit.: Ludlow, ii. 407.

and looks as well; only, something appears to be under his periwig on the crown of his head.[1]　So home by water and there find my wife gone abroad to her tailor's; and I dined alone with W Hewers and then to the office to draw up a Memoriall for the Duke of York this afternoon at the Council about Lanyon's business.[2]　By and by we met by appointment at the office upon a reference of Carcasse's business to us again from the Duke of York; but a very confident cunning rogue we shall find him at length.　He carried himself very uncivilly to Sir W. Batten this afternoon, as heretofore, and his silly Lord[3] pleaded for him; but all will not nor shall not do, for out he shall go – though I love the man as a man of great parts and abilities.　Thence to White-hall by water (only, asking Betty Michell by the way how she did) and there came too late to do anything at the Council; so by coach to my periwig-maker's*a* and tailor's, and so home, where I find my wife with her flagellete-master,[4] which I wish she would practise.　And so to the office, and then to Sir W. Batten's, and then to Sir W. Penn's, talking and spending time in vain a little while; and then home up to my chamber, and so to supper and to bed – vexed at two or three things – *viz*. that my wife's watch proves so bad as it doth – the ill state of the office and Kingdom's business – at the charge which my mother's death for mourning will bring me when all paid.

4.　Up; and going down, found Jervas the barber with a periwig which I had the other day cheapened at Westminster; but it being full of nits, as heretofore his work used to be, I did now refuse it, having bought elsewhere.　So to the office till noon, busy; and then (which I think I have not done three times in my

---

a repl. 'barbers'

---

1. For his recent operation (by trepanning), see above, p. 41 & n. 1.

2. The Tangier victualling. The Clerk of the Cheque at Plymouth (Waltham) had refused to sign the accounts, alleging that Lanyon had not allowed inspection of them. But Waltham was said to be a drunken and unreliable official, who used the brandy-shop as his office: *CSPD 1667*, pp. 18, 32, 35. Lanyon was later paid: below, p. 318 & n. 2.

3. Brouncker: for the Carkesse case, see above, p. 64, n. 1.

4. Greeting. (E).

life) left the board upon occasion of a letter from Sir W. Coventry; and meeting Balty at my house, I took him with me by water, and to the Duke of Albemarle to give him an account of that business; which was the shipping off of some soldiers for the manning of the few ships now going out with Harman to the West Indies;[1] which is a sad consideration, that at the very beginning ⟨of the year⟩, and few ships abroad, we should be in such want of men; but they do hide themselfs and swear they will not go to be killed and have no pay. I find the Duke of Albemarle at dinner with sorry company, some of his officers of the Army – dirty dishes and a nasty wife at table[2] – and bad meat; of which I made but an ill dinner. Pretty, to hear how she talked against Captain Du Tel, the Frenchman that the Prince and her husband put out the last year; and how, says she, the Duke of York hath made for his good services his cup=bearer; yet fired more shot into the Prince's ship, and others[a] of the King's ships, then of the enemy.[3] And the Duke of Albemarle did confirm it, and that somebody in[b] the fight did cry out that a little Dutchman by his ship did plague him more then any other; upon which they were going to order him to be sunk, when they looked and found it was Du Tell, who, as the Duke of Albemarle says, had killed several men in several of our ships. He said, but for his interest which he knew he had at Court, he had hanged him at the yard's-arm without staying for a Court Martiall. One Collonell Howard at the table magnified the Duke of Albemarle's fight in June last,[4] as being a greater action then ever was done by Cæsar; the Duke of Albemarle did say it had been no great action, had all his number fought, as they should have done, to have beat the Dutch; but of his 55 ships, not above 25 fought.[5] He did give an account that it was a fight he was forced to; the Dutch being come in his way and he being ordered to the buoy of the

---

a   repl. 'those'   *b*   repl. 'there'

---

1. The Board was to arrange for the transport of 180 soldiers to the Hope: *CSPD 1667*, p. 10.

2. She was known as 'Our Dirty Besse': above, vii. 354.

3. This was in the Four Days Battle, June 1666: see above, vii. 163

& n. 1. At that time Du Teil was already a gentleman waiter in the Queen-Mother's household.

4. In the same battle.

5. Cf. his similar complaints above, vii. 154, 177.

Nore, he could not pass by them without fighting, nor avoid them with[out] great disadvantage and dishonour. (And this, Sir G. Carteret, I afterward giving him an account of what he said, says that it is true: that he was ordered up to the Nore); "but I remember," he said, "had all his captains fought, he would no more have doubted to beat the Dutch, with all their*a* number, then to eat the apple that lay on his trencher."

My Lady Duchesse, among other things, discoursed of the wisdom of dividing the fleet; which the Generall said nothing to, though he knows well that it come from themselfs in the fleet and was brought up hither by Sir Edw. Spragge.[1] Collonell Howard asking how the Prince did, the Duke of Albemarle answering, "Pretty well," the other replied, "But not so well as to go to sea again." "How!"*b* says the Duchesse, "what should he go for if he were well, for there are no ships for him to command. And so you have brought your hogs to a fair market!" said she. ⟪It was*c* pretty to hear the Duke of Albemarle himself to wish that they would come on our ground, meaning the French – for that he would pay them, so as to make them glad to go back to France again – which was like a General, but not like an Admiral.⟫[2] One at the table told an odd passage in this*d* late plague: that at Petersfield (I think he said) one side of the street had every house almost infected through the town; and the other, not one shut up.[3] Dinner being done, I brought Balty to the Duke of Albemarle to kiss his hands and thank him for his kindness the last year to him and take leave of him. And then Balty and I to walk in the park; and out of pity to his father, told him what I had in my thoughts to do for him about the money – that is, to make him Deputy-Treasurer of the fleet, which I have done by getting Sir G. Carteret's consent and an order from the Duke of York for 1500*l* to be paid to him. He promises the whole profit to be paid to my wife, for to be disposed on as she sees fit for her father and mother's relief. So, mightily pleased

a repl. 'the'   *b* repl. 'Why'   *c* repl. 'it was'   *d* MS. 'the this'

---

1. See above, vii. 179, n. 4.
2. Albemarle was well known for the landlubberly expressions he used at sea (e.g. 'Wheel to the right!'); cf. Aubrey, ii. 74.

3. Petersfield was hit by the plague (VCH, *Hants.*, iii. 120), but this story has not been traced.

with our walk, it being mighty pleasant weather, I back to Sir G. Carteret's and there he had newly dined; and talked and find that he doth*a* give everything over for lost, declaring no money to be raised; and let Sir W. Coventry name the man that persuaded the King to take the Land Tax on promise of raising present money upon it: he will, he says, be able to clear himself enough of it. I made him merry with telling him how many land-Admiralls[1] we are to have this year – Allen at Plymouth, Holmes at Portsmouth, Spragg for Medway, Teddyman at Dover, Smith to the North, and Harman to the South. He did defend to me Sir W. Coventry as not guilty of the dividing of the fleet the last year. And blesses God, as I do, for my Lord Sandwiches absence; and tells me how the King did lately observe to him how they have been perticularly punished that were enemies to my Lord Sandwich. Mightily pleased I am with his family; and my Lady Carteret was on the bed today, having been let blood, and tells me of my Lady Jem's being big-bellied. Thence with him to Lord Treasurer's, and there walked during Councilsitting with Sir St. Fox, talking of the sad condition of the King's purse, and affairs thereby – and how sad the King's life must be, to pass by his officers every hour that are four years behindhand unpaid. And my Lord Barkely I met with there, and fell into talk with him on the same thing, wishing to God that it might be remedied; to which he answered with an oath, that it was as easy to remedy it as anything in the world, saying that there is himself and three more would venture their Carcasses upon it to pay all the King's debts in three year, had they the managing his revenue and putting 300000*l* in his purse as a stock. But Lord, what a thing is this to me, that do know how likely a man my Lord Berkely of all the world is to do such a thing as this. Here I spoke with Sir W. Coventry, who tells me plainly that to all future complaints of lack of money he will answer but with a shrugg of his shoulder; which methought did come to my heart, to see him to begin to abandon the King's affairs and let them sink or swim, so he do his own part; which I confess I believe he

a repl. 'do'

---

1. Because of the decision to divide the fleet into squadrons instead of having a battle-fleet.

doth, beyond any officer the King hath; but unless he do endeavour to make others do theirs, nothing will be done. The consideration hereof did make me go away very sad; and so home by coach and there took up my wife and Mercer (who had been today at White-hall to*a* the Maundy, it being Maundy Thursday; but the King did not wash the poor people's feet himself, but the Bishop of London did it for him; but I did not see it)[1] and with them took up Mrs. Anne Jones at her mother's door; and so to take the ayre to Hackny, where good neat's tongue and things to eat and drink, and very merry, the weather being mighty pleasant; and here I was told that at their church they have a fair pair* of Organs, which plays while the people sing; which I am mighty glad of, wishing the like at our church at*b* London, and would give 50*l* towards it.[2] So, very pleasant and hugging of Mercer in*c* our going home, we home; and there I to the office to do a little business, and so to supper at home and to bed.

5. Up, and troubled with Mr. Carcasse's coming to speak with me, which made me give him occasion to fall into a heat and he begun to be ill-mannered to me, which made me angry. He gone, I to Sir W. Penn about the business of Mrs. Turners Son to keep his ship in imployment;[3] but so false a fellow as Sir W. Penn is, I never did nor hope shall ever know again.

---

a repl. 'at'   *b* repl. 'here'   *c* repl. 'back'

1. Charles II occasionally performed the washing himself. James II is said to have been the last English ruler to have done so. The Bishop of London (Humphrey Henchman) was Lord Almoner. For the Maundy ceremony, see *Merc. Pub.*, 18 April 1661, p. 225; *Rawdon Papers* (ed. E. Berwick, 1819), pp. 175–6 (1665); E. Chamberlayne, *Angl. Not.* (1669), pp. 297–8; H. Misson, *Mémoires*, etc. (1698), pp. 343–4; cf. also A. R. Wright, *Brit. cal. customs* (Engl., ed. Lones), i. 61+.

2. The organ at St Olave's had been removed in 1644 and was not replaced until 1783: A. Povah, *Annals St Olave*, pp. 42, 62; GL, MS 858. The congregation sang unaccompanied, led by the parson or the parish clerk: cf. above, v. 320.

3. Frank Turner (naval captain, and son of Thomas Turner of the Navy Office) had been forced to transfer men from his ship to Harman's fleet; cf. Penn to Pepys, 7 April: *CSPD 1667*, p. 17. In 1668 he entered the service of the E. India Company.

So to the office and there did business till dinner-time – and then home to dinner, wife and I alone. And then down to the Old Swan and drank with Betty[1] and her husband, but no opportunity para besar la. So to White-hall to the Council-chamber, where I find no Council held till after the holidays. So to Westminster-hall and there bought a pair of snuffers and saw Mrs. Howlett after her sickness come to the Hall again. And so by coach to the New Exchange and Mercer's and other places to take up bills for what I owe them – and to Mrs. Pierce, to invite her to dinner with us on Monday, but stayed not with her. In the street met with Mr. Sanchy, my old acquaintance at Cambrige, reckoned a great minister here in the City, and by Sir Rd. Ford perticularly, which I wonder at, for methinks in his talk he is but a mean man.[2] I set him down in Holburne, and I to the Old Exchange and there to Sir Rob. Viners and made up my accounts there to my great content; but I find they do not keep them so regularly as to be*a* able to do it easily and truly and readily, nor would it have been easily stated by anybody on*b* my behalf but myself, several things being to be recalled to memory which nobody else could have done; and therefore it is fully necessary for me to even accounts as often with these people as I can. So to the Change, and there met with Mr. James Hubland; but no hopes, as he sees, of peace, whatever we pretend; but we shall be abused by the King of France. Then home to the office,*c* and busy late; and then to Sir W. Batten, where Mr. Young[3] was talking about the building of the City again and he told me that those few churches that are to be new built are plainly not chosen with regard to the convenience of the City, they stand a great many in a cluster about Cornhill; but that all of them are either*d* in the gift of the Lord Archbishop or Bishop of London or Lord Chancellor or gift of the City – thus all things, even to the

---

a MS. 'to' *b* repl. 'but'
c repl. 'officy' (? a mixture of 'office' and 'busy')
d repl. same symbol badly formed

---

1. Betty Mitchell
2. Cf. above, p. 17 & n. 5.

3. John Young, flagmaker, Cornhill.

building of churches, are done in this world.[1]   And then he says
(which I wonder at that I should not in all this time see) that
Moore Fields have houses two storeys high in them, and paved
streets, the City having let leases for seven years; which he doth
conclude will be very much to the hindering the building of the
City; but it was considered that the streets[a] cannot be passable in
London till a whole street be built, and several that had got
ground of the City for charity, to build sheds on, had got the
trick presently to sell that for 60l which did not cost them 20l[b]
to put up; and so the City, being very poor in stock, thought it as
good to do it themselfs, and therefore lets leases for seven years
of that ground in Moorefields; and a good deal of this money
thus advanced hath[c] been imployed for the enabling them to find
some money for Comissioner Taylor and Sir W. Batten, towards the charge of the *Loyall London*,[2] or else it is feared it had
never been paid; and Taylor having a bill to pay, wherein
Alderman Hooker was concerned, it was his invention to find
out this way of raising money, or else[d] this had not been thought
on neither.   So home to supper and to bed.   This morning came
to me the Collectors for my Pole mony; for which I paid for my
title as Esquire and place of Clerk of Acts, and my head and
wife's, and servants' and their wages, 40l. 17s. 00d.[3]   And though
this be a great deal, yet it is a shame I should pay no more;
that is, that I should not be assessed for my pay, as in the Victualling business and Tanger, and for my money, which of my own

a   repl. same symbol badly formed   b   repl. '21' repeated
c   repl. 'is emply'-   d   repl. 'it'

1. This does not tally with the facts.
In 1665 there were some 109 parish
churches in the city, of which 84 had
been destroyed in the Fire, three
heavily damaged and two partially
damaged. Rebuilding could not start
until funds had been collected, stone
and labour made available and agreement reached on which should be left
unbuilt.   When parliamentary sanc-
tion was at last obtained, in 1670, 35
of the 'burnt' churches were suppressed.   The sites of some (e.g. St

Mary Woolchurch, St Michael le
Querne and St Gabriel Fenchurch)
were required for urgent street and
market improvements.   Others had
parishes of only a few acres in extent.
Suppressions were made in all parts of
the city and Cornhill does not seem
to have been unduly favoured.   See
Bell, *Fire*; T. F. Reddaway, *Rebuilding
of London*.   (R).
2. The ship built in 1666 and paid
for by the city.
3. Cf. above, p. 30 & n. 1.

accord I had determined to charge myself with 1000*l* money,[1]
till coming to the Vestry and seeing nobody of our ablest merchants, as Sir Andrew Rickard, to do it, I thought it not decent
for me to*a* do it; nor*b* would it be thought wisdom to do it
unnecessarily, but vainglory.

6. Up, and betimes in the morning down to the Tower
wharfe, there to attend the shipping of soldiers to go down to
man some ships going out; and pretty to see how merrily some
and most go and how sad others, the leave they take of their
friends, and the tears*c* that some wifes and others' wenches shed
to part with them: a pretty mixture. So to the office, having
stayed as long as I could, and there sat all the morning; and then
home at noon to dinner; and then abroad, Balty with me, and
to White-hall by water to Sir G. Carteret about Balty's 1500*l*
contingent money for the fleet to the West Indys; and so away
with him to the Exchange and mercers and drapers, up and down,
to pay all my scores occasioned*d* by this mourning for my mother
– and emptied a 50*l* bag; and it was a joy*e* to me to see that I am
able to part with such a sum without much inconvenience – at
least, without any trouble of mind. So [to] Captain Cocke's
to meet Fenn[2] to talk about this money for Balty; and there
Cocke tells me that he is confident there will be a peace, whatever
terms*f* be asked us; and he confides that it will take, because
the French and Dutch will be jealous* one of another which shall
give the best terms, lest the other should make the peace with us
alone, to the ruin of the third – which is our best defence, this
jealousy, for aught I at present see. So home and there very late,
very busy; and then home to supper and to bed – the people
having got their house very clean against Mondy*g* dinner.

---

a repl. 'nor'   b MS. 'and'   c MS. 'terms'
d repl. 'which I did'   e repl. symbol rendered illegible
f repl. 'peace'   g repl. 'to'-

---

1. At 31 December 1665 Pepys
estimated his 'estate' at £4,400, and at
30 April 1667 at £6,700. See above,
s.d.

2. Paymaster to the Navy
Treasurer.

7. *Easter day.* Up; and when dressed, with my wife (in*ᵃ* mourning for my mother) to church both, where Mr. Mills; a lazy sermon. Home to dinner, wife and I and W. Hewer; and after dinner, I by water to White-hall to Sir G. Carteret's, there to talk about Balty's money; and did present Balty to him to kiss his hand. And then to walk in the park, and heard the Italian music at the Queen's chapel; whose composition* is fine, but yet the voices of the Eunuches I do not like like our women, nor am more pleased with it at all then with English voices, but that they do jump most excellently with themselfs and their instrument – which is wonderful pleasant; but I am convinced more and more, that as every nation hath a perticular accent and tone in discourse, so as the tone of one not to agree with or please the other, no more can the fashion of singing to words; for that the better the words are*ᵇ* set, the more they take in of the ordinary tone of the country*ᶜ* whose language the song speaks; so that a song well composed by an Englishman must be better to an Englishman then it can be to a stranger, or then if set by a stranger in foreign words. Thence back to White-hall and there saw the King come out of chapel after prayers in the afternoon; which he is never at but after having received the Sacrament; and the Court, I perceive, is quite out of mourning,[1] and some very fine; among others, my Lord Gerard in a very rich vest and Coate. Here I met with my Lord Bellasses; and it is pretty to see what a formal story he tells me of his leaving his place upon the death of my Lord Cleveland, by which he is become Captain of the Pentioners, and that the King did leave it to him to keep the other or take this, whereas I know the contrary, that they had a mind to have him away from Tanger.[2] He tells me he is commanded by the King to go down to the North to satisfy the Deputy Lieutenants of Yorkeshire who have desired to lay down their commissions, upon pretence of having no profit by their places, but charge; but endeed is upon the Duke of Buckinghams

---

a repl. 'she'   *b* MS. 'or'   *c* repl. 'countr'-

1. For the death of the Queen's mother: see above, vii. 84, n. 2.
2. Belasyse had been Governor of Tangier since 1665. The Earl of Cleveland had died on 25 March.

being under a cloud (of whom there is yet nothing heard), so
that the King is apprehensive of their discontent and sends him to
pacify them;[1] and I think he is as good a dissembler as any man
else; and a fine person he is for person, and proper to lead the
Pensioners, but a man of no honour nor faith I doubt. So to
Sir G. Carteret's again to talk with him about Balty's money, and
wrote a letter to Portsmouth about part of it; and then in his
coach with his little daughter Poopott (as he used to nickname
her)[2] and saw her at home, and her*a* maid and another little
gentlewoman; and so I walked into Moore fields*b* and, as is said,
did find houses built two storeys high, and like to stand, and
must become a place of great trade till the City be built, and the
street is already paved as London streets used to be – which is a
strange, and to me an unpleasing sight. So home, and to my
chamber about sending an express to Portsmouth about Balty's
money; and then comes Mrs. Turner to enquire after her son's
business, which goes but bad; which led me to show her how
false Sir W. Penn is to her, whereupon she told me his obligations
to her and promises for her, and how a while since he did show
himself dissatisfied in her son's coming to the table and applying
himself to me[3] – which is a good note, and a note I will make use
of. She gone, I to other business in my chamber and then to
supper and to bed. The Swedes Imbassadors and our Commissioners are making all the haste they can over to the treaty for
peace; and I find at Court, and perticularly Lord Bellasses says,
there will be a peace. And it is worth remembering what Sir

a repl. 'then'   *b* repl. 'mor'-

---

1. Buckingham was Lord Lieutenant of the W. Riding, and several
of the deputy-lieutenants he had appointed had resigned when he was
disgraced – and their militia officers
with them. They were now replaced, though not completely: Sir
John Reresby, *Memoirs* (ed. Browning), pp. 64–5; A. Browning, *Danby*,
i. 46–7. The government feared a
Dutch landing on the Yorkshire
coast; it was therefore important for
Belasyse to go north – he was both
Governor of Hull and Lord Lieutenant of the E. Riding. By 28 April he
was in Hull: *CSPD 1667*, p. 59;
Reresby, op. cit., pp. 67–8.

2. He had five daughters: Anne,
Caroline, Louisa-Margaret, Rachel
and Elizabeth.

3. See above, p. 150. For Penn's
alleged obligations to the Turners, see
below, pp. 226–9.

W. Coventry did tell me (as a secret though), that whereas we are afeared Harmans fleet to the West Indys will not be got out before the Dutch come and block us up, we shall have a happy pretext to get out our ships, under pretence of attending the Imbassadors and Commissioners; which is a very good, but yet a poor shift.

8.   Up; and having dressed myself, and to the office a little and out, and expecting to have seen the pretty daughter of the Ship tavern at the hither end of Billiter lane (whom I never yet have opportunity to speak to), I in there to drink my morning draught of a half pint of Rhenish wine, but a mi dolor ella and their family are going away thence and a new man come to the house.   So I away to the Temple to my new bookseller's,[1] and there I did agree for Rycaut's late history of the Turkish Policy,* which costs me 55s; whereas it was sold plain before the late fire for 8s, and bound and coloured as this is for 20 – for I have bought it finely bound and truly coloured, all the figures;   of which there was but six books done so, whereof the King and Duke of York and Duke of Monmouth and Lord Arlington had four – the 5th was sold, and I have bought the 6th.[2]   So to enquire out Mrs. Knepp's new lodging, but could not;   but do hear of her at the Playhouse, where she was practising, and I sent for her out by a porter, and the jade came to me all undressed, so cannot go home to my house to dinner as I had invited her;   which I was not much troubled at, because I think there is a distance[a] between her and Mrs. Pierce, and so our company would not be so pleasant.   So I home and there find all things in good readiness for a good

a   repl. 'difference'

---

1. John Starkey, whose shop was on the s. side of Fleet St, near Middle Temple Gate. Pepys's old bookseller, Joseph Kirton of St Paul's Churchyard, had been put out of business by the Fire.

2. Paul Rycaut, *The present state of the Ottoman empire* . . . (1667): PL 2372; bound in acid-stained calf, now much pitted. The coloured prints are charming. There is a note in Pepys's hand on the back of the title-page repeating this information about the prices, together with a receipt (8 April) for 55s. written by Pepys and signed by John Ford, servant of Starkey. Cf. above, vii. 326 & n. 1.

dinner; and here unexpectedly I find little Mis Tooker, whom my wife loves not from the report of her being already naught;[1] however, I do show her countenance, and by and by come my guests, Dr. Clerke and his wife, and Mrs. Worshipp and her daughter, and then Mr. Pierce and his wife and boy, and Betty, and then I sent for Mercer; so that we had, with my wife and I, twelve at table; and very good and pleasant company, and a most neat and excellent, but dear dinner; but Lord, to see with what envy they looked upon all my fine plate was pleasant, for I made the best show I could, to let them understand me and my condition, to take down the pride of Mrs. Clerke, who thinks herself very great.[2] We sat long, and very merry and all things agreable; and after dinner went out by coaches, thinking to have seen a play, but came too late to both houses and then they had thoughts of going abroad somewhere; but I thought all the charge ought to be mine, and therefore I endeavoured to part the company, and so ordered it to set them all down at Mr. Pierces; and there my wife and I and Mercer left them in good humour, and we three to the King's house and saw the latter end of *The Surprizall*;[3] wherein was no great matter I thought, by what I saw. Thence away to *Polichenelli*,[4] and there had three times more sport then at the play; and so home and there, the first night we have been this year, in the garden late, we three and our Barker singing very well; and then home to supper; and so broke up and to bed, mightily pleased with this day's pleasure.

9. Up and to the office a while, none of my fellow-officers coming to sit, it being holiday;[5] and so towards noon, I to the Exchange and there do hear mighty cries for peace, and that

---

1. See above, p. 79 & n. 1.
2. Her husband, already physician to the King's Household, was this year appointed physician to the King's person.
3. A comedy by Sir Robert Howard, first acted in 1662 and published in 1665 in *Four new plays*. Nell Gwyn acted Samira; Mrs Knepp, Emilia. (A).
4. Pepys probably saw this popular Italian puppet-play at Moorfields, though there was also a puppet theatre at Charing Cross at this time. (A).
5. The first day of the Easter law term.

otherwise we shall be undone, and yet do suspect the badness of the peace we shall make. Several do complain of abundance of land flung up by tenants out of their hands, for want of ability to pay their rents; and by name, that the Duke of Buckingham hath 6000*l* so flung up. And my father writes that Jesper Trice, upon this pretence of his tenants' dealing with him, is broke up housekeeping, and gone to board with his brother Naylor at Offord – which is very sad.[1] So home to dinner; and after dinner I took coach and to the King's house; and by and by comes after me my wife, with W. Hewer and his mother and Barker, and there we saw *The Tameing of a Shrew*; which hath some very good pieces in it, but generally is but a mean play; and the best part, Sawny, done by Lacy, hath not half its life, by reason of the words I suppose not being understood, at least by me.[2] After the play was done, as I came, so I went away alone; and had a mind to have taken out Knepp to have taken the ayre with her, and to that end sent a porter in to her that she should take a coach and come to me to the piatza in Covent-garden; where I waited for her, but was doubtful I might have done ill in doing it if we should be visto ensemble; sed ella was gone out, and so I was eased of that care; and therefore away to Westminster to the Swan, and there did bezar la little mosa[3] and hazer tocar mi thing ⟨through mi chemise⟩ con su mano, at which she was enojado; but I did donar ella

1. Corn prices had been low since 1663, and 'the decay of rents' became a matter of national concern around 1667-70. Clarendon (*Life*, ii. 220-1) thought it the worst fall of rents ever known; several politicians (including Ashley and Sir W. Coventry) wrote on it; an act limiting the import of foreign corn still further was passed in 1669, and a committee of the Lords reported on the subject in November 1669. See esp. N. S. B. Gras, *Evolution Engl. corn market*, pp. 409+; J. E. T. Rogers, *Hist. agric. and prices*, vi. 73+. Cf. below, 31 January 1668.

2. *Sawney the Scot, or The taming of a shrew* was John Lacy's alteration of Shakespeare's comedy. This is the first record of a performance; it was not published until 1698. Lacy, specialising in dialect roles, converted Shakespeare's Grumio into Sawney, an officious Scots servant – which probably explains why Pepys found his diction hard to follow. Lacy is represented in the role of Sawney in Michael Wright's picture of him (c.1668-70) at Hampton Court. (A).

3. Sarah Udall's sister, Frances ('Frank').

algo,*ᵃ* and so all well and drank; and then by water to the Old Swan and there found Betty Michell*ᵇ* sitting at the door; it being darkish, I stayed and talked a little with her, but no osais bezar la, though she was to my thinking at this time una de las plus pretty mohers that ever I did ver in my vida. And God forgive me, my mind did run sobra ella all the vespre and night and la day suivante. So home and to the office a little, and then to Sir W. Batten's; where he tells me how he hath found his Lady's Jewells again, which have been so long lost, and a servant imprisoned and arraigned; and they were in her closet under a China Cup, where he hath servants will swear they did look in searching the house. But Mrs. Turner and I and others do believe that they were only disposed of by my Lady, in case she had died, to some friends of hers, and now laid there again.

So home to supper, and to read the book I bought yesterday of the Turkish Policy, which is a good book, well writ; and so owned by Dr. Clerke yesterday to me, commending it mightily to me for my reading as the only book of that subject that ever was writ, yet so designedly. So to bed.

10. Up, and to my office a little; and then in the garden find Sir W. Penn, and he and I to Sir W. Batten, where he tells us news of the new disorders of Hogg and his men in taking out of 30 Tons of wine out of a prize of ours,[1] which makes us mad; and that, added to the unwillingness of the men to go longer abroad without money, doth lead us to conclude not to keep her abroad any longer; of which I am very glad, for I do not like our doings with what we have already got, Sir W. Batten ordering the disposal of our wines and goods, and he leaves it to Morrice the Cooper, who I take to be a cunning proud knave – so that I am very desirous to adventure no further. So away by water from the Old Swan to White-hall; and there to Sir W. Coventry's, with whom I stayed a great while longer then I have

---

a repl. same symbol badly formed   *b* name in s.h.

---

1. The *Lindenbaum*: see above, p. 130 & n. 2. The theft had taken place at Portsmouth, but Hogg (cap- tain of the privateer which had captured the prize) denied responsibil- ity: PRO, HCA 14/54.

done these many months, and had opportunity of talking with him; and he doth declare himself troubled that he hath anything left him to do in the Navy, and would be glad to part with his whole profits and concernments in it, his pains and care being wholly ineffectual during this lack of money – the expense growing infinite, the service not to be done, and discipline and order not to be kept; only from want of money.*a* I begun to discourse with him the business of Tanger, which by the removal of my Lord Bellasses is now to have a new Governor; and did move him that at this season all the business of reforming the garrison might be considered, while nobody was to be offended. And I told him it is plain that we do overspend our revenue – that the place is of no more profit to the King then it was the first day, nor in itself of better credit; no more people of condition willing to live there, nor anything like a place likely to turn his Majesty to account – that it hath been hitherto, and for aught I see, likely only to be used as a jobb to do a kindness to some Lord, or he that can get to be Governor. Sir W. Coventry agreed with me, so as to say that unless the King hath the wealth of the Mogull, he would be a beggar to have his businesses ordered in the manner they now are, that his garrisons must be made places only of convenience to perticular persons. That he hath moved the Duke of York in it, and that it was resolved to send no Governor thither till there had been Commissioners sent to put the garrison in order, so as that he that*b* goes may go with limitations and rules to fallow, and not to do as he please, as the rest have hitherto done.[1] That he is not afeared to speak his mind, though to the displeasure of any man; and that I know well

a repl. 'br'-   *b* repl. 'may'

1. After the conclusion of peace with the Berbers in 1666, the Tangier Committee were now planning to reorganise the government of the town to convert it into a colony as well as a naval station and garrison, and to reduce its cost. The plan to send out civil commissioners to act alongside the governor seems to have died an early death (cf. below, pp. 207, 210), but a civil constitution was conferred by the grant of a charter in June 1668. See Routh, esp. ch. vii; cf. above, v. 274, n. 3. The Governor-designate was the Earl of Middleton, but his appointment and departure were delayed until 1668: see below, p. 167, n. 1.

enough. But that when it is come (as it is now) that to speak the truth in behalf of the King plainly doth no good, but all things are done by other measures then by what is best for the King, he hath no temptation to be perpetually fighting of battles, it being more easy to him on those terms to suffer things to go on without giving any man offence, then to have the same thing done and he contract the displeasure of all the world – as he must do that will be for the King. I did offer him to draw up my thoughts in this matter to present to the Duke of York, which he approved of, and I do think to do it.[1] So away; and by coach going home, saw Sir G. Carteret going toward White-hall; so light and by water met him, and with him to the King's little chapel and afterward to see the King heal the King's Evil (wherein no pleasure, I having seen it before),[2] and then to see him and the Queen and Duke of York and his wife at dinner in the Queen's lodgings;[3] and so with Sir G. Carteret to his lodgings*a* to dinner, where very good company; and after dinner he and I to talk alone, how things are managed and to what ruin we must come if we have not a peace. He did tell me one occasion: how Sir Tho. Allen (which I took for a man of known courage and service on the King's side) was tried for his life in Prince Rupert's fleet in the late times for Cowardize, and condemned to be hanged, and fled to Jerzy, where Sir G. Carteret received him, not knowing the reason of his coming thither; and that thereupon, Prince Rupert wrote to the Queen-Mother his dislike of Sir G. Carteret's receiving a person that stood condemned, and so Sir G. Carteret was forced to bid him betake himself to some other place – this was strange to me.[4] Our Comissioners are preparing to go to Bredah to the treaty, and do design to be going the next week. So away by coach home, where there should have been a meeting

a repl. symbol rendered illegible

---

1. This letter, if ever written, has not been traced.

2. On 13 April 1661: above, ii. 74 & n. 1.

3. For the court's public dinners, see above, i. 299, n. 2.

4. The incident had occurred in November 1650 when Allin lost his own and several other royal ships to Blake off Carthagena, allegedly through his anxiety to protect his cargo. He escaped before being brought to trial. Allin, vol. i, pp. xii–xiii; R. C. Anderson in *Mar. Mirr.*, 21/63–4. Sir John Laughton in the *DNB* dismissed the story as false.

about Carcasse's business, but only my Lord¹ and I met; and so
broke up, Carcasse having only read his answer to his charge;
which is well writ, but I think will not prove to his advantage,
for I believe him to be a very rogue.   So home, and Balty and I
to look Mr. Fenn at Sir G. Carteret's office in Broad-street;
and there missing him and at the banquier's hard by, we home,
and I down by water to Deptford dockyard and there did a little
business; and so home back again, all the way reading a little
piece I lately bought, call[ed] *The Virtuoso or The Stoicke*, proposing
many things paradoxicall to our common opinions; wherein in*ᵃ*
some places he speaks well, but generally is but a sorry man.²
So home, and to my chamber to enter my two last days' journal
and this, and then to supper and to bed.   Blessed be God, I hear
that my father is better and better, and will I hope live to enjoy
some cheerful days more.   But it is strange what he writes me,
that Mr. Weaver of Huntington, who was a lusty, likely, and but
a youngish man, should be dead.³

11.   Up, and to the office, where we sat all the morning; and
(which is now rare, he having not been with us twice I think
these six months) Sir G. Carteret came to us upon some perticular
business of his office and went away again.   At noon, I to the
Change and there hear by Mr. Hublon of the loss of a little East
Indiaman valued at about 20000*l*, coming home alone and safe
to within*ᵇ* ten leagues of Scilly and there snapped by a French
caper.⁴   Our merchants do much pray for peace, and he tells

---

a repl. 'in'   *b* MS. 'without'

---

1. Brouncker: for the case, see
above, p. 64 & n. 1.
2. This was a discourse on religion
by George Mackenzie, a Scottish
lawyer and writer.   'There are some
thoughts in this piece', he wrote (ed.
1665, p. 144), 'which may seem to
rebell against the empire of the
Schools; yet, who know but my
Watch goes right, albeit it agree not
with the publick Clock of the City?'
A memorable thought (amid much
which is merely turgid) is at p. 46:

'Churches do, like coy maids, lace
their bodies so strait, that they bring
on them a consumption.'   The title
Pepys gives is the running title only.
The book was published (anonymous-
ly) as *Religio Stoici, with a friendly
addresse to the phanaticks of all sects and
sorts* (Edinburgh 1663; 12°; reissued
twice 1665; not in the PL).
3. Richard Weaver, an attorney,
had been buried on the 5th.
4. See the report (Lyme, 13 April)
in *CSPD 1667*, p. 31.

me that letters are come that the Dutch have stopped the fitting of their great ships and the coming out of a fleet of theirs of 50 sail that was ready to come out; but I doubt the truth of it yet.[1] Thence to Sir G. Carteret by his invitation to his office, where my Lady was, and dined with him and very merry, and good people they are when pleased as any I know. After dinner, I to the office, where busy till evening; and then with Balty to Sir G. Carteret's office and there with Mr. Fenn despatched the business of Balty's 1500*l* he received for the contingencies of the fleet, whereof he received about 253*l* in pieces-of-eight at a goldsmith's there hard by; which did puzzle me, and him to tell, for I could not tell the difference by sight, only by bigness, and that is not always discernible between a whole and half-piece and quarter-piece.[2] Having received this money, I home with Balty and it; and then abroad by coach with my wife and set her down at her father's; and I to White-hall, thinking there to have seen the Duchesse of Newcastle's coming this night to Court to make a visit to the Queen, the King having been with her yesterday to make her a visit since her coming to town. The whole story of this Lady is a romance, and all she doth is romantic. Her footmen in velvet coats, and herself in an antique* dress,[3] as they say; and was the other day at her own play, *The Humourous Lovers*; the most ridiculous thing that ever was wrote, but yet she and her Lord mightily pleased with it,[4] and she at the end made her respect to the players from her box and did give them thanks. There is as much expectation of her coming to Court, that so [many]

---

1. See below, p. 186 & n. 5.
2. Coins from Spanish-American mints were often of irregular shape, although accurate in weight.
3. She herself remarks (*Life of W. Cavendish*, ed. Firth, pp. 174, 175) that as a child she preferred 'variety of fine clothes' to toys, attiring herself in fashions of her own design. 'I did dislike any should follow my fashions, for I always took delight in a singularity, even in accoutrements of habits'. Cf. below, pp. 186–7, 196. Evelyn met her on 18 April and was

'much pleasd, with the extraordinary fancifull habit, garb, & discourse of the Dutchesse . . .'. Her biographer in the *DNB* (Joseph Knight) concludes that 'her occasional appearances in theatrical costume, and her reputation for purity of life . . . contributed to gain her a reputation for madness'. (She was known as 'Mad Madge of Newcastle'.) Cf. *Letters of D. Osborne* (ed. Parry), p. 83.
4. The play, staged at the LIF, was actually by the Duke of Newcastle; see above, p. 137 & n. 4. (A).

people may come to see her, as if it were the Queen of Sweden.[1]
But I lost my labour, for she did not come this night; so meeting
Mr. Brisband, he took me up to my Lady Jemimah's chamber,
who is let blood today;[2] and so there we sat and talked an hour
I think, very merry and one odd thing or other; and so away,
and I took up my wife at her tailor's (whose wife is brought
to bed, and my wife must be godmother) and so with much ado
got a coach to carry us home, it being late; and so to my chamber,
having little left to do at my office, my eyes being a little sore by
reason of my reading a small printed book the other day after it
was dark; and so to supper and to bed. It comes in my head to
set down that there hath been two fires in the City, as I am told for
certain, and it is so, within this week.

12. Up; and when ready, I[a] to my office to do a little business; and coming homeward again, saw my door and hatch open,
left so by Luce our cookmaid; which so vexed me, that I did give
her a kick in our entry and offered a blow[b] at her, and was seen
doing so by Sir W. Penn's footboy, which did vex me to the
heart because I know he will be telling their family of it, though
I did put on presently a very pleasant face to the boy and spoke
kindly to him as one without passion, so as it may be he might not
think I was angry; but yet I was troubled at it.
So away by water to White-hall and there did our usual
business before the Duke of York; but it fell out, that discoursing
of matters of money, it rose to a mighty heat, very high words
arising between Sir G. Carteret and W. Coventry, the former
in his passion saying that the other should have helped things if
they were so bad; and the other answered, so he would, and
things should have been better had he been Treasurer of the
Navy. I was mightily troubled at this heat, and it will breed ill

a MS. 'and'   *b* repl. 'c'-

---

1. Ex-Queen Christina, who had
abdicated in 1654. Her flamboyant
dress and flamboyant behaviour in
exile had attracted much public attention. She had made 'state-entries'
into Rome and Paris in 1655 and 1656,
and at this moment crowds were
flocking to witness her progress
through Germany. She and the
Duchess had a similar gift for eccen-
tricity.
2. She was pregnant: see below,
p. 208.

blood I fear; but things are in that bad condition that I do daily expect when we shall all fly in one another's faces, when we shall be reduced everyone to answer for himself. We broke up; and I soon after to Sir G. Carteret's chamber, where I find the poor man telling his lady privately; and she weeping, I went into them and did seem, as endeed I was, troubled for this and did give the best advice I could; which I think did please them, and they do apprehend me their friend, as indeed I am, for I do take the Vice chamberlain for a most honest man. He did assure me that he was not, all expenses and things paid, not clear in estate 15000*l* better then he was when the King came in; and that the King and*ᵃ* Lord Chancellor did know that he was worth, with the debt the King owed him, 50000*l* ⟨(I think he said)⟩ when the King came into England.¹ I did pacify all I could; and then away by water home, there to write letters and things for the despatch of Balty away this day to sea; and after dinner he did go, I having given him much good counsel, and I have great hopes that he will make good use of it and be a good man – for I find him willing to take pains and very sober. He being gone, I close at my office all the afternoon, getting off of hand my papers, which by the late holidays and my laziness were grown too many upon my hands, to my great trouble; and therefore at it as late as my eyes would give me leave; and then by water down to Redriffe, meaning to meet my wife, who is gone with Mercer,*ᵇ* Barker, and the boy (it being most sweet weather) to walk; and I did meet with them and walked back, and then by the time we got home it was dark, and we stayed singing in the garden till supper was ready, and there with great pleasure. But I tried my girls, Mercer and Barker singly, one after another, a single song, *At dead=low Ebb*, &c.;² and I do clearly find that as to manner of singing, the latter doth much the better, the other

---

a repl. 'did'   *b* repl. 'these'

---

1. The debts arose mainly from his services as Governor of Jersey. Later this summer he exchanged his post as Navy Treasurer for that of Vice-Treasurer of Ireland.

2. A setting by Henry Lawes of words by an anonymous author.

Printed in John Playford, *Select ayres and dialogues . . . the second book* (1669), pp. 5–6, under the title 'A tale out of Anacreon'. Pepys's source here was probably the earlier edition of *Select ayres* known only from newspaper advertisements of February 1663. (E).

thinking[a] herself, as I do myself, above taking pains for a manner of singing, contenting ourselfs with the judgment and goodness of eare.   So to supper, and then parted and to bed.

13.   Up, and to the office, where we sat all the morning; and strange how that false fellow Comissioner Pett was eager to have had Carcasse's business brought on today, that he might give my Lord Brouncker (who hates him I am sure, and hath spoke as much against him to the King in my hearing as any man[b]) a cast of his office in pleading for his man Carcasse; but I did prevent its being brought on today, and so broke up and I home to dinner; and after dinner, with a little singing with some pleasure, alone with my poor wife, and then to the office, where sat all the afternoon till late at night; and then home to supper and to bed, my eyes troubling me still after candle-light; which troubles me.   Wrote to my father, who I am glad to hear is at some ease again; and I long to have him in town, that I may see what can be done for him here, for I would fain do[c] all I can, that I may have him live and take pleasure in my doing well in the world.   ⟨This afternoon came Mrs. Lowther[1] to me to the office, and there yo did tocar su mamelles and did bezar them and su boca, which she took fort willingly, and perhaps yo posse in time a hazer mas to her.⟩[a]

14.   *Lords day.*   Up, and to read a little in my new History of Turky;[2] and so with my wife to church, and then home to dinner, where is little Michell and my pretty Betty and also Mercer; and very merry, a good dinner of roast beef.   After dinner, I away to take water at the Tower; and thence to Westminster, where Mrs. Martin was not at home; so to White-hall and there walked up and down; and among other things, visited Sir G. Carteret, and much talk with him; who is discontented, as he hath reason, to see how things are like to come all to naught.   And it is very much that this resolution of having of country-Admirals[3] should not come to his eares till I told it him

a   repl. 'thing'   b   repl. 'main'   c   repl. 'have'
d   addition crowded into end of paragraph

1. *Née* Peg Penn.   3. See above, p. 149 & n. 1.
2. See above, p. 156, n. 2.

the other day, so that I doubt who manages things. From him to Margaret Church, and there spied Martin and home with her, who had those, so could have ninguno placer; but fell out to see her expensefulness, having bought Turkey work chairs &c; by and by away home, and there took out my wife and the two Mercers and two of our maids, Barker and Jane, and over the water to the Jamaica-house, where I never was before; and there the girls did run for wagers over the bowling-green. And there with much pleasure, spent little, and so home; and they home, and I to read with satisfaction in my book of Turky and so to bed.

15. Lay long in bed – and by and by called up by Sir H. Chumbly, who tells me that my Lord Middleton is for certain chosen Governor of Tanger; a man of moderate understanding, not covetous, but a soldier-of-fortune and poor.[1] Here comes Mr. Sanchy with an impertinent* business to me of a ticket, which I put off. But by and by comes Dr Childe by appointment, and sat with me all the morning, making me Bases and inward parts to several songs that I desired of him – to my great content. Then dined and then abroad by coach, and I set him down at Hatton Guarden and I to the King's house by chance, where a new play; so full as I never saw it, I forced to stand all the while close to the very door, till I took cold, and many people went away for want of room. The King and Queen and Duke of York and Duchesse there and all the Court, and Sir W. Coventry. The play called *The Change of Crownes*, a play of Ned Howard's,[2] the best that I ever saw at that House, being a great play and serious; only, Lacy did act the country gentleman come up to

---

1. The Earl of Middleton (a Scotsman and one of the most successful military leaders to emerge during the Civil War) had been Commander-in-Chief in Scotland 1660–3, but since then had lived quietly in semi-retirement in Surrey. He served at Tangier until his death there in 1674. His patent as Governor was not issued until 22 May 1668 and he did not sail to his post until September 1669.

Pepys's view of him is confirmed by Clarendon (*Hist.*, v. 237), and Burnet (i. 363).

2. Entered on the Stationers' Register on 7 August 1667 (*Trans. Stat. Reg.*, ii. 380), but not printed until 1949, when F. S. Boas published a text based on a prompt copy licensed for the present performance by Sir Henry Herbert, Master of the Revels, on 13 April. (A).

Court, who doth abuse the Court with all the imaginable wit and plainness, about selling of places and doing everything for money.[1] The play took very much. Thence I to my new book-seller's and there bought Hookers *Policy*, the new edition,[2] and Dugdale's history of the Inns of Court, of which there was but a few saved out of the Fire[3] – and Playfords new ketch-book,[4] that hath a great many new fooleries in it. Then home; a little at the office, and then to supper and to bed, mightily pleased with the new play.

16. Up, and to the office, where sat all the morning; at noon home to dinner; and thence in haste to carry my wife to see the new play I saw yesterday, she not knowing it. But there, contrary to expectation, find *The Silent Woman*,[5] however, in; and there Knip came into the pit. I took her by me, and here we met with Mrs. Horsly, the pretty woman, an acquaintance of Mercer's, whose house is burnt. Knipp tells me the King was so angry at the liberty taken by Lacy's part to abuse him to his face, that he commanded they should act no more, till Moone went and got leave for them to act again; but not this*a* play.[6]

a repl. 'let'

1. John Lacy played Asinello. The topical satire in this part had serious consequences for Lacy and the Theatre Royal: see below, p. 173 & n. 1. (A).

2. Richard Hooker, *Works . . . in eight books of ecclesiastical polity* (1666); PL 2499. The bookseller was John Starkey.

3. The *Origines Juridiciales*; for its destruction in the Fire, see above, vii. 297 & n. 7. Pepys retained the 3rd edition of 1680 (PL 2552).

4. John Playford's collection, *Catch that catch can, or The musical companion* (1667); see above, vii. 381 & n. 4. This contained 228 songs; previous editions (1652, 1658 and 1663) had contained 144–184. (E).

5. Jonson's comedy: see above, i. 171, n. 2. (A).

6. In *The change of crownes* Lacy played the part of a country gentle-man who sells his estate on the assumption that he will be able to obtain preferment at court by bribery. According to a contemporary news-letter, Lacy added some comic gags to his already indiscreet role: see *The change of crownes* (ed. Boas), p. 9. Boas's text is based upon a ms. prompt-copy which has most of Lacy's scenes enclosed in black lines which were probably inserted after Charles had expressed his displeasure with Lacy's role. Michael Mohun was a leading actor and a shareholder at the Theatre Royal. (A).

The King mighty angry; and it was bitter endeed, but very true and witty.   I never was more taken with a play then I am with this *Silent Woman*, as old as it is – and as often as I have seen it. There is more wit in it then goes to ten new plays.   Thence with my wife and Knepp to Mrs. Pierce's; and saw her closet again and liked her picture.[1] Thence took them all to the Kakehouse in Southampton market-place, where Pierce told us the story how in good earnest [the King] is offended with the Duke of Richmond marrying, and Mrs. Steward's sending the King his jewels again.   As she tells it, it is the noblest romance and example of a brave lady that ever I read in my life.   Pretty, to hear them talk of yesterday's play and I durst not own to my wife to have seen it.   Thence home and to W. Batten, where we have made a bargain for the ending some of the trouble about some of our prizes for 1400*l*.[2]   So home*ª* to look on my new books that I have lately bought; and then to supper and to bed.

17.   Up, and with the two Sir Wms. by coach to the Duke of York, who is come to St. James's, the first time we have attended him there this year.[3]   In our way, in Tower-street we saw Desbrough walking on foot; who is now no more a prisoner, and looks well, and just as he used to do heretofore.[4]   When we came to the Duke of York's, I was spoke to by Mr. Brouncker in behalf of Carcasse.[5]   Thence by coach to Sir G. Carteret's in

a   repl. 'own'

---

1. By Hayls: see above, vii. 93, n. 1. (OM).

2. See above, pp. 135–6.

3. The Duke usually moved from Whitehall to St James's Palace for the summer.

4. John Desborough, Cromwell's brother-in-law and one of his major-generals, had been released from the Tower a few weeks before.   At the Restoration he had suffered nothing worse than exclusion from public office and brief imprisonment, because he had taken no part in the King's trial.   Since then he had lived abroad, mostly in Holland.   But he had returned in July 1666 in obedience to a proclamation, and was held in the Tower.   After examination by a committee of council on 23 February 1667, he was released unconditionally: *CSPD 1666–7*, p. 531.   He survived undisturbed until his death at Hackney in 1680.

5. Henry Brouncker was a Groom of the Bedchamber in the Duke's Household, and brother of Lord Brouncker, whom Carkesse served as clerk.

London,[1] there to pass some accounts of his, and at it till dinner; and then to work again a little, and then go away; and my wife being sent for by me to the New Exchange, I took her up and there to the King's playhouse (at the door met with W. Joyce in the street, who came to our coach-side, but we in haste took no notice of him; for which I was sorry afterward, though I love not the fellow, yet for his wife's sake) and saw a piece of *Rollo*, a play I like not much, and[a] much good acting in it.[2]   The house very empty.   So away home; and I a little to the office and then to Sir Rob. Viner's; and so back and find my wife gone down by water to take a little ayre, and I to my chamber and there spent the night in reading my new book, *Origines Juridiciales*,[3] which pleases me.   So to supper and to bed.

18.   Up, and to read more in the *Origines*; and then to the office, where the news is strong that not only the Dutch cannot set out a fleet this year, but that the French will not; and that he[4] hath given that answer to the Dutch Imbassador, saying that he is for the King of England's having an honourable peace – which, if true, is the best news we have heard a good while.[5]   At the office all the morning; and there pleased with the little pretty Deptford woman I have wished for long,[6] and she hath occasion given her to come again to me.   After office, I to the Change a little and then home and to dinner; and then by coach with my wife to the Duke of York's House and there saw *The Wits*,

a   ? slip for 'but'

---

1. I.e. to the Navy Treasury in Broad St.
2. *The bloody brother, or Rollo, Duke of Normandy* was a tragedy by John Fletcher and others; see above, ii. 62 & n. 1.   According to Downes (pp. 5–6), Hart played Rollo; Kynaston, Otto; Mohun, Aubrey; Burt, Latorch; Mrs Corey, the Duchess; and Mrs Marshall, Edith.   (A).
3. See above, p. 168 & n. 3.

4. Louis XIV.
5. See Louis' letter of 19/29 April to his ambassador in Holland to this effect: D'Estrades, *Lettres* (1709), iv. 167–8.   He had made a secret arrangement with the English a few days before: Feiling, p. 218.   The Dutch ambassador referred to here was van Beuningen.
6. Presumably the unnamed 'jolie femme' mentioned above at 1 April.

a play I formerly loved and is now corrected and enlarged[1] – but though I like the acting, yet I find not much in the play now. The Duke of York and W. Coventry gone to Portsmouth makes me thus to go [to] plays.   So home; and to the office a little and then home, where I find Goodgroome and he and I did sing several things over and tried two or three three-parts in Playford's new book,[2] my wife pleasing me in singing her part of the things she knew; which is a comfort to my very heart.   So he being gone, we to supper and to bed.

19.   Up, and to the office all the morning, doing a great deal of business.   At noon to dinner betimes; and then my wife and I by coach to the Duke's House, calling at Lovetts, where I find my Lady Castlemaynes picture not yet done, which has lain so many months there;[3] which vexes me, but I mean not to trouble them more after this is done.   So to the playhouse, where not[a] much company come, which I impute to the heat of the weather, it being very hot.   Here we saw *Macbeth*, which though I have seen it often, yet is it one of the best plays for a stage, and variety of dancing and music, that ever I saw.[4]   So being very much pleased, thence home by coach with young Goodyer and his own sister, who offered us to go in their coach – a good-natured youth I believe he is, but I fear will mind his pleasures too much; she is pretty, and a modest,[b] brown[c] girl.[5]   Set us down; so my wife and I into the garden, a fine moonshine evening, and there talking; and among other things, she tells me that she finds by W. Hewer that my people do observe my minding my pleasure more then usual; which I confess and am ashamed of, and so from this day take upon me to leave it till

---

a repl. 'much much m'-   b repl. 'most'   c repl. 'and'

---

1. A comedy by Davenant: see above, ii. 155 & n. 1. According to Genest (i. 40), the dialogue had been improved and two short scenes added. (A).

2. See above, p. 168, n. 4. The second section contained part-songs. (E).

3. See above, p. 23, n. 3. (OM).

4. This was the spectacular musical adaptation of *Macbeth* devised by Davenant; see above, v. 314 & n. 3. The music was composed by Matthew Locke. (A).

5. Aaron (about 18) and Hester (about 13) were children of Moses and Hester Goodyear, neighbours of Pepys.

Whit-Sunday. While we were setting there in the garden, comes Mrs. Turner to advise about her son,*a* the Captain; which I did give her the best advice I could, to look out for some land imployment for him – a peace being at hand, when few ships will be imployed, and very many, and those old Captains, to be provided for[1] – which she thanked me for. Then to other talk: and among the rest, about Sir W. Penn's being to buy Wanstedhouse of Sir Rt. Brookes,[2] but hath put him off again; and left him the other day to pay for a dinner at a tavern, which she says our parish[ioner] Mrs. Hollworthy[3] talks of. And I dare be hanged if ever he could mean to buy that great house, that knows not how to furnish one that is not the tenth part so big. Thence I to my chamber to write a little; and then to bed, having got a mighty cold*b* in my right eare and side of my throat, and in much trouble with it almost all the night.

20. Up, with much pain in my eare and palate. To the office, out of humour all the morning. At noon dined; and with my wife to the King's house, but there found the bill torn down and no play acted; and so being in the humour to see one, went to the Duke of York's house and there saw *The Witts* again; which likes me better then it did the other day, having much wit in it. Here met with Rolt, who tells me the reason of no play today at the King's house – that Lacy had been committed to the porter's lodge for his acting his part in the late new play;[4] and that being thence released, he came to the King's house and there met with Ned Howard, the poet of the play, who congratulated his release; upon which, Lacy cursed him as that it was the fault of

a MS. 'some'   MS. 'gold'

---

1. Turner's ship had been laid up: *CSPD 1667*, p. 17. Half-pay for unemployed naval officers had not yet been introduced: see above, vii. 410, n. 2.
    2. See below, p. 197 & n. 2.
    3. Mrs Hollworthy was a neigh-

bour of Pepys. At 21 November 1667 he recorded that Sir Robert Brookes was 'mighty . . . taken with her'.
    4. *The change of crownes* by Edward Howard; see above, pp. 167, 168 & nn. 2, 6. (A).

his nonsensical*a* play that was the cause of his ill usage;[1] Mr. Howard did give him some reply, to which Lacy [answered] him that he was more a fool then a poet; upon which Howard did give him a blow on the face*b* with his glove; on which Lacy, having a cane in his hand, did give him a blow over the pate. Here, Rolt and others that discoursed of it in the pit this after-noon[2] did wonder that Howard did not run him through, he being too mean a fellow to fight with – but Howard did not do anything but complain to the King of it; so the whole House is silenced – and the gentry seem to rejoice much at it, the House being become too insolent. Here was many fine ladies this afternoon at this House as I have at any time seen; and so after the play, I home and there wrote to my father; and then to walk in the garden with my wife, resolving by the grace of God to see no more plays till Whitsuntide,[3] I having now seen a play every day this week, till I have neglected my business, and that I am ashamed of, being found so much absent – the Duke of York and Sir W. Coventry having been out of town at Ports-mouth did the more*c* imbolden me thereto. So home; and having brought home with me from Fanchurch-street a hundred of sparrowgrass, cost 18*d*, we had them and a little bit of salmon which my wife had a mind to, cost 3*s*; so to supper, and my pain being somewhat better in my throat, we to bed.

21. *Lords day.* Up, and John, a hackney-coachman whom of late I have much used, as being formerly Sir W. Penn's coach-man, coming to me by my direction to see whether I would use him today or no, I took him to our back-gate to look upon the ground which is to be let there, where I have a mind to buy*d*

---

a	repl. 'play'	
c	MS. 'for'	
b	repl. same symbol badly formed	
d	repl. 'build'	

---

1. Lacy attributed his imprisonment to what Howard had written, not to the gags he himself had added to his part: see above, p. 168 & n. 6. (A).

2. Patrons of the Restoration play-houses often used them in this way as a kind of club in which they could gossip or play cards for an hour or two before the performance began. Plays usually began at 3.30 p.m. (A).

3. His resolution held firm until 1 May: but by Whit Sunday he had been four times to the theatre. (A).

enough to build a coach-house and stable; for I have had it much
in my thoughts lately that it is not too much for me now, in
degree or cost, to keep a coach; but contrarily, that I am almost
ashamed to be seen in a hackney; and therefore, if I can have
the conveniency, I will secure the ground at least till peace
comes, that I do receive encouragement to keep a coach or else
that I may part with the*a* ground again.   The place I like*b* very
well, being close by my own house, and so resolve to go about it.[1]
And so home and with my wife to church; and then to dinner,
Mercer with us, with design to go to Hackney to church in the
afternoon.*c*   So after dinner she and I sung *Scio Moro*,[2] which is
one of the best pieces of music to my thinking that ever I did
hear in my life; then took coach and to Hackny church, where
very full; and found much difficulty to get pews, I offering the
sexton money and he could not help me – so my wife and Mercer
ventured into a pew, and I into another.   A knight and his lady
very civil to me when they came, and the like to my wife in hers,
being Sir George*d* Viner's; and his lady*e* rich in Jewells, but most
in beauty; almost the finest woman that ever I saw.[3]   That which
we went chiefly to see was the young ladies of the schools,[4]
whereof there is great store, very pretty; and also the organ,
which is handsome and tunes the psalm and plays with the
people; which is mighty pretty and makes me mighty earnest to
have a pair at our church, I having almost a mind to give them a
pair* if they would settle a maintenance on them for it[5] – I am
mightily taken with them.   So church done, we to coach and
away to Kingsland and Islington and there eat and drank at the

---

a   repl. 'it'   b   repl. 'l'-   c   repl. 'after dinner'
        d   repl. 'Je'-   e   MS. 'lady's'

---

1. See below, p. 205 & n. 2.
2. *Sio* [*S'io*] *Moro*: a short part-
song (author and composer unknown)
in J. Playford, *Catch that catch can,
or The musical companion* (1667), pp.
162–3. (E).
3. She was Abigail, daughter of Sir
John Lawrence, Lord Mayor 1664–5;
aged about 22.   Her husband, a member of the well-known family of
goldsmith-bankers, was a baronet.
4. In the 1690s advertisements of
schools in Hackney out-numbered
those in other London suburbs in
John Houghton's *Coll. for improvement of husbandry and trade.*
5. Cf. above, p. 150 & n. 2.

old house;[1] and so back, it raining a little; which is mighty welcome, it having not rained in many weeks,[2] so that they say it makes the fields just now mighty sweet; so with great pleasure home by night. Set Mercer down,[a] and I to my chamber and there read a great deal in Rycaut's Turks book[3] with great pleasure, and so eat and to bed – my sore throat still troubling me, but not so much. This night I[b] do come to full resolution of diligence for a good while, and I hope God will give me the grace and wisdom to perform it.

22. Up pretty betimes, my throat better; and so dressed me and to White-hall to see Sir W. Coventry, returned from Portsmouth; whom I am almost ashamed to see, for fear he should have been told how often I have been at plays; but it is better to see him at first then afterward.[c] So walked to Old Swan and drank at Michells, and then to White-hall and over the park to St. James's to W. Coventry; where well received, and good discourse. He seems to be sure of a peace – that the King of France doth not intend to set out a fleet, for that he doth design Flanders[4] – our Imbassadors set out this week.[5] Thence I over the park to Sir G. Carteret; and after him by coach to [my] Lord Chancellors house,[6] the first time I have been therein; and it is very noble, and brave pictures of the ancient and present nobility; never saw better.[7] Thence with him[8] to London, mighty merry

---

a repl. 'home'   *b* repl. 'day'   *c* repl. 'at last'

---

1. The King's Head: see above, ii. 125, n. 2.
2. At Oxford no such dry summer had been known since 1633, according to Wood (*L & T*, ii. 106). A hot dry summer ensued.
3. See above, vii. 326, n. 1.
4. He invaded the Spanish Netherlands in May, and his fleet played no part in the naval campaign of 1667.
5. See below, p. 189.
6. Clarendon House, Piccadilly.
7. This – probably the finest, and most personal, collection assembled at that period – consisted mostly of the great men (particularly lawyers)

of the age of James I and Charles I, and of Clarendon's own colleagues and contemporaries. They included originals by Van Dyck and Lely, but a number were copies of standard portraits by Van Dyck, and assistants in Lely's studio helped in the production of the later portraits. Evelyn was greatly interested in it: cf. Evelyn, iii. 520 & n. 3; Evelyn, *Diary and Corr.* (ed. Bray), ii. 234–5, 435–56. For its later history and value, see BM, Add. 19027, ff. 35–6; Lady T. Lewis, *Lives of friends of Clarendon*; Whinney and Millar, pp. 9–10. (OM).
8. Carteret.

in the way. Thence home, and find the boy out of the house and office, and by and by comes in and hath been at Mercer's; I did pay his coat for him. Then to my chamber; my wife comes home with linen she hath been buying of.*a* I then to dinner; and then down the river to Greenwich, and the watermen would go no further – so I turned them off, giving them nothing, and walked to Woolwich; there did some business, and met with Captain Cocke and back with him. He tells me our peace is agreed on; we are not to assist the Spanyard against the French for this year – and no restitution – and we are likely to lose Poleroone.[1] I know not whether this be true or no, but I am for peace on any terms. He tells me how the King was vexed the other day for having no paper laid him at the Council-table as was usual; and that Sir Rd. Browne did tell his Majesty he would call the person whose work it was to provide it[2] – who being come, did tell His*b* Majesty that he was but a poor man, and was out 4 or 500*l* for it, which was as much as he is worth; and that he cannot provide it any longer without money, having not received a penny since the King's coming in. So the King spoke to my Lord Chamberlaine; and many such Mementos the King doth nowadays meet withal, enough to make an ingenuous [man] mad. I to Deptford, and there scolded with a master for his ship's not being gone. And so home to the office and did business till my eyes are sore again; and so home to sing and then to bed, my eyes failing me mightily.

a followed by symbol rendered illegible   *b* MS. 'is'

---

1. This report is confusing. No public treaty had yet been concluded, but on 8 April Britain had reached a secret agreement with France by which each promised not to succour the enemies of the other for one year. The principle of restitution was not applied: Acadia (Nova Scotia) was to be given up by England, and St Kitt's by France. The question of restitution also concerned Britain and Holland in their disputes over territory captured during the war. Here the French had urged 'no restitution' and this was the arrangement made at the peace in August: Pulo Run (in the E. Indies) was in fact lost because although the Dutch had surrendered it in 1665, it had been recaptured.

2. Browne was a Clerk to the Council. The officer responsible was John Woolley, underkeeper of Council records: below, pp. 182–3.

23. *St. George's day.* The feast being kept at White-hall, out of design, as it is thought, to make the best countenance we can to the Swedes Imbassadors before their leaving us to go to the treaty abroad, to show some jollity.[1] We sat at the office all the morning. Word is brought me that young Michell is come to call my wife to his wife's labour; and she went and I at the office, full of expectation what to hear from poor Betty Michell. This morning, much to do with Sir W Warren,[a] all whose applications now are to Lord Brouncker; and I am against him now, not professedly but apparently in discourse, and will be. At noon home to dinner, where alone, and after dinner to my music papers; and by and by comes in my wife, who gives me the good news that the midwife and she alone have delivered poor Betty of a pretty girl, which I am mighty glad of – and she in good condition – my wife as well as I mightily pleased with it. Then to the office to do things towards the post; and then my wife I set down at her mother's; and I up and down to do business, but did little, and so to Mrs. Martin's and there did hazer what I would con her; and then called my wife, and to little Michell's, where we saw the little child; which I like mightily, being I think very pretty, and asked her how she did, being mightily glad of her doing well; and so home to the office and then to my chamber, and so to bed.

24. Up, and with Sir W. Penn to St. James's; and there the Duke of York was preparing to go to some further ceremonies about the Guarter, that he could give us no audience. Thence I to Westminster-hall, the first day of the term, and there joyed Mrs. Michell,[2] who is mightily pleased with my wife's work yesterday. And so away to my barber's about my periwigs, and then to the Exchange, there to meet Fen about some money to be borrowed of the Office of the Ordinance to answer a great pinch. So home to dinner, and in the afternoon met by agreement (being

a   repl. 'W. Coventry'

---

1. Description in *London Gazette,* 25 April. The Garter-day ceremonies were (and are) normally held at St George's Chapel, Windsor.

The Swedes acted as mediators in the Anglo-Dutch treaty negotiations.
2. Mother-in-law of Betty.

Carcas it by Harry Brouncker's frighting us into a despatch of
Battense's business);[1] Brouncker, T. Harvey, J. Mennes, W.
put on, and I (Sir W. Penn keeping out of the way still), where a
great many high words from Brouncker and as many from me
and others to him, and to better purpose, for I think we have
fortified ourselfs to overthrow his man Carcasse and to do no
honour to him.   We rose with little done, but great heat; not
to be reconciled I doubt, and I care not, for I will be on the right
side and that shall keep me.   Thence by coach to Sir Jo. Duncomb's lodging in the Pell Mell in order to the money spoken of
in the morning; and there awhile sat and discoursed; and I
find him that he is a very proper man for business, being very
resolute and proud and industrious.[2] He told me what reforma-
tion they had made in the office of the Ordnance, taking away
Legg's fees.[3]   Have got an order that no Treasurer after him
shall ever sit at the Board, and it is a good one – that no maister
of the Ordinance here shall ever sell a place.   He tells me they
have not paid any encrease of price for anything during this war,
but in most have paid less.   And at this day have greater stores
then they know where to lay, if there[a] should be peace, and then
ever was any time this war.   That they pay every man in course,
and have notice of the disposal of every farding.   Every man
that they owe money to hath his share of every sum they receive.
Never borrowed all this war but 30000l by the King's express
command, but do usually stay until their assignments become
payable in their own course; which is the whole mystery, that
they have had assignments for a fifth part of whatever was assigned

---

a   repl. symbol rendered illegible

---

1. For this case, see above, p. 64
& n. 1.
2. Duncombe was Master of the
Ordnance Office and was shortly
afterwards appointed one of the
Treasury Commissioners. Cf. Burnet's verdict on him (i. 478): a 'judicious, but very haughty . . . and able
parliament man, but could not go in

to all the doings of the court; for he
had a sense of religion and a zeal for
the liberty of his country'.
3. William Legge, Lieutenant and
Treasurer of the Ordnance, had had
his poundage reduced, not taken
away, by a royal warrant of 11 March:
CSPD 1666–7, pp. 467, 556.

to the Navy.[1] They have power of putting out and in of all officers. Are beginning upon a building that will cost them 12000*l*.[2] That they out of their stock of tallies have been forced to help the Treasurer of the Navy at this great pinch. Then to talk of news: that he thinks the want of money hath undone the King, for the Parliament will never give the King more money without calling all people to account; nor, as he believes, will ever make war again but they will manage it themselfs – unless, which I proposed, he would visibly become a severer inspector into his own business and accounts, and that would gain upon the Parliament yet – which he confesses and confirms as the only [means] left to set him upon his legs; but says that it is not in his nature ever to do. He says that he believes but four men (such as he could name) would do the business of both offices, his and ours; and if ever the war were to do again, it should be so he believes. He told me to my face that I was a very good Clerk, and did understand the business and do it very well, and that he would never desire a better. He doth believe that the Parliament, if ever they meet, will offer some alterations to the King, and will turn some of us out. And I protest I think he is in the right, that either they or the King will be advised to some regulation; and therefore I ought to beware – as it is easy for me to keep myself up if I will. He thinks that much of our misfortune hath been for want of an active Lord Treasurer, and that such a man as Sir W. Coventry would do the business thoroughly.[3] This talk being over, comes his boy and tells us W. Coventry is come in; and so he and I to him, and there told the difficulty of getting this money; and they did play hard upon Sir G. Carteret as a man moped and stunned, not knowing which way to turn himself. Sir W. Coventry cried that he was disheartened, and I do think that there is much in it; but J. Duncomb doth charge him with mighty neglect in the pursuing of his business, and that

---

1. Pepys had on 14 March told the King that the solvency of the Ordnance Office was largely due to their 'liberty in demanding': *Further Corr.*, p. 163.

2. The New Armouries: a series of alterations and additions to their offices and storehouses in the Tower: *CSPD 1667*, p. 52.

3. On Southampton's death a month later both Coventry and Duncombe were included in the commission which replaced him. For Southampton's inefficiency, see above, vi. 218 & n. 1.

he doth not look after it himself, but leaves it to Fenn; so that I do perceive they are resolved to shove at bringing the business into a better way of execution; and I think it needs [it], that is the truth of it. So I away to Sir G. Carteret's lodgings about this money; and contrary to expectation, I find he hath prevailed with Legg on his own bond to lend him 2000*l*, which I am glad of; but poor man, he little sees what observations people do make upon his management, and he is not a man fit to be told what one hears. Thence by water at 10 at night from Westminster-bridge, having kissed little Frank;[1] and so to the Old Swan, and walked home by moonshine; and there to my chamber a while, and supper and to bed.

25. Received a writ from the Exchequer this morning of distrain for 70000*l*, which troubled me, though it be but matter of form.[2] To the office,*a* where sat all the morning. At noon, my wife being to Unthankes christening, I to Sir W. Batten's to dinner, where merry, and the rather because we are like to come to some good end in another of our prizes. Thence by coach to Lord Treasurer's; and there being come too soon, I to the New Exchange, but did nothing; and back again and there find my Lord Brouncker and T. Harvy and walked in*b* a room, very merrily discoursing. By and by comes my Lord Ashly and tells us my Lord Treasurer is ill and cannot speak with us now. Thence away, Sir W. Penn and I and*c* Mr. Lewes, who came thither after us, and Mr. Gawden in the last man's coach. Set me down by the Poultry,*d* and I to Sir Rob. Viner's and there had my account stated and took it home to review. So home to the office and there late writing out something, having been a little at Sir W. Batten's to talk, and there vexed to see them give order for Hogg's[3] [going] further abroad. And so home and to bed.

a MS. 'morning'   *b* repl. 'up'   *c* repl. 'to L'-   *d* MS. 'poultry'

---

1. The serving maid at the Swan, New Palace Yard.
2. This writ of distraint was used by the Exchequer court to call on government treasurers to render their accounts. In this case Pepys was re-

quired to declare his account of Tangier money to the Exchequer. Cf. below, 27 April 1669.
3. Commander of the privateer, the *Flying Greyhound*.

26. Up, and by coach with W. Batten and W. Penn to White-hall and there saw the Duke of Albemarle, who is not well and doth grow crazy.*[1] Thence I to St. James's, there to meet Sir G. Carteret, and did, and Lord Berkely, to get them (as we would have done the Duke of Albemarle) to the meeting of the Lords of Appeale in the business of one of our prizes.[2] With them to the meeting of the Guinny Company, and there stayed; and went with Lord Berkely. While I was waiting for him in the Matted Gallery, a young man was most finely working in Indian Inke the great picture of the King and Queen sitting, by van Dike, and did it very finely.[3] Thence to Westminster-hall to hear our cause, but did not come before them today; so went down and walked below in the Hall and there met with Ned Pickering, who tells me the ill news of his nephew Gilbert ⟨who is turned a very rogue⟩.[4] And then I took a turn with Mr. Eveling, with whom walked two hours, till almost one of the clock – talking of the badness of the Government, where nothing but wickedness, and wicked men and women command the King. That it is not in his nature to gainsay anything that relates to his pleasures. That much of it arises from the sickliness of our Ministers of State,[5] who cannot be about him as the idle companions are, and therefore give way to the young rogues; and then from the negligence of the Clergy, that a Bishop shall never be seen about him, as the King of France hath always.[6]

1. Albemarle was 59. He retired from public life at the end of 1668.

2. The *Lindenbaum*: see above, p. 130 & n. 2; below, p. 231.

3. The picture was of Charles I and his Queen seated, with their two eldest children, Prince Charles and Princess Mary ('*The greate peece of o*ʳ *royall selfe, Consort and children*'); Van Dyck's first important royal commission after his arrival in London. He was paid £100 for it by a warrant of 8 August 1632. It is now at Buckingham Palace (see O. Millar, *Tudor, Stuart and Early Georgian pictures in coll. H.M. Queen* (1963), no. 150). No 17th-century drawings from the complete composition are known. (OM).

4. Gilbert may well be the 'Mr. Pickering' (also a nephew of Sandwich) whom Pepys recommended for employment as a volunteer in 1674. He had then been at sea for five or six years. *Cat.*, ii. 391.

5. Evelyn was referring to Clarendon and Southampton, the elder statesmen in the King's service.

6. Charles had been alienated from most of his bishops since the failure of his indulgence scheme in the spring of 1663. Several of Louis XIV's bishops held office at court.

That the King would fain have some of the same gang to be Lord Treasurer; which would be yet worse, for now some delays are put to the getting gifts of the King, as that whore my Lady Byron, who had been, as he called it, the King's seventeenth whore abroad, did not leave him till she had got him to give her an order for 4000*l* worth of plate to be made for her; but by delays, thanks be to God, she died before she had it.[1] He tells me mighty stories of the King of France, how great a prince he is.[2] He hath made a Code to shorten the law.[3] He hath put out all the ancient commanders of castles that were become hereditary.[4] He hath made all the Fryers subject to the Bishops, which before were only subject to Rome and so were hardly the King's subjects. And that none shall become religious but at such an age – which he thinks will in few years ruin the pope and bring France into a patriarchate.[5] He confirmed to me the business of the want of paper at the Council-table the other day, which I have observed – Wooly being to have found it, and did, being

1. Lady Byron had died in January 1664. She had contrived to get £15,000 from the King during his exile (GEC, ii. 455 n.), but after the Restoration only with difficulty secured payment of a pension of £500 p.a.: *CTB*, i. 255, 597. As for her being Charles's 'seventeenth whore abroad', there have been several attempts at counting them, but none giving such a high total for this early period.

2. Evelyn had not been in France since 1652. Much of the news which follows may have come from his cousin Sir Samuel Tuke, diplomatist and playwright (who had twice been on diplomatic missions to France since Richard Browne (Resident at the French court for Charles I and Charles II, 1641–60).

3. Colbert's *ordonnance* (April 1667) reforming civil procedure; the first of a series of important legal reforms: F. A. Isambert, *Receuil . . . des anciennes lois françaises*, xviii (1829), no. 503.

4. There had been a large-scale reorganisation of commands of castles and garrisons in 1666: L. André, *Michel le Tellier*, esp. pp. 534–5.

5. An edict (December 1666) had forbidden the establishment of new orders without the King's consent, and a parliamentary *arrêt* (April 1667) had reformed the four mendicant orders. The proposal to put an age limit on monks was abandoned at the behest of the Nuncio. See Isambert, op. cit., xviii, no. 496; C. Gérin, *Louis XIV et le Saint-Siège*, ii. 126–8. Cf. D. de Repas to Sir R. Harley (London, 8 December 1666): 'I hope to see all France cast off the authority of the Pope, which they do by degrees . . . in twenty or thirty years there will not be any monastery left . . .' (HMC, *Portland*, iii. 303).

called, tell the King to his face the reason of it.[1] And Mr. Eveling tells me that several of the menial servants of the Court lack[a] bread, that have not received a farding wages since the King's coming in. He tells me the King of France hath[b] his Maistresses, but laughs at the foolery of our King, that makes his bastards princes, and loses his revenue upon them – and makes his mistresses his maisters. And the King of France did never grant Lavaliere anything to bestow on others; and gives a little sub-sistence, but no more, to his bastards.[2] He told me the whole story of Mrs. Stewarts going away from Court,[3] he knowing her well and believes her, to her leaving the Court, to be as virtuous as any woman in the world; and told me, from a Lord that she told it to but yesterday with her own mouth, and a sober[c] man, that when the Duke of Richmond did make love to her, she did ask the King and he did the like also; and that the King did not deny it; and told this Lord that she was come to that pass as to resolve to have married any gentleman of 1500*l* a year that would have had her in honour – for it was come to that pass, that she could not longer continue at Court without prostituting herself to the King, whom she had so long kept off, though he had liberty more then any other had,[d] or he ought to have, as to dalliance. She told this Lord that she had reflected upon the occasions she [had] given the world to think her a bad woman, and that she had no way but to marry and leave the Court, rather in this way of discontent then otherwise – that the world might see that she sought not anything but her honour; and that she will never come to live at Court, more then when she comes to town to come to kiss the Queen her mistress's hand; and hopes, though she hath little reason to hope, she can please her Lord so as to reclaim him, that they may yet live comfortably in the country on his estate. She told this Lord that all the jewels she ever had given her at Court, or any other presents[e] (more then the King's

---

a   MS. 'lacking'   *b*   repl.? 'of'-   *c*   repl. 'sober'
d   repl. 'ought'   *e*   repl. same symbol badly formed

---

1. See above, p. 176. Evelyn's father-in-law, Sir Richard Browne, was Clerk to the Council.
2. In fact Louis' bastards were given titles, land and offices, and La Vallière obtained favours both for herself and her relatives.
3. See above, p. 145 & n. 4.

allowance of 700*l* per annum out of the Privy-purse for her clothes) was: at her first coming, the King did give her a necklace of pearl of about 1100*l*; and afterward, about seven months since, when the King had hopes to have obtained some*ᵃ* courtesy of her, the King did give her some jewels, I have forgot what, and I think a pair of pendants. The Duke of York, being once her Valentine, did give her a jewell of about 800*l*; and my Lord Mandeville, her valentine this year, a*ᵇ* ring of about 300*l*; and the King of France, who would have had her mother (who he says is one of the most cunning women in the world) to have let her stay in France, saying that he loved her not as a mistress but as one*ᶜ* that he could marry as well as any lady in France, and that if she might stay, for the honour of his Court he would take care she should not repent.[1]   But her mother, by command of the Queene-mother, thought rather to bring her into England, and the King of France did give her a Jewell; so that Mr. Eveling believes she may be worth in jewells about 6000*l*, and that that is all that she hath in the world – and a worthy woman, and in this hath done as great an act of honour as ever was done by woman. That now the Countesse Castlemayne doth carry all before her; and among other arguments to prove Mrs. Stewart to have been honest to the last, he says that the King's keeping in still with my Lady Castlemaine doth show it, for he never was known to keep two mistresses in his life – and would never have kept to her had he prevailed anything with Mrs. Steward.   She is gone yesterday with her Lord to Cobham.   He did tell me of the ridiculous humour of our King and Knights of the Garter the other day; who, whereas heretofore their Robes were only to be worn during their ceremonies and service, these, as proud of their coats, did wear them all day till night, and then rode into the park with them on.   Nay, and he tells me he did see my

a   repl. 'her'   *b*   repl. 'a'   *c*   repl. 'a'

---

1. Her father, Walter Stewart, seems to have been a physician in the service of Henrietta-Maria.   She had been given a present by Louis XIV when she left for England in January 1662 to enter the service of Catherine of Braganza, but nothing appears to be known of his desire to prevent her going.

Lord Oxford and Duke of Monmouth [in] a hackney-coach with two footmen in the park, with their robes on; which is a most scandalous thing, so as all gravity may be said to be lost among us. By and by we discoursed of Sir Tho. Clifford, whom I took for a very rich and learned man, and of the great family of that name.[1] He tells me he is only a man of about seven-score pound a year[2] – of little learning,[3] more then the law of a Justice of Peace, which he knows well – a parson's son, got to be Burges in a little borough in the West[4] and here fell into the acquaintance of my Lord Arlington, whose creature he is and never from him. A man of virtue, and comely and good parts enough; and hath come into his place with a great grace, though with a great skip over the heads of a great many, as Chichly and Dunkum and some Lords that did expect it.[a] By the way he tells me that of all the great men of England, there is none that endeavours more to raise those that he takes into favour then my Lord Arlington; and that on that score, he is much more to be made one's patron then my Lord Chancellor, who never did nor will do anything

a The following 27 lines of printed text written in a very small hand.

---

1. He had been appointed Comptroller of the Household in November 1666; and was soon (22 May) to be a Treasury Commissioner. Evelyn knew him as a colleague on the Commission for the Sick and Wounded. His account of Clifford, as Pepys reports it, is similar to the account in his own diary at 18 August 1673: cf. also ib., 27 November 1666. It has several inaccuracies. His family (the Cliffords, Earls of Westmorland) was one with which Pepys's wife claimed relationship: see above, v. 118 & n. 1. Sir Thomas belonged to a cadet branch which had settled in Devon.

2. His patrimony was of about that value: for an account of his property

(1659) see C. H. Hartmann, *Clifford*, pp. 14–23. But he had married well and been given offices and perquisites by the King, and was now employing a financial expert to look after his affairs to whom he paid £40 p.a.: ib., pp. 45, 124–5.

3. He always regretted his lack of languages, but he had a flair for finance and a command of both the spoken and written word.

4. Totnes, Devon, which he had represented since 1660. It was his grandfather (Thomas Clifford, d. 1634), not his father, who was a parson. (He had taken orders when a country gentleman of 38: Hartmann, p. 6.) Burnet (i. 402) falls into the same error.

but for money.[1]   After having this long discourse, we parted
about one of the clock; and so away by water home, calling on
Michell, whose wife and girl is pretty well; and I home and to
dinner, and after dinner with Sir W. Batten to White-hall, there
to attend the Duke of York before council, where we all met at his
closet and there did the little business we had; and[a] here he did
tell us how the King of France is intent upon his design against
Flanders, and hath drawn up a remonstrance of the cause of the
war,[2] and appointed the 20th of the next month for his Rendez-
vouz, and himself to depart for the Campagne the 30th – so that
this we are in hopes will keep him in imployment.   Turin[3] is to
be his Generall.   Here was Carcasse's business unexpectedly
moved by him, but what was done therein appears in my account
of his case in writing by itself.[4]   Certain news of the Dutch being
abroad on our coast with 24 great ships.[5]   This done, Sir W.
Batten and I back again to London; and in the way met my Lady
Newcastle, going with her coaches and footmen all in velvet;
herself (whom I never saw before) as I have heard her often
described (for all the town-talk is nowadays of her extravagancies),
with her velvet-cap, her hair about her ears, many black patches
because of pimples about her mouth, naked necked, without

---

a   repl. 'and had design upon a remonstrance'

---

1. Arlington (Bennet) had since
1663 deliberately formed (or pre-
sided over) a parliamentary party in
rivalry to Clarendon.   Clifford, with
whom his friendship dated from c.
1662, was its 'bribe-master-general'.
Clarendon (often accused of receiving
money for offices: e.g. *CJ*, ix. 16) had
always refrained from using government resources to form a political
clientèle around him.   Burnet (i. 402)
states that Clifford turned to Bennet
only after he had failed to engage the
interest of Clarendon.   See A. Browning in *TRHS* (ser. 4), 30/22+ ; cf.
M. H. Nicolson (ed.), *Conway Letters*,
p. 240.

2. Published as *Traitté des droits de la
reyne tres-chrestienne sur divers estats de
la monarchie d'Espagne* (Paris, 1667).
3. Turenne.
4. Not traced: for the dispute, see
above, p. 64, n. 1.
5. The Dutch plan this year was to
attack shipping in the Thames, and
their main fleet left the Dutch coast
for this purpose on 4 June.   The
ships mentioned here were those of
the diversionary squadron under van
Ghent which now came out and, after
convoying a merchant fleet to the
North, made raids and took prizes in
the Firth of Forth.

anything about it, and a black juste-au-corps; she seemed to me a very comely woman – but I hope to see more of her on May-day.[1] My mind is mightily of late upon a coach. At home to the office, where*a* late, spending all the evening upon entering in longhand our late passages with Carcasse for memory sake; and so home, in great pain in my back by the uneasiness of Sir W. Batten's coach driving hard this afternoon over the stones to prevent coming too late. So at night to supper in great pain, and to bed, where lay in great pain, not able to turn myself all night.

27. Up, with much pain, and to the office, where all the morning. At noon home to dinner, W. Hewer with us. This noon I got in some coals at 23s per chaldron, a good bargain*b* I thank God, having not been put to buy a coal all this dear time, that during this war poor people have been forced to give 45s and 50s and 3l.[2] In the afternoon (my wife and people busy these late days, and will be for some time, making of shirts and smocks) to the office, where late; and then home, after letters, and so to supper and to bed with much pleasure of mind, after having despatched business. This afternoon I spent some time walking with Mr. Moore in the garden – among other things, discoursing of the condition of my Lord Sandwiches family,* which he tells me is in a very bad condition for want of money and management – my Lord charging them with bills, and no body nor thing provided to answer them; he did discourse of his hopes of being supplied with 1900l to answer a present bill from me, but I took no notice of it, nor will do it.[3] It seems Mr.

---

a repl. 'sp'-   *b* MS. 'hearing

---

1. When the beauty and chivalry of the town paraded in Hyde Park in carriages.

2. For coal prices, see above, p. 98 & n. 5.

3. Henry Moore, as Sandwich's London steward, made many similar complaints in this and the following years: e.g. below, 17 October 1668.

Pepys clearly believed that Sandwich was mainly to blame. Sandwich's secretary at Madrid, William Godolphin, thought that Moore, though honest, was too slow in money affairs: W. Godolphin to Sandwich, 8 June 1668 (Sandwich MSS, Letters from Mins., ii, f. 127).

Sheply doubts that^a his accounts are ill kept¹ and everything else in that family out of order; which I am grieved to hear of.

28. *Lords day.* Lay long, my pain in my back being still great, though not so great as it was. However, up and to church, where a lazy sermon; and then home and to dinner, my wife and I alone, and Barker. After dinner by water, the day being mighty pleasant and the tide serving finely – I up (reading in Boyles book of Colours)² as high as Barne Elmes; and there took one turn alone and then back to Putny church, where I saw the girls of the schools,³ few of which pretty. And there I came into a pew and met with little James Pierce; which I was much pleased at, the little rogue being very glad to see me – his maister, Reader to the church. Here was a good sermon and much company, but I sleepy and a little out of order for my hat falling down through a hole underneath the pulpit; which however, after sermon, by a stick and the help of the clerk, I got up again. And then walked out of the church with the boy, and then left him, promising him to get him a play another time. And so by water, the tide being with me again, down to Deptford; and there I walked down the yard, Shish and Cox with me, and discoursed about cleaning of the wet-Docke;⁴ and heard (which I had before) how when the Docke was made, a ship of near 500 ⟨Tons⟩ was there found, a ship supposed of Queen Elizabeth's time and well wrought, with^b a great deal of stone-shot in her of 18-inch Diameter, which was shot then in use; and afterward meeting with Captain Perriman and Mr. Castle at Half-way Tree, they tell me of stone-shot of 36-inches Diameter which they shot out of mortar-pieces.⁵ Thence walked to^c Half-way Tree,

---

a MS. 'and'   *b* repl. 'with'   *c* repl. full stop and 'Thence'

---

1. Edward Shipley was Moore's opposite number at Hinchingbrooke. Two years later Shipley was relieved of his post, 'age and good-fellowship' having made him incompetent: below, 8 March 1669.

2. Robert Boyle, *Experiments and considerations touching colours . . .*; a small octavo. Pepys retained a copy of the first edition (1664): PL 798. It was the first book in any language to deal with the phenomena of colours.

3. Evelyn in 1649 (ii. 555) mentions the *Schooles* or *Colledges* of the Young Gentlewomen' at Putney.

4. For the dock, see above, iii. 18 & n. 1.

5. These would be land guns.

and there stopped and talk with Mr. Castle and Captain Perriman, and so to Redriffe and took boat again; and so home, and there to write down my Journall, and so to supper and to read, and so to bed – mightily pleased with my reading Boyles book of Colours today; only, troubled that some part of it, endeed the greatest part, I am not able to understand for want of study. My wife this night troubled at my leaving her alone so much and keeping her within doors; which endeed I do not well nor wisely in.

29. Up, being visited very early by Creed, newly come from Hinchingbrooke; who went thither without my knowledge, and I believe only to save his being taxed to the Poll Bill. I did give him no very good countenance nor welcome, but took occasion to go forth and walked (he with me) to St. Dunstan's; and thence I to Sir W. Coventry's, where a good while with him; and I think he pretty kind, but that the nature of our present condition affords not matter for either of us to be pleased with anything.*a* We discoursed of Carcasse, whose Lord,[1] he tells me, doth make complaints that his clerk should be singled out; and my Lord Berkely doth take his part. So he advises we would sum up all we have against him and lay it before the Duke of York, he condemning my Lord Brouncker. Thence to Sir G. Carteret and there talked a little while about office business; and thence by coach home, in several places paying my debts in order to my evening my accounts this month. And thence by and by to White-hall again to Sir G. Carteret to dinner, where very good company and discourse; and I think*b* it my part to keep in there now more then ordinary, because of the probability of my Lord's coming soon home. Our commissioners for the treaty[2] set out this morning betimes down the River. Here I hear that the Duke of Cambrige, the Duke of York's son, is very sick[3] – and my Lord Treasurer very bad of the stone, and hath been so some days.[4] After dinner, Sir G. Carteret and I alone in

a repl. 'one another'   *b* repl. 'keep'

---

1. Brouncker.
2. Lord Holles and Henry Coventry, plenipotentiaries to the Breda conference.

3. He died on 20 June at the age of four.
4. Southampton died on 16 May at the age of 59.

his closet an hour or more, talking of my Lord Sandwiches coming
home; which, the peace being likely to be made here, he expects,
both for my Lord's sake and his own (whose interest he wants)
it will be best for him to be at home, where he will be well
received by the King he is sure, and his service well accepted,
though the business of Spain doth fall by this peace.[1] He tells
me my Lord Arlington hath done like a gentleman by him in all
things. He says, if my Lord were here, he were the fittest man
to be Lord Treasurer of any man in England. And he thinks it
might be compassed, for he confesses that the King's matters do
suffer through the inability of this man, who is likely to die;
and he will propound him to the King – it will remove him from
his place at sea, and the King will have a good place to bestow.
He says to me that he could wish, when my Lord comes, that he
would think fit to forbear playing, as a thing below him and
which will lessen him, as it doth my Lord St. Albans,[2] in the
King's esteem. And as a great secret, tells me that he hath made
a match for my Lord Hinchingbrooke, to a daughter of my Lord
Burlington's; where there is great alliance, 10000*l* portion, a
civil family, and relation to my Lord Chancellor, whose son
hath married one of the daughters;[3] and that my Lord Chancellor
doth take it with very great kindness, so that he doth hold himself
obliged by it. My Lord Sandwich hath referred it to my Lord
Crew, Sir G. Carteret, and Mr. Mountagu[4] to end it – my Lord

1. The French attack on the Span-
ish Netherlands, however, gave Sand-
wich's mission a new importance.
He concluded a trade treaty with
Spain on 3 May, mediated in the
peace between Spain and Portugal in
January 1668, and did not return to
England until September 1668.

2. St Albans is said to have lost vast
sums at the gaming-table. In 1683
Evelyn speaks of him (iv. 338) as old
and blind but still playing – 'having
one that sets by him to name the spot
in the Chards'.

3. Laurence Hyde, second son of
Clarendon and later Earl of Rochester,
had married Lady Henrietta Boyle,

fifth daughter of the 1st Earl of Burlington, in 1665. Viscount Hinchingbrooke married Lady Anne Boyle,
Burlington's fourth daughter, in January 1668.

4. William Mountagu, Sandwich's
cousin and legal adviser. Henry
Moore was also to be consulted.
Sandwich's note of his committing
the negotiations to these advisers (c.
March 1667) is in Sandwich MSS,
Journals, iii. 694. The settlement was
a poor bargain: see below, 5 February
1668. For Carteret's letters to Sandwich urging the match, see Harris, ii.
178.

Hinchingbrooke and the lady know nothing yet of it. It will, I think, be very happy. Very glad of this discourse, I away, mightily pleased with the confidence I have in this family; and so away, took up my wife, who was at her mother's, and so home; where I settled to my chamber about my accounts, both Tanger and private, and up at it till 12 at night with good success, when news is brought me that there is a great fire in Southworke;[1] so we up to the leads, and then I and the boy down to the end of our lane and there saw it, it seeming pretty great but nothing to the fire of London, that it made me think little of it. We could at*a* that distance see an engine play;[2] that is, the water go out, it being moonlight. By and by it began to slacken, and then I home and to bed.

30. Up, and Mr. Madden[3] came to speak with me; whom my people not knowing, have made to wait long without doors, which vexed me. Then comes Sir Jo. Winter to discourse with me about the Forest of Deane[4] and then about my Lord Treasurer; and asking me whether, as he had heard, I had not been cut of the stone, I took him to my closet and there showed it him;[5] of which he took the dimensions and had some discourse of it, and I believe will show my Lord Treasurer it. Thence to the office, where we sat all the morning, but little to do; and then to the Change, where for certain I hear, and the newsbook declares, a peace between France and Portugal.[o] Met here with

a MS. 'that'

---

1. Near the Spur Inn; over 40 families lost their homes. It was said to have been started deliberately by three Frenchmen. Accounts in *N. & Q.*, 1 February 1862, p. 99; *CSPD 1667*, pp. 337, 338.

2. For fire-engines, see above, i. 264, n. 1.

3. John Madden, Surveyor of the Woods on this side Trent.

4. Winter had a lease of the wood and ironworks in the Forest of Dean: see above, iii. 112 & n. 2. He was at about this time involved in disputes

with the Treasury both about his timber nursery and the ship timber he had contracted for: see above, p. 114; *CTB*, ii. 5, 56.

5. The stone was kept in a leather case: above, v. 247 & n. 1.

6. *London Gazette*, 29 April. This was an offensive and defensive alliance which France concluded with Portugal in preparation for her attack on the Spanish Netherlands. It led to the Anglo-Spanish trade treaty which Pepys reports below at 1 June.

Mr. Pierce, and he tells me the Duke of Cambrige is very ill and full of spots about his body, that Dr. Frazier knows not what to think of it. Then home and to dinner, and then to the office, where all the afternoon; we met about Sir W. Warren's business and accounts, wherein I do rather oppone then forward him; but not in declared terms, for I will not be at enmity with him. But I will not have him find any friendship so good as mine.[1] By and by rose, and by water to White hall, and then called my wife at Unthankes; and so home and to my chamber to my accounts, and finished them to my heart's wish and admiration, they being very great and intricate, being let alone for two months; but I brought them together all naturally, within a few shillings; but to my sorrow, the pole Mony I paid this month, and mourning, have made me 80*l* a worse man then at my last balance, so that I am worth now but 6700*l*; which is yet an infinite mercy to me – for which God make me thankful. So late to supper, with a glad heart for the evening of my accounts so well, and so to bed*a*.

a Following this a leaf has been cut out.

---

1. Pepys was jealous of Warren's association with Brouncker: see above, p. 31 & n. 3.

MAY

1. Up, it being a fine day; and after doing a little business in my chamber, I left my wife to go abroad with W. Hewer and his mother in a hackney-coach incognit[1] to the park, while I abroad to the Excize Office first, and there met the Cofferer and Sir St. Fox about our money matters there, wherein we agreed; and so to discourse of my Lord Treasurer, who is a little better then he was of the stone, having rested a little this night. I there did acquaint them with my knowledge of that disease, which I believe will be told my Lord Treasurer. Thence to Westminster, in the way meeting many milk-maids with their garlands upon their pails, dancing with a fiddler before them,[2] and saw pretty Nelly standing at her lodgings door in Drury-lane[3] in her smock-sleeves and bodice, looking upon one – she seemed a mighty pretty creature. To the Hall and there walked a while, it being term; and thence home to the Rose and there had Doll Lane*a* vener para me; but it was in a lugar mighty ouvert, so as we no poda*b* hazer algo; so parted and then met again at the Swan, where for la misma reason we no pode hazer, but put off to recontrar anon, which I only used as a put-off; and so parted and to my Lord Crew's, where I found them at dinner; and among others, Mrs. Bocket, which I have not seen a long time, and two little dirty children, and she as idle a prating, impertinent woman as ever she was. After dinner my Lord took me alone, walked with me, giving me an account of the meeting of the

a name in s.h. *b* repl. 'pez'-

---

1. I.e. in a closed coach.
2. They collected tips from their customers. This May-day custom lasted in varied forms into the 19th century: see esp. W. Hone, *Every-day Book* (1838), i. 570. The milkmaids, probably from nearby farms, may have been on their way to the May-

pole in the Strand. For descriptions of country milkmaids and their music, see above, iii. 221 & n. 2. Households used milk mainly for cooking; to drink it was dangerous.
3. Nell Gwyn's lodgings are said to have been opposite Wych St. (A).

Commissioners for Accounts, whereof he is one.[1] How some of the gentlemen, Garraway, Littleton and others, did scruple at their first coming there, being called thither to act as Members of Parliament, which they could not do by any authority but that of the Parliament, and therefore desired the King's direction in it; which was sent for by my Lord Bridgewater, who brought answer very short, that the King expected[a] they should obey his Commission. Then they went on and missed a power to be given them of administering and framing an oath, which they thought they could not do by any power but Act of Parliament; and the whole Commission did think fit to have the judges' opinion in it; and so drawing up their scruple in writing, they all attended the King, who told them he would send to the judges to be answered, and did so; who have, my Lord tells me, met three times about it, not knowing what answer to give to it; and they have met this week, doing[b] nothing but expecting the solution of the judges in this point.[2] My Lord tells me he doth believe this Commission will do more hurt then good; it may undo some accounts if these men shall think fit, but it can never clear an accountant,* for he must come into the Exchequer for all this. Besides, it is a kind of Inquisition that hath seldom, if ever, been granted in England; and [he] believes it will never besides give any satisfaction to the people or Parliament, but be looked upon as a forced, packed business of the King, especially if these Parliament men that are of it shall not concur with them –

a repl. 'expr'-   *b* repl. 'too'

1. The Commissioners had been appointed by the King on or before 21 March: *CSPD 1666-7*, p. 676. The Commons had in January objected to an enquiry by royal commissioners.

2. Pepys's report is confirmed by the information sent to Williamson, c. May 1667 (incorrectly ascribed to November 1666): *CSPD 1666-7*, p. 305. Cf. also ib., *1667*, pp. 32, 122. A new commission was issued on

8 May which added the judges to the commission, and provided for administration of oaths and for trial of offenders by jury: *CTB*, vol. ii, pp. xlviii–xlix. But after a few preliminary meetings it broke up. A statutory commission (the Brooke House Committee) was later appointed to undertake the enquiry, in December 1667, and reported in October 1669: see below, p. 559 & n. 2.

which he doubts they will not – and therefore wishes much that the King would lay hold of this fit occasion, and let the Commission fall. Then to talk of my Lord Sandwich, whom my Lord Crew hath a great desire might get to be Lord Treasurer if the present Lord should die, as it's believed he will in a little time – and thinks he can have no competitor but my Lord Arlington, who it is given out desires [it].[1] But my Lord thinks it is not so, for that the being Secretary doth keep him a great[er] interest with*a* the King then the other would do – at least, doth believe that if my Lord would surrender him his Wardrobe place, it would be a temptation to Arlington to assist my Lord in getting the Treasurer['s]. I did object to my Lord that it would be no place of content nor safety, nor honour for my Lord – the State being*b* so indigent as it is and the [King] so irregular, and those about him, that my Lord must be forced to part with anything to answer his warrants; and that therefore I do believe the King had rather have a man that may be one of his vicious cabal, then a sober man that will mind the public, that so they may sit at cards and dispose of the revenue of the kingdom. This my Lord was moved at, and said he did not indeed know how to answer it, and bid me think of it and so said he himself would also do. He*c* doth mightily cry out of the bad management of our monies, the King having had so much given him; and yet when the Parliament do find that the King should have 900000*l* in his purse by the best account of issues they have yet seen, yet we should report in the Navy a debt due from the King of 900000*l*;[2] which I did confess I doubted was true in the first, and knew to be true in the last, and did believe that there was some great miscarriages in it; which he owned to believe also, saying that at this rate it is not in the power of the kingdom to make a war nor answer the King's wants. Thence away to the King's playhouse by agreement; met Sir W. Penn and saw *Love in a Maze*; but a sorry play, only Lacy's clowne's part, which he did most admirably

a repl. 'then'   *b* repl. 'b'-   *c* repl. 'it'

---

1. Southampton, the Lord Treasurer, died on 16 May; a commission was appointed to succeed him. For Arlington's hope of attaining the office, see above, p. 96, n. 2.

2. Cf. above, vii. 294 & n. 1.

endeed; and I am glad to find the rogue at liberty again.¹   Here
was but little, and that ordinary company.   We sat at the upper
bench next the boxes;² and I find it doth pretty well – and hath
the advantage of seeing and hearing the great peopleᵃ, which may
be pleasant when there is good store.   Now was only Prince
Rupert and my Lord Lauderdale, and my Lord   ,³
(the naming of whom puts me in mind of my seeing at Sir Robt.
Viner's two or three great silver flagons made with inscriptions,
as gifts of the King to such and such persons of quality as did
stay in town the late great plague for the keeping things in order
in the town; which is a handsome thing);⁴ but here was neither
Hart, Nell, nor Knepp; therefore the play was not likely to
please me.   Thence Sir W. Penn and I in his coach, Tiburne
way, into the park; where a horrid dust and number of coaches,
without pleasure or order.   That which we and almost all went
for was to see my Lady Newcastle; which we could not, she
being fallowed and crowded upon by coaches all the way she
went, that nobody could come near her; only, I could see she
was in a large black coach, adornedᵇ with silverᶜ instead of gold,
and so with the curtains and everything black and white, and
herself in her cap; but other parts I could not make.   But that
which I did see and wonder at, with reason, was to find Pegg Penn
in a new coach, with only her husband's pretty sister⁵ with her,
both patched and very fine, and in much the finest coach in the
park and I think that ever I did see, one or other, for neatness
and richness in gold and everything that is noble – my Lady
Castlemaine, the King, my Lord St. Albans, nor Mr. Germin

---

a repl. 'Lords'   *b* repl. 'adord'   *c* repl. 'silk'

---

1. The play was Shirley's comedy:
see above, iii. 88 & n. 4.   John Lacey
played the part of Johnny Thump.
For his arrest, see above, p. 172. (A).

2. I.e. the back row of the pit,
which was just in front of the boxes at
the rear of the auditorium. (A).

3. Probably Lord Craven, soldier
and courtier, is meant. For his services
during the Plague, when he acted as
Albemarle's principal assistant, see T.

Skinner, *Life of Monck* (1723), p. 365.

4. Vyner was the King's goldsmith.   Tankards – smaller ones –
were also presented to J.P.'s, physicians and apothecaries for their
services: PRO, PC2/59, ff. 16*v*–17*r*;
N. & Q., 13 December 1873, p. 471.

5. Margaret Lowther (now about
19) who in 1668 married Capt. John
Holmes.

have so neat a coach that ever I saw – and Lord, to have them have this, and nothing else that is correspondent, is to me one of the most ridiculous sights that ever I did see, though her present dress was well enough; but to live*ᵃ* in the condition they do at home, and be abroad in this coach, astonishes me. When we had spent half an hour in the park, we went out again, weary*ᵇ* of the dust and despairing of seeing my Lady Newcastle; and so back the same way and to St. Jones's,¹ thinking to have met my Lady Newcastle before she got home; but we staying by the way to drink,*ᶜ* she got home a little before us, so we lost our labours; and then home, where we find the two young ladies come home and their patches off (I*ᵈ* suppose Sir W. Penn doth not allow of them in his sight) and going out of town tonight, though late, to Walthamstow. So to talk a*ᵉ* little at Sir W. Batten's, and then home to supper, where I find Mrs. Hewer and her son, who have been abroad with my wife in the park; and so after supper to read and then to bed. Sir W. Penn did give me an account this afternoon of his design of buying Sir Rob. Brookes's fine house at Wanstead,² which I so wondered at; and did give him reasons against it, which he allowed of and told me that he did intend to pull down that house and build a less, and that he should get 1500*lᶠ* by the old house, and I know not what fooleries; but I will never believe he ever intended to buy it for my part, though he troubled Mr. Gawden to go and look upon it and advise him in it.

2. To the office, where all the morning. At noon home to dinner, and then abroad to my Lord Treasurer's, who continues so ill as not to be troubled with business; so Mr. Gawden and I to my Lord Ashly's and spoke with him, and then straight home; and there I did much business at the office, and then to my

---

a repl. same symbol badly formed   *b* repl. 'weary of'
c MS. 'drinking'   *d* repl. 'and'   *e* MS. 'at'
        f repl. 'money'

---

1. St John's, Clerkenwell. The London house of the Duke and Duchess was in Clerkenwell Close.
2. For the house, see above, vi. 102

& n. 4. Penn did not buy it, but later lived at a house in High St, Wanstead, known eventually as Sheridan House, The Mall.

chamber and did the like there, to my great content but to the
pain of my eyes; and then to supper and to bed – having a song
with my wife with great pleasure, she doing it well.

3. Up, and with Sir J. Mennes, W. Batten and W. Penn in
the last man's coach to St. James's; and thence up to the Duke of
York's chamber (which, as it is now fretted at the top and the
chimney-piece made handsome, is one of the noblest and best-
proportioned rooms that ever I think I saw in my life); and
when ready, into his closet*a* and did our business – where among
other things, we have a proposition of Mr. Pierce's for being
continued in pay, or something done for him, in reward of his
pains as Chyrurgeon Generall, forasmuch as Troutbecke, that was
never a Doctor before, hath got 200*l* a year settled on him for
nothing but the one voyage with the Duke of Albemarle;[1] the
Duke of York and the whole company did show most perticular
kindness to Mr. Pierce, everybody moving for him and the Duke
himself most, that he is likely to be a very great man I believe.
Here also we had another mention of Carcasse's business,[2] and
we directed to bring in a report of our opinion of his case –
which vexes us that such a rogue shall make us so much trouble.
Thence I presently to the Excise Office, and there met the Cofferer
and Sir St. Fox by agreement and agreed upon a method for our
future payments. And then we three to my Lord Treasurers,
who continues still very ill. I had taken my stone with me on
purpose,[3] and Sir Ph. Warwicke carried it in to him to see,
but was not in condition to talk with me about it, poor man.
So I with them to Westminster by coach, the Cofferer telling us
odd stories: how he was dealt with by the men of the church at
Westminster in taking a lease of them at the King's coming in;

a repl. 'cham'-

---

1. James Pearse, Surgeon-in-ordinary to the Duke of York, had been
appointed Surgeon-general to the
navy at the beginning of the war.
An order was made this day for him
to be paid until notice to the contrary:
PRO, Adm. 106/3520, f. 36*r*. Trout-
beck had served as an army surgeon
but never (until 1666) in the navy.
For his naval service, see above, vii. 79
and n. 1. His pension was granted
(on 3 April 1667) as a mark of Albemarle's favour: *CSPD 1665-6*, pp.
386, 567; *CTB*, ii. 182, 210.
2. See above, p. 64 & n. 1.
3. See above, p. 191, n. 5.

and perticularly the devilish covetousness of Dr. Busby.[1] Sir
St. Fox in discourse told him how he is selling some land he hath,
which yields him not above three per cent, if so much, and
turn[ing] it into money, which he can put out at ten per cent;
and as times go, if they be like to continue, it is the best way for[a]
me to keep money going so, for aught I see.[2] I to Westminster
hall and there took a turn with[b] my old acquaintance Mr. Pechell,
whose red nose makes me ashamed to be seen with him,[3] though
otherwise a good-natured man; so away, I not finding of Mr.
Moore, with whom I should have met and spoke about a letter
I this day received from him from my Lord Hinchingbrooke,
wherein he desires me to help him to 1900*l* to pay a bill of
exchange of his father's; which troubles me much, but I will
find some way if I can to do[c] it; but not to bring myself in bonds
or disbursements for it, whatever comes of it. So home to
dinner, where my wife hath *ceux là* upon her; and is very ill
with them, so forced to go to bed, and I sat by her a good while.
Then down to my chamber and made an end of Rycauts *History
of the Turkes*,[4] which is a very good book. Then to the office
and did some business; and then, my wife being pretty well,
by coach to little Michell's and there saw my poor Betty and her
little child, which slept so soundly we could hardly wake[d] it in an

---

a repl. 'to doing it'   *b* repl. 'of'   *c* MS. 'day'
d repl. 'ap'-

---

1. The house referred to by the
Cofferer (William Ashburnham) was
in the cloisters of Westminster Abbey
and became known as Ashburnham
House. Richard Busby (d. 1695) had
been Headmaster of Westminster
School since 1640 and a Prebendary of
Westminster since July 1660. There
is no evidence that he was personally
covetous (in fact much evidence to the
contrary), but the Church in general
was often alleged at this time (probably wrongly) to have been too
severe in the terms made for the
recovery of its property at the
Restoration – more severe, for instance, than the King in similar cases:
Burnet, i. 329–30; cf. Clarendon,
Life, ii. 7–10.
2. For the decline in land values,
see above, p. 158 & n. 1. The maxi-
mum legal rate for interest was 6%,
but an extra 4% was under various
guises often charged.
3. Rev. John Peachell was a Fellow
of Magdalene well-known for his
drinking. At the close of his life
(when he was Master of his college)
Archbishop Sancroft rebuked him for
his bad example His death is said to
have been brought on by four days'
abstinence.
4. See above, p. 121, n. 2.

hour's time without hurting it; and they tell me what I did not know, that a child (as this doth) will hunt and hunt up and down with its mouth, if you touch the cheek of it with your finger's end, for a nipple, and fit its mouth for suckeing; but this hath not sucked yet, she having no nipples. Here sat a while; and then my wife and I, it being most curious* clear evening after some rain today, took a most excellent tour by coach to Bow,*a* and there drank and back again; and so a little at the office and home, to read a little and to supper and bed, mightily refreshed with this evening's tour, but troubled that it hath hindered my doing some business which I would have done at the office. This day the news is come that the fleet of the Duch, of about 20 ships, which came upon our coasts upon design to have intercepted our Colliers (but by good luck failed), is gone to the Frith[1] and there lie, perhaps to trouble the Scotch*b* privateers which have galled them of late very much, it may be more then all our last year's fleet.

4. Up and to the office, where sat all the morning. Among other things, a great conflict I had with Sir W. Warren, he bringing a letter to the Board, flatly in words*c* charging them with ⟨their delays in⟩*d* passing his accounts, which have been with them these two years[2] – part of which I said was not true, and the other undecent. The whole Board was concerned to take notice of it, as well as myself, but none of them had the honour to do it, but suffered me to do it alone; only Sir W. Batten, which did what he did out of common spite to him. So I writ in the margin of the letter, "Returned as untrue," and by consent of the Board did give it him again – and so parted. Home to dinner, and there came a woman whose husband I sent for, one Fisher, about the business of Perkins and Carcasse; and I do think by her that I shall find that business as bad as ever it was, and that we shall find Comissioner Pett a rogue, and using foul play in behalf of Carcasse. After dinner, to the office

a MS. 'bow'   *b* repl. 'their'   *c* repl. 'word'
                       d repl. 'not'

1. The Firth of Forth. Cf. the reports in *CSPD 1667*, pp. 56, 58; Rawl. A 195, ff. 152r, 181r.   2. The delays continued until 1675; see below, 29 November 1668 & n.

again and there late all the afternoon, doing much business; and with great content, home*ª* and to supper and to bed.

5. *Lords day.* Up; and going down to the waterside, I met Sir Jo. Robinson, and so with him by coach to White-hall – still a vain, prating, boasting man as ever I know, as if the whole City and Kingdom had all its work done by him. He tells me he hath now got a street ordered to be continued, 40 feet broad, from Paul's through Cannon-street to the Tower, which will be very fine.[1] He, and others this day where I was in the afternoon, doth tell me of at least six or eight fires within these few days, and continually stories of fires; and real fires there have been in one place or other almost ever since the late great fire, as if there was a fate over people for fire. I walked over the park to Sir W. Coventry; among other things, to tell him what I hear of people's being forced to sell their bills before September for 35 and 40 per cent loss; and which is worst, that there are some Courtiers that have made a knot to buy them, in hopes of some ways to get money of the King to pay them – which Sir W. Coventry is amazed at, and says we are a people made up for destruction; and will do what he can to prevent all this, by getting the King to provide wherewith to pay them. We talked of Tanger, of which he is ashamed; also that it should put the King to this charge for no good in the world, and now a man going over that is a good Souldier but a debauched man,[2] which that place needs not to have. And so used these words: "That this place was to the King as my Lord Carnarvan says of Wood; that it is an Excrescence of the earth provided by God for the payment of debts."[3] Thence away to Sir G. Carteret, whom I find taking

---

a repl. same symbol badly formed

---

1. See the Lord Mayor's proclamation (29 April) and the King's proclamation (8 May) approving it: Steele, nos 3491–2. Robinson, Lieutenant of the Tower, had been Lord Mayor, 1663–4. For a similar project of his made during his mayoralty, see above, iv. 77 & n. 3.

2. The new Governor, the Earl of Middleton, was reputedly a drunkard.

3. The maxim applied particularly to owners of entailed estates. The 2nd Earl of Carnarvon's estate (at Wing, Bucks.) had suffered from his father's royalism and his own hospitality. Cf. VCH, *Bucks.*, ii. 308, 311, etc.

physic; I stayed talking with him but a little, and so home to church and heard a dull sermon; and most of the best women of our parish gone into the country, or at least not at church. So home and find my boy not there, nor was at church; which vexed me, and when he came home I enquired; he tells me he went to see his mother; I sent him back to her to send me some token that he*a* was with her; so there came a man with him back of good fashion; he says he saw him with her; which pacified me, but I did soundly threaten him before him. And so to dinner, and then had a little scolding with my wife for not being fine enough to go to the christening today; which she excused by being ill, as she was endeed, and cried; but I was in an ill humour, and ashamed endeed that she should not go dressed. However, friends by and by, and we went by water to Michell's; and there his little house full of his father and mothers and the kindred, hardly any else, and mighty merry in this innocent company; and Betty mighty*b* pretty in bed, but her head akeing, not very merry; but the company mighty merry, and I with them; and so the child was christened, my wife, his father, and her mother the witnesses, and the child's name Elizabeth. So we had gloves and wine and wafers, very pretty, and talked and tattled; and so we away by water and up with the tide, she and I and Barker, as high as Barne Elmes, it being a fine evening; and back again to pass the bridge at standing-water between 9 and 10 at night; and then home and to supper, and then to bed with much pleasure. This day Sir W. Coventry tells me the Dutch fleet hath shot some shot, 4 or 500, into Burnt Iland[1] in the Frith, but without any hurt; and so are gone.

6.*c* Up; and angry with my maids for letting in watermen and I know not who, anybody that they are acquainted with, into the kitchen*d* to talk and prate with them, which I will not endure. Then out and by coach to my Lord Treasurer's, who

---

a repl. 'she was'   *b* MS. 'my'   *c* repl. '5'
d repl. 'kitch'-

---

1. Burntisland, Fife, on the north of the Firth of Forth: the attack took place on 29–30 April, causing no casualties. Account in *CSPD 1667*, p. 62.

continues still very ill. Then to Sir Ph. Warwicke's house and there did a little business about my Tanger tallies; and so to Westminster-hall and there to the Exchequer to consult about some way of getting our poor creditors of the Navy (who served in their goods before the last session of Parliament) paid out of the Eleven Months Tax, which seems to relate only for goods to be then served in[1] – and I think I have found out a way to bring them into the act; which if it doth, I shall think a good service done. Thence by coach home with Captain Cocke, in our way talking of my Lord Brouncker and his Lady, who are mighty angry with us all of the office about Carcasse's business, but especially with me; and in great confidence he bids me have a care of him, for he hath said that he would wound me with the person where my greatest interest is. I suppose he means Sir W. Coventry, and therefore I will beware of him; and am glad, though vexed, to hear it. So home to dinner, where Creed came, whom I vexed devilishly with telling him a wise man, and good friend of his and mine, did say that he lately went into the country to Hinchingbrooke, and at his coming to town again hath shifted his lodging, only to avoid paying to the pole bill; which is*a* so true, that he blushed and could not in words deny it, but the fellow did think to have not had it discovered. He is so devilish a subtle false rogue that I am really weary and afeared of his company; and therefore after dinner left him in the house and to my office, where busy all the afternoon, despatching much business; and in the evening to Sir R. Viner's to adjust accounts there; and so home, where some of our old Navy Creditors came to me by my direction, to consider of what I have invented for their help, as I have said in the morning, and like it mighty well; and so I to the office, where busy late; then home to supper and sing with my wife, who doth begin to give me real pleasure with her singing; and so to bed.

7. Up betimes and by coach to St. James; but there find W. Coventry gone out betimes this morning on horseback with

a MS. 'he is'

---

1. For examples, see *CTB*, ii. 254, 279, 289–90.

the King and Duke of York to Putny-heath to run some horses, and so back again to the office – where some witnesses from Chatham which*a* I sent for are come up, and do give shrowd testimonies against Carcasse; which*b* put my Lord into a new flame, and he and I to high words, and so broke up. Then home to dinner, where W. Hewer dined with us; and he and I after dinner to my chamber to discourse of Carcasses business, wherein I apparently*c* now do manage it wholly against my Lord Brouncker, Sir W. Penn like a false rogue shrinking out of the collar, and Sir J. Mennes, a fool, being easily led either way, and Sir W. Batten, a malicious fellow that is not able to defend anything, so that the whole odium must fall on me; which I will therefore beware how I manage, that I may not get enemies to no purpose. It vexes me to see with what a company I am mixed, but then it pleases me to see that I am reckoned the chief mover among them – as they do confess and esteem me in everything.

Thence to the office and did business; and then by coach to St. James's again, but W. Coventry not within, so I wrote something to him and then straight back again and to Sir W. Batten's; and there talked with him and J. Mennes, who are mighty hot in Carcasse's business, but their judgments not to be trusted. However, I will go through with it, for otherwise we shall be all slaves to my Lord Brouncker and his man's impudence. So to the office a little; and then home to supper and to bed – after hearing my wife sing, who is manifestly come to be more musical in her eare then ever I thought she could have been made; which rejoices me to the heart, for I take great delight now to hear her sing.

8. Up pretty betimes and out of doors; and in Fanchurch-street met Mr. Lovett going with a picture to me, but I could not stand to discourse*d* or see it; but on to the next hackney-coach and so to Sir W. Coventry, where he and I alone a while, dis-coursing of some businesses of the office; and then up to the Duke of York to his chamber with my fellow Brethren who are come, and so did our usual weekly business, which was but little today; and I was glad that the business of Carcasse was not mentioned,

_a_ repl. 'came'　　　_b_ MS. 'where'　　　_c_ repl. 'apper'-
_d_ repl. 'discourse' badly formed

because our report was not ready, but I am resolved it shall against the next coming*a* to the Duke of York. Here was discourse about a way of paying off ⟨our⟩ old Creditors, which did please me, there being hopes of getting them comprehended within the Eleven-Months Tax; and this did give occasion for Sir G. Carteret's and my going to Sir Robt. Long to discourse it, who doth agree that now the King's Council do say that they may be included in that Act;[1] which doth make me very glad, not so much for the sake of the poor men as for the King – for it would have been a ruin to him and his service not to have had a way to have paid that debt. There parted with Sir G. Carteret and into Westminster hall; and there I met with Sir H. Cholmly and he and I to Sir Ph. Warwicks to speak a little about our Tanger business, but to little purpose, my Lord Treasurer being so ill that no business can be done. Thence with Sir H Cholmly to find out Creed, from one lodging to another, which he hath changed so often that there is no finding him; but at last do come to his lodging that he is entering into this day, and do find his goods unloading at the door by*b* Scotland-yard; and there I set down Sir H. Cholmly, and I away to the Change, where spoke about several things; and then going home did meet Mr. Andrews our neighbour, and did speak with him to enquire about the ground behind our house, which I have a mind to buy enough to make a stable and coach-house – for I do see that my condition doth require it, as well as that it is more charge to my purse to live as I do then to keep one; and therefore I am resolved before winter to have one, unless some extraordinary thing happens to hinder me.[2] He promises me to look after it for me; and so I home to dinner, where I find my wife's Flagilette-master; and I am so pleased with her proceeding, though she hath lost time by not practising, that I am resolved for the encouragement of the man to learn myself a little, for a month or

a repl. 'sitting'   *b* repl. 'there'

---

1. Arrears of this sort had not been covered by the previous parliamentary grant, the Additional Aid of 1665. Cf. above, vi. 311 & n. 2.

2. There were difficulties in the acquisition of a coach house, and the coach itself was not bought until November 1668.

so¹ – for I do foresee, if God send my wife and I to live, she will become very good company for me.   He gone, comes Lovett with my little print of my dear Lady Castlemayne, varnished and the frame prettily done like gold, which pleases me well.² He dined with me, but by his discourse I do still see that he is a man of good wit, but most strange experience and acquaintance with all manner of subtleties and tricks, that I do think him not fit for me to keep any acquaintance with him, lest he some time or other show me a slippery trick.   After dinner, he gone, I to the office, where all the afternoon very busy; and so in the evening to Sir R. Viner, thinking to finish my accounts there, but am prevented; and so back again home and late at my office at business; and so home to supper and sing a little with my dear wife, and so to bed.

9.   Up, and to the office and at noon home to dinner; and then with my wife and Barker by coach and left them at Charing Cross; and I to St. James's and there found Sir W. Coventry alone in his chamber, and sat and talked with him more then I have done a great while, of several things – of the Navy, how our debts and wants do unfit us for doing anything.   He tells me he hears stories of Commissioner Pett of selling Timber to the Navy under other names; which I told him I believe is true, and did give him an instance.³   He told me also how his clerk Floyd he hath put away for his common idlenesse and ill company; and perticularly, that yesterday he was found not able to come to attend him, by being run into the arme in a squable, though he pretends it was done in the street by strangers, at 9 at night by the Maypole in the Strand.   Sir W. Coventry did write to me this morning to recommend him another;

---

1. Pepys could already play the flageolet: above, i. 19.   For the arranging of these lessons, see below, p. 221.   The master was Thomas Greeting.   (E).

2. Cf. above, p. 23, n. 3.   (OM).

3. For this case, see below, pp. 230–1 & n.   Pepys, defending his office before the Brooke House Committee two years later, denied that Pett had ever dealt in any navy goods except one parcel of Albemarle's timber, and adduced this as a proof of the improved efficiency of the Board as compared with that of the Cromwellian administrators, under whom Pett had been able to conduct a busy trade: PL 2874, p. 403.

which I could find my heart to do W Hewers for his good,[a] but do believe he will not part with me, nor have I any mind to let him go. I would my brother were fit for it; I would adventure him there. He insists upon an unmarried man – that can write well – and hath French enough to transcribe it only from a copy, and may write shorthand if it may be. Thence with him to my Lord Chancellors at Clarendon-house to a Committee for Tanger, where several things spoke of and proceeded on; and perticularly sending Commissioners thither[b] before the new Governor goes,[1] which I think will signify as much good as everything else that hath been done about the place; which is, none at all. I did again tell them the badness of their credit by[c] the time their tallies took, before they become[d] payable, and their spending more then their fond. They seem well satisfied with what I[e] said, and I am glad that I may be remembered I do tell them the case plain. But it troubled me that I see them hot upon it that the Governor shall not be paymaister, which will force me either to the providing one there to do it (which I will never undertake) or leave the imployment, which I had rather do.

Mightily pleased with the nobleness of this house and the brave furniture and pictures, which endeed is very noble.[2] And being broke up, I with Sir G Carteret in his coach into Hyde park[f] to discourse of things, and spent an hour in this manner with great pleasure; telling me all his concernments, and how he is gone through with the purchase for my Lady Jemimah and her husband.[3] How the Treasury is like to come into the hands of a committee;[4] but that not that, nor anything else, will do our business, unless the King himself will mind his business; and how his servants do execute their parts. He doth fear an utter ruin in the state, and that in a little time, if the King do not mind his business soon. That the King is very kind to him and to my Lord Sandwich; and that he doubts not but at his coming home,

---

a MS. 'goods'   b repl. 'to'   c repl. 'and'
d repl. 'were'   e repl. 'they'   f repl. 'park'

---

1. See above, p. 160 & n. 1.   3. See below, p. 221 & n. 2.
2. For the house, see above, vii. 32,   4. See below, pp. 229-30 & n.
n. 2; for the pictures, see above,
p. 175, n. 6.

which he expects about Michaelmas, he will be very well received. But it is pretty strange how he begun again the business of ⟨the intention of⟩ a marriage of my Lord Hinching-brooke to a daughter of my Lord Burlington's to my Lord Chancellor; which he now tells me as a great secret, when he told it me the last Sunday but one. But it may be the poor man hath forgot, and I do believe he doth make it a secret, he telling me that he hath not told it to any but myself, and this day to his daughter my Lady Jemimah – who looks to lie down about two months hence. After all this discourse, we turned back and to White-hall, where we parted; and I took up my wife at Un-thankes and so home; and in our street, at the Three Tuns tavern door, find a great hubbub, and what was [it] but two brothers have fallen out and one killed the other; and who should they be but the two Fieldings, one whereof, Bazill, was page to my Lady Sandwich; and he hath killed the other, himself being very drunk, and so is sent to Newgate.[1] I to the office and did as much business as my eyes would let me, and so home to supper and to bed.

10. Up and to the office, where a meeting about the Victual-lers' accounts all the morning; and at noon all of us to Kent's at the Three Tun tavern and there dined well at Mr. Gawden's charge. There the constable of the parish did show us the pick-locks and dice that were found in the dead man's pockets, and but 18d in money – and a table-book, wherein were entered the names of several places where he was to go; and among others, his house, where he was to dine, and did dine yesterday. And after dinner went into the church, and there seed his Corps with the wound in his left breast; a sad spectacle, and a wide wound, which makes my hand now shake to write of it.[a] His brother entending, it seems, to kill the coachman, who did not please

a The handwriting is however steady at this point. See above, Intro., vol. i, p. c & n. 11.

---

1. It was in fact Christopher Field-ing who had killed his brother Basil: below, p. 321 & n. 3. They were both soldiers (and Irish): *CSPD 1667*, pp. 368, 555. Their father, George Fielding, 17th Earl of Desmond (d. 1666) had fought a duel in 1631: GEC, iv. 258 n. (c).

him, this fellow stepped in and took away his sword; who thereupon took out his knife, which was in[a] the fashion, with a
Falchon blade and a little cross at the hilt like a dagger, and with
that stabbed him.

So to the office again, very busy; and in the evening to Sir
Rob. Viner's, and there took up[b] all my notes and evened our
balance to the 7th of this month, and saw it entered in their
Leiger and took a receipt for the remainder of my money as the
balance of an account then adjusted. Then to my Lord
Treasurer's, but missed Sir Ph. Warwick; and so back again,
and drove hard towards Clerkenwell, thinking to have overtaken
my Lady Newcastle,[1] whom I saw before us in her coach, with
100 boys and girls running looking upon her; but I could not
and so she got home before I could come up to her, but I will
get a time to see her. So to the office and did more business,
and then home and sang with pleasure with my wife, and to
supper and so to bed.

11. Up; and being called on by Mr. Commander,[2] he and I
out to the ground behind Sir W. Penn's, where I am resolved to
take[c] a lease of some of it for a stable and coach, and so to keep a
coach, unless some change come before I can do it; for I do see it
is a greater charge to me now in hackneys and I am a little dis-
honoured by going in them. We spoke with him that hath the
letting it, and I do believe, when I[d] can tell how much it will be
fit for me to have, we shall go near to agree. So home, and
there find my door open, which makes me very angry with Nell
and do think to put her away for it; though it doth so go against
me to part with a servant, that it troubles me more than anything
in the world. So to the office, where all the morning. At noon
home to dinner, where Mr. Goodgroome and Creed, and I have
great hopes that my wife will come to sing to my mind. After
dinner, my wife and Creed and I being entered a hackney-coach

a repl. 'like a'   *b* repl. 'upon'
c repl. 'buy'   *d* repl. 'we'

---

1. Cf. above, p. 197, n. 1.   He had also been employed to draw
2. Henry Commander, scrivener.   up Pepys's will: above, v. 31.

to go to the other end of the town, we espied The Turner coming
in her coach to see us – which we were surprized at; and so light
and took her and another young lady home, and there sat and
talked with The, she being lately come out of the North after
two or three years absence – she is come to put out her sister
and brothers to school at Putny.¹ After a little talk, I over
Tower-hill with them to a lady's they go to visit; and so away
with my wife, whose being dressed this day in fair hair² did
make me so mad, that I spoke not one word to her in our going,
though I was ready to burst with anger. So to White-hall to
the Committee of Tanger, where they were discoursing about
laws for the civil government of that place;³ but so dull and so
little to purpose, that I fell to slumber; which the fear of being
seen by Sir W. Coventry did trouble me much afterwards, but I
hope he did not. After that broke up, Creed and I into the park
and walked, a most pleasant evening; and so took coach and
took up my wife, and in my way home discovered*ᵃ* my trouble
to my wife for her white locks, swearing by God several times
(which I pray God forgive me for) and bending my fist, that I*ᵇ*
would not endure it. She, poor wretch, was surprized with it,
and made me no answer all the way home. But there we parted,
and I to the office late; and then home, and without supper to
bed, vexed.

12. *Lords day.* Up, and to my chamber to settle some
accounts there; and by and by down comes my wife to me in
her nightgown; and we begun calmly, that upon having money
to lace her gown for*ᶜ* second mourning,⁴ she would promise to
wear white locks no more in my sight; which I, like a severe
fool, thinking not enough, begun to except against and made her
fly out to very high terms, and cry; and in her heat told me of

---

a repl. 'disc'–   *b* repl. 'she'   *c* repl. 'she in'

---

1. Theophila Turner's mother, Jane
was a cousin of Pepys. Her father
had property in Kirkleatham, Yorks.
For the schools at Putney, see above,
p. 188, n. 3.

2. Artificial curls or tufts of hair
mounted on wire: cf. above, vii. 346.
3. See above, p. 160, n. 1.
4. Half-mourning; for Pepys's
mother.

keeping company*a* with Mrs. Knipp, saying that if I would promise never to see her more (of whom she hath more reason to
suspect then I had heretofore of Pembleton), she would never
wear white locks more. This vexed me, but I restrained myself
from*b* saying anything; but do think never to see this woman;
at least, to have her here more. But by and by I did give her
money to buy lace, and she promised to wear no more white
locks while I lived; and so all very good friends as ever, and
I to my business and she to dress herself. Against noon we had a
coach ready for us; and she and I to White-hall, where I went
to see whether Sir G. Carteret was at dinner or no, our design
being to make a visit there, and I found them sat down, which
troubled me, for I would not then go up; but back to the coach
to my wife, and she and I homeward again; and in our way
bethought ourselfs*c* of going alone, she and I, to a French house
to dinner, and so enquired out Monsieur Robins my periwig-
maker, who keeps an ordinary, and in an ugly street in Covent-
garden did find him at the door, and so we in; and in a moment
almost have the table covered, and clean glasses, and all in the
French manner, and a mess of potage first and then a couple
of pigeons *a l'esteuvé*, and then a piece of *bœuf-a-la-mode*,[1] all
exceeding well seasoned and to our great liking; at least, it would
have been anywhere else but in this bad street and in a periwig-
maker's house; but to see the pleasant and ready attendance that
we had, and all things so desirous to please and ingenious in the
people, did take me mightily – our dinner cost us 6*s*; and so my
wife and I away and by coach to Islington, it being a fine day,
and thence to Sir G. Whitmore's house,[2] where we light and
walked over the fields to Kingsland and back again, a walk I
think I have not taken these twenty years but puts me in mind
of my boy's time, when I boarded at Kingsland and used to
shoot with my bow and arrows in these fields.[3] A very*d*

a repl. 'me'   *b* repl. 'and'   *c* repl. 'ours'
d followed by smudge and 'very'

---

1. The French served their courses
consecutively. The pigeons were
stewed and the beef casseroled.
2. See above, v. 272, n. 2.
3. Pepys, with his younger brother

Tom, had for a time boarded – possibly for reasons of health – at the
house of his old nurse, Goody Lawrence: Bryant, i. 11–12.

pretty place it is – and little did any of my friends* think I should come to walk in these fields in this condition and state that I am. Then took coach again and home through Shoreditch; and at home my wife finds Barker to have been abroad, and telling her so many lies about it, that she struck her, and the wench said she would not stay with her; so I examined the wench, and found her in so many lies myself, that I was glad to be rid of her, and so resolved of having her go away tomorrow. So my wife and W. Hewer and I to supper, and then he and I to my chamber to begin the draft of the report from this office to the Duke of York in the case of Mr. Carcasse;[1] which I sat up till midnight to do, and then to bed – believing it necessary to have it done and to do it plainly, for it is not to be endured the trouble that this rascall hath put us to, and the disgrace he hath brought on this office.

13. Up; and when ready, to the office (my wife rising to send away Barker according to our resolution last night; and she did do it with more clothes then have cost us 10*l*, and 20*s*. in her purse;*a* which I did for the respect I bear Mr. Falconbridge,[2] otherwise she had not deserved half of it – but I am the more willing to do it to be rid of one that made work and trouble in the house and had not qualities of any honour or pleasure to me or my family; but which is a strange thing, did alway declare to her mistress and others that she had rather be put to drudgery and to wash*b* the house then to live as she did, like a gentlewoman) – and there I and Gibson*c* all the morning, making an end of my report against Carcasse; which I think will do our business – but it is a horrid shame such a rogue should give me and all of us this trouble. This morning came Sir H Cholmly to me for a tally or two, and tells me that he hears that we are by agreement to give the King of France Nova Scotia, which he

---

a followed by closing bracket struck through   b repl. 'n'-
c MS. 'and I Gibson'

---

1. For the case, see above, p. 64,   old Exchequer colleague, who had
n. 1.   The report has not been traced.   recommended her in October 1666.
2. Her previous employer; Pepys's

doth not like, but I do not know the importance of it.[1] Then abroad with my wife to my Lord Treasurer's, and she to her tailor's. I find Sir Ph. Warwicke, who I perceive doth give over my Lord Treasurer for a man of this world, his pain being grown great again upon him and all the rest he hath is by Nicotiques; and now Sir Ph. Warwick doth please himself like a good man, to tell some of the good ejaculacions of my Lord Treasurer concerning the little*a* worth of this world, to buy it with so much pain, and other things fit for a dying man. So finding no business likely to be done here for Tanger, I having a warrant for tallies to be signed, I away to the New Exchange and there stayed a little ⟨and then to a looking-glass shop to consult about covering the wall in my closet over my chimney, which is darkish, with looking-glasses⟩; and then to my wife's tailor's,[2] but find her not ready to go home but got to buy things; and so I away home to look after my business and finish my report of Carcasse; and then did get Sir W. Batten, J. Mennes, and W. Penn together, and read it over with all the many papers relating to the business; which they do wonder at, and the trouble that I have taken about it, and like the report, so as that they do unanimously resolve to sign it and stand by it. And after a great deal of discourse of the strange deportment of my Lord Brouncker in this business, to withstand the whole board in behalf of such an impudent rogue as this is, I parted; and home to my wife and supped and talked with her; and then to bed, resolving to rise betimes tomorrow to write fair the report.

14. Up by 5 a-clock; and when ready, down to my chamber. And there with Mr. Fist, Sir W. Batten's clerk, who writes mighty well, writing over our report in Mr. Carcasse's business, in which we continued till 9 a-clock that the office met; and then to the office, where all the morning; and so at noon home and to dinner, where Mr. Holliard come and eat with us; who among

---

a repl. 'worthlessness'

---

1. By a 'secret' arrangement with France made on 8 April the English were to exchange Acadia (Nova Scotia) for the whole of St Kitt's.

2. Unthanke's.

other things doth give*a* me good hopes that he shall give my
father some ease as to his rupture when he comes to town, which
I expect tomorrow.   After dinner comes Fist, and he and I to
our report again till 4 a-clock; and then by coach to my Lord
Chancellors, where I met Mr. Povy, expecting the coming of the
rest of the Commissioners for Tanger.   Here I understand how
the two Dukes both, the only sons of the Duke of York, are sick
even to danger, and that on Sunday last they were both so ill
as that the*b* poor Duchesse was in doubt which would die first –
the Duke of Cambrige of some general disease; the other little
Duke, whose title I know not, of the convulsion fits, of which
he had four this morning.[1]   Fear that either of them might be
dead did make us think that it was the occasion that the Duke of
York and others were not come to the meeting of the Commission, which was designed and my Lord Chancellor did expect.
And it was pretty to observe how when my Lord sent down
to St. James's to see why the Duke of York came not, and Mr.
Povy, who went, returned, my Lord did ask (not how the
Princes or the Dukes do, as other people do) but "How do the
children?" which methought was mighty great, and like a great
man and grandfather.   I find everybody mightily concerned for
these children, as a matter wherein the State is much concerned
that they should live.   At last it was found that the meeting did
fail from no known occasion; at which my Lord Chancellor was
angry, and did cry out against Creede that he should give him no
notice.   So Povy and I went forth and stayed at the gate of the
house by the street, and there stopped to talk about the business
of the Treasury of Tanger, which, by the badness of our credit and
the resolution that the Governor shall not be pay-maister,*c* will
force me to provide one there to be my pay-maister; which I
will never do, but rather lose my place, for I will not venture my
fortune to a fellow to be imployed so far off and*d* in that wicked

a   repl. 'tell'   *b*   repl. 'they'
c   repl. 'Treasurer'   *d*   repl. 'in'

1. The Duke of Cambridge (born   was the Duke of Kendal, born in
in 1663) died on 20 June 1667 at Rich-   1666; he died on 22 May 1667 at St
mond Palace. 'The other little Duke'   James's Palace.

place.¹ Thence home; and with Fist presently to the finishing the writing fair of our report. And by and by to Sir W. Batten, and there he and I and J. Mennes and W. Penn did read and sign it with great good liking; and so away to the office again to look over and correct it; and then home to supper and to bed – my mind being pretty well settled, having this report done. And so to supper and to bed.

15. 《This morning my wife had some things brought home by a new woman of the ⟨New⟩ Exchange, one Mrs. Smith, which she would have me see for her fine hand; and endeed, it is a fine hand and the woman I have observed is a mighty pretty-looked woman.》 Up, and with Sir W. Batten and J. Mennes to St. James's, and stopped at Temple Barr for Sir J. Mennes to go into the Devil tavern to shit, he having drunk whey and his belly wrought. Being come, we up to the Duke of York's chamber; who when ready, we to our usual business, and being very glad that we all that signed it, that is, Sir J. Mennes, W. Batten, W. Penn and myself, and then Sir G. Carteret and W. Coventry, Brouncker, and T. Harvy, and the officers of the Ordinance, Sir J. Duncombe and Mr. Chichely*ª* – I presented our report about Carcasse to the Duke of York, and did afterwards read it, with that success that the Duke of York was for punishing him, not only with turning him out of the office but what other punishment he could; which nobody did forward, and so he escaped only with giving security to secure the King against double tickets of his, and other things that he might have wronged the King or subject in before his dismission.*ᵇ*² Yet Lord, to see how our silly Lord Brouncker would have stirred to have justified this rogue, though to the reproach of all us that have signed; which I shall never forget to have been a most malicious or a most silly act, and I do think it is as much the latter as the other, for none but a fool could have done as this silly Lord hath done in

a MS. 'Ch.'   *b* repl. 'discom'-

1. Pepys may have been thinking of the malversations of Vernatty, paymaster to Lord Peterborough: see above, vii. 264 & n.2.

2. For this affair, see above, p. 64 & n. 1.

this business. So the Duke of York did like our report, and ordered his being secured till he did give his security; which did fully content me, and will I hope vindicate the office. It happened that my Lord Arlington, coming in by chance, was at the hearing of all this; which I was not sorry for, for he did move ⟨or did second the Duke of York⟩ that this roguery of his might be put in the news-book, that it might be made public, to satisfy for the wrong the credit of this office hath received by this rogue's occasion.[1] So with utmost content, I away with Sir G. Carteret to London, talking all the way; and he doth tell me that the business of my Lord Hinchingbrooke his marriage with my Lord Burlington's daughter is concluded on by all friends; and that my Lady is now told of it, and doth mightily please herself with it – which I am mighty glad of. So home, and there I find my wife hath been at my desire at the Inne, thinking that my father might be come up with the coach; but he is not come this week, poor man – but will be here the next. At noon to dinner and then to Sir W. Batten's, where I hear the news how our Imbassadors were but ill received at Flushing, nor at Bredah itself, there being only[a] a house and no furniture provided for them, though it be said that they[b] have as much as the French. Here we stayed talking a little, and then I to the office about my business; and thence to the office, where busy about my own papers of my office; and by and by comes the office full to examine Sir W. Warren's account, which I do appear mighty fierce in against him; and endeed am, for his accounts are so perplexed that I am sure he cannot but expect to get many a 1000*l* in it before it passes our hands – but I will not favour him,[2] but save what I can to the King. At his account, wherein I very high against him, till late, and then we broke up with little done; and so broke up, and I to my office, where late doing of business, and then home to supper and to bed. News still that my Lord Treasurer is so ill as not to be any man of this world; and it is said that the Treasury shall be managed by commission. I

---

a repl. 'never'   *b* repl. 'he'

---

1. No notice appeared in the *London Gazette*.

2. Cf. above, p. 31 & n. 3.

would to God Sir G. Carteret or my Lord Sandwich be in it –
but the latter is the more fit for it.[1] This day, going to White-
hall, Sir[a] W. Batten did tell me strange stories of Sir W. Penn:
how[b] he is already ashamed of that fine[c] coach which his son-in-
law and daughter have made; and endeed, it is one of the most
ridiculous things for people of their low, mean fashion to make
such a coach that ever I saw.[2] He tells me how his people comes,
as they do to mine every day, to borrow one thing or other;
and that his Lady hath been forced to sell some coals (in the late
dear time) only to enable her to pay money that she hath
borrowed of Griffin to defray her family expense – which is a
strange story for a rogue that spends so much money on clothes
and other occasions himself as he doth. But that which is most
strange, he tells me that Sir W. Penn doth not give 6000*l*, as is[d]
usually [supposed], with his daughter to him; and that Mr.
Lowder is come to use the Tubb; that is, to bathe and sweat
himself, and that his lady is come to use the Tubb too; which he
takes to be that he hath and hath given her the pox,[3] but I hope
it is not so – "but," says Sir W. Batten, "this is a fair Joynture
that he hath made her;" meaning by that, the costs [of] the
having of a Bath.

16. Up and to the office, where we sat all the morning; and
among other things, comes in Mr. Carcasse and, after many
arguings against it, did offer security as was desired; but who
should this be but Mr. Powell, that is one other of my Lord
Brouncker's clerks; and I hope good use will be made of it.
But then he begin to fall foul upon the injustice of the Board;
which when I heard, I threatened him with being laid by the
heels; which my Lord Brouncker took up as a thing that I could
not do upon the occasion he had given, but yet did own that it
was ill said of him. I made not many words of it, but have let
him see that I can say what I will without fear of him; and so we
broke off, leaving the bond to be drawn by me; which I will do

---

a blotted *b* repl. 'is' *c* repl. 'fine' *d* repl. 'he'

1. A commission was appointed
but neither Carteret nor Sandwich
was included: below, pp. 229–30 &
nn.

2. Cf. above, p. 196.
3. Sweating was a common treatment for syphilis.

in the best manner I can. At noon, this being Holy Thursday, that is, Ascension-day when the boys go on procession round the parish, we were to go to the Three Tuns tavern to dine*ᵃ* with the rest of the parish;¹ where*ᵇ* all the parish almost was, Sir Andrew Rickard and others; and of our house, J. Mennes, W. Batten, W. Penn and myself – and Mr. Mills² did sit uppermost at the table. Here we were informed that the report of our Imbassadors being ill received*ᶜ* in their way to Bredah is not true, but that they are received with very great civility – which I am glad to hear.

But that that did vex me was that among all us there should come in Mr. Carcasse, to be a guest for his money (5s a-piece) as well as any of us. This did vex me, and I would have gone and did go to my house, thinking to dine at home; but I was called away from them, and so we sat down and to dinner. Among other things, Sir Jo. Fredricke and Sir R. Ford did talk of Paul's school, which they tell me must be taken away; and then I fear it will be long before another place, as they say is promised, is found; but they do say that the honour of their company is concerned in the doing of it, and that it is a thing that they are obliged to do.³ Thence home and to my office, where busy; and anon, at 7 at night, I and my wife and Sir W. Penn in his coach to Unthanke's, my wife's tailor's, for her to speak one word; and then we to my Lord Treasurer's, where I find the porter crying, and suspected it was that my Lord is dead; and, poor Lord, we did find that he was dead just now; and the crying of that fellow did so trouble me, that considering that I was not likely to trouble him any more, nor have occasion to give any more anything, I did give him 3s; but it may be, poor man, he hath lost a considerable hope by the death of this Lord, whose

---

a repl. 'dined'   *b* MS. 'which'   *c* repl. 'res'-

---

1. It was customary to hold a parish dinner on Ascension Day: cf. below, 30 April 1668.

2. Daniel Milles, Rector of St Olave's.

3. The Mercers' Company had been trustees of the school since its foundation. The school was not in fact moved from its old site on the e. side of St Paul's Churchyard until 1884. The original building destroyed in the Great Fire was replaced in 1670 'after the same manner and Proportion it was before': Stow, *Survey* (ed. Strype), i. 167.

house will be no more frequented as before – and perhaps I may never come thither again about any business. There is a good man gone; and I pray God that*ᵃ* the Treasury may not be worse managed by the hand or hands it shall now be put into; though, for certain, the slowness (though he was of great integrity) of this man, and remissness, have gone as far to undo the nation as anything else that hath happened;¹ and yet if I knew all the difficulties that he hath lain under, and his instrument Sir Ph. Warwick, I might be brought to another mind. Thence, we to Islington to the old house² and there eat and drank; and then, it being late and a pleasant evening, we home; and there to my chamber and to bed. It is remarkable that this afternoon Mr. Moore came to me and there, among other things, did tell me how Mr. Moyer the Merchant, having procured an*ᵇ* order from the King and Duke of York and Council, with the consent*ᶜ* of Lord Chancellor and by assistance of Lord Arlington, for the releasing out of prison his brother, Samuell Moyer, who was a great man in the late times in Haberdasher's-hall, and was engaged under hand and seal to give the man that obtained it so much in behalf of my Lord Chancellor;³ but it seems my Lady Duchesse of Albemarle had before undertaken it for so much money, but hath not done it – the Duke of Albemarle did the next*ᵈ* day send for this Moyer, to tell him that notwithstanding this order of the King and Council's being passed for release of his brother, yet if he did not consider the pains of some friends of his, he would*ᵉ* stop that order; this Moyer, being an honest, bold man, told him that he was engaged to the hand that had done the thing to give

---

a repl. 'though' b repl. 'by' c repl. 'cons of'
d repl. 'other' e repl. 'he'

---

1. Cf. the similar opinions of Clarendon (*Life*, iii. 234) and Burnet (i. 170–1). Southampton had left most business to his secretary Sir Philip Warwick. For his integrity, see below, p. 222 & n. 2.
2. The King's Head: cf. above, ii. 125, n. 2.
3. Samuel Moyer had been one of the leading London republicans, and under the Commonwealth had been

chairman of the committee which met at Haberdashers' Hall to deal with the composition and sequestration of delinquents' estates. He had been imprisoned since 1661. His brother Laurence, the merchant, now secured an order for his release from Tynemouth Castle (10 May; *CSPD 1667*, p. 139), at the cost, it was said, of £500 (below, p. 325).

him a reward; and more he would not give, nor could own any kindness done by his Grace's interest – and so parted. The next day, Sir Edw. Savage¹ did take the said Moyer in tax about it, giving ill words of this Moyer and his brother; which he not being able to bear, told him he would give to the person that had engaged him what he promised, and not anything to anybody else; and that both he and [his] brother were as honest men as himself or any man else; and so sent*ᵃ* him going and bid him do his worst. It is one of the most extraordinary cases that ever I saw or understood; but it is true.

This day Mr. Sheply is come to town and to see me; and he tells me my father is very well, only for this pain; so that he is not able to stir, but is in great pain; I would to God he were in town, that I might have what help can be got for him – for it troubles me to have him live in that condition of misery if I can help it.

17. Up and to the office, where all the morning upon some accounts of Mr. Gawden's; and at noon to the Three Tuns to dinner with Brouncker, J. Mennes, W. Batten, W. Penn and T. Harvy; where very merry, and my Lord Brouncker in appearance as good friends as ever – though I know he hath a hatred to me in heart. After dinner to my house, where Mr. Sheply dined and we drank and talked together. He, poor man, hath had his arm broke the last frost, slipping in going over Huntington bridge. He tells me that Jesper Trice and Lewis Phillips and Mr. Ashfield are gone from Brampton, and he thinks chiefly from the heighth of Sir Jo. Bernard's carriage, who carries all things before him there, which they cannot bear with and so leave the town; and this is a great instance of the advantage a man of the law hath over all other people, which would make a man to study it a little.² Sheply being gone, there came the Flagilette-

---

a   repl. 'put'

---

1. Gentleman of the Privy Chamber to the King.
2. Bernard was a serjeant-at-law and the Recorder of Huntingdon. He had become a baronet in 1666, and in Brampton owned one manor and was steward of another. He was an M.P. for the county and took a leading part in county politics. Jasper Trice and Lewis Phillips were lawyers too (but not so grand); Sutton Ashfield a landowner.

maister;[1] who having had a bad bargain of teaching my wife by the year, she not practising so much as she should do, I did think the man did deserve some more consideration, and so will give him a opportunity of 20*s* a month more and he shall teach me; and this afternoon I begin, and I think it will be a few shillings well spent. Then to Sir[a] R. Viner's with 600 pieces of gold to turn into silver, for the enabling me to answer Sir G. Carteret's 3000*l*, which he now draws all out of my hand towards[b] the paying for a purchase he hath made for his son and my Lady Jemimah in Northamptonshire of Sir Samuell Luke; in a good place, a good house, and near all her friends – which is a very happy thing.[2] Thence to St. James's, and there spoke with Sir W. Coventry and give him some account of some things; but had little discourse with him, there being company with him, and so directly home again and there to my office, being some business; and so to my house, and with my wife to practice on the flagelette a little, and with great pleasure I see she can readily hit her notes; but only want of practice makes her she cannot[c] go through a whole tune readily. So to supper and to bed.

18. Up and all the morning at the office, and then to dinner; and after dinner to the office to dictate some letters, and then with my wife down to Sir W Turner's to visit The; but she being abroad, we back again home; and then I to the office, finished my letters, and then to walk an hour in the garden talking with my wife, whose growth in music doth begin to please me mightily; and by and by home and there find our Luce drunk, and when her mistress told her of it, would be gone; and so put up some of her things and did go away of her accord, nobody pressing her to it; and the truth is, though she be the dirtiest and homeliest[d] servant that ever I kept, yet I was sorry to have

a repl. 'the office and'   *b* repl. 'for the p'-
c repl. 'doth not'   *d* repl. 'and'

---

1. Thomas Greeting. (E).
2. The manor of Hawnes or Haynes (in Bedfordshire not Northamptonshire) was conveyed at this time by Sir

Samuel Luke and his son Oliver to William Mountagu and Sir Thomas Crew, presumably trustees for Carteret: VCH, *Beds.*, ii. 340-1.

her go, partly through my love to my servants and partly because she was a very drudging, working wench; only, she would be drunk.   But that which did a little trouble me was that I did hear her tell her mistress that she would tell her maister something, before she was aware of her, that she would be sorry to have him know;   but did it in such a silly, drunken manner, that though it trouble me a little, yet not knowing what to suspect she should know, and not knowing well whether she said it to her mistress or Jane, I did not much think of it.   So she gone, we to supper and to bed – my study being made finely clean.

19.   *Lords day.*   Up, and to my chamber to set some papers in order;   and then to church, where my old acquaintance, that dull fellow Meriton,[1] made a good sermon;   and hath a strange knack of a grave, serious delivery, which is very agreeable. After*ᵃ* church, to White-hall and there find Sir G. Carteret just sat down to dinner;   and I dined with them as I entended, and good company, the best people and family in the world I think. Here was great talk of the good end that my Lord Treasurer made;   closing his own eyes and setting his mouth, and bidding Adieu with the greatest content and freedom in the world;   and is said to die with the cleanest hands that ever any Lord Treasurer did.[2]   After dinner,*ᵇ* Sir G. Carteret and I alone;   and there among other discourse, he did declare that he would be content to part with his place of Treasurer of the Navy upon good terms.[3] I did propose my Lord Bellasses as a man likely to buy it;   which he listened to, and I did fully concur and promote his design of parting with it, for though I would have my father live, I would not have him die Treasurer of the Navy, because of the accounts which must be uncleared at his death;   besides many other circumstances making it advisable for him to let it*ᶜ* go –

a repl. 'Home'   *b* repl. 'din'-   *c* repl. 'him go'

---

1. Probably Thomas Meriton, Rector of St Nicholas Cole Abbey, London; a Magdalene acquaintance: see above, vii. 365 & n. 3.

2. He had insisted on taking a fixed salary of £8,000 p.a. instead of fees, and had given the King the disposal of all subordinate offices: Burnet, i. 171; cf. S. B. Baxter, *Devel. Treasury, 1660–1702*, pp. 9–10.

3. See below, p. 295 & n. 3.

he tells me that he fears all will come to naught in the nation soon, if the King doth not mind his business, which he doth not seem likely to do. He says that the Treasury will be managed for a while by a commission, whereof he thinks my Lord Chancellor, for the honour of it, and my Lord Ashly and the two Secretaries will be [members], and some others he knows not.[1]

I took leave of him, and directly by water home; and there to read the Life of Mr. Hooker,[2] which pleases me as much as anything I have read a great while; and by and by comes Mr. How to see us, and after him a little, Mr. Sheply, and so we all to talk; and Mercer being there, we some of us to sing and so to supper; a great deal of silly talk; among other things, W. How told us how the barristers and students of[a] Grays Inne rose in rebellion against the Benchers the other day; who outlawed them, and a great deal of do but now they are at peace again.[3]

They being gone, I to my book again and made an end of Mr. Hooker's Life, and so to bed.

20. Up betimes; and comes my Flagelette man and set me a new tune, which I played presently and shall in a month[b] do as much as I desire at it. He being [gone], I to several businesses in my chamber; and then by coach to the Commissioners of Excise, and so to Westminster-hall and there spoke with several persons I had to do with. Here, among other news, I hear that the Commissioners[c] for the Treasury were named by the King yesterday, but who they are nobody could tell; but the persons are[d] the Lord Chancellor, the two Secretaries, Lord Ashly, and others say Sir W. Coventry and Sir Jo. Duncomb, but all conclude the Duke of Albemarle; but report doth differ – but will be

a repl. 'were rose in'   b repl. 'month'
c repl. 'Com'-   d repl. 'are'

---

1. See below, pp. 229-30 & nn.
2. The life (by Isaak Walton) included in the recent edition of Richard Hooker's *Works* which Pepys had bought on 15 April. It had also been published separately (in a slightly fuller form) in 1665.
3. This and similar disturbances in this period are signs of the breakdown of the old disciplines of the inns of court which had been based on the system of readings: see *Pension Bk of Gray's Inn, 1569-1669* (ed, R. J. Fletcher), p. xliv; F. Cowper, *Prospect of Gray's Inn*, pp. 72+.

known in a day or two.¹ Having done my business, I then homeward and overtook Mr. Comander;² so took him into a coach with me, and he and I into Lincoln's Inne Fields, there to look upon the coach-houses to see what ground is necessary for coach-house and horses, because of that that I am going about to do; and having satisfied myself in this, he and I home and he dined with me all alone, my wife being unfit to be seen: and so after dinner, he and I to Mr. Hides to look upon the ground again behind our house, and concluded upon his going along with us tomorrow to see some stables, he thinking that we demand more room then is necessary. So away home; and then I, it being a broken day and had power by my vows,³ did walk abroad; first through the Minorys (the first time I have been over the Hill⁴ to the postern-gate and seen that place since the houses were pulled down about that side of the Tower since the fire) to find where my young Mercer with my pretty little woman to his wife lives, who lived in Lumbard-street – and I did espy them, but took no notice now of them but may do hereafter.⁵ Thence down to the Old Swan and there saw Betty Michell, whom I have not seen since her christening. But Lord, how pretty she is, and looks so well as ever I saw her; and her child (which I am fain to seem very fond of) is pretty also I think, and will be. Thence by water to Westminster-hall and there walked a while, talking at random with Sir Wm. Doyly; and so away to Mrs. Martin's lodging, who was gone before expecting me; and there yo haze what yo vellem cum her, and drank; and so by coach home (but I have forgot that I did in the morning go to the Swan; and there tumbling of la little fille,⁶ son uncle did trouver her cum su neckcloth off, which I was ashamed of, but made no great matter of it but let*a* it pass with a laugh) and there spent the evening with my wife at our Flagelettes; and so to supper, and after a little

---

a repl. 'it'

---

1. See below, p. 229 for the correct list. The warrant for the issue of the letters patent of appointment was issued on the 22nd; the patent itself on the 24th: *CSPD 1667*, p. 115; *CTB*, ii. 1.

2. Henry Commander, scrivener.

3. See above, pp. 171-2.

4. Tower Hill. (R).

5. See below, 2 June 1668. Their name was Finch.

6. Frances ('Frank') Udall, of the Swan in New Palace Yard. Her uncle was the landlord, William Herbert.

reading, to bed.   My wife still troubled with her cold.   I find it everywhere now to*ᵃ* be a thing doubted whether we shall have peace or no; and the captain of one of our ships that went with the Embassadors doth say that the seamen of Holland, to his hearing, did defy us, and called us English dogs and cried out against peace; and that the great people there do oppose peace, though he says the common people do wish it.

21.   Up and to the office, where sat all the morning.   At noon dined at home with my wife, and find a new girle, a good big girl, come to us, got by Payne to be our girl; and his daughter Nell we make our cook.   This wench's name is Mary – and seems a good likely maid.[1]   After dinner, I with Mr. Comander and Mr. Hide's brother to Lincoln's Inne Fields, and there viewed several coach-houses and satisfied ourselfs now fully in it.   And then there parted, leaving the rest to future discourse between us. Thence, I home; but Lord, how it went against my heart to go away from the very door of the Duke's playhouse, and my Lady Castlemayns coach and many great coaches there to see *The Siege of Rhodes*;[2] I was very near making a forfeit,[3] but I did command myself; and so home to my office and there did much business to my good content, much better then going to a play; and then home to my wife, who is not well with her cold, and sat and read [a] piece of *Grand Cyrus*[4] in English by her; and then to my chamber and to supper, and so to bed.   This morning, the Captain come from Holland did tell us at the board what I have said he reported yesterday.

This evening, after I came from the office, Mrs. Turner came to see my wife and me and sit and talk with us; and so my wife not being well and going to bed, Mrs. Turner and I sat up till 12 at night talking alone in my chamber, and most of our discourse was of our neighbours.[5]   As to*ᵇ* my Lord Brouncker, she

a repl. 'it'   *b* repl. 'he'

---

1. She stayed until 10 July.   Payne, who introduced her, was a waterman.
2. See above, ii. 130, n. 2.   (A).
3. He had vowed not to visit theatres until Whitsuntide: see above, p. 173.   (A).
4. See above, i. 312, n. 2.

5. Thomas Turner (Clerk-General to the Navy Office) and his wife had until recently lived next door to Pepys in the house now occupied by Brouncker and his mistress, Abigail Williams.

says how Mrs. Griffin, our housekeeper's wife, hath it from his maid, that comes to her house often, that they are very poor; that the other day Mrs. Williams was fain to send a jewell to pawn. That their maid hath said herself that she hath got 50*l* since she came thither, and 17*l* by the payment of one bill.[1] That they have a most lewd and nasty family here in the office; but Mrs. Turner doth tell me that my Lord hath put the King to infinite charge since his coming thither, in alterations; and perticularly, that Mr. Harper at Deptford did himself tell her that my Lord hath had of Foly the ironmonger*a* 50*l*-worth in locks and keys for his house, and that it is from the fineness of them, having some of 4 and 5*l* a lock, such as is in ladies*b* closets; that he hath several of these. That he doth keep many of her things from her of her own goods, and would have her bring a bill into the office for them. That Mrs. Griffin doth say that he doth not keep Mrs. Williams now for love, but need, he having another whore that he keeps in Covent-garden. That they do owe money everywhere, almost for everything; even Mrs. Shipman for her butter and cheese about 3*l*, and after many demands cannot get it. Mrs. Turner says she doth believe that their coming hither is only out of a belief of getting purchase*c** by it, and that their servants (which was wittily said of her touching his clerks) do act only as privateers: no purchase, no pay. And in my conscience, she is in the right.

Then we fall to talk of Sir W. Penn and his family and rise. She says that he was a pitiful [fellow] when she first knew them. That his lady was one of the sorriest, dirty women that ever she saw. That they took two chambers, one over another, for themselfs and child in Tower-hill. That for many years together they eat more meals at her house then at their own. Did call brothers and sisters the husbands and wifes. That her husband was god-father to one, and she godmother to another (this Margaret) of their children; by the same token, that she was fain to write with her own hand a letter to Captain Twiddy to stand for a

---

a repl. 'smith'   *b* repl. 'but'   *c* repl. 'p'-

---

1. Cf. above, p. 75.

godfather for her.[1] That she brought my Lady (who then was a dirty slattern, with her stockings hanging about her heels, so that afterward the people of the whole Hill did say that Mrs. Turner had made Mrs. Pen a gentlewoman) first to the knowledge of my Lady Vane (Sir Henry's lady),[2] and him to the knowledge of most of the great people that then he sought to; and that in short, his rise hath been his giving of large Bribes, wherein (and she agrees with my opinion and knowledge before therein) he is very profuse. This made him General; this got him out of the Tower when he was in;[3] and hath brought him into what he is now since the King's coming in. That long ago endeed, he would drink the King's health privately with Mr. Turner; but that when he saw it fit to turn Roundhead, and was offered by Mr. Turner to drink the King's health, he answered no, he was changed, and now he that would make him drink the King's health, or any health but the Protectors and the State's (or to that purpose), he would be the first man should sheath his sword in his guts. That at the King's coming in, he did send for her husband and told him what a great man Sir W. Coventry was like to be; and that he having all the records in his hands of the Navy, if he would transcribe what was of most present use of the practice of the Navy, and give them him to give Sir W. Coventry from him, it would undoubtedly do his business of getting him a Principal Officer's place. That her husband was at 5*l* charge to get these presently writ. That Sir W. Penn*a* did give them W. Coventry as from himself, which did set him up with W. Coventry and made him what he is, and never owned anything of Mr. Turner in them; by which he left him in the lurch, though he did promise the Duke of Albemarle to do all that was possible, and made no question of Mr.*b* Turner's being what he

a MS. 'Coventry'   *b* repl. 'Mr.'

---

1. This was in 1652. Capt. Roger Tweedy had been a parliamentary navy commissioner during the Civil War.

2. Sir Henry Vane, jun., Joint-Treasurer of the Navy and Admiralty Commissioner during the Revolution.

3. Penn, made General and Commander-in-Chief of the W. Indies expedition in 1654–5, was imprisoned in the Tower on his return: cf. above, iv. 376 & n. 2.

desired.¹ And when afterward, too, did propose to him the getting of the Pourveyors place for him, he did tell Mr. Turner it was necessary to present Sir W. Coventry 100 pieces, which he did, and W. Coventry took 80 of them – so that he was W. Coventry's mere broker, as Sir W. Batten and my Lady did once tell my Lady Duchess of Albemarle*ᵃ* in the case of Mr. Falconer, whom W. Penn made to give W. Coventry 200*l* for his place of Clerk of the ropeyard of Woolwich, and to settle 80*l* a year upon his daughter Peg after the death of his wife, and a*ᵇ* gold watch presently to his wife.² Mrs. Turner doth tell me that my Lady and Peg have themselfs owned to her that Sir W. Coventry and W. Penn*ᶜ* had private marks to write to one another by; that when they in appearance writ a fair letter in behalf of anybody, that they had a little mark to show that meant it only in show – this, these silly people did confess themselfs of him.³ She says that their son, Mr.*ᵈ* William Pen, did tell her that his father did observe the commanders did make their addresses to me, and applications, but they should know that his father should be the chief of the office. And that she hath observed that W. Penn never had a kindness to her son⁴ since W. Penn told her son that he had applied himself to me. That his rise hath been her and her husband's means, and that it is a most unconceivable thing how this man can have the face to use her and her family with the neglect that he doth them. That he was the last war⁵ a most devilish plunderer, and that got

a repl. 'Newc'-   *b* repl. 'did give
c repl. 'her'   *d* repl. 'Jacke'

---

1. Turner had hoped to become, with Albemarle's help, Clerk of the Acts. Instead he had been given a senior clerkship and the place of Petty Purveyor. Cf. above, vii. 31 & n. 1.

2. Pepys gives Falconer's wife's version of the same transaction at 3 August 1664; Coventry's *douceur* is there said to have been £150.

3. Their close association persisted. Penn in his will (1670) made Coventry arbitrator in any differences over his estate that might arise between his widow and his elder son and executor, William: PCC, Penn, 130.

4. Frank, the naval officer; see e.g. above, p. 150.

5. The First Dutch War, 1652–4.

him his estate which he hath in Ireland,[1] and nothing else; and that he hath always been a very liberal man in his bribes. That upon his coming into this part of the Controller's business wherein he is, he did send for T. Willson[2] and told him how against his knowledge he was put in, and had so little wit as to say to him, "This will make the pot boyle, will it not, Mr. Willson? will it not make the pot boil?" and doth offer him to come in and do his business for him, and he would reward him. This, Mr. Willson did come and tell her presently, he having been their servant and to this day is very faithful to them. That her husband's not being forward to make him a bill for Rere-admirall's pay and Generalls pay, both at the same time, after he was first made Generall,[3] did first give him occasion of keeping*a* a distance from him; since which they have never been great friends, Pen having by degrees been continually growing higher and higher, till now that he doth wholly slight them and use them only as servants. Upon the whole, she told me stories enough to confirm me that he is the most false fellow that ever was born of woman, and that so she thinks and knows him to be.

22. Up and by water to White-hall to Sir G. Carteret, who tells me now for certain how the Commission for the Treasury is disposed of: *viz.*, to Duke of Albemarle, Lord Ashly, Sir W. Coventry, Sir Jo. Duncum, and Sir Tho. Clifford; at which he says all the whole Court is disturbed, it having been once concluded otherwise, into the other hands formerly mentioned in yesterday's notes;[4] but all of a sudden the King's choice was changed, and these*b* are to be the men; the first of which is only for

---

a repl. 'making'   *b* repl. 'a'

---

1. For his Irish estate, see above, ii. 143 & n. 2; ib., p. 200 & n. 1.
2. Clerk to Batten the Surveyor.
3. In the W. Indian expedition of 1654–5.
4. The entry for 20 May, written on the 21st. Pepys had expected the Chancellor and both Secretaries to be on the commission, precedent being strongly in favour of the appointment of Privy Councillors and high dignitaries. Secretary Williamson, in his Journal (20 May), wrote that membership was 'much different from the forward judgements of the Towne': PRO, SP 29/231, p. 22.

a puppet to give honour to the rest.[1]   He doth presage that these men will make it their business to find faults in the management of the late Lord Treasurer and in discouraging the banquiers; but I am (whatever I in compliance do say to him) of another mind, and my heart is very glad of it; for I do expect they will do much good, and that it is the happiest thing that hath[a] appeared to me for the good of the nation since the King came in.   Thence to St. James's and up to the Duke of York; and there in his chamber Sir W. Coventry did of himself take notice of this business of the Treasury, wherein he is in the Commission, and desired that I would be thinking of anything fit for him to be acquainted with for the lessening of charge and bettering of our credit; and what our expense hath been since the King's coming home, which he believes will be one of the first things they shall enquire into – which I promised him; and from time to time, which he desires, give him an account of what I can think of worthy his knowledge.   I am mighty glad of this opportunity of professing my joy to him in what choices the King hath made, and the hopes I have that it will save the kingdom from perishing, and how it doth encourage me to take pains again, after my having through despair neglected it: which he told me of himself that it was so with him; that he had given himself up to more ease then ever he expected; and that his opinion of matters was so bad, that there was no public imployment in the kingdom should have been accepted by him but this which the King hath now given him; and therein he is glad, in hopes of the service he may do therein – and in my conscience he will.   So into the Duke of York's closet; and there, among other things, Sir W. Coventry did take notice of what he told me the other day, about a report of Comissioner Pett's dealing for timber in the

a   repl. 'hath'

---

1. Arlington, writing to Ormond (22 May), remarked that the fact that members were of 'a lower station than formerly . . . gives occasion of much discourse', but that they were 'not . . . unfitting instruments to ratify the disorders of the Exchequer': Bodl., Carte 46, f. 478v.   The King said he wanted 'rougher hands', 'ill-natured men, not to be moved with civilities': qu. H. Roseveare, Treasury, p. 58. Clarendon (Life, iii. 240+) regretted their lack of 'lustre', but Williamson (op. cit., p. 20) was pleased because all, except Albemarle, were expert administrators.

Navy and selling it*ᵃ* to us in other names;[1] and besides his own proof, did produce a paper I had given him this morning about it, in the case of Widow Murford and Morecocke – which was so handled, that the Duke of York grew very angry, and commanded us presently to fall into the examination of it, saying that he would [not] trust a man for*ᵇ* his sake that lifts up the whites of his eyes.   And it was declared that if he be found to have done so, he should be reckoned unfit to serve the Navy.   And I do believe he will be turned out; and it was methought a worthy saying of W. Coventry to the Duke of York – "Sir," says he, "I do not make this complaint out of any disrespect to Comissioner Pett, but because I do love to do these things fairly and openly."

Thence I to Westminster-hall with Sir G. Carteret to the Chequer-chamber to hear our cause of the *Lindeboome* prize, there before the Lords of Appeal[2] – where was Lord Ashly, Arlington, Barkely, and Sir G. Carteret; but the latter three signified nothing, the former only either minding or understanding what was said.   Here was good pleading of Sir Walt. Walker's, and worthy hearing – but little done in our business. Thence by coach to the Red lyon, thinking to meet my father, but I came too soon; but my wife is gone out of town to meet him.   I am in great pain, poor man, for him, lest he should come up in pain to town.   So I stayed not; but to the Change and there stayed a little, where most of the news is that the*ᶜ* Swedes are likely to fall out with the Dutch; which we wish, but how true I know not.[3]   Here I met my Uncle Wight, the second day

a repl. 'them'   *b* repl. 'that'   *c* repl. 'm'-

---

1. See above, p. 206. Pett replied to these charges on 24 May, alleging, *inter alia*, that 'Murford and Moorcock went two-thirds in Newhall [i.e. Albemarle's] timber': *CSPD 1667*, pp. 116–17. The charges were soon lost sight of in the larger disgrace of the Medway disaster, for which Pett became a scapegoat. Murford referred to his share of the bargain in

his will (June 1666): PCC, Mico, 101.

2. For this case, see above, p. 130 & n. 2. The Lords of Appeal were special commissioners appointed by the Crown under a statute of 1534.

3. See above, vii. 92 & n. 3 for a similar (and similarly untrue) rumour. The Dutch were to make a treaty with Sweden on 18/28 July.

he hath been abroad, having been sick these two months even to death; but having never sent to me even in the greatest of his danger, I do think my aunt had no mind I should come, and so I never went to see him; but neither he took notice of it to me, nor I made any excuse for it to him; but passed two or three "How do you's" and so parted. And so home; and by and by comes my poor father, much better then I expected, being at ease by fits, according as his truss sits, and another time in as much pain. I am mighty glad to see him come well to town. So to dinner, where Creed comes. After dinner, my wife and father abroad; and Creed and I also by water, and parted at the Temple stairs; where I landed and to the King's house, where I did give 18*d* and saw the two last acts of *The Goblins*,[1] a play I could not make anything of by those two acts; but here Knipp spied me out of the tiring-room and came to*ᵃ* the pit door: and I out to her and kissed her, she only coming to see me, being in a country-dress, she and others having it seemed had a country-dance in the play, but she no other part; so we parted, and I into the pit again till it was done. The house full, but I had no mind to be seen; but thence to my cutler's and two or three other places on small errands; and so home, where my father and wife come home; and pretty well, my father, who to supper and betimes to bed at his country hours. I to Sir W. Batten's and there got some more part of my dividend of the prize-money. So home to set*ᵇ* down in writing the state of that account;[2] and then to supper and my wife to her flagelette; wherein she did take out a tune so prettily of herself, that I was infinitely pleased, beyond whatever I expected from her; and so to bed.

This day, coming from Westminster with W. Batten, we saw at White-hall-stairs a fisher-boat with a Sturgeon that he had newly ketched in the River; which I saw, but it was but a little

---

a repl. 'into'   *b* repl. 'my'

---

1. A comedy by Suckling: see above, p. 27, n. 4. 18*d*. was the customary price of admission to the middle gallery, but on this occasion Pepys paid that amount to see the last two acts from a seat in the pit, where the price of a seat for a complete performance was 2*s*. 6*d*. (A).

2. Untraced: concerning prize taken by the *Flying Greyhound*.

one – but big enough to prevent my mistake of that for a colt, if ever I become Mayor of Huntington.¹

23. Up and to the office, where we sat all the morning. At noon home and with my father dined; and poor man, he hath put off his travelling-clothes today and is mighty spruce, and I love to see him cheerful. After dinner, I to my chamber and my wife and father to talk; and by and by they tell Mrs. Daniel would speak with me, so I down to the parlour to her and sat down together and talked about getting her husband a place; and here I did adventure etsi the porta etait operta para put my mano abajo su jupes two or three temps et touch her cosa con great pleasure, ella resisting pretty much, sed never the minus submitted. I do promise, and mean to do what kindness I can to her husband;² and after having been there hasta yo was ashamed, de peur that my people pensaient to pragma de it, or lest they might espy nous through some trees, we parted, and I to the office and presently back home again, and there was asked by my wife, I know not whether simply or with design, how I came to look as I did, car yo was in much calor et de body and of animi; which I put off with the heat of the season, and so to other business, but I had some fear hung upon me lest algo had sido decouvert. So to the office, and then to Sir R Viner's about some part of my accounts now going on with him; and then home and ended my letters; and then to supper and my chamber to settle many things there, and then to bed.

This noon I was on the Change, where I to my astonishment hear, and it is in the gazette, that Sir Jo. Duncum is sworn yester-

---

1. The Huntingdon town authorities were alleged to have seized a drowned colt from the floods in 1624 under the impression it was a sturgeon: see R. C., *Hist. Hunt.* (1824), n.p.; cf. *Huntington Divertisement* (1678), p. 18. It soon became a well-known joke against this town: cf. *Poems of John Cleveland* (ed. Morris and Withington), p. 33; *Harl. Misc.* (1808-13), v. 424; John Philips, *Montelion 1660* (1661), sig. A7.

Pepys later (c. 1685) makes a cryptic reference to the incident in *Naval Minutes*, p. 237. Possibly the Mayor claimed all royal fish taken above the bridge in the same way as the Lord Mayor of London claimed all taken above London bridge.
2. Appointments to the summer fleet were now due; Samuel Daniel(s) appears to have been a lieutenant in the *Royal Charles* in 1666.

day a privy-councillor.[1] This day I hear also that last night the Duke of Kendall, second son of the Duke of York, did die; and that the other[a], Duke of Cambrige, continues very ill still.[2]

This afternoon I had opportunity para jouer with Mrs. Pen,[3] tocando her mamelles and besando ella – being sola in the casa of her pater – and she fort willing.

24. Up and to the office, where by and by, by appointment we met upon Sir W. Warren's accounts;[b] wherein I do appear in everything as much as I can his enemy, though not so far but upon good conditions from him I may return to be his friend[4] – but I do think it necessary to do what I do at present. We broke off at noon without doing much; and then home, where my wife not well; but yet, engaged by invitation to go with Sir W. Penn, I got her to go with him by coach to Islington to the old house,[5] where his lady and Madam Lowder[6] (with her exceeding fine coach and mean horses) and her mother-in-law[7] did meet us and two of Mr. Lowther's brothers; and here dined upon nothing but pigeon pyes – which was such a thing for him to invite all that company to, that I was ashamed of it; but after dinner was all our sport, when there came in a Jugler, who enedeed did show us so good tricks as I have never seen in my life, I think; of Legerdemaine, and such as my wife hath since seriously said that she would not believe but that he did them by the help of the devil. Here, after a bad dinner and but ordinary company (saving that I discern good parts in one of the sons, who me-thought did take me up very prettily in one or two things that I said, and I was so sensible of it as to be a caution to me hereafter

a repl. 'little'   *b* repl. 'accounts'

---

1. *London Gazette*, 23 May. Dun-combe's rise, from a post in the Ord-nance, had been rapid. In Marvell's words: 'Powder ne'er blew man up so soon so high' (*Last Instructions*, l. 796.) Clarendon (*Life*, iii. 244-5) wrongly states that he was a mere private gentleman at the time of his appointment to the Treasury com-mission.

2. See above, p. 214, n. 1.
3. Peg Penn, recently married to Anthony Lowther.
4. For their estrangement, see above, p. 31 & n. 3.
5. The King's Head: cf. above, ii. 125, n. 2.
6. See above, n. 3.
7. Elizabeth, widow of Ald. Robert Lowther.

how [I] do venture to speak more then is necessary in any company, though, as I did now, I do think them uncapable to censure
me), we broke up, they back to Walthamstow and only my wife
and I and Sir W. Penn to the King's playhouse; and there saw
The Mayden Queene,[1] which, though I have often seen, yet pleases
me infinitely, it being impossible, I think, ever to have the
Queen's part, which is very good and passionate, and Floramell's
part, which is the most Comicall that ever was made for woman,
ever done better then they two are by young Marshall and
Nelly.[2] Thence[a] home, where I spent the evening with my
father and wife; and late at night some Flagilette with my wife,
and then to supper and to bed.

25. Up and to the office, where all the morning. At noon
dined at home, and there came Mr. Pierce the surgeon and dined
with me – telling me that the Duke of Cambrige continues very
ill, so as they do despair of his living. So to the office again,
where all the afternoon. About 4 a-clock comes Mrs. Pierce
to see my wife; and I into them, and there find Pierce very fine
and in her own hair, which doth become her, and so says my
wife,[3] ten times better then lighter hair, her complexion being
mighty good. With them talked a little, and was invited by
her to come with my wife on Wednesday next in the evening
to be merry there, which we shall do. Then to the office again,
where despatched a great deal of business till late at night, to my
great content; and then home and with my wife to our flagelettes
a little; and so to supper and to bed, after having my chamber a
little wiped up.

26. *Lords day.* Up sooner then usual on Sundays, and to
walk, it being exceeding hot all night (so as this night I begin to
leave off my waistcoat* this year) and this morning; and so to

a repl. 'then'

1. By Dryden: see above, p. 91,
n. 2. (A).
2. The role of the Queen of Sicily
was taken by Rebecca, younger sister
of Anne Marshall, who also acted at
the Theatre Royal. (A).

3. On 11 May Pepys had objected
to his wife wearing artificial white
'locks'.

walk in the garden till toward church time, when my wife and I to church; where several strangers of good condition came to our pew, where the pew was full. At noon dined at home, where little Michell came, and his wife, who continues mighty pretty. After dinner, I by water alone to Westminster, where not finding Mrs. Martin within, did go toward the parish church[1] and in the way did overtake her, who resolved to go into the church with her that she was going with (Mrs. Hargrave, the little crooked woman, the vintner's wife of the Dog) and then go out again; and so I to the church; and seeing her return, did go to go out again myself, but met with Mr. Howlett, who offering me a pew in the gallery, I had no excuse but up with him I must go, and there, much against my will, stayed out the whole church in pain, while she expected me at home; but I did entertain myself with my perspective glass up and down the church, by which I had the great pleasure of seeing and gazing a great many very fine women; and what with that and sleeping, I passed away the time till sermon was done; and then to Mrs. Martin and there stayed with her an hour or two, and there did what jo would with her[a]. And after having been here so long, I away to my boat, and up with it as far as Barne Elmes, reading of Mr. Eveling's late new book against Solitude, in which I do not find much excess[b] of good matter, though it be pretty for a by-discourse.[2] I walked the length of the Elmes, and with great pleasure saw some gallant ladies and people, come with their bottles and basket[s] and chairs and form[s] to sup under the trees by the waterside, which was mighty pleasant. I to boat again and to my book; and having done that, I took another book, Mr. Boyles of Colours, and there read where I left,[3] finding many

a repl. 'would'   b repl. 'excessness'

---

1. St Margaret's.
2. *Publick employment and an active life . . . prefer'd to solitude . . .*; licensed 13 December 1666, published 15 February 1667 (Evelyn, *Diary*); a small octavo of 120 pp.; PL 461. Evelyn's own views on this book do not differ much from Pepys's:

Diary and corr. (ed. Wheatley), iii. 349; *Misc. Writings* (ed. Upcott), p. 507. For bibliographical information, see Sir G. Keynes, *John Evelyn . . . a bibliography* (1968 ed.), pp. 185+.
3. Sc. where he had left off. He had read it at the same place on 28 April.

fine things worthy observation. And so landed at the Old Swan and so home, where I find my poor father newly come out of an unexpected fit of his pain, that they feared he would have died. They had sent for me to White-hall and all up and down, and for Mr. Holliard also, who did come. But W Hewers being here did I think do the business, in getting my father's bowel,[a] that was fallen down, into his body again. And that which made me the more sensible of it was that he this morning did show me the place where his bowels did use to fall down and swell, which[b] did trouble me to see. But above all things, the poor man's patience under[c] it, and his good heart and humour as soon as he was out[d] of it, did so work upon me, that my heart was sad to think of his condition; but do hope that a way will be found by a steele truss to relieve him. By and by to supper, all our discourse about Brampton, and my intentions to build there if I could be free of my engagement to my Uncle Tho and his son,[1] that they may not have what I have built, against my will, to them, whether I will or no, in case of my and my brothers being without heirs males – which is the true reason[e] why I am against laying out money upon that place, together with my fear of some inconvenience by being so near Hinchingbrooke; being obliged to be a servant to that family, and subject to what expenses they shall cost me, and to have all that I shall buy or do esteemed as got by the death of my Uncle; when endeed, what I have from him is not worth naming. After supper, I to read and then to bed.

27. Up, and there comes Greeting my Flagelette-maister and I practised with him. There came also Richardson the book-binder with one of Ogilby's Bible's[2] in quires for me to see and

---

    a MS. 'body'   *b* repl. 'them'   *c* repl. 'is'
      d repl. 'whole'   *e* repl. 'reas' – that'

---

1. The agreement mentioned at 14 February 1663; see also above, v. 225 & n. 2. For Pepys's plans to build there, see below, p. 469.

2. Published by John Field at the Cambridge Press in two large folios (1660, 1659) and 'illustrated with Chorographical Sculps. by J. Ogilby': A. S. Herbert, *Hist. cat. Engl. Bible*, p. 206. Cf. Aubrey, ii. 102–3. Not in the PL.

buy, it being Mr. Cade's my stationer's; but it is like to be so big, that I shall not use it, it being too great to stir up and down without much trouble, which I shall not like nor do intend it for. So by water to White-hall and there found Sir G. Carteret at home; and talked with him a while and find that the new Commissioners of the Treasury did meet this morning.[1] So I to find out*ᵃ* Sir W. Coventry, but missed; only, I do hear that they have chosen Sir G. Downing for their Secretary; and I think in my conscience they have done a great thing in it – for he is a busy*ᵇ* active man, and values himself upon having of things do well under his hand; so that I am mightily pleased in their choice.[2]   Here*ᶜ* I met with Mr. Pierce, who tells me that he lately met Mr. Carcasse, who doth mightily*ᵈ* inveigh against me, for that all that hath been done against him[3] he lays on me; and I think he is in the right and I do own it; only, I find what I suspected, that he doth report that Sir W. Batten and I, who never agreed before, do now, and since this business agree, none more; which I did fear would be thought, and therefore will find occasion to undeceive*ᵉ* the world in that perticular, by promoting something shortly against W. Batten. So home; and there to sing with my wife before dinner, and then to dinner; and after dinner comes Carcasse to speak with me, but I would not give him way to enlarge on anything; but he would have begun to have made a noise, how I have undone him and used all the wit I could in the drawing up of his report,[4] wherein he told me I had taken a great deal of pains to undo him. To which I did not think fit to enter into any answer, but dismissed him; and so I again up to my chamber, vexed at the impudence of this rogue; but I think I shall be wary enough for him. So to

a repl. 'up'   *b* MS. 'business'   *c* repl. 'Thence'
d repl. same symbol badly formed   *e* repl. 'unperceive'

---

1. They had met for the reading of their commission on the 25th. On this day they held their first business meeting: *CTB*, ii. 1–2.

2. Downing's achievements as a financial administrator proved to be considerable, though not perhaps as considerable as his energy and gift for self-display suggested: see S. B. Baxter, *Devel. Treasury, 1660–1702*, pp. 168–9, 177–81.

3. See above, p. 64, n. 1.

4. Pepys had drafted the Board's report on Carkesse on 12 May.

my chamber and there did some little business; and then abroad by
[water] and stopped at the Bear-garden stairs, there to see a Prize
fought;¹ but the house so full, there was no getting in there; so
forced to [go] through an alehouse into the pit where the bears are
baited, and upon a stool did see them fight, which they did very
furiously, a butcher and a waterman. The former had the better
all along, till by and by the latter dropped his sword out of his
hand, and the butcher, whether not seeing his sword dropped or I
know not, but did give him a cut over the wrist, so as he was dis-
abled to fight any longer. But Lord, to see how in a minute the
whole stage was full of watermen to revenge the foul play, and the
butchers to defend*a* their fellow, though most blamed him; and
there they all fell to it, to knocking down and cutting many of
each*b* side. It was pleasant to see, but that I stood in the pit and
feared that in the tumult I might get some hurt. At last the
rabble broke up, and so I away to White-hall; and so to St.
James's, but found not Sir W. Coventry; so into the park and
took a turn or two, it being a most sweet day; and so by water
home, and with my father and wife walked in the garden, and
then anon to supper and to bed. The Duke of Cambrige very
ill still.

28. Up and by coach to St. James's, where I find Sir W.
Coventry and he desirous to have spoke with me. It was to read
over a draft of a letter which he hath made of his brother-
Commissioners and him to sign to us, demanding an account of
the whole business of the Navy accounts;² and I perceive by the

a repl. 'justify'   *b* repl. 'other'

---

1. The Bear Garden, Southwark,
was the principal centre of prize-
fighting (with swords, etc.). Cf.
above, iv. 167-8.

2. Similar letters were to be sent to
all the principal spending depart-
ments, asking for an account of what
they had spent and what they still
owed for the whole period from the
Restoration to 25 May 1667, when

Coventry and his fellow Commissioners of the Treasury had taken
office: *CTB*, ii. 2. For the letter to
the Navy Board (30 May), see the
abstract (in Gibson's hand) in NMM,
LBK/8, p. 489; printed in *Further
Corr.*, pp. 173-4. On 17 June the
Commissioners wrote to complain
that the Board had not replied: BM,
Add. 36782, f. 45.

way he goes about it, that they will do admirable things.[1] He
tells me they have chosen Sir G Downing their Secretary, which
will be as fit a man as any in the world.   And said by the by,
speaking of the Banquiers being fearful of Sir G. Downing's
being Secretary, he being their enemy, that they did not entend
to be ruled by their Secretary, but do the business themselfs.[2]
My heart is glad to see so great hopes of good to the nation as
will be by these men; and it doth me good to see Sir W. Coventry
so cheerful as he now is on the same score.   Thence home, and
there fell to seeing my office and closet there made soundly clean,
and the windows cleaned – at which all the morning, and so at
noon to dinner.   After dinner, my wife away down with Jane
and W. Hewer to Woolwich in order to a little ayre, and to lie
there tonight and so to gather May dew tomorrow morning,
which Mrs. Turner hath taught her as the only thing in the world
to wash her face with,[3] and I am contented with it.   Presently
comes Creed, and he and I by water to Fox hall and there walked
in Spring-garden; a great deal of company, and the weather and
garden pleasant; that it is very pleasant and cheap going thither,
for a man may go to spend what he will, or nothing, all as one –
but*a* to hear the nightingale and other birds, and here fiddles and
there a harp, and here a jews trump, and here laughing, and there
fine people walking, is mighty divertising.   Among others, there
were two pretty women alone, that walked a great while; which
[being] discovered by some idle gentlemen, they would needs
take them up; but to see the poor ladies, how they were put to
it to run from them, and they after them; and sometimes the

a   repl. 'to'

---

1. They founded the modern Treasury system by making their office
something more than a department of
the Exchequer.   Henceforth the Navy
Board presented its accounts to them
instead of to the Privy Council.   The
Council, until about Anne's reign,
still made decisions of policy.   D. M.
Gill in *EHR*, 46/600+ ; S. B. Baxter,
Devel. Treasury, 1660–1702, esp. chs
ii, iii and iv.

2. Nevertheless Downing came to
dominate business.   His enmity to
the bankers derived from his 1665
scheme for government credit (see
above, vi. 292 & n. 3), but good relations were soon established with them.

3. It was supposed to be an aid to
beauty, as well as having medicinal
properties.   The Royal Society in-
vestigated the matter in May 1665:
Birch, ii. 45, 49.

ladies put themselfs along with other company, then the others drew back; at last, the ladies*a* did get off out of the house and took boat and away.   I was troubled to see them abused so; and could have found my heart,* as little desire of fighting as I have, to have protected the ladies.

So by water; set Creed down at White-hall, and I to Old Swan and so home.   My father gone to bed and wife abroad at Wool-wich, I to Sir W. Penn, where he and his Lady and Pegg, and pretty Mrs. Lowther, her sister-in-law, at supper; where I sat and talked, and Sir W. Penn, half drunk, did talk like a fool and vex his wife, that I was half pleased and half vexed to see so much folly and rudeness from him; and so late home to bed.

29.   Up and by coach to St. James's, where by and by up to the Duke of York; where among other things, our Parson Mills having the offer of another benefice by Sir Rob. Brookes, who was his pupil,*b* he by my Lord Barkely's [desire] – is made one of the Duke's chaplains; which qualifies him for two livings.¹ But to see how slightly such things are done; the Duke of York only taking my Lord Barkely's word upon saying that we, the Officers of the Navy, do say he is a good man and minister of our parish; and the Duke of York admits him to kiss his hand but speaks not one word to him, but so a warrant will be drawn from the Duke of York to qualify him, and there's an end of it. So we into the Duke's closet, where little to do but complaint for want of money and a motion of Sir W. Coventry's that we should all now bethink ourselfs of lessening charge to the King, which he said was the only way he saw likely to put the King out of debt.   And this puts me upon thinking to offer something presently myself, to prevent its being done in a worse manner without me, relating to victualling business – which, as I may

---

a MS. 'last'   *b* MS. 'tutor'

---

1. Milles had presumably been a private tutor to Brookes.   Milles now became non-resident Rector of Wan-stead, Essex (where Brookes was lord of the manor) until his death in 1689.

An act of 1529 exempted chaplains of members of the royal family and of noblemen from the usual rules con-trolling pluralism and non-residence.

order it, I think may be done, and save myself something.[1]

Thence home, and there settle to some accounts of mine in my chamber, all the morning till dinner. My wife comes home from Woolwich but did not dine with me, going to dress herself against night to go to Mrs. Pierces to be merry, where we are to have Knipp and Harris and other good people. I at my accounts all the afternoon, being a little lost in them as to reckonings of interest. Anon comes down my wife, dress[ed] in her second mourning,[2] with her black moyre waistcoat and short petticoat, laced with silver lace so basely that I could not endure to see her, and with laced lining, which is too soon; so that I was horrid angry and went out of doors to the office, and there stayed and would not go to our intended meeting, which vexed me to the blood; and my*a* wife sent twice or thrice to me to direct her any way to dress her but to put*b* on her cloth gown, which she would not venture, which made me mad; and so in the evening to my chamber, vexed, and to my accounts, which I ended to my great content, and did make amends*c* for the loss of our mirth this night by getting this done, which otherwise I fear I should not have done a good while else. So to bed.

30. Up, and to the office, where all the morning. At noon dined at home; being, without any words, friends with my wife, though last night I was very angry, and do think I did give her as much cause to be angry with me. After dinner I walked to Arundell-house, the way very dusty (the day of meeting of the Society being changed from Wednesday to Thursday; which I knew not before*d* because the Wednesday is a Council-day and several of the Council are of the Society, and would come but for their attending the King at Council);[3] where I find much

a repl. 'she'   *b* repl. 'show'   *c* repl. 'a'
d followed by closing bracket struck through

---

1. Pepys resigned as Surveyor-General of Victualling in July: below, p. 367 & n. 1. There appears to be no trace of the project he refers to here.

2. Half-mourning. The family was in mourning for Pepys's mother, who had died in March.

3. The Society's minutes (reporting the vote on 1 February) make no mention of the reason given by Pepys: Birch, ii. 144. Pepys had not attended any meeting since 9 January.

company, endeed very much company, in expectation of the
Duchesse of Newcastle, who had desired to be invited to the
Society, and was, after much debate pro and con, it seems many
being against it, and we do believe the town will be full of ballets
of it.[1]   Anon comes the Duchesse, with her women attending
her; among others, that Ferrabosco[2] of whom so much talk is,
that her lady would bid her show her face and kill the gallants.
She is endeed black and hath good black little eyes, but otherwise
but a very ordinary woman I do think; but they say sings well.
The Duchesse hath been a good comely woman; but her dress so
antic and her deportment so unordinary, that I do not like her at
all, nor did I hear her say anything that was worth hearing, but
that she was full of admiration, all admiration.   Several fine
experiments were shown her of Colours, Loadstones, Micro-
scope, and of liquors: among others, of one that did while she was
there turn a piece of roasted mutton into pure blood – which
was very rare[3] – here was Mr. Moore of Cambrige, whom I
had not seen before,[4] and I was glad to see him[a] – as also a very
pretty black* boy that run up and down the room, somebody's
child in Arundell-house.   After they had shown her many
experiments, and she cried still she was "full of admiration," she
departed, being led out and in by several Lords that were there;
among others, Lord George Barkely and the Earl of Carlisle
and a very pretty young man, the Duke of Somersett.

a MS. 'her'

1. For a ballad apparently by Evelyn, see Evelyn, iii. 483, n. 2.   The
decision to invite the Duchess to the
Royal Society was made on 23 May.
Lord Berkeley proposed it, saying that
she wished to be invited officially, and
the Earl of Carlisle and Dr Charleton
seconded it: Birch, ii. 176.   She sat
at the President's right hand: HMC,
Le Fleming, p. 49.
   2. See above, v. 262, n. 1.   (E).
   3. The 'experiments appointed for
her entertainment' (which had been
in preparation for a week) included
'the mixing of cold liquors, which
upon their infusion grew hot', 'a

terrella driving away the steel-dust at
its poles', and 'the dissolving of meat
in the oil of vitriol': Birch, ii. 177–8.
The result of the last was not, of
course, 'pure blood', but perhaps
looked like it.   Birch's list of the
experiments does not tally very well
with Pepys's. Cf. Evelyn, s.d.;
M. H. Nicolson, *Pepys' diary and the
new science*, pp. 107+.
   4. Henry More, Fellow of Christ's
(the college from which Pepys's
brother John had graduated); one of
the most important theologians of the
century.

She gone, I by coach home and there busy at my letters till night; and then with my wife in the evening, singing with her in the garden with great pleasure. And so home to supper and to bed.

31. Up, and there came young Mrs. Daniel in the morning as I expected, about business of her husband's; I took her into the office to discourse with her about getting some imployment for him. And there I did*ᵃ* put my hand to her belly, so as to make myself do, but she is so lean*ᵇ* that I had no great pleasure with her.*ᵃ* So parted and I by water to White-hall to the Lords Commissioners of the Treasury, the first time I ever was there, and I think the second that they have met at the Treasury chamber there. Here I saw Duncomb look so big, and takes as much state on him, as if he had been born a lord. I was in with him about Tanger; and at present received but little answer from them,[1] they being in a cloud of business yet; but I doubt not but all will go well under them. Here I met with Sir H Cholmly, who tells that he is told this day by Secretary Morris that he believes we are, and shall be, only fooled by the French; and that the Dutch are very high and insolent, and do look upon us as come over only to beg a peace – which troubles me very much, and*ᶜ* do fear it is true. Thence to Sir G. Carteret at his lodgings, who I perceive is mightily displeased with these*ᵈ* new Treasurers; and he hath reason, for they*ᵉ* will eclipse him; and he tells me that my Lord Ashly says they understand nothing; and he says he believes the King doth not entend they shall sit long. But I believe no such thing, but that the King will find such benefit by them as he will desire to have them continue; as we see he hath done in the late new Act,[2] that was so much decried

---

a–a Garbled s.h. From this point onwards to the end of the diary Pepys usually garbles the s.h. in passages of this kind by inserting extra letters, especially *r, l, m* or *n*. Thus, here: 'dild punt mini harand toli hemr benleri, so as to malak mimi senelf do; but shere ilis somo leanen that I had no greaset plelesonure with hener.' For the reader's comfort, these passages are transcribed into ordinary spelling.
b repl. ungarbled 'so'   *c* repl. 'but'   *d* MS. 'this'   *e* MS. 'it'

---

1. The Treasury minute runs: 'Mr Pepys to be speedily considered for 30,000*l*. for Tangiers' (*CTB*, ii. 3).   2. The Additional Aid of 1665: see above, vi. 292 & n. 3.

about the King, but yet the King hath since permitted it and found good by it. He says, and I believe, that a great many persons at Court are angry at the rise of this Duncomb, whose father he tells me was a Long Parliament man and a great committee-man,[1] and this fellow used to carry his papers to committees after him – he was a kind of an Atturny. But for all this, I believe this man will be a great man in spite of all. Thence I away to Holborne to Mr. Gawden, whom I met at Bernards Inne gate, and straight we together to the Navy Office, where we did all meet about some victualling business; and so home to dinner and to the office, where the weather so hot nowadays that I cannot but sleep before I can do any business. And in the evening home; and there to my unexpected satisfaction did get my intricate accounts of interest (which have been of late much perplexed by mixing of some moneys of Sir G. Carteret's with mine) evened and set right; and so late to supper, and with great quiet to bed – finding by the balance of my account that I am Creditor 6900*l*,[2] for which the Lord of Heaven be praised.[a]

---

a From about this point onwards Pepys uses much less l.h. In the five last MS. pages for this month there are only 17 words in l.h. (as against, e.g., 28 in a single page of January 1662). Even personal names and place names are now often in s.h. – and not only in compromising passages.

1. Carteret was misinformed: Duncombe's father, Sir Edward (of Battlesden, Beds.) had died in 1638, before the Long Parliament was summoned (VCH, *Beds.*, iii. 344), and Duncombe himself had been in France throughout most of the Interregnum. The Duncombes were a many-branched family and possibly the mistake was due to confusion with, e.g., Robert Duncombe of Suffolk whose name often appears in the lists of committee-men for his county in the 1650s. (Firth and Rait, passim). For the Bedfordshire branch, see *Beds. N. & Q.*, ii. 40+. For the resentment against Duncombe's recent rise, see above, p. 234, n. 1.

2. 'Private Accompt made up May.31.1667': Rawl. A 185, ff. 17–27; an abstract (with rough notes and some later items added), in Pepys's hand. The exact amount of his credit was £6948 12*s*. 0*d*.

JUNE

1. Up; and there comes to me Mr. Commander, whom I imploy about*a* hiring of some ground behind the office for the building of me a stable and Coach-house, for I do find it necessary for me, both in respect to honour and the profit of it also (my expense in hackney-coaches being now so great) to keep a coach, and therefore will do it.[1] Having given him some instructions about it, I to the office, where we sat all the morning – where we have news that our peace with Spaine as to trade is wholly concluded, and we are to furnish him with some men for Flanders against the French;[2] how that will agree with the French, I know not, but they say that he also hath liberty to get what men he pleases out of England. But for the Spaniard, I hear that my Lord Castlehaven is raising a Regiment of 4000 men, which he is to command there,[3] and several young gentlemen are going over in commands with him. And they say the Duke of Monmouth is going over only*b* as a Travailer, not to engage on either side but only to see the Campagne – which will be becoming him much more then to live whoreing and rogueing of it here, as he now does.[4] After dinner to the office, where after a little nap I fell to business and did very much, with infinite joy to myself, as it always is to me when I have despatched much business; and therefore it troubles me to see how hard it is for me to settle to it sometimes, when my*c* mind is upon pleasure. So home late to supper and to bed.

---

a MS. 'but' *b* repl. 'to' *c* repl. 'they'

---

1. Cf. above, p. 205, n. 2.
2. For the trade treaty, see below, p. 453, n. 2. Negotiations for an offensive–defensive alliance were now begun but never completed. See Sandwich to Clarendon, Madrid, 14/24 May (Lister, iii. 465–6); J. O. McLachlan, *Trade and peace with Old Spain*, ch. i.

3. I.e. in Flanders, against the French: cf. HMC, *Rep.*, 14/4/79. For Castlehaven's military enterprises, see above, iv. 349 & n. 2.
4. He appears not to have gone but to have served in the troops defending Harwich against a Dutch attack: below, p. 255; *CSPD 1667*, pp. 171, 172.

2. *Lords day.* Up betimes, and down to chamber, without trimming myself or putting on clean linen, thinking only to keep to my chamber to do business today; but when I came there, I find that without being shaved I am not fully awake nor ready to settle to business, and so was fain to go up again and dress myself; which I did, and so down to my chamber and fell roundly to business, and did to my satisfaction by dinner go far in the drawing up a state of my accounts of Tanger for the new Lords Comissioners. So to dinner, and then to my business again all the afternoon close, when Creed came to visit me; but I did put him off, and to my business; till anon I did make an end and wrote it fair, with a letter to the Lords to accompany my account; which I think will be so much satisfaction, and so soon*a* done (their order*b* for my doing it being dated but May. 30),[1] as they will not find from any hand else. Being weary and almost blind with writing and reading so much today, I took boat at the Old Swan, and there up the River all alone, as high as Puttny almost; and then back again, all the way reading and finishing Mr. Boyle's book*c* of Colours,[2] which is so Chymicall that I can understand but little of it, but understand enough to see that he is a most excellent man. So back and home, and there to supper and so to bed.

3. Up; and by coach to St. James's and with Sir W. Coventry a great while, talking about several businesses – but especially about accounts and how backward our Treasurer is in giving them satisfaction; and the truth is, I do doubt he cannot do better. But it is strange to see, that being conscious of our doing little at this day nor for some time past in our office, for want of money, I do hang my head to him and cannot be so free with him as I used to be, nor can be free with him, though of all men I think I have the least cause to be so, having taken so much more pains (while I could do anything) then the rest of my fellows. Parted with him; and so going through the park, met Mr. Mills our parson, whom I went back with to bring him to W. Coventry

a repl. 'so' *b* repl. same symbol badly formed
c 'book' repeated

1. *CTB*, ii. 3. Pepys's statement 2. See above, p. 188, n. 2.
and letter have not been traced.

to give him the form of a Qualificacion for the Duke of York
to sign to, to enable him to have two livings; which was a
service I did, but much against my will, for a lazy, fat priest.[1]
Thence to Westminster*-hall and there walked a turn or two with
Sir Wm. Doyly, who did lay a wager with me the Treasurership
would be in one hand (notwithstanding this present Commission) before Christmas; on which we did lay a pole of ling,
a brace of carps, and a pottle of wine, and Sir W. Penn and Mr.
Scowen to be at the eating of them. Thence down by water
to Deptford, it being Trinity Monday, when the Maister is
chosen.[2] And there finding them all at church, and thinking they
dined as usual at Stepny, I turned back, having a good book in my
hand (the Life of Cardinal Wolsey, wrote by his own servant)[3],
and to Ratcliffe; and so walked to Stepny and spent my time in
the churchyard looking over the gravestones, expecting when the
company would come; but finding no company stirring, I sent
to the house to see, and it seems they dine[b] not there, but at
Deptford; so I back again to Deptford and there find them just
sat down; and so I down with them and we had a good dinner
of plain meat, and good company at our Table; among others,
my good Mr. Evelyn, with whom after dinner I stepped aside
and talked upon the[c] present posture of our affairs; which is,
that the Dutch are known to be abroad with 80 sail of ships ⟨of
war and 20 fireships⟩ and the French come into the Channell
with 20 sail of men-of-war and 5 fireships,[4] while we have not a

<hr>

a repl. 'white'-   b repl. 'dined'   c repl. 'our'

<hr>

1. Cf. above, p. 241 & n. 1.
2. Penn was chosen (but Pepys
does not mention it).
3. *The life and death of Thomas
Woolsey, Cardinal . . . written by one
of his own servants, being his gentleman
usher* (1667); small octavo; PL 794.
The author (unidentified at this time)
was George Cavendish.
4. The Dutch had left the Texel
and were to appear off the Suffolk
coast a few days later: see below, p.
254. Coventry sent to the Navy
Board on this day a report (received
from Holland) giving the numbers

exactly as Pepys here records them:
CSPD Add. 1660–85, p. 187. The
Dutch fleet was in fact slightly smaller
and consisted of 51 warships, 3 frigates, 6 armed yachts and 14 fireships:
J. C. de Jonge, *Geschiedenis van het
nederlandsche zeewesen*, ii. 177. (For
the numbers in general, see also *CSPD
1667*, pp. 144, 146, 157; Clowes, ii.
295.) The French operated from
Brest and did not come into the Channel. For a report about the French
similar to Pepys's, see the newsletter
(4 June) in HMC, *Le Fleming*, p. 49.

ship at sea to do them any hurt with, but are calling in all we can, while our Imbassadors are treating at Bredah and the Duch look upon them as come to beg peace, and use them accordingly. And all this through the negligence of our Prince; who hath power, if he would, to maister all these with the money and men that he hath had the command of, and may now have if he would mind his business. But for [aught] we see, the Kingdom is likely to be lost, as well as the reputation of it is, for ever – notwithstanding so much reputation got and preserved by a Rebell that went before him.[1] This discourse of ours ended with sorrowful reflections upon our condition, and so broke up; and Creed and I got out of the room and away by water to Whitehall; and there he and I waited in the Treasury-chamber an hour or two, where we saw the country Receivers and accountants for money come to attend; and one of them, a brisk young fellow (with his hat*a* cocked like a fool behind, as the present fashion among the blades is) committed to the Serjeant.[2] By and by, I upon desire was called in and delivered in my report of my accounts: present, Lord Ashly, Clifford, and Duncomb; who being busy, did not read it but committed it to Sir G Downing, and so I was dismissed.[3] But Lord, to see how Duncomb doth take upon him is an eysore, though I think he deserves great honour; but only, the suddenness of his rise and his pride. But I do like the way of these Lords, that they admit nobody to use many words; nor do they spend many words themselfs, but in great state do hear what they see necessary, and say little themselfs but bid withdraw. Thence Creed and I by water up to Fox hall; and over against it stopped, thinking to see some cockfighting, but it was just being done; and therefore back again

a repl. 'c'-

---

1. For the growth of Cromwell's reputation (as a diplomatist and war-leader) at this time, see below, p. 332 & n. 2; p. 382 & n. 2.
2. 'Country Receivers' had charge in the counties of the collection of the land-taxes recently voted. Warrants for the arrest and prosecution of several were ordered this day. The 'brisk young fellow' may have been Mr Price, receiver for Herefordshire, who was granted leave to go in the custody of the serjeant to get in his moneys: *CTB*, ii. 6.
3. Pepys's report is not mentioned in Downing's minute of the meeting: *CTB*, ii. 5–7.

to the other side and to Spring-garden and there eat and drank a little; and then to walk up and down the garden, reflecting upon the bad management of things now compared with what it was in*a* the late rebellious times, when men, some for fear and some for religion, minded their business; which none now do, by being void of both. Much talk of this and other kinds, very pleasant; and so when it was almost night, we home, setting him in at White-hall, I to Old Swan; and thence home, where to supper and then to read a little; and so to bed.

4. Up and to the office; and there busy all the morning putting in order the answering*b* the great letter sent to the office by the new Commissioners of the Treasury, who demand an account from the King's coming in to this day;[1] which we shall do in the best manner we can. At noon home to dinner; and after dinner comes Mr. Commander to me and tells me after all, that I cannot have a lease of the ground for my coach-house and stable till a suit in law be ended about the end of the old stable now standing, which they and I would have pulled down to make a better way for a coach. I am a little sorry that I cannot presently have it, because I am pretty full in my mind of keeping a coach; but yet when I think on it again, the Dutch and French both at sea and we poor, and still out of order, I know not yet what turns there may be, and besides, I am in danger of parting with one of my places (which relates to the Victualling, that brings me by accident in 800*l* a year; that is, 300*l* from the King and 500*l* from D. Gawden), I ought to be well contented to forbear*c* awhile, and therefore am contented. To the office all the afternoon, where I despatched much business to my great content; and then home in the evening, and there to sing and pipe with my wife; and that being done, she fell all of a sudden to discourse about her clothes and my humours in not suffering her to wear them as she pleases, and grew to high words between us. But I fell to read a book (Boyle's *Hydrostatickes*)[2] aloud in

a repl. 'before'   *b* repl. 'answering'   *c* repl. 'hope'

1. Strictly speaking, to 25 May. For the reply, see below, pp. 372 & n. 1, 373 & n. 2.   2. Robert Boyle, *Hydrostatical Paradoxes* . . . (1666); PL 790.

my chamber and let her talk till she was tired, and vexed that I would not hear her; and so become friends and to bed together, the first night after four or five that she hath lain from me by reason of a great cold she had got.

5. Up, and with Mr. Kenaston[1] by coach to White-hall to the Commissioners of the Treasury about getting money for Tanger, and did come to speak with them after long waiting (and there I find them all sat; and among the rest, Duncomb, lolling with his heels upon another chair, by that that he sat upon) and had an answer good enough;[2] and then away home (it being a most windy day and hath been so all night, South-West, and we have great hopes that it may have done the Dutch or French fleets some hurt); and having got some papers in order, I back to St. James's, where we all met at Sir W. Coventry's chamber and dined and talked of our business, he being a most excellent man; and endeed, with all his business, hath more of his imployed upon the good of the service of the Navy then all of us, that makes me ashamed of it. This noon Captain Perriman brings us word how the *Happy Returne* below in the Hope, ordered to carry the Portugall Embassador to Holland (and the Embassador I think on board), refuse to go till paid;[3] and by their example, two or three more ships are in a mutiny – which is a sad consideration, while so many of the enemy's ships are at this day triumphing in the sea. Here a very good and neat dinner after the French manner,[4] and good discourse; and then up after dinner to the Duke of York and did our usual business, and are put in hopes by Sir W. Coventry that we shall have money. And so away, Sir G. Carteret and I, to my Lord Crew to advise about Sir G. Carteret's carrying his accounts tomorrow to the Comissioners appointed to examine them and all others accounts since the war; who at last, by the King's calling them to him yesterday

1. Edward Kinaston, merchant; apparently concerned with the victualling of Tangier.
2. 'Mr Pepys called in about Tangier moneys. Warrant ordered for charging the 30,000*l.* on the Privy Seal for the 200,000*l.* for the king on the Eleven Months' Tax': *CTB*, ii. 8.
3. The ship was a man-of-war

detailed for the purpose. An order for pay was issued on the 6th and she sailed soon afterwards: *CSPD 1667*, pp. 147, 154, 187. The ambassador was Francisco de Mello, ambassador-extraordinary from Portugal to the United Provinces. A pass had been issued on 31 May: ib., p. 135.
4. Cf. above, p. 211, n. 1.

and chiding them, will sit; but Littleton and Garraway much
against their wills. And the truth of it is, it is a ridiculous thing,
for it will come to nothing nor do the King nor kingdom good
in any manner I think.[1] Here they talked of my Lord Hinchingbrooke's match with my Lord Burlington's daughter, which is
now gone a pretty way forward, and to great content; which I
am infinitely glad of. So from thence to White-hall; and in the
street Sir G. Carteret showed me a gentleman coming by in his
coach, who hath been sent for up out of Lincolneshire; I think
he says he is a Justice of Peace there, that the Council have laid
by the heels here, and here lies in a messenger's hands for saying
that a man and his wife are but one person and so ought to pay
but 12d for both to the Pole bill; by which others were led to do
the like, and so here he lies prisoner.[2] To White-hall, and there
I attended to speak with Sir W. Coventry about Lanyon's
business,[3] to get him some money out of the Prize-Office from
my Lord Ashly. And so home and there to the office a little;
and thence to my chamber to read and supper, and to bed. My
father, blessed be God, finds great ease by his new steel Trusse
which he put on yesterday. So to bed. The Duke of Cambrige
past hopes of living still.

6. Up, and to the office all the morning, where (which he
hath not done a great while) Sir G. Carteret came to advise with
us for the disposing of 10000*l*, which is the first sum the new
Lords-Treasurers have provided us; but unless we have more,
this will not enable us to cut off any of the growing charge,
which they seem to give it us for and expect we should discharge
several ships quite off with it. So home and*a* with my father

a repl. 'to dinner'

---

1. The Medway disaster of the
following week seems to have ended
the work of this commission: *CTB*,
vol. ii, p. xlix. For its revival (as a
parliamentary commission), see below, pp. 566–7.

2. Two Lincolnshire justices acting
as commissioners for poll-tax (William Wolley and George Sanderson)

had been summoned to the Council
for this offence in mid-May, and were
released by an order of 7 June: PRO,
PC 2/59, ff. 191r, 224v. They had
also claimed exemption for children
under 16.

3. Lanyon was one of the Tangier
victuallers.

and wife to Sir W. Penn's to dinner, which they invited us to out of their respect to my father, as a stranger; though I know them as false as the devil himself, and that it is only that they think it fit to oblige me; wherein I am a happy man, that all of my fellow-officers are desirous of my friendship. Here as merry as in so false a place and where I must dissemble my hatred, I could be. And after dinner, my father and wife to a play and I to my office; and there busy all the afternoon till late at night; and then my wife and I sang a song or two in the garden, and so home to supper and to bed. This afternoon comes Mr. Pierce to me about some business and tells me that the Duke of Cambrige is yet living, but every minute expects to die and is given over by all people – which endeed is a sad loss.

7. Up and after with my flagelette and Mr. Townsend, whom I sent for to come to ⟨me to⟩ discourse about my Lord Sand-wich's business*a* for whom I am in some pain, lest the accounts of the Wardrobe may not be in so good order as may please the new Lords-Treasurer's (who are quick-sighted, and under obliga-tions of recommending themselfs to the King and the world by their finding and mending of faults, and are most of them not the best friends to my Lord); and to the office and there all the morning. At noon home to dinner, my father, wife and I, and a good dinner; and then to the office again, where busy all the afternoon also, I having a desire to despatch all business that hath lain long on my hands; and so to it till the evening, and then home and to sing and pipe with my wife; and then to supper and to bed – my head full of thoughts how to keep, if I can, some part of my wages as Surveyor of the Victualling, which I see must now come to be taken away, among the other places that have been occasioned by this war – and the rather because I have of late an inclination to keep a coach. Ever since my drinking, two days ago, some very coole drink at Sir W. Coven-try's table, I have been full of wind and with some pain, and I was afeared the last night that it would amount to much; but blessed be God, I find that the worst is past, so that I do clearly see all the indisposition I am liable today as to sickness is only the Collique. This day I read (shown*b* me by Mr. Gibson) a dis-

---

a followed by opening bracket   *b* repl. 'give'

course newly come forth, of the King of France his pretence to Flanders;[1] which is a very fine discourse, and the truth is, hath so much of the Civil Law in it that I am not a fit judge of it; but as it appears to me, he hath a good pretence to it by right of his Queene. So to bed.

8. Up and to the office, where all the news this morning is that the Duch are come with a fleet of 80 sail to Harwich,[2] and that guns were[a] heard plain by Sir W Rider's people at Bednall Greene all yesterday noon. So to the office we all, and sat all the morning; and then home to dinner – where our dinner, a ham of French Bacon boiled with pigeons – an excellent dish. Here dined with us only W Hewers and his mother. After dinner to the office again, where busy till night; and then home and to read a little and then to bed. The news is confirmed that the Dutch are off[b] of Harwich, but had done nothing last night. The King hath sent down my Lord of Oxford to raise the country there;[3] and all the Westerne Barges are taken up to make a bridge over river about the Hope, for horse to cross the river if there be occasion.[4]

a MS. 'can'   *b* repl. 'at'

---

1. *A dialogue concerning the rights of His Most Christian Majesty* (1667), which summarises the arguments of the government's recently published *Traité* on the subject (q.v. above, p. 186 & n. 2). In it a French *avocat* makes the case for Louis XIV's claim to the Spanish Netherlands at the death of Philip IV of Spain. Louis' Queen (Maria Theresa, Philip's daughter) claimed the territory by virtue of a local law (the law of 'devolution') by which the inheritance devolved upon the children of a first marriage, their father having only a life interest. The argument is developed through 78 pages, with many marginal citations of legal authorities and local custumals. For other pamphlets in the controversy, see below, 27 January, 10 February 1668 & nn. The

French had invaded Flanders on 14/24 May.

2. Cf. the reports in *CSPD 1667*, pp. 156–7; Rawl. A 195a, f. 157r.

3. The Earl of Oxford was Colonel of the Royal Regiment of Horse (the Oxford Blues), and also Lord Lieutenant of Essex, Oxfordshire and Hertfordshire. He had arrived in Harwich on the 7th: *CSPD 1667*, pp. 157, 167.

4. Western barges plied between the upstream ports (Windsor, Maidenhead etc.) and the capital. Many brought corn and market produce to Queenhithe. They had been used before for the building of bridges – in 1588 at Tilbury, and 1642 at Putney: H. Humpherus, *Hist. Watermen's Co.*, i. 140, 245, 401.

9. *Lords day.* Up and by water to White-hall; and so walked to St. James's, where I hear that the Duke of Cambrige,[a] who was given over long since by the Doctors, is now likely to recover; for which God be praised. To Sir W. Coventry and there talked with him a great while; and mighty glad I was of my good fortune to visit him, for it keeps in my acquaintance with him, and the world sees it and reckons[b] my interest accordingly. In comes my Lord Berkely,[1] who is going down to Harwich also to look after the Militia there; and there is also the Duke of Monmouth, and with him a great many young Hectors, the Lord Chesterfield, my Lord Mandevill, and others; but to little purpose, I fear, but to debauch the country-women thereabouts. My Lord Berkely wanting some[c] maps and Sir W. Coventry recommending the six maps of England that are bound up for the pocket,[2] I did offer to present my Lord with them, which he accepted and so I will send them him. Thence to White-hall and there to the Chapel, where I met Creed; and he and I stayed to hear who preached, which was a man that begun dully, and so we away by water and[d] landed in Southworke; and to a church[3] in the street where we take water beyond the bridge, which was so full and the weather hot we could not stand there; so to my house, where we find my father and wife at dinner. And after dinner, Creed and I by water to White-hall; and there we parted and I to Sir G. Carteret's; where, he busy, I up into the house and there met with a gentleman, Captain Aldrige, that belongs to my Lord Berkely and I did give him the book of maps for my Lord. And so I to Westminster church[4] and there stayed a good while, and saw Betty Michell there. So away thence; and after church time to Mrs. Martins and there haze what[e] jo

a   repl. 'Duke of York'   *b*   repl. 'thinks'   *c*   repl. 'a b'-
                              d   repl. 'to'
e   repl. ungarbled 'what' in passage of garbled s.h. ('haze' to 'would'). See above, p. 244, note *a*.

1. Berkeley of Stratton; he was now made Lieutenant-General of the militia in Suffolk, Cambridgeshire and the Isle of Ely: *CSPD 1667*, p. 167.
2. Wenceslaus Hollar, *The King-dome of England, & Principality of Wales, exactly described whith every* *sheere and the small towns in every one of them in six mappes. Portable for euery mans pocket . . . Usefull for all commanders for quarteringe of souldiers . . .* (1644); not in the PL.
3. Presumably St Olave's, Southwark. (R).
4. St Margaret's.

would with her. And then took boat and up all alone, a most
excellent evening, as high as Barn-elmes and there took a turn;
and then to my boat again and home, reading and making an end
of the book I*a* lately bought, a merry Satyr called *The Visions*,
translated from Spanish by Le Strange; wherein there are many
very pretty things, but the translation is, as to the rendering it in
English expression, the best that ever I saw, it being impossible
almost to conceive that it should be a translation.[1] Being come
home, I find an order come for the getting some fireships presently
to annoy the Dutch, who are in the King's Channel and expected
up higher.[2] So W. Batten and W. Penn being come this evening
from their country houses to town, we did issue orders about it;
and then home to supper and to bed.

10. Up; and news brought us that the Dutch are come up as
high as the Nore, and more pressing*b* orders for fireships.[3]
W. Batten, W. Penn and I to St. James, where the Duke of
York gone this morning betimes to send away some men down
to Chatham. So we three to White-hall and met Sir W.
Coventry, who presses all the possible for fireships; so we three
to the office presently, and thither comes Sir Fr. Hollis, who is to
command them all in some exploits he is to do with them on the
enemy in the river.[4] So we all down to Deptford and pitch

a repl. 'of'   *b* repl. 'pro'-

1. *The visions of Dom Francisco de
Quevedo . . . made English by* R[oger]
L['Estrange]; licensed 26 March
1667. Pepys retained a copy (3rd ed.
1668; PL 730) but kept no copy of the
original, if he ever had one. L'Estrange's translations generally were –
in the fashion of the time – loose but
spirited: G. Kitchin, *L'Estrange*, pp.
376–8.

2. Cf. Coventry to Navy Board,
9 June, 7 p.m. (PRO, SP 46/136, no.
485; *CSPD Add. 1660–85*, p. 188)
reporting the Dutch to be in the
King's Channel (south of Harwich;
now the East Swin) and ordering
fireships to be organised, as 'the most
probable way to annoy them'.

3. The orders are in *CSPD 1667*,
pp. 166–7; the Board were urged not
to wait for warrants or forms, and to
send at least six fireships.

4. Sir Frescheville Holles, captain
of the *Cambridge*, had been summoned
with his ship from Portsmouth, supplied with blank press-warrants, and
put in command of the fireships in the
river: *CSPD 1666–7*, pp. 166, 167.
He had held an army commission in
1663 but his first naval commission
dated only from 1666. Pepys and
Coventry came to take a low view of
him.

upon ships and set men at work; but Lord, to see how backwardly things move at this pinch, notwithstanding that by the enemy's being now come up as high as almost the Hope, Sir J. Mennes (who was gone down to pay some ships there)*ᵃ* hath sent up the money; and so we are possessed of money to [do] what we will with.¹ Yet partly ourselfs, being used to be idle and in despair, and partly people, that have been used to be deceived by us as to money, won't believe us; and we know not, though we have it, how almost*ᵇ* to promise it; and our wants such, and men out of the way, that it is an admirable thing to consider how much the King suffers, and how necessary it is in a State to keep the King's service always in a good posture and credit. Here I eat a bit; and then in the afternoon took boat and down to Greenwich, where I find the stairs*ᶜ* full of people, there being a great Riding there today for a man, the*ᵈ* constable of the town, whose wife beat him.² Here I was with much ado fain to press two watermen to make me a galley; and so to Woolwich to give order for the despatch of a ship I have taken under my care to see despatched; and orders being so given, I, under pretence to fetch up the ship, which lay at Grays (the *Golden hand*),³ did do that in my way; and went down to Gravesend, where I find the Duke of Albemarle just come, with a great many idle lords and gentlemen with their pistols and fooleries,⁴ and the Bulworke⁵ not

---

a MS. has closing bracket after 'money'   b repl. 'to'
    c repl. 'people'   d repl. 'that'

---

1. On the 13th Albemarle ordered Mennes to spend the £5000 (sent down to pay off Chatham Yard) on the defence of the river, according to the orders of the Earls of Carlisle and Middleton: Tanner 45, f. 195r. Cf. also Rawl. A 195a, f. 159r.

2. Marvell describes the incident in *Last Instructions*, ll. 375–89. Mock-processions of this sort, aimed especially against shrewish wives, and known under a variety of names ('ridings', 'skimmington rides', 'rough music', etc.), lasted until the early 20th century in rural England. There

is a famous one in Hardy's *Mayor of Casterbridge* (chs 36, 39). For discussion and bibliography, see N. Davis in *Past and Present*, no. 50 (1971), esp. p. 56, n.

3. Pepys had been ordered to arrange for the *Golden Hand* to convey the Swedish ambassadors' goods and horses to Holland: *CSPD 1667*, pp. 15, 18.

4. Cf. Marvell, *Last Instructions*, ll. 597–8: 'Our feather'd gallants, which came down that day / To be spectators safe of the new play.'

5. The defences of Gravesend.

able to have stood half an hour had they come up; but the Dutch
are fallen down from the Hope and Shell haven as low as the
Sheernesse, and we do plainly at this time hear the guns play.
Yet I do not find the Duke of Albemarle entends to go thither,
but stays here tonight and hath (though the Dutch are gone)
ordered our frigates to be brought in a line between the two
block-houses[1] – which I took then to be a ridiculous thing.   So
I away into the town and took a Captain or two of our ships
(who did give me an account of the proceedings of the Dutch
fleet in the river)[2] to the tavern and there we eat and drank;
and I find the town had removed most of their goods out of the
town, for fear of the Duch coming up to them; and Sir Jo.
Griffen[3] [told me] that last night there was not twelve men to
be got in the town to defend it – which the master of the house
tells me is not true; but that the men of the town did entend to
stay, though they did endeed,and so had he[a] (at the Ship), removed
their goods.   Thence went off to an Ostend man-of-war, just
now come up, who met the Dutch fleet, who took three ships
that he came convoying hither from him – says they are as low
as the Nore or thereabouts.   So I homeward, as long as it was
light reading Mr. Boyles book of *Hydrostatickes*,[4] which is a
most excellent book as ever I read; and I will take much pains
to understand him through if I can, the doctrine being very useful.
When it grew too dark to read, I lay down and took a nap, it
being a most excellent fine evening; and about one a-clock got
home, and after having wrote to Sir W. Coventry an account of
what I had done and seen (which is entered in my letter-book)[5],
I to bed.

a　MS. 'he at'

---

1. At Gravesend.

2. Pepys summarised this in s.h.:
NMM, LBK/8, p. 491 (translated and
printed in *Shorthand Letters*, p. 92).

3. Sir John Griffith, in charge of the
blockhouses at Gravesend.

4. See above, p. 250, n. 2.

5. NMM, LBK/8, p. 491, 11 June,
in Pepys's hand (partially printed in
Further Corr. pp. 176–7). The original is in Longleat, Coventry MSS
97, f. 73r. The letter adds a few
details to the account in the diary:
there were said to be 26 Dutch men-
of-war, and 'the offall of some Mut-
tons drove up the River the last flood
shews what they had been doeing'.

11. Up, and more letters still from Sir W. Coventry about more*a* fireships; and so W. Batten and I to the office, where Brouncker came to us; who is just now going to Chatham upon a desire of Commissioner Pett's, who is in a very fearful stink for fear of the Dutch, and desires help for God and the King and kingdom's sake.[1] So Brouncker goes down, and Sir J. Mennes also, from Gravesend. This morning Pett writes us word that Sherenesse is lost last night, after two or three hours' dispute – the enemy hath possessed himself of the place; which is very sad and puts us into great fears of Chatham. Sir W. Batten and I down by water to Deptford, and there Sir W. Penn and we did consider of several matters relating to the despatch of the Fire-shipps; and so W. Batten and I home again – and there to dinner, my wife and father having dined. And after dinner, by W. Hewer's lucky advice, went to Mr. Fenn and did get him to pay me above 400*l* of my Wages,[2] and*b* W. Hewer received it for me and brought it home this night. Thence, I meeting Mr. Moore, went toward the other end of the town by coach; and spying Mercer in the street, I took leave of Moore and light and fallowed her; and at Pauls overtook her and walked with her through the dusty street almost to home; and there in Lumbard-street met The Turner in coach, who had been at my house to see us, being to go out of town tomorrow to the Northward, and so I promised to see her tomorrow; and then home and there to our business, hiring some fireships and receiving every hour almost

a repl. 'fire' *b* repl. 'and brought it'

---

1. Cf. Pett's two letters to the Navy Board, Chatham, 10 June: PRO, SP 46/136, nos 488, 489 (summaries in *CSPD Add. 1660–85*, p. 189). In these letters he asks for help but does not use the words which Pepys appears to quote later in the entry. For an account (with bibliography) of the Dutch raid on the Medway, see P. G. Rogers, *Dutch in Medway*. Pepys kept two detailed accounts by observers at Chatham among his papers: Rawl. A 195a, ff. 159–61 (by Mennes, 16 June), and ib., ff. 128–31 (by Edward Gregory, 20 July).

2. The figure is presumably a mistake for £100. According to the Navy Treasurer's ledger, Pepys received for the quarter ending on 24 June £100 for his clerks' wages and £75 as Surveyor-General of Victualling: PRO, Adm. 20/9, pp. 153, 154, 157.

letters from Sir W. Coventry, calling for more Fireshipps[1] – and an order from Council to enable us to take any man's ships;[2] and Sir W. Coventry in his letter to us says he doth not doubt but at this time (under an Invasion, as he owns it to be) the King may by law take any man's goods. At this business late, and then home, where a great deal of serious talk with my wife about the sad state we are in, and especially from the beating-up of drums this night for the train-bands, upon pain of death to appear in arms tomorrow morning, with bullet and powder and money to supply themselfs with victuals for a fortnight – which, considering the soldiers drawn out to*ᵃ* Chatham and elsewhere, looks as if they had a design to ruin the City and give it up to be undone – which I hear makes the sober citizens to think very sadly of things. So to bed after supper, ill in my mind. ⟨This afternoon Mrs. Williams sent to me to speak with her, which I did, only about news. I had not spoke with her many a day before by reason of Carcasse's business.⟩*ᵇ*³

12. Up very betimes to our business at the office, there hiring of more fireships; and at it close all the morning. At noon home, and Sir W. Penn dined with us. By*ᶜ* and by, after dinner, my wife out by coach to see her mother; and I in another (being afeared at this busy time to be seen with a woman in a coach, as if I were idle) toward The*Turners; but met Sir W. Coventry's boy, and there in his letter find that the Dutch had made no motion since their taking Sherenesse; and the Duke of Albemarle writes that all is safe as to the great ships against any assault – the boom

a repl. 'into'   *b* addition crowded into end of paragraph
　　　　c repl. 'Then to business again'

---

1. Four letters of this date (headed 9.30, 1 p.m., 3.30 p.m. and 'evening') are in PRO, SP 29/136, nos 491–4 (summaries in *CSPD Add. 1660–85*, pp. 189–91).

2. PRO, PC 2/59, f. 227*v*; an order (11 June) authorising the Board to impress any ships in the Thames. The Board, in one of their several letters on this subject to Coventry this day, took the view that violent

proceedings would not reduce the capacity of shipowners to obstruct the King's service: Longleat, Coventry MSS 97, f. 75*r*; cf. ib., ff. 77–9. They had six fireships and the promise of three more.

3. Brouncker, with whom she lived, had supported Carkesse in his quarrel with the Board: cf. above, p. 83.

The Dutch Raid on the Medway, by Romeyn de Hooghe

(National Maritime Museum, London)

and Chaine being so fortified; which put my heart into great joy.[1]

When I came to Sir W. Coventry's chamber, I find him abroad; but his clerk Powell doth tell me that ill news is come to Court of the Dutch breaking the Chaine at Chatham, which struck me to the heart, and to White-hall to hear the truth of it; and there, going up the park stairs, I did hear some lackeys speaking of sad news come to Court, saying that hardly anybody in the court but doth look as if they cried; and would not go into the house for fear of being seen, but slunk out and got into a coach, and to The Turner to Sir W Turner's, where I met Roger Pepys, newly come out of the country (he and I talked aside a little, he offering a match for Pall, one Barnes,[2] of whom we shall talk more the next time; his father married a Pepys). In discourse, he told me further that his grandfather, my great grandfather, had 800*l* per annum in Queen Elizabeth's time in the very town of Cottenham[3] – and that we did certainly come out of Scotland with the Abbot of Crowland.[4]   More talk I had, and shall have more with him, but my mind is so sad and head full

---

1. Albemarle's news was in Coventry's letter to the Board (of this date): *CSPD Add. 1660–85*, pp. 191–2. Two ships had been sunk outside the boom across the Medway; the *Unity* had been stationed there and batteries set up at either end.

2. William Barnes of Cottenham, Cambs., grandson of George Pepys, also of Cottenham. Nothing came of the proposal.

3. John Pepys (d. 1589), of Cottenham and Impington. He acquired the manor of Impington in 1579: W. C. Pepys, *Geneal. Pepys family* (1952 ed.), pp. 77–8.

4. Roger Pepys probably derived his information from '*Liber Talboti Pepys*', a MS. commonplace book on the history of his family inherited from his father Talbot Pepys (d. 1666). It was probably drawn up by Talbot; among the extracts printed in W. C. Pepys (op. cit. – the book is now untraced) is one (p. 78) which runs: 'William Pepys died at Cotten-ham 10 Hen. VIII was brought up by the Abbot of Crowland in Huntingdon, and he was born in Dunbar in Scotland, a gentleman whom the said Abbot did make his bayliffe of all his lands in Cambridgshire . . .'. But this was certainly not the beginning of the family story. The Pepyses are to be traced as villeins in Cottenham in the thirteenth century, and from at least 1290, members of the family had held office in the service of the Benedictine house of Crowland. See F. M. Page, *Estates of Crowland Abbey*, esp. pp. 71–2. Dr Page suggests that a younger branch of the family may have returned to Cottenham from Scotland in the reign of Henry VIII. There was a Benedictine house at Coldingham, south of Dunbar. Pepys's nephew and heir, John Jackson, made enquiries in 1707 about the possible Scottish ancestry of both the Pepyses and the Jacksons: PL, Jackson MSS, 10 (b).

of this ill news, that I cannot now set it down. A short visit
here, my wife coming to me, and took leave of The; and so
home, where all our hearts do now ake; for the news is true,
that the Dutch have broke the Chain and burned our ships, and
perticularly the *Royall Charles*; other perticulars I know not,
but most sad to be sure.[1] And the truth is, I do fear so much
that the whole kingdom is undone, that I do this night resolve to
study with my father and wife what to do with the little that I[a]
have in money by me, for I give all the rest that I have in the
King's hands for Tanger for lost. So God help us, and God
knows what disorders we may fall into and whether any violence
on this office, or perhaps some severity on our persons, as being
reckoned by the silly people, or perhaps may by policy of State
be thought fit to be condemned by the King and Duke of York,
and so put to trouble; though God knows I have in my own
person done my full duty, I am sure. So having with much ado
finished my business at the office,[2] I home to consider with my
father and wife of things; and then to supper and to bed with a
heavy heart. The[b] manner of my advising this night with my
father was: I took him and my wife up to her chamber, and shut
the door and there told them the sad state of the times; how we
are like to be all undone – that I do fear some violence will be
offered to this office, where all I have in the world is. And resolved upon sending it away – sometimes into the country, sometimes my father to lie in town and have the gold with him at
Sarah Giles's; and with that resolution went to bed – full of fear
and fright; hardly slept all night.

13. No sooner up but hear the sad news confirmed, of the
Royall Charles being taken by them and now in fitting by them

a repl. 'the'
b The rest of this entry, with many others during the next few weeks, is in
a smaller hand. This day Pepys committed his journals into safe keeping:
below, p. 264. Like the Fire sequence, therefore, the Dutch Invasion sequence
must have been entered later in space left for the purpose. Presumably it was
entered in July: see below, p. 271, note *a*.

---

1. The *Royal Charles* was a first-
rate, one of the principal ships of the
English navy. It was captured, not
burnt, and was towed away in
triumph on the 14th.

2. There is a letter from Pepys and
Batten to Coventry (about fireships)
headed '12 June, ¾ past 9 at night' in
Longleat, Coventry MSS 95, f. 325r.

The Capture of the *Royal Charles*, by Ludolf Bakhuyzen

(*National Maritime Museum, London*)

(which Pett should have carried up higher by our several orders, and deserves therefore to be hanged for not doing it) and burning several others, and that another fleet is come up into the Hope;[1] upon which news the King and Duke of York have been below* since 4 a-clock in the morning, to command the sinking of ships at Barking Creeke and other places, to stop their coming up higher; which put me into such a fear that I presently resolved of my father's and wife's going into the country; and at two hours' warning they did go by the coach this day – with about 1300*l* in gold in their night-bag; pray God give them good passage and good care to hide it when they come home, but my heart is full of fear. They gone, I continued in frights and fear what to do with the rest. W. Hewer hath been at the banquiers and hath got 500*l* out of Backewell's hands of his own money; but they are so called upon that they will be all broke,[2] hundreds coming to them for money – and their answer is, "It is payable at twenty days; when the days are out, we will pay you;" and those that are not so, they make tell over their money, and make their bags false on purpose to give cause to retell it and so spend time; I cannot have my 200 pieces of gold[3] again for silver, all being bought up last night that were to be had – and sold for 24 and 25*s* a-piece. So I must keep the silver by me, which sometimes I think to fling into the house of office – and then again, know not how I shall come by it if we be made to leave the office. Every minute some[one] or other calls for this order or that order; and so I forced to be at the office most of the day about the fireships which are to be suddenly fitted out; and it's a most strange thing that we hear nothing from any of my Brethren at Chatham; so that we are wholly in the dark, various being the reports of what is done there – insomuch, that I sent ⟨Mr.⟩ Clapham[4] express thither to see how matters go. I did about noon resolve to send Mr. Gibson away after my wife with another 1000 pieces, under colour of an express to Sir Jer: Smith, who is, as I hear, with some ships at Newcastle;[5] which I did

1. This was a reconnaissance force only: Clowes, ii. 294.

2. None in fact went bankrupt: see below, p. 450 & n. 3.

3. Probably guineas: cf. above, vii. 346 & n. 3.

4. John Clapham of the Ticket Office: see his letter to Pepys, Chatham, 14 June, in *CSPD 1667*, p. 185.

5. Smith was by now in Leith Roads: ib., p. 173. Richard Gibson was one of Pepys's clerks.

really send to him, and may possibly prove of good use to the
King; for it is possible, in the hurry of business they may not
think of it at Court, and the charge of express is not considerable
to the King. So though I entend Gibson no further then to
Huntington, yet I direct him to send the packet forward. My
business the most of the afternoon is listening to everybody that
comes to the office, what news, which is variously related, some
better, some worse, but nothing certain. The King and Duke of
York up and down all the day here and there; some time on
Tower-hill, where the City Militia was; where the King did make
a speech to them that they should venture themselfs no further
then he would himself.[1] I also sent (my mind being in pain)
Saunders after my wife and father, to overtake them at their
night's lodging to see how matters go with them. In the evening
I sent for my cousin Sarah and her husband; who came and I
did deliver them my chest of writings about Brampton, and my
brother Tom's papers and my Journalls, which I value much[2] –
and did send my two silver flagons to Kate Joyce's: that so,
being scattered what I have, something might be saved. I have
also made a girdle, by which with some trouble I do carry about
me 300l in gold about my body, that I may not be without something in case I should be surprized; for I think, in any nation
but ours, people that appear (for we are not endeed so) so faulty as
we would have their throats cut. In the evening comes Mr.
Pelling[3] and several others to the office, and tell me that never
were people so dejected as they are in the City all over at this
day, and do talk most loudly, even treason; as, that we are
bought and sold, that we are betrayed by the papists and others
about[a] the King – cry out that the Office of the Ordinance hath

---

a   repl. 'people'

---

1. According to the *London Gazette*
(17 June), the King (replying to an
address from the City corporation)
said that he left it to 'their Prudence to
do . . . what shall be necessary and
effectual . . .'.

2. Certain of the Brampton papers
(concerning the property inherited
from Robert Pepys) were later (October 1681) kept 'loose' in his 'Chatham Chest-Box': Rawl. A 183, f. 240r.
Many survive; see *Comp.*: 'Pepys,
Robert'. Tom's papers were probably those in Rawl. A 182, ff. 300–51
(see above, v. 122, n. 3). The journals now occupied over four volumes.
'Sarah' was Sarah Giles of St Giles's,
Cripplegate.

3. Probably Walter Pelling, apothecary.

been so backward as no powder to have been at Chatham nor Upner Castle till such a time, and the carriages all broken – that Legg is a papist[1] – that Upner, the old good castle built by Queen Elizabeth, should be lately slighted[2] – that the ships at Chatham should not be carried up higher. They look upon us as lost; and remove their families and rich goods in the City and do think verily that the French, being come down with his army to Dunkirke, it is to invade us – and that we shall be invaded. Mr. Clerke the solicitor comes to me about business, and tells me that he hears that the King hath chosen Mr. Pierpoint and Vaughan of the West privy*a* councillors[3] – that my Lord Chancellor was affronted in the Hall this day by people telling him of his Dunkirke house[4] – and that there are Regiments ordered to be got together, whereof to be commanders my Lord Fairfax, Ingolsby, Bethell, Norton, and Birch and other presbyters;[5] and that Dr. Bates will have liberty to preach.[6] Now whether this be true or not, I know not; but do think that nothing but this will unite*b* us together. Late at night comes Mr. Hudson the cooper, my neighbour, and tells me that he came from

a repl. 'his'   *b* l.h. repl. s.h. 'invite'

---

1. William Legge (Lieutenant-General of the Ordnance) was wrongly suspected of being a secret Papist – because of his Irish birth, his Catholic friends, and (later) his attachment to the Duke of York's interest. The rumour was now rife that he had replaced Robinson as Governor of the Tower: *CSPD 1667*, p. 207.

2. For the castle, see above, iii. 155, n. 1. Its garrison had been reduced in 1666: *CSPD 1666–7*, p. 328.

3. This was untrue. William Pierre-pont, the 'Presbyterian' politician, had been out of politics since his defeat at the elections of 1661. John Vaughan (M.P. for Cardiganshire) was a prominent critic of the government.

4. His newly-built house allegedly paid for by French bribes given him in return for the sale of Dunkirk in 1662.

5. On the 13th some colonelcies were granted to 'Presbyterians' and ex-parliamentarians such as Fairfax, Manchester and Norton: *CSPD 1667*, pp. 179, 181, 182, 199. For other forms of the rumour, see newsletter (15 June): ib., p. 189.

6. Dr William Bates, a moderate Presbyterian (who had taken the oath required under the Five Mile Act of 1665) seems to have received some concession at about this time: cf. *Somers Tracts* (ed. Scott), viii. 11–12.

Chatham this evening at 5 a clock and saw this afternoon the
Royall James, *Oake*, and *London* burnt by the enemy with their
fireships; that two or three men-of-war came up with them, and
made no more of Upner castle's shooting then of a fly – that
these ships lay below Upner Castle (but therein I conceive he is in
an error)[1] – that the Dutch are fitting out the *Royall Charles* –
that we shot so far as from the yard thither, so that the shot did
no good, for the bullets grazed on the water – that Upner played
hard with their guns at first, but slowly afterward, either from
the men being beat off or their powder spent.   But we hear that
the fleet in the Hope is not come up any higher the last flood.
And Sir W. Batten tells me that ships are provided to sink in the
River about Woolwich, that will prevent their coming up higher
if they should attempt it.   I made my will also this day, and did
give all I had equally between my father and wife – and left copies
of it in ⟨each of⟩ Mr. Hater and W. Hewer's hands, who both
witnessed the will;[2] and so to supper and then to bed; and slept
pretty well, but yet often waking.

14.   Up, and to the office; where Mr. Fryer comes and tells
me that there are several Frenchmen and Flemish ships in the
River, with passes from the Duke of York for carrying of
prisoners, that ought to be parted from the rest of the ships and
their powder taken, lest they do fire themselfs when the enemy
comes and so spoil us; which is good advice I think, and will
give notice of it – and did[a] so.[3]   But it is pretty odd to see how
everybody, even at this high time of danger, puts business off of
their own hands.   He says that he told this to the Lieutenant of
the Tower (to whom I for the same reason was directing him
to go) and the Lieutenant of the Tower bade him come to us,
for he had nothing to do with it – and yesterday comes Captain
Crow off one of the fireships and told me that the officers of the

----

a repl. 'did so'

----

1. They lay above Upnor, off
Chatham dockyard.
2. This will has not survived.   For
Pepys's wills, see above, i. 90 & n. 1.

3. Cf. PRO, PC 2/59, f. 210r.
Fryer appears to have been employed
in Chatham dockyard.

Ordinance would deliver his gunner's materials but not compound them,[1] but that we must do it; whereupon I was forced to write to them about it – and one that like a great many comes to me this morning. By and by comes Mr. Willson[2] and, by direction of his, a man of Mr. Gawden's who came from Chatham last night and saw the three ships burnt, they lying all dry, and boats going from the men-of-war and fire them. But that that he tells me of worst consequence is that he himself (I think he said) did hear many Englishmen on board the Dutch ships, speaking to one another in English, and that they did cry and say, "We did heretofore fight for tickets; now we fight for Dollers!" and did ask how such and such a one did, and would commend themselfs to them – which is a sad consideration.[3] And Mr. Lewes (who was present at this fellow's discourse to me) did tell me that he is told that when they took the *Royall Charles*, they said that they had their tickets signed (and showed some) and that now they came to have them paid, and would have them paid before they parted. And several seamen came this morning to me to tell me that if I would get their tickets paid, they would go and do all they could against the Dutch; but otherwise they would not venture being killed and lose all they have already fought for – so that I was forced to try what I could do to get them paid. This man tells me that the ships burnt last night did lie above Upner Castle over against the Docke; and the boats came from the ships*a* of war and burnt them – all which is very sad; and maisters of ships that we are now taking up do keep from their ships all their stores, or as much as they can, so that we can despatch them – having not time to appraise them nor

a repl. 'fire'

---

1. The Ordnance normally supplied ready-mixed gunpowder. The Navy Office supplied the gun-wadding.
2. Thomas Wilson, newly appointed storekeeper at Chatham.
3. English deserters and ex-prisoners of war were serving in the Dutch forces. An act had been passed to recall them in 1665. Cf. *CSPD 1667*, p. 323; and Marvell's comment in *Last Instructions* (ll. 601-4): 'Our Seamen, whom no Dangers shape could fright, / Unpaid, refuse to mount our Ships for spight: / Or to their fellows swim on board the Dutch, / Which show the tempting metal in their clutch.' Cf. also *Naval Minutes*, p. 251.

secure their payment.   Only, some little money we have, which we are fain to pay the men we have with every night, or they will not work.   And endeed, the hearts as well as affections of the seamen are turned away; and in the open streets in wapping, and up and down, the wifes have cried publicly, "This comes of your not paying our husbands; and now your work is undone, or done by hands that understand it not;" and Sir W. Batten told me that he was himself affronted with a woman in language of this kind himself on tower-hill publicly yesterday; and we are fain to bear it – and to keep one at the office-door to let no idle people in, for fear of firing of the office and doing us mischief. The City is troubled at their[1] being put upon duty: summoned one hour and discharged two hours after and then again summoned two hours after that, to their great charge as well as trouble; and Pelling the pothecary tells me the world says all over that less charge then what the kingdom is put to, of one kind or other, by this business, would have set out all our great ships. It is said they did in open streets yesterday, at Westminster, cry, "A Parliament! a Parliament!"; and do believe it will cost blood to answer for these miscarriages.   We do not hear that the Duch are come to Gravesend, which is a wonder; but a wonderful ⟨thing⟩ it is that to this day we have not one word yet from Brouncker or P. Pett or J. Mennes of anything at Chatham; the people that come hither to hear how things go make me ashamed to be found unable to answer them, for I am left alone here at the office; and the truth is, I am glad my station is to be here – near my own home and out of danger, yet in a place of doing the King good service.   I have this morning good news from Gibson; three letters, from three[a] several stages, that he was safe last night as far as Royston at between 9 and 10 at night. The dismay that is upon us all in the business of the kingdom and Navy at this day, is not to be expressed otherwise then by the condition the citizens were in when the City was on fire, nobody knowing which way to turn themselfs, while everything concurred to greaten the fire; as here, the easterly gale and spring-tides, for coming up both rivers and enabling them to break the

a repl. 'his'

----

1. The trainbands.

chain. D. Gawden did tell me yesterday that the day before at the Council, they were ready to fall together by the ears at the council-table, arraigning one another of being guilty of the counsel that brought us into this misery, by laying up all the great ships.[1] Mr. Hater tells me at noon that some rude people have been, as he hears, at my Lord Chancellor's, where they have cut down the trees before his house and broke his windows; and a Gibbet either set up before or painted upon his gate, and these[a] words writ – "Three sights to be seen; Dunkirke, Tanger, and a barren Queen."[2] It gives great matter of talk that it is said there is at this hour in the Exchequer as much money as is ready to break down the floor. This arises, I believe, from Sir G. Downing's late talk of the greatness[b] of the sum lying there of people's money that they would not fetch away, which he showed me and a great many others. Most people that I speak with are in doubt how we shall do to secure our seamen from running over to the Duch; which is a sad but very true consideration at this day. At noon am told that my Lord Duke of Albemarle is made Lord High Constable; the meaning whereof at this time I know not, nor[c] whether it be true or no.[3] Dined, and Mr. Hater and W. Hewer with me; where they do speak very sorrowfully of the posture of the times, and how people do cry out in the streets of their being bought and sold; and both they and everybody that come to me do tell me that people make nothing of talking treason in the streets openly: as, that we are bought and sold and governed by Papists and that we are betrayed by people about the King and

---

a MS. 'these three'   *b* repl. 'greatest'   *c* repl. 'and'

---

1. For this decision, see above, p. 98 & n. 1.
2. Clarendon was accused of having been responsible for selling Dunkirk to the French and for acquiring a useless colony in Tangier. He had also allegedly arranged that the King should marry a barren Queen so that the succession should pass to the Duke of York who was married to the Chancellor's daughter. The report about his windows and his trees is confirmed by *CSPD 1667*, p. 189.
3. Cf. the similar report (newsletter, 15 June) in *CSPD 1667*, p. 189. It was not true. The office of Constable (once the greatest military office of the kingdom) had been extinct since the reign of Henry VIII, and was by this time revived only at coronations, and for the constitution of Courts of Chivalry.

shall be delivered up to the French, and I know not what. At
dinner we discoursed of Tom of the Wood, a fellow that lives
like a Hermit near Woolwich, who as they say (and Mr. Bodham,
they tell me, affirms that he was by at the Justice's when some
did accuse him there for it) [did] foretell the burning of the City,
now says that a greater desolation is at hand.[1] Thence we read
and laughed at Lillys prophecies this month – in his almanac this
year.[2] So to the office after dinner; and thither comes Mr.
Pierce, who tells me his condition: how he cannot get his money
(about 500*l*, which he says is a very great part of what he hath
for his family and children) out of Viner's hand – and endeed, it
is to be feared that this will wholly undo the banquiers. He says
he knows nothing of the late affronts to my Lord Chancellors
house as is said, nor hears of the Duke of Albemarle's being made
High Constable; but says that they are in great distraction at
White-hall – and that everywhere people do speak high against
Sir W. Coventry;[3] but he agrees with me that he is the best
Minister of State the King hath, and so from my heart I believe.
At night came home Sir W. Batten and W. Penn, who only can
tell me that they have placed guns at Woolwich and Deptford
and sunk some ships below Woolwich and Blackwall, and are in
hopes that they will stop the enemy's coming up. But strange
our confusion; that among them that are sunk[a] they have gone
and sunk without consideration the *Franckin*, one of the King's
ships, with stores to a very considerable value, that hath been
long loaden for supply of the ships and the new ship at Bristoll,
and much wanted there[4] – and nobody will own that they

a repl. 'stopped'

---

1. William Bodham was Clerk of
the Ropeyard, Woolwich. The story
of Tom of the Wood has not been
traced elsewhere.

2. William Lilly, in his *Merlini
Anglici Ephemeris* (1666), had forecast
for June 1667: 'great expectation of
Peace . . . a most strange and unusual
loss at Sea (for Holland), if they shall
dare to fight His Majesties Forces. . . .
Strange news out of Holland, as if all
were in an uproar; we believe they

are now in a sad and fearful condition.' (Pepys preserved in his library
four of Lilly's miscellaneous works on
astrology, but none of his almanacks.)

3. Coventry was (unfairly) blamed
for the decision not to fit out a battle-
fleet this year: Evelyn, 29 July.

4. The ship now sunk was one of
the three put in charge of the river
defences: *CSPD 1667*, p. 193. The
new ship at Bristol was probably the
Edgar: see below, 13 June 1668 & n.

directed it, but do lay it on Sir W Rider; they speak also of
another ship, loaden to the value of 80000*l,ᵃ* sunk with the goods
in her, or at least was mightily contended for by him, and a
foreign ship that had the faith of the nation for her security;
this Sir R. Ford tells us. And it *ᵇ* is too plain a truth, that both
here and at Chatham the ships that we have sunk have many,
and the first of them, been ships completely fitted for fireships
at great charge. But most strange, the backwardness and disorder of all people, especially the King's people in pay, to do any
work (Sir W. Penn tells me), all crying out for money. And it
was so at Chatham, that this night comes an order from Sir
W. Coventry to stop the pay of the wages of that Yard, the Duke
of Albemarle having related that not above three of 1100 in pay
there did attend to do any work there.¹ This evening, having
sent a messenger to Chatham on purpose, we have received a
dull* letter from my Lord Brouncker and P. Pett how matters
have gone there this week;² but not so much, or so perticular
as we knew it by common talk before, and as true. I doubt
they will be found to have been but slow men in this business;
and they say the Duke of Albemarle did tell my Lord Brouncker
to his face that his discharging of the great ships there was the
cause of all this; and I am told that it is become common talk
against my Lord Brouncker, but in that he is to be justified, for
he did it by verball order from Sir W. Coventry, and with good
intent; and was to good purpose, whatever the success* be, for
the men would have but spent the King so much the more in
wages, and yet not attended on board to have done the King any
service [*ᶜ*and as an evidence of that just now, being the 15th
day in the morning that I am writing yesterday's passages, one
is with me, Jacob Bryan, purser of the *Princesse*, who confesses to
me that he hath above 180 men borne at this day in victuals and

---

a The following six pages are headed 'July' and corrected to 'June'.
b repl. 'for'   *c* The bracket (square altered from round) is Pepys's.

---

1. Coventry to Navy Board, 14
June: PRO, SP 29/205, no. 59; summary in *CSPD 1667*, p. 185. Coventry reported Albemarle's words in
this letter.

2. Summary in *CSPD Add. 1660–
85*, p. 193 (Chatham, 14 June).

wages on that ship lying at Chatham, being lately brought in thither; of which 180 there was not above five appeared to do the King any service at this late business. And this morning also, some of the *Cambriges* men came up from Portsmouth by order from Sir Fre. Hollis,[1] who boasted to us the other day that he had sent for 50, and would be hanged if 100 did not come up, that would do as much as twice the number of other men: I say some of them, instead of being at work at Deptford where they were intended, do come to the office this morning to demand the payment of their tickets, for otherwise they would, they said, do no more work; and are, as I understand from everybody that[a] have do with them, the most debauched, damning, swearing rogues that ever were in the Navy, just like their profane commander].[b] So to W. Batten's to sit and talk a little; and then home to my flagelette, my heart being at pretty good ease by a letter from my wife, brought by Saunders, that my father and wife got well last night to their Inne and out again this morning, and Gibson's being got safe to Caxton[2] at 12 last night. So to[c] supper, and then to bed. No news today of any motion of the enemy, either upwards towards Chatham or this way.

15. All the morning at the office. No news more then last night; only, Purser Tyler comes and tells me that he being at all the passages in this business at Chatham, he says there have been horrible miscarriages, such as we shall shortly hear of.[3] That the want of boats hath undone us; and it is commonly said, and Sir J. Mennes under his hand tells us, that they were imployed by the men of the Yard to carry away their goods;[4] and I hear that

a MS. 'they' *b* The bracket (square altered from round) is Pepys's.
c repl. 'home'

---

1. Sir Frescheville Holles, recently placed in command of the river defences. For his order, see *CSPD 1667*, p. 204. The *Cambridge* had just been paid off: ib., pp. 164, 204.

2. Nine miles west of Cambridge.

3. A report by Richard Tyler (undated, but shortly after the 13th) was summarised by Hewer in the form of a list of ships lost and saved: Rawl. 195a, f. 163r.

4. Mennes to Navy Board, 15 June: *CSPD Add. 1660–85*, pp. 193–4. He refrained from accusing any individuals. This alleged misuse of the boats was later one of the principal charges in the parliamentary impeachment of Pett.

Comissioner Pett will be found the first man that begun to remove; he is much spoken against – and Brouncker is complained of and reproached for discharging the men of the great ships heretofore. At noon Mr. Hater[1] dined with me, and tells me he believes that it will hardly be the want of money alone that will excuse to the Parliament the neglect of not setting out a fleet, it having never been[harbour-] bound in our greatest straits; but how[ever] unlikely that*a* it appeared, yet when it was gone about, the State or King did compass it; and there is something in it. In like manner, all the afternoon busy, vexed to see how slowly things go on for want of money. At night comes (unexpectedly so soon) Mr. Gibson, who left my wife well and all got down well with them, but not with himself, who (which I was afeared of and cannot blame him, but must myself be wiser against another time) had one of his bags broke through his breeches. And some pieces dropped out, not many (he thinks but two, for he light and took them up, and went back and could find no more); but I am not able to tell how many, which troubles*b* me; but the joy of having the greatest part safe there makes me bear with it, so as not to afflict*c* myself for it. This afternoon, poor Betty Michell, whom I love, sent to tell my wife her child was dying; which I am troubled for, poor girl. At night home and to my flagelette; played with pleasure, but with a heavy heart; only, it pleased me to think how it may please God I may live to spend my time in the country with plainness and pleasure, though but with little glory. So to supper and to bed.

16. *Lords day.* Up, and called on by several on business of the office. Then to the office to look out some of my old letters to W. Coventry, in order to preparing for justifying this office in our frequent foretelling the want of money.*d* By and by comes Roger Pepys and his son Talbott, whom he had brought to town to settle at the Temple; but by reason of our present stirs will carry him back again with him this week. He seems

a MS. 'they'   *b* repl. 'trouble' badly formed
   c repl. 'afk'-   *d* repl. 'this office'

---

1. Thomas Hayter, one of Pepys's clerks.

to be but a silly lad.¹ I sent them to church this morning, I staying at home at the office busy. At noon home to dinner, and much good discourse with him, he being mighty sensible of our misery and maladministration. Talking of these straits we are in, he tells me that my Lord Arlington did the last week take up 12000*l* in gold; which is very likely, for all was taken up that could be. Discoursing afterward with him of our family, he told me that when I come to his house he will show me a decree in Chancery, wherein there was 26 men, all housekeepers, in the town of Cottenham in Queen Elizabeth's time, of our name.² He to church again in the afternoon; I stayed at home busy. And did show some dalliance to my maid Nell, speaking to her of her sweetheart, which she owned, silly girl. After sermon R. Pepys comes again; I spent the evening with him, much troubled with the thoughts of the evils of our time, whereon we discoursed. By and by occasion offered for my writing to Sir W. Coventry a plain bold letter touching lack of money;³ which when it was gone, I was afeared might give offence, but upon two or three readings over again the copy of it, I was satisfied it was a good letter; only, Sir W. Batten signed it with me, which I could wish I had done alone. R. Pepys gone, I to the garden and there dallied a while all alone with Mrs. Markham, and then home to my chamber and to read and write; and then to supper and to bed.

17. Up and to my office, where busy all the morning. Perticularly, setting my people to work in transcribing pieces of letters public and private, which I do collect against a black day, to defend the office with and myself.⁴ At noon dined at home, Mr. Hater with me alone, who doth seem to be confident that this nation will be undone, and with good reason. Wishes

1. He was now aged 20. Son and heir of Roger Pepys, he was admitted to the Middle Temple in January 1663 and called to the bar in May 1670.

2. Roger Pepys probably got his information from the MS. mentioned above, p. 261, n. 4. The Chancery case concerned a dispute about the marriage contract of John Pepys (d. 1589). See the (fragmentary) petition of 1558 in PRO, C3/136/29. The decree has not been traced.

3. Longleat, Coventry MSS 97, f. 85; headed 16 June 'neare 5 afternoone'. 'We thinke it will be little lesse than to betray his Majesty's Service to give his R.H. ground to expect that any thing can redeeme the Honour or support the Service of his Majesty but a supply of praesent Mony (publiquely declared). . . .'.

4. These letter-books have not been traced: above, iii. 281, n. 2.

himself at Hambrough, as a great many more, he says, he believes do – but nothing but the reconciling of the presbyterian party will save us, and I am of his mind.[1] At the office all the afternoon, where every moment business of one kind or other about the fireships and other businesses; most of them vexatious[a] for want of money, the commanders all complaining that if they miss to pay their men a night, they run away – seamen demanding money of them by way of advance, and some of Sir Hollis's men, that he so bragged of, demanding their tickets to be paid or they would not work.   This Hollis, Sir W. Batten and W. Penn say, proves a very wind-fucker, as Sir W. Batten terms him; and the other called him a conceited, idle, prating, lying fellow.   But it was pleasant this morning to hear Hollis give me the account, which he says he told the King in Commissioner Pett's presence, whence it was that his ship[2] was fit sooner then others, telling the King how he dealt with the several commissioners and agents of the ports where he comes, offering Lanyon to carry him a ton or two of goods to the Straights – giving Middleton an hour or two's hearing of his stories of Berbados[3] – going[b] to prayer with Taylor; and standing bare and crying, "If it please your Honour" to Pett.   But W. Penn says that he tells this story to everybody, and believes it to be a very lie.   At night comes Captain Cocke to see me, and he and I an hour in the garden together; he tells me there have been great endeavours of bringing in the presbyterian interest, but that it will not do.   He named to me several of the insipid * Lords that are to command the army that are to be raised.[4]   He says the King and Court are all troubled, and the gates of the Court were shut up upon the first coming of the Dutch to us; but do mind the business no more then ever. That the Banquiers, he fears, are broke as to ready money, though

a repl. same symbol badly formed   *b* repl. 'Praying'

---

1. This view soon became widespread, according to Pepys. Hayter was a nonconformist: cf. above, iv. 129, n. 1. Hamburg (which was both Lutheran and tolerant) does not appear in fact to have been a city of refuge for English nonconformists.

2. The *Cambridge*.

3. Cf. below, ix. 500 & n. 1.

4. For the new troops, see above, p. 265 & n. 5.   The list of commanders (including several peers) is given in *CSPD 1667*, pp. 179–83.

Viner had 100000*l* by him when our troubles begun.[1]   That he and the Duke of Albemarle have received into their own hands of Viner, the former 10000*l* and the latter*ᵃ* 12000*l*, in tallies or assignments to secure what was in his hand of theirs.   And many other great men of our maisters have done the like – which is no good sign, when they begin to fear the main.   He and everybody cries out of the Office of the Ordinance for their neglects, both at Gravesend and Upner and everywhere else.   He gone, I to my business again; and then home to supper and to bed.   I have lately played the fool much with our Nell, in playing with her breasts.   This night late comes a porter with a letter from Monsieur Pratt[2] to borrow 100*l* for my Lord Hinchingbrooke, to enable him to go out with his Troop in the country as he is commanded, but I did find an excuse to decline it.   Among other reasons to myself, this is one: to teach him the necessity of being a good husband and keeping money or credit by him.

18.   Up, and did this morning dally*ᵇ* with Nell*ᶜ* and touch her thing,*ᵇ* which I was afterward troubled for.   To the office, and there all the morning.   Peg Penn came to see me, and I was glad of it; and did resolve to have tried her this afternoon, but that there was company with*ᵈ* ella at my house, whither I got her.   Dined at home, W. Hewer with me; and then to the office and to my Lady Penn's, and did find occasion for Peg to go home with me to my chamber; but there being an idle gentleman with them, he went with us and I lost my hope.   So to the office; and by and by word was brought me that Comissioner Pett is brought to the Tower and there laid up close prisoner[3] –

a   repl. same symbol badly formed
b–b   garbled s.h., with garbled 'dally' repl. ungarbled 'dally'.   See above, p. 244, note *a*.

c   MS. 'Nerel'   *d*   repl. 'mit ella'

1. Sir Robert Vyner, unlike his rival Backwell, was unable to lend to the Treasury on the Eleven Months Tax: *CSPD 1667–8*, p. 113. By December 1667 he was obliged to petition the King for assistance in maintaining his credit: ib., loc. cit.

2. Du Prat, who had been Hinchingbrooke's tutor in Paris.

3. The news was sent to the Navy Board in the postscript of a letter (17 June) from Brouncker and Mennes at Chatham: *CSPD Add. 1660–85*, p. 195.   The arrest had been made on the previous day.

which puts me into a fright, lest they may do the same with us
as they do with him. This puts me upon hastening what I am
doing with my people, and collecting out of my papers our
defence. Myself got Fist, Sir W. Batten's clerk, and busy with
him writing letters late; and then home to supper and to read
myself asleep, after piping; and so to bed. Great news tonight
of the blowing up of one of the Duch greatest ships while a
council-of-war was on board; the latter part, I doubt, is not so,
it not being confirmed since; but the former, that they had a
ship blown up, is said to be true.[1] This evening comes Sir G.
Carteret to the office to talk of business at Sir W. Batten's;
where all to be undone for want of money, there being none to
pay the Chest at their public pay the 24th of this month, which
will make us a scorn to the world.[2] After he had done there,
he and I into the garden and walked; and the greatest of our
discourse is his sense of the requisiteness of his parting with his
being Treasurer of the Navy if he can on any good terms. He
doth harp upon getting my Lord Brouncker to take it on half-
profit, but that he is not able to secure him in paying him so
much. But the thing I do advise him to do by all means; and
he resolves on it, it being but the same counsel which I intend to
take for myself. My Lady Jem goes down to Hinchingbrooke to
lie down – because of the troubles of the times here. He tells
me he is not sure that the King of France will not annoy us this
year, but that the Court seems [to] reckon upon it as a thing
certain; for that is all that I and most people are afeared of this
year. He tells me now the[a] great Question is, whether a Parliament or no Parliament; and says the Parliament itself cannot be
thought able at present to raise money, and therefore it will be
to no purpose to call one. I hear this day poor Michell's child[3]
is dead.

a repl. 'is'

---

1. A Chatham observer, writing on
27 July, reported that at about this
time the Dutch in their withdrawal
blew up one of their ships: Rawl. A
195a, f. 131r. Cf. also the report
(18 June) of the Dutch burning two
of their ships which had been crippled:
HMC, *Le Fleming*, p. 50.

2. Cf. Pepys to Officers of the
Chest (1 June): NMM, LBK/8, pp.
487–8 (printed *Further Corr.*, p. 176);
a statement of Batten's indebtedness
to the Chest (c. £5400).

3. Elizabeth, born on 23 April.

19. Up and to the office, where all the morning busy with Fist again, beginning early to overtake my business in my letters, which for a post or two have by the late and present troubles been interrupted. At noon comes Sir W. Batten and W. Penn, and we to W. Penn's house and there discoursed of business an hour; and by and by comes an order from Sir R. Browne, commanding me this afternoon to*a* attend the Council-board with all my books and papers touching the Medway.[1] I was ready [to fear] some mischief to myself, though that that appears most reasonable is that it is to inform them about Comissioner Pett. I eat a little bit in*b* haste at W. Batten's without much comfort, being fearful, though I show it not; and to my office and did get up some papers and find out the most material letters and orders in our books. And so took coach and to the Council-chamber lobby, where I met Mr. Eveling, who doth miserably decry our follies that brings all this misery upon us. While we were discoursing over our public misfortunes, I am called in to a large committee of the Council: present, the Duke of Albemarle, Anglesy, Arlington, Ashly, Carteret, Duncomb, Coventry, Ingram, Clifford, Lauderdale, Morice, Manchester, Craven, Carlisle, Bridgewater; and after Sir W. Coventry's telling them what orders his Royal Highness had made for the safety of the Medway, I told them to great full content what*c* we had done, and showed them our letters. Then was P. Pett call[ed] in with the Lieutenant of the Tower. He is in his old clothes, and looked most sillily. His charge was chiefly the not carrying up of the great ships, and the using of the boats in carrying away his goods; in which he answered very sillily – though his faults to me seem only great omissions.*d* Lord Arlington and Coventry very severe against him; the former saying that if he was not guilty, the world would think them all guilty. The latter urged that there must be some fault, and that the Admiral must be found to have done his part. I did say an unhappy word, which

a repl. 'board'   *b* repl. 'at'   *c* repl. 'we'
d repl. 'amission'

---

1. The order is in *CSPD Add. 1660–85*, p. 197. Copies of some of the papers were enclosed in a letter from Pepys to Coventry, 16 June: Longleat, Coventry MSS 97, f. 83.

I was sorry for, when he complained of want of oares for the boats; and there was it seems enough, and good enough to carry away all the boats with from the King's occasions. He said he used never a boat till they were all gone but one – and that was to carry away things of great value, and those were his models of ships; which when the Council, some of them, had said they wished that the Dutch had had them instead of the King's ships, he answered he did believe the*a* Dutch would have made more advantage of the models then of the ships, and the King have had greater loss thereby. This they all laughed at. After having heard*b* him for an hour or more, they bid him withdraw, I all this while showing him no respect, but rather against him; for which God forgive me, for I mean no hurt to him, but only find that these Lords are upon their own purgation, and it is necessary I should be so in behalf of the office. He being gone, they caused Sir Rd. Browne to read over his minutes; and then my Lord Arlington moved that they might be put into my hands to put into form, I being more acquainted with such business; and they were so.¹ So I away back*c* with my books and papers; and when I got into the Court, it was pretty to see how people gazed upon me – that I thought myself obliged to salute people and to smile, lest they should think I was a prisoner too; but afterward I found the most did take me to be there to bear evidence against P. Pett. But my fear was such, at my going in, of the success* of the day, that at my going in I did think*d* fit to give T. Hater (whom I took with me to wait the event) my closet-key and directions where to find 500*l* and more in silver and gold, and my tallies, to remove in case of any misfortune to me. Thence to Sir G. Carteret's to take my leave of my Lady Jem, who is going into the country tomorrow; but she being now at prayers with my Lady and family, and hearing here by Yorke the carrier that my wife was coming to town, I did make haste home to see her, that she might not find*e* me abroad, it being the first minute I have been abroad since yesterday

a repl. 'he would'   *b* repl. 'hear him'   *c* repl. 'tack'
     d repl. 'give'   *e* repl. 'think'

---

1. Being committee minutes, they were not recorded in the Council Register.

was sennit. It is pretty to see how strange it is to be abroad to
see people, as it used to be after a month or two's absence; and
I have brought myself so to it, that I have no great mind to be
abroad – which I could not have believed *a* of myself. I got home;
and after being there a little, she came, and two of her fellow-
travellers with her, with whom we drunk – a couple of merchant-
like men I think, but have friends in our country. They being
gone, I and my wife to talk; who did give me so bad an account
of her and my father's method in burying of our gold, that made
me mad – and she herself is not pleased with it, she believing that
my sister knows of it. My father and she did it on Sunday when
they were gone to church, in open daylight in the midst of the
garden, where for aught they knew, many eyes might see them;
which put me into such trouble, that I was almost mad about it,
and presently cast about how to have it back again to secure it
here, the times being a little better now; at least, at White-hall
they seem as if they were – but one way or other, I am resolved
to free them from the place if I can get them. Such was my
trouble at this, that I fell out with my wife; that though new
come to town, I did not sup with her nor speak to her tonight,
but to bed and sleep.

20. Up, without any respect to my wife, only answering her
a question or two, without any anger though; and so to the
office, where all the morning busy; and among *b* other things,
Mr. Barber came to me (one of the clerks of the Ticket Office)
to get me to sign some tickets, and told me that all the discourse
yesterday about that part of the town where he was, was that
Mr. Pett and I were in the Tower; and I did hear the same
before. At noon home to dinner; and there my wife and I
very good friends, the care of my gold being somewhat over,
considering it was in their hands that have as much cause to
secure it as myself almost. And so if they will be mad, let
them; but yet I do intend to send for it away. Here dined
Mercer with us, and after dinner she cut my hair; and then I
into my closet and there slept a little, as I do now almost every day
after dinner; and then after dallying a little with Nell, which I am
ashamed to think of, I away to the office – busy all the afternoon;

a repl. 'my'-   *b* MS. 'after'

in the evening did treat with and in the end agree, but by some kind of compulsion, with the owners of six merchant ships to serve the King as men-of-war. But Lord, to see how against the hair it is with these men and everybody to trust us and the King, and how unreasonable it is to expect they should be willing to lend their ships and lay out 2 or 300*l* a man to fit their ships for new voyages, when we have not paid them half of what we owe them for their old services. I did write so to Sir W. Coventry this night.[1]   At night, my wife and I to walk and talk again about our gold, which I am not quiet in my mind to be safe; and therefore will think of some way to remove it, it troubling me very much.   So home with my wife to supper and to bed – miserable hot weather all night it was.

21.   Up and by water to White-hall, there to discourse with G. Carteret and Mr. Fenn about office business. I find them all aground, and no money to do anything with. Thence homewards, calling at my tailors to bespeak some colour[ed] cloth[e]s;[2] and thence to Hercules pillers all alone and there spent 6*d* on myself; and so home and busy all the morning. At noon to dinner, home; where my wife shows me a letter from her father, who is going over sea and this afternoon would take his leave of her; I sent him by her three Jacobus's in gold – having real pity for him and her.[3] So I to my office, and there all the afternoon. This day comes news from Harwich that the Duch fleet are all in sight, near 100 sail great and small they think, coming towards them; where they think they shall be able to oppose them, but do cry out of the falling back of the seamen, few standing by them, and those with much faintness.[4] The[a]

a MS. 'They'

---

1. Longleat, Coventry MSS 97, f. 91*r*; '20 June, ½ 9 at night'; giving the names of the ships.

2. Possibly because the period of mourning for Pepys's mother (who had died in March) was now ending.

3. Alexandre St Michel now went to Paris, where his wife joined him for a while: below, 28 January 1668.

4. Three letters sent to Pepys from Harwich on 20 June bearing news of the Dutch approach are in Rawl. A 195a, ff. 153–8. In that written by Anthony Deane (ib., f. 153*r*) is the sentence: 'We have a strang turne of seamens spirrits that out of 800 men which weare on board Colliers . . . now to be found not so many as will man eight Fierships . . .'.

like they write from Portsmouth,[1] and their letters this post[a] are worth reading. Sir H. Cholmly came to me this day, and tells me the Court is as mad as ever and that the night the[b] Duch burned[c] our ships, the King did sup with my Lady Castlemayne at the Duchess of Monmouth, and there were all mad in hunting of a poor moth. All the Court afeared of a Parliament; but he thinks nothing can save us but the King's giving up all to a Parliament.[d] Busy at the office all the afternoon and did much business, to my great content. In the evening, sent for home; and there I find my Lady Pen and Mrs. Lowther and Mrs. Turner and my wife eating some victuals, and there I sat and laughed with them a little, and so to the office again; and in the evening walked with my wife in the garden, and did give Sir W Pen at his lodgings (being just come from Deptford from attending the despatch of the fireships there) an account of what passed the other day at Council touching Comissioner Pett. And so home to supper and to bed.

22. Up, and to my office, where busy, and there came Mrs. Daniel; and it is strange how merely the putting my[e] hand to[f] her belly through[g] her coats did make me do.[e] At the office, I all the morning busy. At noon home to dinner, where Mr. Lewes Phillips[2] by invitation of my wife comes,[h] he coming up to town with her in the coach this week; and she expected another gentleman, a fellow-traveller, and I perceive the feast was for him,[i] though she doth not say it; but by some mistake he came not, so there was a good dinner lost. Here we had the two Mercers, and pretty merry. Much talk with Mr. Phillips about country business; among others, that there is no way for me to purchase any severall lands[3] in Brampton, or making any several

---

a MS. 'most'   b repl. 'our'   c 'burned' repeated
d The preceding part of this entry and the latter part of the preceding entry (from 'But Lord' onwards) are crowded into the bottom half of the page. The following leaf has been cut out.
      e–e garbled s.h. : see above, p. 244, note a   f repl. 'in'
      g repl. 'dimid' (='did')   h repl. 'coming'   i repl. 'f'-

---

1. Sc. about the unwillingness of the seamen to fight. There were no Dutch ships before Portsmouth as there were before Harwich.

2. Lawyer, of Brampton.
3. Enclosed lands; usually pastures enclosed from the common.

that is not so without much trouble and cost, and it may be not do it neither – so that there is no more ground to be laid to our Brampton house. After dinner I left them, and to*ᵃ* the office and thence to Sir W. Penn's, there to talk with Mrs. Lowther and by and by, we hearing Mercer and my boy singing at my house, making exceeding good music, to the joy of my heart that I should be the maister of it, I took her to my house and there merry a while; and then I left them and at the office, busy all the afternoon and sleepy after a great dinner. In the evening came Captain Hart and Hayword to me about the six Merchant-ships now taken up for men-of-war, and in talk they told me about the taking of *Royall Charles*; that nothing but carelessness lost the ship, for they might have saved her the very tide that the Duch came up, if they would have but used means and had had but boats, and that the want of boats plainly lost all the other ships. That the Dutch did take her with a boat of nine Men, who found not a man on board her (and her laying so near them was a main temptation to them to come on); and presently a man went up and struck her flag and Jacke, and a trumpeter sounded upon her "Joan's placket is torn."¹ That they did carry her down at a time, both for tides and wind, when the best pilot in Chatham would not have undertaken it, they heeling her on one side to make her draw little water, and so carried her away safe. They being gone, by and by comes Sir W Pen home, and he and I together talking. He hath been at Court; and in the first place, I hear the Duke of Cambrige is dead,² which is a great loss to the nation, having I think never an heyre male now of the King's or Duke's to succeed to the Crown. He tells me that they do begin already to damn the Dutch and call them cowards at White-hall, and think of them and their business no better then they used to do; which is very sad. The King did tell him himself (which is so, I was told here in the City) that the City hath lent him 10000*l*, to be laid out towards securing of the River of Thames;

a repl. 'home'

---

1. The original ballad is untraced. For the tune, see C. M. Simpson, *Brit. broadside ballad and its music,* pp. 388–90. (E).

2. See above, p. 214 & n. 1.

which methinks is a very poor thing, that we should be reduced
to borrow by such mean sums.[1]   He tells me that it is most
manifest that one great thing making it impossible for us to have
set out a fleet this year (if we could have done it for money or
stores) was the liberty given the beginning of the year for the
setting out of merchant-men, which did take up, as is said, above
10 if not 15000 seamen (and this the other day Captain Cocke
tells me appears in the council-books; that is, the number of
seamen required to man the merchant ships that had passes to go
abroad);[2] by and by, my wife being here, they sat down and eat
a bit of their nasty victuals, and so parted and we to bed.

23.   *Lords day.*   Up, and I to my chamber, and there all the
morning reading in my Lord Cooke's *Pleas of the Crowne*,[3]
very fine noble reading.   After church-time comes my wife and
Sir W. Penn his lady and daughter and Mrs. Markham and
Captain Hannum (who came to dine with them) by invitation
and dined with me, they as good as inviting themselfs.   I confess
I hate their company and tricks, and so had no great pleasure in
[it], but a good dinner lost.   After dinner they all to church and
I by water alone down to Woolwich; and there called on Mr.
Bodham[4] and he and I to see the Batterys newly raised; which
indeed are good works to command the River below the ships
that are sunk, but not above them.   Here I met with Captain
Cocke and Matt Wren, Fen and Charles Porter, and Temple and
his wife.   Here I fell in with these, and to Bodhams with them;
and there we sat and laughed and drank in his arbour – Wren
making much and kissing all the day of Temples wife.   It is a
sad sight to see so many good ships there sunk in the River, while

1. The Lord Mayor and Aldermen
had been summoned to a Privy Council meeting on the 21st, and had
agreed to make this loan for the erec-
tion of a fort at Sheerness and other
works: *CSPD 1667*, p. 247; Sharpe,
ii. 436–7; cf. above, p. 98 & n. 3.
The smallness of the loan was said to
be due to the City's losses in the fire.

2. The passes are listed in the Privy
Council registers.   Pepys (and others)

received fees for their issue: see the
minute (19 May) in PRO, PC
1/1/8.

3. *The third part of the Institutes of
the Laws of England: concerning High
Treason, and other pleas of the Crown*, by
Sir Edward Coke: see above, vi. 70,
n. 3.

4. Clerk of the Ropeyard, Woolwich.

we would be thought to be maisters of the Sea. Cocke says the Banquiers cannot, till peace returns, ever hope to have credit again; so that they can pay no more money, but people must be contented to take public security, such as they[1] can give them; and if so, and they do live to receive the money thereupon, the banquiers will be happy men. Fen read me an order of council passed the 17th instant, directing all the Treasurers of any part of the King's revenue to make no payments but such as shall be approved by the present Lords Commissioners;[2] which will, I think, spoil the credit of all his Majesty's service, when people cannot depend upon payment anywhere. But the King's Declaracion in behalf of the Banquiers, to make good their assignments for money, is very good, and will I hope secure me.[3] Cocke says that he hears it is come to it now, that the King will try what he can soon do for a peace; and if he cannot, that then he will cast all upon the Parliament to do as they see fit; and in doing so, perhaps he may save us all. The King of France, it is believed, is engaged for this year,[4] so that we shall be safe as to him. The great misery the City and kingdom is like to suffer for want of coals in a little time is very visible, and is feared will breed a mutiny; for we are not in any prospect to command the sea for our colliers to come; but rather, it is feared the*a* Dutch may go and burn all our Colliers at Newcastle; though others do say that they lie safe enough there.[5] No news at all of late from Bredagh what our Treaters do. By and by all by water in three boats to Greenwich, there to Cockes, where we supped well; and then late, Wren, Fenn, and I home by water, set me in at the

a repl. 'they may'

---

1. The departmental treasurers or cashiers, such as Pepys and Fenn.
  2. PRO, PC 2/59, pp. 457–8; *CTB*, ii. 12–13. On the 21st Fenn had taken Carteret's certificates of payment to the Treasury.
  3. Steele, no. 3493 (18 June). For its effects in stopping a run on the banks, see [Thomas Turnor,] *The case of the bankers and their creditors . . .* (1675).

4. In the Flanders campaign against the Spaniards.
  5. The Dutch fleet blockaded the Thames until the end of July when peace was signed. Fear for the Newcastle colliers was widespread: see e.g. *CSPD 1667*, p. 190; *Savile Corr.* (ed. W. D. Cooper), pp. 16, 17.

Tower and they to White-hall; and so I home, and after a little
talk with my wife, to bed.

24. Up, and to the office, where much business upon me by
the coming of people of all sorts about the despatch of one
business or other of the fireships or other ships to be set out now.
This morning Greeting came, and I with him at my flagelette.
At noon dined at ⟨home⟩ with my wife alone; and then in the
afternoon, all the day at my office – troubled a little at a letter
from my father which tells me of an idle companion, one Coleman, who went down with him and*a* my wife in the coach and
came up again with my wife, a pensioner of the King's Guard
and one that my wife, endeed, made the feast for on Saturday
last, though he did not come; but if he knows nothing of our
money,*b* I will prevent any other inconvenience. In the evening
comes Mr. Povy about business, and he and I to walk in the
garden an hour or two and to talk of State matters; he tells me
his opinion that it is out of possibility*c* for us to escape being
undone, there being nothing in our power to do that is necessary
for the saving us – a lazy prince – no council – no money; no
reputation at home or abroad. He says that to this day the King
doth fallow the women as much as ever he did. That the Duke
of York hath not got Mrs. Middleton, as I was told the other day;
but says that he wants not her, for he hath others and hath alway
had, and that he hath known them brought through the Matted
Gallery at White-hall into his closet. Nay, he hath come out of
his wife's bed and gone to others laid in bed for him. That Mr.
Brouncker is not the only pimp, but that the whole family is of
the same strain, and will do anything to please him. That,
besides the death of the two princes lately, the family* is in
horrible disorder by being in debt, by spending above 60000*l* per
annum when he hath not 40000*l*.[1] That the Duchesse is not

a repl. 'in'   *b* repl. 'brom'-   *c* repl. 'supposable'

1. Povey had been Treasurer of the   of Kendal and Cambridge, had died
Duke's Household, 1660–66. The   on 22 May and 20 June respectively.
Duke of York's infant sons, the Dukes

only the proudest woman in the world, but the most expenseful;[1] and that the Duke of York's marriage with her hath undone the kingdom by making the Chancellor so great above reach, who otherwise would have been but an ordinary man, to have been dealt with by other people, and he would have been careful of managing things well, for fear of being called to account; whereas now, he is secure and hath let things run to wrack, as they now appear. That at a certain time Mr. Povy did carry him an account of the state of the Duke of York's estate, showing[a] in faithfulness how he spent more then his estate would bear, by above 20000*l* per annum, and asked my Lord's opinion of it; to which he answered that no man that loved the King or kingdom durst own the writing of that paper; at which Povy was started and reckoned himself undone for this good service, and found it necessary then to show it to the Duke of York's commissioners,[2] who read, examined and approved of it, so as to cause it to be put into form, and signed to it and gave it the Duke. Now the end of the Chancellor was for fear that his daughter's ill house-wifery should be condemned. He tells me that the other day, upon this ill news of the Duch being upon us, White-hall was shut up and the Council called and sat close (and by the way he doth assure me, from the mouth of some privy-councillors, that at this day the Privy-council in general doth know no more what the state of the kingdom as to peace and war is then he or I, nor knows who manages it nor upon whom it depends); and there my Lord Chancellor did make a speech to them, saying that they knew well that he was no friend to the war from[b] the beginning,[3] and therefore

a repl. 'that'   *b* repl. 'fr'-

---

1. Cf. Povey's similar story of her below, 27 January 1668. Burnet (i. 298, 299) says that she was 'generous and friendly', but that she 'took state on her, rather too much'.

2. The commissioners appointed to manage the Duke's estates and revenues: for their names (December 1667), see HMC, *Rep.*, 8/1/2, p. 280a.

3. Clarendon had regarded the war, from the autumn of 1664 onwards, as

a regrettable necessity, caused by Dutch provocations: Lister, iii. 238–40, 245, 266–7, 346–7; *Life*, ii. 303; cf. Coventry's account in Longleat, Coventry MSS 102, f. 5*r*. He seems to have taken little or no part in its direction. Until the time of the preparations against a Dutch attack in the summer of 1667 he had never even heard of Sheerness: *Life*, iii. 193–4.

had concerned himself little in, nor could say much to it; and a great deal of that kind, to discharge himself of the fault of the war – upon which, my Lord Anglesy rose up and told his Majesty that he thought their coming now together was not to enquire who was or was not the cause of the war, but to enquire what was or could be done in the business of making a peace, and in whose hands that was and where it was stopped or forwarded; and went on very highly to have all made open to them (and by the way, I remember that Captain Cocke did the other day tell me that this Lord Anglesy hath said, within few days, that he would willingly give 10000*l* of his estate that he was well secured of the rest,*a* such apprehensions he hath of the sequel of things, as giving all over for lost): he tells me, speaking of the horrid effeminacy* of the King, that the King hath taken ten times more care and pains making friends between my Lady Castlemayne and Mrs. Steward when they have fallen out, then ever he did to save his kingdom; nay, that upon fallings-out between my Lady Castlemayne's nurse and her woman, my Lady hath often said she [would] make the King to make them friends, and*b* they would not be friends and be quiet – which the King hath been fain to do.   That the King is at this day every night in Hyde-park with the Duke of Monmouth or with my Lady Castlemaine.   That he[1] is concerned of late by my Lord Arlington in the looking after some buildings that he is about in Norfolke, where my Lord is laying out a great deal of money;[2] and that he (Mr. Povy), considering*c* the unsafeness of laying*d* out money at such a time as this, and besides the enviousness of that particular county, as well as all the Kingdom, to find him building and imploying workmen while all the ordinary people of the country are carried*e* down to the sea-sides for securing

---

   a repl. closing bracket *b* repl. 'and would'
 c repl. 'concer'- *d* repl. 'l'- *e* repl. ? 'warned'

---

1. Povey.

2. At Euston Hall, Norf., which Arlington had bought in 1665: W. A. Copinger, *Manors of Suff.*, i. 293. For his lavish building there c. 1666–70, see Evelyn, iii. 591–2, iv. 116–20; *Country Life*, 10 January 1957, pp. 58+. It appears that he did not yet live in the house, but was about to start reconstructing it: *CSPD 1667–8*, p. 602. Pepys kept a copy of a later memorandum written by Povey to Arlington (28 October 1668): 'Considerations touching the Purchase of the Parke and wood neare Euston' (Rawl. A 195a, ff. 58–9).

the land, he thought it becoming him to go to my Lord Arlington (Sir Tho. Clifford by) and give it as his advice to hold his hand a little. But my Lord would not, but would have him go on; and so Sir Tho. Clifford advised also, which one would think (if he were a statesman worth a fart) should be a sign of his foreseeing that all shall do well; but I do forbear concluding any such thing from them. He tells me that there is not so great confidence between any two men of power in the nation at this day, that he knows of, as between my Lord Arlington and Sir Tho. Clifford; and that it arose by accident only, there being no relation nor acquaintance between them; but only Sir Tho. Clifford's coming to him and applying himself to him for favours when he came first up to town to be a Parliament-man.[1] He tells me that he doth not think there is anything in the world for us possibly to be saved by but the King of France's generousnesse to stand by us against the Duch, and getting us a tolerable peace, it may be, upon our giving him Tanger and the islands[2] he hath taken, and other things, what he shall please to ask. He confirms me in the several grounds I have conceived of fearing that we shall shortly fall into mutinies and outrages among ourselfs, and that therefore he as a Treasurer (and therefore much more myself, I say, as being not only a Treasurer[3] but an Officer of the Navy,* on whom, for all the world knows, the fault of all our evils are to be laid) do fear to be seized on by some rude hands, as having money to answer for – which will make me the more desirous to get off of this Treasurership as soon as I can, as I had before in my mind resolved. Having done all this discourse and concluded the Kingdom in a desperate condition, we parted; and I to my wife, with whom was Mercer and Betty Michell, poor woman, come with her husband to see us after the death of her little girl; we sat in the garden together a while, it being night; and then Mercer and I a song or two, and then in (the Michells home), my wife, Mercer and I, to supper; and then parted and to bed.

25. Up, and with Sir W Pen in his new chariot (which endeed is plain, but pretty and more fashionable in shape then any coach

---

1. Cf. above, p. 185 & nn.
2. In the W. Indies.
3. Of Tangier.

he hath, and yet doth not cost him, harness and all, above 32*l*)[1]
to White-hall, where stayed a very little; and thence to St.
James's to W. Coventry, whom I have not seen since before the
coming of the Duch into the River, nor did endeed know how
well to go see him, for shame either to him or me, or both of us,
to find ourselfs in so much misery. I find that he and his fellow-
Treasurer's are in the utmost want of money, and do find fault
with Sir G. Carteret, that having kept the mystery of borrowing
money to himself so long (to ruin of the nation, as W. Coventry
said in words to W. Penn and me), he should now lay it aside
and come to them for money for every penny he hath, declaring
that he can raise no more – which I confess doth appear to me the
most like ill-will of anything that I have observed of W. Coventry, when he himself did tell us on another occasion at the same
time, that the Banquiers who used to furnish them money are not
able to lend a farding; and he knows well enough that that was
all the mystery G. Carteret did use; that is, only his credit with
them.[2] He told us*a* the maisters and owners of two ships that I
had complained of, for not readily setting forth their ships, which
we had taken up to make [men]-of-war, had been yesterday with
the King and Council,[3] and had made their case so well understood, that the King did owe them for what they had earned
the last year, that they could not set them out again without
some money or stores out of the King's yards; the latter of which
W. Coventry said must be done, for that they were not able to
raise money for them, though it was but 200*l* a ship; which doth
show us our condition to be so bad, that I am in a total despair of
ever*b* having the nation do well. After talking awhile, and all out

a repl. opening bracket   *b* repl. 'every'

---

1. In 1668 Pepys paid £53 for his
coach (apart from the painting): below, 24 October 1668.
2. In a parliamentary debate, 17
November 1669, Carteret claimed to
have borrowed £280,000 for the navy
on his own credit: Grey, i. 170.
Previous Treasurers had done much
the same: cf. *Journal of Sir S. D'Ewes*
(ed. W. Notestein), pp. 518–19.
3. Arnold Browne, master of the

Loyal Subject and Capt. Dunch, of the
Baltimore, had attended the Council
Committee at 4 p.m. on the 24th:
PRO, PC 2/59, f. 237*v*. They had
been impressed under the council
order of 11 June: *CSPD 1667*, p. 227.
See Pepys to Coventry, 22 June (Long-
leat, Coventry MSS 97, f. 93) and
Coventry to Pepys, 23 June (*CSPD
Add. 1660–85*, p. 199).

of heart with stories of want^a of seamen, and seamen's running
away, and their demanding a month's advance, and our being
forced to give seamen 3s a day to go hence to work at Chatham,[1]
and other things that shows nothing but destruction upon us;
for it is certain, that as it now is, the seamen of England in my
conscience would, if they could, go over [and] serve the King
of France or Holland rather then us – up to the Duke of York to
his chamber, where he seems to be pretty easy, and now and then
merry; but yet one may perceive in all their minds there, there is
something of trouble and care – and with good reason. Thence
to White-hall with Sir W. Penn by chariot, and there in the
Court met with my Lord Anglesy; and he to talk with Sir
W. Penn and told him of the maisters of ships being with the
Council yesterday, and that we were not in condition, though
the men were willing, to furnish them with 200*l* of money
(already due to them as earned by them the last year) to enable
them to set out their ships again this year for the King – which he
is amazed at; and when I told him, "My Lord, this is a sad
instance of the condition we are in," he answered that it was so
endeed, and sithed; and so parted, and he up to the Council-
chamber, where I perceive they sit every morning, and I to
Westminster-hall, where it is term-time. I met with none I
knew, nor did desire it, but only passed through the Hall; and
so back again and by coach home to dinner, being weary endeed
of seeing the world, and thinking it high time for me to provide
against the foul weather that is certainly coming upon us. So to
the office, and there W. Penn and I did do some business; and
then home to dinner – where my wife pleases me mightily with
what she can do upon the flagelette; and then I to the office
again, and busy all the afternoon. And it is worth noting that
the King and Council, in their order of the 23rd instant for
unloading three merchant-ships taken up for the King's service for

a repl. 'men and'

---

1. The normal rate for dockyard
workers was 12*d*. or 18*d*. a day.
Now they were demanding 3s. See
report from Chatham, 24 June,
CSPD Add. 1660–85, p. 200. Seamen serving on board ship mostly got
24s. a month: above, iv. 432, n. 2.

men-of-war, do call the late coming of the Duch "An invasion".[1]
I was told yesterday that Mr. Oldenburgh, our Secretary at
Gresham College, is put into the Tower for writing news to a
Virtuoso in France with whom he constantly corresponds[a] in
philosophical matters; which makes it very unsafe at this time to
write, or almost do anything.[2]   Several captains came to the
office yesterday and today, complaining that their men come and
go when they will and will not be commanded, though they are
paid every night, or may be.   Nay, this afternoon comes Harry
Russell[3] from Gravesend, telling us[b] that the money carried down
yesterday for the Chest at Chatham had like to have been seized
upon yesterday, in the barge there, by seamen who did beat our
watermen; and what[c] men should these be but the boat's Crew
of Sir Fr. Hollis, who used to brag so much of the goodness and
order of his men and his command over them.

   Busy all the afternoon at the office.   Towards night, I with
Mr. Kinaston to White-hall about a Tanger Order, but lost our
labour; only met Sir H Cholmly there, and he tells me great
news: that this day in Council, the King hath declared that he
will call his Parliament in 30 days – which is the best news I have
heard a great while, and will, if anything, save the Kingdom.[4]
How the King came to be advised to this, I know not; but he
tells me that it was against the Duke of York's mind flatly, who

---

a MS. 'correspondents'   *b* repl. 'me'   *c* repl. 'whose

---

1. PRO, PC 2/59, p. 466: the
Royal Exchange, Society and *Lewis*
were taken up 'in regard to the invasion of the Dutch'.   A full list of all
the merchantmen hired for the royal
service during the war is in PL 2589,
ff. 84–8.

2. Henry Oldenburg had been arrested on 20 June, and was released in
late August: *CSPD 1667*, pp. 214,
215, 418.   He had corresponded on
political as well as scientific subjects
with French and Dutch virtuosi
during the war, and had in fact passed
on some of his news to Williamson,

Arlington's secretary. The precise
occasion of his disgrace is uncertain,
but Arlington may have objected to
his connections with the French
Huguenot scholar Henri Justel.   See
A. R. and M. Hall (ed.), *Corresp. H.
Oldenburg*, vol. iii, p. xxvi; D. McKie
in *Notes and Records Roy. Soc.*, vi.
28+.

3. Waterman to the Navy Board.

4. A proclamation (26 June) recalled Parliament on 25 July, but it
met only to be prorogued again until
10 October: Steele, no. 3495; *CJ*,
viii. 692.

did rather advise the King to raise money as he pleased; and against the Chancellors, who told the King that Queen Elizabeth did do all her business in 88 without calling a Parliament, and so might he do for anything he saw;[1] but blessed be God, it is done, and pray God it may hold, though some of us must surely go to the pot, for all must be flung up to them or nothing will be done. So back home, and my wife down the water; I sent her with Mrs. Hewers and her son, W. Hewers, to see the sunk ships, while I stayed at the office; and in the evening was visited by Mr. Roberts, the merchant by us, about the getting him a ship cleared from serving the King as a man-of-war, which I will endeavour to do.[2] So home to supper and to bed.

26. Up; and in dressing myself in my dressing-chamber, comes up Nell and I did*a* play with her and touch her belly and thing, but did not kiss her.*a* So being ready, I to White-hall by water, and there to the Lords Treasurers chamber and there wait; and here it [is] everybody's discourse that the Parliament is ordered to meet the 25th of July; being, as they say, St. James's day[3] – which every creature is glad of.*b* But it is pretty to consider, how walking to the Old Swan from my house, I met Sir Tho. Harvy;[4] whom asking the news of the Parliament's meeting, he told me it was true and they would certainly make a great rout among us. I answered, I did not care of my part though I was ruined, so the Commonwealth might escape ruin by it. He answered, "That is a good one, in faith!*c* For you know

a–a   garbled s.h.: see above, p. 244, note *a*
b   followed by 'it' (struck through)   *c*   repl. symbol rendered illegible

1. This advice was one of the justifications for Parliament's impeachment of Clarendon in the following autumn. His contention, according to his autobiography, was that the occasion called for a 'more contracted council' than a Parliament, and that there were legal difficulties in now recalling a Parliament which had been prorogued to a later date (20 October): *Life*, iii. 252–60. Carteret, as well as the Duke of York and Clarendon, is said to have been against

summoning Parliament: *Savile Corr.* (ed. W. D. Cooper), p. 17.
2. This was probably the *Lewes*, a merchantman in which William Roberts had a quarter-share. She had served as a frigate since 1664 and was paid off and released at the end of the summer. *CSPD 1667*, pp. 239, 292; PL 2265, no. 19; PL 2871, p. 663.
3. James, Duke of York, had opposed the summons of parliament.
4. Navy Commissioner.

yourself to be secure, in being necessary to the office; but for my part," says he, "I must look to be removed; but then," says he, "I doubt not but I shall have amends made me, for all the world knows upon what terms I came in" – which is a saying that a wise man would not unnecessarily have said, I think, to anybody; meaning, his buying his place of my Lord Berkely.[1] So we parted; and I to White-hall as I said before, and there met with Sir St. Fox and Mr. Scowen, who both confirm the news of the Parliament's meeting. Here I stayed for an order for my Tanger money (30000*l*) upon the Eleven Months Tax;[2] and so away to my*ᵃ* Lord Arlington's office, and there spoke to him about Mr. Lanyons business[3] and received a good answer; and thence to Westminster-hall and there walked a little; and there met with Collonell Reames, who tells me of a letter come last night ⟨or the day before⟩ from my Lord St. Albans out of France, wherein he says that the King of France did lately fall out with him, giving him ill names; saying that he had belied him to our King by saying that he had*ᵇ* promised to assist our King and to forward the peace; saying that endeed he had offered to forward the peace at such a time, but it was not accepted of, and so he thinks himself not obliged, and would do what was fit for him;[4] and so made him to go out of his sight in great displeasure; and he hath given this account to the King, which Collonell Reemes tells me puts them into new melancholy at Court, and he believes hath forwarded the resolution of calling the Parliament – wherewith,

a repl. 'Secr'-　　　　*b* repl. 'would'

---

1. He was said to have paid £3000 to Berkeley for his place in 1665: Clarendon, *Life*, ii. 333. He sold it for £2000 in February 1668: *CSPD 1667-8*, p. 227. Pepys's opinion of him was always low.

2. Warrant (25 June) in *CTB*, ii. 166. £15,000 was added in July: see below, p. 344 & n. 3. Cf. above, p. 52.

3. The victualling of Tangier.

4. St Albans had been in Paris as envoy-extraordinary since February:

C. H. Firth and S. C. Lomas, *Notes on diplom. relations Engl. and France, 1603-88*, pp. 18-19. Despite the delaying tactics of the French, a peace treaty was signed on 21/31 July. The letter here mentioned does not appear to be among either St Albans's despatches to Arlington (PRO, SP 78/123) or his letters to Clarendon (Bodl., Clar. MSS). Bullen Reymes, M.P., was a Gentleman of the Privy Chamber to the King.

for all this, I am very well contented; and so parted and to the Exchequer, but Mr. Burges was not in his office; so alone to the Swan, and thither came Mr. Kinaston[1] to me, and he and I into a room and there drank and discoursed, and I am mightily pleased with him for a most diligent and methodical man in all his business. By and by to Burges and did as much as we could with him about our Tanger order, though we met with unexpected delays in it; but such as are not to be avoided, by reason of the form of the Act and the disorders which the King's necessities do put upon it;[2] and therefore away by coach and at White-hall espied Mr. Povy, who tells me as a great secret, which none knows but himself, that Sir G. Carteret hath parted with his place*a* of Treasurer of the Navy by consent,*b* to my Lord Anglesy, and is to be Treasurer of Ireland in his stead;[3] but upon what terms it is, I know not; but Mr. Povy tells me it is so, and that it is in his power to bring me to as great a friendship and confidence in my Lord Anglesy as ever I was with W. Coventry, which I am glad of; and so parted, and I to my tailor's about turning my old silk suit and cloak into a suit and vest;[4] and thence with Mr. Kinaston (whom I had set down in the Strand and took up again at the Temple gate) home and there to dinner, mightily pleased with my wife's playing on the flagelette; and so after dinner to the office. Such is the want already of coals and the despair of having any supply, by reason

a repl. 'of'   *b* symbol smudged

---

1. See above, p. 251, n. 1.
2. Delays followed from the 'form' of the act (for the Eleven Months Tax) in that funds were reserved for naval charges. 'Disorders' followed from the King's recouping himself for advances made out of his ordinary income.
3. Carteret and Anglesey were both under attack and hoped (in vain) to save themselves by changing places. The warrant to the Attorney-General to prepare a surrender by Carteret

and a grant of the office to Anglesey was issued this day: *CSPD 1667*, p. 235. Anglesey's office was that of Vice-Treasurer and Receiver-General, not Treasurer, of Ireland. But knowledgeable persons (according to Sandwich) put the Irish post's profits at £5000 p.a. – about double those of the Navy Treasurership in peacetime: Sandwich MSS, Journals, v. 60.
4. The new (1666) fashion: cf. above, vii. 315.

of the enemy's being abroad and no fleet of ours to secure, that they are come, as Mr. Kinaston tells me, at this day to 5*l.* 10*s.* 00*d* per chaldron.[1] All the afternoon busy at the office; in the evening, with my wife and Mercer took coach, and to Islington to the old house,[2] and there eat and drank and sang with great pleasure, and then round by Hackeny home with great pleasure; and when come home, to bed, my stomach not being well pleased with the cream we had tonight.

27.   Wakened this morning about 3 a-clock by Mr. Griffin, with a letter from Sir W. Coventry to W. Penn[3] (which W. Penn sent me to see) that the Dutch are come up to the Nore again, and he knows not whether further or no – and would have, therefore, several things done: ships sunk, and I know not what; which Sir W. Penn (who it seems is very ill this night, or would be thought so) hath directed Griffin to carry to the Trinity-house; so he went away with the letter, and I tried and with much ado did get a little sleep more; and so up about 6 a-clock, full of thought what to do with the little money I have left, and my plate, wishing with all my heart that that was all secured. So to the office, where much business all the morning, and the more by my Brethren being all out of the way: Sir W. Penn this night taken so ill, cannot stir – W. Batten ill at Walthamstow – Sir J. Mennes the like at Chatham; and my Lord Brouncker there also upon business – horrible trouble with the backwardness of the merchants to let us have their ships, and seamen's running away and not to be got or kept without money. It*a* is worth turning to our letters this day to Sir W. Coventry about these matters.[4]   At noon to dinner, having a haunch of venison boiled,

a MS. 'is'

---

1. This was apparently the highest price reached: cf. above, p. 98, n. 5. By mid-September it had fallen steeply: below, p. 435.

2. The King's Head: cf. above, ii. 125, n. 2.

3. 27 June, 'past 2 a.m.'; 'in his absence to be opened by any officers

of the Navy': PRO, SP 46/136, no. 518; summary in *CSPD Add. 1660–85*, pp. 200–01.

4. See e.g. Longleat, Coventry MSS 95, f. 359*r*; a letter from Pepys and Penn reporting that Trinity House could get no more cash from the bankers.

and all my clerks at dinner with me; and mightily taken with Mr. Gibson's discourse of the faults of this war in its management compared [with] that in the last war, which I will get him to put into writing.[1] Thence after dinner to the office again, and there I saw the proclamations come out this day for the Parliament to meet the 25th of next month;[2] for which God be praised – and another to invite seamen*a* to bring in their complaints of their being ill-used in the getting their tickets and money – there being a committee of the Council appointed to receive their complaints.[3]

This noon W. Hewer and T Hater both tell me that it is all over the town, and Mr. Pierce tells me also, this afternoon coming to me, that for certain Sir G. Carteret hath parted with his Treasurer's place, and that my Lord Anglesy is in it upon agreement and change of places, though the latter part I do not think. This Povy told me yesterday, and I think it is a wise act of G. Carteret. Pierce tells me that he hears for certain, fresh at Court, that France and we shall agree – and more, that yesterday was damned at the Council the Canary Company;[4] and also that my Lord Mordant hath laid down his commission[5] – both good things to please the Parliament, which I hope will do good. Pierce tells me that all the town doth cry out of our office for a pack of fools and knaves, but says that everybody speaks either

a repl. 'people'

---

1. Richard Gibson was a Navy Office clerk. His memorandum (undated; in his own and Pepys's hand) survives as 'The Charge of the Dutch Warrs in the Yeares 1653 and 1666 Compared'; BM, Add. 11602, f. 93. It shows that the Board had been more economical in 1666. Pepys sent a copy (in his own hand) to Coventry: Longleat, Coventry MSS 98, f. 236*r*. Cf. below, 16 March 1669.

2. See above, p. 292 n. 4.

3. 25 June: Steele no. 3494.

4. For this affair, see above, vii. 314 & n. 2. A committee of Council was appointed on the 28th to consider the patent, and the charter was withdrawn on 18 September: *EHR*, 31/540. The vote was a victory for the enemies of Clarendon, who was blamed for having authorised the issue of the patent.

5. This was untrue: for the attack made on him in parliament, see above, vii. 386 & n. 2. Mordaunt did not resign his commission in the army or give up his government of Windsor Castle until September 1668: *CSPD 1667–8*, p. 608.

well, or at least the best, of me, which is my great comfort and I
do think I do deserve it and shall show I have; but yet do think,
and he also, that the Parliament will send us all going; and I
shall be well contented with it, God knows. But he tells me
how Matt Wren should say that he was told that I should say
that W. Coventry was guilty of the miscarriage at Chatham;
though I myself, as he confesses, did tell him otherwise, and that
it was wholly Pett's fault.[1] This doth trouble me; not only
as untrue, but as a design in some or other to do me hurt; for as
the thing is false, so it never entered into my mouth or thought,
nor ever shall. He says that he hath rectified Wren in his belief
of this, and so all is well. He gone, I to business till the evening;
and then by chance home and find the fellow that came up with
my wife, Coleman, late from Brampton; a silly rogue, but one
that would seem a gentleman, but I did not stay with him. So to
the office, where late, busy; and then to walk a little in the garden,
and so home to supper and to bed. News this tide, that about
80 sail of Duch, great and small, were seen coming up the River
this morning;[2] and this tide, some of them to the upper end of
the Hope.

28. Up, and hear Sir W. Batten is come to town; I to see
him; he*a* is very ill of his Feaver, and come to town only for
advice. Sir J. Mennes I hear also*b* is very ill all this night, worse
then before. Thence, I going out, met at the Gate Sir H. Cholmly
coming to me, and I to him in the coach and both of us presently
to St. James's, by the way discoursing of some Tanger business
about money, which the want of I see will certainly bring the
place into a bad condition. We find the Duke of York and
W. Coventry gone this morning by 2 a-clock to Chatham, to
come home tonight; and it is fine to observe how both the
King and Duke of York have, in their several late journeys to
and again*c*, done them in the night for coolenesse. Thence with

---

a repl. 'is'   *b* repl. 'is'   *c* repl. 'ago'

---

1. Wren was Remembrancer to
the Lord Chancellor; in September
he succeeded to Coventry's post as
Secretary to the Admiral.

2. R. Elkin to Pepys, Gravesend,
27 June: *CSPD Add. 1660–85*, p. 201.

him to the Treasury-chamber, and then to the Exchequer to inform ourselfs a little about our warrant for 30000*l* for Tanger, which vexes us that it is so far off in time of payment.[1] Having walked two or three turns with him in the Hall, we parted, and I home by coach and did business at the office till noon; and then by water to White-hall to dinner to Sir G. Carteret, but he not at home; but I dined with my Lady, and good company and good dinner. My Lady and the family in very good humour upon this business of his parting with his place of Treasurer of the Navy; which I perceive they do own, and we did talk of it with satisfaction. They do here tell me that the Duke of Buckingham hath surrendered himself to Secretary Morrice and is going to the Tower.[2] Mr. Fenn at the table says that he hath been taken by the Wach two or three times of late at unseasonable hours, but so disguised that they could not know him (and when I came home by and by, Mr. Lowther tells me that the Duke of Buckingham doth dine publicly this day at Wadlow's at the Sun tavern and*a* is mighty merry, and sent word to the Lieutenant of the Tower that he would come to him as soon as he had dined). Now, how sad a thing it is when we come to make sport of proclaiming men traitors and banishing them, and putting them out of their offices and Privy Council, and of sending to and going to the Tower: God have mercy on us. At table, my Lady and Sir Phill. Carteret have great and good discourse of the greatness of the present King of France; what great things he hath done, that a man may pass at any hour in the night all over that wild city, with a purse in his hand and no danger.[3] That there is not a beggar to be seen*b* in it, nor dirt

---

a repl. closing bracket   *b* repl. 'sun'

---

1. See above, p. 294 & n. 2.
2. For Buckingham's disgrace, see above, pp. 86, 92–3. His letter of surrender, addressed to the King (28 June) is in *CSPD 1667*, p. 240. Cf. HMC, *Le Fleming*, p. 51.
3. Cf. a similar view of conditions in Paris (December 1666) in HMC, *Portland*, iii. 303. In 1666–7 a much-improved system of street-lighting

had been introduced and the police reorganised: F. A. Isambert, *Receuil . . . des anciennes lois françaises*, xviii (1829), nos 485, 495, 401. Previously the dangers had been horrifying: cf. Sir W. Petty, *Econ. writings* (ed. Hull), p. 354. See E. Magne, *Images de Paris sous Louis XIV*, pp. 26+.

lying in it.[1]   That he hath married two of Colberts daughters to two of the greatest princes of France, and given them portions.[2] Bought the greatest Dukedome in France and given it to Colbert,[3] and ne'er a prince in France dare whisper against it; whereas here, our King cannot do any such thing but everybody's mouth is open against him for it, and the man that hath the favour also. That to several commanders that had not money to set them out to the present Campagne,[4] he did of his own accord send them 1000*l* sterling apiece to equip themselfs.   But then they did enlarge upon the slavery of the people: that they are taxed more then the real estates they have; nay, it is an ordinary thing for people to desire to give the King all their land that they have, and themselfs become only their tenants and pay him rent to the full value for it, so they may have but their earnings – but this will not be granted; but he shall give the value of his rent, and part of his labour too.   That there is not a petty governor of a province, nay, of a town, but he will take the daughter from the richest man in the town under him that hath got anything, and give her to his footman for a wife if*a* he pleases; and the King of France will do the like to the best man in his Kingdom, take his daughter from him and give her to his footman or whom he pleases.[5]   It is said that he doth make a sport of us now; and says that he knows no reason why his Cosen the King of England should not be as willing to let him have his Kingdom as that the Dutch should take it from him – which is a most wretched thing, that ever we should live to be in this contemptible condition.

a   repl. 'he'

---

1. Colbert, the *premier ministre*, had discouraged mendicancy, and in December 1666 had issued an edict on the subject of the cleanliness of the streets: Isambert, op. cit., no. 495.

2. One, not two, of Colbert's daughters had been married to a duke (Josephine-Marie-Thérèse to the Duc de Chevreuse on 2 February 1667). Two others were later (in 1671 and 1679) to become duchesses by marriage. Each of them had a large

dowry (400,000 livres) from her father.

3. A mistake. He was given large estates (the largest a barony), and in 1668 was created a marquis.

4. In the Spanish Netherlands.

5. These stories about taxation and marriage are exaggerated. But the King did interfere in family affairs: see E. Bertin, *Les mariages dans l'ancienne société française.*

After dinner Sir G. Carteret came in, and I to him and my Lady and there he*a* did tell me that the business was done between him and my Lord Anglesy: that himself is to have the other's place of Deputy Treasurer of Ireland (which is a place of honour and great profit, being far better (I know not by what reason but a reason there is) then the Treasurer's,[1] my Lord of Corke's) and to give the other his of Treasurer of the Navy. That the King, at his earnest entreaty, did with much unwillingness, but with owning of great obligations to him for his faithful and long service to him and his father; and therefore was willing to grant his desire. That the Duke of York hath given him the same kind words, so that it is done with all the good manner that could be; and he I perceive doth look upon it, and so do I I confess, as a great good fortune to him to meet with one of my Lord Anglesy's quality willing to receive it at this time. Sir W. Coventry he hath not yet made acquainted with it; nor doth intend it, it being done purely to ease himself of the many troubles and plagues which he thinks the perverseness and un-kindness of Sir W. Coventry, and others by his means, hath and is likely every day to bring upon him, and the Parliament's envy; and lastly, to put himself into a condition of making up his accounts, which he is, he says,*b* afeared he shall never other-wise be.[2] My Lord Chancellor I perceive is his friend in it. I remember I did in the morning tell Sir H Cholmly of this business and he answered me*c* he was sorry for it, for whatever Sir G. Carteret was, he is confident my Lord Anglesy is one of the greatest knaves in the world[3] – which was news to me, but I shall make my use of it. Having done this discourse with Sir G. Carteret and signified my great satisfaction in it, which they

---

a MS. 'it'   *b* MS. 'rise'   *c* repl. 'him'

---

1. The Treasurer of Ireland held little more than the title; his deputy did the work and received the fees: G. E. Howard, *Treatise of the Ex-chequer . . . of Ireland* (Dublin, 1776), i. 21–5.

2. In 1669 they were still not made up properly: above, p. 48, n. 1.

3. He was wealthy and sancti-monious, and widely (though not altogether justly) suspected of corrupt dealings in Ireland. Cf. Burnet, i. 174; *Poems of State*, vol. i, *1660–1714* (ed. G. deF. Lord), p. 233.

seem to look upon as something, I went away; and by coach home and there find my wife making of Tea, a drink which Mr. Pelling the pothecary tells her is good for her for her cold and defluxions. I to the office⋆ ⟪⋆whither came Mr. Carcasse to me to sue for my favour to him⟫ and Sir W. Penn's, where*a* I find Mr. Lowther come to town after the journey; and after a small visit to him, I to the office to do much business; and then in the evening to Sir W. Batten to see how he did, and is better then he was. He told me how Mrs. Lowther had her train held up yesterday by her page*b* at his house in the country; which is so ridiculous a piece of pride as I am ashamed of. He told me also how he hears by somebody that my Lord Brouncker's maid hath told that her lady, Mrs. Williams, had sold her jewels and clothes to raise money for something or other; and endeed, the*c* last night a letter was sent from her to me to send to my Lord, with about five pieces of gold in it, which methought at the time was*d* but a poor supply. I then to Sir W Pen, who continues a*e* little ill, or dissembles it, the latter of which I am apt to believe; here I stayed but little, not meaning much kindness in it; and so to the office and despatched more business, and then home at night and to supper with my wife; and who should come in but Mr. Pelling and supped with us, and told us the news of the town, how the Officers of the Navy⋆ are cried out upon, [and] a great many greater men; but doth think that I shall do well enough, and I think, if I have justice, I shall. He tells me of my Lord Duke of Buckingham his dining today at the Sun, and that he was mighty merry; and which is strange, tells me that really he is at this day a very popular man, the world reckoning him to suffer upon no other account then that he did propound ⟨in Parliament⟩ to have all men questioned that had to do with the receipt of the Taxes and prizes;[1] but they must be very silly that do think he can do anything out of good intention. After a

----

a MS. 'which'   *b* repl. 'chamber'-   *c* repl. 'this night'
d repl. 'what'   *e* repl. 'ill'

----

1. Buckingham was in disgrace at this time: see above, p. 299 & n. 2. He had several times made accusations of this sort: above, loc. cit., and vii. 309 & n. 1.

great deal of tittle-tattle with this honest man, he gone, we to bed. We hear that the Dutch are gone down again; and thanks be to God, the trouble they give us this second time is not very considerable.

29. Up, having had many ugly dreams tonight – of my father and my sister and mother's coming to us and meeting my wife and me at the gate of the office going out – they all in laced suits, and come, they told me, to be with me this May-day. My mother told me she lacked a pair of gloves, and I remembered a pair of my wife's in my chamber and resolved she should have them. But then recollected how my mother came to be here when I was in mourning for her; and so thinking it to be a mistake in our thinking her all this while dead, I did contrive that it should be said to any that enquired, that it was my mother-in-law, my wife's mother, that was dead and we in mourning for. This dream troubled me and I waked. Then I dreamed that I had great pain of the stone in making water, and that once I looked upon my yard in making water at the steps before my door, and there I took hold of the end of a thing and pulled it out, and it was a turd; and it came into my mind that I was in the same condition with my aunt Pepys, my uncle Roberts wife. And by and by, on the like occasion, I pulled out something and flung on the ground – it looked like slime or snot, and presently it swelled and turned into a gray kind of Bird, and I would have taken it in my hand and it run from me to the corner of the door, going into the garden in the entry by Sir J. Mennes's; and so I waked. These dreams did trouble me mightily all night.

Up, and by coach to St. James's and there find Sir W. Coventry and W. Penn above stairs, and then we to discourse about making up our accounts against the Parliament; and Sir W. Coventry did give us the best advice he could, for us to provide for our own justification, believing, as everybody doth, that they will fall heavily upon us all, though he lays all upon want of money; only, a little he says (if the Parliament be in any temper*) may be laid*a* upon themselfs for not providing money sooner, they being expressly*b* and industriously warned thereof by him, he says, even to the troubling them, that some of them did afterward tell him

---

a repl. same symbol badly formed   *b* symbol blotted that he had frighted them.¹ He says he doth prepare to justify himself, and that he hears that my*ᵃ* Lord Chancellor, my Lord Arlington, the Vice Chamberlain and himself are reported all up and down the Coffee-houses to be the four sacrifices that must be made to attone the people.

Then we to talk of the loss*ᵇ* of all affection and obedience now in the Seamen, so that all power is lost. He told us that he doth concur in thinking that want of money doth do the most of it, but that that is not all; but the having of gentlemen Captaines, who discourage*ᶜ* all Tarpaulins² and have given out that they would in a little time bring it to that pass that a Tarpaulin should not dare to aspire to more then to be a bosun or a gunner – that this makes the sea-captains to lose their own good affections to the service and to instil it into the seamen also, and that the seamen do see it themselfs and resent it. And tells us that it is notorious, even to his bearing of great ill will at Court, that he hath been the opposer of gentlemen-captains; and Sir*ᵈ* W. Pen did put in and said that he was esteemed to have been the man that did instil it into Sir W. Coventry; which Sir W. Coventry did own also – and says that he hath alway told the gentlemen-captains his opinion of them; and that himself, who had now served to the business of the sea six or seven years, should know a little, and as much as them that had never almost been at sea; and that yet he found himself fitter to be a Bishop or Pope then to be a sea-commander, and so endeed he is. I begun to tell him of the experience I had of the great brags made by Sir Hollis the other day, and the little proof either of the command or interest he had in his men; which Sir W. Penn seconded by saying Sir Fr. Hollis had told him that there was not a pilot to be got the other day for his fireships, and so was forced to carry them down himself³ – which Sir W. Coventry [says] "In my conscience, he knows no more to do, nor understands the River no more, then he doth Tiber or Ganges." Thence I away with W. Penn to

---

a repl. 'himself and'   b repl. 'want of affection'
     c repl. 'discourse'   d repl. 'that'

---

1. Cf. above, v. 330 & n. 2.   3. See above, p. 256 & n. 4.
2. Cf. above, vii. 10–11 & n.

White-hall to the Treasury-chamber, but to no purpose; and so by coach home and there to my office to business; and then home to dinner and to pipe with my wife; and so to the office again, having taken a resolution to take*ᵃ* a turne to Chatham tomorrow; endeed, to do business of the King's, but also to give myself the satisfaction of seeing the place after the Duch have been here – I have sent to and got Creed to go with me by coach betimes tomorrow morning. After having done my business at the office, I home and there I find Coleman¹ come again to my house and with my wife in our great chamber, which vexed me, there being a bed*ᵇ* therein; I stayed there a while and then to my study, vexed, showing no civility to the man. But he comes on a compliment to receive my wife's commands into the country, whither he is going; and it being Saturday, my wife told me there was no other room for her to bring him in, and so much is truth. But I stayed vexed in my closet, till by and by my cousin Tho. Pepys of Hatcham came to see me, and he up to my closet and there sat talking an hour or two of the sad state of the times; whereof we did talk very freely, and he thinks nothing but a union of religious interests will ever settle us;² and I do think that, and the Parliament's taking the whole management of things into their hands, and severe inquisitions into our miscarriages will help us. After we had bewailed ourselfs and the Kingdom and very freely one to another (wherein I do a little blame myself for my freedom of speech to anybody), he gone (and Coleman gone also before), I to the office; whither Creed came by my desire, and he and I to my wife, to whom I now propose the going to Chatham; who, mightily pleased with it, sent for Mercer to go with her, but she could not go, having friends at home, which vexed my wife and me; and the poor wretch would have had anybody else to have gone, but I would like nobody else; so was contented to stay at home, on condition to go to Epsum next Sunday, which I

---

a repl. 'go'   *b* MS. 'ala bemed.' Cf. above, p. 244, note *a*

---

1. The army officer Mrs Pepys had met on her recent coach journey from Brampton.

2. Thomas Pepys was a noncon-

formist. The government attempted such a union a few months later: below, 20 January 1668.

will do.   And so I to the office to despatch my business, and then home to supper with Creed; and then Creed and I together to bed, very pleasant in discourse. This day, talking with Sir W. Batten, he did give me an account how ill[a] the King and Duke of York was advised, to send orders for our frigates and fire-ships to come from Gravesend as soon as ever news came of the Dutch being returned into the River (wherein no seamen, he believes, was advised with); "for," says he, "we might have done just as Warwicke did when he (W. Batten)[b] came with the King and the like fleet in the late wars into the River[b][1] – for Warwicke did not run away from them,[c] but sailed before them when they sailed and came to anchor when they came to anchor, and alway kept in a small distance from them, so as to be able to take any opportunity of any of their ships running aground or change of wind, or anything else to his advantage. So might we have done with our fireships; and we have lost an opportunity of taking or burning a good ship of theirs which was run aground about Holehaven," I think he said, "with the wind, so as their ships could not get her away; but we might have done what we would with her and it may be done them mischief, too, with that wind." This seems very probable – and I believe was not considered.

30. *Lords day.*   Up about 3 a-clock, and Creed and I got ourselfs ready and took coach at our gate, it being very fine weather and the cool of the morning; and with much pleasure, without any stop, got to Rochester about 10 of the clock – all the way having mighty pleasant talk of the fate that is over[d] all we do, that it seems as if we were designed in everything, by land, by sea, to undo ourselfs. At the foot of Rochester bridge, at the landing-place, I met my Lord Bruncker and my Lord Douglas and all the officers ⟨of the soldiers⟩ in the town, waiting there for the Duke of York, whom they heard was coming thither this day; and by and by comes my Lord Middle-ton (the first time I remember to have seen him) well mounted,

---

a l.h. repl. s.h. 'the ill'   *b* MS. has closing bracket after 'River
         c repl. 'him'   *d* repl. 'our'

---

1. In 1648; see above, v. 169 & n. 1.

View of Chatham from the West, by Jacob Esselens

(*Austrian National Library, Vienna*)

who had been to meet him but came back without him. He seems a fine soldier, and so everybody says he is; and a man like my Lord Tiviott, and endeed most of the scotch gentry (as I observe), of few words.[1]   After staying here by the waterside and seeing the boats come up from Chatham with them that rowed with bandoleeres about their shoulders and muskets in their boats, they being the workmen of the yard who*ª* have promised to redeem their credit, lost by their deserting the service when the Dutch were there – my Lord Brouncker went with Lord Middleton to his Inne, the Crowne,[2] to dinner; which I took unkindly, but he was slightly invited; so I and Creed down by boat to Chatham yard (our watermen having their bandoliers about them all the way) and to Comissioner Pett's house, where my Lord Brouncker told me that I should meet with his dinner, two dishes of meat, but did not; but however, by the help of Mr. Wiles[3] had some beer and ale brought me, and a good piece of roast beef from somebody's table, and eat well we two; and after dinner, into the garden to show Creed; and I must confess, it must needs be thought a sorrowful thing for a man that hath taken so much pains to make a place neat,* to lose it, as Comissioner Pett must now this.[4]   Thence to*ᵇ* see the Batterys made; which endeed are very fine, and guns placed so as one would think the River should be very secure.   I was glad, as also it was new to me, to see so many fortifications as I have of late seen; and so up to the top of the hill there to look, and could see towards Sheerenesse, to espy the Dutch fleet; but could make none but one vessel, they being all gone.   But here I was told that in all the late attempt there was but one man that they know

a repl. 'are'
b repl. 'it raining down by barge to' (followed by some four words rendered illegible)

---

1. Pepys had known Teviot (Rutherford) as Governor of Tangier, 1663–4.   Middleton was the Governor-designate.
   2. See above, iii. 153, n. 2.
   3. George Wild, Deputy-Governor of the Tower.
   4. For Pepys's admiration of both the house and the garden, see above, ii. 69 & n. 7.   The 'neatness' of the houses of dockyard officials was suspected of having some connection with the excellence of the materials they stole from official stores.   Cf. J. Hollond, *Discourses* (ed. Tanner), pp. 97, 151.

killed on shore; and that was a man that had laid*a* upon his belly, upon one of the hills on the other side of the River, to see the action; and a bullet*b** came and took the ground away just under his belly, and ripped up his belly, and so was killed. Thence back to the*c* Docke, and in my way saw how they are fain to take the deals off of the rope-house to supply other occasions; and how sillily the country troopers look that stand upon the passes there, and methinks as if they were more willing to run away then to fight; and it is said that the country soldiers did first run at Sherenesse, but that then my Lord Douglas's men did run also; but it is excused that there was no defence for them towards the sea, that so the very Beach did fly in their faces as the bullets came and annoyed* them, they having, after all this preparation of the officers of the ordinance, only done something towards the land and nothing at all towards the sea. The people here everywhere do speak very badly of Sir Edw. Spragge,[1] as not behaving himself as he should have done in that business, going away with the first; and that old Captain Pyne (who I am here told, and no sooner, is Maister-Gunner of England)[2] was the last that stayed there. Thence by barge, it raining hard, down to the Chain; and in our way did see the sad wrackes of the poor *Royall Oake*, *James*, and *London*, and several other of our ships by us sunk; and several of the enemy's, whereof three men-of-war, that they could not get off and so burned. We did also see several*d* dead bodies lie by the sides of the water. I do not see that Upner Castle hath received any hurt by them, though they played long against it, and they themselfs shot till they have hardly a gun left upon the carriages, so badly provided they were; they have now made two batteries on that side, which will be very good

---

a　MS. 'laid upon self'　　　*b*　repl. 'bult'
　　c　repl. 'see'　　　*d*　repl. 'many'

---

1. A young Vice-Admiral, influential with the Duke of York, but an Irish papist and unpopular: cf. *CSPD 1667*, p. 206. Pepys has several other critical references to him at this time. In 1666 he was said to have been one of those most responsible for the dividing of the fleet.

2. Valentine Pyne did not receive the appointment until January 1668, but for some time he had performed the duties of the office while holding the post of deputy-master.

and do good service. So to the Chain,[1] and there saw it[a] fast at the end on Upner side of the River; very fast, and borne[b] up upon the several stages across the River – and where it is broke, nobody can tell me.[2] I went on shore on Upner side to look upon the end of the Chain; and caused the link to be measured, and it was 6 inch and a quarter in circumference.[3] They have burned the Crane-house that was to haul it tought. It seems very remarkable to me, and of great honour to the Dutch, that those of them that did go on shore to Gillingham, though they went in fear of their lives and were some of them killed, and notwithstanding their provocation at Scelling,[4] yet killed none of our people nor plundered their houses; but did take some things of easy carriage and left the rest, and not a house burned; and which is to our eternal disgrace, that what[c] my Lord Douglasse's men, who come after them, found there, they plundered and took all away. And the watermen that carried us did further tell us that our own soldiers are far more terrible to those people of the country-towns then the Dutch themselfs. We were told at the Batterys, upon my seeing of the field-guns that were there, that had they come a day sooner they had been able to have saved all; but they had no orders, and lay lingering upon the way and did not come forward for want of direction. Comissioner Pett's house was all unfurnished, he having carried away all his goods. I met with no satisfaction whereabouts the Chain was broke, but do confess I met with nobody that I could well expect to have satisfaction, it being Sunday, and the[d] officers of the Yard, most of them abroad or at the Hill house at

---

a repl. 'the several'   *b* repl. 'burn'   *c* repl. 'what'
              d repl. 'people'

---

1. This ran on pulleys which turned on wheels, and was stretched across the Medway in Gillingham Reach, lying for most of the distance about 9 ft below the surface. It was guarded by batteries at either end.

2. There was at the time some doubt whether it had been broken at all or whether it had been sunk by the dislodging of the stages supporting it: Brouncker to Pepys, 3 July: Rawl. A 195a, f. 142. It seems probable that it was in fact broken by a Dutch fire-ship. For this exploit, see P. R. Rogers, *Dutch in Medway*, pp. 93+.

3. It was however of inferior (Spanish) iron: Rawl. A 195a, loc. cit.

4. See above, vii. 247 & n. 1.

the pay of the Chest, which they did make use of today to do part in. Several complaints I hear of the *Monmouth*'s coming away too soon from the Chaine, where she was placed with the two guard-ships to secure it; and Captain Rob. Clerke, my friend, is blamed for so doing there, but I hear nothing of him at London about it. But Captain Brookes's running aground with the *Sancta Maria*, which was one of the three ships that were ordered to be sunk to have dammed up the River at the Chain, is mightily cried against;[1] and with reason, he being the chief man to approve of * the abilities of other men, and the other two ships did get safe thither and he run aground; but yet I do hear that though he be blameable, yet if she had been there, she nor two more to them three would have been able to have command[ed] the River all over. I find that here (as it hath been in our River) fireships, when fitted, have been sunk afterwards; and perticularly those here at the Mussle,[2] where they did no good at all. Our great ships that were run aground and sunk are all well raised but the *Vantguard*, which they go about[a] to raise tomorrow. The *Henery*, being let loose to drive up the River of herself, did run up as high as the bridge and broke down some of the rails of the bridge, and so back again with the tide and up again, and then birthed himself so well, as no pilot could ever have done better; and Punnett[3] says he would not for his life have undertaken to have done it, with all his Skill. I find[b] it is true that the Dutch did heele the *Charles* to get her down, and yet run aground twice or thrice; and yet got her safe away and have her (with a great many good guns in her), which none of our pilots would ever have undertaken.[4] It is very considerable, * the quantities of goods which the making of these platforms and Batterys do take out of the King's stores; so that we shall have little left there, and God knows no credit to buy[c] any – besides the

a repl. 'a'   b repl. 'fire'
c repl. same symbol badly formed

---

1. John Brookes was Master-Attendant at Chatham. For the grounding of his ship (a large one), see *CSPD 1667*, p. 188.
2. Mussel (Muscle) Bank in Long Reach in the Medway.

3. Augustine Punnett, an experienced pilot. Cf. *Naval Minutes*, p. 343.
4. Her sternpiece is now displayed in the Rijksmuseum, Amsterdam.

taking away and spending of (it is possible) several goods that would have been either rejected or abatements made for them before used. It is a strange thing to see, that while my Lord Douglas and Middleton do ride up and down upon single horses, my Lord Brouncker doth go up and down with his hackney-coach and six horses at the King's charge; which will, for all this time and the time that he is likely to stay, must amount to a great deal. But I do not see that he hath any command over the sea[men], he being affronted by three or four seamen before my very face; which he took sillily methought, and is not able to do so much good as a good bosun*a* in this business. My Lord Brouncker, I perceive, doth endeavour to speak well of Comissioner Pett, saying that he did exercize great care and pains while he was there – but doth not undertake to answer for his not carrying*b* up of the great ships. Back again to Rochester, and there walked to the Cathedrall as they were beginning of the service, but would not be seen to stay to church there; besides, had no mind, but rather to go to our Inne, the White hart,[1] where we drank and were fain (the town being so full of soldiers) to have a bed corded[2] for us to lie in, I being unwilling to lie at the Hill-house[3] for one night, being desirous to be near our coach to be gone betimes tomorrow morning. Here in the streets I did hear the Scotch march beat by the drums before the soldiers, which is very odde. Thence to the Castle[4] and viewed it with Creed, and had good satisfaction from him that showed it us, touching the history of it. Then into the fields, a fine walk, and there saw Sir Fr. Clerke's house, which is a pretty seat,[5] and

a repl. 's'-   *b* repl. 'undertaking for'

---

1. A late fourteenth-century inn on the e. side of High St, near the bridge; slept in by Queen Elizabeth; still surviving. Account in *Arch. Cant.*, 21/315.

2. Beds were usually framed with cords or 'bed-lines' on which was placed a mat or mattress.

3. Close by Chatham dockyard.

4. See above, vi. 249 & nn.

5. Clerke was M.P. for Rochester and a colleague of Pepys on the Chatham Chest. The house was Elizabethan, of red brick, in Crow Lane, and is now known as Restoration House from the fact that the King slept there on 28–9 May 1660 on his way from Dover to London. Illust. in Frederick F. Smith, *Hist. Rochester*, pl. 55.

then back to our Inne and bespoke supper; and so back to the
fields and into the Cherry-garden, where we had them fresh
gathered; and here met with a young, plain, silly shopkeeper
and his wife, a pretty young woman, the man's name Hawkins;
and I did kiss her and we talked (and the woman of the house,
one May, is a very talking bawdy jade) and eat cherries together;
and then to walk in the fields till it was late; and did kiss her, and
I believe, had I had a fit*a* time and*a* place, I might have done what
I would with her.*b* Walked back and left them at their house
near our Inne; and then to our Inne, where I hear my Lord
Brouncker hath sent for me to speak with me before I go; so I
took his coach, which stands there with two horses, and to him
and to his bedside, where he was in bed – and hath a watchman
with a Halbert at his door. And to him and did talk a little;
and find him a very weak man for this business that he is upon.
And do pity the King's service that is no better handled, and his
folly to call away Pett before we could have found a fitter man
to have stayed in his stead. Took leave of him,[1] and with Creed
back again, it being now about 10 at night; and to our Inne to
supper, and then to bed, being both sleepy; but could get no
sheets to our bed, only linen to our mouths; and so to sleep,
merrily talking of Hawkins and his wife, and I troubled that
Creed did see so much of my dalliance, though very little.

a–a garbled s.h.: see above, p. 244, note *a*   *b* repl. garbled 'to to'

1. On 3 July Brouncker wrote to
Pepys: 'I found in my Chamber an
Indian staffe which I suppos'd was
yours' (Rawl. A 195a, f. 142*r*).

JULY.

1. Up betimes about 4 a-clock, waked by a damned[a] noise between a sow gelder and a cow and a dog, nobody after we were up being able to tell us what it was. After being ready, we took coach; and being[b] very sleepy, drouzed most part of the way to gravesend; and there light and down to the new Battery[1] which are like to be very fine, and there did hear a plain fellow cry out upon the folly of the King's officers above, to spend so much money in works at Woolwich and Deptford and sinking of good ships loaden with goods, when if half the charge had been laid out here, it would have secured all that, and this place too, before now – and I think it is not only true in this, but that the best of the actions of us all are so silly, that the meanest people do begin to see through them and contemn them. "Besides," says he, "they spoil the river by it." Then informed ourselfs where we might have some Creame, and they guided us to one Goody Best's, a little out of the town towards London-road; and thither we went with the Coach and find it a mighty clean, plain house, and had a dish of very good cream to our liking; and so away presently, very merry, and fell to reading[c] of the several *Advices to a Painter*,[2] which made us good sport; and endeed, are very witty; and Creed[d] did also repeat to me some of the substance of letters of old Burleigh in Queen Elizabeth's time which he hath of late read in the printed *Cabbala*,[3] which is a very fine style at this day and fit to be imitated. With this, and talking and laughing

a repl. ? 'madded'   *b* repl. 'with'   *c* repl. 'rea-ing'   *d* repl. 'then'

---

1. The batteries had been set up and manned in late June: PRO, SP 46/136, nos 518, 520; *CSPD 1667*, p. 193.

2. [Anon.,] *The second and third advice to a painter, for drawing the history of our navall actions, the two last years . . .* (1667); see above, vii. 407 & n. 4.

3. These were letters written (1566–70) to Sir Henry Norris, ambassador to France, now printed in *Cabala, sive Scrinia Sacra* (1663; PL 2261), pp. 134–79. They had not been printed in the 1654 edition.

at the folly of our maisters in the management of things at this day, we got home by noon, where all well.   And then to dinner, and after dinner both of us laid down upon the Couch and chairs and to sleep; which I did for an hour or two, and then to the office, where I am sorry to hear that Sir J. Mennes is likely to die*ᵃ* this night or tomorrow.[1]   I forgot to set down that we met this morning upon the road with Mrs. Williams, going down to my Lord Brouncker; we bowed without speaking one to another, but I am ashamed at the folly of the man, to have*ᵇ* her down at this serious busy time, when the town and country is full of people and full of censure, and against him perticularly.   At Sir W. Batten's my Lady tells me that she hears for certain that my Lord's maid of his lodgings here doth give out that Mrs. Williams hath been fain of late to sell her best clothes and Jewells to get a little money upon – which is a sad condition.   Thence to the office and did write to my Lord Brouncker to give me a little satisfaction about the certainty of the Chaines being broke, which I begin to doubt, and the more from Sir W Pen's discourse; it is worth while to read my letter to him entered in my letter book.[2]   Home in the evening to supper; and so pretty betimes, about 10 a-clock, to bed, and slept well.   This day letters are come that my sister is very ill.

2.   Up, and put on my new silk Camelott suit, made of my cloak, and suit now made into a vest.   So to the office, where W. Penn and myself and Sir T. Harvy met, the first time we have had a meeting since the coming of the Dutch upon the coast.   Our only business (for we have little else to do, nobody being willing to trust us for anything) was to speak with the owners of

---

a MS. 'day'   *b* repl. 'bring'

---

1. He did not die until February 1671.

2. NMM, LBK/8, p. 493 (dated this day; in Pepys's hand); printed in *Further Corr.*, pp. 177–8. It pointedly asked whether any trial of the chain had been made by sailing ships against it.   The polite tone of the letter is in marked contrast to Pepys's entries in the diary about Brouncker at this time.   In reply (3 July), Brouncker wrote: 'Not only in my own opinion is the Chain broke, but in the opinion of I think all who have been with me there at any time' (Rawl. A 195, f. 142r).

six merchantmen which we have been taking*a* up this fortnight, and are yet in no readiness, they not fitting their*b* ships without money advanced to them, we owing them for what their ships have earned the last year. So everything stands still for money, while we want money to pay for some of the most necessary things that we promised ready money for in the heighth of our wants – as grapnells, &c.; at noon home to dinner; and after dinner, my wife and Jane (mighty fine the girle) to go to see Jane's old mistress, who was to see her, and did see my wife the other day.[1] And it is pleasant to hear with what kindness her old mistress speaks of this girl, and how she would still have her, and how the wench cried when she told her that she must come to her old mistress, my wife. They gone, I to my chamber, and there dallied a little with my maid*c* Nell to touch her thing,*c* but nothing more. And so to the office, where busy till night; and then comes Mrs. Turner and walks with me in the garden, to talk with me about her husband's business[2] and to tell me how she hears at the other end of the town how bad our office is spoken of by the King and Prince and Duke of Albemarle; and that there is not a good word said of any of us but of me, and me they do all speak mightily of – which, whether true or no, I am mighty glad to hear. But from all put together that I hear from other people, I am likely to pass as well as anybody. So she gone, comes my wife and to walk in the garden, Sir J. Mennes being still ill and so keeping us from singing; and by and by Sir W Pen came and walked with us, and gave us a bottle of cider; and so we home to supper, and I to read myself asleep and so to bed. ⟨This day I am told that poor Tooker,[3] is dead, a very painful poor man as ever I knew.⟩

3. Up, and within most of the morning, my tailor's boy coming to alter something in my new suit I put on yesterday.

---

a repl. same symbol badly formed   *b* repl. 'of they'
     c–c garbled s.h.: see above, p. 224, note *a*.

---

1. Jane Birch had been out of the Pepyses' service between 1663 and 1666. The name of the mistress here mentioned is unknown.

2. See above, p. 63 & n. 1.

3. John Tooker, the Navy Board's shipping agent on the river.

Then to the office and did business, and then (my wife being a little ill of those in the bed) I to Sir W. Batten's and dined, and there comes in Sir Rd. Ford and tells us how he hath been at the Session's-house, and there it is plain that there is a combination of rogues in the town that do make it their business to set houses on fire, and that one house they did set on fire in Aldersgate-street last Easter,[1] and that this is proved by two young men, whom one[a] of them debauched by degrees to steal their father's plate and clothes, and at last to be of their company, and they had their places to take up what goods were flung into the streets out of the windows when the houses were on fire; and this is like to be proved to a great number[b] of rogues, whereof five are already found, and some found guilty this day.   One of these boys is the son of a Mountagu, of my Lord Manchester's family; but whose son, he could not tell me.[2]   This is a strange thing methinks, but I am glad that it is proved so true and discovered.   So home, and to enter my Journall of my late journy to this hour; and then to the office – where to do a little business; and then by water to White-hall (calling at Michells in my way, but the rogue would not invite me in, I having a mind para ver his wife[c]); and there to the Council-chamber to deliver a letter to their Lordships about the state of the six merchantmen which we have been so long fitting out.[3]   When I came, the King and the whole tableful of Lords were hearing of a pitiful cause of a complaint of an old man, with a great gray beard,[d] against his son, for not allowing himself something to live on; and at last came to the ordering the son to allow his father 10*l* a year.[4]   This cause lasted them near two hours; which methinks, at this time to be the work of the Council-board of England, is a

---

a   repl. 'they'   b   repl. symbol rendered illegible
c   'his wife' in garbled s.h.   d   repl. 'bird'

---

1. For this case, see LRO, Sessions Minute Bk and File, s.d.
2. He was a son of James Mountagu of Lackham, Wilts., third son of the 1st Earl of Manchester: Braybrooke (1854), iii. 180, n. 1.

3. See above, pp. 281, 285 & nn.
4. This case is not recorded in the Privy Council Register, and must have been heard in committee. After the Restoration hearings of private cases were rare.

scandalous thing, and methought Sir W. Coventry to me did own as much. Here I find all the news is the enemy's landing 3000 men near Harwich, and attacquing Langnerfort[1] and[a] being beat off thence with our great guns, killing some of their men and they leaving their lathers behind them;[2] but we had no Horse in the way on Suffolke side,[3] otherwise we might have galled their Foot. The Duke of York is gone down thither this day,[4] while the Generall sat sleeping this afternoon at the Council-table. The news so much talked of this Exchange, of a peace, I find by Sir Rd. Browne arises from a letter the Swedes agent hath received from Bredah, and showed at Court today, that they are come very near it, but I do not find anybody here relying on it. This cause being over, the Trinity-house men, whom I did not expect to meet, were called in; and there Sir W Pen[5] made a formal speech in answer to a Question of the King's, whether the lying of the sunk ships in the River would spoil the River; but Lord, how gingerly he answered it, and with a deal of do, that he did not know whether it would be safe as to the enemy to have them taken up, but that doubtless it would be better for the River to have them taken up.[6] Methought the Council found them answer like fools, and it ended in bidding them think more of it and bring their answer in writing. Thence I to Westminster-hall and there hear how they talk against[b] the present management of things, and against Sir W. Coventry for

---

a repl. 'after two'   b repl. 'how'

---

1. Landguard Fort, on the n. side of the Orwell estuary, opposite Harwich.

2. This was on the late afternoon of the 2nd. About 3000 men (led by 'a tall English Lieutenant-Colonel') were landed in boats near Felixstowe. Two unsuccessful attacks were made on the port, the Dutch losses being about 150. The militia dealt with the main body of invaders, and by 2 a.m. had driven them back to their boats: *CSPD 1667*, pp. 259, 263, 266. See also Deane to Pepys, 3 June [*sic*], 11 July: Rawl. A 195a, ff. 148, 135-7.

3. The Dutch had prevented Sir Philip Parker from crossing the river at Woodbridge with his troop of horse.

4. He arrived at Harwich at 7 a.m. on the 4th: *CSPD 1667*, p. 266.

5. Newly-elected Master of Trinity House.

6. In addition to those already sunk, ships were now ordered to be sunk first at Galleons' Reach and then at Blackwall Point. For the part played by Trinity House, see HMC, *Rep.*, 8/1/253b.

his bringing in of new commanders and casting out the old sea-men; which I did endeavour to rectify Mr. Michell and them in, letting them know that he hath opposed it all his life, the most of any man in England.   After a deal of this bibble babble, I to Mrs. Martins and there she was gone in before; but when I came, contrary to my expectation, I find her all in trouble, and what was it for but that I have *a* got her with child, for those do not venir upon her as they should have done; and is in *b* exceed-ing grief, and swears that the child is mine; *a* which I do not believe, but yet do comfort her that either it can[not] be so; or if it be, that I will take care to send for her husband, though I do hardly see how I can be sure of that, the ship [1] being at sea and as far as Scotland; but however, I must do it, and shall find some way or other of doing it, though it doth trouble me not a little. Thence, not pleased, away to White-hall to Mr. Williamson and by and by my Lord Arlington about Mr. Lanyon's business; [2] and it is pretty to see how Mr. Williamson did altogether excuse himself that my business was not done, and when I came to my Lord and told him my business, – "Why," says my Lord, "it hath [been] done, and the King signed it several days ago;" and so it was, and was in Mr. Williamson's hand, which made us both laugh; and I in innocent mirth, I remember, said, "It is pretty to see in what a condition we are, that all *c* our matters nowadays are undone we know not how, and done we know not when.*d*" He laughed at it, but I have since reflected on it and find it a severe speech, as it might be taken by a chief minister of state, as endeed Mr. Williamson is, for he is endeed the Secretary. [3] But we fell to other pleasant talk, and a fine gentleman he is; and so gave him 5*l* for his fee, and away home and to Sir W. Batten's to talk a little; and then to the office to do a little business, and so home to supper and to read myself asleep, and then to bed.

a–a garbled s.h.: see above, p. 244, note *a*.   *b* MS. 'in is'
       c repl. 'our business is'   *d* repl. 'when'

---

1. Pepys's privateer, the *Flying Greyhound*, in which Samuel Martin served as purser.
    2. This concerned a warrant for the payment of £9000 for Tangier victualling: see above, p. 146 & n. 2.

3. Joseph Williamson was Arling-ton's principal secretary. He did himself become Secretary of State, 1674–8.

4. Up; and in vain expecting Sir*ᵃ* Rd. Ford's calling on me, I took coach and to the Sessions-house, where I have a mind to hear Bazill Fielding's case tried;[1] and so got up to the Bench, my Lord Chief Justice Keeling being Judge. Here I stood bare, not challenging, though I might well enough, to be covered.[2] But here was several fine trials. Among others, several brought in for making it their trade to set houses on fire, merely to get plunder, and all proved by the two little boys spoken of yesterday by Sir R. Ford, who did give so good account of perticulars that I never heard children in my life; and I confess, though I was unsatisfied*ᵇ* with the force given to such little boys to take away men's lives, yet when I was told that my Lord Chief-Justice did declare that there was no law against taking the oath of children above twelve years old, and then heard from Sir R. Ford the good account which the boys had given of their understanding the nature and consequence of an oath, and now my own observation of the sobriety and readiness*ᶜ* of their answers, further then of any man of any rank that came to give witness this day, though some men of years and learning, I was a little amazed, and fully satisfied that they ought to have as much credit as the rest. They*ᵈ* proved against several, their consulting several times at a bawdy-house in Moore-Fields called the Russia House, among many other rogueries, of setting houses on fire, that they might gather the goods that were flung into the streets; and it is worth considering how unsafe it is to have children play up and down this lewd town, for these two boys, one is my Lady Mountagus (I know not what Lady Mountagu) son and the other of good condition, were playing in Moore-Fields, and one rogue, Gabr. Holmes, did come to them and teach them to drink, and then to bring him plate and clothes from their fathers' houses and carry him into their houses, and leaving open the doors for him; and at last were made of their conspiracy, and were at the very burning

---

a repl. 'Sir **W. P.**'	*b* repl. 'willing'
c repl. 'w'-	*d* MS. 'that'

---

1. See above, p. 208, n. 1.
2. Pepys had the right to be covered since he was himself a Justice of the Peace.

of this*a* [house] in Aldersgate-street on Easter Sunday at night last, and did gather up goods as they had resolved before. And this Gabriel Holmes did advise to have had two houses set on fire, one after another, that while they were quenching of one, they might be burning another. And it is pretty that G Holmes did tell his*b* fellows, and these boys swore it, that he did set fire to a box of linen in the Sheriffs, ⟨Sir Joseph⟩ Shelden's, house[1] while he was attending the fire in Aldersgate-street, and the Sheriffe himself [said] that there*c* was a fire in his house, in a box of linen, at the same time, but cannot conceive how this fellow should do it. The boys did swear against one of them, that he had made it his part to pull out the plug out of the engine while it was a-playing; and it really was so. And goods they did carry away, and the*d* manner of the setting the house on*e* fire was that Holmes did get to a Cockepitt (where it seems there was a public cockpit)[2] and set fire to the straw in it, and hath a fire-ball at the end of the straw which did take fire, and so it prevailed and burned the house; and among other things they carried away, he took six of the cocks that were at*f* the cockpit, and afterward the boys told us how they had one dressed; by the same token, it was so hard they could not eat it. But that which was most remarkable was the impudence of this Holmes, who hath been arraigned often and got still away; and on this business was taken, and broke loose just at Newgate gate and was last night luckily taken about Bow; who got loose and run into the River and hid himself in the Rushes, and they pursued him with a dog, and the dog got him and held him till he was taken; but the impudence of this fellow was such, that he denied he ever saw the boys before, or ever knew the Russia-house, or

---

	a repl. 'these'	*b* repl. 'them'
c repl. 'his'	*d* repl. 'they say'	*e* MS. 'of' *f* repl. 'in'

---

1. Sheldon seems at this date to have lived in the house of his uncle the Archbishop of Canterbury on the w. side of Aldersgate St, opposite Thanet House, having moved there after the Fire from St Paul's Churchyard, s. side. (R).

2. On the n. side of Horn Alley (now Edmund Place) east of Aldersgate St: LRO, Hustings Rolls 341, mb. 115. (R).

that the people knew him; and by and by the mistress of the Russia-house was called in, being indicted at the same time about another thing, and she denied that the fellow was of her acquaintance; when it was pretty to see how the little boys did presently fall upon her, and ask her how she durst say so, when she was always with them when they met at her house, and perticularly when she came in in her smock before a dozen of them – at which the court laughed and put the woman away. Well, this fellow Holmes was found guilty of the *a* act of burning the house, and other things that he stood indicted for;[1] and then there were other good cases, as of a woman that came to serve a gentlewoman, and in three days run away, betimes *b* in the morning, with a great deal of plate and rings and other good things. It was time very well spent to be here. Here I saw how favourable the judge [was] to a young gentleman that struck one of the officers for not making him room; told him he had endangered the loss of his hand, but that he hoped he had not struck him, and would suppose that he had not struck him.[2] About [noon] the court rose, and I to dinner with my Lord Mayor and Sheriffs – where a good dinner and good discourse, the Judge being there. There was also tried this morning Fielding (which I thought had been Bazill, but it proved the other, and Bazill was killed) that killed his brother; who was found guilty of murther, and nobody pitied him.[3] The Judge seems to be a worthy man and able, and doth entend of these rogues that burned this house, to be hung in some conspicuous place in the town, for an example. After dinner to the court again, where I hear some more causes, but with so much trouble because of the hot weather, that I had no pleasure in it. Anon the court rose and I walked to Fleetstreete for my

a repl. 'more too'   *b* repl. 'besides'

---

1. Gabriel Holmes and Thomas Arnold were both sentenced to death, and the former was hanged on 11 July: Richard Smyth, *Obituary*, p. 75.

2. Offences of this sort could be punished with brutal severity: cf. below, pp. 428–9 & n. Lord Chief Justice Kelyng was not noted for leniency.

3. LRO, Sessions of Gaol Delivery commencing 3 July 1667: Sessions Minute Bk and File. Christopher Fielding was sentenced to death for the murder (by stabbing) of his brother Basil. Cf. above, p. 208 & n. 1.

belt at the Beltmakers; and so home and to the office, wrote some letters, and then home to supper and to bed.

5. Up and to the office, where Sir W. Batten, W. Penn, T. Harvy and I met upon Mr. Gawden's accounts, and was at it all the morning. This morning Sir G. Carteret did come to us and walked in the garden; it was to talk*a* with me about something of my Lord Sandwiches; but here he told us that the great Seale is passed to my Lord Anglesy*b* for Treasurer of the Navy, so that now he doth no more belong to us – and I confess, for his sake I am glad of it – and do believe the other will have little content in it.[1] At noon I home to dinner with my wife; and after dinner to sing, and then to the office a little and Sir W. Batten's, where I am vexed to hear that Nan Wright, now Mrs. Marckham, Sir W. Penn's maid and whore, is come to sit in our pew at church, and did so while my Lady Batten was there – I confess I am very much vexed at it and ashamed. By and by out with W. Penn to White-hall, where I stayed not; but to the New Exchange to buy gloves and other little errands, and so home and to my office, busy till night; and then walked in the garden with my wife, and then to supper and to sing, and so to bed. No news, but that the Dutch are gone clear from Harwich Northward and have given out they are going to Yarmouth.[2]

6. Up and to the office, where some of us sat busy*c* all the morning. At noon home to dinner, whither Creed came to dine with us and brings the first word I hear of the news of a peace, the King having letters come to him this noon, signifying that it is concluded on and that Mr. Coventry is upon his way, coming over for the King's ratification.[3] The news was so good and sudden, that I went with great joy to W. Batten and then to

---

a MS. 'tak' (phonetic)   *b* MS. 'Annesly'   *c* repl. 'late'

---

1. Anglesey's patent was issued on 2 July. He retained office just over a year, falling victim to the Buckingham faction in the autumn of 1668.

2. In fact, they had turned south off Aldeburgh on the 4th. There was a fleet of colliers at Yarmouth

for whose safety the Navy Board was anxious: *CSPD 1667*, pp. 270, 275.

3. Henry Coventry arrived at Dover on the evening of this day for consultations. For his mission, see below, p. 326 & n.3. The treaty was signed on 11/21 July.

W. Penn to tell it them; and so home to dinner, mighty merry
and light at my heart only on this ground, that a continuing of
the war must undo us, and so, though peace may do the like, if
we do not make good use of it to reform ourselfs and get up
money, yet there is an opportunity for us to save ourselfs – at
least, for my own perticular, we shall continue well till I can get
my money into my hands, and then I will shift for myself.
After dinner away, leaving Creed there, by coach to Westminster, where to the Swan and drank; and then to the Hall and
there talked a little, with great joy of the peace; and then to Mrs.
Martins, where I met with the good news que esta no es con child*a*
⟨she having de estos upon her⟩*a* – the fear of which, which she
did give me the other day, had troubled me much. My joy in
this made me send for wine, and thither came her sister and Mrs.
Cragg and I stayed a good while there. But here happened the
best instance of a woman's falseness in the world; that her sister
Doll, who went for a bottle of wine, did come home all blubber-
ing and swearing against one Captain Vandena, a Dutchman of
the Rhenish wine-house, that pulled*b* her into a stable by the
Dog tavern and there did tumble her and toss her; calling him
all the rogues and toads in the world, when she knows that ella
hath suffered me*c* to do anything with her*c* a hundred times.
Thence with joyful heart to White-hall to ask Mr. Williamson
the news; who told me that Mr. Coventry is coming over with
a project of a peace; which, if the States agree to and our King,
when their ministers on both sides have showed it them, we shall
agree, and that is all; but the King I hear doth give it out plain
that the*d* peace is concluded. Thence by coach home and there
wrote a few letters; and then to consult with my wife about going
to Epsum tomorrow, sometimes designing to go and then again
not; and at last it grew late and I bethought myself of business to
imploy me at home tomorrow, and so I did not go. This
afternoon I met with Mr. Rolt, who tells me that he is going
Cornett under Collonell Ingoldsby, being his old acquaintance,
and Ingoldsby hath a troop now from under the King;[1] and I

---

a–a garbled s.h.: see above, p. 244, note *a*.   *b* repl. 'would'
c–c garbled s.h.   *d* repl. 'there'

1. For Ingoldsby's appointment,
see above, p. 265. Edward Rolt was
a relative of his, and like him had
once served in the Cromwellian
army. He came of a family Pepys
knew in Brampton.

think it is a handsome way for him.   But it was an ominous thing methought, just as he was bidding me his last Adieu, his nose fell a-bleeding, which run in my mind a pretty while*a* after.   This afternoon Sir Alex. Frazier,[1] who was of counsel for Sir Jo. Minnes and had given him over for a dead man, said to me at White-hall: "What," says he, "Sir Jo. Minnes is dead."   I told him no, but that there is hopes of his life.   Methought he looked very sillily after it, and went his way.   Late home to supper, a little troubled at my not going to Epsum tomorrow as I had resolved, especially having the Duke of York and W. Coventry out of town; but it was my own fault, and at last my judgment to stay; and so after supper, to bed.   ⟨This day, with great satisfaction I hear that my Lady Jemimah is brought to bed at Hinchingbrooke of a boy.⟩[2]

7.   *Lords day.*   Up; and to my chamber, there to settle some papers; and thither comes Mr. Moore to me and talked till church-time of the news of the times*b* about the peace, and the bad consequences of it if it be not improved to good purpose of fitting ourselfs for another war.   He tells me he hears that the discontented Parliament-men are fearful that the next sitting*c* the King will put for a general Excize, by which to raise him money, and then to fling off the Parliament, and raise a land-army and keep them all down like slaves;[3] and it is gotten among them that Bab. May, the Privy-purse, hath been heard to say that 300*l* a year is enough for any country gentleman; which makes them mad, and they do talk of 6 or 800000*l* gone into the privy-purse this war, when in King James's time it arose but to 5000*l* and in King Charles's but 10000*l* in a year.[4]   He tells me that a goldsmith in town told him, that being with some plate with my Lady Castlemaine lately, she directed her woman (the great

a repl. 'wh'-   *b* repl. 'of the time'   *c* repl. 'Parliament'

---

1. Physician to the King.
2. George Carteret, later 1st Baron Carteret.
3. Roger Pepys, sending parliamentary news to his Norfolk friend John Hobart (2 July), wrote that the Chatham disaster was part of a deep plot to impoverish the country and make it subject to 'arbitrary power, as it is in France': Tanner 45, f. 202r.
4. For these figures, see below, p. 331 & n. 2.

beauty), "Willson," says she, "make a note for this and for that to the Privy-purse for money." He tells me a little more of the basenesse of the courses taken at Court in the case of Mr. Moyer,[1] who is at liberty and is to give 500*l* for his liberty; but now the great ones are divid[ed] who shall have the money, the Duke of Albemarle on one hand, and another Lord on the other; and that it is fain to be decided by having the person's name put into the King's warrant for his liberty, at whose intercession the King shall own that he is set at liberty; which is a most lamentable thing, that we do professedly own that we do these things, not for right and justice sake, but only to gratify this or that person about the King.[a] God forgive us all.

Busy till noon and then home to dinner and Mr. Moore come and dined with us, and much more discourse at and after dinner of the same kind; and then he[b] gone, I to my office, busy till[c] the evening; and then with my wife and Jane over to Half-way house, a very good walk, and there drank; and in the cool of the evening back again, and sang with pleasure upon the water and were mightily pleased in hearing a boat full of spaniards sing; and so home to supper and to bed. Jane of late mighty fine, by reason of a laced whiske her mistress hath given her, which makes her a very gracefull servant. But above all, my wife and I were the most surprized in the beauty of a plain girle which we met in the little lane going from Redriffe-stairs into the fields, one of the prettiest faces that we think we ever saw in our lives.

8. Up and to my chamber; and by and by comes Greeting, and to my flagelette with him with a pretty deal of pleasure; and then to the office, where W. Batten, W. Penn and I met about putting men to work for the weighing of the ships in the River sunk. Then home again and there heard Mr. Cæsar play some very good things on the lute, together with myself on the viall and Greeting on the viallin. Then with my wife abroad by

a MS. 'me'   *b* repl. 'home'   *c* repl. full stop

1. See above, p. 219 & n. 3.

coach, she to her tailor's, I to Westminster to Burges[1] about my Tanger business; and thence to White-hall, where I spoke with Sir John[a] Nicholas,[2] who tells me that Mr. Coventry is come from Bredah as was expected; but contrary to expectation, brings with him two or three Articles which do not please the King – as, to retrench the Act of Navigation, and then to ascertaine what are contraband goods.   And then, that those exiled persons who are or shall take refuge in their country may be secure from any further prosecution.   Whether these will be enough to break the peace upon or no, he cannot tell; but I perceive the certainty of peace is blown over.[3]   So called on my wife and met Creed by the way, and they two and I to Charing-cross, there to see the great Boy and Girle that are lately come out of Ireland; the latter, eight, the former but four years old, of most prodigious bigness for their age.[4]   I tried to weigh them in my arms, and find them twice as heavy as people almost twice their age; and yet I am apt to believe they are very young – their father a little sorry fellow, and their mother an old Irish woman.   They have had four children of this bigness and four of ordinary growth, whereof two of each are dead.   If (as my Lord Ormond certifies) it be true that they are no older, it is very monstrous.   So home and to dinner with my wife, and to pipe.   And then I to the office, where busy all the afternoon till the evening; and then with my wife by coach abroad to Bow and Stratford, it being so[b] dusty weather, that there was little pleasure in it; and so home and to walk in the garden, and thither comes Pelling to us to talk; and so in and to supper, and then to bed – all the world being, as I hear, very much damped that their hopes of peace is become[c] uncertain again.

    a repl. 'Edwd.'   *b* repl. 'most'   *c* repl. 'over'

1. William Burgess, clerk to Sir Robert Long, Auditor of the Exchequer.

2. A Clerk of the Privy Council.

3. Certain clauses of the draft treaty infringed the English Navigation Acts, and the Dutch were insisting on postponing consideration of the contraband question to a later treaty. The Privy Council, after long debates on 10–11 July, gave in to the Dutch on all these points: Feiling, p. 225.

4. These children (born in Limerick) had been presented to the King on 10 May. The boy was four-and-a-half feet tall; the girl nearly six feet tall 'and in thickness proportionable'. HMC, *Le Fleming*, p. 48 (newsletter, 14 May).

9. Up pretty betimes and to the office, where busy till office time; and then we sat, but nothing to do but receive clamours about money. This day my Lord Anglesy, our new Treasurer, came the first time to the Board, and there sat with us*a* till noon; and I do perceive he is a very notable man and understanding, and will do things regular and understand them himself, not trust Fenn as Sir G. Carteret did, and will solicit soundly for money; which I do fear was Sir G. Carteret's fault, that he did not do that enough, considering the age we live in, that nothing will do but by solicitation – though never so good for the King or Kingdom; and a bad business well solicited shall for peace sake speed,*b* when a good one shall not. But I do confess I do think it a very bold act of him to take upon him the place of Treasurer of the Navy at this time; but when I consider that a regular accountant never ought to fear anything, nor have reason, I then do cease to wonder. At noon home to dinner and to play on the flagelette with my wife; and then to the office, where very busy, close at my office till late at night; at night walked and sang with my wife in the garden, and so home to supper and to bed. This evening news comes for certain that the Dutch are with their fleet before Dover, and that it is expected they will attempt something there.[1] The business of the peace is quite dashed again, so as now it is doubtful whether the King will condescend to what the Dutch demand, it being so near the Parliament, it being a thing that will, it may be, recommend him to them when they shall find that the not having of a peace lies on his side, by denying some of their demands.

This morning Captain Clerke (Robin Clerke) was at the table, now commands the *Monmouth* and did when the enemy passed the Chain at Chatham the other day, who said publicly at the table that he did admire at the order when it was brought him, for sinking of the *Monmouth* (to the endangering of the ship and spoiling of all her provisions) when her number of men were upon her, that he could have carried her up the River whither he

---

a repl. 'him'   *b* repl. 'succeed sp'-

---

1. But they sailed southwards from Dover on the 9th without firing a gun: *CPSD 1667*, p. 281.

pleased and have been a guard to the rest, and could have sunk her at any time. He did carry some 100 barrels of powder out of the ship, to save it, after the order came for the sinking her. He knew no reason at all, he declares, that could lead them to order the sinking her, nor the rest of the great ships that were sunk; but above all, admires they would burn them on shore and sink them there, when it had been better to have sunk them long way in the middle of the River, for then they could not have burned them so low as now they did.

10. Up, and to the office betimes; and there all the morning very busy, causing papers to be entered and sorted, to put the office in order against the Parliament. At noon home to dinner and then to the office again, close all the afternoon, up[on] the same occasion, with great pleasure till late; and then with my wife and Mercer in the garden and sung; and then home and sung, and to supper with great content, and so to bed. The Duke of York is come back last night from Harwich, but [what] news he brings I know not – nor hear anything today from Dover whether*a* the enemy have made any attempt there, as was expected. This day our girle Mary, whom Payne helped us to, to be under his daughter when that she came to be our cook-maid, did go away, declaring that she must be*b* where she might earn something one day, and spend it and play away the next – but a good civil wench, and one neither wife nor I did ever give angry word to; but she hath this silly vanity that she must play.

11. Up betimes and to my office, and there busy till the office (which was only Sir T. Harvy and myself) met; and did little business and then broke up. He tells me that the Council last night did sit close, to determine of the King's answer about the peace; and that though he doth not certainly know, yet by all discourse yesterday, he doth believe it is peace; and that the King had said it should be peace and had bidden*c* Alderman Backewell to declare upon the Change. It is high time for us to have peace, that the King and Council may get up their credits and have time to do it, for that endeed is the bottom of all our

---

a repl. 'what'   *b* repl. 'have'   *c* MS. 'bin'

misery, that nobody hath any so good opinion of the King and his Council and their advice, as to lend money, or venture their persons or estates or*a* pains upon people that they know cannot thrive with all that we can do, but either by their corruption or negligence must be undone.   This endeed is the very bottom of every man's thought, and the certain ground that we must be ruined, unless the King change his course, or the Parliament come and alter it.   At noon dined alone with my wife.   All the afternoon close at the office, very hard at gathering papers and putting things in order against the Parliament; and at night home with my wife to supper, and then to bed, in hopes to have all things in my office in good condition in a little time for anybody to examine, which I am sure none else will.

12.   Up betimes and to my chamber, there doing business; and by and by comes Greeting, and begun a new month with him, and now to learn to set anything from the notes upon the flagelette;[1] but Lord, to see how like a fool he goes about to give me direction would make a man mad.   I out,*b* and by coach to White-hall and to the Treasury-chamber, where did a little business; and thence to the Exchequer to Burges about Tanger business; and so back again, stepping into the Hall a little, and then homeward by coach and met at White-hall with Sir*c* H. Cholmly; and so into his coach, and he with me to the Excise Office, there to do a little business also – in the way, he telling me that undoubtedly the peace is concluded, for he did stand yesterday where*d* he did hear part of the discourse at the Council-table, and there did hear the King argue for it; among other things, that the spirits of the seamen were down, and the forces of our enemies are grown too great and many for us, and he would not have his subjects overpressed, for he knew an Englishman would do as much as any man upon hopeful terms,

---

a MS. 'and or'	*b* repl. 'then home'
c repl. 'Mr.'	*d* repl. 'at'

---

1. Thomas Greeting's flageolet tutor, *The pleasant companion* (1680, 1682) uses a dot tablature to illustrate the fingering.   The new lessons may have been based on ordinary notation.   (E).

but where he sees he is overpressed, he despairs as soon as any other; and besides that, they have already such a load of dejection already upon them, that they will not be in temper*ᵃ* a good while again.   He heard my Lord Chancellor say to the King, "Sir," says he, "the whole world doth complain publicly of treachery, that things have been managed falsely by some of his great ministers; Sir," says he, "I am for your Majesty's falling into a speedy enquiry into the truth of it, and where you meet with it, punish it – but at the same time, consider what you have to do, and make use of your time for having a peace; for more money will not be given without much trouble, nor is it I fear to be had of the people, nor will a little do it, to put us into condition of doing our business."   But the other day Sir H. Cholmly tells me, he¹ did say the other day at his table – "Treachery?" says he, "I could wish we could prove there was anything of that in it, for that would imply some wit and thoughtfulness; but we are ruined merely by folly and neglect."   And so Sir H. Cholmly tells me they did all argue for peace, and so he doth believe that the King hath agreed to the three points Mr. Coventry brought over, which I have mentioned before,² and is gone with them back.   He tells me further, that the Duke of Buckingham was before the Council the other day,³ and there did carry it very submissively and pleasingly to the King; but to my Lord Arlington, who doth prosecute the business, he was most bitter and sharp, and very slighting.   As to the letter about his imploying a man to cast the King's nativity,⁴ says he to the King, "Sir," says he, "this is none of my hand, and I refer it to your Majesty whether you do not know this hand."   The King answered that it was endeed none of his,*ᵇ* and that he knew whose it was, but could not recall it presently – "Why," says he, "it is my sister of Richmonds,⁵ some frolic or other of hers of some

a repl. 'mood'   *b* repl. 'is'

---

1. Clarendon.
2. See above, p. 326 & n. 3.
3. For his examination on 1 July (at the Tower), see BM, Add. 27872, ff. 13+.
4. See above, pp. 93–4 & n.

5. Mary, Duchess of Richmond, widow of the 1st Duke, Buckingham's only sister; Lady of the Bedchamber to the Queen since March 1662. Clarendon (*Life*, iii. 280) has a similar account.

certain person; and there is nothing of the King's name in it, but it is only said to be his by supposition, as is said." The King, it seems, seemed not very displeased with what the Duke had said; but however, he is still in the Tower, and no discourse of his being out in haste – though my Lady Castlemayne hath so far solicited for him, that the King and she are quite fallen out; he comes not to her nor hath for some three or four days, and parted with very foul words, the King calling*a* her a whore, and a jade that meddled with things she had nothing to do withal. And she calling him fool; and told him, if he was not a fool, he would not suffer his businesses to be carried by fellows that did not understand them, and cause his best subjects, and those best able to serve him, to be imprisoned, meaning the Duke of Buckingham; and it seems she was not only for his liberty, but to be restored to all his places; which it is thought he will never be. While we were at the Excise office talking with Mr. Ball, it was computed that the Parliament had given the King, for this war only, besides all prizes and besides the 200000*l* which he was to spend of his own revenue to guard the sea, above five millions and odd 100000*l*'s; which is a most prodigious sum.¹ Sir H. Cholmly, as a true English gentleman, doth decry the King's expenses of his privy-purse; which in King James's time did not rise to above 5000*l* a year and in King Charles's to 10000*l*, do now*b* cost us above 100000*l*² – besides the great charge of the Monarchy; as, the Duke of York 100000*l*³ of it, and other limbs of the Royall

---

a repl. 'telling her to her face that she was'   *b* MS. 'here'

---

1. These grants are listed in *CTB*, vol. ii, pp. l, lxiv. They were those which could legitimately be the subject of the enquiry instituted by the King in May. Their actual yield was rather less than the figures given here.

2. These figures are wildly wrong. Charles II's annual privy purse expenditure averaged c. £20,000 in the 1660s; about £5800 less than James I's in 1603–8. That of Elizabeth at the end of her reign was c. £5000 p.a. *CTB*, vol. i, pp. xxxii–iii; F. C. Dietz, *Engl. pub. finance*, pp. 110–11.

3. Probably an exaggeration, but the exact figure has not been worked out. The Duke received in cash from the Exchequer some £63,500 in 1666–7, but that was probably not his net income: *CTB*, vol. ii, p. xv. The evidence is briefly examined by F. C. Turner in his *James II* (p. 69, n. 2), who suggests a figure much nearer £50,000 p.a. An account presented to Clarendon in September 1660 put it at £40,000 p.a.: Lister, iii. 507.

family, and the guards, which for his part, says he, "I would have all disbanded; for the King is not the better by them and would be as safe without them, for we have had no rebellions to make him fear anything." But contrarily, he is now raising of a land-army, which this Parliament and Kingdom will never bear; besides, the commanders they put over them are such as will never be able to raise or command them. But the design is, and the Duke of York he says is hot for it, to have a land army, and so to make the government like that of France; but our princes have not brains, or at least care and forecast enough, to do that.[1] It is strange how he and everybody doth nowadays reflect upon Oliver and commend him, so brave things he did and made all the neighbour princes fear him;[2] while here a prince, come in with all the love and prayers and good liking of his people, and have given greater signs of loyallty*a* and willingness to serve him with their estates then ever was done by any people, hath lost all so soon, that it is a miracle what way a man could devise to lose so much in so little time. Thence he set me down at my Lord

a l.h. repl. s.h. 'loyal'

---

1. Cf. below, pp. 355, 361. Clarendon (*Life*, iii. 252–60) describes the difficulties which arose from the levy of troops and appointment of commanders, and justifies the King's action on the ground that peace was not yet concluded and the kingdom still in danger. He says that the privy council was divided, but does not mention James's attitude. James, in his memoirs, claims that he was merely preventing a few hot-heads like Northumberland from disbanding the guards: *Life* (ed. J. S. Clarke, 1816), i. 427. Some members of the government and most of its critics saw danger in the King's unwillingness to recall parliament, which stood prorogued until 10 October.

2. The Medway disaster had heightened Cromwell's posthumous reputation, although none of this admiration was allowed to appear in print: below, p. 382 & n. 2; W. C. Abbott, *Conflicts with oblivion*, pp. 149+. Sorbière in 1664 had reported that the coffee-house talk consisted of complaints about taxes, and regrets for the achievement of Cromwell: 'la puisance de leurs flottes ... la gloire ... la pompe de la République, vers laquelle il venoit des Ambassadeurs de tous costez ...' (*Relation d'un voyage en Angleterre*, Cologne, 1667, p. 94). Magalotti (p. 407) remarked in almost the same terms in 1669 that people 'cannot refrain from odiously comparing the present government with the late one of Cromwell, magnifying the power of the fleets, the alliances, and the reputation of their nation in those times, with many other reflections of a like nature ....'.

Crew's and away, and I up to my Lord, where Sir Tho. Crew[1]
was; and by and by comes Mr. Cæsar, who teaches my Lady's
page[a] upon the Lute, and here Mr. Cæsar did play some very fine
things endeed, to my great liking. Here was my Lord Hinchingbrooke also, newly come from Hinchingbrooke, where all well;
but methinks, I knowing in what case he stands for money, by his
demands to me and the report Mr. Moore gives of the management of the family, makes me, God forgive me, to contemn him,
though I do really honour and pity them; though they deserve it
not, that have so good an estate and will live beyond it. To
dinner, and very good discourse with my Lord; and after dinner,
Sir Tho. Crew and I alone, and he tells me how I am mightily in
esteem with the Parliament, there being harangues made in the[b]
House to the Speaker of Mr. Pepys's readiness and civility to
show them everything; which I am at this time very glad of.
He tells me the news of the King and my Lady Castlemaine
which I have wrote already this day – and the design of the
Parliament to look into things very well before they give any
more money, and I pray God they may. Thence after dinner to
St. James's, but missed Sir W. Coventry; and so home and there
find my wife in a dogged humour for my not dining at home,
and I did give her a pull by the nose and some ill words, which
she provoked me to by something she spoke, that we fell extra-
ordinarily out; insomuch, that I going to the office to avoid
further anger, she fallowed me in a devilish manner thither, and
with much ado I got her into the garden out of hearing, to
prevent shame; and so home, and by degrees I found it necessary
to calme her, and did; and then to the office, where pretty late,
and then to walk with her in the garden, and so to supper and
pretty good friends; and so to bed – with my mind very quiet.

13. Up pretty betimes, it being mighty hot weather and I
lying this night (which I have not done I believe since a boy;
I am sure not since before I had the stone before) with only a
rugg and a sheet upon me. To my chamber, and my wife up to
do something and by chance we fell out again; but I to the

a repl. 'pach'   b repl. 'Mr. P'-

office, and there we did at the board much business, though the most was the dividing of 5000*l* (which the Lords-Comissioners have with great difficulty found upon*a* our letter to them this week that would have required 50000*l*)[1] among a great many occasions. After rising, my Lord Anglesy, this being the second time of his being with us, did take*b* me aside and asked me where I lived, because he would be glad to have some discourse with me. This I liked well enough, and told him I would wait upon him, which I will do; and so all broke up, and I home to dinner, where Mr. Pierce dined with us; who tells us what troubles me, that my Lord Buckhurst hath got Nell away from the King's House, lies with her, and gives her 100*l* a year, so as she hath sent her parts to the House and will act no more.[2] And yesterday Sir Tho. Crew told me that Lacy lies a-dying of the pox,[3] and yet hath his whore by him; whom he will have to look on, he says, though he can do no more; nor would receive any ghostly advice from a Bishop, an old acquaintance of his that went to see him. He says there is a strangeness between the King and my Lady Castlemayne, as*c* I was told yesterday.

After dinner, my wife and I to the New Exchange to pretty maid Mrs. Smith's shop, where I left my wife; and I to Sir W. Coventry's and there had the opportunity of talk with him; who I perceive doth not like our business of the change of the Treasurer's hand, and he tells me he is entered the lists with this new Treasurer before the King, in taking away the business of the victualling money from his hand,[4] and the Regiment,[5] and declar-

---

a repl. 'after my'   *b* repl. 'privately'   *c* repl. full stop

---

1. The letter has not been traced. The warrant for the payment of £5000 was issued on the 11th: *CTB*, ii. 34.

2. He bought her from the actor Charles Hart and for a while she abandoned the Theatre Royal: John H. Wilson, *Nell Gwynn*, pp. 61–3.

3. John Lacy was the leading comedian in the King's Company; far from dying, he lived on till 1681. (A).

4. Coventry's aim was to transfer the victualling business from the Navy Treasurer to the Exchequer: cf. below, p. 378 & n. 2.

5. The Admiral's regiment was later reconstituted as the Royal Marines. It had hitherto been paid by the Navy Treasurer; the arrangement was now under review: *CTB*, ii. 33.

Nell Gwyn, by Simon Verelst

(Private Collection)

ing that he hath no right to the 3*d* per cent by his patent, for
that it was always heretofore given by perticular Privy Seal;
and that the King and Council just upon his coming in had
declared 2000*l* a year sufficient.¹ This makes him angry, but
Sir W. Coventry I perceive cares not, but doth every day hold
up his head higher and higher. And this day I have received
an order from the Comissioners of the Treasury to pay no more
pentions for Tanger, which I am glad of² – and he tells me they
do make bold with all things of that kind. Thence I to White-
hall, and in the street I espied Mrs. Burroughs and took a means
to meet and salute her and talk a little; and then parted, and I
home by coach, taking up my wife at the Exchange; and there
am mightily pleased with this Mrs. Smith, being a very pleasant
woman. So home, and resolved upon going to Epsumm tomorrow, only for Ayre, and got Mrs. Turner to go with us;
and so home and to supper (after having been at the office) to
bed. It is an odd and sad thing to see, that though this be a peace
worse then we had before, yet everybody's fear almost is that the
Dutch will not stand by their promise, now the King hath consented to all they would have. And yet no wise man that I
meet with, when he comes to think of it, but wishes with all his
heart a war; but that the King is not a man to be trusted with
the management of it. It was pleasantly said by a man in the
City, a stranger, to one that told him that peace was concluded,
"Well," says he, "and have you a peace?" "Yes," says the
other. "Why, then," says he, "hold your peace!" – partly reproaching us with the disgracefulness of it, that it is not fit to be
mentioned; and next, that we are not able to make the Dutch
keep it when they have a mind to break it.

Sir Tho. Crew yesterday, speaking of the King of France,
how great a man he is, "Why," says he, "all the world thought

---

1. This was the figure fixed by
Council order on 4 July 1660. Until
August 1662 Carteret had received
this amount in salary, and had fore-
gone fees. The same amount was
awarded to the Treasurer in 1671–4,
after which it was raised to £3000:
Cat., i. 8 & n.
   2. On 9 July the Treasury had

ordered a list to be drawn up of all
pensions payable by departmental
treasurers: *CTB*, ii. 31. Pepys, as
Treasurer for Tangier, had had much
troublewith the case of Peterborough,
who had received a pension of £1000
p.a. after only eight months' service
as Governor.

that when the last pope died, there would have been such bandying between the Crownes of France and Spain; whereas, when he was asked what he would have his Ministers at Rome do, 'Why,' says [he], 'let them choose who they will – if the Pope will do what is fit, the Pope and I will be friends; if he will not, I will take a course with him; therefore, I will not trouble myself;' and thereupon the election was despatched in a little time, I think in a day, and all ended."[1]

14. *Lords day.* Up, and my wife, a little before 4, and to make us ready; and by and by Mrs. Turner came to us by agreement, and she and I stayed talking below while my wife dressed herself; which vexed me that she was so long about it, keeping us till past 5 a-clock before she was ready. She ready, and taking some bottles of wine and beer and some cold Fowle with us into the Coach, we took coach and four horses which I had provided last night, and so away – a very fine day; and so towards Epsum, talking all the way pleasantly, and perticularly of the pride and ignorance of Mrs. Lowther in having of her train carried up.[2] The country very fine; only, the way very dusty. We got to Epsum by 8 a-clock to the Well, where much company; and there we light and I drank the water; they did not, but do go about and walk a little among the women, but I did drink four pints and had some very good stools by it. Here I met with divers of our town; among others, with several of the tradesmen of our office, but did talk but little with them, it growing hot in the sun; and so we took coach again and to the Towne to the King's Head,[3] where our coachman carried us; and there had an ill room for us to go into, but the best in the

---

1. The conclave for the election of the successor to Alexander VII (d. 12/22 May 1667) had assembled on 23 May/2 June, and had in fact taken 18 days to choose Giulio Rospigliosi (Clement IX), during which Louis XIV's influence had been exerted quite strenuously. Crew's story may perhaps refer to the events of the final day of the conclave, when Rospigliosi had only five votes in the

morning, and 61 (out of 64) in the evening. See L. Pastor, *Hist. Popes* (trans.), xxxi. 314-18; C. Gérin, *Louis XIV et le Saint-Siège*, ii. 179-205.

2. See above, p. 302.

3. For long, one of the three principal inns: *Some particulars relating to ... Epsom ... By an Inhabitant* (1825), p. 117.

house that was not taken up; here we called for drink and bespoke dinner. And hear that my Lord Buckhurst and Nelly is lodged at the next house, and Sir Ch. Sidly with them, and keep a merry house. Poor girl, I pity her; but more the loss of her at the King's House. Here I saw Gilsthrop, Sir W. Batten's clerk that hath been long sick; he looks like a dying man, with a consumption* got, as is believed, by the pox; but God knows that, but the man is in a sad condition, though he finds himself much better since his coming thither he says.[1] W Hewers rode with us, and I left him and the women, and myself walked to church, where few people (contrary to what I expected) and none I knew but all the Houblons brothers; and them after sermon I did salute and walk with towards my Inne, which was in their way to their lodgings. They came last night to see their elder brother, who stays here at the waters, and away tomorrow. James did tell me that I was the only happy man of the Navy; of whom, he says, during all this freedom the people have taken of speaking treason, he hath not heard one bad word of me – which is a great joy to me, for I hear the same of others; but do know that I have deserved as well as most. We parted, to meet anon; and I to my women into a better room, which the people of the house borrowed for us; and there to dinner, a good dinner, and were merry; and Pendleton came to us, who happened to be in the house, and there talked and were merry. After dinner, he gone, we all lay down after dinner (the day being wonderful hot) to sleep, and each of us took a good nap and then rose; and Tom Willson came to see me and sat and talked an hour, and I perceive he hath been much acquainted with Dr. Fuller (Tom) and Dr. Pierson and several of the great Cavalier parsons during the late troubles;[2] and I*a* was glad to hear him talk of them, which he did very ingeniously, and very much of Dr. Fullers art of memory,[3] which he did tell me several

a repl. 'hear'

---

1. He died in the following December.

2. Fuller was the author, and John Pearson the Cambridge theologian – after 1662 Master of Trinity and after 1672 Bishop of Chester. They had both been active as preachers in London during the 1650s.

3. Cf. above, ii. 21 & n. 2.

instances of. By and by he parted, and we took coach and to take the ayre, there being a fine breeze abroad; and I went and carried them to the Well and there filled some bottles of water to carry home with me. And there talked with the two women that farm the well of the lord of the manor, Mr. Eveling (who with his lady and also my Lord George Berkely's lady, and their fine daughter that the King of France liked so well and did dance so rich in Jewells before the King at the Ball I was at, at our Court last Winter, and also their son, a Knight of the Bath,[1] were at church this morning), at 12*l* per annum. Here W. Hewer's horse broke loose, and we had the sport to see him taken again. Then I carried them to see my Cosen Pepys's house;[2] and light and walked round about it, and they like it (as endeed it deserves) very well, and is a pretty place; and then I walked them to the wood hard by and there got them in in the thickets, till they had lost themselfs and I could not find the way into any of the walks in the wood, which endeed are very pleasant if I could have found them. At last got out of the wood again; and I, by leaping down the little bank coming out of the wood, did sprain my right foot, which brought me great present pain; but presently, with walking, it went away for the present, and so the women and W. Hewer and I walked upon the Downes, where a flock of sheep was, and the most pleasant and innocent sight that ever I saw in my life; we find a shepheard and his little boy reading, far from any houses or sight of people, the Bible to him. So I made the boy read to me, which he did with the forced Tone that children do usually read, that was mighty pretty; and then I did give him something and went to the father and talked with him; and I find he had been a servant in my Cosen Pepys's house, and told me what was become of their old servants. He did content himself mightily in my liking his boy's reading and

---

1. For the ball, see above, vii. 371–3. Richard Evelyn of Woodcote Park was brother of the diarist. Lord George Berkeley was the 9th Baron Berkeley; the daughter (whose association with the King of France has not been traced) was probably Elizabeth, his eldest; his son was Charles, later the 10th Baron and 2nd Earl.

The Berkeleys had a house, Durdans, nearby.

2. At Ashtead. The cousin was John Pepys, brother of Mrs Turner, one of Pepys's companions on this jaunt. He had been secretary to Chief Justice Coke and had died in about 1652.

did bless God for him, the most like one of the old Patriarchs
that ever I saw in my life, and it brought those thoughts of the
old age of the world in my mind for two or three days after.
We took notice of his woolen knit stockings of two colours
mixed, and of his shoes shod with Iron shoes, both at the toe and
heels, and with great nails in the soles of his feet, which was
mighty pretty; and taking notice of them, "Why," says the
poor man, "the Downes, you see, are full of stones, and we are
fain to shoe ourselfs thus; and these," says he, "will make the
stones fly till they sing before me." I did give the poor man
something, for which he was mighty thankful, and I tried to cast
stones with his Horne Crooke. He values his dog mightily, that
would turn a sheep any way which he would have him when he
goes to fold them. Told me there was about 18 Scoare sheep in
his flock, and that he hath 4s a week the year round for keeping
of them. So we parted thence, with mighty pleasure in the
discourse we had with this poor man; and Mrs. Turner, in the
common fields here, did gather one of the prettiest nosegays
that ever I saw in my life. So to our coach, and through Mr.
Minnes's wood and looked upon Mr. Eveling's house;[1] and so
over the common and through Epsum towne to our Inne[a], in the
way stopping a poor woman with her milk-pail and in one of
my gilt Tumblers did drink our bellyfuls of milk, better then any
Creame; and so to our Inne and there had a dish of creame, but
it was sour and so had no pleasure in it; and so paid our reckoning
and took coach, it being about 7 at night, and passed and saw
the people walking with their wifes and children to take the ayre;
and we set out for home, the sun by and by going down, and we
in the cool of the evening all the way with much pleasure home,
talking and pleasing ourselfs with the pleasure of this day's
work; and Mrs. Turner mightily pleased with my resolution,
which I tell her is never to keep a country-house, but to keep a

a repl. 'Lod'-

1. Woodcote Park, since 1663
owned by Elizabeth, wife of Richard
Evelyn and daughter of George
Mynne, on whose death in 1663 she
had inherited the property. Pepys
had known the wood as 'Mr Minnes's'
in his youth. VCH, *Surrey*, iii.
375–6; O. W. Manning and W. Bray,
Hist. Surrey (1804–14), ii. 612–13.

coach and with my wife on the Saturday and to go sometimes
for a day to this place and then quite to another place; and there
is more variety, and as little charge and no trouble, as there
is in a country-house.[1]   Anon it grew dark, and as it grew dark
we had the pleasure to see several Glow wormes, which was
mighty pretty.   But my foot begins more and more to pain me;
which Mrs. Turner, by keeping her warm hand upon it, did much
ease; but so that when we came home, which was just at 11 at
night, I was not able to walk from the lane's end to my house
without being helped, which did trouble me; and therefore to
bed presently; but thanks be to God, found that I had not been
missed nor any business happened in my absence; so to bed and
there had a cere-cloth laid to my foot; and lay alone, but in
great pain all night long, so as I was not able to go today to
《15》 wait on the Duke of York with my fellows; but was
forced in bed to write the perticulars for their discourse
there, and kept my bed all day; and anon comes Mrs. Turner
and new-dressed my foot, and did it so, that I was at much ease
presently and so continued all day, so as I slept much and well
in the daytime and in the evening rose and eat something.
Where our poor Jane very sad for the death of her poor brother,[2]
who hath left a wife and two small children.   I did give her 20s
in money, and what[a] wine she needed for the burying him.
After supper I was willing to go to bed to ease my foot again;
which I did, and slept well all night ⟨this evening came to see me
《16》 Pelling and we did sing together; and he sings well
endeed⟩ and in the morning I was able to put on a wide
shoe on that foot; and to the office without much pain and there
sat all the morning.   At noon home to dinner, where Creed to
discourse of our Tanger business, which stands very bad in the
business of money – and therefore we expect to have a committee called soon, and to acquaint them, among other things,

a repl. 'wine to'

---

1. From 1677 to 1681 Pepys in
fact joined with his friends the Houblons in renting a country villa at
Parson's Green, a few miles west of
Chelsea: Rawl. A 194, f. 261;
Bryant, ii. 183. Cf. above, vol. i,
p. xvii.

2. Probably 'Will the groom',
mentioned at 27 December 1662.

with the order come to me for the not paying of any more pensions. We dined together; and after dinner, I to the office and there very late, very busy, doing much business endeed; and so with great comfort home to supper, and so to bed to ease my foot, which toward night begun to ake.

17. Up, and to my chamber to set down my Journall of Sunday last with much pleasure; and my foot being pretty well, but yet I am forced to limp. Then by coach; set my wife down at the New Exchange, and I to White-hall to the Treasury-chamber, but to little purpose; so to Mr. Burges,[1] to as little. There to the Hall and talked with Mrs. Michell, who begins to tire me about doing something for her elder son; which I am willing to do, but know not what. Thence to White-hall again, and thence away and took up my wife at Unthankes and left her at the Change; and so I to Bennets to take up a bill for the last silk I had for my vest and coat, which I owe them for; and so to the Excise Office and there did a little business, and so to Temple Barr and stayed at my bookseller's[2] till my wife calls me; and so home, where I am saluted with the news of Hogg's bringing a rich Canary Prize to*a* Hull,[3] and Sir W. Batten doth offer me 1000*l* down for my perticular share, besides Sir Rd. Ford's part; which doth tempt me, but yet I would not take it, but will stand and fall with the company.[4] He and two more, the *Panther* and *Fanfan*,[5] did enter into consortship; and so they have all brought in each a prize, though ours worth as much as both theirs, and more. However, it will be well worth having, God be thanked for it. This news makes us all very glad. I at Sir W. Batten's did hear the perticular of it; and there for joy he did give the company that were there a bottle or two of his own last year's

a repl. 'with'

---

1. Of the Exchequer.
2. Probably John Starkey, by Temple Bar.
3. See Thomas Pointer to Pepys, Hull, 15 July: *CSPD 1667*, p. 298; cf. ib., pp. 295, 296. She was a ship of 400 tons, laden with sack and log-wood, taken by the privateer owned by Pepys and his partners. See also Lord Belasyse to Pepys, Hull, 16 July: HMC, *Eliot Hodgkin*, pp. 168–9.
4. But see below, p. 385.
5. Privateers owned by Prince Rupert.

wine, growing at Walthamstow,[1] then which the whole company said they never drank better foreign wine in their lives.

Home and to dinner; and by and by comes Mr. Pierce, who is interested in the *Panther*, for some advice; and then comes Creed, and he and I spent the whole afternoon, till 8 at night, walking and talking of sundry things, public and private, in the garden; but most of all, of the unhappy state of this nation at this time by the negligence of the King and his Council. The Duke of Buckingham is it seems set at Liberty,[2] without any further charge against him or other clearing of him, but let to go out; which is one of the strangest instances of the fool's play with which all public things are done in this age that is to be apprehended. And it is said that when he was charged with making himself popular (as*a* endeed he is, for many*b* of the discontented Parliament, Sir Robt. Howard and Sir Tho. Meres and others, did attend at the Council-chamber when he was examined), he should answer that whoever was committed to prison by my Lord Chancellor or my Lord Arlington could not want being popular.[3] But it is worth considering the ill state a Minister of State is in under such a prince as ours is; for undoubtedly, neither of those two great men would have been so fierce against the Duke of Buckingham at the Council-table the other day had they [not] been assured of the King's good liking and supporting them therein; whereas, perhaps at the desire of my Lady Castlemayne[4] (who I suppose hath at last overcome the King), the Duke of Buckingham is well received again, and now these men delivered up to the interest he can make for his revenge. He told me over the story of Mrs. Stewart, much after the manner which I was told it long since and have entered it in this book, told me

---

a repl. 'he should answer'   *b* repl. 'most'

---

1. For English-grown wine, see *Comp.*: 'Drink'.
2. By a warrant of the 14th: *CSPD 1667*, p. 294.
3. Cf. the French ambassador's despatches (6, 10 October) qu. V. Barbour, *Arlington*, pp. 113, 114 nn.; and Baxter's remarks in M. Sylvester, *Reliq. Baxt.* (1696), pt iii. 21. Buckingham had joined in the demand, e.g., for parliamentary examination of accounts.
4. She was anxious to gain an ally against Clarendon.

by Mr. Eveling.[1] Only, he says it is verily believed that the King did never intend*a* to marry her to any but himself, and that the Duke of York and Lord Chancellor were jealous of it;[2] and that Mrs. Stewart might be got with child by the King or somebody else, and the King own a marriage before his contract (for it is but a contract, as he tells me, to this day) with the Queene,[3] and so wipe their noses of the Crown; and that therefore the Duke of York and Chancellor did do all they could to forward the match with my Lord Duke of Richmond, that she might be married out of the way. But above all, it is a worthy part that this good lady hath acted. Thus we talked till night and then parted; and so I to my office and did business, and so home to supper and there find my sister Michell come from Lee[4] to see us; but doth tattle so much of the late business of the Duch coming thither, that I was weary of it. Yet it is worth remembering what she says: that she hath heard both seamen and soldiers swear they would rather serve the Dutch then the King, for they should be better used. She saw the *Royal Charles* brought into the River by them, and how they shot off their great guns for joy when they got her out of Chatham River. I would not forget that this very day, when we have nothing to do almost but five merchantmen to man in the River, which have now been about it some weeks, I was asked at Westminster what the matter was that there was such ado kept in pressing of men, as it seems there is thereabouts at this day. So after supper, we all to bed. My foot very well again, I thank God.

18. Up and to the office*b*, where busy all the morning, and most*c* of our time taken up with Carcasse, upon some complaints

---

a repl. 'pre'-   *b* repl. same symbol   *c* repl. 'a'

---

1. See above, p. 184.
2. I.e. in order to promote the claims to the succession of the Duchess of York, Clarendon's daughter.
3. The story about the marriage contract was baseless. There had also been two religious ceremonies –
one Roman Catholic and the other Anglican at Portsmouth on 21 May 1661. The allegation that Charles had been previously married (to Lucy Walter) was untrue.
4. Esther St Michel; from Leigh-on-Sea, Essex.

brought in against him.[1]   And many other petitions about tickets lost, which spends most of our time.   Home to dinner and then to the office again, where very well imployed at the office till evening; and then being weary, took out my wife and Will Batelier by coach to Islington; but no pleasure in our going, the way being so dusty that one durst not breathe.   Drank at the old house[2] and so home; and then to the office a little and so home to supper and to bed.

19.   Up, and comes the flagelette-maister[a] and brings me two new great Ivory pipes, which cost me 32s.   And so to play; and he being done and Balty's wife taking her leave of me, she going back to Lee today, I to Westminster and there did receive 15000l orders out[b] of the Exchequer, in part of a bigger sum upon the Eleven Months Tax for Tanger[3] – part of which I presently delivered to Sir H. Cholmly who was there; and thence with Mr. Gawden to Auditor Woods and Beales to examine some precedents in his business of the victualling[4] on his behalf, and so home; and in my way by coach down Marke[c]-lane, mightily pleased and smitten to see, as I thought in passing, the pretty woman, the Line-maker's wife that lived in Fanchurch-street; and I had great mind to have gone back to have seen, but yet would correct my nature and would not.   So to dinner with my wife and then to sing; and so to the office, where busy all the afternoon late, busy; and to Sir W. Batten and Sir R Fords we all, to consider about our great prize at Hull; being troubled at our being likely to be troubled with Prince Rupert, by reason of Hogg's consorting himself with two privateers of the Prince's – and so we study how to ease or secure ourselfs.   So to walk in

a   repl. 'maister   *b*   repl. 'upon'
        c   l.h. repl. s.h. 'the'

---

1. For examples, see *CSPD 1667*, pp. 153, 298–9. For this case, see above, p. 64, n. 1.

2. The King's Head: above, ii. 125, n. 2.

3. A warrant for 24 orders amounting to £15,300 was issued on 16 July: *CTB*, ii. 171. For the grant of £30,000 in June, see above, p. 294.

4. Cf. above, p. 334 & n. 4.

the garden with my wife, and then to supper and to bed.   One
tells me that by letter from Holland, the people there are made
to believe that our condition in England is such as they may have
whatever they will ask.   And that so they are mighty high, and
despise us or a peace with us – and there is ⟨too⟩ much reason
for them to do [so].

The Duch fleet are in great squadrons everywhere still*a* about
Harwich.   And were lately at Portsmouth; and the last letters
say at Plymouth, and now gone to Dartmouth to destroy our
Straights-fleet, lately got in thither; but God knows whether
they can do it any hurt or no.[1]   But it was pretty news came
the other day so fast, of the Duch fleets being in so many places,
that Sir W. Batten at table cried, "By God!" says he, "I think the
Devil shits Dutchmen."

20.*b*   Up and to the office, where all the morning; and then
toward the Change at noon, in my way observing my mistake
yesterday in Mark-lane: that the woman I saw was not the
pretty woman I meant, the line-maker's wife, but a new-married
woman, very pretty, a strong-water seller.   And in going by,
to my content I find that the very pretty daughter at the Ship
tavern at the end of Billiter-lane is there still, and in the bar;
and I believe is married to him that is new come and hath new-
trimmed the house.   Home to dinner, and then to the office,
we having despatched away Mr. Oviatt[2] to Hull about our prizes
there; and I have wrote a letter*c* of thanks by him to my Lord
Bellasses, who had writ to me to offer all his service for my

---

a repl. 'else'   *b* repl. '16'   *c* repl. 'I'-

---

1. For the news of de Ruyter's
movements, see *CSPD 1667*, pp.
295-6, 301-2, 309; Deane to Pepys,
Harwich, 13 July: Rawl. A 195a,
f. 138r. The militia was out both in
Devon and Cornwall, but no serious
attack was made anywhere (the worst

that happened being a few shots fired
at Torquay), and the Straits fleet
escaped damage.

2. John Oviatt, merchant; son-in-
law of Sir Richard Ford, one of the
partners in the privateering enter-
prise.

interest there; but I dare not trust him.[1] In the evening, late, walking in the garden with my wife; and then to bed.

21. *Lords day.* Up betimes, and all the morning [in my chamber]; and then to dinner with my wife alone, and then all the afternoon in like manner in my chamber, making up my Tanger accounts and drawing a letter, which I have done at last to my full content, to present to the Lords-Commissioners for Tanger tomorrow.[2] And about 7 at night, when finished my letter and weary, I and my wife and Mercer up by water to Barne elmes, where we walked by Moone-shine; and called at Lambeth and drank, and had cold meat in the boat, and did eat and sang, and down home by almost 12 at night, very fine and pleasant; only, could not sing ordinary songs with that freedom that otherwise I would. Here Mercer tells me that the pretty maid of the Ship tavern I spoke of yesterday is married there, which I am glad of. So having spent this night with much serious pleasure, to consider that I am in a condition to fling away an angell in such a refreshment to myself and family, we home and to bed, leaving Mercer by the way at her own door.

22. Up, and with Sir W. Batten and J. Mennes to St. James's, where the first time I have been there since the enemy's being with us. Where little business but lack of money, which now is so professed by Sir W. Coventry as nothing is more, and the King's whole business owned to be at a stand for want of it. So up to my Lord Chancellors, where was a Committee of

---

1. For Belasyse's letter (16 July) and Pepys's draft reply (20 July), see NMM, MS 55/040; printed in HMC, *Eliot Hodgkin*, pp. 168–9. It would be difficult to detect in Pepys's letter any signs of his mistrust of Belasyse. 'But, my lord, I esteeme it a part of my good Fortune equall to all the rest that shee [the ship] happens to bee brought in to a Port, where I have so noble a friend as your Lordship . . . your Lordship will pardon mee if I adventure to

begg the full advantage of your Lordship's kindnesse towards mee, which you have beene pleased soe nobly to offer mee, and esteeming it my very great happiness to have fallen into your Lordshipp's protection at a time of my soe much needing it . . .' and so on.

2. The letter has not been traced. The Tangier accounts for November 1664 to December 1667 are summarised in Routh, p. 366.

Tanger in my Lord's Roome where he is to hear causes, where all
the Judges' pictures hang up very fine.[1] Here I read my letter
to them, which was well received and they did fall seriously to
discourse the want of money and other perticulars, and to some
pretty good purpose. But to see how Sir W. Coventry did
oppose both my Lord Chancellor and the Duke of York himself,
about the order of the Commissioners of the Treasury to me for
not paying of Pensions,[2] and with so much reason and eloquence,
so natural, was admirable – and another thing, about his pressing
for the reduction of the charge of Tanger, which they would
have put off to another time; "But," says [he], "the King suffers
so much by the putting off of the consideration of reductions[a] of
charge, that he is undone; and therefore I do pray you, Sir," (to
his Royal Highness) "that when anything offers of that kind,
you will not let it scape you." Here was a great bundle of letters
brought hither, sent up from sea from a vessel of ours that had
taken them after they had been flung over by a Duchman –
wherein, among others, the Duke of York did read the super-
scription of one to De Witt, thus – "To the most[b] wise, foreseeing[c]
and discreet Here,* &c;" which I thought with myself I could have
been glad might have been duly directed to any one of them at
the table, though the greatest men in this kingdom – the Duke
of York – Lord Chancellor – my Lord Duke of Albemarle,
Arlington, Ashly, Peterburgh, and Coventry (the best of them all
for parts). I perceive they do all profess their expectation of a
peace, and that suddenly; and do advise of things accordingly –
and do all speak of it (and expressly I remember the Duke of
Albemarle) saying that they hoped for it. Letters were read at
the table from Tanger, that Guildand is wholly lost, and that he
doth offer Arzill to us to deliver it to us;[3] but Sir W. Coventry
did declare his opinion that we should have nothing to do with

a repl. 'redussion' *b* repl. 'the' *c* repl. 'pre'-

1. For Clarendon's collection of pictures, see above, p. 175, n. 7. (OM).
2. See above, p. 335 & n. 2.
3. Guyland, the old enemy of the English garrison at Tangier, was now besieged in Azila by his overlord Taffiletta. In April and May he had appealed for help to 'my beloved friend the king of Great Britain': Routh, p. 93. Cf. above, vii. 214 & n. 2.

it, and said that if Tanger were offered us now, as the King's
condition is, he would advise against the taking it; saying that
the King's charge is too great, and must be brought down (it
being like the fire of this City, never to be mastered till you
have brought it under you); and that these places abroad are
but so much charge to the King, and we do rather hitherto *a* strive
to greaten them then lessen them; and then the King is forced to
part with them, "As," says he, "he did with Dunkirke, by my
Lord Tiviotts making it so chargeable to the King as he did that;
and would have done Tanger if he had lived." I perceive he is
the only man that doth seek the King's profit and is bold to
deliver what he thinks on every occasion.

Having broke up here, I away with Mr. Gawden in his coach
to *b* the Change; and there a little, and then home and dined, and
then to the office; and by and by with my wife to White-hall
(she to Unthankes) and there met Creed and did a little business
at the Treasury chamber; and then to walk into Westminster-
hall an hour or two with much pleasure, reflecting upon our
discourse today at the Tanger meeting and crying up the worth
of Sir W. Coventry. He tells me of the Fray between the Duke
of Buckingham at the Duke's playhouse the last Saturday (and
it is the first day I have heard that they have acted at either the
King's or Duke's houses this month or six weeks) and Henry
Killigrew; whom the Duke of Buckingham did soundly beat
and take away his sword and make a fool of, till the fellow prayed
him to spare his life.[1] And I am glad of it, for it seems in this
business the Duke of Buckingham did *c* carry himself very
innocently and well – and I wish he had paid this fellow's coat

a repl. 'here'   b repl. 'home'   c repl. 'had'

---

1. They had quarrelled over the
Countess of Shrewsbury, whom
Killigrew (one of her ex-lovers) had
insulted. Killigrew was committed
to the Tower on the 20th, but on the
22nd the punishment was changed to
confinement at his house, because of
his head injuries. On 9 August, on
the recommendation of the council,
the King ordered him to be arrested
and banished from the court for ever.
He managed to escape to France.
See Gramont, pp. 350–1; C. H.
Hartmann (ed.), *The King my brother*,
pp. 202–3; HMC, *Le Fleming*, pp. 51,
52. For brawls in theatres (which
were not uncommon), see M. Summers, *Restoration Theatres*, pp. 78–82.

well. I heard something of this at the Change today; and it is pretty to hear how people do*a* speak kindly of the Duke of Buckingham, as one that will enquire into faults, and therefore they do mightily favour him; and it puts me in mind that this afternoon, Billing the Quaker meeting me in the hall, came to me, and after a little discourse did say, "Well," says he, "now you will be all called to an account;" meaning the Parliament is drawing near. This done, I took coach and took up my wife, and so home; and after a little at the office, I home to my chamber a while, and then to supper and to bed.

23. Up betimes and to the office, doing something towards our great account to [the]*b* Lords Commissioners of the Treasury; and anon the office sat, and all the morning doing business. At noon home to dinner and then close to my business all the afternoon. In the evening Sir R Ford is come back from the Prince and tells Sir W. Batten and me how basely Sir W. Penn received our letter we sent him about the prizes at Hull, and slyly answered him about the Prince's leaving all his concerns to him; but the Prince did it afterward, by letter brought by Sir R Ford to us, which Sir W. Penn knows not of – but a very rogue he is.

By and by comes sudden news to me, by letter from the Clerk of the Cheque at Gravesend, that there was 30 sail of Duch men-of-war coming up into the Hope this last tide;[1] which I told Sir W. Penn of, but he would not believe it, but laughed and said it was a fleet of Billanders, and that the guns that were heard was the saluting of the Swedes Imbassador that comes over with them; but within half an hour comes another letter from Captain Proud, that 8 of them were come into the Hope, and 30 more fallowing them, at 10 this morning.[2] By and by comes order from White-hall to send down one*c* of our number to

a MS. 'to'   *b* MS. has symbol rendered illegible   *c* repl. 'a'

---

1. Richard Elkins to Pepys, 23 July, PRO, SP 29/210, no. 112; summary in *CSPD 1667*, p. 319. The Dutch (under van Nes) retired downriver on the 24th.

2. Capts John Prowd and William Haddock to the Navy Board, Gravesend, 'past 12', 23 July, in *CSPD Add. 1660–85*, p. 207.

Chatham, fearing that, as they did before, they may make a show first up hither, but then go to Chatham; so my Lord Brouncker doth go, and we here are ordered to give notice to the merchant men-of-war, gone below the Barracado at Woolwich,[1] to come up again. So with much trouble, to supper, home and to bed.

24. Betimes this morning comes a letter from the Clerk of the Cheque [at] Gravesend to me, to tell me that the Dutch fleet did come all into the Hope yesterday noon and held a fight with our[a] ships from thence till 7 at night; that they had burned 12 fireships, and we took one of theirs and burned 5 of their[b] fireships.[2] But then rising and going to Sir W. Batten, he tells me that we have burned one of their men-of-war, and another of theirs is blown up;[3] but how true this is, I know not. But these fellows are mighty bold, and have had the fortune of the wind Easterly this time to bring them up and prevent our troubling them with our fireships; and endeed have had the winds at their command from the beginning, and now do take the beginning of the spring [tide] as if they had some great design to do.

I to my office, and there hard at work all the morning, to my great content, abstracting the contract-Booke in into my abstract book; which I have by reason of the war omitted for above two years,[4] but now am endeavouring to have all my books ready and perfect against the Parliament comes, that upon examination I may be in condition to value myself upon my perfect doing of my own duty.

At noon home to dinner, where my wife mighty musty, but I took no notice of it; but after dinner to the office, and there with Mr. Harper did another good piece of work about my late

a repl. 'all'   *b* MS. 'our'

---

1. A 60-gun battery erected after the Dutch raid on the Medway: *CSPD 1667*, pp. 179, 215.

2. Richard Elkins to Pepys, 23 July: Rawl. A 195a, f. 126r.

3. The *London Gazette*, 25 July,

gives the story of two Dutch men-of-war destroyed in this way.

4. For the contract books, see above, iii. 65, n. 2. The abstract-book should have been entered up monthly: above, vi. 43.

collection of the accounts of the Navy presented to the Parliament at their last session, which was left unfinished[1] and now I have done it, which sets my mind at my ease. And so having tired myself, I took a pair of oares about 5 a-clock, which I made a gally at Redriffe; and so with very much pleasure down to*a* Gravesend, all the way with extraordinary content reading of Boyl's *Hydrostatickes*;[2] which the more I read and understand, the more I admire as a most excellent piece of philosophy.* As we come nearer Gravesend, we hear the Dutch fleet and ours a-fighting, their guns most distinctly and loud; but before we got to Gravesend they ceased, and it grew darkish, and so I landed only (and the flood being come) and went up to the Shipp and discoursed with the landlord of the house, who undeceives me in what I heard this morning about the Dutch having lost two men-of-war, for it is not so, but several of their fireships. He doth say that this afternoon they did force our ships to retreat, but that now they are gone down as far as Shield Haven;[3] but what the event hath been of this evening's guns they know not, but supposes not much, for they have all this while shot at good distance one from another. They seem confident of the security of this town and the River above it if the enemy should come up so high – their fortifications being so good, and guns many. But he doth say that people do complain of Sir Edwd. Spragg that he hath not done extraordinary; and more of Sir W Jenings, that he came up with his Tamkins in his guns. Having discoursed thus a little with him, and eat a bit of cold venison and drank, I away, took boat, and homeward again with great pleasure, the moon shining and it being a fine pleasant cool evening; and got home by half-past 12 at night, and so to bed.

25. Up, and to the office, where we sat all the morning. At noon*b* home to dinner and there sang with much pleasure with my wife; and so to the office again and busy all the afternoon. At night, Sir W. Batten, W. Penn and myself and Sir R. Ford

---

     a   MS. 'to down'   *b*   repl. 'home'

---

1. See above, p. 71 & n. 1.   3. Shell Haven, Essex.
2. See above, p. 250, n. 2.

did meet in the garden to discourse about[a] our prizes at Hull; it appears that Hogg is the veriest rogue, the most observable embezzler, that ever was known. This vexes us, and made us very free and plain with Sir W. Penn, who hath been his great patron, and as very a rogue as he; but he doth now seem to own that his opinion is changed of him and that he will joyne with us in our strictest enquiries; and did sign to the letters we had drawn, which he had refused before, and so seemingly parted good friends. And then I demanded of Sir R Ford and the rest what passed today at the meeting of the Parliament – who told me, that contrary to all expectation by the King that there would be but a thin meeting,[1] there met above 300 this first day, and all the discontented party; and endeed, the whole House seems to be no other almost. The Speaker told them, as soon as they were sat, that he was ordered by the King to let them know he was hindered by some important business to come to them and speak to them as he intended; and[b] therefore ordered him to move that they would adjourn themselfs till Monday next (it being very plain to all the House that he expects[c] to hear by that time of the sealing of the peace, which by letters, it seems from my Lord Hollis, was to be sealed the last Sunday); but before they would come to the Question whether they would adjourne, Sir Tho. Tomkins steps up and tells them that all the country is grieved at this new-raised standing army, and that they thought themselfs safe enough in their Traynbands, and that therefore he desired the King might be moved to disband them.[2] Then rises Garraway and seconds him; only, with this explanation (which he said he

---

a 'about' repeated　　　*b* repl. 'but'　　　*c* repl. 'intends'

---

1. Parliament had been prorogued on 8 February to 10 October, and there had been some doubt whether it could properly be reconvened before that date: cf. above, p. 293, n. 1. Moreover most M.P.'s normally expected to be at home for the harvest at this time of the year.
2. Tomkins was M.P. for Weobley, Heref., and an old Cavalier. His speech, delivered amid excitement, became famous. (Cf. Marvell's comment: 'Not so! quoth Tomkins, and straight drew his tongue,/Trusty as steel, that always ready hung': *Last Instructions*, ll. 841-2.) The trainbands had been raised during the Dutch raid on the Medway.

believed the other meant): that as soon as peace should be concluded, they might be disbanded. Then rose*a* Sir W Coventry and told them that he did approve of what the last gentleman said; but also that at the same time he did no more then what, he durst be bold to say, he knew to be the King's mind, that as soon as peace was concluded he would do of himself. Then rose Sir Tho. Littleton and did give several reasons, from the uncertainty of their meeting again but to adjourne (in case news comes of the peace being ended before Monday next), and the possibility*b* of the King's having some about him that may endeavour to alter his own, and the good part of his Council's, advice for the keeping up of the land-army; and therefore it was fit that they did present it to the King as their desire, that as soon as peace was concluded, the land-army might be laid down, and that this their request might be carried to the King by them of their House that were privy-councillors; which was put to the vote, and carried *nemine contradicente.*[1] So after this vote passed, they adjourned; but it is plain what the effects of this Parliament will be if they be suffered to sit, that they will fall foul upon the faults of the government; and I pray God they may be permitted to do it, for nothing else I fear will save the King and Kingdom then the doing it betimes.

They gone, I to walk with my wife in the garden, and then home to supper and to bed.

26. Up, and betimes to the office, where Mr. Hater and I together all the morning about the perfecting of my*c* Abstract-book of contracts and other things, to my great content. At noon home to dinner and then to the office again all the afternoon, doing of other good things there; and being tired, I then abroad with my wife and left her at the New Exchange, while I by water thence to Westminster to the Hall, but shops were shut up; and so to*d* White-hall by water, and thence took up my

---

    a repl. 'came'   *b* repl. 'sup'-
    c repl. 'the'   *d* repl. 'back'

---

    1. *CJ*, viii. 692. Pepys's account of this debate is confirmed by (and in point of detail superior to) that in   Milward, pp. 82–4. Another good account is in Bodl., Carte 35, ff. 649–50.

wife at Unthankes and so home, mightily tired with the dust in riding in a coach, it being mighty troublesome; so home and to my office, and there busy very late; and then to walk a little with my wife and then to supper and to bed. No news at all this day what we have done to the enemy, but that the enemy is fallen down[1] and we after them, but to little purpose.

27. Up and to the office, where I hear that Sir John Coventry is come over from Bredagh (a nephew I think of Sir W. Coventry's); but what message he brings I know not.[2] This morning, news is come that Sir Jos. Jordan is come from Harwich with 16 fireships and 4 other little ships[a]-of-war; and did attempt to do some execution upon the enemy, but did it without discretion as most do say, so as that they have been able to do no good, but have lost 4 of their fireships.[3] They attempted, it seems, when the wind was too strong, that our grapplings would not hold; others say we came to leeward of them, but all condemn it as a foolish management. They are come to Sir Edwd.[b] Spragg about Lee, and the Duch are below at the Noure. At the office all the morning; and at noon to the Change, where I met Fenn[4] and he tells me that Sir Jo. Coventry doth bring the confirmation of the peace; but I do not find the Change at all glad of it, but rather the worse, they looking upon it as a peace made only to preserve

a repl. 'vessels'　　　*b* repl. 'Jer.'

---

1. i.e. sailed away down the Thames.

2. He was the son of John, elder brother of Sir William and Henry Coventry, and had been in the service of the latter in the negotiations at Breda. He came with official news of the peace signed on the 11th/21st, and travelled to Dover in a ship wearing a white flag: *CSPD 1667*, p. 328.

3. See ib., pp. 328–9 for this report. There were seven, not four, small men-of-war: Tedder, p. 189. The action took place on the 26th off the mouth of the Thames, and goes by the name of the Second Battle of the N. Foreland. Jordan had sailed hurriedly and with mutinous men on board. His losses amounted all told to 15 fireships. Several burned uselessly without damaging the enemy. Pepys kept an account of the fight sent to him on 3 August by Capt. James Jenifer: Rawl. A 195a, ff. 264–5. Cf. also *CSPD 1667* (Preface); J. C. de Jonge, *Geschiedenis van het nederlandsche zeewesen*, ii. 208+.

4. Paymaster to the Navy Treasurer.

the King for a time in his lusts and ease, and to sacrifice trade and his kingdoms only to his own pleasures; so that the hearts of merchants are quite down. He tells me that the King and my Lady*ᵃ* Castlemayne are quite broke off and she is gone away, and is with child and swears the King shall own it; and she will have it christened in the Chapel at White-hall as, and owned for the King's as other Kings have done; or she will bring it into White-hall gallery and dash the brains of*ᵇ* it out before the King's face.¹

He tells me that the King and Court were never in the world so bad as they are now for gaming, swearing, whoring, and drinking, and the most abominable vices that ever were in the world – so that all must come to naught. He told me that Sir G. Carteret was at this end of the town; so I went to visit him in Broad-street,² and there he and I together; and he is mightily pleased with my Lady Jem's having a son, and a mighty glad man he is. He tells me, as to news, that the peace is now confirmed and all that over. He says it was a very unhappy motion in the House the other day about the land-army; for whether the King hath a mind of his own to do the*ᶜ* thing desired or no, his doing it will be looked upon as a thing done only in fear of the Parliament. He says that the Duke of York is suspected to be the great man that is for raising of this army and bringing things to be commanded by an army; but he believes that he is wronged, and says that he doth know that he is wronged therein.³ He doth say that the Court is in a way to ruin all for their pleasures; and says that he himself hath once taken the liberty to tell the King the necessity of having at*ᵈ* least a show of religion in the government, and sobriety; and that it was that that did set up and keep up Oliver, though he was the greatest rogue in the world. And that it is so fixed in the nature of the common Englishman, that it will not out of him. He*ᵉ* tells me that while all should be

---

a MS. 'Lord'   *b* repl. 'out'   *c* repl. 'good'   *d* MS. 'a'
    e repl. 'that while'

---

1. For this quarrel (caused by Castlemaine's affair with Henry Jermyn), see below, pp. 366, 368. Between 1661 and 1672 the King acknowledged six children of hers, but none born at about this time: GEC, vi. 707.

2. At the Navy Treasury.

3. Cf. above, p. 332 & n. 1.

labouring to settle the Kingdom, they are at Court all in factions, some for and others against my Lord Chancellor, and another for and against another man; and the King adheres to no man, but this day delivers himself up to this and the next to that, to the ruin of himself and business. That he is at the command of any woman like a slave, though he be the best man to the Queene in the world, with so much respect and never lies a night from her; but yet cannot command himself in the presence of a woman he likes. Having had this discourse, I parted and home to dinner, and thence to the office all*a* the afternoon to my great content, very busy. It raining this day all day to our great joy, it having not rained I think this month before, so as the ground*b* was everywhere as burned and dry as could be – and no travelling in the road or streets in London for dust.[1] At night, late*c* home to supper and to bed.

28. *Lords day.* Up, and to my chamber, where all the morning close, to draw up a letter to Sir W. Coventry upon this tidings of peace, taking occasion (before I am forced to it) to resign up to his Royal Highness my place of the Victualling and to recommend myself to him by promise of doing my utmost to improve this peace in the best manner we may, to save the Kingdom from ruin.[2] By noon I had done this to my good content; and then with my wife all alone to dinner, and so to my chamber all the afternoon to write my letter fair; and sent it away, and then to talk with my wife and read, and so by daylight (the only time I think I have done it this year) to supper; and then to my chamber to read, and so to bed – my mind very much eased after what I have done today.

29. Up, and with Sir W. Batten to St. James's to Sir W. Coventry's chamber; where among other things, he came to me

a repl. 'in'   *b* repl. 'grad'   *c* repl. 'm'-

1. Cf. above, p. 175 & n. 2. According to Wood, Oxford had in the first half of July the hottest weather within memory – 'several scolars mad, with heat and strong drink' (*L & T*, ii. 115).

2. Copy (in Gibson's hand) in NMM, LBK/8, pp. 498–9; printed in *Further Corr.*, pp. 178–80. Cf. also *CSPD Add. 1660–85*, pp. 208, 210.

and told me that he had received my yesterday's letters and that
we concurred*a* very well in our notions; and that as to my place
which I had offered to resign of the Victualling, he had drawn
up a letter at the same time, for the Duke of York's signing for
the like places in general raised during this war,[1] and that he had
done me right to the Duke of York, to let him know that I had
of my own accord offered to resign mine. The letter doth bid
us to do all things, perticularizing several, for the laying up of
the ships and easing the King of charge; so that the war is now
professedly over. By and by up to the Duke of York's chamber;
and there all the talk was about Jordan's coming with so much
indiscretion,*b* with his 4 little frigates and 16 fireships from
Harwich, to annoy the enemy.[2] His failures were of several
sorts, I know not which the truest – that he came with so strong
a gale of wind that his grapplings would not hold – that he did
come by their lee, whereas if he had come thwart their hawse,
they would have held – that they did not stop a tide and came
up with a windward tide, and then they would not have come so
fast. Now, there happened to be Captain Jenifer by, who commanded the *Lilly* in this business, and thus says: that finding
the Duch not so many as they expected, they did not know but
that there were more of them above, and so were not so earnest
to the setting upon these. That they did do what they could
to make the fireships fall in among the enemy; and for their
lives, Sir J Jordan nor others could by shooting several times at
them make them go in; and it seems they were commanded by
some idle fellows, such as they could of a sudden gather up at
Harwich;[3] which is a sad consideration, that at such a time as this,
where the saving the reputation of the whole nation lay at stake,
and after so long a war, the King had not credit to gather a few
able*c* men to command these vessels. He says that if they had

a repl. 'concern'   b MS. 'indescription'
repl. 'but able'

---

1. Duke of York to Navy Board, 29 July: PRO, Adm. 2/1745, ff. 161r–162r; BM, Add. 36782, ff. 45v–46r (copies).
2. See above, p. 354 & n. 3.

3. William Howe of the *Virgin* was later shot, and three other commanders ignominiously dismissed: Clowes, ii. 297.

come up slower, the enemy would, with their boats and their
great Sloops, which they have to row with a great many men,
they would and did come and cut up several of our fireships, and
would certainly have taken most of them, for they do come
with a great provision of these boats on purpose and to save their
men; which is bravely done of them, though they did on this
very occasion show great fear, as they say, by some men leaping *a*
overboard out of a great ship (as these were all of them of 60 *b*
and 70 guns apiece) which one of our fireships laid on board,
though the fire did not take; but yet it is brave to see what
care they do take to encourage their men to provide great stores
of boats to save them, while we have not credit to find one boat
for a ship. And further, he told us that this new way used by
Deane (and this Sir W. Coventry observed several times) of
preparing of fireships[1] doth not do the work, for the fire, not
being strong and quick enough to flame up, so as to take the
rigging and sails, lies smothering a great while, half an hour
before it flames; in which time they can get her off safely, though
(which is uncertain, and did fail in one or two this bout) it doth
serve to burn our own ships. But what a shame it is, to consider
how two of our ships' companies did desert their ships for fear of
being taken by their boats, our little frigates being forced to leave
them, being chased by their greater; and one more company did
set their ship on fire and leave her, which *c* afterward a Feversham
fisherman came up to and put out the fire and carried safe into
Feversham, where she now is; which was observed by the Duke
of York and all the company with him, that it was only want of
courage and a general dismay and abjectness of spirit upon all our
men; and others did observe our ill management and God
Almighty's curse upon all that we have in hand, for never such
an opportunity was of destroying so many good ships of theirs
as we now had; but to see how negligent we were in this

a repl. 'over of'   *b* repl. '67'   *c* repl. 'with'

---

1. Anthony Deane used simply
broom and resin, 'with a few shav-
ings and brimstone', without any
fireballs to prime the train: Rawl.
A 195a, f. 264*v*. He sent his own
account of the fireships' action in a
letter to Pepys, 1 August: ib., ff.
116+.

business, that our fleet of Jordan should not have any notice where Spragg was, nor Spragg of Jordan's, so as to be able to meet and join in the business and help one another; but Jordan, when he saw Spragg's fleet above,[1] did think them to be another part of the enemy's fleet – while on the other side, notwithstanding our people at Court made such a secret of Jordan's design, that nobody must know it, and even this Office itself must not know it, nor for my part I did not, though Sir W. Batten says by others' discourse to him he had heard something of it; yet De= Ruiter (or he that commanded this fleet)[2] had notice of it, and told it to a fisherman of ours that he took and released on Thursday last, which was the day before our*ᵃ* fleet came to him. But then, that that seems most to our disgrace, and which the Duke of York did take special and vehement notice of, is that when the Duch saw so many fireships provided for them, themselfs lying I think about the Nore, they did with all their great ships, with a North-East wind (as I take they said; but whatever it was, it was a wind that we should not have done it with) turned down to the Middleground;[3] which the Duke of York observed, never was nor would have been undertaken by ourselfs; and whereas some of the company answered it was their great fear, not their choice, that made them do it, the Duke of York answered that it was, it may be, their fear and wisdom that made them do it; but yet their fear did not make them mistake, as we should have done, when we have had no fear upon us and have run our ships on ground. And*ᵇ* this brought it into my mind that they managed their retreat down this difficult passage, with all their fear, better then we could do ours in the main sea when the Duke of Albemarle run away from the Duch when the *Prince* was lost and the *Royal Charles* and the other great ships come on ground upon the Galloper.[4] Thus, in all things; in wisdom – courage – force –

a repl. 'they'   *b* repl. 'so'

---

1. Higher up the river.
2. Lieut.-Admiral Aert Jansz van Nes.
3. In the Thames estuary, opposite the mouth of the Medway.

4. In June 1666: see above, vii. 153–4.

knowledge of our own streams – and success, the Duch have the best of us, and do end the war with victory on their side.

The Duke of York being ready, we into his closet; but being in haste to go to the Parliament House, could not stay, so we parted and to Westminster-hall, where the Hall full of people to see the issue of the day, the King being to come to speak to the House today. One thing extraordinary was this day, a man, a Quaker, came naked through the Hall, only very civilly tied about the privities to avoid scandal, and with a chafing-dish of fire and brimstone burning upon his head did pass through the Hall, crying, "Repent! Repent!"[1] I up to the Painted Chamber, thinking to have got in to have heard the King's speech, but upon second thoughts did not think it would be worth the crowd, and so went down again into the Hall and there walked with several; among others, my Lord Rutherford, who is come out of Scotland, and I hope I may get some advantage by it in reference to the business of the interest of the great sum of money I paid him long since without interest[2] – but I did not now move him in it; but presently comes down the House of Commons, the King having made them a very short and no pleasing speech to them at all, not at all giving them thanks for their readiness to come up to town at this busy time; but told them that he did think he should have had occasion for them, but had none and therefore did dismiss them to look after their own occasions till October; and that he did wonder any should offer to bring in a suspicion that he intended to rule by an army or otherwise then by the laws of the land, which he promised them he would not; and so bade

1. This was Solomon Eccles. In 1662 on the day after a savage raid on a Quaker conventicle he had gone through Bartholomew Fair, as a 'sign' – 'naked with a pan on his head full of fire and brimstone, flaming up in the sight of the people, crying repentance among them, and bade them remember Sodom': *A brief relation of the persecution* . . . (1662; qu. W. C. Braithwaite, *Second period Quakerism*, p. 25). In the plague years he went round London stripped to the waist with a brazier on his head. Defoe called him 'the famous *Solomon Eagle* . . . not infected at all, but in his Head'. On the occasion which Pepys refers to here he wore a seaman's neckcloth and cried 'Repent and remember Sodom, Gomorrah, that was burnt with fire and brimstone from Heaven!': HMC, *Hastings*, ii. 154.

2. See above, vi. 221 & n. 2; ib., p. 250 & n. 3.

them go home and settle the minds of the country in that per-ticular; and only added that he hath had made a peace, which he did believe they would find reasonable and a good peace, but did give them none of the perticulars thereof.[1] Thus, they are dismissed again, to their general great distaste, I believe the greatest that ever Parliament was, to see themselfs so fooled and the nation in certain condition of ruin, while the King, they see, is only governed by his lust and women and rogues about him. The Speaker, they found, was kept from coming in the morning to the House on purpose, till after the King was come to the House of Lords,[2] for fear they should be doing anything in the House of Commons to the further dissatisfaction of the King and his courtiers. They do all give up the kingdom for lost that I speak of, and do hear what the King says, how he and the Duke of York do do what they can to get up an army, that they[a] may need no more Parliaments. And how my Lady Castle-mayne hath, before the late breach between her and the King, said to the King that he must rule by an Army or all would be lost. And that Bab May hath given the like advice to the King to crush the English gentlemen, saying that 300*l* a year was enough for any man but them that lived at Court. I am told that many petitions were provided for the Parliament, complaining of the wrongs they have received from the Court and courtiers in City and Country, if the Parliament had but sat; and I do perceive they all do resolve to have a good account of the money spent before ever they give a farding more; and the whole Kingdom is everywhere sensible of their being abused, insomuch that they forced their Parliament-men to come up to sit; and my Cousin Roger told me that (but that was in mirth) he believed, if he had not come up he should have had his house burned. The kingdom never in so troubled a condition in this[b] world as now; nobody

a repl. 'he   *b* MS. 'the this'

1. See *LJ*, xii. 114: Milward, p. 84. He prorogued parliament until 10 October.

2. Milward (p. 84) has an account. The Commons were summoned by Black Rod to the Lords in indecent haste. Cf. Marvell (*Fifth Advice*, ll. 857–8): 'The Speaker summon'd to the Lords repairs, / Nor gave the Commons leave to say their pray'rs'.

pleased with the peace, and yet nobody daring to wish for the continuance of the war, it being plain that nothing doth nor can thrive under us.   Here I saw old good Mr. Vaughan and several of the great men of the Commons, and some of them old men, that are come 200 mile and more to attend this session of Parliament, and been at great charge and disappointments in their other private business; and now all to no purpose, neither to serve their country, content themselfs, nor receive any thanks*a* from the King.   It is verily expected by many of them that the King will continue the prorogacion in October, so as, if it be possible, never to have Parliament more.   My Lord Bristoll took his place in the House of Lords this day, but not in his robes; and when the King came in, he withdrew.[1] But my Lord of Buckingham was there, as brisk as ever, and sat in his robes; which is a monstrous thing, that a man proclaimed against, and put in the Tower and all, and released without any trial, and yet not restored to his places.   But above all, I saw my Lord Mordant, as merry as the best; that it seems hath done such further indignities to Mr. Taylor since the last sitting of Parliament as would hang if there were nothing else, would the King do what were fit for him – but nothing of that is now likely to be.[2] After having spent an hour or two in the hall, my Cosen Roger and I and Creed to the Old Exchange, where I find all the merchants sad at this peace and breaking up of the Parliament, as men despairing of any good to the nation – which is a grievous consideration.   So home, and there Cosen Roger and Creed to dinner with me, and very merry.   But among other things, they told me of the strange bold sermon of Dr. Creeton yesterday before the King; how he preach against the sins of the Court, and perticularly against adultery, over and over instancing how for that single sin in David, the whole nation was undone.[3]

a   repl. 'thing'

---

1. He was included amongst those present in the official list: *LJ*, xii. 113.   For his disgrace, see above, iv. 271 & n. 1.

2. For Mordaunt's impeachment in the Tayleur affair, see above, vii. 386 & n. 2.

3. Dr Robert Creighton was Dean of Wells and perhaps the most outspoken of the court preachers: cf. above, iii. 42 & n. 5.   None of his sermons appears to have been printed.

And of our negligence in having our castles without ammunition
and powder when the Duch come upon us; and how we have no
courage nowadays, but let our ships be taken out of our Harbour.
Here Creed did tell us the story of the Duell last night in Covent-
garden, between Sir H. Bellasses and Tom Porter.[1] It is worth
remembering the silliness of the quarrel, and is a kind of
emblem of the general complexion of this whole Kingdom at
present. They two, it seems, dined yesterday at Sir Robt. Carrs,[2]
where it seems people do drink high, all that come. It happened
that these two, the greatest friends in the world, were talking
together and Sir H. Bellasses talked a little louder then ordinary
to T. Porter, giving of him some advice: some of the company
standing by said, "What, are they quarrelling, that they talk so
high?" Sir H. Bellasses hearing it, said, "No!", says he, "I would
have that you know I never quarrel but I strike; and take that
as a rule of mine." "How!" says T. Porter, "strike! I would I
could see that man in England that durst give me a blow!" With
that, Sir H. Bellasses did give him a box of the eare[a] and so they
were going to fight there, but were hindered; and by and by
T. Porter went out, and meeting Dryden the poet, told him of
the business and that he was resolved to fight Sir H. Bellasses
presently, for he knew if he did not, they should be made friends
tomorrow and then the blow would rest upon him; which he
would prevent, and desired Dryden to let him have his boy to
bring him notice which way Sir H. Bellasses goes. By and by
he is informed that Sir H. Bellasses's coach was coming, so
T. Porter went down out of the Coffee-house, where he stayed
for the tidings, and stopped the coach and bade Sir H. Bellasses
come out: "Why," says H. Bellasses, "you will not hurt me
coming out, will you?" – "No," says T. Porter. So out he

---

a l.h. repl. l.h. 'ayre'

---

1. Tom Porter (son of Endymion,
the poet and art connoisseur) was a
man of ability – he wrote plays – and
quick with his sword. In 1655 he had
killed his man in a duel. Belasyse
(q.v. above, iii. 34, n. 2), his victim on
this occasion, died on 11 August, but
the coroner's jury was directed to find
that he died from causes unknown:
HMC, *Le Fleming*, p. 52; ib., *Rep.*,
14/4/79; *CSPD 1667*, p. 377.
2. M.P. for Lincolnshire. Belasyse was also from Lincolnshire.

went, and both drew; and H. Bellasses having drawn and flung
away his scabbard, T. Porter asked him whether he was ready;
the other answering he was, they fell to fight, some of their
acquaintance by; they wounded one another, and H. Bellasses
so much, that it is feared he will die; and finding himself sorely
wounded, he called to T. Porter and kissed him and bade him
shift for himself – "For," says [he], "Tom, thou hast hurt me, but
I will make shift to stand upon my legs till thou mayest withdraw;
and the world*a* not take notice of you, for I would not have
thee troubled for what thou hast done."   And so whether he did
fly or no I cannot tell, but T. Porter showed*b* H. Bellasses that he
was wounded too; and they are both ill, but H. Bellasses to fear
of life.   And this is a fine example; and H. Bellasses a Parliament-
man too, and both of them most extraordinary friends.

Among other discourse, my Cosen Roger told us as a thing
certain, that the Archbishop of Canterbury that now is doth keep
a wench, and that he is as very a wencher as can be.[1]   And tells
us it as a thing publicly known, that Sir Ch. Sidly hath had got
away one of the Archbishop's wenches from him, and the Archbishop sent to him to let him know that she was his kinswoman,
and did wonder that he would offer any dishonour to one related
to him.   To which Sir Ch. Sidly is said to answer, "A pox take
his Grace! Pray tell his Grace that I believe he finds himself too
old, and is afeared that I should outdo him among his girls and
spoil his trade."   But he makes no more of doubt to say that the*c*
Archbishop is a wencher, and known to be so – which is one of
the most astonishing things that I have heard of – unless it be,
what for certain he says is true, that my Lady*d* Castlemayne hath
made a Bishop lately; namely, her un[c]le Dr. Glenham, who I
think they say is Bishop of Carlisle; a drunken, swearing rascal

a MS. 'hurt'   *b* repl. 'should'
c repl. 'all'   *d* MS. 'Lord'

---

1. This and other baseless slanders
about Sheldon – a bachelor – were
current among critics of the government, such as Roger Pepys; they
were probably put about by Buckingham and Lady Castlemaine. Marvell relished the scandals, in his *Last*
Instructions (ll. 813–14) accusing him
of having affairs with two court
beauties, Katherine Boynton and Mrs
Charles Myddleton, and remarking
in *The loyall Scot* (ll. 218–19): ' 'Tis
necessary Lambeth never wed, / Indifferent to have a Wench in bed.'

and a scandal to the Church, and doth now pretend to be Bishop of Lincolne in competition with Dr. Raynbow, who is reckoned as worthy a man as most is in the Church for piety and learning [1] – which are things so scandalous to consider, that no man can doubt but we must be undone that hears of them.

After dinner comes W How and a son of Mr. Pagetts to see me, with whom I drank but could not stay; and so by coach with Cosen Roger (who before his going did acquaint me in private with an offer made of his marrying of Mrs. Elizabeth Wiles; whom I know, a kinswoman of Mr. Honiwoods,[2] an ugly old maid but good housewife, and is said to have 2500*l* to her portion; but if I can find that she hath but 2000*l*, which he prays me to examine, he says he will have her, she being one he hath long known intimately, and a good housewife and discreet woman – though I am against it in my heart,[a] she being not handsome at all – and it hath been the very bad fortune of the Pepyses that ever I knew, never to marry an handsome woman, excepting Ned Pepys[3]) and Creed; set the former down at the Temple, resolving to go to Cambrige tomorrow, and Creed and I to White-hall to the Treasury-chamber, there to attend, but in vain; only, here looking out of the window into the garden, I saw the King (whom I have not had any desire to see since the Duch came upon the coast first to Sheerness, for shame that I should see him, or he me methinks, after such a dishonour)

a MS. 'never'

---

1. Henry Glemham (Lady Castle-maine's great-uncle) had through her influence been made Bishop of St Asaph (not of Carlisle) in February, but was not yet consecrated. He seems to have deserved Pepys's censure: see Wood, *Ath. Oxon.* (ed. Bliss), iv. 837. Benjamin Laney of Lincoln had been translated to Ely on 24 May; he was succeeded not by Edward Rainbowe (once Master of Magdalene, now Bishop of Carlisle, 1664–84), but by Pepys's friend William Fuller, now Bishop of Limerick.

2. Elizabeth Wyld was a niece of the Honywood brothers who had lodged with Pepys's father in Salisbury Court. Roger Pepys's third wife had died some time before May 1663. This match did not come off; in 1669 he married Esther Dickenson, a widow 'wonderfull merry, good-humoured, fat but plain': below, 4 January 1669.

3. Edward Pepys of Brooms-thorpe, Norf. (d. 1663), had married Elizabeth Walpole of Broomsthorpe – 'the only handsome woman of our name': above, iv. 421.

come upon the garden; with him two or three idle Lords, and instantly after him, in another walk, my Lady Castlemayne, led by Bab May; at which I was surprized, having but newly heard the stories of the King's and her being parted for ever. So I took Mr. Povy, who was there, aside, and he told me all – how imperious this woman is, and hectors*ᵃ* the King to whatever she will. It seems she is with child, and the King says he did not get it; with that, she made a slighting "puh!" with her mouth and went out of the house, and never came in again till the King went to Sir Dan. Harvy's[1] to pray her; and so she is come today – when one would think his mind should be full of some other cares, having but this morning broken up such a Parliament, with so much discontent and so many wants upon him, and but yesterday heard such a sermon against adultery. But it seems she hath told the King that whoever did get it, he should own it; and the bottom of the quarrel is this: she is fallen in love with young Jermin, who hath of late lain with her oftener then the King and is now going to marry my Lady Falmouth.[2] The King, he is mad at her entertaining Jermin, and she is mad at Jermin's going to marry from her, so they are all mad; and thus the kingdom is governed. And they say it is labouring to make breaches between the Duke of Richmond and his lady, that the King may get her to him. But he tells me for certain, that nothing is more sure then that the King and Duke of York and the Chancellor are desirous and labouring all they can to get an army,[3] whatever the King says to the Parliament. And he

a　repl. 'halters'

---

1. Harvey lived in Covent Garden. His wife (a relative of Sandwich) was said to have been a mistress of the Duke of York and 'a very witty and intriguing *wench*': James Macpherson, *Orig. Papers* (1776), i. 49.

2. Henry Jermyn (Master of the Horse to the Duke of York) did not marry until eight years later and then not Lady Falmouth, but Jane, daughter of Sir Edmund Pooley. For his

affair with Lady Castlemaine, see Gramont, pp. 252–6.

3. This was an unfair aspersion on the King and on Clarendon, though not far from the truth about James: Clarendon, *Life*, iii. 253+: About Clarendon, Baxter wrote that 'bad as he was, he was the chief means of hindering' rule by the army. M. Sylvester, *Reliq. Baxt.* (1696), pt iii. 20.

believes that they are at last resolved to stand and fall all three together. So that he says in terms, that the match of the Duke of York with the Chancellor's daughter hath undone the nation. He tells me also that the King hath not greater enemies in the world then those of his own family,* for there is not an officer*a* in the house almost but curses him for letting them starve, and there is not a farding of money to be raised for the buying them bread.

Having done talking with him, I to Westminster-hall and there talked and wandered up and down till the evening, to no purpose there; and to the Swan and so till the evening; and so home and there to walk in the garden with my wife, telling her of my losing 300 a year by my place that I am to part with;[1] which doth a little trouble me, but we must live with somewhat more thrift; and so home to supper and to play on the flagelette, which [she] doth do very prettily, and so to bed.

Many guns were heard this afternoon, it seems,*b* at White-hall and in the Temple-garden, very plain; but what it should be nobody knows, unless the Duch be driving our ships up the River. Tomorrow we shall know.

30. Up and to the office, where we sat busy all the morning. At noon home to dinner, where Daniel and his wife with us, come to see whether I could get him any imployment.[2] But I am so far from it, that I have the trouble upon my mind how to dispose of Mr. Gibson and one or two more I am concerned for in the victualling business, which are to be now discharged. After dinner by coach to White-hall, calling on two or three tradesmen and paying their bills; and so to White-hall to the Treasury-chamber, where I did speak with the Lords and did my business about getting them to assent to 10 per cent interest on the Eleven Months Tax – but find them mightily put to it for money. Here I do hear that there are three Lords more to be added to them; my Lord Bridgewater, my Lord Anglesy, and

a repl. same symbol   *b* MS. 'sums'

---

1. That of Surveyor-General of Victualling.
2. Samuel Danerell had served as

captain of a frigate in 1666. Pepys was fond of his wife: cf. above, vi. 336.

my Lord Chamberlaine.[1] Having done my business, I to Creeds chamber and thence out to White-hall with him, in our way meeting with Mr. Cooling, my Lord Chamberlaines secretary, on horseback, who stopped to speak to us; and he proved very drunk and did talk and would have talked all night with us, I not being able to break loose from him, he holding me so by the hand. But Lord, to see his present humour; how he swears at every word and talks of the King and my Lady Castleman in the plainest words in the world. And from him I gather that the story I learned yesterday is true – that the King hath declared that he did not get the child of which she is conceived at this time, he having not as he says lain with her this half year; but she told him – "God damn me! but you shall own it." It seems he is jealous of Jermin and she loves him, so that the thoughts of his marrying of my Lady Falmouth puts her into fits of the mother. And he, it seems, hath lain with her from time to time continually, for a good while; and once, as this Cooling says, the King had like to have taken him a-bed with her, but that he was fain to creep under the bed into her closet. He says that for a good while the King's greatest pleasure hath been with his fingers, being able to do no more. But it is a pretty thing he told us: how the King, once speaking of the Duke of Yorke's being maistered by his wife, said to some*a* of the company by, that he would go no more abroad with this Tom Otter[2] (meaning the Duke of York) and his wife. Tom Killigrew, being by, answered, "Sir," says he, "pray, which is the best for a man to be, a Tom Otter to his wife or to his mistress?" – meaning the King's being so to my Lady Castlemayne. Thus he went on; and speaking then of my Lord Sandwich, whom he professed to love exceedingly, says Cooling*b*, "I know not what, but he is a

---

a repl. 'one' *b* MS. 'Creed'

---

1. They were not added to the Treasury commission, but, together with the two Secretaries of State and the Treasury Commissioners, were appointed on 29 July to form a committee of council for the retrenchment of expenditure – 'his Majesty being resolved to practise the rules of thrift and good husbandry': *CSPD 1667*, p. 338.

2. The henpecked husband in Ben Jonson's comedy, *Epicoene*. (A).

man methinks that I could love for himself, without other regards;
and by your favour," says he, "by God, there is nothing to be
beloved *propter se*[a] but a cunt.[b]" And so he talked very lewdly.
And then took notice of my kindness to him on shipboard seven
years ago, when the King was coming over, and how much he
was obliged to me[1]; but says, "Pray look upon this acknowledgement of a kindness in me to be a miracle; for," says [he], "it is
against the law at Court for a man that borrows money of me,
even to buy his place with, to own it the next Sunday." And
then told us his horse was a Bribe, and his boots a bribe;[c] and told
us he was made up of bribes, as a Oxford scholar is set out
with other men's goods when he goes out of town, and that he
makes every sort of tradesman to bribe him; and invited me
home to his house to taste of his bribe-wine. I never heard so
much vanity from a man in my life. So being now weary of
him, we parted, and I took coach and carried Creed to the Temple,
there set him down, and to my office, where busy late till my
eyes begun to ake; and then home to supper: a pullet, with good
sauce, to my liking; and then to play on the flagelette with my
wife, which she now does very prettily, and so to bed.

31. Up; and after some time with Greeting upon my
flagelette, I to the office and there all the morning busy. Among
other things, Sir W. Batten, W. Penn, and myself did examine
a fellow of our private man-of-war, who we have found come
up from Hull with near[d] 500*l* worth of pieces-of-eight, though
he will confess but 100 pieces. But it appears that there have
been fine doings there.[2] At noon dined at home and then to
the office, where busy again till the evening, when[e] Major Halsey
and Kinaston to adjust matters about Mrs. Rumbalds bill of

---

  a l.h. repl. s.h. 'for itself'   *b* garbled to 'cunut'
  c l.h. repl. s.h. 'br'-   *d* repl. 'the'   *e* repl. 'where'

---

1. The incident does not appear to
be noticed in the diary. When
Pepys was imprisoned in the Marshal-
sea in 1679, Cooling wrote to his
cousin, the prison-keeper, asking him
to show kindness to Pepys: Bryant,
ii. 274.

2. See above, p. 341 & n. 3.

exchange;[1] and here Major Hallsy, speaking much of my doing business and understanding business, told me how my Lord Generall doth say that I am worth them all – but I have heard that Hallsy hath said the same behind my back to others. Then abroad with my wife by coach to Marrowbone, where my Lord Mayor and Aldermen, it seems, dined today[2] and were just now going away, methought in a disconsolate condition compared with their splendour they formerly had when the City was standing. Here my wife and I drank at the gate, not lighting; and then home with much pleasure, and so to my chamber, and my wife and I to pipe; and so to supper and to bed.[a]

a　followed by one blank page

---

1. The transaction has not been traced elsewhere. But possibly the bill was drawn by Henry Rumbold, storekeeper of Tangier, on Edward Kinaston (a merchant concerned in the Tangier victualling) for the benefit of William Rumbold, his uncle, who had died in May. Halsey was an executor of the latter's will, and may have been acting on behalf of the widow.

2. The corporation of the city of London had for some centuries piped water from the Tyburn to augment the city's supplies, acquiring the Conduit Mead Estate, where Stratford Place now stands, as a water-head. This was inspected periodically by the Lord Mayor and Aldermen, whose dinners there gave it the name of the banqueting house. (R).

AUGUST.

1. Up, and all the morning at the office. At noon my wife and I dined at Sir W Pen's, only with Mrs. Turner and her husband, on a damned venison pasty that stunk like a devil; however, I did not know it till dinner was done. We had nothing but only this and a leg of mutton and a pullet or two. Mrs. Markeham was here, with her great belly. I was very merry; and after dinner, upon a motion of the women, I was got to go to a play with them, the first I have seen since before the Duch coming upon our Coast; and so to the King's House to see *The Custome of the Country*.[1] The house mighty empty – more than ever I saw it – and an ill play. After the play, we into the House and spoke with Knepp, who went abroad with us by coach to the Neat-houses[2] in the way to Chelsy; and there in a box in a tree we sat and sang and talked and eat – my wife out of humour, as she always is when this woman is by. So after it was dark, we home; set Knepp down at*a* home, who told us the story how Nell is gone from the King's House and is kept by my Lord Buckhurst.[3] Then we home, the gates of the City shut, it being so late; and at Newgate we find them in trouble, some thiefs having this night broke open prison. So we through and home; and our coachman was fain to drive hard from two or three fellows, which he said were rogues, that he met at the end of Blowblather-street, next Cheapside. So set Mrs. Turner home, and then we home and I to the office a little; and so home and to bed, my wife in an ill Humour still.

2. Up, but before I rose my wife fell into angry discourse of my kindness yesterday to Mrs. Knip, and leading her and sitting in the coach hand-in-hand and my arm about her middle, and in some bad words reproached me with it. I was troubled; but having much business in my head, and desirous of peace, rose and did not provoke her. So she up and came to me and added

a repl. 'who'

1. A comedy by Fletcher and Massinger; see above, v. 280, n. 2. (A).   2. See above, ii. 158, n. 2
3. See above, p. 334 & n. 2.

more, and spoke basely of my father, who I perceive did do
something in the country, at her last being there, that did not
like her; but I would not enquire into anything, but let her talk;
and when ready, away to the office I went – where all the morning I was; only, Mr. Gawden come to me and he and I home to
my chamber and there reckoned; and there I received my profits
for Tanger of him and 250*l* on my victualling score.   He is a
most noble-minded man as ever I met with.   And seems to own
himself much obliged to me, which I will labour to make him,
for he is a good man also.   We talked on many good things
relating to the King's service; and in fine, I had much matter of
joy by this morning's work, receiving above 400*l* of him on one
account or other – and a promise that though I lay down my
victualling place, yet as long as he continues victualler*ᵃ* I shall be
the better by him.

To the office again and there evened all our business with Mr.
Kinaston about Collonell Norwood's bill of exchange from
Tanger; and am glad of it, for though he be a good man, yet his
importunity tires me.

So home to dinner, where Mr. Hater with me and W. Hewer,
because of their being in the way after dinner; and so to the
office after dinner, where, and with my Lord Brouncker at his
lodgings all the afternoon and evening, making up our great
account for the Lords Commissioners of the Treasury;[1] but not
so as pleases me yet.

So at 12 at night home to supper and to bed, my wife being
gone in an ill humour to bed before me.

This noon, my wife comes to me alone and tells me she had
those upon her and bid me remember it.   I asked her why,
and she said she had a reason.   I*ᵇ* do think by something too she
said today, that she took notice that I had not lain*ᶜ* with her this

---

a   repl. 'is'   *b*   'I' repeated
c   garbled s.h. to 'somebody' (p. 373): cf. above, p. 244, note *a*

---

1. Copy (in unidentified clerical
hand) in BM, Add. 9311, ff. 144–9,
dated 5 August: 'The Expence of the
Navy from his Majesties Restauration
1660 to the 25th May 1667.'   On 27
July Pepys had written to Coventry
explaining that he had completed his
own accounts a month before, but
was held up by Brouncker's delay in
completing his: Longleat, Coventry
MSS 97, f. 101*r*.

half-year,*ᵃ* that she thinks that I have some doubt that she might be with child by somebody else – which God knows never entered into my head, or whether my father observed anything at Brampton with Coleman¹ I know not. But I do not do well to let these beginnings of discontents take*ᵇ* so much root between us.

3. Up and to the office, where very busy all the morning. Then at noon to dinner and to the office again, there to enable myself, by finishing our general account, to go to the Lords Commissioners of the Treasury; which I did, and there was called in to them – to tell them only the total of our Debt of the Navy on the 25 of May last – which is above 950000*l.ᶜ*² Here I find them mighty hot in their answer to the Council-board about our Treasurer's three-pences of the Victualling,³ and also against the present farm of the Customes, which they do most highly inveigh against.⁴ So home again by coach, and there hard to work till very late and my eyes begin to fail me, which now upon every little overworking them they do; which grieves me much. Late home to supper and to bed.

4. *Lords day.* Busy at my office from morning till night in writing with my own hand fair our large general account of the expense and debt of the Navy⁵ – which lasted me till night to do, that I was almost blind; and Mr. Gibson with me all day long,

a   'yemer' repl. same symbol twice misformed
b   repl. 'grow so'   *c*   repl. 'is above 590'-

---

1. The army officer in whose company she had recently travelled home from Brampton: above, p. 286.

2. Cf. the Treasury minute: 'Mr. Pepys called in; and is desired to take care to insert the prices of goods in the Navy certificates. Mr. Papys [*sic*] offers a state of the Navy debt, which is 951,000*l* to May 25 last' (*CTB*, ii. 53). For details of the debt, see BM, Add. 36782, f. 60*v*.

3. The Treasury objected that the recent patent appointing Anglesey

Navy Treasurer had allowed him the usual poundage, although the Poll Tax and Eleven Months Tax had reduced it: *CSPD 1667*, p. 235; *CTB*, ii. 36; above, p. 30 & n. 3.

4. Arrangements for the new customs farm were not concluded until 6 September. The Treasury (not fully consulted) objected to the rent fixed by the Privy Council: Carte 35, f. 624*r*.

5. See above, p. 372 & n. 1.

and dined with me; and excellent discourse I had with him, he understanding all the business of the Navy most admirably.[1] To walk a little with my wife at night in the garden, it being very hot weather again, and so to supper and to bed.

5. Up, and with Sir W. Batten in the morning to St. James's – where we did our ordinary business with the Duke of York, where I perceive they have taken the highest resolution in the world to become good husbands and to retrench all charge; and to that end we are commanded to give him an account of the Establishment in the seventh year of the late King's[a] reign, and how offices and salaries have been encreased since.[2]   And I hope it will end in the taking away some of our Commissioners, though it may be to the lessening of some of our salaries also. After done, with the Duke of York; and coming out through his dressing-room, I there espied Seignor Francisco[3] tuning his Gittar, and Monsieur De Puy[4] with him, who did make him play to me; which he did most admirably, so well as I was mightily troubled that all that pains should have been taken upon so bad an instrument.[5]   Walked over the park with Mr. Gawden, and with him by coach home; and thence to the Exchange, where I hear the ill news of our loss lately of four rich ships, two from Genoa, one from gallipoly, all with rich oyles; and the other from Berbados, worth, as is guessed, 80000*l*.[6]   But here is strong talk as if Harman had taken some of the Duch Eastindia ships (but I

a repl. 'year'

---

1. Richard Gibson (now one of Pepys's clerks) had been a ship's purser.
2. A committee of council for the retrenchment of expenses had been appointed on 29 July and on 3 August had written to the Duke asking for this information: Longleat, Coventry MSS 96, f. 267*r*. The test year was 1632, when Charles I had for the second time put the admiralty into commission. See below, pp. 383, 391-2 & nn.
3. Francesco Corbetta, court musi-

cian; author of *La guitarre royale* (1670). (E).
4. Lawrence Du Puy, servant of the Duke and a friend of Corbetta.
5. Pepys later became fonder of the guitar, and the PL contains four MS. volumes of songs with guitar tablature, the work of Morelli, his domestic musician in the late 1670s. (E).
6. See the letter to the Navy Board from Plymouth (2 August): *CSPD 1667*, p. 354. The capture was made by the Dutch.

dare not yet believe it) and brought them into Lisbon.¹ Home, and dined with my wife at Sir W. Penn's, where a very good pasty of venison, better then we expected, the last stinking basely. And after dinner, he and my wife and I to the Duke of York's House and there saw *Lovetrickes, or The School of Compliments,* a silly play; only, Mis's dancing in a shepherd's clothes did please us mightily.² Thence, without much pleasure home*ᵃ* and to my office; so home to supper and to bed. My wife mighty angry with Nell, who is turned a mere gossip and gads abroad as soon as our backs are turned – and will put her away tomorrow, which I am not sorry for.

6. Up, and to the office, where all the morning very full of business; a full Board. Here talking of news, my Lord Anglesy did tell us that the Dutch do make a further bogle with us about two or three things, which they will be satisfied in, he says, by us easily; but only in one, it seems they do demand that we shall not interrupt their East Indiamen coming home, and of which they are in some fear, and we are full of hopes that we have light upon some*ᵇ* of them and carried them into Lisbon by Harman; which God send. But they (which doth show the low esteem they have of us) have the confidence to demand that we shall have a cessation on our parts, and yet they at liberty to take what they will; which is such an affront, as another cannot be devised greater.

At noon home to dinner, where I find Mrs. Wood (Bab. Shelden) and our Mercer, who is dressed today in a paysan dress that looks mighty pretty. We dined and sang and laughed, mighty merry; and then I to the office (only, met at the door with Mrs. Martin and Burroughs, who I took in and drank with;

---

a repl. 'to'   *b* repl. 'sm'-

---

1. A canard: there were no English men-of-war in the Straits at this time. The rumour possibly originated with the story of Jeremy Smith's capturing two Dutch Indiamen off the Irish coast: *CSPD 1667*, p. 358.

2. The play was a comedy by James Shirley, acted in 1625, and published in 1631. By 'Mis's' Pepys refers to Mary Davis in the role of Selina, who, when she is disguised as a shepherd, dances with Antonio, who is dressed as a woman. (A).

but was afeared my wife should see them, they being, especially
the first, a twattling gossip; and so after drinking with them,
parted); and I to the office, busy as long as my poor eyes would
endure, which trouble me mightily; and then into the garden
with my wife, and to Sir W. Batten's with W. Penn and J. Mennes
and there eat a melon and talked; and so home to supper and to
bed. My wife, as she said last night, hath put away Nell today
for her gossiping abroad and telling of stories. Sir W. Batten
did tell me tonight that the Council have ordered a hearing before
them of Carcasse's business;[1] which doth vex me mightily, that
we should be troubled so much by an idle rogue, a servant of our
own, and all my thoughts tonight have been how to manage the
matter before the Council.

7. Up, and at the office very busy, and did much business all
the morning. My wife abroad with her maid Jane and Tom all
the afternoon, being gone forth to eat some pasties at*a* the Bottle
of Hay in St. John's-street, as you go to Islington, of which she
is mighty fond; and I dined at home alone, and at the office
close all the afternoon, doing much business to my great content.
This afternoon, Mr. Pierce the surgeon comes to me about business and tells me that though the King and my Lady Castlemaine
are friends again, she is not at White-hall but at Sir D. Harvys,[2]
whither the King goes to her; and he says she made him ask her
forgiveness upon his knees, and promised to offend her no more
so. That endeed, she did threaten to bring all his bastards to his
closet-door, and hath nearly*b* hector'd him out of his wits.

I at my office till night, and then home to my pipe, * my wife
not coming home, which vexed me; I then into the garden and
there walked alone in the garden till 10 at night, when she came
home, having been upon the water and could not get home
sooner. So to supper and to bed.

---

repl. 'masties'   *b* MS. 'merely'

---

1. For this case, see above, p. 64,
n. 1. On 26 July Carkesse had
petitioned the King against his dismissal.

2. See above, p. 366 & n. 1.

8. Up, and all the morning at the office – where busy; and at noon home to dinner, and Creed dined with us; who tells me that Sir Henry Bellasses is dead of the Duell he fought about ten days ago with Tom Porter;[1] and it is pretty to see how the world talk of them as of a couple of fools, that killed one another out of Love. After dinner to the office a while; and then with my wife to the Temple, where I light and sent her to her tailor's. I to my bookseller's, where by and by I met Mr. Eveling and talked of several things, but perticularly of the times; and he tells me that wise men do prepare to remove abroad what they have, for that we must be ruined – our case being past relief, the Kingdom so much in debt, and the King minding nothing but his lust,*a* going two days a week to see my Lady Castlemaine at Sir D. Harvy's. He gone, I met with Mr. Moore, who tells me that my Lord Hinchingbrooke is now with his mistress,[2] but not that he is married as W Howe came and told us the other day. So by*b* coach to White-hall and there stayed a little, thinking to see Sir G. Carteret, but missed him; and so by coach, took up my wife, and so home and as far as Bow, where we stayed and drank; and there passing by Mr. Lowther and his lady, they stopped and we talked a little with them, they being in their gilt coach, and so parted; and presently came to us Mr. Andrews, whom I had not seen a good while, who, as other merchants do, doth all give over any hopes*c* of things doing well, and so he spends his time here most, playing at Bowles; after drinking together at the coach-side, we with great pleasure home; and so to the office, where I despatched my business, and home to supper and to bed.

9. Up, and betimes with Sir H. Cholmly upon some accounts of Tanger; and then he and I to Westminster to Mr. Burges[3] and then walked in the Hall. And he and I talked, and he doth

a repl. 'lost'
b repl. 'down to the Temple-stairs and there took boat to Westminster'
c repl. 'thing'

---

1. He died on the 11th: above, p. 363, n. 1.
2. Lady Anne Boyle; see above, p. 190 & n. 3.

3. William Burgess, clerk to Sir Robert Long, Auditor of the Receipt in the Exchequer.

really declare that he expects that of necessity this Kingdom will fall back again to a commonwealth;[1] and other wise men are of the same mind, this family* doing all that silly men can do to make themselfs unable to support their Kingdom – minding their lust and their pleasure, and making their government so chargeable, that people do well remember better things were done, and better managed and with much less charge, under a commonwealth then they have been by this King.   And doth seem to resolve to wind up his businesses and get money in his hand against the turn doth come.   After some talk, I by coach and there dined, and with us Mr. Batelier, by chance coming in to speak with me; and when I came home and find Mr. Goodgroome my wife's singing-master there, I did soundly rattle him for neglecting her so much as he hath done, she having not learned three songs these three months and more.   After dinner, my wife abroad with Mrs. Turner and I to the office, where busy all the afternoon; and in the evening by coach to St. James's, and there met Sir W. Coventry and he and I walked in the park an hour; and then to his chamber, where he read to me the heads of the late great dispute between him and the rest of the Commissioners of the Treasury and our new Treasurer of the Navy: where they have over-throwne him, the last Wednesdy, in the great dispute touching his having the payment of the Victualler; which is now settled by Council that he is not to have it.[2]   And endeed, they have been most just, as well as most severe and bold, in the doing this against a man of his quality.   But I perceive he doth really make no difference between any man.   He tells me this day it is supposed the peace is ratified at Bredah, and all that matter over.[3] We did talk of many retrenchments of charge of the Navy which he will put in practice, and everywhere else; though he tells me he despairs of being able to do what ought to be done for the saving of the Kingdom (which I tell him, as endeed all the world is

---

1. Pepys reports this view several times: below, pp. 390–1, 556. Cf. the prophecy said to have been made in mid-February 1660 by James Harrington, the republican writer: 'Well, the King will come in. Let him come in, and call a Parliament of the greatest Cavaliers in England, so they be men of estates, and let them sett but 7 years, and they will all turn Commonwealthe's men': Aubrey, i. 291.

2. Cf. above, p. 373 & n. 3. For the council order, see PRO, PC 2/59, f. 265r. The victualler was now paid by the Exchequer: *CTB*, ii. 181.

3. See below, p. 396 & n. 2.

almost in hopes of, upon the proceeding of these gentlemen for the regulating of the Treasury)[1] it being so late, and our poverty grown so great, that they want where to set their feet to begin to do anything. He tells me how weary he hath for this year and a half been of the Warr; and how in the Duke of York's bedchamber at Christchurch at Oxford, when the Court was there,[2] he did labour to persuade the Duke to fling off the care of the Navy and get it committed to other hands; which if he had done, would have been much to his honour, being just come home with so much honour from sea as he did.[3] I took notice of the sharp letter he wrote[a] (which he sent us to read yesterday[b]) to Sir Edwd. Spragg,[c] where he is very plain about his leaving his charge of[d] the ships at Gravesend when the enemy came last up, and several other things; a copy whereof I have kept.[4] But it is done like a most worthy man; and he says it is good, now and then, to tell these gentlemen their duties, for they need it; and it seems, as he tells me, all our Knights are fallen out one with another, he and Jenings and Hollis, and (his words were) "they are disputing which is the Coward among them; and yet men that take the greatest liberty of censuring others." Here with him very late – till I could hardly get a coach or link willing to go through the ruines; but I do, but will not do it again; it being, endeed, very dangerous. So home and to supper and bed – my head being full of an answer I have drawn this afternoon[e] to the committee of the Council, to whom Carcasse's business is referred to be examined again.[5]

---

  a followed by 'the other day' (struck through)   *b* repl. 'on the'
  c followed by closing bracket (struck through)   *d* repl. 'he'
                 e MS. 'answer noon'

---

1. The council committee appointed on 29 July: see above, pp. 367–8 & n.

2. The Court was at Oxford from late September 1665 until January–February 1666, the Duke occupying the lodgings of Dr Richard Allestry, Canon of Christ Church and Regius Professor of Divinity.

3. After the Battle of Lowestoft, June 1665.

4. Rawl. A 195a, ff. 108–9 (clerical copies of Coventry's letter to the Board, 8 August, with Spragge's reply and Coventry's rejoinder). Cf. *CSPD 1667*, p. 351.

5. Untraced; for the case, see above, p. 64, n. 1. Carkesse had petitioned the King on 26 July against his dismissal.

10. Up, and to the office and there finished the letter about Carcasse and sent it away; I think well writ, though it troubles me we should be put to trouble by this rogue so much. At the office all the morning, and at noon home to dinner, where I sang and piped with my wife with great pleasure, and did hire a coach to carry us to Barnett tomorrow. After dinner, I to the office and there wrote as long as my eyes would give me leave, and then abroad and to the New Exchange to the bookseller's there, where I hear of several new books coming out – Mr. Pratts history of the Royal Society and Mrs. Phillips's poems.[1] Sir Jo. Denhams poems are going to be all printed together; and among others, some new*a* things, and among them he showed me a copy of verses of his upon Sir Jo. Minnes's going heretofore to Bulloigne to eat a pig.[2] Cowly, he tells me, is dead; who it seems was a mighty civil, serious man, which I did not know before.[3] Several good plays are also likely to be abroad soon – as, *Mustapha* and *Henry the 5th*.[4] Here having stayed and divertized myself a good while, I home again and to finish my letters by the post; and so home, and betimes to bed with my wife because of rising betimes tomorrow.

11. *Lords day.* Up by 4 a-clock and ready with Mrs. Turner to take coach before 5; which we did, and set on our Journy

a repl. 'th'-

1. Thomas Sprat's *History of the Royal Society of London* had been licensed on 25 July, and Katherine Philips's *Poems* on 21 January 1667: *Trans. Stat. Reg.*, ii. 373. Pepys later acquired the first, but not, apparently, the second. See below, pp. 387, 439. The bookseller was Henry Herringman, publisher of the Philips.

2. 'To Sir John Mennis being invited from Calice to Bologne to eat a Pig': Denham, *Poems and translations . . .* (pub. by Herringman, 1668; PL 824), pp. 73–6. Mennes, with his two companions (one of whom was Denham), had ridden in a cart 'with a

fat Dutch Woman who broke wind all along'.

3. Abraham Cowley had died on 28 July at Chertsey, Surrey, had lain in state at Wallingford House, and had been buried in Westminster Abbey on 3 August. Evelyn at Sayes Court heard of his death on 1 August, possibly because the poet's brother, Thomas (lately Clerk of the Cheque, Deptford) lived near by. Herringman had published several of Cowley's poems, and brought out a collection of them in 1668.

4. Two plays by Roger Boyle, Earl of Orrery; above, vi. 73 & n. 1; v. 240 & n. 2. (A).

and got to the Wells at Barnett[1] by 7 a-clock, and there found
many people a-drinking; but the morning is a very cold morning,
so as we were very cold all the way in the coach. Here we met
Joseph Batelier and I talked with him, and here was W Hewers
also and his uncle Steventon. So after drink[ing] three glasses,
and the women nothing, we back by coach to Barnett, where to
the Red Lyon;[2] where we light and went up into the Great
Room and there drank and eat some of the best cheese-cakes that
ever I eat in my life; and so took coach again, and W Hewers on
horseback with us, and so to Hatfield to the inn[3] next my Lord
Salsbury's house, and there we rested ourselfs and drank and
bespoke dinner; and so to church, it being just church-time,
and there we find my Lord and my Lady Sands[4] and several fine
ladies of the family and a great many handsome faces and gentile
persons more in the church, and did hear a most excellent good
sermon, which[a] pleased me mightily; and very devout, it being
upon the signs of saving grace where it is in a man; and one
sign, which held him all this day, was that where that grace was,
there is also the grace of prayer; which he did handle very
finely. In this church lies the former Lord of Salsbury, Cecill,
buried in a noble tomb.[5] So the church being done, we to our
inn and there dined very well and mighty merry; and as soon
as had dined, we walked out into the park, through the fine walk
of trees and to the vineyard, and there showed them that;[6] which
is in good order, and endeed a place of great delight; which
together with our fine walk through the park, was of as much
pleasure as could be desired in the world for country pleasure,
and good ayre. Being come back, and weary with the walk,

a MS. 'with'

1. For the wells, see above, v. 201,
n. 1.
2. In the High St.
3. The Salisbury Arms, Fore St.
4. The 6th Baron Sandys had
married Mary, daughter of the 2nd
Earl of Salisbury.
5. In the Salisbury chapel of the
church of St Etheldreda, Maximilian

Colt's effigy of Robert Cecil, 1st Earl
of Salisbury (d. 1612) lies on a marble
slab supported by four figures repre-
senting Faith, Justice, Fortitude and
Prudence. Account and photograph
in Sir N. Pevsner, *Buildings of England: Herts.*, pp. 108-9; pl. 33.
6. Cf. above, ii. 139, n. 1.

for as I made it it was pretty long, being come back to our Inne, there the women had pleasure in putting on some straw hats, which are much worn in this country;[1] and did become them mightily, but especially my wife. So after resting a while, we took coach again and back to Barnett, where W Hewers took us into his lodging, which is very handsome, and there did treat*a* us very highly with cheesecakes, cream, tarts, and other good things; and then walked into the garden, which was pretty, and there filled my pockets full of Filberts, and so with much pleasure (among other things, I met in this house with a printed book of the life of O. Cromwell,[2] to his honour as a soldier and politician, though as a rebell, the first of that kind that ever I saw, and it is well done) took coach again; and got home with great content, just at day shutting in; and so as soon as home, eat a little, and then to bed with exceeding great content at our day's work.

12. My wife waked betimes to call up her people to washing, and so to bed again; whom I then hugged, it being cold now in the mornings, and then did la otra cosa con her, which I had not done con clla for these tres meses past, which I do believe is a great matter towards the making her of*b* late so indifferent towards me, and with good reason; but now she*c* had much pleasure,*c* and so to sleep again. Up by and by, and I with Mr. Gawden*d* by coach to St. James's, where we find the Duke gone a-hunting with the King but found Sir W. Coventry within; with whom

---

a repl. same symbol badly formed	*b* repl. 'of'
c-c garbled s.h.: see above p. 244, note *a*	*d* repl. 'Sir Jo. Minnes'

---

1. For the manufacture of hats, etc., from straw plaits in Hertford-shire, see VCH, *Herts.*, iv. 251-6.
2. The book was probably the anonymous *The perfect politician: or A full view of the life and actions military and civil of Oliver Cromwel . . .* (1660); doubtfully attributed to Henry Fletcher or William Raybould; royalist, but appreciative; by far the best of the early biographies of Cromwell, and unusual among them for being neither a diatribe nor a pane-gyric. In PL 793 (nos 1 and 2) are two of the panegyrics: S. Carrington, *The history of . . . Oliver . . .* (1659), and H. D., *Historie and policie reviewed in the heroick transactions of . . . Oliver* (1659). Cf. above, p. 332 & n. 2.

we discoursed, and he did largely discourse with us about our speedy falling upon considering of retrenchments in the expense of the Navy;[1] which I will put forward as much as I can. So having done there, I to Westminster to[a] Burges and then walked to the New Exchange; and there to my bookseller's there and did buy Scotts discourse of Witches,[2] and do hear Mr. Cowly mightily lamented his death by Dr. Ward the Bishop of Winchester and Dr. Bates, who were standing there – as the best poet of our nation, and as good a man.[3]

Thence I to the print=sellers over against the Exchange towards Covent-garden, and there bought a few more prints of Cittys[4] and so home with them; and my wife and maids being gone over the water to the Whitsters with their clothes, this being the first time of her trying this way of washing her linen,[5] I dined at Sir W Batten's; and after dinner, all alone to the King's playhouse, and there did happen to sit just before Mrs. Pierce and Mrs. Knepp, who pulled me by the hair, and so I addressed myself to them and talked to them all the intervalls of the play, and did give them fruit. The play is *Breneralt*,[6] which I do find but little in for my part. Here was many fine ladies; among others, the German Baron with his Lady, who is Envoyé from the

---

a s.h. repl. l.h. 'hall'

---

1. Cf. above, p. 374, n. 2. Coventry's suggestions were contained in a letter sent to the committee this day by the Duke: *CSPD 1667*, p. 383 (copy in BM, Add. 40839, ff. 73*v*+); summary in *Cat.*, i. 103–4. See below, pp. 391–2.

2. Reginald Scot, *The discovery of witchcraft*, first published in 1584; PL 2046 (3rd ed., 1665). The bookseller was Henry Herringman.

3. For Cowley's death, see above, p. 380, n. 3. His reputation was now at its height, and he was buried in Westminster Abbey near to Chaucer and Spenser. Seth Ward was Bishop of Exeter, not Winchester (he was in fact translated to Salisbury a few weeks later). William Bates, a friend of Ward, was one of the leading Presbyterian ministers in London.

4. A favourite genre with Pepys. The printseller was probably Richard Tompson of Bedfordbury St.

5. A bleacher ('whitster') would probably bleach the clothes by soaking them in a solution of lye (made from vegetable ashes). The open spaces of Lambeth Marsh or Southwark would in this case be used for drying. The process took a day or two.

6. *Brennoralt, or The discontented colonel*, a tragicomedy by Sir John Suckling; see above, ii. 139 & n. 4. (A).

Emperour, and their fine daughter, which hath travelled all Europe over with them it seems, and is accordingly accomplished; and endeed is a wonderful pretty woman.[1] Here Sir Ph. Frowd, who sat next to me, did tell me how Sir H. Belasses is dead, and that the quarrel between him and Tom[a] Porter (who is fled) did arise in the ridiculous fashion that I was first told it;[2] which is a strange thing between two so good friends. The play being done, I took the women, and Mrs. Corbett who was with them, by coach, it raining, to Mrs. Manuell's the Jew's wife, formerly a player, who we heard sing with one of the Italian's that was there; and endeed, she sings mighty well and just after the Italian manner, but yet doth not please me like one of Mrs. Knepps songs to[b] a good English tune, the manner of their ayre not pleasing me so well as the fashion of our own, nor so natural. Here I sat a little and then left them; and then by coach home, where my wife not come home; so to the office a little and then home, and my wife came; and so saying nothing where I had been, we to supper and pipe,* and so to bed.

13. Up, and to the office, where we sat busy all the morning. At noon home to dinner all alone, my wife being again at the Whitster's. After dinner, I with Sir W. Penn to St. James's, where the rest came and attended the Duke of York with our usual business; who, upon occasion, told us that he did expect this night or tomorrow to hear from Breda of the consummation of the peace. Thence Sir W Penn and I to the King's House and there saw *The Comittee*; which I went to with some præjudice, not liking [it] before, but I do now find it a very good play and a great deal of good invention in it; but Lacy's part is so well performed that it would set off anything.[3] The play being

a repl. 'Perr'- *b* repl. full stop

---

1. Franz Paul de Lisola, envoy-extraordinary from Leopold I, had arrived in England only a few days earlier to promote an Anglo-Dutch accord which would isolate France: *CSPD 1667*, p. 375; *CSPVen. 1666–8*, pp. 99–100. For the popularity of his daughter Eleonora, see

G. de Chavagnac, *Mémoires*, (n.d.), p. 258.
2. See above, pp. 363–4.
3. The play was a comedy by Sir Robert Howard, in which John Lacy played Teague, the comical Irish footman: see above, iv. 181 & n. 1. (A).

done, we with great pleasure home; and there I to the office to finish my letters, and then home to my chamber to sing and pipe till my wife comes home from her washing, which was 9 at night, and a dark and rainy night, that I was troubled at her staying out so long. But she came well home, and so to supper and to bed.

14. Up and to the office, where we hold a meeting extraordinary upon some perticular businesses, and there sat all the morning. At noon, my wife being gone to the Whitster's again to her clothes, I to dinner to Sir W. Batten, where much of our discourse touching Carcasse,[1] who it seems doth find success before the Council and doth everywhere threaten us[a] with what he will prove against us – which doth vex us, to see that we must be subjected to such a rogue of our own servants as this is. By and by to talk of our prize at Hull; and Sir W. Batten offering, again and again, seriously how he would sell his part for 1000*l*, and I considering the knavery of Hogg and his company, the trouble we may have with the Prince Rupert about the consortship,[2] and how we are linked with Sir Rd. Ford, whose son-in-law[3] too is got thither and there we intrust him with all our concerns, who I doubt is of the same breed with his father-in-law for a knave, and then the danger of the sea if it shall be brought about, or bad debts contracted in the sale, but chiefly to be eased of my fears about all or any of this, I did offer my part to him for 700*l*—with a little beating the bargain, we come to a perfect agreement for 666*l*. 13*s*. 04*d*, which is two-thirds of 1000*l*, which is my proportion[b] of the prize. I went to my office full of doubts and joy concerning what I had done; but however, did put into writing the heads of our agreement, and returned to Sir W. Batten and we both signed them – and Sir R. Ford, being come thither since, witnessed them. So having put it past further dispute, I away satisfied; and took coach and to the King's playhouse and

a repl. 'him'   *b* repl. 'proper'

---

1. See above, p. 64, n. 1.
2. The *Fanfan*: see *CSPD 1667*, p. 296.
3. John Oviatt: see above, p. 345 & n. 2.

there saw *The Country Captain*[1] – which is a very ordinary play methinks; I had no pleasure therein at all. And so home again and to my business hard, till my wife came home from her clothes; and so with her to supper and to bed. No news yet come of the ratification of the peace, which we have expected now every hour since yesterday.

15. Up and to the office betimes, where busy and sat all the morning, vexed with more news of Carcasse's proceedings at the Council. Insomuch as we four, J. Mennes, W. Batten, W. Penn and myself, did make an appointment to dine with Sir W. Coventry today to discourse it with him; which we did by going thither as soon as the office was up; and there dined and very merry, and many good stories. And after dinner to our discourse about Carcasse and how much we are troubled that we should be brought, as they say we shall, to defend our report before the Council-board with him, and to have a clerk imposed on us. He tells us in short, that there is no intention in the Lords for the latter; but wholly the contrary. That they do not desire neither to do anything in disrespect to the Board; and he will endeavour to prevent, as he hath done, our coming to plead at the table with our clerk; and doth believe the whole will amount to nothing at the Council; only what he shall declare in behalf of the King against the office, if he offers anything, will and ought to be received; to which we all show a readiness, though I confess even that (though I think I am as clear as the clearest of them), yet I am troubled to think what trouble a rogue may without cause give a man, though it be only by bespattering a*ᵃ* man. And therefore could wish that over, though I fear nothing to be proved. Thence with much satisfaction, and Sir W. Penn and I to the Duke's House, where a new play; the King and Court there, the house full, and an act begun; and so we went to the King's and there saw *The Merry Wifes of Windsor*,[2] which did not please me at all – in no part of it; and so after the play done, we to the Duke's House, where my wife was by

a repl. 'of'

1. A comedy by the Duke of New-   2. Cf. above, i. 310. (A).
castle; see above, ii. 202 & n. 2. (A).

appointment in Sir W. Penn's coach; and she*a* home and we home, and I to my office, where busy till letters done; and then home to supper and to bed.

16. Up, and at the office all the morning; and so at noon to dinner. And after dinner, my wife and I to the Duke's play-house, where we saw the new play acted yesterday, *The Feign Innocence or Sir Martin Marr=all*, a play made by my Lord Duke of Newcastle, but as everybody says corrected by Dryden.[1] It is the most entire piece of Mirth, a complete Farce from one end to the other, that certainly was ever writ. I never laughed so in all my life; I laughed till my head [ached] all the evening and night with my laughing, and at very good wit therein, not fooling. The house full, and in all things of mighty*b* content to me. Thence to the New Exchange with my wife, where at my bookseller's I saw the *History of the Royall Society*,[2] which I believe is a fine book and I have bespoke one in quires. So home, and I to the office a little; and so to my chamber and read the history of 88*c* in Speede,[3] in order to my seeing the play thereof acted tomorrow at the King's House. So to supper, in some pain by the sudden change of the weather cold and my drinking of cold drink; which I must I fear begin to leave off,

a repl. 'they'   *b* MS. 'my'   *c* repl. 'the'

---

1. *Sir Martin Mar-all, or The feign'd innocence*, a comedy acted for the first time on 15 August and pub-lished in 1668, was an adaptation of Molière's *L'Etourdi*. According to Downes (p. 28), Harris played War-ner; Smith, Sir John Swallow; Mrs Norris, Lady Dupe; Mrs Davis, Mrs Millicent. Downes states that Dry-den worked on a bare translation by the Duke of Newcastle, adding a sub-plot and elaborating the role of Sir Martin with the comic gifts of James Nokes in mind, but the play was entered in the Stationers' Register on 24 June 1668 as a comedy written by Newcastle: *Trans. Stat. Reg.*, ii. 387.

No author's name appears in the editions of 1668 and 1678, and it was not until 1691, fifteen years after Newcastle's death, that Dryden put his own name on the title-page of a new edition. For evidence of a comic detail added to the plot by Dryden, see below, p. 468, n. 2. This comedy was one of the most profitable productions of the Duke's Company and so popular that it was occasionally acted until 1728. (A).

2. Thomas Sprat's *History*, just published; PL 1529. Cf. above, p. 380, n. 1.

3. John Speed, *The history of Great Britaine* (1650), pp. 885-90; PL 2906.

though I shall try it as long as I can without much pain. But I find myself to be full of wind, and my anus to be knit together, as it is always with cold. Everybody wonders that we have no news from Bredah of the ratification of the peace, and do suspect that there is some stop in it. So to bed.

17. Up and all the morning at the office, where we sat. And my head was full of the business of Carcasse, who hath a hearing this morning before the Council and hath summoned at least 30 persons; and which is wondrous, a great many of them I hear do declare more against him then for him, and yet he summons people without distinction – sure, he is distracted.[1] At noon home to dinner; and presently my wife and I and Sir W. Penn to the King's playhouse, where the house extraordinary full; and there was the King and Duke of York to see the new play, *Queen Elizabeths Troubles, and the History of Eighty-Eight.*[2] I confess I have sucked in so much of the sad story of Queen Elizabeth from my cradle, that I was ready to weep for her sometimes. But the play is the most ridiculous that sure ever came upon stage, and endeed is merely a show; only, shows the true garbe of the queens in those days, just as we see Queen Mary and Queen Elizabeth painted[3] – but the play is merely a puppet-play acted by living puppets. Neither the design nor language better; and one stands by and tells us the meaning of things. Only, I was pleased to see Knipp dance among the milkmaids, and to hear her sing a song to Queen Elizabeth[4] – and to see her come

1. He later went mad in earnest, and in 1679 published from the madhouse a book of verse (*Lucida intervalla . . . miscellaneous poems, written at Finsbury and Bethlem by the doctors patient extraordinary*), which included an incoherent attack on Pepys. 'Him I must *Praise*, who open'd hath my *Lips*, / Sent me from *Navy*, to the *Ark*, by *Pepys*; / By Mr *Pepys*, who hath my *Rival* been / For the *Dukes* favour, more than years *thirteen*: / But I excluded, he High and Fulcinate . . .'.

2. *If you know not me, you know nobody, or, The troubles of Queen Elizabeth*, a history play by Thomas Heywood, first acted c. 1605, and published in that year. This was probably an adaptation. (A).

3. Historically accurate costuming was very rare on the Restoration stage; though Queen Mary and Queen Elizabeth evidently wore Elizabethan costumes, the remainder of the cast probably wore contemporary dress. (A).

4. There are neither milkmaids nor a song to Elizabeth in the original version of this play; the episode evidently formed part of an addition to it in this production. (A).

out in her night-gowne,* with no locks on, but her bare face and hair only tied up in a knot behind; which is the comeliest dress that ever I saw her in to her advantage.   Thence home and went as far as Mile-end with Sir W. Penn, whose coach took him up there for his country-house;[1] and after having drunk there at the Rrse and Crowne, a good house for Alderman Bides Ale,[2] we parted; and we home, and there I finished my letters and then home to supper and to bed.

18. *Lords day.* Up; and being ready, walked up and down into the streets to Creed Church[3] to see it how it is, but I find no alteration there, as they say there was, for my Lord Mayor and Aldermen to come to sermon as they do every Sunday, as they did formerly to Paul's. Walk back home and to our own church, where a dull sermon and our church empty of the best sort of people, they being at their country-houses; and so home, and there dined with me Mr. Turner and his daughter Betty (her mother should, but they were invited to Sir J. Mennes's, where she dined and the others here with me); Betty is grown a fine lady as to carriage and discourse; I and my wife are mightily pleased with her. We had a good haunch of venison, powdered and boiled, and a good dinner and merry. After dinner comes Mr. Pelling the pothecary, whom I had sent for to dine with me, but he was engaged. After sitting an hour to talk, we broke up, all leaving Pelling to talk with my wife, and I walked toward White-hall; but being weary, turned into St. Dunstan's church, where I hear an able sermon of the Minister[4] of the place. And stood by a pretty, modest maid, whom I did labour to take[a] by the hand and the body; but she would not, but got further and further from me, and at last I could perceive her to take pins out of her pocket to prick me if I should touch her again;[a] which seeing, I did forbear, and was glad I did espy her[b] design. And then I fell to gaze upon another pretty[c] maid[d] in a pew close to me,

---

a–a garbled s.h.: see above, p. 244, note *a*   b repl. 'it'
  c garbled s.h.   d garbled s.h.

---

1. At Walthamstow, Essex.
2. Ald. John Bide (d. 1665) was a Shoreditch brewer.
3. St Catherine Cree Church,

which had survived the Fire. (R).
4. Joseph Tompson (d. 1678), Vicar of St Dunstan-in-the-West, 1662–78.

and she*ᵃ* on me; and I did go about to take her by the hand,*ᵃ*
which she suffered a little and then withdrew. So the sermon
ended and the church broke up, and my amours ended also;
and so took coach and home, and there took up my wife and to
Islington with her, our old road; but before we got to Islington,
between that and Kingsland, there happened an odd adventure;
one of our coach-horses fell*ᵇ* sick of the staggers, so as he was ready
to fall down. The coachman was fain to light and hold him up
and cut his tongue to make him bleed, and his tail – the horse
continued shaking every part of him, as if he had been in an ague
a good while, and his blood settled in his tongue, and the coachman thought and believed he would presently drop down dead.
Then he blew some tobacco[1] in his nose; upon which the horse
sneezed, and by and by grows well and draws us the rest of our way
as well as ever he did; which was one of the strangest things of a
horse I ever observed – but he says it is usual. It is the staggers.

Stayed and eat and drank at Islington at the old house,[2] and so
home and to my chamber to read; and then to supper and to bed.

19. .Up and at the office all the morning, very busy. Towards
noon, I to Westminster about some tallies at the Exchequer and
then straight home again and dined; and then to sing with my
wife with great content; and then I to the office again, where
busy. And then out and took coach and to the Duke of York's
House all alone, and there saw *Sir Martin Marr=all* again, though
I saw him but two days since, and do find it the most comical
play that ever I saw in my life. As soon as the play done, I
home and there busy till night; and then comes Mr. Moore to
me, only to discourse with me about some general things touching
the badness of the times, how ill they look; and he doth agree
with most people that I meet with, that we shall fall into a
commonwealth in a*ᶜ* few years, whether we will or no;[3] for the
charge of a Monarchy is such as the Kingdom cannot be brought
to bear willingly, nor are things managed so well nowadays

---

a–a garbled s.h.: see above, p. 244, note *a*
  b repl. symbol rendered illegible   *c* repl. same symbol

---

1. For the use of tobacco to clear   2. The King's Head: above, v.
the head, see R. Hooke, *Diary* (ed.   101.
Robinson and Adams), p. 17.   3. Cf. above, p. 378 & n. 1.

under [it] as it was heretofore. He says everybody doth think that there is something extraordinary that keeps us so long from the news of the peace being ratified – which the King and the Duke of York have expected these six days. He gone, my wife and I and Mrs. Turner walked in the garden a good while, till 9 at night, and then parted; and I home to supper and to read a little (which I cannot refrain, though I have all the reason in the world to favour my eyes, which every day grow worse and worse by over-useing them) and then to bed.

20. Up, and to my chamber to set down my journall for the last three days; and then to the office – where busy all the morning. At noon home to dinner and then with my wife abroad; set her down at the Exchange and I to St. James's, where find Sir W. Coventry alone and fell to discourse of retrenchments; and thereon he tells how he hath already propounded to the Lords' committee of the Council[1] how he would have the Treasurer of the Navy a less man, that might not sit at the Board but be subject to the Board.[2] He would have two Controllers to do his work, and two Surveyors, whereof one of each to take it by turns to reside at Portsmouth and Chatham, by a kind of Rotation.[3] He would have but only one Clerk of the Acts. He doth tell me he hath propounded how the charge of the Navy in peace shall come within 200000*l*, by keeping out*a* 24 ships in summer and 10 in the winter.[4] And several other perticulars we

a repl. 'how'

1. The committee for retrenchments appointed on 29 July.
2. The Treasurer was responsible directly to the Lord Admiral.
3. There was always to be one surveyor in London.
4. The suggestions for the reorganisation of the Board were shelved, but the new figure for the annual charge was adopted by council order on 16 March 1669. It was the figure proposed before the war (see above, iv. 81), and was half of what Pepys was to suggest as a reasonable minimum in 1685–6:

Memoires of the royal navy, 1679–88 (ed. Tanner), pp. 19+. Coventry's present proposals (12 and 27 August) are in PRO, SP 29/213, no. 65; ib./215, no. 35 (summaries in *CSPD 1667*, pp. 383, 420–1); partial copies in PL 2265, nos 102, 104 (in Hayter's hand); NMM, LBK/8, pp. 567–8 (printed *Further Corr.*, pp. 217–19; Penn, ii. 528–30); Longleat, Coventry MSS 99, ff. 184, 186 (in Coventry's hand); Rawl. A 477, ff. 41–2 (dated 1668). Account in *Cat.*, i. 24–6, 103–5.

went over of retrenchment; and I find I must provide some things to offer, that I may be found studious to lessen the King's charge. By and by comes my Lord Brouncker; and then we up to the Duke of York and there had a hearing of our usual businesses, but no money to be heard of; no, not 100*l* upon the most pressing service that can be imagined, of bringing in the King's timber from Whittlewood,[1] while we have the utmost want of it, and no credit to provide it elsewhere. And as soon as we had done with the Duke of York, Sir W. Coventry did single Sir W. Penn and me, and desired us to lend the King some money out of the prizes we have taken by Hogg; he did not much press it, and we made but a merry answer thereto, but I perceive he did ask it seriously, and did tell us that there never was so much need of it in the world as now, being brought to lowest*ª* straits that can be in the world. This troubled me much. By and by Sir W. Batten told me that he heard how Carcasse doth now give out that he will hang me, among the rest of his threats of him and Pen; which is the first word*ᵇ* I ever heard of that kind from him concerning me. It doth trouble me a little, though I know nothing he can possibly find to fasten on me. Thence with my Lord Brouncker to the Duke's playhouse (telling my wife so at the Change, where I left her) and there saw *Sir Martin Marr=all* again; which I have now seen three times, and it hath been acted but four times, and still find it a very ingenious play and full [of] variety. So home and to the office, where my eyes would not suffer me to do anything by candlelight; and so called my wife and walked in the garden; she mighty pressing for a new pair of cuffs – which I am against the laying out of money upon yet, which makes her angry. So home to supper and to bed.

21. Up, and my wife and I fell out about the pair of cuffs, which she hath a mind to have to go to see the ladies dancing tomorrow at Betty Turner's school tomorrow; and doth vex me

a repl. 'their'   *b* repl. illegible symbol

---

1. On 10 August Christopher Pett had written to the Board hoping (for the sake of the ships now building) that Mr Langrack would 'be en- couraged with some money' to send in timber from Whittlewood, Nor- thants.: *CSPD 1667*, p. 374.

so, that I am resolve[d] to deny them her. However, by and by a way was found that she had them; and I well satisfied, being unwilling to let our difference grow higher upon so small an occasion and frowardness of mine. Then to the office, my Lord Brouncker and I all the morning answering petitions, which now by the King and Council's order we are commanded to set a day in a week apart for.[1] And we resolve to do it by turns, my Lord and I one week, and two others another. At noon home to dinner; and then my wife and I mighty pleasant abroad, she to the New Exchange and I to the Commissioners of the Treasury, who do sit very close and are bringing the King's charge as low as they can; but Sir W. Coventry did here again tell me that he is very serious in what he said to Sir W. Penn and me yesterday about our lending*a* of money to the King; and says that people do talk that we had had the King's ship at his cost to take prizes, and that we ought to lend the King money more then other people. I did tell him I will consider it, and so parted; and do find I cannot avoid it. So to Westminster-hall and there stayed a while; and thence to Mrs. Martin's and there did take a little pleasure both*b* with her and her sister.*b* Here sat and talked, and it is a strange thing to see the impudence of the woman, that desires by*c* all means to have her marido come home, only that she might be at liberty to have me para tocar her*c*; which is a thing I do not so much desire. Thence by coach, took up my wife, and home and out to Mile end and there drank; and so home, and after some little reading in my chamber, to supper and to bed.

This day I sent my Cosen Roger a Tierce of claret which I gave him.

This morning came two of Captain Cookes boys, whose voices are broke and*d* are gone from the Chapel, but have extraordinary

---

a repl. 'King'   *b–b* garbled s.h.: see above, p. 244, note *a*
    c–c garbled s.h.   *d* repl. 'by the'

---

1. The order (14 August; PRO, PC 2/59, f. 269*v*) concerned petitions about pay-tickets, and required them to be heard regularly by the Board (of which Brouncker and Pepys were on this occasion a quorum). The fact that Brouncker had in December 1666 heard them alone was a source of grievance: PL 2874, pp. 468–9.

skill; and they and my boy, with his broken voice, did sing three parts (their names were Blaeu and Loggings);[1] but notwithstanding their skill, yet to hear them sing with their broken voices, which they could not command to keep in tune, would make a man mad, so bad it was.

22.   Up and to the office; whence Lord Brouncker, J. Mennes, W. Penn and I went to examine some men that are put in there for rescueing of men that were pressed into the service; and we do plainly see that the desperate condition that we put men into for want of their pay makes them mad, they being as good men as ever were in the world, and would as readily serve the King again, were they but paid.   Two men leapt overboard, among others, into the Thames out of the vessel into which they were pressed, and were shot by the soldiers placed there to keep them, two*a* days since;[2] so much people do avoid the King's service. And then these men are pressed without money and so we cannot punish them for anything, so that we are forced only to make a show of severity, by keeping them in prison, but are unable to punish them.   Returning to the office, did ask whether we might visit Commissioner Pett (to which I confess I have no great mind); and it was answered that he was close prisoner and we could not; but the Lieutenant of the Tower would send for him to his lodgings if we would, so we put it off to another time.[3]   Returned to the office, where we sat all the morning: and at noon I to Captain Cocke's to dinner, where Lord Brouncker and his Lady, Matt Wren and Bulteale and Sir Allen Apsly; the last of which did make good sport, he being already fallen under

---

a repl. 'upon'

---

1. John Blow and John Loggins had received their leaving present of clothes ('retirement liveries') from the Great Wardrobe on 17 May 1665 and 4 December 1666 respectively: PRO, LC 5/61, pp. 246, 349. Blow (now aged about 19) was the composer; in 1674 he became Master of the Children at the Chapel Royal.

2. The incident has not been traced elsewhere. Pepys noted in June 1666 that pressed men were leaping overboard into the Thames: NWB, p. 113.

3. For Pett's imprisonment, see above, p. 276 & n. 3.

the retrenchments of the new committee, as he is maister-Falconer; [1] which makes him mad, and swears that we are doing that that Parliament would have done; that is, that we are now endeavouring to destroy one another. But it was well observed by some at the table, that they do not think this retrenching of the King's charge will be so acceptable to the Parliament, they having[a] given the King a revenue of so many 100000*l*'s a year more then his predecessors had, that he might live in pomp like a king. After dinner, with my Lord Brouncker and his mistress to the King's[b] playhouse and there saw The[c] *Indian Emperour*; where I find Nell come again, which I am glad of, but was most infinitely displeased with her being put to act the Emperours daughter; which is a great and serious part, which she doth most basely.[2] The rest of the play, though pretty good, was not well acted by most of them methought, so that I took no great content in it. But that that troubled me most was that Knipp sent by Mall[d][3] to desire to speak with me after the play; and she beckoned to me at the end of the play, and I promised to come; but it was so late, and I forced to step to Mrs. Williams' lodgings with my Lord and her (where I did not stay however, for fear of her showing me her closet, and thereby forcing me to give her something);[4] and it was so late, that for fear of my wife's coming home before me, I was forced to go straight home, which troubled me. Home and to the office a little, and then home and to my chamber to read; and anon, late, comes home my wife with Mr. Turner and Mrs. Turner, with whom she supped,

---

a 'having' repeated   *b* repl. 'Duke of York's'
c repl. 'again *Sir Martin Marral*'   *d* repl. 'Mrs.'

---

1. Apsley was not himself dismissed, but the establishment of his department, along with others, was reduced by the committee for retrenchments: *CTB*, ii. 104, 194, 572; *CSPD 1667*, p. 433.

2. Nell Gwyn had abandoned the stage for a few months to be Lord Buckhurst's mistress; see above, p. 334. She played Cydaria in this revival (Downes, p. 9) but may not

have been in the original cast. It is generally agreed that she was a mediocre tragedienne. The play was a tragedy by Dryden; see above, p. 14 & n. 2. (A).

3. Mary Meggs, the chief seller of oranges at the Theatre Royal, who frequently acted as a messenger in this way. (A).

4. Cf. above, vii. 237.

having been with Mrs. Turner today at her daughter's school to
see her daughter's dancing and the rest, which she says is fine.
They gone, I to supper and to bed. My wife very fine today
in her new suit of laced cuffs*a* and perquisites.

This evening Pelling came to me and tells me that this night
the Dutch letters are come, and that the peace was proclaimed
there the 19th instant, and that all is finished;[1] which, for my
life, I know not whether to be glad or sorry for, a peace being so
necessary and yet the peace is so bad in its terms.[2]

23. Up; and Greeting comes, who brings me a tune for two
flagelettes, which we played, and is a tune played at the King's
playhouse;[3] which goes so well that I will have more of them,
and it will be a mighty pleasure for me to have my wife able to
play a part with me – which she will easily,*b* I find, do. Then
abroad to White-hall in a hackney-coach with Sir W. Penn;
and in our way, in the narrow street near Pauls (going the back-
way by tower-street) and the coach being forced to put*c* back,
he was turning himself into a cellar;[4] which made people cry out
to us, and so we were forced to leap*d* out; he out of one and I out
of the other boate* (*Question*: whether a glass-coach[5] would have
permitted us to have made that escape), neither of us getting any
hurt; nor could the coach have got much hurt had we been in it;
but however, there was cause enough for us two to do what we
could to save ourselfs. So being all dusty, we put into the Castle
tavern by the Savoy and there brushed ourselfs; and then to
White-hall with our fellows to attend the Council by order, upon

| *a* MS. 'cups' | *b* repl. full stop |
| *c* repl. 'go' | *d* MS. 'leaped' |

1. Pelling (probably John Pelling, apothecary) was presumably report-ing the arrival of Dutch newsletters in the city. The peace had been ratified at Breda on the 14th/24th, and proclaimed in the principal cities of the United Provinces shortly after-wards. The news was officially pub-lished in England in the *London Gazette* of the 26th.

2. England was forced to abandon most of W. Africa, Pulo Run and Surinam, and to give way on certain other controversial points.

3. Theatre music sometimes circu-lated in MS.: cf. above, iii. 36 & n. 2. (E).

4. The buildings being in ruins after the Fire.

5. A coach with glass windows: see below, p. 446 & n. 1.

some propositions of my Lord Anglesey. We were called in, the*a* King there; and it was about considering how the fleet might be discharged at their coming in shortly (the peace being now ratified and takes place on Monday next,[1] which Sir W. Coventry said would make some clashing between*b* some of us, twenty to one, for want of more warning, but the wind hath kept back the boats from coming over), whether by money or ticket, and cries out against tickets; but the matter was referred for us to provide an answer to, which we must do in a few days;[2] and so we parted, and I to Westminster to*c* the Exchequer to see what sums of money other people lend upon the Act;[3] and find of all sizes from 1000*l* to 100*l*; nay, to 50; nay, to 20*l*; nay to*d* 5*l*; for I find that one Dr. Reade, Doctor of Law, gives no more, and others of them 20*l*;[4] which is a poor thing methinks, that we should stoop so low as to borrow such sums. Upon the whole, I do think to lend (since*e* I must lend) 300*l*;[5] though God knows it is much against my will to lend any, unless things were in better condition and like to continue so.

Thence home and there to dinner; and after dinner, by coach out again, setting my wife down at Unthankes; and I to the Treasury-chamber, where I waited, talking with Sir G Downing till the Lords met. He tells me how he will make all the

---

a repl. 'it'   *b* repl. 'if'   *c* repl. 'hall'
    d repl. 'to 5 '   *e* repl. 'if'

---

1. 26 August was the date agreed on for the cessation of hostilities in the seas around Britain and Holland. Any ships or goods taken after then had to be restored.

2. See PRO, PC 2/59, f. 275. The Navy Board was requested to give an answer on the 28th. On the 30th the Council forbade payment by ticket: ib., f. 281.

3. The Eleven Months Tax. The committee of council in charge of the loans was now pressing government

servants to make their contributions: see the letter to the Duke of York (22 August) in Longleat, Coventry MSS 96, f. 277r.

4. Pepys's account is confirmed by the register of orders on the Eleven Months Tax: PRO, E 403/2430. Dr Thomas Reade lent £5 on 22 July. Between then and 23 August there were a number of unusually small loans (of £10–£50) at a time when most were of over £100.

5. See below, p. 407 & n. 1.

Exchequer-officers, of *a* one side and t'other,[1] to lend the King money *b* upon the act, and that the least clerk shall lend money; and he believes the least will 100*l*[2] – but this I do not believe. He made me almost ashamed that we of the Navy had not in all this time lent any – so that I find it necessary I should, and so will speedily do it before any of my fellows begin and lead me to a bigger sum.

By and by the Lords came; and I perceive Sir W. Coventry is the man, and nothing done till he comes. Among other things, I hear him observe, looking over a paper, that Sir John Shaw is a miracle of a man, for he thinks he executes more places then any man in England, for there he finds him a Surveyor of some of the King's woods; and so reckoned up many other places, the most inconsistent in the world.[3]

Their business with me was to consider how to assigne such of our commanders as will take assignements upon the Act for their Wages; and the consideration thereof was referred to me to give them an answer the next sitting[4] – which is a horrid poor thing, but they scruple at nothing of Honour in the case.

So away thence and called my wife; and to the King's House and saw *The Mayden Queene*,[5] which pleases us mightily; and then away and took up Mrs. Turner at her door, and so to Mile end and there drank; and so back to her house, it being a fine evening, and there supped – the first time I ever was there since they lived there;[6] and she hath all things so neat and well done, that I am mightily pleased with her and all she doth. So here very merry; and then home and to bed – my eyes being very bad.

I find most people pleased *c* with their being at ease and safe of a peace, that they may know no more charge or hazard of an ill-managed war; but nobody speaking of the peace with any

---

a repl. 'one'   *b* repl. 'up'   *c* repl. 'at'

---

1. I.e. of the Upper and Lower sides of the office: the Exchequer of Account and of Receipt respectively.

2. See the Treasury circular (30 August): *CTB*, ii. 181–2.

3. Shaw was one of the greatest London merchants of his day and sat on several government committees.

His main public office was that of a customs farmer.

4. The matter, again deferred on the 26th, was settled on the 28th: *CTB*, ii. 70, 71.

5. By Dryden; see above, p. 91 & n. 2. (A).

6. See above, p. 63 & n. 1.

content or pleasure, but are silent in it, as of a thing they are
ashamed of – no, not at Court; much less in the City.

24. *St. Bartholomew's day*. This morning was proclaimed the
peace between us and the States of the United Provinces, and also
of the King of France and Denmarke, and in the afternoon the
proclamations were printed and came out.[1] And at night the
bells rung, but no bonfires that I hear of anywhere, partly from
the dearness of firing but principally from the little content most
people have in the peace.

All the morning at the office. At noon dined, and Creed
with me, at home. After dinner, we to a play and there saw
The Cardinall at the King's House, wherewith I am mightily
pleased; but above all with Becke Marshall.[2] But it is pretty to
observe how I look up[a] and down for and did espy Knepp;
but durst not own it to my wife that I saw her, for fear of angering
her, who doth not like my[b] kindness to her – and so I was forced
not to take notice of her. And so homeward, leaving Creed
at the Temple: and my belly now full with Plays, that I do
entend to bind myself to see no more till Michaelmas. So with
my wife to Mile end and there drank of Bides ale,[3] and so home;
most of our discourse about[c] our keeping a coach the next year,
which pleases my wife mightily; and if I continue as able as now,
it will save us money.[4]

This day came a letter from the Duke of York to the Board,
to invite us, which is as much as to fright us, into the lending the
King money;[5] which is a poor thing and most dishonourable –

a repl. 'upon'   *b* MS. 'not'   *c* repl. 'of'

---

1. Steele, nos 3500-2; summaries
in *CSPD 1667*, pp. 414-15. Description of ceremony in *London
Gazette*, 26 August.

2. Rebecca Marshall, the younger
of two sisters who acted at this theatre,
played the part of the Duchess
Rosaura in this production. The
play was a tragedy by James Shirley:
see above, iii. 211 & n. 2. (A).

3. Cf. above, p. 389 & n. 2.

4. See below, 28 November 1668
& n.

5. The letter (24 August) asked for
a list of names and sums, so that the
Duke could give His Majesty an
account of their zeal for his service:
copy in PRO, Adm. 2/1745, f. 166r.
He enclosed a copy of the letter of
the committee of council to him:
see above, pp. 397-8.

and shows in what a case we are at the end of the war to our neighbours. And the King doth now declare publicly to give 10 per cent to all lenders;[1] which makes some think that the Dutch themselfs will send over money and lend it upon our public faith, the*ᵃ* Act of Parliament.[2] So home and to my office; wrote a little and then home to supper and to bed.

25. *Lords day.* Up, and to church and thence home; and Pelling comes by invitation to dine with me, and much pleasant discourse with him. After dinner, away by water to Whitehall, where I landed Pelling, who is going to his wife where she is in the country at parson's greene;[3] and myself to Westminster and there at the Swan I did besar Frank. And to the parish church, thinking to see Betty Michell, and did stay an hour in the crowd, think[ing] by the end of a nose that I saw that it had been her; but at last the head turned toward me and it was her mother – which vexed me; and so I back to my boat, which had broke one of her oares in rowing and had now fastened it again; and so I up to Putny and there stepped into the church to look upon the fine people there, whereof there is great store, and the young ladies;[4] and so walked to Barne Elmes, whither I sent Russell,[5] reading of Mr. Boyles *Hydrostatickes*,[6] which are of infinite delight. I walked in the Elmes a good while, and then to my boat and leisurely home, with great pleasure to myself; and there supped and W. Hewer with us – with whom a great deal of good talk touching the office, and so to bed.

26. Up; and Greeting came and I reckoned with him for his teaching of my wife and me upon the Flagielette to this day, and so paid him off, having as much as he can teach us. Then to the

a repl. full stop

---

1. See the council order (22 August): PRO, PC 2/59, f. 298. To the interest of 6% allowed by the act (q.v. above, p. 397 & nn. 3, 4) was to be added a gratuity of 4% on all sums lent before 1 November. The gratuity was to be reduced to 2% after that date.

2. The Dutch kept interest rates on government stock low throughout the century.

3. In Fulham, Mdx. (R).

4. From the schools: cf. above, p. 188.

5. Waterman to the Navy Board.

6. See above, p. 250, n. 2.

office, where we sat upon a perticular business all the morning, and my Lord Anglesey with us; who, and my Lord Brouncker, do bring us news how my Lord Chancellors seal is to be taken*a* away from him today.[1] The thing is so great and sudden to me, that it put me into a very great admiration what should be the meaning of it; and they do not own that they know what it should be. But this is certain: that the King did resolve it on Saturday, and did yesterday send the Duke of Albemarle (the only man fit for those works) to him for his purse; to which the Chancellor answered that he received it from the King, and would deliver it to the King's own hand, and so civilly returned the Duke of Albemarle without it; and this morning my Lord Chancellor is to be with the King, to come to an end in that business.[2] After sitting, we rose; and my wife being gone abroad with Mrs. Turner to her washing at the whitster's,[3] I dined at Sir W. Batten, where Mr. Boreman[4] was, who came from White-hall; who tells us that he saw my Lord Chancellor come in his coach with some of his men, without his Seal, to White-hall to his chamber; and thither the King and Duke of York came, and stayed together alone an hour or more.[5] And it is said that the King doth say that he will have the Parliament meet, and that it will prevent much trouble by having of him out of their envy,*b* by his place being taken away – for that all their envy will be at him.[6] It is said also that my Lord Chancellor answers that he desires he may be brought to his trial if he have done anything to lose his office; and that he will be willing, and is most desirous, to lose that and his head both together. Upon*c*

---

a repl. 'take'   *b* repl. 'e'-   *c* repl. 'how'

---

1. Pepys's account of the fall of Clarendon in this and succeeding entries confirms on the whole Clarendon's own version in his *Life*, and is greatly superior to the Duke of York's brief treatment in his memoirs. The best modern account is in Clayton Roberts, *Growth of responsible government in Stuart Engl.*, ch. 5.
2. According to Clarendon, the Duke of York had already told him of the King's decision before Albe-

marle's visit: *Life*, iii. 282–6; cf. Arlington to Ormond, 27 August (Carte 46, f. 540).
3. Cf. above, p. 383 & n. 5.
4. George Boreman, Keeper of the Privy Lodgings, Greenwich.
5. Cf. Clarendon, *Life*, iii. 286; the interview began at 10 a.m. Clarendon delivered up his seal to Secretary Morice on the 30th: ib., p. 294; Lister, iii. 470.
6. Clarendon.

what terms they parted nobody knows; but the Chancellor looked sad he says. Then in comes Sir Rd. Ford and says he hears that there is nobody more presses to reconcile the King and Chancellor then the Duke of Albemarle and Duke of Buckingham; the latter of which is very strange, not only that he who was so lately his enemy should do it, but that this man, that but the other day was in danger of losing his own head, should so soon come to be a mediator*a* for others.[1] It shows a wise government. They all say*b* that he is but a poor man, not worth above 3000*l* a year in land, but this I cannot believe; and all do blame him for having built so great a house, till he had got a better estate.[2] Having dined, Sir J. Mennes and I to White-hall, where we could be informed in no more then we were told*c* before, nobody knowing the result of the meeting but that the matter is suspended. So I walked to the King's playhouse, there to meet Sir W. Penn; and we saw *The Surprizall*,[3] a very mean play I thought, or else it was because I was out of humour and but very little company in the house. But there Sir W. Penn and I had a great deal of discourse with Mall,[4] who tells us that Nell is already left by my Lord Buckhurst, and that he makes sport of her and swears she hath had all she could get of him; and Hart,[5] her great admirer, now hates her; and that she is very poor and hath lost my Lady Castlemayne, who*d* was her great friend, also. But she is come to the House, but is neglected by them all.

Thence with Sir W. Penn home, and I to my office, where late about business; and then home to supper and so to bed.

a repl. 'm'-   *b* repl. 'so'   *c* repl. 'told'   *d* repl. 'by'

---

1. According to Clarendon (*Life*, iii. 297–8), Buckingham remained his enemy in the business throughout. For Buckingham's recent disgrace, see above, p. 86, n. 3.

2. Clarendon's own statement, made later in answer to his impeachment (*Life*, iii. 339) was that his estate in land was, after payment of debts, worth less than £2000 p.a.

For Clarendon House, Piccadilly, see above, vii. 32 & n. 2.

3. A comedy by Sir Robert Howard; see above, p. 157 & n. 3. (A).

4. The orange-seller. (A).

5. Charles Hart, the leading actor at the Theatre Royal, reputedly one of Nell Gwyn's lovers – her 'Charles I' as she called him. (A).

27. Up, and am invited betimes to be godfather tomorrow to Captain*ᵃ* Poole's child, with my Lady Pen and Lady Batten, which I accepted out of complaisance to them.¹ And so to the office, where we sat all the morning. At noon dined at home; and then my wife and I with Sir W. Penn to the New Exchange, set her down, and he and I to St. James's, where Sir J. Mennes and W. Batten and we waited upon the Duke of York, but did little business; and he, I perceive, his head full of other business and of late hath not been very ready to be troubled with any of our business. Having done with him, Sir J. Mennes, W. Batten and I to White-hall and there hear how it is like to go well enough with my Lord Chancellor; that he is like to keep his Seal, desiring that he may stand his*ᵇ* trial in Parliament if they will accuse him of anything. Here Sir J. Mennes and I looking upon the pictures, and Mr. Chevins² being by, did take us of his own accord into the King's closet to show us some pictures; which endeed is a very noble place, and exceeding great variety of brave pictures and the best hands.³ I could have spent three or four hours there well; and we had great liberty to look and Chevins seemed to take pleasure to show us and commend the pictures.

Having done here, I to the Exchange and there find my wife gone with Sir W. Penn; so I to visit Collonell Fitzgerald,⁴ who hath been long sick at Woolwich, where most of the officers*ᶜ* and soldiers quartered there since the Duch being in the River have died or been sick, and he among the rest; and by the growth of his beard and gray [hair], I did not know him.*ᵈ* His desire to speak with me was about the late command for my paying no more pensions for Tanger.⁵

Thence home and there did business, and so in the evening home to supper and to bed. This day Mr. Pierce the surgeon

---

a repl. 'Mr.'   *b* repl. 'his'   *c* repl. 'of'   *d* repl. 'not'

---

1. Jonas Poole was a brother-in-law of Lady Penn. Pepys was forced to buy a gift in silver plate: Rawl. A 185, f. 23*v*.
2. Will Chiffinch, Keeper of the King's Closet.
3. See above, i. 258 & n. 1; v. 188 & n. 5. (OM).
4. John Fitzgerald, Deputy-Governor of Tangier.
5. See above, p. 335, n. 2.

was with me; and tells me how this business of my Lord Chancellors was certainly designed in my Lady Castlemaine's chamber,
and that when he went from the King on Monday morning, she
was in bed (though about 12 a-clock) and*ᵃ* ran out in her smock
into her Aviary looking into White-hall-garden, and thither her
woman brought her her nightgown,* and stood*ᵇ* joying herself
at the old man's going away.¹   And several of the gallants of
White-hall (of which there was many staying to see the Chancellor return) did talk to her in her Bird cage; among others,
Blanckford,² telling her she was the Bird of paradise.

28. Up; and stayed undressed till my tailor's boy did mend
my vest, in order to my going to the christening anon.   Then
out and to White-hall to attend the Council by their order, with
an answer to their demands touching our advice for the paying-off
of the seamen – when the ships shall come in; which answer is
worth seeing, showing the badness of our condition.³   There
when I came, I was forced to stay till past 12 a-clock in a crowd
of people in the lobby, expecting the hearing of their great
cause of Alderman Barker against my Lord Deputy of Ireland
for his ill-usage in his business of land there.⁴   But the King and
Council sat so long, as they neither heard them nor me; so when
they rose, I into the House and saw the King and Queen at
dinner and heard a little of their viallins music; and so home and
there to dinner; and in the afternoon*ᶜ* with my Lady Battin, Pen

---

a   repl. 'bed'   *b*   repl. ? 'of joying her'-   *c*   repl. 'do'

---

1. Clarendon, describing his return
on 26 August from a final interview
with the King at Whitehall, wrote
that Lady Castlemaine, Arlington and
May 'looked together out of her open
window with great gaiety and
triumph, which all people observed':
Life, iii. 291.   Nathaniel Crew adds
that Clarendon 'looked up and said "O
Madam, is it you? Pray remember
that if you live, you will grow old" ':
Mem. (Camden Misc., ix), p. 9.
Cf. also Sir J. Bramston, *Autobiog.*,

p. 256.   For her share in Clarendon's
fall, see Clarendon, *Life*, iii. 286–91;
Duke of York, *Life* (ed. J. S. Clarke),
i. 428.
    2. Marquis de Blanquefort; a
naturalised Frenchman; later (1677)
Earl of Feversham; recently appointed colonel of the Duke of York's
troop of Guards.
    3. Cf. above, p. 397 & n. 2.   The
answer has not been traced.
    4. For this case, see below, p. 420
& n. 2.

and her daughter, and my wife to Mrs. Poole's,[1] where I mighty merry among the women, and christened the child, a girl, Elizabeth; which though a girl, yet my*a* Lady Batten would have me to give the name. After christening comes Sir W. Batten, W. Penn and Mr. Lowther, and mighty merry there, and I forfeited for not kissing the two godmothers presently after the christening, before I kissed the mother – which made*b* good mirth. And so anon away, and my wife and I took coach and went round twice Bartholomew fayre, which I was glad to see again, after two years missing it by the plague.[2] And so home and to my chamber a little, and so to supper and to bed.

29. Up, and Mr. Moore comes to me and, among other things, tells me that my Lord Crew and his friends takes it very ill of me that my Lord Sandwiches Sea=fee[3] should be retrenched, and so reported from this office and I gave them no notice of it. The thing, though I know to be false, at least that nothing went from our office towards it, yet it troubled me; and therefore after the office rose, I went and dined with my Lord Crew, and before dinner I did enter into the discourse and laboured to satisfy; but found, though he said little, yet that he was not yet satisfied, but after dinner did pray me to go and see how it was, whether true or no. Did tell me, if I was not their friend, they could trust to nobody; and that he did not forget my service and love to my Lord and adventures for him in dangerous times, and therefore would not willingly doubt me now, but yet asked my pardon if, upon this news, he did begin to fear it. This did mightily trouble me, so I away thence to White-hall but could do nothing; so home and there wrote all my letters, and then in the evening to White-hall again and there met Sir Rd. Browne, Clerk to the Committee for Retrenchments, who assures me no one word was ever yet mentioned about my Lord's Salary. This pleased me, and I to Sir G Carteret, who I found in the same

---

a repl. 'the woman' *b* repl. 'made'

---

1. For private christenings, see above, i. 42, n. 3.

2. For the fair, see above, ii. 166, n. 2. It had been cancelled in 1665 and 1666.

3. As Vice-Admiral of the Kingdom, he received £1 a day for himself, and an allowance for servants: PRO, C 66/2962, no. 26.

doubt about it, and assured me he saw it in our original report, my Lord's name with a discharge against it; this, though I know to be false or that it must be a mistake in my clerk, I went back to Sir R Browne and got a sight of their paper, and find how the mistake arose: by the ill copying of it out for the Council from our paper sent to the Duke of York;[1] which I took away with me and showed Sir G. Carteret, and thence to my Lord Crew and the mistake ended very merrily and to all our contents, perticularly my own; and so home and to the office, and then to my chamber late, and so to supper and to bed.

I find at Sir G. Carteret's that they do mightily joy themselfs in their hopes of my Lord Chancellor's getting over this trouble; and I make them believe (and so endeed I do believe he will) that my Lord Chancellor is become popular by it. I find by all hands that the Court is at this day all to pieces, every man of a[a] faction of one sort or other, so as it is to be feared what it will come to. But that that pleases me is, I hear tonight that Mr. Brouncker[2] is turned away yesterday by the Duke of York, for some bold words he was heard by Collonell Werden[3] to say in the garden, the day the Chancellor was with the King: that he believed the King would be hector'd out of everything. For this, the Duke of York, who all say hath been very strong for his father-in-law at this trial, hath turned him away; and everybody I think is glad of it, for he was a pestilent rogue, an Atheist, that would have sold his King and country for 6d almost – so covetous and wicked a rogue he is by all men's report.[4] But one observed

a repl. 'his f'-

---

1. PRO, SP 29/213, no. 65 (2 August). Appended to it is a list of offices and salaries in which some of the latter (but not Sandwich's) are marked 'discharged'. Cf. Navy Board to Committee for Retrenchments, 29 August (*Further Corr.*, pp. 216–17).

2. Henry Brouncker (brother of Pepys's colleague, Lord Brouncker), one of the commissioners of the Duke's Household, and Groom of the Bedchamber to the Duke.

3. Robert Werden, Groom of the Bedchamber to the Duke.

4. No contemporary had a good word for Brouncker, except Gramont who said (p. 262) that he played a good game of chess. The same authority stated that 'he kept . . . a little country-house . . . always well stocked with several working-girls'. He was impeached in April 1668 for his disastrous part in the Battle of Lowestoft.

to me that there never was the occasion for men's holding their tongue at Court and everywhere else as there is at this day – for nobody knows which side[a] will be uppermost.

30. Up, and to Whitehall, where at the Council-chamber I hear Barker's business is like to come to a hearing today, having failed the last day. I therefore to Westminster to see what I could do in my Chequer business about Tanger; and finding nothing to be done, returned, and in the Lobby stayed till almost noon, expecting to hear Barker's business;[1] but it was not called and so I came away. Here I met with Sir G Downing, who tells me of Sir W. Penn's offering to lend 500*l*, and I tell him of my 300*l*; which he would have me to lend upon the credit of the latter part of the Act, saying that by that means my 10 per cent will continue[b] to me the longer; but I understand better and will do it upon the 38000*l*,[2] which will come to be paid the sooner, there being no delight in lending money now, to be paid by the King two year hence. But here he and Sir Wm. Doyly were attending the Council as commissioners for sick and wounded and prisoners, and they told me their business, which was to know how we shall do to release our prisoners; for it seems the Dutch have got us to agree in the treaty (as they fool us in anything) that the Dyett[c] of the prisoners on both sides shall be paid for before they be released[3] – which they have done, knowing ours to run high; they having more prisoners of ours then we have of theirs – so that they are able and most ready to discharge that debt of theirs, but we are neither able nor willing to do that of ours – the debt, of those in Zeland only, amounting to above 5000*l* – for men taken in the King's own ships; besides others

---

a repl. 'sight'   *b* repl. 'come'   *c* repl. 'eating of'

---

1. See below, p. 420 & n. 2.
2. This was the sum reserved in the Eleven Months Tax for the payment of seamen, and loans to provide it had been recommended to 'such as desire an early repayment': *CTB*, ii. 182. Other repayments under the act did

not fall due until February 1669. There is no trace either in the diary or in the Exchequer records of any loan by Pepys at this time.
3. Article X, Treaty of Breda: J. Dumont, *Corps univ. diplom.* (1731), vol. vii, pt i. 45.

taken in merchantmen, which expect, as is usual, that the King should redeem them; but I think he will not, by what Sir G. Downing says.[1] This our prisoners complain of there, and say in their letters, which Sir G. Downing showed me, that they have made a good fight, that they should be taken in the service of the King and the King not pay for their victuals while prisoners for him. But so far they are from doing thus with their men, as we do to discourage ours, that I find in the letters of some of our prisoners there, which he showed me, that they have with money got our men that they took to work and carry their ships home for them; and they have been well rewarded, and released when they came into Holland; which is done like a noble, brave, and wise people.

Having stayed out my time that I thought fit for me to return home, I home; and there took coach, and with my wife to Walthamstow to Sir W. Penn's by invitation, the first time I have been there; and there find him and all their guests (of our office only) at dinner, which was a very bad dinner, and everything suitable, that I never knew people in my life, that make their flutter, that do things so meanly – I was sick to see it; but was merry at some ridiculous humours of my Lady Batten, who, as being an ill-bred woman, would take exceptions at anything anybody said, and I made good sport at it.

After dinner, into the garden and wilderness, which is like the rest of the house, nothing in order nor looked after. By and by comes news that my Lady Viner was come to see Mrs. Lowther, which I was glad of and was all the pleasure I had here, to see her; which I did, and saluted her and find is pretty (though not so eminently so as people talked of her) and of very pretty carriage and discourse.[2] I sat with them and her an hour, talking and pleasant; and then slunk away alone without taking leave, leaving my wife there to come home with them, and I to Bartholomew-fair to walk up and down; and there, among

---

1. Arrangements were made in fact for their release in December, and Downing was paid the £5000 about a year later: *CTB*, ii. 75, 148, 160, 482.

2. Abigail, wife of Sir George Vyner. Cf. above, p. 174, n. 3.

other things, find my Lady Castlemayne at a puppet-play (*patient*[a] *Grizill*)[1] and the street full of people expecting[b] her coming out. I confess I did wonder at her courage to come abroad, thinking the people would abuse her; but they, silly people, do not know her work she makes, and therefore suffered her with great respect to take coach; and she away without any trouble at all, which I wondered at[c] I confess.

I only walked up and down; and among others, saw Tom Pepys the turner, who hath a shop and I think lives in the fair when the fair is not. I only asked how he did, as he stood in the street, and so up and down sauntering till late; and then home and there discoursed with[d] my wife of our bad entertainment today, and so to bed.[e]

I met Captain Cocke today at the Council-chamber and took him with me to Westminster; who tells me that there is yet expectation that the Chancellor will lose the Seal, and that he is sure the King hath said it to him who told it him – and he fears we shall be soon broke in pieces. Assures me that there have been high words between[f] the Duke of York and Sir W. Coventry, for his being so high against the Chancellor – so as the Duke of York would not sign some papers that he brought, saying that he could not endure the sight of him. And that Sir W. Coventry answered that what he did was in obedience to the King's commands; and that he did not think any man fit to serve a prince that did not know how to retire and live a country life.[2] This is all I hear.

31. At the office all the morning – where by Sir W. Penn I do hear that the Seal was fetched away to the King yesterday from the Lord Chancellor, by Secretary Morrice – which puts me

a l.h. repl. s.h. 'patient' *b* repl. 'expr'-
   c MS. 'it' *d* repl. 'w'-
   e repl. 'bad' repl. 'beyond'

1. The story of Patient Griselda, as told by Boccaccio, Petrarch and Chaucer; still the theme of a puppet play in 1770: Thomas Warton, *Hist. Engl. poetry* (1871 ed.), ii. 350, n. 5. (A).

2. For Coventry's part in the fall of Clarendon, see below, pp. 414–15; and cf. Clarendon, *Life*, iii. 256; Duke of York, *Life* (ed. J. S. Clarke), i. 431. Coventry retired to Oxfordshire in 1668.

into a great horror, to have it done after so much debate and confidence that it*a* would not be done at last. When we rose I took a turn with Lord Brouncker in the garden, and he tells me that he hath of late discoursed about this business with Sir W. Coventry, who he finds is the great man in the doing this business of the Chancellors, and that he doth persevere in it, though against the Duke of York's opinion; to which he says that the Duke of York was once of the same mind, and if he hath thought fit since, for any reason to alter his mind, he hath not found any to alter his own; and so desires to be excused, for it is for*b* the King's and Kingdom's good. And it seems that the Duke of York himself was the first man that did speak to the King of this, though he hath since altered his mind.[1] And that W. Coventry did tell the Duke of York that he was not fit to serve a prince that did not know how to retire and live a private life;*c* and that he was ready for that, if it be his and the King's pleasure. After having wrote my letters at the office in the afternoon, I in the evening to White-hall to see how matters go; and there I met with Mr. Ball of the Excise-Office and he tells me that the Seal is delivered to Sir Orlando Bridgeman, the man of the whole nation that is the best*d* spoken of and will please most people;[2] and therefore I am

---

a repl. 'd'-　　　*b* repl. 'by'　　　*c* MS. 'live'　　　*d* repl. 'best'

---

1. A more plausible version of this story is given below, p. 415. The evidence is obscure. It seems unlikely that the Duke would ever have proposed to sacrifice Clarendon in order to placate parliament, but he may have reported to the King that he knew Clarendon to be weary of office. Brouncker was probably repeating the story of what was alleged to have happened at Whitehall on 26 August when the King broke the news to Clarendon that he was going to be dismissed in order to protect him from parliamentary impeachment. According to Clarendon's later account of the interview (*Life*, iii. 287) the King 'entered upon a relation of all that had passed between

him and the duke, and "that he really thought his brother had concurred with him in his opinion . . ." In that discourse the duke sometimes positively denied to have said somewhat, and explained other things as not said to the purpose his majesty understood, or that he ever implied that himself thought it fit'.

2. Bridgeman (Chief Justice of Common Pleas) now became Lord Keeper, an inferior office to that of Chancellor which Clarendon had held. According to Roger North he was a 'very good' common law judge, but proved a 'very bad' Chancery judge: *Life of . . . Guildford* (1742), p. 198.

mighty glad of it. He was then at my Lord Arlington's, whither I went, expecting to see him come out; but stayed so long, and Sir W. Coventry coming thither, whom I had not a mind should see me there idle upon a post-night, I went home without seeing him; but he is there with his Seal in his hand. So I home; took up my wife, whom I left at Unthankes, and so home; and after signing my letters, to bed.

This day, being dissatisfied with my wife's learning so few songs of Goodgroome,[1] I did come to a new bargain with him, to teach her songs at so much, *viz.*, 10s a song; which he accepts of and will teach her.

1. Three in three months: above, p. 378. (E).

SEPTEMBER

1. *Lords day.* Up, and betimes by water from the Tower; and called at the Old Swan for a glass of strong water and sent word to have little Michell and his wife come and dine with us today; and so, taking in a gentleman and his lady that wanted a boat,[1] I to Westminster, setting them on shore at Charing-cross; I to Mrs. Martin's, where I had two pair of cuffs which I bespoke, and there did sit and talk with her and*[a]* no mas, ella having aquellos upon her; and here I did see her little girl my god-daughter, which will be pretty. And there having stayed a little, I away to Creeds chamber; and when he was ready, away to White-hall, where I met with several people and had my fill of talk. Our new Lord Keeper, Bridgeman, did this day the first time attend the King to chapel with his Seal. Sir H. Cholmly tells me there is hopes that the women also will have a rout, and perticularly that my Lady Castleman is coming to a composition with the King to be gone; but how true this is, I know not. Blancfort is made privy-purse to the Duke of York. The Atturny-general is made Chief Justice in the room of my Lord Bridgeman. The Solicitor-general is made Atturney-general; and Sir Ed. Turner made Solicitor-general.[2] It is pretty to see how strange everybody looks, nobody knowing whence this arises; whether from my Lady Castlemaine, Bab May and their faction, or from the Duke of York, notwithstanding his great appearance of defence of the Chancellor, or

a repl. 'et'

---

1. Boats were hard to come by on Sundays, except for officials.

2. This news about appointments was inaccurate. Blanquefort appears to have held no financial office and was not included on the list of commissioners appointed in December to manage the Duke's revenue: HMC, *Rep.*, 8/1/2, p. 280*a*. Bridgeman's successor as Chief Justice of Common Pleas was Sir John Vaughan, who was not appointed until May 1668. The Attorney-General (Sir Geoffrey Palmer) continued in that office until his death in May 1670; and the Solicitor-General (Sir Heneage Finch) did not resign in Turnor's favour until 1670, when he was made Lord Keeper.

from Sir W. Coventry and some few with him – but greater changes are yet expected. So home by water to dinner, where comes Pelling and young Michell and his wife, whom I have not seen a great while, poor girl. And then comes Mr. How, and all dined with me very merry; and spent all the afternoon, Pelling, How, I and my boy, sing[ing] of Locke's Response to the Ten Commandments, which he hath set very finely, and was a good while since sung before the King and spoilt in the performance – which occasioned his printing them for his vindication, and are excellent good.[1] They parted, in the evening my wife and I to walk in the garden; and there scolded a little, I being doubtful that she had received a couple of fine pinners (one of point-de-Gesne),[2] which I find she hath from some[one] or other of a present; but on the contrary, I find she hath bought them for me to pay for them, without my knowledge. This doth displease me much; but yet doth so much please me better then if she had received them the other way,[a] that I was not much angry, but fell to other discourse; and so to my chamber, and got her to read to me for saving of my eyes; and then having got a great cold, I know not how, I to bed and lay ill at ease all the night.

2. This day is kept in the City as a public fast for the fire this day twelve months.[3] But I was not at church, being commanded with the rest to attend the Duke of York; and therefore with Sir J. Mennes to St. James's, where we had much business before the Duke of York; and observed[b] all things to be very kind between the Duke of York and W. Coventry, which did mightily joy me. When we had done, Sir W. Coventry called

---

a repl. 'wise'   b repl. 'after having done with'

---

1. The book was Matthew Locke's *Modern church musick, pre accus'd, censur'd, and obstructed vindicated by the author* (1666). The 'spoilt' perform-ance had occurred on 1 April 1666, at the Chapel Royal, when, in protest against the novelty of a different setting for each repetition of the Kyrie, the choristers had deliberately sabotaged the singing. (E).

2. The pinners were in this case probably gorgets worn over a low *décolletage*, though the word could also be applied to caps or to the decorative aprons worn at this period.

3. The fast (to be held every year 'for ever') was established by the Rebuilding Act of 1667: 18–19 Car. II c. 8, sect. xxvi.

me down with him to his chamber and there told me that he is leaving the Duke of York's service, which I was amazed at; but he tells me that it is not with the least unkindness on the Duke of York's side, though he expects (and I told him he was in the right) it will be interpreted otherwise, because done just at this time. "But," says he, "I did desire it a good while since, and the Duke of York did with much entreaty grant it, desiring that I would say nothing of it, that he might have time and liberty to choose his successor without being importuned for others whom he should not like"[1] – and that he hath chosen Mr. Wren;[2] which I am glad of, he being a very ingenious man, and so W. Coventry says of him, though he knows him little; but perticularly commends him for the book he writ in answer to Harrington's *Oceana*,[3] which for that reason I intend to buy. He tells me the true reason is that he being[a] a man not willing to undertake more business then he can go through, and being desirous to have his whole time to spend upon the business of the Treasury and a little for his own ease, he did desire this of the Duke of York. He assures me that the kindness with which he goes away from the Duke of York is one of the greatest joys that ever he had in the world. I used some freedom with him, telling him how the world hath discourse of his having offended the Duke of York about the late business of the Chancellor; he doth not deny it, but says that perhaps the Duke of York might have some reason for it, he opposing him in a thing wherein he was so earnest; but tells me that notwithstanding all that, the Duke of York doth not now, nor can blame him – for he tells me that he was the man that did propose the removal of the Chancellor; and that he did still persist in it, and at this day

a repl. 'is'

---

1. Coventry, writing to Savile on 3 September, was at pains to point out that his decision to resign was taken 'befor anything of my Ld Chancellor's businesse broke forthe': H. C. Foxcroft, *Halifax*, i. 54. Clarendon's suggestion to the contrary (*Life*, iii. 292) is contradicted both by Coventry's letter and Pepys's report.

2. Matthew Wren, M.P., F.R.S., son of the late Bishop of Ely and cousin of the architect, had served as Clarendon's secretary. He now served the Duke until 1672.

3. Either his *Considerations on Mr. Harrington's Oceana* (1657) or its sequel, *Monarchy Asserted . . .* (1659). Neither survives in the PL.

publicly owns it and is glad of it; but that the Duke of York knows that he did first speak of it to the Duke of York, before he spoke to any mortal creature besides, which was fair dealing; and that the Duke of York was then of the same mind with him and did speak of it to the King, though since, for reasons best known to himself, he was*ᵃ* afterward altered.*ᵇ* I did then desire to know what was the great matter that grounded his desire of the Chancellor's removal; he told me many things not fit to be spoken, and yet not anything of his being unfaithful to the King;[1] but, *instar omnium*, he told me that while he was so great at the Council-board and in the administration of matters, there was no room for anybody to propose any remedy to what was amiss or to compass anything, though never so good for the Kingdom, unless approved of by the Chancellor, he managing all things with that greatness which now will be removed, that the King may have the benefit of others' advice.[2] I then told him that the world*ᶜ* hath an opinion that he hath joined himself with my Lady Castlemayn's faction in this business; he told me he cannot help it, but says they are in an errour: but for first, he will never while he lives truckle under anybody or any faction, but do just as his own reason and judgment directs; and when he cannot use that freedom, he will have nothing*ᵈ* to do in public affairs: but then he added that he never was the man that ever had any discourse with my Lady Castlemaine, or with others from her, about this or any public business, or ever made her a visit, or at least not this twelvemonth, or been in her lodgings but when*ᵉ* called on any business to attend the King there, nor hath had anything to do in knowing her mind in this business. He ended all with telling me that he knows that he that serves*ᶠ* a Prince must expect and be contented to stand all fortunes and be*ᵍ* provided to retreat; and that that he is most willing to do

a repl. 'is' *b* repl. 'al'- *c* MS. 'would'
d repl. 'have' *e* repl. 'what' *f* repl. 'must'
g repl. 'prov'-

1. This view that no reason was alleged is important, in view of the nature of the impeachment charges made against him a few weeks later: see below, p. 526 & n. 3.

2. This was one of the principal charges against Clarendon at his impeachment: cf. Milward, p. 101. Cf. also Foxcroft, *Halifax*, i. 54–5.

whenever the King shall please. And so we parted, he setting me down out of his coach at Charing-cross, and desired me to tell Sir W. Penn what he had told me of his leaving the Duke of York's service, that his friends might not be the last that know it. I took a coach and went homeward; but then turned again and to White-hall, where I met with many people; and among other things, do learn that there is some fear that Mr. Brouncker is*a* got into the King's favour and will be cherished there; which will breed ill will between the King and Duke of York, he lodging at this time in White-hall since he was put away from the Duke of York;[1] and he is great with Bab May, my Lady Castlemaine, and that wicked crew. But I find this denied by Sir G. Carteret, who tells me that he is sure he hath no kindness from the King. That the King at first, endeed, did endeavour to persuade the Duke of York from putting him away; but when, besides this business of his ill words concerning his Majesty in the business of the Chancellor, he told him that he hath had a long time a mind to put him away for his ill offices done between him and his wife, the King held his peace and said no more, but wished him to do what he pleased with him – which was very noble. I met with Fenn[2] and he tells me, as I do hear from some others, that the business of the Chancellor's had proceed[ed] from something of a mistake, for the Duke of York did first tell the King that the Chancellor had a desire to be eased of his great trouble; and that the King, when the Chancellor came to him, did wonder to hear him deny it, and the Duke of York was forced to deny to the King that ever he did tell him so in those terms;[3] but the King did answer that he was sure that he did say some such thing to him; but however, since it had gone so far, did desire him to be contented with it, as a thing very convenient for him as well as for himself (the King); and so matters proceeded as we find. Now it is likely the Chancellor might some time or other, in a compliment or vanity, say to the Duke of York that he was weary of this burden, and I know not what; and this comes of it.

a repl. 'the'

1. See above, p. 406 & n. 2.
2. John Fenn, Paymaster to the Navy Treasurer, whose late master (Carteret) was a friend of Clarendon.
3. Cf. above, p. 410 & n. 1.

Some people, and myself among them, are of good*a* hope from this change that things are reforming; but there are others that do think it no but[1] that it is a hit of chance, as all other our greatest matters are, and that there is no general plot or contrivance in any number of people what to do next (though I believe Sir W. Coventry may in himself have further designs); and so, that though other changes may come, yet they shall be accidental and laid upon [no] good principles of doing good.

Mr. May showed me the King's new buildings,[2] in order to their having of some old sails for the closing of the windows this winter. I dined with Sir G. Carteret, with whom dined Mr. ⟨Jack⟩ Ashburnham and Dr. Creeton[3] (who I observe to be a most good man and humble). In discourse at dinner concerning the change of men's humours and fashions touching meats, Mr.*b* Ashburnham told us that he remembers since the only fruit in request, and eaten by the King and Queen at table as the best fruit, was the Katharine payre,[4] though they knew at that time other fruits of France and our own country. After dinner comes in Mr. Townsend;[5] and there I was witness of a horrid rateing, which Mr. Ashburnham, as one of the Grooms of the King's Bedchamber, did give him for want of linen for the King's person; which he swore was not to be endured, and that the King would not endure it, and that the King his father would have hanged his wardrobe-man should he have been served so; the King having at this day no handkerchers and but three bands to his neck, he swore. Mr. Townsend answered want of money and the owing of the linendraper 5000*l*; and that he hath of late got many rich things made, beds and sheets*c* and saddles, and all without money, and that he can go no further; but still this old

---

a repl. 'hope from this'   *b* repl. 'he tells us'   *c* MS. 'states'

---

1. ? nobbut (nothing else than).
2. These may have been the 'new lodgings' (May 1667) in the Volary Garden: PRO, Works 5/10. Payment for some such work (December 1668) is recorded in *CTB*, ii. 639. Hugh May was the architect in charge of the King's Works.
3. Robert Creighton, Dean of Wells and chaplain to the King.

4. A small and early English variety, of which Evelyn noted two sorts, the Red and the King: *Kalendarium Hortense* (1664), p. 72. According to T. Moffett, *Healths Improvement* (1655), it was the 'best relished' of all pears.
5. Thomas Townshend, sen., Clerk of the Great Wardrobe.

man (endeed, like an old loving servant) did cry out for the King's person to be neglected.   But when he was gone, Townsend told me that it is the grooms taking away the King's linen at the Quarter's end, as their Fees, which makes this great want: for whether the King can get it or no, they will run away at the Quarter's end with what he hath had,*a* let the King get more as he can.   All the company gone, Sir G. Carteret and I to talk; and it is pretty to observe*b* how already he says that he did alway look upon the Chancellor endeed as his friend, though he never did do him any service at all, nor ever got anything by [him], nor was a man apt (and that I think is true) to do any man any kindness of his own nature – though I do know he was he that was believed by all the world to be the greatest support of Sir G. Carteret with the King of any man in England – but so little is now made of it.   He observes that my Lord Sandwich will lose a great friend of him.   And I think so too, my Lord Hinchingbrooke being about a match calculated purely out of respect to my Lord Chancellor's family.[1]   By and by, Sir G. Carteret and Townsend and I to consider of an answer to the Commissioners of the Treasury about my Lord*c* Sandwiches profits in the Wardrobe; which seem, as we make them, to be very small, not 1000*l* a year; but only the difference in measure which he buys at and delivers out to the King, and then 6*d* in the pound from the tradesman for what money he receives of him.   But this, it is believed, these Commissioners will endeavour to take away.[2]

From him I went to see a great match at tennis between Prince Rupert and one Captain Cooke against Bab. May and the elder Chichly,[3] where the King was and Court, and it seems are the

a repl. 'his'   *b* repl. 'observe'   *c* repl. 'Lord'

---

1. See above, p. 190 & n. 3.
2. See the enquiries into the payments of Wardrobe fees in *CTB*, ii. esp. 237, 245, 249.   Occasionally 12*d*. in the pound seems to have been paid, but Sandwich's allowance for the Household was badly in arrears.   In August 1669 his fees and allowances were abolished, and a fixed salary of £2000 p.a. substituted: *CTB*, iii (pt i), p. 131.   Cf. above, iii. 287 &

n. 2;   Sandwich MSS, Letters to Mins., ff. 43*v*–45*r* (Sandwich to Arlington, 20/30 November 1667, Madrid: a long and submissive letter on the proposals for retrenchment).
3. Capt.   Thomas   Cooke   was master   of   the   Tennis   Court   at Whitehall;   Baptist May a courtier; and Thomas Chicheley a Commissioner of the Ordnance.

best players at tennis in the nation. But this puts me in mind of what I observed in the morning; that the King, playing at tennis, had a Steele yard*a* carried to him, and I was told it was to weigh him after he had done playing; and at noon Mr. Ashburnham told me that it is only the King's curiosity, which he usually hath, of weighing himself before*b* and after his play, to see how much he loses in weight*c* by playing; and this day he lost 4½ lb.

Thence home and took my wife out to Mile-end-green and there drank; and so home, having a very fine evening. Then home, and I to Sir W. Batten and W. Penn and there discoursed of Sir W. Coventry's leaving the Duke of York and Mr. Wren's succeeding him; they told me both seriously, that they had long cut me out for Secretary to the Duke of York if ever W. Coventry left him; which, agreeing with what I have heard from other hands heretofore, doth make me*d* not only think that something of that kind hath been thought on, but doth comfort me to see that the world hath such an esteem of my qualities as to think me fit for any such thing – though I am glad with all my heart that I am not so, for it would never please me to be forced to the attendance that that would require, and leave my wife and family to themselfs, as I must do in such a case; thinking myself now in the best place that ever man was in to please his own mind in, and therefore I will take care to preserve it. So to bed,*e* my cold remaining, though not so much, upon me. ⟨This day, Nell, an old tall maid, came to live with us, a cook maid recommended by Mr. Batelier.⟩

3. All the morning, business at the office. Dined at home. Then in the afternoon set my wife down at the Exchange, and I to St. James's and there attended the Duke of York about the list of ships that we propose to sell;[1] and here there attended Mr. Wren the first time, who hath not yet I think received the Duke of York's seal and papers. At our coming hither we

---

a repl. 'payr'   *b* repl. 'self'   *c* MS. 'weigh'
     d repl. 'men'   *e* repl. 'sup'-

---

1. The Admiral had been authorised on 9 June to sell unserviceable men-of-war, the proceeds going to the navy. Twenty-six were sold on 27 November. *CSPD 1667*, p. 451; PRO, Adm. 106/3520, f. 37*v*.

found the Duke and Duchesse all alone at dinner, methought melancholy, or else I thought so from the late occasion of the Chancellors fall – who they say, however, takes it very contentedly. Thence I to White-hall a little; and so took up my wife at the Change and so home and at the office late, and so home to supper and to bed. Our boy ill.

4. By coach to White-hall to the Council-chamber; and there met with Sir W. Coventry going in, who took me aside and told me that he was just come from delivering up his seal and papers to Mr. Wren; and told*a* me he must now take his leave of me*b* as a naval man, but that he shall always bear respect to his friends there, and perticularly*c* to myself, with great kindness, which I returned to him with thanks; and so with much kindness parted, and he into the Council. I met with Sir Sam. Moreland, who showed me two orders upon the Exchequer, one of 600*l* and another of 400*l*, for money*d* assigned to him, which he would have me lend him money upon and he would allow 12 per cent. I would not meddle with them, though they are very good; and would, had I not so much money out already on public credit.[1] But I see by this, his condition will alway be bad. I stayed and heard Alderman Barker's case of his being abused by the Council of Ireland touching his lands there.[2] All I observed

----

a repl. 'told'   *b* repl. 'him'   *c* repl. 'perf'-
                          d repl. 'many'

----

1. For the use of Treasury orders as negotiable instruments, see below, p. 520 & n. 2. At 31 May 1667, when Pepys made up his accounts, he had Treasury orders drawn on the Eleven Months Tax for £824 2s. 6d., and tallies drawn on Tangier funds for £5375: Rawl. A 185, ff. 17*v*, 23*r*.

2. This case was promoted by Ormond's enemies, particularly Buckingham. It was the first blow in an attack which led to Ormond's dismissal in March 1669 from his office

as Lord Lieutenant. William Barker and others had adventured £7000 in the purchase of Irish lands, but on 12 June 1667 the Council of Ireland had adjudged their claims invalid, mainly on the ground that the money had not been paid. Barker now brought the case on appeal to the King and Privy Council, but lost it, the lands being granted to others in July 1669. *CSP Ireland 1666–9*, passim, esp. pp. 408–10, 766; T. Carte, *Ormond* (1851), iv. 314+.

there is the silliness of the King, playing with his dog all the while,[1] or his codpiece, and not minding the business, and what he said*ᵃ* was mighty weak; but my Lord Keeper I observe to be a mighty able man. The business broke off without any end to it, and so I home and thence with my wife and W. Hewer to Bartholomew fayre and there saw *Polichinelli*[2] (where we saw Mrs. Clerke and all her crew); and so to a private house and sent for a side of pig[3] and eat it at an acquaintance of W. Hewer's, where there was some learned physique and Chymical Bookes; and among others, a natural Herball,[4] very fine. Here we stayed not; but to the Duke of York's playhouse and there see *Mustapha*, which the more I see, the more I like; and is a most admirable poem – and bravely acted; only, both Batterton and Harris could not contain from laughing in the midst of a most serious part, from the ridiculous mistake of one of the men upon the stage – which I did not like.[5] Thence home, where Batelier and his sister Mary came to us and sat and talked; and so they gone, we to supper and to bed.

5. Up, and all the morning at the office, where we sat till noon; and then I home to dinner, where Mary Batelier and her brother dined with us, who grows troublesome in his talking so much of his going to Marseillis, and what commissions he hath to execute as a factor,[6] and a deal of do of which I am weary. After dinner, with Sir W. Penn, my wife, and Mary Batelier to the Duke of York's House and there saw *Heraclius*,[7] which is a

ᵃ repl. 'was'

---

1. Cf. Rochester, *The Restauration* (*Coll. Works*, ed. Hayward, p. 87): 'His very dog at Council Board, / Sits grave and wise as any Lord.'

2. The popular Italian puppet play which Pepys had already seen several times. The puppeteer was probably Antonio Devoto: G. Speight, *Hist. Engl. puppet theatre*, pp. 75–7. (A).

3. Pork was the traditional dish at Bartholomew Fair: cf. Jonson, *Barth. Fair*, Act I, 5.

4. A book of dried and pressed plants. Cf. above, vi. 289 & n. 6.

5. The play was a tragedy by Orrery: see above, ᵥi. 73 & n. 1. Betterton and Harris played the leading roles of Solyman and Mustapha. It was unusual for Betterton to violate artistic discipline in this way. (A).

6. Joseph Batelier was a wine merchant.

7. A translation of Pierre Corneille's *Heraclius*: see above, v. 78 & n. 1. (A).

good play; but they did so spoil it with their laughing and being all of them out,[1] and with the noise they made within the Theater, that I was ashamed of it and resolve not to come thither again a good while, believing that this negligence, which I never observed before, proceeds only from their want of company in the pit,[2] that they have no care how they act.   My wife was ill, and so I was forced to go out of the house with her to Lincoln's-Inn-walks, and there in a corner[a] she did her business and was by and by well; and so into the House again, but sick of their ill acting. So home and to the office, where busy late; then home to supper and to bed.

This morning, was told by Sir[b] W. Batten that he doth hear from Mr. Grey, who hath good intelligence, that our Queene is to go into a nunnery, there to spend her days.   And that my Lady Castlemayne is going into France and is to have a pension of 4000*l* a year.[3]   This latter I do more believe then the other, it being very wise in her to do it and save all she hath, besides ease the King and kingdom of a burden and reproach.

6.   Up, and to Westminster to the Exchequer and then into the Hall; and there bought Guillim's *Heraldry* for my wife.[4] And so to the Swan, and thither came Doll Lane and yo did tocar her and drank and so away; I took coach and home, where I find

a repl. 'priv'-   *b* repl. 'my'

---

1. I.e. they had not memorised their parts properly. (A).
2. The pit usually contained the most discriminating of the playgoers. (A).
3. Batten's informant was probably Thomas Grey, M.P., a member of several committees of Council. According to the Duke of York's account, Buckingham and Bristol were now plotting to have the Queen divorced: *Life* (ed. J. S. Clarke), i. 438. Burnet (i. 474) says that the King tried (through her confessor) to persuade her to take the veil, 'upon which the parliament would have been easily prevailed on to pass a

divorce . . . but what steps were made in it were never known'.   See also Reresby, *Memoirs* (ed. Browning), pp. 80–1, 161, 204–5; cf. below, p. 438.   There was no truth in the rumour about Lady Castlemaine.
4. John Guillim, *A display of heraldry*, first published in 1610; a 5th edition had appeared in 1664. For Mrs Pepys's interest in English heraldry (because of her alleged descent from the Cliffords), see above, v. 118 & n. 1.   Pepys preserved a copy of the enlarged 5th edition of 1679 (PL 2576), in which the arms of 'Samuel Pepys, Esquire', are given for the first time: see above, iii. 50, n. 3.

my wife gone to Walthamstow by invitation with Sir W. Batten; and so I fallowed, taking up Mrs. Turner, and she and I much discourse all the way touching the baseness of Sir W. Penn and sluttishness of his family – and how the world doth suspect that his son Lowther, who is sick of a sore mouth, hath got the pox. So we came to Sir W. Batten's, where Sir W. Penn and his Lady and we and Mrs. Shipman, and here we walked and had*ᵃ* an indifferent good dinner; the victuals very good and cleanly dressed, and good linen, but no fine meat at all. After dinner we went up and down the house, and I do like it very well, being furnished with a great deal of very good goods.¹ And here we stayed, I tired with the company, till almost evening; and then took leave, Turner and I together again, and my wife with W. Batten. At Allgate I took my wife into our coach, and so to Bartholomew-fair and there, it being very dirty and now night, we saw a poor fellow, whose legs were tied behind his back, dance upon his hands with his arse above his head, and also dance upon his crutches, without any legs upon the ground to help him; which he did with that pain, that I was sorry to see it, and did pity him and give him money after he had done. Then we to see a piece of Clocke-work made by an Englishman;² endeed, very good, wherein all the several states of man's age, to 100 year old, is shown very pretty and solemne, and several other things more cheerful; and so we ended and took a link, the women resolving to be dirty, and walked up and down to get a coach; and my wife, being a little before me, had been like to be taken up by one, whom we saw*ᵇ* to be Sam Hartlib. My wife had her vizard on – yet we cannot say that he meant any hurt, for it was as she was just by a coach-side, which he had or had a mind to take up; and he ask[ed] her, "Madam, do*ᶜ* you go in this coach?" but as soon as he*ᵈ* saw a man come to her (I know not whether he knew me) but he departed away apace. By and by did get a coach, and so away home and there to supper and to bed.

a repl. 'every'   *b* repl. 'found'   *c* repl. 'will'
d repl. symbol rendered illegible

---

1. For Batten's house, see above, i. 279, n. 2.
2. For clockwork automata, see

above, iv. 298. They were usually German.

7. Up and to the office, where all the morning. At noon home to dinner, where Goodgroome was teaching my wife, and dined with us, and I did tell him of my intention to learn to trill;* which he will not promise I shall obtain, but he will do what can be done, and I am resolved to learn. All the afternoon at the office, and towards night out by coach with my wife, she to the Change and I to see the price of a Copper Cesterne for the table, which is very pretty; and they demand 6 or 7*l* for one, but I will have one. Then called my wife at the Change, and thence bought a nightgown for my wife, cost but 24*s*, and so out to mile end to drink, and so home to the office to end my letters, and so home to supper and to bed.

8. *Lords day.* Up, and walked to St. James's, but there I find Sir W. Coventry gone from his chamber and Mr. Wren not yet come thither. But I up to the Duke of York and there, after being ready, my Lord Brouncker and I had an audience. And thence with my Lord Brouncker to White-hall, and he told me in discourse how that though it is true that Sir W. Coventry did long since propose to*a* the Duke of York the leaving his service, as being unable to fulfil it as he should do now he hath so much public business, and that the Duke of York did bid him say nothing of it, but that he would take*b* time to please himself in another to come in his place, yet the Duke of York's doing it at this time, declaring that he hath found out another, and this one of the Chancellor's servants, he cannot but think was done with some displeasure, and that it could not well be otherwise that the Duke of York should keep one in that place that had so eminently opposed him in the defence of his father-in-law, nor could the Duchesse ever endure the sight of him, to be sure. But he thinks that the Duke of York and he are parted upon clear terms of friendship. He tells me he doth believe that my Lady Castlemayne is compounding with the King for a pension, and to leave the Court; but that her demands are mighty high. But he believes the King is resolved, and so doth everybody else I speak with, to do all possible to please the Parliament; and he doth declare that he will deliver everybody up to them to give

a repl. 'his leaving the'　　　*b* repl. 'think of'

an account of their actions.[1] And that last Friday, it seems, there was an act of Council passed to put out all papists in office and to keep out any from coming in.[2]

I went to the King's Chapel to the closet, and there I hear Cresset[3] sing a Tenor part along with the Church music; very handsomely, but so loud that people did laugh at him – as a thing done for ostentacion. Here I met Sir G Downing, who would speak with me; and first, to enquire what I paid for my Kids-leather gloves I had on my hands, and showed me others on his, as handsome, as good in all points, cost him but 12*d* a pair, and mine me 2*s*. He told me he had been seven years finding out a man that could dress English sheep-skin as it should be; and endeed, it is now as good in all*a* respects as Kidd, and he says will save 100000*l* a year that goes out to France for Kids-skins.[4] Thus he labours very worthily to advance our own trade, but doth it with mighty vanity and talking. But then he told me of our base condition, in the treaty with Holland and France, about our prisoners; that whereas before we did clear one another's prisoners man for man, and we upon the publication of the peace did release all ours, 300 at Leeth and others in other places for nothing, the Dutch do keep theirs and will not discharge them with[5] paying their debts according to the treaty.[6] That

a repl. 'real'

---

1. See below, p. 476 & n. 1.
2. The Council in fact on 6 September simply gave consideration to the parliamentary resolutions of 31 October 1666 to this effect: an order enforcing them was not passed until the 18th. All officers, civil and military, refusing the oaths of allegiance and supremacy were to be removed and replaced. The order was not effective. PRO, PC 2/59, ff. 286*v*, 297*v*–298; cf. *CJ*, viii. 644. See also below, p. 476 & n. 2.
3. Possibly Francis Cresset, Groom of the Privy Chamber from 1660.
4. Nothing more seems to be

known of this scheme. Downing had been a keen promoter of protective legislation in 1660–3, and in October 1666 had been appointed chairman of a parliamentary committee for the advancement of English manufactures: *CJ*, viii. 632. He had attempted to introduce a new plough design from Spain and methods of pottery making from Holland: Arlington, *Letters* (1701), ii. 48; Bodl., Clar. 108, f. 102*r*. Gloves in England were mostly made by domestic outworkers in Wiltshire and Somerset.
5. I.e. discharge them from.
6. Cf. above, p. 407 & n. 2.

his instruments in Holland writing to our Imbassadors about this to Bredagh, they answer them that they do not know of anything that they have done therein, but left it just as it was before – to which, when they answer that by the treaty their Lordships had bound our countrymen to pay their debts in prison, they answer they cannot help it, and we must get them off as cheap as we can. On this score they demand 1100*l* for Sir G. Ascue and 5000*l* for the one province of Zealand the prisoners that we have therein. He says that this is a piece of shame that never any nation committed, and that our very Lords here of the Council, when he related this[a] matter to them, did not remember that they had agreed to this article.   And swears that all their articles are alike; as, the giving away Polleroon and Seranam and Nova Scotia, which hath a River 300 miles up the country, with copper mines more then Swedeland and Newcastle coals, the only place in America that hath coals that we know of.[1]   And that Cromwell did value[b] these places and would for ever have made much of them; but we have given them away for nothing, besides a debt to the King of Denmarke;[2] but which is most of all, they have discharged those very perticular demands of merchants of the Guinny Company and others, which he, when he was there, had adjousted with the Dutch and come to agreement in writing and they undertaken to satisfy; and that this was done in black and white under their hands,[3] and yet we have forgiven all these, and not so much as sent to Sir G. Downing to know what he had done or to confer with him about any one point of the treaty,

a repl. 'the'   *b* repl. 'value'

---

1. The river was the St John. The copper deposits were probably those in the Gaspé peninsula; the coal probably those on the coast of Cape Breton Is. near the modern Sydney. Very little was then known about these regions. (Downing had been brought up in New England and knew a little more than most English-

men.) Nova Scotia, acquired in 1654, had been restored to the French by the recent peace, and became British again only in 1713.
2. The treaty with Denmark cancelled a debt due to the English traders with Hamburg.
3. The *règlements* concluded in 1664: Lister, iii. 317–18, 330.

but signed to what they would have; and we here signed to whatever in grosse was brought over by Mr. Coventry. And tells me, just in these words, "My Lord Chancellor had a mind to keep himself from being questioned,*a* by clapping up a peace upon any terms." When I answered that there was other privy-councillors to be advised with besides him, and that therefore this whole peace could not be laid to his charge, he answered that nobody durst say anything at the Council-table but himself,[1] and that the King was as much afeared of saying anything there as the meanest privy-councillor; and says more, that at this day the King in familiar talk doth call the Chancellor "that insolent man," and says that he would not let him speak himself*b* in Council – which is very high – and doth show that the Chancellor is like to be in a bad state unless he can defend himself better then people think. And yet Creed tells me that he doth hear that my Lord Cornbury doth say that his father doth long for the coming of the Parliament, in order to his own vindication, more then any one of his enemies. And here it comes into my head to set down what Mr. Rawlinson (whom I met in Fanchurch-street on Friday last, looking over his ruines*c* there) told me: that he was told by one of my Lord Chancellors gentlemen*d* (by name) lately, that a grant coming to him to be sealed, wherein the King hath given her,[2] or somebody by her means, a place which he did not like well of, he did stop the grant, saying that he thought this woman would sell everything shortly[3] – which she hearing of, she sent to let him know that she had disposed of this place, and did not doubt in a little time to dispose of his. This, Rawlinson*e* doth tell me my Lord Chancellors own gentleman did tell him himself.

Thence, meeting Creed, I with him to the parke, there to walk a little, and to the Queen's Chapel and hear their music, which I liked in itself pretty well as to the composition, but their voices

---

a l.h. repl. illegible l.h.   b   MS. 'himself speak'
c   l.h. repl. s.h. 'building'   d   repl. 'serv'-   e   repl. 'he did'

---

1. Cf. above, p. 415 & n. 2.   3. See below, p. 434 & n. 3.
2. Lady Castlemaine.

are very harsh and rough, that I thought it was some instruments they had that made them sound so.

So to White-hall and saw the King and Queen at dinner; and observed (which I never did before) the formality, but it is but a formality, of putting a bit of bread*ᵃ* wiped upon each dish into the mouth of every man that brings a dish – but it should be in the sauce.[1]   Here were some Russes come to see the King at dinner;[2] among others, the Interpreter, a comely Englishman, in the Envoy's own clothes; which the Envoy, it seems in vanity, did send to show his fine clothes upon this man's back, which is one it seems of a comelier presence then himself.   And yet it is said that none of their clothes are their own, but taken out of the King's own Wardrobe; and which they dare not bring back dirty or spotted, but clean, or are in danger*ᵇ* of being beaten as they say – insomuch that Sir Ch. Cotterell[3] says, when they are to have an Audience, they never venture to put on their clothes till he appears to come to fetch them, and as soon as ever they come home, put them off again.

To Sir G. Carterets to dinner, where Mr. Cofferer Ashburnham – who told a good story of a prisoner's being condemned at Salsbury for a small matter; while he was on the bench with his father⟨-in-law⟩, Judge Richardson, and while they were considering to transport him to save his life, the fellow flung a great stone at the Judge,*ᶜ* that missed him but broke through the wainscoat.   Upon this, he had his hand cut off and was hanged

---

a repl. same symbol badly formed   *b* MS. 'endanger'
   c 'the Judge' repl. two illegible smudged symbols

---

1. Since 7 August, the Dutch war having ended, the King and Queen had dined in public three times a week in the Queen's presence chamber, 'with the usual solemnities and the band of violins': newsletter in HMC, *Le Fleming*, p. 52; Evelyn, 7 August. The tasting or 'assay' was meant to ensure that no food was poisoned: cf. above, ii. 85 & n. 1. Men of rank still occasionally had their drink tasted in this way; but it was usually only for royalty that the control was extended to food.

2. Two envoys (Mikhail Golovin and Fedka Akichov) had been sent to announce the peace recently made by the Tsar with Poland: I. Lubimenko, *Relations commerciales . . . de l'Angleterre avec la Russie*, pp. 243–4 & n.

3. Master of the Ceremonies; a friend of Sandwich.

presently.[1]   Here was a gentleman, one Sheres, one come lately from my Lord Sandwich with an express.[2]   But Lord, I was almost ashamed to see him, lest he should know that I have not yet wrote one letter to my Lord since his going.   I had no discourse with him.   But after dinner, Sir G. Carteret and I to talk about some business of his; and so I to Mrs. Martin, where was Mrs. Burroughs; and also fine Mrs. Noble, my partener in the christening of Martin's child, did come to see it; and there we sat and talked an hour, and then all broke up; and I by coach home and there find Mr. Pelling and How and we to sing, and good music till late and then to supper, and How lay at my house; and so after supper, to bed with much content; only, my mind a little troubled at my late breach of vows;[3] which however I will pay my forfeits, though the badness of my eyes making me unfit to read or write long is my excuse, and doth put me upon other pleasures and imployment which I should refrain from in observation of my vows.

9.   Up and to the office, where all the morning; and at noon comes Creed to dine with me.   After dinner, he and I and my wife to the Bear-garden to see a prize fought there; but coming too soon, I left them there and went on by water to White-hall and there did some business with the Lords of the Treasury; and here do hear by Tom. Killigrew and Mr. Progers[4] that for

---

1. The incident occurred at the summer assizes of 1631. Cf. the MS. note by Chief Justice Treby in his copy of Sir James Dwyer's *Reports* (qu. E. Foss, *Judges of Engl.*, vi. 361; perhaps of doubtful authenticity): 'The prisoner ject un Brickbat a le dit Justice, que narrowly mist. Et pur ceo immediately fuit Indictment drawn pur Noy envers le Prisoner, et son dexter manus ampute et fixe al Gibbet, sur que luy mesme immediatement hange in presence de Court.' (For punishments of contempt, see Sir W. Holdsworth, *Hist. Engl. law*, iii. 319+.) The judge happened to be leaning on his elbow – 'If I had been an upright Judge', he is reported to have said, 'I had been slain': W. J. Thomas, *Anecdotes and traditions* (1839), p. 53. He was Sir Thomas Richardson (d. 1635), Chief Justice of Common Pleas, 1626-31, and of King's Bench, 1631-5. He had married (as his second wife) Ashburnham's mother.

2. Henry Sheeres, mathematician and engineer; now in Sandwich's service in Spain; later a friend of Pepys.

3. In going to the theatre on 4 and 5 September. For his vow, see above, p. 399. (A).

4. Killigrew (manager of the Theatre Royal) and Edward Progers were both grooms of the King's Bedchamber.

certain news is come of Harman's having spoilt 19*ᵃ* of 22 French ships, somewhere about the Berbados I think they said; but wherever it is, it is a good service and very welcome.¹ Here I fell in talk with T. Killigrew about music, and he tells me that he will bring me to the best music in England (of which endeed he is master), and that is two Italians and Mrs. Yates,² who he says is come to sing the Italian manner as well as ever he heard any. Says that Knepp won't take pains enough, but that she understands her part so well upon the stage that no man nor woman in the House doth the like.   Thence I by water to the Bear-garden, where now the yard was full of people, and those most of them seamen, striving by force to get in, that I was afeared to be seen among them; but got into the alehouse and so a' back-way was put into the Bull-house, where I stood a good while all alone among the bulls, and was afeared I was among the bears, too; but by and by the door opened and I got into the common pit; and there, with my cloak about my face, I stood and saw the prize fought, till one of them, a shoemaker, was so cut in both his wrists that he could not fight any longer, and then they broke off – his enemy was a butcher.   The sport very good, and various humours to be seen among the rabble that is there.   Thence carried Creed to White-hall, and there my wife and I took coach and home, and both of us to Sir W. Batten's to invite them to dinner on Wednesday next, having a whole buck come from Hampton Court by the warrant which Sir St. Fox did give me. And so home to supper and to bed – after a little playing on the Flagelette with my wife, who doth out-do thereon whatever I expected of her.

10.   Up, and all the morning at the office, where little to do but bemoan ourselfs under the want of money – and endeed,

---

a repl. '2'-

---

1. Sir John Harman's victory took place off Martinique at the end of June. He had sailed up and down the coast trying to tempt the French commanders into action; then destroyed the enemy ships piecemeal at their moorings.   British power in the Caribbean was restored. See the reports from Plymouth and Lyme, 7 September, in *CSPD 1667*, pp. 447–8.
2. Of the Theatre Royal. (A).

little is or can be done for want of money, we having not now received one penny for any service in many weeks, and none in view to receive, saving for paying of some seamen's wages. At [noon] sent to by my Lord Brouncker to speak with him, and it was to dine with him and his Lady Williams (which I have not now done in many months at their own table) and Mr. Wren, who is come to dine with them, the first time he hath been at the office since his being the Duke of York's Secretary. Here we sat and eat and talked, and of some matters of the office, but his discourse is yet but weak in that matter; and no wonder, he being new in it; but I fear he will not go about understanding with the impatience that Sir W. Coventry did. Having dined, I away and with my wife and Mercer; set my wife down at the Change and the other at White Hall, and I to St. James's, where we all met and did our usual weekly business with the Duke of York. But Lord, methinks both he and we are mighty flat and dull over what we used to be when W. Coventry was*a* among us. Thence I into St. James's park and there met Mr. Povy; and he and I to walk an hour or more in the Pell Mell, talking of the times. He tells me, among other things, that this business of the Chancellor doth breed a kind of inward*b* distance between the King and the Duke of York, and that it cannot be avoided – for though the latter did at first move it through his folly, yet he is made to see that he is wounded by it, and is become much a less man then he was, and so will be. But he tells me that they are, and have always been, great dissemblers one towards another; and that their parting heretofore in France is never to be thoroughly reconciled between them.[1] He tells me that he believes there is no such thing like to be as a composition with my Lady Castlemayne, and that she shall be got out of the

a repl. 'with' *b* repl. 'inw'-

---

1. They had quarrelled (in 1656) in the Spanish Netherlands, not in France. Charles had forced James to leave the French army against his will, and James against the King's wishes had insisted on having Sir John Berkeley accompany him to Bruges. James had taken himself off to Holland for a few months until tempers cooled. See his account in *Life* (ed. J. S. Clarke), i. 275+.

way before the Parliament comes.   For he says she is as high as ever she was, though he believes the King is as weary of her as is possible, and would give anything to remove her; but he is so weak in his passion that he dare not do it.   That he doth believe that my Lord Chancellor will be doing some acts in the Parliament*a* which shall render him popular; and that there are many people now do speak kindly of him that did not before; but that if he doth do this, it must provoke the King and the party that removed him.   He seems to doubt what the King of France will do in case an accommodation shall be made between Spain and him for Flanders, for then he will have nothing more easy to do with his army then to subdue us.   Parted with him at White-hall, and there I took coach and took up my wife and Mercer and so home; and I to the office, where ended my letters, and then to my chamber with my boy*b* to lay up some papers and things that lay out of order against tomorrow, to make it clean against*c* the feast that I am to have.   Here Mr. Pelling came to sit with us, and talked of Musique and the musicians of the town; and so to bed after supper.

11.   Up, and with Mr. Gawden to the Exchequer.   By the way he tells me this day he is to be answered whether he must hold Sheriffe or no – for he would not hold unless he may keep it at his office, which is out of the City (and so my Lord Mayor must come with his sword down whenever he comes thither), which he doth because he cannot get a house fit for him in the City, or else he will fine for it.[1]   Among others that they have in nomination for Sheriffe, one is little Chaplin, who was his servant and a very young man to undergo that place,[2] but as the City is now, there is no great honour nor joy to be had in being a public officer.   At the Exchequer I looked after my business;

a   repl. symbol rendered illegible
b   repl. 'wife'   *c*   repl. 'for'

---

1. I.e. pay a fine and so avoid the burden of office.   Denis Gauden had been chosen Alderman for Dowgate Ward on or before 18 July 1667; he did in fact serve as Sheriff in 1667–8.

His office in Smithfield (that of the Navy Victualler) was in Middlesex.

2. Francis Chaplin, Sheriff in 1668–9, cannot have been much older than Pepys himself.

and when done, went home to the Change and there bought a[a] case of knifes for dinner and a dish of fruit of 5s and bespoke other things, and then home; and here I find all things in good order, and a good dinner towards. Anon comes Sir W. Batten and his Lady, and Mr. Griffith their Ward, and Sir W. Penn and his Lady, and Mrs. Louther (who is grown, either through pride or want of manners, a fool, having not a word to say almost all dinner; and as a further mark of a beggarly proud fool, hath a bracelet of diamonds and rubies about her wrist and a sixpenny necklace about her neck and not one good rag of clothes upon her back); and Sir Jo Chichly in their company – and Mrs. Turner. Here I had an extraordinary good and handsome dinner for them, better then any of them deserve or understand (saving Sir Jo. Chichly and Mrs. Turner); and not much mirth, only what I by discourse made, and that against my genius. After dinner I took occasion to break up the company – as soon as I could, and all parted. Sir W. Batten and I by water to White-hall, there to speak with the Commissioners of the Treasury, who are mighty earnest for[b] our hastening all that may be the paying-off of the seamen now there is money,[1] and are considering many other things for easing of charge; which I am glad of, but vexed to see that J. Duncomb should be so pressing in it, as if none of us had like care with him. Having done there, I by coach to the Duke of York's playhouse and there saw part of *The Ungratefull Lovers*;[2] and sat by Beck Marshall,[3] who is very handsome near-hand. Here I met Mrs. Turner and my wife as we agreed, and together home; and there my wife and I part[c] of the night at the Flagilette, which she plays now anything upon almost, at first sight and in good time. But here came Mr.[d] Moore and sat and discoursed with me of public matters; the

a	repl. 'some'	*b*	repl. 'to pay'
c	repl. 'and in the evening'	*d*	repl. 'Mr.'

---

1. The Treasury minute runs: 'The principal officers of the Navy called in (and inform my Lords) that about 12,000*l* or 14,000*l* per week will serve to pay off the seamen' (*CTB*, ii. 81).

2. No play with this title has been found; Pepys may be referring to Davenant's tragedy, *The unfortunate lovers*, q.v. above, v. 77 & n. 2. (A).

3. Rebecca Marshall, the younger of two sisters who acted at the other London playhouse, the Theatre Royal. (A).

sum of which is that he doth doubt that there is more at the bottom then the removal of the Chancellor; that is, he doth verily believe that the King doth resolve to declare the Duke of Monmouth legitimate[1] – and that we shall soon see it. This I do not think the Duke of York will endure without blows; but his poverty,[2] and being lessened by having the Chancellor fallen and W. Coventry gone from him, will disable him from*a* being able to do anything almost, he being himself almost lost in the esteem of people; and will be more and more, unless my Lord Chancellor (who is already begun to be pitied by some people, and to be better thought of then was expected) doth recover himself in Parliament. He would seem to fear that this difference*b* about the Crowne (if there be nothing else) will undo us. He doth say that*c* it is very true, that my Lord did lately make some stop of some grants of 2000*l* a year to my Lord Grandison, which was only in his name for the use of my Lady Castlemayn's children; and that this did incense her, and she did speak very scornful words and sent a scornful message to him about it.[3] He gone after supper, I to bed – being mightily pleased with my wife's playing so well upon the flagelette, and I am resolved she shall learn to play upon some instrument – for though her eare be bad, yet I see she will*d* attain anything to be done by her hand.

12. Up and at the office all the morning till almost noon; and then I rose from the office (which I have not done five times I think since I come thither) and to the Exchequer*e* for some

a repl. 'all'   *b* repl. 'differ'-   *c* 'that' repeated
        d repl. 'of'   *e* repl. 'checking'

---

1. This rumour was recurrent since the Queen was childless and the Duke of York (the heir presumptive) unpopular. Cf. above, iii. 238, n. 4. Soon there was a strong rumour that the King would get a divorce: below, pp. 438, 518.

2. Cf. above, pp. 286–7.

3. Clarendon, by his own account, did all he could to reduce Lady Castlemaine's influence: *Life*, iii. 267. In May of this year Grandison (with Baptist May) had been granted

£1000 p.a. out of Post Office revenues for 99 years. He was Lady Castlemaine's uncle, and several times acted as her man of straw in this way. PRO, Docquets Bk, vol. xvi (Ind. 6815), p. 102; *CTB*, ii. 264, 277. Bridgeman, Clarendon's successor, also made difficulties on the same score: *DNB*. So too (in the matter of Irish patronage) did Ormond: T. Carte, *Ormonde* (1736), ii. 276.

tallies for Tanger; and that being done, to the Dog tavern and there I spent half a piece upon the clerks and so away; and I to Mrs. Martin's, but she not at home, but stayed and drunk with her sister and landlady; and by that time it was time to go to a play, which I did to the Duke of York's House, where *Tu quoque*[1] was the first time acted, with some alterations of Sir W Davenant's; but the play is a very silly play methinks, for I and others that sat by me, Mr. Povy and Mr. Progers, were weary of it; but it will please the citizens. My wife also was there, I having sent for her to meet me there, and W Hewers. After the play, we home; and there I to the office and despatched my business, and then home and mightily pleased with my wife's playing on the Flagilette, she taking out any tune almost at first sight and keeping time to it – which pleases me mightily. So to supper and to bed.

13. Called up by people come to deliver in ten chaldron of coals, brought in one of our prizes from Newcastle; the rest we intend to sell, we having above ten chaldron between us. They sell at about 28 or 29s per chaldron; but Sir W. Batten hath sworn that he was a cuckold that sells under 30s, and that makes us lay up all but what we have for our own spending; which is very pleasant, for I believe we shall be glad to sell them for less.[2] To the office and there despatched business till 10*ᵃ* a-clock, and then with Sir W. Batten and my wife and Mrs. Turner to Walthamstow by hackney-coach to Mrs. Shipman's to dinner, where Sir W. Penn and my Lady and Mrs. Lowther (the latter of which hath got a sore nose, given her I believe from her husband,[3] which made me I could not look upon her with any pleasure); and here a very good and plentiful wholesome dinner and above all thing, such plenty of milke-meats (she keeping a great dairy) and so good as I never met with. Afternoon proved

a repl. '10'

---

1. A comedy by John Cooke, first acted about 1611 and published in 1614 with the title, *Greene's tu quoque, or The city gallant*, because of the popularity of Thomas Greene in the role of Bubble. (A).

2. For the movements in the price of coal, see above, p. 296 & n. 1.

3. Cf. above, p. 423.

very foul weather, the morning fair. We stayed talking till evening, and*ᵃ* then home and there to my flagelette with my wife; and so to bed*ᵇ* without any supper, my belly being full and dinner not digested. It vexed me to hear how Sir W. Penn, who came alone from London, being to send his coachman for his wife and daughter and bidding his coachman in much anger to go for them (he being vexed, like a rogue, to do anything to please his wife), his coachman Tom*ᶜ* was heard to say, "A pox of God rot her! Can she [not] walk hither?" These words do so mad me, that I could find in my heart to give him or my Lady notice of them.

14. Up and to the office, where all the morning busy. At noon comes Mr. Pierce and dined with me, to advise about several matters of his relating to the office and his purse;[1] and here he told me that the King and Duke of York and the whole Court is mighty joyful at the*ᵈ* Duchesse of York's being brought to bed this day or yesterday of a son[2] – which will settle men's minds mightily; and he tells me that he doth think that what the King doth, of giving the Duke of Monmouth the command of his Guards and giving my Lord Gerald 12000*l* for it, is merely to find an imployment for him upon which he may live, and not out of any design to bring him into any title to the Crowne[3] – which Mr. Moore did the other day put me into great fear of. After dinner, he gone, my wife and I to the King's playhouse to see *The Northerne Lasse*,[4] which I think I never did

a   repl. 'them'   b   repl. 'su'-
c   l.h. repl. s.h. 'who'   d   repl. 'the news which'

---

1. James Pearse was Surgeon-General to the fleet, as well as surgeon to the Duke of York.

2. Edgar, Duke of Cambridge, born on the 14th just before 7 a.m. – 'the least and leanest childe the Dutchesse ever had, but its very lively': Sir J. Nicholas to Sir E. Nicholas, 17 September (BM, Egerton 2539, f. 112). He died in 1671. Of the eight children of this marriage only two, Mary and Anne, survived infancy.

3. Monmouth succeeded Gerard in command of the 1st Life Guards only, in fact, a year later. He then paid him £8000 for it and gave him a preferential bargain of a house and land at Chiswick: below, 16 September 1668 & n.; *CSPD 1667–8*, pp. 553, 560.

4. Richard Brome's comedy, first acted in 1629 and published in 1632. (A).

see before. Knipp acted it and did her part very extraordinary well, but the play is but a mean sorry play; but the House very full of gallants; it seems it hath not been acted a good while. Thence to the Exchange for something for my wife, and then home and to the office; and then home to our flagelette, and so to bed – being mightily troubled in mi[nd] at the liberty I give myself of going to plays,*a* 1 upon pretence of the weakness of my eyes that cannot continue so long together at work at my office; but I must remedy it.

15. *Lords day.* Up to my chamber, there to set some papers to rights. By and by to church, where I stood in continual fear of Mrs. Markham's coming to church and offering to come into our pew;2 to prevent which, as soon as ever I heard the great door open, I did step back and clapped my breech to our pew-door, that she might be forced to shove me to come in; but as God would have it, she did not come. Mr. Mills preached; and after sermon, by invitation he and his wife came to dine with me (which is the first time they have been in my house I think these five years), I*b* thinking it not amiss, because of their acquaintance in our country,3 to show them some respect. Mr. Turner and his wife and their son the Captain dined with me, and I had a very good dinner for them – and very merry; and after dinner he was forced to go, though it rained, to Stepny to preach. We also to church, and then home, and there comes Mr. Pelling with two men by promise, one Wallington and Piggott;4 the former whereof, being a very little fellow, did sing a most excellent bass, and yet a poor fellow, a working goldsmith, that goes without gloves to his hands. Here we sung several good things,

a repl. 'pl'-   *b* repl. 'b'-

---

1. Cf. above, p. 429 & n. 3. (A).
2. Cf. above, p. 322.
3. Milles owned property near to Brampton, Hunts., and his wife was the daughter of a neighbour of Pepys's uncle, Robert Pepys of Brampton: *Occ. Papers Pepys Club,* ii. 97; above, ii. 28.
4. In Playford's *Catch that catch*

can, or The musical companion (1667) there is mention of 'the late Musick Society *and* Meeting, *in the* Old-Jury, London', which included John Pelling, citizen, Benjamin Wallington, citizen, George Piggot, gentleman, and Francis Piggot, citizen. Wallington and Francis Piggot are known to have composed songs. (E).

but I am more and more confirmed that singing with many voices is not singing, but a sort*a* of Instrumentall music, the sense of the words being lost by not being heard, and especially as they set them with Fuges of words, one after another; whereas singing*b* properly, I think, should be but with one or two voices at most, and that counterpoint. They supped with me; and so broke up, and then my wife and I to my chamber, where through*c* the badness of my eyes she was forced to read to me, which she doth very well; and was Mr. Boyle's discourse upon the Style of the Scripture,[1] which is a very fine piece. And so to bed.

16. Up, and several came to me, among others Mr. Yeabsly of Plymouth, to discourse about their matters touching Tanger, and by and by Sir H. Cholmly, who was with me a good while; who tells me that the Duke of York's child is christened, the Duke of Albemarle and the Marquis of Worcester godfathers and my Lady Suffolke godmother, and they have named it Edgar, which is a brave name.[2] But it seems they are more joyful in*d* the Chancellor's family at the birth*e* of this Prince then in wisdom they should, for fear it should give the King cause of jealousy. Sir H. Cholmly doth*f* not seem to think there is any such thing can be in the King's intention as that of raising the Duke of Monmouth to the Crown, though he thinks there may possibly [be] some persons that would, and others that would be glad to have the Queen removed to some monastery or somewhere or other, to make room for a new wife, for they will all be unsafe under the Duke of York.[3] He says the King and Parliament will agree; that is, that the King will do anything that they will

---

a repl. 'bad'   *b* repl. symbol rendered illegible   *c* repl. 'for'
    d MS. 'and'   *e* repl. 'death'   *f* repl. 'doth s'-

---

1. Robert Boyle, *Some considerations touching the style of the Holy Scriptures*, first published 1661; PL 832 (1663 ed.).
2. The christening was on the 15th. The Marquess of Worcester, writing to his wife on 17 September, explained that the Duke of York 'fancied' Edgar as a name 'because he

was the first King that had the dominion of the seas, which hee went upon about the Kingdom every year with a thousand ships': HMC, *Beaufort*, p. 64. On the growing vogue for the name, see above, vi. 81, n. 1.
3. Cf. above, p. 434 & n. 1.

have him. We together to the Exchequer about our Tanger orders, and so parted at the New Exchange, where I stayed reading Mrs. Phillips's poems[1] till my wife and Mercer called me to Mrs. Pierce's by invitation to dinner; where I find her painted (which makes me loathe her)[2] and the nastiest poor dinner, that made me sick. Only, here I met with a fourth *Advice to the painter*,[3] upon the coming in of the Dutch to the River and end of the war, that made my heart ake to read, it being too sharp and so true. Here I also saw a printed account of the examinations taking touching the burning of the City of London, showing the plots of the papists therein; which it seems hath[a] been ordered and hath been burnt[b] by the hands of the hangman in Westminster Palace – I will try to get one of them.[4] After dinner she showed us her closet, which is pretty with her James's picture, done by Hales but with a mighty bad hand, which is his[c] great fault, that he doth do negligently, and the drapery also not very good.[5] Being tired of being here, and sick of their damned sluttish dinner, my wife and Mercer and I away to the King's playhouse

---

a repl. 'is'   *b* repl. 'ordered'   *c* repl. 'is'

---

1. Probably at Henry Herringman's; he had just published this first collected edition of Katherine Philips's *Poems*: above, p. 380, n. 1.

2. Pepys disliked cosmetic paint: cf. e.g. below, p. 454. Mrs Pearse was described in 1678 as having a complexion 'florid and pure red without paint': J. Yonge, *Journal* (ed. Poynter), p. 156.

3. *Directions to a painter for describing our naval business . . . by an unknown author* (1667); usually attributed to Marvell; a sequel to the *Second and third advices to a painter*. Cf. above, vii. 407 & n. 4.

4. The book was *London's Flames, or The discovery of such evidence as were deposed before the Committee of Parliament etc., with the insolences of the Popish party* (1667; not in the PL) – an unauthorised version of the evidence taken by the Commons'

committee which had reported (January 1667) that the Fire had been planned by the French Catholics, the Jesuits and the Duke of York. Several impressions appeared, maliciously put out by critics of the government who suspected that the King had prorogued parliament in February in order to suppress the evidence. For the government's measures against the book, see *CSPD Add. 1660–85*, pp. 205–6; ib., *1667*, pp. 290, 393, 401. (There appears to be no trace of any order to burn it.) Cf. another version: *A true and faithfull account of the several informations* etc. (1667); repr. in F. Grose and T. Astle, *Antiq. Repert.*, ii (1808), pp. 123+ ; *State Trials* (ed. Howell), vi. 807+ . See Bell, *Fire*, pp. 200–3.

5. This portrait is not known to survive. (OM).

to see *The Scornfull Lady*; but it being now 3 a–clock,[1] there was not one soul in the pit; whereupon, for shame we would not go in, but against our wills went all to see *Tu quoque*[2] again, where there is pretty store of company; and going with a prejudice, the play appeared better to us. Here we saw Madam Morland, who is grown mighty fat but is ⟨very⟩ comely. But one of the best parts of our sport was a mighty pretty lady that sat behind us, that did laugh so heartily and constantly that it did me good to hear her. Thence to the King's House, upon a wager of mine with my wife that there would be no acting there today, there being no company: so I went in[3] and found a pretty good company there, and saw their dance at the end of the play; and so to the coach again and to the Cock ale–house and there drank in our coach; and so home and I to the office; and then home and my wife read to me as last night, and so to bed – vexed with our dinner today, and myself more with being convinced that Mrs. Pierce paints, so that henceforth to be sure I shall loathe her.

17.   Up and at the office all the morning – where Mr. Wren came to us and sat with us, only to learn; and doth entend to come once or twice a week and sit with us. In the afternoon I walked to the Old Swan, the way mighty dirty; and there called at Michell's and there had opportunity para kiss su moher, but ella did receive it with a great deal of seeming regret, which did vex*a* me. But however, I do not doubt overcoming her as I did the moher of the menusier at Deptford.*a* So thence by water to Westminster to Burges, and there did receive my orders for 15000*l* more for Tanger.[4] Thence to the Hall and there talked a little with Mrs. Michell, and so to Mrs. Martin's to pay for my cuffs and drink with her, and did hazer la cosa with her. And by and by, away by coach and met with Sir H Cholmly, and with him to the Temple and there in Playfords shop did give

---

a–a   garbled s.h.: see above, p. 244, note *a*

1. Performances at public theatres usually began at 3.30 p.m. The play was a comedy by Beaumont and Fletcher; see above, i. 303 & n. 3. (A).
2. See above, p. 435 & n. 1. (A).
3. At this time theatregoers claimed the privilege of seeing the fourth or fifth act of a play without payment, despite a prohibition issued by the Lord Chamberlain's office on 7 December 1663. (A).
4. *CTB*, ii. 183 (5 September).

him some of my Exchequer orders and took his receipts; and so parted and home and there to my business hard at the office; and then home, my wife being at Mrs. Turner's, who and her husband came home with her and here stayed and talked, and stayed late and then went away, and we to bed.

But that which vexed me much this evening is that Captain Cocke and Sir W. Batten did come to me and sat and drank a bottle of wine, and told me how Sir W. Pen hath got an order for the *Flying greyhound*[1] for himself – which is so false a thing and the part of a knave as nothing almost can be more. This vexed me, but I resolve to bring it before the Duke and try a pull for it.

18. Up betimes and to Captain Cocke in his coach, which he sent for me; and he not being ready, I walked in the Exchange,[2] which is now made pretty by having windows and doors before all their shops, to keep out the cold. By and by to him; and he being ready, he and I out in his coach to my Lord Chancellors; there to Mr. Wren's chamber – who did tell us the whole of Sir W Pen's having the order for this ship of ours; and we went with him to St. James's and there I did see the copy of it, which is built upon a Suggestion of his, having given the King a ship of his, the *Prosperous*;[3] wherein is such a cheat as I have the best advantage in the world over him, and will make him do reason or lay him on his back. This I was very glad of; and having done as far as I could in it, we returned, and I home and there at the office all the morning; and at noon with my Lord Brouncker to the Treasurer's office to look over the clerks, who are there making up the books, but in such a manner as it is a shame to see. Then home to dinner; and after dinner, my mind mighty full of this business of Sir W Pen's, to the office and there busy all the afternoon. This evening Sir W. Batten and W. Penn and I met at W. Batten's house, and there I took an opportunity to break the business, at which W. Penn is much disturbed and

1. The privateer Penn had shared with Pepys, Batten and Ford. The order has not been traced.
2. Now temporarily housed in Gresham College.

3. Possibly the horseboat of that name (built at Chatham in 1665), burnt by the Dutch in the raid on Medway this year.

would excuse it the most he can; but doth it so basely, that though he do offer to let go his pretence to her, and resign up his order for her and come in only to ask his share of her (which doth very well please me, and gives me present satisfaction), yet I shall remember him for a knave while I live. But thus my mind is quieted for the present, more then I thought I should be, and am glad that I shall have no need of bidding him open defiance, which I would otherwise have done and made a perpetual war between us. So to the office, and there busy pretty late; and so home and to supper with my wife, and so to bed.

19. Up, and all the morning at the office. At noon home to dinner, W. Hewer and I and my wife, when comes my Cosen Kate Joyce and an aunt*a* of ours, Lettice, formerly Hanes and now Howlett,[1] come to town to see her friends, and also Sarah Kite, with her little boy in her armes, a very pretty little boy. The child I like very well, and could wish it my own. My wife, being all unready, did not appear. I made as much of them as I could such ordinary company; and yet my heart was glad to see them, though their condition was a little below my present state to be familiar with. She tells me how the Lifeguard, which we thought a little while since was sent down into the country about some insurrection, was sent to Winchcombe to spoil the Tobacco there, which it seems the people there do plant contrary to law and have always done, and still been under force and danger of having it spoiled; as it hath been oftentimes, and yet they will continue to plant it.[2] The place, she says, is a miserable poor place.

---

a l.h. repl. l.h. 'ant'

1. She was a sister of Pepys's mother.

2. Winchcombe, Glos., was the most important centre in England of tobacco cultivation. The government's prohibition, designed to protect the valuable Virginia trade, had begun with a proclamation of 1619; many similar orders had been issued since, including statutes in 1660 and 1663, but to no effect. The use of troops had begun under the Interregnum, and on this occasion six-score

horse of the Guards had been sent on 14 August (the local J.P.'s being unable or unwilling to act): HMC, *Le Fleming*, p. 52. Cf. *CSPD 1661–2*, p. 602; Tanner 47, f. 119*v*. There is evidence of English-grown tobacco being sold in Virginia in 1621. Large-scale cultivation ended towards the close of the century. W. J. Hardy in *Archaeologia*, 51 (pt i)/157+; E. Lipson, *Econ. hist. Engl.* (1934 ed.), iii. 169–71; W. B. Willcox, *Gloucestershire 1590–1640*, pp. 158–62.

They gone, I to the office, where all the afternoon very busy; and at night, when my Eyes were weary*ᵃ* of the light, I and my wife to walk in the garden, and then home to supper and pipe* and then to bed.

20. At the office doing business all the morning. At noon expected Creed to have come to dine with me and brought Mr. Sheeres (the gentleman lately come from my Lord Sandwich) with him; but they came not, so there was a good dinner lost. After dinner, my wife and Jane about some business of hers abroad; and then I to the office, where having done my business, I out to pay some debts; among others, to the Taverne at the end of Billiter-lane, where my design was to see the pretty mistress of the house, which I did; and endeed is, as I always thought, one of the modest, prettiest, plain women that ever I saw. Thence was met in the street by Sir W. Penn, and he and I by coach to the King's playhouse and there saw *The Madd Couple*,[1] which I do not remember that I have seen; it is a pretty pleasant play. Thence home, and my wife and I to walk in the garden, she having been at the same play with Jane, in the 18*d* seat,[2] to show Jane the play; and so I home to supper and to bed.

21. All the morning at the office. Dined at home and expected Sheres again; but he did not come, so another dinner lost by the folly of Creed. After having done some business at the office, I out with my wife to Sheres's lodging and left an invitation for him to dine with me tomorrow; and so back and took up my wife at the Exchange and there kissed Mrs. Smith's[3] pretty hand; and so with my wife by coach as far to take some ayre (but the way very dirty) as far as Bow; and so drinking (as usual) at Mile end of Bydes ale,[4] we home and there busy at my letter till late; and so to walk by moonshine*ᵇ* with my wife, and

a repl. 'very'   *b* repl. 'moonm'-

1. *All Mistaken, or The mad couple*, a comedy by James Howard, published in 1672. This is the first record of a performance. (A).

2. In the middle gallery. (A).
3. A sempstress.
4. See above, p. 389, n. 2.

so to bed.   The King, Duke of York, and the men of the Court have been these four or five days a-hunting at Bagshott.[1]

22.   *Lords day*.   At my chamber all the morning, making up some accounts to my great content.   At noon comes Mr. Sheres,[2] whom I find a good engenious man, but doth talk a little too much of his travels.   He left my Lord Sandwich well, but in pain to be at home for want of money, which comes very hardly. Most of the afternoon talking of Spain and informing him against his return how things are here.   And so spent most of the afternoon, and then he parted.   And then to my chamber busy, till my eyes were almost blind with writing and reading and I was fain to get the boy to come and write for me.   And then to supper, and Pelling come to me at supper and then to sing a Psalm with him; and so parted and to bed – after my wife had read something to me (to save my eyes) in a good book. This night I did even my accounts of the house, which I have (to my great[a] shame) omitted now above two months or more; and therefore am content to take my wife's and maids' accounts as they give them, being not able to correct them, which vexes me; but the fault being my own, contrary to my wife's frequent desires, I cannot find fault; but am resolved never to let them come to that pass again.   The truth is, I have indulged myself more to pleasure for these last two months then ever I did in my life before since I came to be a person concerned in business – and I doubt when I come to make up my accounts, I shall find it so by the expense.

23.   Up, and walked to the Exchange, there to get a coach; but failed, and so was forced to walk a most dirty walk to the Old Swan; and there took boat and so to the Exchequer[b] and there took coach to St. James's and did our usual business with the Duke of York.   Thence I walked over the park to White-hall and took water to Westminster; and there, among other things,

a '23' struck through in margin   *b* MS. 'Exchange'

1. They went on the 17th and returned on the 20th: BM, Egerton 2539, ff. 112*v*, 120*r*.

2. See above, p. 429, n. 2.

bought the examinations of the business about the fire of London, which is a book that Mrs. Pierce tells me hath been commanded to be burnt.[1] The examinations endeed are very plain. Thence to the Excise Office, and so to the Exchange and did a little business; and so home and took up my wife, and so carried her to the other end, where I light at my Lord Ashly's,[2] by invitation to dine there; which I did, and Sir H. Cholmly, Creed and Yeabsly, upon*a* occasion of the business of Yeabsly, who God knows doth bribe him very well for it;[3] and it is pretty to see how this great man doth condescend to these things and doth all he can in his examining of his business to favour him, and yet with great cunning, not to be discovered but by me that am privy to it. At table, it is worth remembering that my Lord tells us that the House of Lords is the last Appeale that a man can make upon a poynt of interpretation of the law – and that therein they are above the Judges; and that he did*b* assert this in the Lords' House upon the late occasion of the quarrel between my Lord Bristoll and Chancellor; when the former did accuse the latter of treason and the Judges did bring it in not to be treason, my Lord Ashly did declare that the judgment*c* of the Judges was nothing in the presence of their Lordships, but only as far as they were the properest men to bring precedents; but not to interpret the law to their Lordships, but only the inducements of their persuasions: and this the Lords did concur in.[4] Another pretty

a repl. 'up'-   *b* repl. 'd'-   *c* repl. 'vote'

---

1. See above, p. 439 & n. 4.
2. Exeter House, Strand.
3. See above, vii. 128, n. 3.
4. Bristol had brought articles of impeachment against Clarendon in July 1663 (cf. above, iv. 222–4 & nn.). The judges had unanimously declared them invalid and the peers had then accepted their opinion *nem. con.*: LJ, xi. 560. I have not found any other record than Pepys's of Ashley's speech. He was fond of pronouncing on the law of the constitution, and on this occasion had been anxious to have

Bristol succeed. Sir Matthew Hale (a better authority) took the same view as Ashley on the general issue of the status of the judges' advice in these matters. He pointed out that the peers normally (as in this case) did not differ from the judges; but that exceptions might occur in cases concerning the succession, parliamentary privilege, or the liberty of the subject. Hale, *Jurisdiction of the Lords House* (1790 ed.), pp. 59, 94–5, 158–9; cf. *Law Quart. Rev.*, 66/70–1.

thing was my Lady Ashly's speaking of the bad qualities of glass-coaches; among others, the flying open of the doors upon any great shake: but another was that my Lady Peterborough, being in her glass-coach with the glass up and seeing a lady pass by in a coach whom she would salute,*a* the glass was so clear that she thought it had been open, and so run her head through the glass and cut all her forehead.[1] After dinner, before we fell to the examination of Yeabsly's business, we were put into my Lord's room before he could come to us, and there had opportunity to look*b* over his state of his accounts of the prizes;[2] and there saw how bountiful the King hath been to several people, and hardly any man almost, commander of the Navy of any note, but hath had some reward or other out of it – and many sums to the privy-purse, but not so many, I see, as I thought there had been;[3] but we could*c* not look quite through it – but several Bedchamber-men and people about the Court had good sums – and among others, Sir John Minnes and Lord Brouncker have 200*l* apiece for looking to the East India prizes[4] while I did their work for them. By and by my Lord came, and we did look over Yeabsly's business a little and I find*d* how prettily this cunning Lord can be partial and dissemble it in this case, being privy to the bribe he is to receive.[5] This done, we away and I with Sir H. Cholmly to Westminster, who by the way told me how merry the King and Duke of York and Court were the other day when they were abroad a-hunting; they came to Sir G. Carteret's house at Cranborne and there were entertained and all made drunk; and that being all drunk, Armerer*e*[6] did come to the King and

---

a repl. 'salt'-   *b* repl. 'exam'-   *c* repl. 'did'   *d* repl. 'was'
e name inserted by Pepys later into blank space; cf. above, vol. i, p. cii & n. 28

---

1. The use of glass in coach windows was a recent innovation, and plate-glass as clear as this was unusual: E. W. Hulme in *The Antiquary*, 31 (1895)/134+; J. Parkes, *Travel in Engl. in 17th cent.*, pp. 64+.

2. Ashley was Treasurer of the Prize Office. For the accounts, see PRO, PRO 30/24/40/39; summary in K. H. D. Haley, *Shaftsbury*,

p. 175.

3. The amount paid to the privy purse was £7000 in all, out of a total of over £400,000.

4. See above, vi. 234 & n. 2.

5. See above, vii. 128, n. 3.

6. ? Sir William Armourer, Equerry of the Great Horse to the King.

swore to him, "By God, Sir," says he, "you are not so kind to the Duke of York of late as you used to be." "Not I", says the King, "why so?" "Why," says he, "if you are, let us drink his health;" "Why, let us," says the King.*a* Then he fell on his knees and drank it; and having done, the King begun to drink it. "Nay, Sir," says Armerer*b*, "by God, you must do it on your knees." So*c* he did, and then all the company; and having done it, all fell a-crying for joy, being all Maudlin and kissing one another, the King the Duke of York and the Duke of York the King, and in such*d* a maudlin pickle as never people were; and so passed that day. But Sir H. Cholmly tells me that the King hath this good luck: that the next day he hates to have anybody mention what he had done the day before, nor will suffer anybody to gain upon [him] that way – which is a good quality. Parted with Sir H. Cholmly at White-hall; and there I took coach and took up my wife at Unthankes, and so out for ayre, it being a mighty pleasant day, as far as Bow, and so drank by the way and home; and there to my chamber, till by and by comes Captain Cocke about business, who tells me that Mr. Brouncker is lost for ever,[1] notwithstanding that my Lord Brouncker hath advised with him (Cocke) how he might make a peace with the Duke of York and Chancellor, upon promise of serving him in the Parliament: but Cocke says that is base to offer,*e* and will have no success neither. He says that Mr. Wren hath refused a present of Tom Willson's for his place of Store-keeper of Chatham, and is resolved never to take anything;[2] which is both wise in him and good to the King's service. He stayed with me very late, here being Mrs. Turner and W. Batelier, drinking and laughing; and then to bed.

24. Up; and to the office, where all the morning very busy. At noon home, where there dined with me Anth. Joyce and his

---

a MS. 'thing'   *b* name inserted by Pepys later into blank space
c repl. 'So all'   *d* MS. 'some'   *e* MS. 'over'

1. See above, p. 406 & n. 2.
2. Wren had succeeded Coventry as secretary to the Duke of York earlier in the month, and was anxious to avoid the charge of selling places brought against his predecessor. Cocke was his close friend.

wife, and Will and his wife, and my aunt Lissett[1] that was here the other day, and Sarah Kite. And I had a good dinner for them, and were as merry as I could be in that company where W Joyce is, who is still the same impertinent fellow that ever he was. After dinner I away to St. James's, where we had an audience of the Duke of York of many things of weight; as the confirming an establishment of the numbers of men on ships in peace[2] and other things – about which we stayed till past candle-light, and so Sir W. Batten and W. Penn and I fain to go all in a hackney-coach round by London Wall for fear of cellars[3] – this being the first time that I have been forced to go that way this year, though now I shall begin to use it. We tired one coach upon Holborne-Conduit hill and got another, and made it a long journey home – where to the office; and then home and at my business till 12 at night, writing [in] shorthand the draft of a report to make to the King and Council tomorrow about the reason of not having the book of the Treasurer made up.[4] This I did finish tonight, to the spoiling of my eyes I fear. This done, then to bed.

This evening my wife*a* tells me that W. Batelier hath been here today and brought with him the pretty girl he speaks of, to come to serve my wife as a woman, out of the School at Bow.[5] My wife says she is extraordinary handsome and enclines to have her, and I am glad of it – at least, that if we must have one, she should be handsome. But I shall*b* leave it wholly to my wife to do what she will therein.

a repl. same symbol   *b* MS. 'am'

---

1. See above, p. 442 & n. 1.
2. The establishment in its final form (27 September) covered both peacetime and wartime: PRO, SP 29/146/218, no. 9; *CSPD 1667*, p. 486.
3. After the Fire, all that remained of many buildings was their cellars, now dangerously close to the traffic.
4. The draft has not been traced. The Board had been directed on 19 August to prepare a final statement of the accounts of Carteret, the late Treasurer. On 23 September they had been asked to hasten it, and to prepare 'distinct accounts' for the war. On receiving their excuses on the 25th, the Council ordered the employment of extra clerks and accountants. *CSPD 1667*, p. 470; PRO, PC 2/59, ff. 302r, 304r. Carteret did not finish his accounts until August 1668: HMC, *Rep.*, 8/1/130.
5. See below, p. 451 & n. 2.

25. Up as soon as I could see, and to the office to write over fair with Mr. Hater my last night's work, which I did by 9 a-clock and got it signed; and so with Sir H. Cholmly (who came to me about his business) to White-hall, and thither came also my Lord Brouncker; and we by and by called in and our paper read, and much discourse thereon by Sir G. Carteret, my Lord Anglesy, Sir W. Coventry, and my Lord Ashly, and myself, but I could easily discern that they none of them understood the business; and the King at last ended it with saying lazily, "Why," says he, "after all this discourse, I now come to understand it; and that is, that there can nothing be done in this more then is possible" (which was so silly as I never heard), "and therefore," says he, "I would have these gentlemen to do as much as is possible to hasten the Treasurer's accounts; and that is all." And so we broke up; and I confess I went away ashamed to see how slightly things are advised upon there.   Here I saw the Duke of Buckingham sit in Council again, where he was re-admitted it seems the last Council-day;[1] and it is wonderful to see how this man is come again to his places, all of them, after the reproach and disgrace done him – so that things are done in a most foolish manner quite through.   The Duke of Buckingham did second Sir W. Coventry in the advising the King that he would not concern himself[a] in the owning or not owning any man's accounts, or anything else wherein he had not the same satisfaction that there would satisfy the Parliament, saying that nothing would displease the Parliament more then to find him defending anything that is not right, and justifiable to the utmost degree.   But methought he spoke it but very poorly.   After this I walked up and down the Gallery till noon; and here I met with Bishop Fuller, who to my great joy is made (which I did not hear before) Bishop of Lincolne.[2]

***

a repl. symbol rendered illegible

---

1. On 23 September, when he was restored to the Council and to his place in the Bedchamber: PRO, PC 2/59, f. 301r. For his disgrace, see above, p. 86 n. 3.

2. William Fuller (Bishop of Limer-ick) was an old acquaintance of Pepys. The *congé d'élire* for his appointment to Lincoln was issued on 4 September, and the election held on the 17th: *CSPD 1667*, p. 466.

At noon I took coach and to Sir G. Carteret's in Lincolnes Inn-
fields to the house that is my Lord's, which my Lord lets him
have,[1] and this is his first day of dining there; and there dined
with him and his Lady my Lord Privy Seale,[2] who is endeed a
very sober man; who, among other talk, did mightily wonder at
the reason of the growth of the Credit of Banquiers (since it is so
ordinary a thing for citizens to break, out of knavery); upon this
we had much discourse, and I observed therein, to the honour of
this City, that I have not heard of one citizen of London broke
in all this war – this plague – this fire, and this coming up of the
enemy among us[3] – which he owned to be very considerable.*
After dinner, I to the King's playhouse, my eyes being so bad
since last night's straining of them that I am hardly able to see;
besides the pain which I have in them. The play was a new
play; and infinitely full, the King and all the Court almost there.
It is *The Storme*,[4] a play of Fletchers – which is but so so methinks;
only, there is a most admirable dance at the end, of the ladies in a
Military manner,[5] which endeed did please me mightily. So it
being a mighty wet day and night, I with much ado got a coach,
and with 20 stops which he made I got him to carry me quite
through, and paid dear for it; and so home, and there comes my
wife home from the Duke of York's playhouse, where she hath
been with my aunt and Kate Joyce; and so to supper and betimes
to bed, to make amends for my last night's work and want of
sleep.

26. Up and to my chamber, whither Jonas Moore[6] comes;
and among other things, after our business done, discoursing of
matters of the office, I showed him my varnishd things; which he

1. The present nos 57 and 58, Lincoln's Inn Fields, leased by Sandwich.
(R).
2. Lord Robartes.
3. Cf. the similar observation
above: vii. 287 & n. 2. For the help
which the government found it
necessary to give to bankers in dis-
tress, see above, vi. 150 & n. 1.
4. I.e. *The sea voyage*, a comedy by
Fletcher and Massinger, acted in 1622

and published in 1647. This is the
first record of a post-Restoration performance. (A).
5. An addition to the play; none
is required by the original text. (A).
6. The mathematician and military
engineer, employed by the Ordnance
Office. He had written to Pepys on
the 24th about plank: *CSPD 1667*,
p. 468.

says he can outdoe much, and tells me the mighty use*a* of Napiers bones;[1] so that I will have a pair presently. To the office, where busy all the morning sitting; and at noon home to dinner, and then with my wife abroad to the King's playhouse to show her yesterday's new play, which I like as I did yesterday, the principal thing extraordinary being the dance, which is very good. So to Charing-cross by coach about my wife's business; and then home round by London Wall, it being very dark and dirty; and so to supper and, for the ease of my eyes, to bed, having first ended all my letters at the office.

27. Up and to the office, where very busy all the morning. While I was busy at the office, my wife sends for me to come to home,*b* and what was it but to see the pretty girl which she is taking to wait upon her; and though she seems not altogether*c* so great a beauty as she had before told me, yet endeed she is mighty*d* pretty; and so pretty, that I find I shall be too much pleased with it, and therefore could be contented as to my judgment, though not to my passion, that she might not come, lest I may be found too much*e* minding her, to the discontent of my wife.[2] She is to come next week. She seems by her discourse to be grave beyond her bigness and age, and exceeding well-bred as to her deportment, having been a scholar in a school at Bow these seven or eight year. To the office again, my [mind] running on this pretty girl; and there till noon, when Creed and Sheres come and dined with me; and we had a great deal of pretty discourse of the ceremoniousness of the Spaniards – whose*f* ceremonies are so many and so known, that he tells me, upon all occasions of joy or sorrow in a grandee's family, my Lord Embassador is fain to send one with an *en hora buena* (if it be upon a marriage or birth of a child) or a *pesa me*, if it be upon the

---

a repl. 'ut'-   *b* repl. same symbol badly formed   *c* repl. 'q'-
     d MS. 'my'   *e* repl. 'like'   *f* repl. 'which'

---

1. A calculating instrument made of rods, used for multiplication and division, so-called after its inventor, John Napier (d. 1617), the Scottish mathematician. Pepys's 'varnishd things' were papers marked out with arithmetical tables: see above, vii. 120, n. 1.

2. Pepys's forecast proved only too accurate. The girl was Deborah Willet. She was now just 17.

death of*ᵃ* a child or so.   And these ceremonies are so set, and the words of the compliment, that he hath been sent from my Lord when he hath done no more then send in word to the grandee that one was there from the Embassador; and he knowing what was his errand, that hath been enough, and he hath never spoken with him.   Nay, several grandees, having been to marry a daughter, have wrote letters to my Lord*ᵇ* to give him notice and out of the greatness of his wisdom to desire his*ᶜ* advice, though people he never saw; and then my Lord, he answers by commending the greatness of his discretion in making so good an alliance &c., and so ends.   He says that it is so far from dishonour to a man to give private revenge for an affront, that the contrary is a disgrace; they holding that he that receives an affront is not fit to appear in the sight of the world till he hath revenged himself; and therefore, that a gentleman there that receives an affront oftentimes*ᵈ* never appears again in the world till he hath by some private way or other revenged himself; and that on this account, several have fallowed their enemy privately to the Indys, thence to Italy, thence to France and back again, watching for an opportunity to be revenged.   He says my*ᵉ* Lord was fain to keep a letter from the Duke of York to the Queen of Spain a great while in his hands before he could think fit to deliver it, till he had learnt whether the Queen would receive it, it being directed to his "Cosen."[1]   He says that many ladies in Spain,*ᶠ* after they are found to be with child, do never stir out of their beds or chambers till they are brought to bed – so ceremonious they are in that point also.   He tells of their wooing by serenades at the window, and that their friends do alway make the match; but yet that they have opportunities to meet at Masse at church, and there they make love.   That the Court there hath no dancings, nor visits at night to see the King or Queene, but is alway just like a Cloyster, nobody stirring in it.[2]   That my Lord Sandwich

---

a 'of'repeated   *b* MS. 'letter'   *c* repl. symbol rendered illegible
       d repl. 'never appears'   *e* repl. 'he'   *f* repl. 'Spain'

---

1. This mode of address was normally reserved for the exclusive use of reigning sovereigns.

2. For an English account (1665) of Spain, see *Memoirs of Lady Fanshawe* (1829), esp. pp. 241+.

wears a beard* now, turned up in the Spanish manner.[1] But that which pleases me most endeed, is that the peace which he hath made with Spain is now printed here, and is acknowledged by all the merchants to be the best peace that ever England had with them; and it appears that the King thinks it so, for this is printed before the Ratification is gone over;[2] whereas that with France and Holland was not in a good while after, till Copys came over of it ⟨in English⟩ out of Holland and France, that it was a reproach not to have it printed here.[3] This I am mighty glad of; and is the first and only piece of good news, or thing fit to be owned, that this nation hath done several years.

After dinner, I to the office; and they gone and anon, comes Pelling, and he and I to Greys Inne-fields, thinking to have heard Mrs. Knight[4] sing at her lodgings by a friend's means of his; but we came too late, so must*a* try another time. So lost our labour, and I by coach home and there to my chamber and did a great deal of good business about my Tanger accounts; and so with pleasure discoursing with my wife of our Journy shortly to Brampton, and of this little girle, which endeed runs in my head

a MS. 'much'

---

1. This does not appear in any of the extant portraits of Sandwich.

2. The treaty (ratified by the Spaniards on 11/21 September) was published both in the original Latin and in English: *Tractatus pacis et amicitiæ inter coronas Magnæ Britanniæ et Hispaniæ conclusus Matriti., 13/23 die Maii, A.D. 1667*, and *Articles of peace, commerce and alliance etc.* See also J. Dumont, *Corps univ. diplom.* (1731), vii (pt i), pp. 27-33. It was the greatest achievement of Sandwich's embassy, and established the English trading interest in Spain for over a century. It was of particular advantage to the carrying trade and to the woollen and fishing industries, as well as providing for

the protection of English merchants in Spanish territory. See J. O. McLachlan, *Trade and peace with Old Spain, 1667-1750*, pp. 20-2; Harris, ii. 102+.

3. The peace had been concluded on 31 July and proclaimed in London on 24 August, but complaints were still being made in mid-October that copies in English were difficult to come by: *CSPD 1667*, pp. 414-15, 525-6.

4. Mary Knight; a pupil of Henry Lawes and probably the best-known English soprano of her day. Her vocal range was remarkable: see Evelyn, iii. 230, iv. 49 & nn. Pepys does not appear to have heard her during the diary period.

and pleases me mightily, though I dare not own it; and so to supper and to bed.

28. Up, having slept not so much tonight as I used to do, for my thoughts being so full of this pretty little girl that is coming to live with us, which pleases me mightily. All the morning at the office, busy upon an Order of Council, wherein they are mightily at a loss what to advise*a* about our discharging of seamen by ticket, there being no money to pay their wages before January.[1] Only there is money to pay them since*b* January provided by the Parliament, which will be a horrid disgrace to the King and Crown of England, that no man shall reckon himself safe but where the Parliament takes care; and this did move Mr. Wren at the table today to say that he did believe, if ever there be occasion more to raise money, it will become here as it is in Poland, that there is two Treasurer's, one for the King and the other for the Kingdom.[2] At noon dined at home and Mr. Hater with me, and Mr. Pierce the surgeon dropped in, who I feared did come to bespeak me to be godfather to his son;[3] which I am unwilling now to be, having ended my liking to his wife since I find she paints.[4]

After dinner comes Sir Fr. Hollis to me about business; and I with him by coach to the Temple, and there I light – all the way, he telling me romantic lies of himself and his family: how they have been Parliament-men for Grimsby, he and his forefathers, this 140 years – and his father is now; and himself at this day stands for [to] be*c* with his father, by the death of his fellow-burgess; and that he believes it will cost him as much as it did his predecessor, which was 300*l* in ale and 52*l* in buttered-ale –

---

a repl. 'do'　　*b* repl. 'since'　　*c* repl. 'the other'

---

1. The order (27 September) required the Navy Board to work out the method of payment in detail by the 30th: BM, Add. 36782, ff. 64–5. Cf. below, p. 481 & n. 3.
2. The foundation of the Bank of England and the introduction of the Civil List in the 1690s achieved this effect. For the Polish 'royal' and 'state' treasuries, see *Cambridge Hist. Poland . . . to 1696* (ed. W. F. Reddaway *et al.*), pp. 430–2.
3. John, baptised in fact over a week before, on 17 September at St Paul's, Covent Garden: *Harl. Soc. Reg.*, 30/27.
4. Cf. above, p. 439 & n. 2.

which I believe is one of his devilish lies.[1]   Here I light, and to
the Duke of York's playhouse and there saw a piece of *Sir
Martin Marr=all*[2] with great delight, though I have seen it so often;
and so home and there busy late, and so home*a* to my supper*b*
and bed.

29.   *Lords day.*   Up, and put off*c* first my summer's silk suit
and put on a cloth one.   Then to church and so home to dinner,
my wife and I alone to a good dinner.   All the afternoon talking
in my chamber with my wife about my keeping a coach the next
year,[3] and doing something to my house which will cost money –
that is, furnish our best chamber with tapestry – and other rooms
with pictures.   In the evening read [a] good book, my wife to
me; and I did even my kitchen accounts.   Then to supper, and
so to bed.

30.   By water to White-hall – there to a committee of Tanger;
but they not met yet, I went to St. James, there thinking to have
opportunity to speak to the Duke of York about the petition I
have to make to him for something in reward for my service
this war,[4] but I did want it.   Thence to White-hall and*d* there a

---

a repl. 'to my'   *b* repl. ? 'prayer'
c l.h. repl. s.h. 'on'   *d* repl. 'to sp'-

---

1. Sir Frechville Holles was elected
on 24 October in place of the late Sir
Henry Belasyse (killed in a duel), and
thus became fellow member for
Grimsby with his father Gervase
Holles, who had sat for the town in
three parliaments since 1640.   That
was the extent of the family's parliamentary service for Grimsby.   The
first Holles to be an M.P. was
William, member for Nottingham-
shire in 1553; Sir Frechville was perhaps enlarging on that fact.   Or he
may have been misled by the fact that
his family had lived in or near Grimsby since 1558.   But he should have
been under no misapprehensions:
his father was an antiquary and in the

1650s had written a history of the
family and dedicated it to Frechville
himself.   See Gervase Holles, *Memorials of the Holles family* (ed. Wood),
esp. pp. 61, 194.   Pepys himself later
had cause to complain of election
expenses: in 1673 his disputed election to Castle Rising, Norf. (a smaller
constituency than Grimsby, which
had c. 100 voters) cost him £700
instead of the £60 he had been led to
expect: *Further Corr.*, p. 287.

2. Dryden's comedy: see above,
p. 387 & n. 1.   Pepys had already
seen it three times.   (A).

3. See above, p. 205, n. 2.

4. See below, pp. 464–5 & n.

Committee met, where little was done; and thence to the Duke of York to Council, where we the Officers of the Navy* did attend about the business of discharging the seamen by ticket;[1] where several of the Lords spoke, and of our number none but myself; which I did in such manner as pleased the King and Council. Speaking concerning the difficulty of pleasing of seamen and giving them assurance[a] to their satisfaction that they should be paid their arreares of wages, my Lord Ashly did move that an Assignement for money on the Act might be put into the hands of the East India Company or City of London; which he thought the seamen would believe.[2]   But this my Lord Anglesea did very handsomely oppose, and I think did carry it that it will not be: and it is endeed a mean thing that the King should so far own his own want of credit as to borrow theirs in this manner.   My Lord Anglesey told him that this was the way endeed to teach[b] the Parliament to trust the King no more for the time to come, but to have a Kingdom's Treasurer distinct from the King's. Home at noon to dinner, where I expected to have had our new girle, my wife's woman, but she is not yet come.   I abroad after dinner to White-hall and there, among other things, do hear that there will be Musique tomorrow night before the King.   So to Westminster, where to the Swan ; and there I did fling down[c] the fille there[3] upon the chair and did tocar her thigh with my hand; at which she begin to cry[c] out, so I left off and drank, and away to the Hall and thence to Mrs. Martin's to bespeak some linen, and there yo did hazer algo with ella and drank and away, having first promised my god-daughter a new coat, her first coat.   So by coach home, and there find our pretty girl, Willet, come, brought by Mr. Batelier; and she is very pretty, and so grave as I never saw little thing in my life.   Endeed, I think her a little

a repl. 'make'   *b* repl. 'assurance'
c–c garbled s.h.: see above, p. 244, note *a*

---

1. Cf. above, p. 454, n. 1. The Navy Board proposed that the tickets be paid twice a week, in the order in which the ships were discharged, and that seamen be informed by a notice put up at the Treasury Office gate: BM, Add. 9303, f. 175r.

2. The proposal was defeated: Downing's bill for the registration of assignments (q.v. below, p. 520 & n. 2) served much the same purpose. The act was that for the Eleven Months Tax.

3. Frances ('Frank') Udall.

too good for my family, and so well-carriaged as I hardly ever saw – I wish my wife may use her well.   Now I begin to be full of thought for my journey the next week, if I can get leave, to Brampton.   Tonight came and sat with me Mr. Turner and his wife, and tell me of a design of sending their son Francke to the East Indys Company's service if they can get him entertained; which they are promised by Sir Andr. Rickard, which I do very well like of.   So the company broke up and to bed.[a]

a   followed by one blank page

1. All the morning busy at the office. Pleased mightily with my girl that we have got to wait on my wife. At noon dined with Sir G. Carteret and the rest of our officers at his house in Broad-street, they being there upon his accounts. After dinner took coach and to my wife, who was gone before into the Strand, there to buy a night-gowne; where I found her in a shop with her pretty girl, and having bought it, away home; and I thence to Sir G. Carteret's again, and so took coach alone, it now being almost night, to White-hall and there in the Boarded-gallery*a* did hear the music with which the King is presented this night by Monsieur Grebus,[1] the master of his music – both instrumental (I think 24 violins) and vocall, an*b* English song upon peace; but God forgive me, I was never so little pleased with a consort of music in my life – the manner of setting of words and repeating them out of order, and that with a number of voices, makes me sick, the whole design of vocall music being lost by it. Here was a great press of people, but I did not see many pleased with it; only, the instrumental music he had brought by practice to play very just. So thence late, in the dark round by the Wall home by coach; and there to sing and sup with my wife and look upon our pretty girl, and so to bed.

2. Up, and very busy all the morning upon my accounts of Tanger to present to the Commissioners of the Treasury in the afternoon, and the like upon the accounts of the office.[2] This morning came to me Mr. Gawden about business, with his gold chain about his neck, as being Sheriffe of the City this year. At noon to the Treasury Office again and there dined and did business; and then by coach to the New Exchange and there met

a repl. 'gallery'   *b* repl. 'a s'-

---

1. See above, p. 73 & n. 3. (E).
2. See *CTB*, ii. 98; apart from the Tangier business, Pepys was arrang-

ing the transfer of Navy Office accounts from Carteret to Anglesey, and the payment of seamen's tickets.

my wife and girl and took them to the King's House to see*a* *The
Traytor*,[1] which still I like as a very good play; and thence round
by the wall home, having drunk at the Cock alehouse, as I of
late have used to do. And so home and to my chamber to
read, and so to supper and to bed.

3. Up; and going out of doors, I understand that Sir W.
Batten is gone to bed on a sudden again this morning, being
struck very ill. And I confess I have observed him for these last
two months to look very ill*b* and to look worse and worse.
I to St. James's (though it be a sitting day) to the Duke of York
about [the] Tanger Committee, which met this morning; and
he came to us, and the charter for the city of Tanger was read
and the form of the Court Merchant.[2] That being done, Sir W.
Coventry took me into the gallery and walked with me an
hour, discoursing of Navy business, and with much kindness to
and confidence in me still; which I must endeavour to preserve –
and will do; and good man, all his care how to get the Navy paid
off and that all other things therein may go well. He gone, I
thence to my Lady Peterburgh, who sent for me, and with her
an hour, talking about her husband's pension and how she hath
got an order for its being paid again; though I believe, for all
the order, it will hardly be[3] – but of that I said nothing. But her
design is to get it paid again and how to raise money upon it,
to clear it from the engagement which lies upon it to some
citizens who lent her husband money (without her knowledge)
upon [it], to vast loss. She entends to force them to take their

---

a   three following pages headed 'September' and corrected
b   repl. 'w'-

---

1. A tragedy by James Shirley;
see above, i. 300 & n. 1. (A).
2. The charter (establishing civil
government in what had been a garrison town entirely controlled by its
Governor) was not sealed until 4 June
1668: PRO, C 66/3104. (Pepys kept
a copy: Rawl. A 341, ff. 197–9.)

The court-merchant was the most
important of the civil courts established under it. Routh, pp. 117–21.
3. A Treasury warrant for payment
of the pension (q.v. above, iv. 94,
n. 1) was issued on 21 April 1668:
CTB, ii. 304.

money again and release her husband of those hard terms. The
woman is a very wise woman and is very plain in telling me how
her plate and jewels are at pawne for money, and how they are
forced to live beyond their estate and do get nothing by his
being a Courtier.[1]   The lady I pity, and her family – having done
with her and drunk two glasses of her Meade which [she] did
give me.   And so to the Treasurer's office and there find my
Lord Brouncker and W. Penn at dinner with Sir G. Carteret
about his accounts, where I dined and talked and settled some
business; and then home and there took out my wife and Willet,
thinking to have gone to a play; but both houses were begun,
and so we to the Change and thence to my tailor's; and there,
the coachman desiring to go home to change his horses, we went
with him into a nasty end of all St. Giles's and there went into a
nasty room, a chamber of his where he hath a wife and child,
and there stayed (it growing dark too, and I angry thereat)
till he shifted his horses; and then home apace and there I to
business late, and so home to supper and walk in the garden with
my wife and girl, with*a* whom we are mightily pleased.   And
after talking and supping, to bed.   ⟨This noon, going home, I
did call on Will Lincolne[2] and agree with him to carry me to
Brampton.⟩

    4.   Up,*b* and to White-hall to attend the Council about Com-
issioner Pett's business[3] – along with my Lord Brouncker and
Sir W. Penn; and in the Robe-chamber, the Duke of York came
to us, the officers of the Navy, and there did meet together about
Navy business – where Sir W. Coventry was with us; and among
other things did remember his Royal Highness, now the prizes
were disposing, to remember Sir John Harman to the King for

----

    1. Cf. her similar complaints above,   ships in the Medway disaster in the
vii. 355.   Peterborough was an officer   previous June.   Pett had already been
of the Duke of York's Household.   dismissed from his post as Navy Com-
    2. Stable-keeper, Cow Lane.   missioner in the same month.
    3. An enquiry into the loss of the

some bounty,[1] and also for my Lady Minnes;[2] which was very nobly done of him. Thence all of us to attend the Council; where we were anon called on and there was a long hearing of Comissioner Pett, who was there, and there was the two Maisters-Attendant of Chatham[3] called in, who do deny their having any order from Comissioner Pett about bringing up the great ships, which gives the lie to what he says; but in general, I find him to be but a weak, silly man, and that is guilty of horrid neglect in this business all along. Here broke off without coming to an issue, but that there should be another hearing on Monday next. So the Council rose, and I stayed walking*a* up and down the galleries till the King went to dinner and then I to my Lord Crews to dinner; but he having dined, I took a very short leave, confessing I had not dined; and so to an ordinary hard by the Temple-gate, where I have heretofore been, and there dined; cost me 10*d*. And so to my Lord Ashly's, where after dinner, Sir H. Cholmly, Creed and I with his Lordship about Mr. Yeabsly's business[4] – where having come to agreement with him, abating him 1000*l* of what he demands for ships lost, I to Westminster to Mrs. Martin's lodging, whither I sent for her and there hear that her husband is come from sea, which is sooner then I expected. And here I stayed and drank, and so did tocar ella and away; and so by coach to my tailor's, and thence to*b* my Lord Crews and there did stay with him an hour till almost night, discoursing about the ill state of my Lord Sandwich, that he can neither be*c* got to be called home nor money got to maintain him there, which will ruin his family: and the truth is, he doth almost deserve it, for by all relation he hath in a little more then a year and a half spent 20000*l* of the King's money

---

a repl. 'walk'   *b* repl. 'through'   *c* repl. 'to'

---

1. Presumably because of his service this year as Commander-in-Chief, West Indies. He had beaten the French fleet off Martinique on 25 June, and on 15 September had taken Cayenne.

2. Widow of Sir Christopher Myngs, the admiral, killed in action in 1666.

3. John Brooke and William Rand: *CSPD 1667*, p. 353. They had charge (under the Commissioner) of the yard. The hearing (being in committee) is not recorded in the Privy Council register.

4. The Tangier victualling: see above, vii. 162 & n. 2.

and the best part of 10000*l* of his own; which is a most prodigious expense, more then ever Embassadors spent there and more then these Commissioners of the Treasury will or do allow; and they[a] demand an account before they will give him any more money; which puts all his friends to a loss what to answer – but more money we must get him, or to be called home.[1]   I offer to speak to Sir W. Coventry about it; but my Lord will not advise to it without consent of Sir G Carteret.   So home, and there to see Sir W. Batten, who fell sick yesterday morning.   He is asleep and so I could not see him; but in an hour after, word is brought me that he is so ill, that it is believed he cannot live till tomorrow; which troubles me and my wife mightily, partly out of kindness, he being a good neighbour, and partly because of the money he owes me upon our bargain of the late prize.[2]   So home and to supper and to bed.

5.   Up, and to the office and there all the morning, none but my Lord Anglesy and myself.   But much surprized[b] with the news of the death of Sir W. Batten, who died this morning, having been but two days sick.   Sir W. Penn and I did despatch a letter this morning to Sir W. Coventry to recommend Collonell Middleton, who we think a most honest and understanding man, and fit for that place.[3]   Sir G. Carteret did also come this morning, and walked with me in the garden and concluded not to concern or have any advice made to Sir W. Coventry in behalf of my Lord Sandwiches business; so I do rest satisfied, though I do think they are all mad, that they will judge Sir W. Coventry an enemy, when he is endeed no such man to anybody, but is severe and just, as he ought to be, where he sees things ill done. At noon home, and by coach to Temple-bar to a India shop and there bought a gown and Shash, which cost me 26*s*.   And

---

a MS. 'their'   b repl. 'discomp'-

---

1. For Sandwich's debts, see esp. below, 8 February 1669 & n. Embassies were notoriously expensive.

2. See above, p. 385.

3. Thomas Middleton, who had done excellent service as Navy Com-

missioner at Portsmouth, was appointed Surveyor of the Navy and took up his duties on 19 December: *CSPD 1667-8*, p. 55; cf. above, p. 143, n. 1.

so she and Willett away to the Change, and I to my Lord Crew and there met my Lord Hinchingbrooke and Lady Jemimah, and there dined with them and my Lord – where pretty merry. And after dinner, my Lord Crew and Hinchingbrooke and myself went aside to discourse about my Lord Sandwiches business, which is in a very ill state for want of money; and so parted, and I to my tailors and there took up my wife and Willet, who stayed there for me, and to the Duke of York's playhouse; but the House so full, it being a new play *The Coffee-House,*[1] that we could not get in, and so to the King's House; and there going in, met with Knipp and she took us up into the Tireing-rooms and to the women's Shift,[2] where Nell[3] was dressing herself and was all unready; and is very pretty, prettier then I thought; and so walked all up and down the House above, and then below into the Scene-room,[4] and there sat down and she gave us fruit; and here I read the Qu's to Knepp while she answered me, through all her part of *Flora's Figarys,*[5] which was acted today. But Lord, to see how they were both painted would make a man mad – and did make me loath them[6] – and what base company of men comes among them, and how lewdly they talk – and how poor the[a] men are in clothes, and yet what a show they make on the stage by candle-light, is very observable. But to see how Nell cursed for having so few people in the pit was pretty, the other House carrying away all the people at the new play, and is said nowadays

a repl. 'they all'

---

1. *Tarugo's wiles or The coffee house,* a comedy by Sir Thomas St Serfe, published in 1668. This is the first reference to a performance. (A).

2. Actresses in the Restoration play-houses could not – and did not – expect any privacy in their dressing-rooms. (A).

3. Nell Gwyn. (A).

4. The scene-room or scene-house was that part of the stage in which scenery in the form of painted wings and back-flats was exhibited. It was framed by the proscenium arch. Most of the acting, however, took place on the apron stage in front of the proscenium arch. (A).

5. *Flora's Vagaries,* a comedy by Richard Rhodes; see above, v. 236 & n. 2. The cast listed by Genest (i. 70) for this performance includes Mrs Knepp as Otrante, Nell Gwyn as Flora, Mohun as Alberto, and Burt as Francisco. (A).

6. Cf. above, p. 439 & n. 2.

to have generally most company, as being better players.[1] By
and by into the pit and there saw the play; which is pretty good,
but my belly was full of what I had seen in the House; and so
after the play done, away home and there to the writing my
letters; and so home to supper and to bed.

6. *Lords day.* Up, and dressed myself and so walked out
with the boy to Smithfield to Cow-lane to Lincolnes, and there
spoke with him and agree upon the hour tomorrow to set out
toward Brampton; but vexed that he is not likely to go himself,
but sends another[a] for him.   Here I took a hackney-coach, and
to White-hall and there met Sir W. Coventry and discoursed
with him; and then with my Lord Brouncker and many others
to end my matters, in order to my going into the country
tomorrow for five or six days, which I have not been for now
above three years.   Walked with Creed into the park a little,
and at last went into the Queen's side[2] and there saw the King
and Queen and saw the ladies, in order to my hearing any news
stirring, to carry into the country; but met with none, and so
away home by coach and there dined; and W How came to see
me and after dinner parted; and I to my writing to my Lord
Sandwich, which is the greatest business I have to do before my
going into the country.   And in the evening to my office to set
matters to rights there.   And being in the garden, Sir W. Penn
did come to me and fell to discourse about the business of the
Flying greyhound;[3] wherein I was plain to him and he to me,
and at last concluded upon my writing a petition to the Duke of
York for a certain ship, the *Maybolt* gallyott, and he offers to
give me 300*l* for my successe, which however I would not oblige
him to, but will see the issue of it by fair play; and so I did
presently draw a petition, which he undertakes to proffer to the
Duke of York and solicit for me, and will not seem to doubt of

---

a repl. 'a'

---

1. It is generally agreed that the
Duke's Company, headed by Thomas
Betterton, was superior to the King's
Company. For the pit, see above,
p. 422, n. 2. (A).

2. Of Whitehall Palace.
3. See above, p. 441 & n. 1.

his success.[1] So I wrote and did give it him and left it with him; and so home to supper, where Pelling comes and sits with me andthe re tells us how old Mr. Batelier[2] is dead this last night in the night, going to bed well; which I am mightily troubled for, he being a good man. Supper done and he gone, I to my chamber to write my Journall to this night, and so to bed.

7. Up betimes, and did do several things towards the settling all matters, both of house and office, in order for my journey this day; and did leave my chief care, and the key of my closet, with Mr. Hater, with direction what papers to secure in case of fire or other accident; and so about 9 a-clock, I and my wife and Willett set out in a coach I have hired, with four horses, and W. Hewer and Murford[3] rode by us on horseback; and so, my wife and she in their morning gowns, very handsome and pretty and to my great liking, we set out; and so out at Allgate and so to the Greenman and so on to Enfield, in our way seeing Mr. Louther and his lady in a coach going to Walthamstow, and he told us that he would overtake us at night, he being to go that way. So we to Enfield and there bayted, it being but a foul, bad day; and there Louther and Mr. Burford, an acquaintance of his, did overtake us, and there drank and eat together; and[a] by and by we parted, we going before them; and very merry, my wife and girl and [I], talking and telling tales and singing; and before night did come[b] to Bishop=stafford, where Louther

a   repl. 'and they went away before us, being to go further then us and I [illegible] them'
b   repl. 'come'

---

1. A copy of the petition (7 October, in Gibson's hand) is in NMM, LBK/8, p. 501; printed in *Further Corr.*, p. 181. In it Pepys claimed that alone of the principal officers he had received no war bounty. He was granted the *Maybolt* – 'towards satisfaction for disbursements' (*Cat.*, i. 289) – but it proved to be a poor reward. She was a prize taken from

the Dutch in 1666, and had recently come to the notice of the Board because her master had died and the mate and crew fallen sick. *CSPD 1667*, p. 461; *Cat.*, i. 288–9.

2. Joseph Batelier, sen. His son Will and his two daughters were friends of Pepys.

3. Will Murford, Navy Office messenger.

and his friend did meet us again and carried us to the Rayne-deere, where Mrs. Aynsworth (who lived heretofore at Cambrige and whom I knew better then they think for, doth live[1] – it was the woman that, among other things, was great with my Cosen Barmston[2] of Cottenham, and did use to sing to him and did teach me *Full forty times over*,[3] a very lewd song) doth live, a woman they are very well acquainted with, and is here what she was at Cambridge, and all the goodfellows of the country come hither. Louther and his friend stayed and drank and then went further this night, but here we stayed and supped and lodged. But as soon as they were gone and my supper getting ready, I fell to write my letter to my Lord Sandwich, which I could not finish before my coming from London; so did finish it to my good content, and a good letter, telling him[a] the present state of all matters;[4] and did get a man to promise to carry it tomorrow morning to be there at my house by noon, and I paid him well for it. So that being done and my mind at ease, we to supper and so to bed, my wife and I in one bed and the girl in

---

a repl. 'them'

---

1. Elizabeth Aynsworth had been banished from Cambridge by the university authorities and had settled at the Reindeer Inn at Bishop's Stortford, Herts., a well-known stopping place on the road between London and Newmarket. There she throve until she became involved in a duelling affray in 1677. On one occasion the proctor who had sent her away from Cambridge dined there. He was served with a 'most elegant supper all in plate' which he and his party 'were afraid to touch lest they should have a lord's reckoning to pay. Upon which the woman appeared, and said it was the least she could do in return of that Gentleman's whipping her out, by which she had so much advanced herself'. [A gentleman,] *New and complete hist. Essex* (1770), iii. 130–1.

2. Probably George, son of Henry Barnardiston and his wife Anne (*née* Trice).
3. Probably the song in *Wit and drollery* (1656), pp. 58–60; ib. (1661), pp. 60–2. (E).
4. Pepys's draft-copy (in s.h.), dated 7 October at the Navy Office, is in Rawl. A 195a, ff. 90–1; printed Smith, i. 117–22; *Letters*, pp. 29–30. The letter, *inter alia*, touched on the 'unsatisfactory' peace with the Dutch, parliament's enquiries into expenditure, the King's measures of economy, Clarendon's fall, and the work of the new Treasury commission. It also pleaded for better relations between Sandwich and Coventry.

another in the same room. And lay very well, but there was so much tearing company in the house, that we could not see my landlady, so I had no opportunity of renewing my old acquaintance with her. But here we slept very well.

8. Up pretty betimes, though not so soon as we entended, by reason of Murford's not rising and then not knowing how to open our door; which, and some other pleasant simplicities of the fellow, did give occasion to us to call him Sir Martin Marr=all; and W Hewers being his helper and counsellor, we did call him all this journey, Mr. Warner, which did give us good occasion of mirth now and then.[1] At last rose, and up and broke our fast, and then took coach and away; and at Newport did call on Mr. Louther, and he and his friend and the maister of the house, their friend where they were (a gentleman), did presently get a-horse-back and overtook us, and went with us to Audly end and did go along with us all over the house and garden; and mighty merry we were. The house endeed doth appear very fine, but not so fine as it hath heretofore to me.[2] Perticularly, the ceilings[3] are not so good as I alway took them to be, being nothing so well wrought as my Lord Chancellors are; and though the figure of the house without be very extraordinary good, yet the stayre case is exceeding poor; and a great many pictures, and not one good one in the house but one of Harry the 8th done by Holben;[4] and not one good suit of hangings in all the house, but all most ancient things, such as I would not give the hanging-up of in my house; and the other furniture, beds and other things, accordingly. Only, the gallery[5] is good; and above all things, the cellars, where we went down and drank of much good liquor, and endeed the cellars are fine; and here my wife and I

<hr />

1. Sir Martin Mar-all was the central character in Dryden's play of that name (q.v. above, p. 387, n. 1). Warner, his man, calls him (I, 1) 'a Coxcomb . . . that has no more brains than just those I carry for him'.
2. Cf. above, i. 69 & n. 3.
3. Probably the Jacobean ceilings of the Great Hall and of the saloon, attributed to Bernard Jansen, the architect. Description and illust. in R. Comm. Hist. Mon., *Essex*, i. 236+.
4. Presumably one of the standard derivations from Holbein's prototypes. The portrait seen by Pepys cannot be identified. (OM).
5. Evelyn (1 September 1654) thought this 'most cherefull, and I thinke, one of the best in England'.

did sing to my great content[1] and then to the garden and there
eat many grapes, and took some with us; and so away thence,
exceeding well satisfied, though not to that degree that by my
old esteem of the house I ought and did expect to have done –
the situation of it not pleasing me.   Here we parted with Louther
and his friends, and away to Cambrige, it being foul, rainy
weather; and there did take up at the Rose, for the sake of Mrs.
Dorothy Drawwater, the vintener's daughter, which*a* is mentioned in the play of *Sir Martin Marr=all*.[2]   Here we had a good
chamber and bespoke a good supper; and then I took my wife
and W. Hewer and Willett (it holding up a little) and showed
them Trinity College and St. Johns Library, and went to King's
College chapel[3] to see the outside of it only, and so to our Inne;
and with much pleasure did this, they walking in their pretty
morning gowns, very handsome, and I proud to find myself in
condition to do this; and so home to our lodging, and there by
and by to supper with much good sport, talking with the drawers
concerning matters of the town and persons whom I remember;
and so after supper to cards and then to bed, lying, I in one bed
and my wife and girl in another in the same room; and very
merry talking together and mightily pleased both of us with the
girl.   Saunders, the only*b Viallin in my time, is I hear dead of
the plague in the late plague there.[4]

a repl. 'where'   *b* repl. same symbol badly formed

1. Pepys had played his flageolet
in these cellars, 'there being an
excellent echo', on 27 February 1660:
above, i. 70. (E).

2. Dryden's play has a reference
(V, 1) to a bastard begot by Old
Moody 'when he was a *Cambridge-*
scholar'. The mother was '*Dorothy*,
Daughter to one *Draw-water*, a vintner at the Rose'. (The surname may
well have been fictional.) Dryden
and Pepys had been at Cambridge
together: above, v. 37. (A).

3. The same sights as those chosen
on the previous visit: see above, iii.
224 & nn.

4. Possibly Saunders was one of
the family of musicians of that name
whose house in Green St, Cambridge,
had been shut up in the plague in
October 1665: see J. R. Wardale
(ed.), *Clare College letters*, pp. 69–
70. He was the violinist to whose
performances a double-edged compliment was paid by the Cambridge
poet, Nicholas Hookes (a contemporary of Pepys at the university):
'O' the' *Violin / Saunders* plays well /
where' [mentioning two well-known
London players] '*Magge* or *Mel* han't
been' (*Amanda*, 1653, p. 58).

Magdalene College, Cambridge, engraving by David Loggan

9. Up, and got ready and eat our breakfast and then took coach; and the poor, as they did yesterday, did stand at the coach to have something given them, as they do*a* to all great persons, and I did give them something; and the town musique did also come and play; but Lord, what sad music they made – however, I was pleased with them, being all of us in very good humour; and so set forth and through the town, and observed at our College of Magdalen the posts new-painted, and understand that the Vice-Chancellor is there this year.[1] And so away for Huntington,*b* mightily pleased all along the road to remember old stories; and came to Brampton at about noon and there find my father and sister and brother all well; and here laid up our things, and up and down to see the garden with my father, and the house, and do altogether find it very pretty – especially the little parlour and the summer-houses in the garden.[2] Only, the wall doth want greens upon it and the house is too low-roofed; but that is only because of my coming from a house with higher ceilings; but altogether is very pretty and I bless God that I am like to have such a pretty place to retire to. And I did walk with my father without doors and do find a very convenient way of laying out money there in building, which will make a very good seat; and the place deserves it, I think, very well. By and by to dinner, and after dinner I walked up to Hinchingbrooke, where my Lady expected me, and there spent all the afternoon with her; the same most excellent, good, discreet lady that ever she was; and among other things, is mightily pleased with the lady that is like to be her son Hinchingbrooke's wife;[3] which I am mightily glad of. By and by my wife comes with Willett, my wife in her velvett vest, which is mighty fine and becomes her

a repl. 'did'   *b* repl. 'Cambrige'

---

1. John Howorth, Master of Magdalene, 1664–8, was Vice-Chancellor, 1667–8, and died in office. The posts dated from 1585 (when the gate was built) and bore the arms of the college's Visitor, Lord Howard de Walden (later Earl of Suffolk, d. 1626). They have now disappeared.

See David Loggan, *Cantab. Illust.* (1690), pl. xxviii; cf. E. K. Purnell, *Hist. Magdalene Coll.*, p. 15.

2. Cf. the alterations made in 1662: above, iii. 94, etc.

3. Lady Anne Boyle; they were married in January 1668.

exceedingly. I am pleased with my Lady Paulina and Anne, who are both grown very proper ladies, and handsome enough. But a thousand questions my Lady asked me, till she could think of no more almost, but walked up and down the house with me; but I do find by her, that they are reduced to great straits for money, having been forced to sell her plate, 8 or 900*l* worth, and is now going to sell a suit of her best hangings, of which I could almost wish to buy a piece or two, if the pieces will be broke.   But the house is most excellently furnished, and brave rooms and good pictures, so that it doth please*a* me infinitely, beyond Audly-End.[1]   Here we stayed till night, walking and talking and drinking, and with mighty*b* satisfaction, my Lady with me alone most of the day, talking of my Lord's bad condition to be kept in Spain without money and at a great expense, which (as we will save the family) we must labour to remove.   Night being come, we took leave with all possible kindness, and so home; and there Mr. Sheply[2] stayed with us and supped, and full of good country discourse; and when supper done, took his leave and we all to bed – only, I a little troubled that my father tells me that he is troubled that my wife shows my sister no countenance, and him but very little, but is as a stranger in the house; and I do observe she doth carry herself very high, but I perceive there was some great falling-out when she was here last,[3] but the reason I have no mind to enquire after, for vexing myself, being desirous to pass my time with as much mirth as I can while I am abroad.   So all to bed – my wife and I in the high bed in our chamber, and Willet in the trundle-bed, which she desired to lie in, by us.

a repl. 'pl'-   *b* MS. 'my'

---

1. Horace Walpole wrote an account of the pictures in 1763: see *Pub. Walpole Soc.*, xvi. 49–50. There is a *catalogue raisonné* (MS., 1840) at Mapperton, Dorset. For a list c. 1910, see [8th Earl of Sandwich,] *Hinchingbrooke* (priv. ptd, 1910), pp. 33+. Celia Fiennes in 1697 remarked on 'a fine picture of Venus were it not too much uncloth'd': *Journeys* (ed. Morris), pp. 66–7. The collection was partially dispersed at Sotheby's, 4 December 1957.

2. Edward Shipley, Sandwich's steward.

3. In June.

10. Waked in the morning with great pain I, of the Collique, by cold taken yesterday, I believe with going up and down in my shirt; but with rubbing my belly, keeping of it warm, I did at last come to some ease, and rose;[a] and up to walk up and down the garden with my father, to talk of all our concernments – about a husband for my sister, whereof there is at present no appearance. But we must endeavour to find her one now, for she grows old and ugly.[1] Then for my brother; and resolve he shall stay here this winter, and then I will either send him to Cambridge for a year, till I get him some church promotion, or send him to sea as a chaplain – where he may study and earn his living.[2] Then walked round about our Greene to see whether, in case I cannot buy out my uncle Tho. and his son's right in this house,[3] that I can buy another place as good thereabouts to build on, and I do not see that I can; but this, with new building, may[b] be made an excellent pretty thing, and I resolve to look after it as soon as I can and Goody Gorrum dies.[4] By this time it was almost noon, and then my father and I and wife and Willett abroad by coach round the Towne of Brampton to observe any other place as good as ours, and find none; and so back with great pleasure and thence went all of us, my sister and brother and W. Hewer, to dinner to Hinchingbrooke, where we had a good plain country dinner, but most kindly used; and here dined the Minister of Brampton[5] and his wife, who is reported a very good, but poor man. Here I spent alone with my Lady, after dinner, the most of the afternoon; and anon the

---

a repl. 'did'   *b* repl. 'm'-

---

1. Paulina Pepys was now 27. She married John Jackson of Ellington, Hunts., in the following year.

2. He did neither. In 1670 John was made Clerk of Trinity House (on Pepys's recommendation), and in 1673 joint-Clerk of the Acts to the Navy Board.

3. See above, v. 225 & n. 1.

4. By Robert Pepys's will, ownership of the alehouse kept in Brampton by Mrs Gorham was to pass to Pepys's father at her death, and to Pepys after his father's death.

5. John Rowley; after 1669 also Vicar of Hemingford Abbots, Hunts.

two Twins were sent for ⟨from Schoole at Mr. Taylors⟩[1] to come to see me; and I took them into the garden and there in one of the Summer-houses did examine them; and do find them so well advanced in their learning, that I was amazed at it, they repeating a whole Ode without book out of Horace, and did give me a very good account of anything almost, and did make me very readily very good Latin and did give me good account of their Greek grammer, beyond all possible expectation; and so grave and manly as I never saw, I confess, nor could have believed – so that they will be fit to go to Cambridge in two years at most. They are but little, but very like one another; and well-looked children. Then in to my Lady again, and stayed till it was almost night again; and then took leave for a great while again, but with extraordinary kindness from my Lady, who looks upon me like one of her[a] own family and interest. So thence, my wife and people [by] the highway, and I walked over the park with Mr. Sheply and through the grove, which is mighty pretty as is imaginable; and so over their drawbridge to Nun's Bridge[2] and so to my father's, and there sat and drank and talked a little and then parted; and he being gone, and what company there was, my father and I with a dark lantern, it being now night, into the guarden with my wife and there went about our great work to dig up my gold.[3] But Lord, what a tosse I was for some time in, that they could not justly tell where it was, that I begun heartily[b] to sweat and be angry that they should not agree better

a repl. 'her'   b repl. 'time'

---

1. Thomas Taylor was master of the grammar school at Huntingdon (where Pepys himself had been a pupil for a time) from 1641 to 1679. The twins (now aged 12) were Oliver and John, third and fourth sons of Sandwich. It was usual for the children of landed families to go to the local grammar schools at this period, at least for a time. Both these boys went on afterwards to Westminster School and Cambridge.

They had distinguished careers – John becoming Master of Trinity and Dean of Durham; Oliver a Queen's Counsel, a Bencher of the Middle Temple and Solicitor-General to Queen Mary.

2. At the foot of Hinchingbrooke Hill; the house was built on the site of a nunnery.

3. Hidden there by Pepys's wife and father in the previous June during the invasion scare: above, p. 280.

upon the place, and at last to fear*ᵃ* that it was gone; but by and by, poking with a spit, we found it, and then begun with a spudd to lift up the ground; but good God, to see how sillily they did it, not half*ᵇ* a foot under ground and in the sight of the world from a hundred places if anybody by accident were near-hand, and within sight of a neighbour's*ᶜ* window and their hearing also, being close by; only, my father says that he saw them all gone to church before he begun the work when he laid the money, but that doth not excuse it to me; but I was out of my wits almost, and the more from that upon my lifting up the earth with the spud, I did discern that I scattered the pieces of gold round about the ground among the grass and loose earth; and taking up the Iron head-pieces wherein they were put, I perceive the earth was got among the gold and wet, so that the bags were all rotten, all the notes, that I could not tell what in the world to say to it, not knowing how to judge what was wanting or what had been lost by Gibson in his coming down; which, all put together, did make me mad; and at last was forced to take up the head-pieces, dirt and*ᵈ* all, and as many of the scattered pieces as I could with the dirt discern by the candlelight, and carry them up into my brother's chamber and there lock them up till I had eat a little supper; and then all people going to bed, W. Hewer and I did all alone, with several pales of water and basins, at last wash the dirt off of the pieces and parted the pieces and the dirt, and then begun to tell;* and by a note which I had of the value of the whole (in my pocket) do find that there was short above 100 pieces, which did make me mad; and considering that the neighbour's house was so near, that we could not suppose we could speak one to another in the garden at the place where the gold lay (especially by*ᵉ* my father being deaf) but they must know what we had been doing on, I feared that they might in the night come and gather some pieces and prevent us the next morning; so W. Hewer and I out again about midnight (for it was now grown so late) and there by candlelight did make shift to gather 45 pieces more – and so in and to cleanse them,

---

a repl. 'fear'- *b* repl. 'above' *c* repl. 'nibours'
   d repl. 'an' *e* repl. 'be'

and by this time it was past 2 in the morning; and so to bed, with my mind pretty quiet to think that I have recovered so many.   And then to bed, and I lay in the trundle-bed, the girl being gone to bed to my wife.   And there lay in some disquiet all night, telling of the clock till it was daylight; and then rose and called W. Hewer, and he and I, with pails and a Sive, did lock*a* ourselfs into the garden and there gather all the earth about the place into pails, and then Sive those pails in one of the summer-houses (just as they do for Dyamonds in other parts of the world); and there to our great content did with much trouble by 9 a-clock, and by that time we emptied several pails and could not find one, we did make the last night's 45 up 79; so that we are come to about 20 or 30 of*b* what I think the true number should be, and perhaps within less; and of them I may reasonably think that Mr. Gibson might lose some, so that I am pretty well satisfied that my loss is*c* not great and do bless God that it is so well; and do leave my father to make a second examination of the dirt – which he promises he will do; and poor man, is mightily troubled for this accident. But I declared myself very well satisfied, and so endeed I am and my mind at rest in it, it being but an accident which is unusual; and so gives me some kind of content to remember how painful it is sometimes to keep money, as well as to get it, and how doubtful I was how to keep it all night and how to secure it to London.   And so got all my gold put up in bags; and so having the last night wrote to my Lady Sandwich to lend me John Bowles to go along with me my Journy, not telling her the reason, but it was only to secure my gold, we to*d* breakfast; and then about 10 a-clock took coach, my wife and I, and Willett and W. Hewer, and Murford and Bowles (whom my Lady lent me), and my brother John on horseback; and with these four I thought myself pretty safe.   But before we went out, the Huntington music came to me and played, and it was better then that of Cambridge.   Here I took leave of my father, and did give my sister 20s.   She cried at my going; but whether it was at her unwillingness for my going or any unkindness of my

《11》

---

a repl. 'go'	*b* MS. 'or'
c repl 'in.'	*d* repl. 'to'

wife's or no, I know not;[a] but God forgive me, I take her to be so cunning and ill-natured that I have no great love for her; but only, is my sister and must be provided for. My gold, I[b] put into a basket and set under one of the seats; and so my work every quarter of an hour was to look to see whether all was well, and did ride in great fear all the day; but it was a pleasant day and good company, and I mightily contented. Mr. Sheply saw me beyond St. Neotts and there parted, and we straight to Stevenage, through Baldock lanes, which are[c] already very bad. And at Stevenage we came well before night, and all safe;[d] and there with great care I got the gold up to the chamber, my wife carrying one bag and the girl another and W. Hewer the rest in the basket, and set it all under a bed in our chamber; and then sat down to talk and were very pleasant, satisfying myself, among ⟨other⟩ things from[e] Jo. Bowles, in some terms of Hunting and about deere, bucks, and does; and so anon to supper, and very merry we were and a good supper; and after supper to bed. Brecocke[1] alive still, and the best Host I know almost.

12. Up, and eat our breakfast and set out about 9 a-clock; and so to Barnett, where we stayed and baited (the weather very good all day and yesterday) and by 5 a-clock got home, where I find all well; and did bring my gold, to my heart's content, very safe home, having not this day carried it in a basket but in our hands: the girl took care of one and my wife another bag, and I the rest – I being afeared of the bottom of the coach, lest it should break; and therefore was at more ease in my mind then I was yesterday. At home do find that Sir W. Batten's buriall was today; carried from hence with a hundred or two of coaches to Walthamstow and there buried. Here I hear by Mr. Pierce the surgeon, and then by Mr. Lewes and also by Mr. Hater, that the

---

a repl. 'not'   b repl. two symbols rendered illegible
c repl. 'are'   d MS. 'sat'   e repl. 'by'

---

1. Richard Bowcocke; the inn was the Swan: J. E. Cussans, *Hist. Herts.* (Broadwater Hundred), p. 92.

Parliament hath met on Thursday last and adjourned to Monday next. The King did make them a very kind speech, promising them to leave all to them to do, and call to account what and whom they pleased;[1] and declared by my Lord Keeper how many gracious acts he had done since he saw them; among others, disbanding the army, and putting all papists out of imployment, and displacing persons that had managed their business ill[2] – that the Parliament is mightily pleased with the King's speech, and voted giving him thanks for what he said and hath done; and among other things, would by name thank him for displacing my Lord Chancellor, for which a great many did speak in the House, but was opposed by some, and perticularly Harry Coventry, who got that it should be put to a committee to consider what[a] perticulars to mention in their thanks to the King, saying that it was too soon to give thanks for the displacing of a man, before they knew or had examined what was the cause of his displacing.[3] And so it rested; but this doth show that they are and will be very high. And Mr. Pierce doth tell me that he fears, and doth hear, that it hath been said among them that they will move for the calling my Lord Sandwich home, to bring him to account – which doth trouble me mightily; but I trust it will not be so. Anon comes home Sir W. Penn from the buriall, and he and I to walk in the garden, where he did confirm the most of this news; and so to talk of our perticular concernments; and among the rest, he says that my Lady Batten and her children-in-law are all broke in

a repl. symbol rendered illegible

1. This refers to the examination of the war finances; the words were used by the Lord Keeper, not by the King: see *LJ*, xii. 115–16. Cf. Milward, p. 85.

2. These particulars were not in the Lord Keeper's speech but in the address of thanks (delivered on the 14th) which the Commons was now drawing up: Marvell, ii. 57; *CJ*, ix. 1, 2. Pepys's inaccuracies here are

perhaps due to the number of his informants.

3. This speech has not been traced. His brother, Sir William, promoting the impeachment, spoke in the opposite sense in this debate: Milward, p. 329. For Henry Coventry's criticism of the proceedings against Clarendon, see below, p. 533 & n. 2. To Clarendon he was 'a much wiser man than his brother': *Life*, ii. 207.

pieces, and that there is but 800*l* found in the world of money,[1] and is in great doubt*ᵃ* what we shall do toward the doing ourselfs right with them about the prize-money.[2] This troubles me, but we will fall to work upon that next week close. Then he tells me he did deliver my petition[3] into the hands of Sir W. Coventry, who did take it with great kindness and promised to present it to the Duke of York, and that himself hath since seen the Duke of York, but it was in haste, and thinks the Duke of York did tell him that the thing was done; but he is confident that either it is or will be done. This doth please me mightily. So after a little talk more, I away home to supper with Jo. Bowles and brother and wife (who I perceive is already a little jealous of my being fond of Willett, but I will avoid giving her any cause to continue in that mind, as much as possible); and before that, did go with Sir W. Penn to my Lady Batten, whom I had not seen since she was a widow; which she took unkindly but I did excuse it. And the house being full of company and of several factions, she against the children and they against one another and her, I away and home to supper; and after supper to bed.

13. *Lords day.* Up, and by water to White-hall and thence walked to Sir W. Coventry's lodgings, but he was gone out; so I to St. James's and there to the Duke of York's chamber; and there he was dressing and many Lords and Parliament-men come to kiss his hands, they being newly come to town. And there the Duke of York did of himself call me to him and tell me that he had spoke to the King and that the King had granted me the ship I asked for; and did moreover say that he was

a MS. 'down'

---

1. Batten's will (PCC, Carr 144) shows the principal assets as land in Easton St George's, Somerset (inherited from his father and now left, with the mortgages redeemed, to his second son, Benjamin), and the dues payable under his patent for the two lighthouses at Harwich. He left £10 to each of his two daughters and the same to their children, Mary Leming (Lemon) and William Castle.

2. Pepys had sold to Batten his share of the prize taken recently by their privateer the *Flying Grey-hound:* see above, p. 341 & n. 3, p. 385. Batten had died owing Pepys £666 13s. 4d.

3. Asking for the grant of a ship; see above, p. 465, n. 1.

mightily satisfied with my service, and that he would be willing to do anything that was in his power for me; which he said with mighty kindness; which I did return him thanks for and departed with mighty joy – more then I did expect; and so walked over the park to White-hall and then met Sir H. Cholmly, who walked with me and told me most of the same I heard last night of the Parliament, and thinks they will do all things very well; only, they will be revenged of my Lord Chancellor; and says, however, that he thinks there will be but two things*a* proved on him; and the one is that he may have said to the King, and to others, words to breed in the King an ill opinion of the Parliament, that they were factious*b* and that it was better to dissolve them; and this he thinks they will be able to prove, but what this will amount to, he knows not: and next, that he hath taken money for several bargains that have been made with the Crown; and did instance in one that is already complained of,[1] but*c* there are so many more involved in it, that should they unravell things of this sort, everybody almost will be more or less concerned. But these are the two great points which he thinks they will insist on and prove against him. Thence I to the Chapel and there heard the sermon and a pretty good anthemne; and so home by water to dinner, where Bowles and brother, and a good dinner; and in the afternoon to make good my Journall to this day, and so by water again to White-hall. And thence only walked to Mrs. Martin's and there sat with her and her sister and Burroughs and did tocar la prima, and there drank and talked and away by water home; and there walked with Sir W. Penn and told him what the Duke of York told me today about the ship I begged, and he was knave enough of his own accord (but, to be sure, in order to his own advantage)[2] to offer me to send for the maister of the vessel, the *Maybolt* galliott, and bid him to get her furnished as for a long voyage (and I to take no notice of it), that she might be the more worth to me; so that here he is a very knave to the King – and I doubt not his being the same to

a MS. 'thinks'   *b* repl. 'faction'   *c* repl. 'it'

---

1. Probably the Canary Company   2. See above, p. 441 & n. 1.
patent: see above, vii. 314 & n. 2.

me on occasion. So in a-doors and supped with my wife and brother, W. Hewer and Willett, and so evened with W. Hewer for my expenses upon the road this last journey; and do think that the whole journey will cost me little less then 18 or 20*l* one way or other, but I am well pleased with it; and so after supper to bed.

14. Up and by water to White-hall; and thence walked to St. James's and there to Mr. Wren's, and he told me that my business was done about my Warrant on the *Maybolt* galliott;[1] which I did see, and though it was not so full in the reciting of my services as the*a* other was in that of Sir W. Penn's, yet I was well pleased with it and do entend to fetch ⟨it⟩ away anon. Thence with Sir Tho. Allen, in a little sorry coach which he hath set up of late, and Sir Jer. Smith to White-hall; and there I took water and went to Westminster-hall and there hear that the House is this day again upon the business of giving the King the thanks of the House for his speech and, among other things, for laying aside of my Lord Chancellor. Thence I to Mrs. Martin's, where by appointment comes to me Mrs. Howlett, which I was afeared was to have told me something of my freedom with her daughter; but it was not so, but only to complain to me of her son-in-law,[2] how he abuses and makes a slave of her, and his mother is one that encourages him in it, so that they are at this time upon very bad terms one with another; and desires that I would take a time to advise him and tell him what becomes him to do; which office I am very glad of, for some ends of my own also con su filia; and there drank and parted, I mightily satisfied with this business. And so I home by water with Sir W Warren, who happened to be at Westminster, and there I pretty strange to him, and little discourse;[3] and there at the office Brouncker, W. Penn, T. Harvey and I did some business, and so home to dinner; and thence I out to visit Sir G. Carteret and

a repl. 'it was of S'-

1. Summary in PRO, Ind. 10704/1, p. 11 (order no. 795, 14 October: 'To deliver the Mayboltt Galliot unto Samuel Pepys Esquire as of His Majestie's bounty').

2. Michael Mitchell, who kept a strong-water house at the Old Swan, Fish St.

3. For their estrangement, see above, p. 31 & n. 3.

ladies there, and from him do understand that the King himself
(but this he told me as a great secret) is satisfied that this thanks
which he expects from the House for the laying aside of my Lord
Chancellor, is a thing irreguler; but since it is come into the
House, he doth think it necessary to carry it on and will have it,
and hath made his mind known to be so to some of the House.
But Sir G. Carteret doth say he knows nothing*a* of what my
Lord Brouncker told us today, that the King was angry with the
Duke of York yesterday and advised him not to hinder what he
had a mind to have done touching this business; which is news
very bad, if true. Here I visited my Lady Carteret, who hath
been sick some time but now pretty well, but laid on her bed.
Thence to my Lord Crew, to see him after my coming out of the
country, and he seems satisfied with some steps they have made
in my absence towards my Lord Sandwiches relief for money;[1]
and so I have no more to do, nor will trouble myself more about
it – till they send for me. He tells me also that the King will
have the thanks of the House go on. And commends my Lord
Keepers speech for all but what he was forced to say about the
reason of the King's sending away the House so soon the last
time when they were met, but this he was forced to do.[2] Thence
to Westminster-hall and there walked with Mr. Scowen, who
tells me that it is at last carried in the House that the thanks shall
be given to the King; among other things, perticularly for the
removal of my Lord Chancellor; but he tells*b* me it is a strange
act, and that which he thinks would never have been, but that
the King did insist upon it, that since it came into the House, it

---

a repl. 'not'　　　*b* repl. 'tells'

---

1. See above, p. 187 & n. 3.
2. Bridgeman, the Lord Keeper, in
his speech on 10 October (*LJ*, xii.
115–16), had announced that the King
would allow parliament to enquire
into war-expenditure and would not
protect any of his officers guilty of
malpractice. At the same time he
had made what was to Crew an
unconvincing explanation of why
parliament had been allowed to sit
for only two days (25 and 29 July)
during the summer. Parliament had
been summoned, he said, to meet the
danger of the enemy's attacks on the
Thames, but by the end of July peace
negotiations had made their meeting
unnecessary.

might not be let*a* fall.[1]   After walking there a while, I took coach and to the Duke of York's House; and there went in for nothing into the pit at the last Act, to see *Sir Martin Marrall*;[2] and met my wife, who was there, and my brother and W. Hewer and Willett, and carried them home, still being pleased with the humour of [the] play, almost above all that ever I saw.   Home, and there do find that John Bowles is not yet come thither; I suppose he is playing the goodfellow in the town.   So to the office a while and then home to supper and to bed.

15.   Up, and to the office; where Sir W. Penn being ill of the gout, we all of us met there in his parlour and did the business of the office, our greatest business now being to manage the pay of the ships in order and with speed, to satisfy the Commissioners of the Treasury.[3]   This morning my brother set out for Brampton again, and is gone.   At noon home to dinner; and thence my wife and I and Willett to the Duke of York's House, where after long stay the King and Duke of York came, and there saw *The Coffee house*, the most ridiculous, insipid play that ever I saw in my life – and glad we were that Baterton had*b* no part in it.[4] But here, before the play begin, my wife begin to complain to me of Willetts confidence in sitting cheek by jowl by us; which was a poor thing, but I perceive she is already jealous of my kindness to her, so that I begin to fear this girl is not likely to stay long with us.   The play done, we home by coach, it being moonlight; and got well home, and I*c* to my chamber to settle some papers, and so to supper and to bed.

a   repl. 'removed'   *b*   repl. symbol rendered illegible
          c   repl. 'after'

---

1. The whole morning had been spent in debating whether it was appropriate to include this in the general address of thanks to the King. Some members objected, since Clarendon had not yet been legally charged or condemned; others argued that the King should be thanked since he had dismissed him 'to gratify the people': *CJ*, ix. 2; cf. Milward, pp. 86, 328–9.

2. One act of a performance could be seen without payment; see above, p. 440; below, 7 January 1668.   For the play, see above, p. 387 & n. 1.   (A).

3. On 2 October the Treasury had granted £10,000 to pay tickets dating from before the previous January: *CTB*, ii. 98.

4. Thomas Betterton was Pepys's favourite actor.   For the play, see above, p. 463 & n. 1.   (A).

16. Up, and at*ᵃ* home most of the morning with Sir H. Cholmly about some accounts of his;¹ and for news, he tells me that the Commons and Lords have concurred, and delivered the King their thanks, among other things, for his removal of the Chancellor – who took their thanks very well; and among other things, promised them (in these words) "never in any degree to entertain the Chancellor [in] any imployment again."² And he tells me that it is very true, he hath it from one that was by, that the King did give the Duke of York a sound reprimende; told him that he had lived with him with more kindness then ever any brother-King lived with a brother, and that he lived as much like a monarch as himself, but advised him not to cross him in his designs about the Chancellor. In which the Duke of York doth very wisely acquiesce*ᵇ* and will be quiet, but as the King bade him; but presently commands all his friends to be silent in the business of the Chancellor, and they were so.³ But that the Chancellor hath done all that is possible to provoke the King, and to bring himself to lose his head by enraging of people. He gone, I to the office, busy all the morning. At noon to Broad-street to Sir G. Carteret and Lord Brouncker, and there dined with them; and thence after dinner with Brouncker to White-hall (where the Duke of York is now newly come for this winter) and there did our usual business, which is but little; and so I away to the Duke of York's House, thinking, as we appointed, to meet my wife there, but she was not; and more, I was vexed to see Young (who is but a bad actor at best) act Macbeth in the room of Baterton, who poor man is sick.⁴ But Lord, what a prejudice it wrought in me against the whole play, and everybody else agreed in disliking this fellow. Thence home,

a repl. 'to my ch'-   *b* MS. 'acquiesh'

---

1. For the Tangier mole.
2. The two houses waited on the King at Whitehall with their address at 3 p.m. on the 15th. The King's reply, according to the official report, ran: 'I assure you I will never employ him again in any publick Affairs whatsoever' (*LJ*, xii. 119; *CJ*, ix. 4).

3. Sc. in the debates in parliament.
4. The casts of plays listed by Downes (pp. 20–9) show that Young usually played secondary roles. What Pepys saw was probably Davenant's spectacular adaptation: see above, v. 314, n. 3. (A).

and there find my wife gone home; because of this fellow's acting of the part, she went out of the house again. There busy at my chamber with Mr. Yeabsly, and then with Mr. Lewes about public business late; and so to supper and to bed.

17. Up; and being sent for by my Lady Batten, I to her and there she found fault with my not seeing her since her being a widow; which I excused as well as I could, though it is a fault, but it is my nature not to be forward in visits. But here she told me her condition (which is good enough, being sole executrix, to the disappointment of all her husband's children)[1] and prayed my friendship about the accounts of the prizes, which I promised her. And here do see what creatures widows are in weeping for their husbands, and then presently leaving off; but I cannot wonder at it, the cares of the world taking place of all other passions. Thence to the office – where all the morning busy; and at noon home to dinner, where Mr. John Andrews[2] and his wife came and dined with me, and pretty merry we were; only, I out of humour the greatest part of the dinner, by reason that my people had forgot to get wine ready (I having none in my house, which I cannot say now these almost three years I think, without having two or three sorts), by which we were fain to stay a great while while some*a* could be fetched. When it came, I begun to be merry, and merry we were; but it was an odd, strange thing to observe of Mr. Andrews what a fancy he hath to raw meat, that he eats it with no pleasure unless the blood run about his chops; which it did now, by a leg of mutton that was not above half-boiled; but it seems, at home all his meat is dressed so, and beef and all, and eats it so at nights also. Here most of our discourse is of the business of the Parliament, who run on mighty*b* furiously, having yesterday been almost all the morning complaining against some high proceedings of my Lord Chief Justice Keeling, that the gentlemen of the country did

a repl. 'som'-   b MS. 'my'

---

1. The children by his first wife.   2. Timber merchant of Bow.

complain against him in the House and run very high.¹ It is
the man that did fall out with my Cosen Roger Pepys once, at
the Assizes there, and would have laid him by the heels² – but it
seems a very able lawyer.

After dinner, I to the office, where we all met with intent to
proceed to the public sale of several prize shipps; but upon
discourse, my [Lord] Anglesy did discover (which troubled me
that he that is a stranger almost should do more then we ourselves
could) that the appraisements made by our officers were not above
half of what he had been offered for one of them, and did make it
good by bringing a gentleman to give us 700*l* for the*ᵃ* *Wildboare*,
which they valued but at 276*l* – which made us all startle and stop
the sale, and I did propose to acquaint the Duke of York with it;
and accordingly we did agree on it, and I wrote a severe letter
about it and we are to attend him with it tomorrow morning.³

This afternoon my Lord Anglesy tells us that the House of
Commons have this morning run into the enquiry in*ᵇ* many

a repl. 'what'   *b* repl. 'in'

---

1. The 'gentlemen of the country'
were the country party – critics of the
court. Kelyng's conduct of two
capital trials (in which he had fined
both juries) had led to the appointment of a committee of investigation
by the Commons on the 16th.
When they reported on 11 December,
it was voted that he had been guilty
of innovations amounting to the
exercise of 'an arbitrary and illegal
Power', that he had vilified Magna
Carta (which he had called 'Magna
Farta'), and that he should be brought
to trial. After he had appeared
before the house on 13 December, it
was resolved to take no further
action against him but a motion was
passed declaring illegal the fining or
imprisoning of juries. See below,
p. 577 & n. 4; *CJ*, ix. 4, 35–6, 37;
Grey, i. 63; J. Hatsell, *Precedents of
proceedings in Commons* (1818), iv.
123–4. Kelyng's high-handedness

was notorious; cf. E. Foss, *Judges of
Engl.* (1848–64), viii. 139–40.
2. In 1665 at the Cambridge assizes
he had bound over Roger Pepys
(Recorder of the borough) for speaking slightingly of Chief Justice Hyde:
Diary Sam. Newton (ed. Foster), p. 10.
3. The sale was due to begin at 3
p.m.: PRO, Adm. 106/3250, f. 37r.
On this same day, in fact, the pur-
chaser (Maj. Henry Nicoll) petitioned
the King for an abatement of his offer
(on the grounds of services he had
rendered to the King at the Restoration), and was granted the ship – a
flyboat – at the Navy Board's valua-
tion of £276 9s. 0d., and given a year
in which to pay. The ship was to be
used to bring over Irish timber for
the rebuilding of London, but she
foundered on her first voyage.
CSPD 1667, pp. 531–2; ib., *1667–8*,
p. 110; BM, Add. 9307, f. 75.

things; as, the sale of Dunkirke, the dividing of the fleet the last year, the business of the prizes with my Lord Sandwich, and many other things; so that now they begin to fall close upon it and God knows what will be the end of it, but a committee they have chosen to inquire into the miscarriages of the Warr.[1]

Having done, and being a little tired, Sir W. Penn and I in his coach out to Mile-end-green and there drank a cup of Bydes ale; and so talking about the high proceedings of Parliament and how little a thing the King is become to be forced to suffer it, though I declare my being satisfied that things should be enquired into, we back again home; and I to my office to my letters and so home to supper and to bed.

18. Up, and by coach with Sir W. Penn to White-hall and there attended the Duke of York; but first we find him to spend above an hour in private in his closet with Sir W. Coventry; which I was glad to see, that there is so much confidence between them. By and by we were called in and did our usual business, and complained of the business yesterday discovered,[a] of our officers abusing the King in the appraisement of the prizes. Here it was worth observing that the Duke of York considering what third-rate ship to keep abroad,[2] the *Rupert* was thought one;[b] but then it was said that Captain Hubbert was commander of her and that the King had a mind for Spragg to command[c] the ship, which would not be well, to be by turning out Hubbert, who is

a repl. 'disclover'- *b* repl. 'of' *c* MS. 'commander'

---

1. *CJ*, ix. 4. This Committee on Miscarriages, consisting of 56 members, conducted the first parliamentary enquiry ever made into the conduct of an entire war. It reported in February 1668, and condemned three naval failures in particular – the failure to pursue the Dutch after the Battle of Lowestoft in June 1665, the division of the fleet in June 1666, and the neglect to fortify Sheerness which had led to the humiliating raid on Chatham in June 1667. It also heavily criticised the Navy Board's payment of seamen by tickets. Its report, together with that of the Committee of Accounts (or Brooke House Committee, q.v. below, p. 559 & n. 2) led to the reorganisation of the Navy Board in 1668.

2. I.e. for the winter guard.

a good man but one that the Duke of York said he did not know whether he did so well conforme, as at this time, to please the people and Parliament.¹ Sir W. Coventry answered, and the Duke of York merrily agreed to it, that it was very hard to know what it was that the Parliament would call conformity at this time, and so it stopped – which I only observe to see how the Parliament's present temper doth amuse* them all.

Thence to several places to buy a hat and books and neck-cloths, and several errands I did before I got home; and among others, bought me two new pair of spectacles*a* of Turlington,² who it seems is famous for them. And his daughter, he being out of the way, doth advise me to very young sights,³ as that that will help me most; and promises me great ease from them, and I will try them. At the Exchange I met Creed and took him home with me and dined; and among other things, he tells me that Sir Rob. Brookes is the man that did mention that business in Parliament yesterday about my Lord Sandwich, but that it was seconded by nobody;*b* but the matter will fall before the Comittee for miscarriages.⁴ Thence after dinner, my wife and he and I and Willett to the King's House and saw *Brenoralt*, which is a good tragedy that I like well.⁵ And parted after the play and

---

a   repl. 'spectacle' badly formed   b   repl. 'b'-

---

1. Sir Edward Spragge had commanded the *Revenge*, now in dry
dock. John Hubbard retained command of the *Rupert. CSPD 1667*, p.
521; ib.*1667-8*, p.16. For Hubbard's
reputation as 'a proud conceited
fellow', see above, vii. 333-4.

2. John Turlington; his shop was
in Cornhill.

3. I.e. concave lenses, suitable for
young people suffering from short-
sight. Turlington himself later confirmed this advice (below, p. 519),
but the spectacles proved unsuitable
and Pepys never bought them. His
trouble appears to have been long-
sight, complicated by astigmatism:

see D'Arcy Power in *Occ. papers
Pepys Club*, i. 64+. Astigmatism
could not be diagnosed at this period,
nor could the cylindrical lenses necessary for its correction be made. The
use of spherical lenses, concave and
convex, for the correction of short-
and long-sight respectively, was
fairly common.

4. Brooke was appointed to the
committee and became its chairman.
Neither Grey nor Milward records
the speech.

5. Suckling's *Brennoralt, or The
discontented colonel* was in fact a tragicomedy; see above, ii. 139 & n. 4.
(A).

so home and there a little at my office; and so to my chamber and spent this night late in telling over all my gold and putting it into proper baggs and my Iron chest, being glad with my heart to see so much of it here again; but cannot yet*ᵃ* tell certainly how much I have lost by Gibson in his Journy and my father's burying of it in the dirt.¹ At this late, but did it to my mind, and so to supper and to bed.

19. At the office all the morning, where very busy; and at noon home to a short dinner, being full of my desire of seeing my Lord Orery's new play this afternoon at the King's house, *The Blacke prince*,² the first time it is acted; where though we came by 2 a-clock, yet there was no room in the pit, but we were forced to go into one of the upper-box at 4*s* apiece, which is the first time I ever sat in a box in my life.³ And in the same box came by and by, behind me, my Lord Berkly and his Lady; but I did not turn my face to them to be known, so that I was excused from giving them my seat.*ᵇ* And this pleasure I had, that from this place the Scenes do appear very fine endeed and much better then in the pit. The house infinite full, and the King and Duke of York was there. By and by the play begin, and in it nothing perticular but a very fine dance for*ᶜ* variety of figures, but a little too long. But as to the contrivance and all that was witty (which endeed was much, and very witty), was almost the same that had been in his two former plays of *Henry*

a repl. 'again'   *b* MS. 'self'   *c* repl. 'only'

---

1. Pepys now had £2720 7s. 3d. in gold. The accounts he made up this evening survive in Rawl. A. 185, f. 23*v*: 'State of Gold after my returne from Brampton. Oct 18 1667 . . . Memd. Soe much as my gold had cost mee less then 22d. and would have sold for more, I have lost of my Profit. Soe much as my praesent Quantity of gold yeeld mee lesse then 22d. I loose out of Purse, the price I then payd for them ariseing at most but to 2720. 07. 03. the 3 jacobus's given my Father in law being included.'

2. A rhymed 'tragedy' with a happy ending by Roger Boyle, Earl of Orrery; now performed for the first time; published in 1669. The cast listed by Downes (p. 14) includes Mohun as Edward III, Kynaston as the Black Prince, Mrs Marshall as Plantagenet, and Nell Gwyn as Alizia. (A).

3. But see above, iii. 211–12.

the 5th and *Mustapha*,[1] and the same points and turns of wit in both; and in this very same play often repeated, but in excellent language. And were so excellent that the whole House was mightily pleased with it all along, till towards the end he comes to discover the ⟨chief⟩ plot of the play by the reading of a long letter; which was so long and some things (the people being set already to think too long) so unnecessary,[a] that they frequently begin to laugh and to hiss twenty times, that had it not been for the King's being there, they had certainly hissed it off of the stage;[2] but I must confess that (as my Lord Berkely said behind me) the having of that long letter was a thing so absurd, that he could not imagine how a man of his parts could possibly fall into it; or if he did, if he had but let any friend read but the friend would have told him of it. And I must confess it is one of the most remarkable instances that ever I did or expect to meet with in my life, of a wise man's not being wise at all times and in all things, for nothing could be more ridiculous then this; though the letter of itself at another time would be thought an excellent letter; and endeed an excellent Romance; but at the end of the play, when everybody was weary of sitting and were already possessed with the effect of the whole letter, to trouble them with a letter of a quarter of an hour long was a most absurd thing. After the play done, and nothing pleasing them from the time of that letter to the end of the play, people being put into a bad humour of disliking (which is another thing worth the noting), I home by coach; and could not forbear laughing almost[b] all the way home, and all the evening to my going to bed, at the ridiculousness of the letter; and the more because my wife was angry with me and the world for laughing, because the King was there, though she cannot defend the length of the letter. So after having done business at the office, I home to supper and to bed.

a repl. 'long'   *b* repl. 'at'

---

1. A rhymed heroic drama and a tragedy respectively. See above, v. 240 & n. 2; vi. 73 & n. 1. (A).

2. Charles Hart in the role of Lord Delaware read this letter in Act V. This episode was afterwards omitted, as Pepys notes on the following 23 October. (A).

20. *Lords day.* Up, and put on my new Tunique of velvett, which is very plain, but good. This morning is brought to me an order for the presenting the committee of Parliament to-morrow with a list of the commanders and ships' names of all[a] the fleets set out since the war, and perticularly of those ships which were divided from the fleet with Prince Rupert;[1] which gives me occasion to see that they are busy after that business – and I am glad of it. So I alone to church and then home, and there Mr. Deane[2] comes and dines with me by appointment; and both at and after dinner, he and I spent all the day till it was dark in discourse of business of the Navy and the ground of the many miscarriages; wherein he doth inform me in many more then I knew, and I had desired him to put them in writing; and many endeed they are, and good ones. And also we discoursed of the business of shipping, and he hath promised me a Draught of the ship he is now building[3] – wherein I am mightily pleased. This afternoon comes to me Captain O Bryan, about a ship that the King hath given him,[4] and he and I to talk of the Parliament and he tells me that the business of the Duke of York's slackening sail in the first fight, at the beginning of the war,[5] is brought into Question, and Sir W Pen and Captain Cox is to appear tomorrow about it. And is thought will at last be laid[b] upon Mr. Brouncker's bringing orders from the Duke of York (which the Duke of York doth not own) to Captain Cox

---

a repl. same symbol badly formed   *b* repl. 'thought'

---

1. For the division of the fleet in the action of June 1666, see above, vii. 144 & n. 1. The committee appointed to enquire into the miscarriages of the war had met for the first time on the afternoon of Saturday the 19th: *CJ*, ix. 45. Pepys's copy of the lists given by the Navy Board to the committee is in Rawl. A 195a, ff. 255–63.

2. Anthony Deane, Master-Shipwright, Harwich dockyard.

3. Possibly the *Resolution*, a third-rate, launched at Harwich in December: *Further Corr.*, p. 186.

4. Charles O'Brien, courtier and gentleman-captain, was a friend of Monmouth and Lady Castlemaine, by virtue, according to Pepys, of his 'quallity and Guift of Daunceing' (NWB, p. 221). He had been granted the *St Jacob* fireship, now put up for sale by the Navy Board. On 20 November he was given another prize-ship, the *St Mary* of St Jean de Luz. *CSPD 1667–8*, pp. 25, 31.

5. The Battle of Lowestoft, June 1665.

to do it; but it seems they do resent this very highly, and are mad in going through all businesses where they can lay any fault.[1] I am glad to hear that in the world I am as kindly spoke of as anybody; for, for aught I see, there is bloody work like to be, Sir W. Coventry having been forced to produce a letter in Parliament wherein the Duke of Albemarle did from Sherenesse write in what good posture all things were at Chatham, and that the Chain was so well placed that he feared no attempt of the enemy.[2] So that, among ⟨other⟩ things, I see everybody is upon his own defence, and spares not to blame another to defend himself; and the same course I shall take. But God knows where it will end. He gone and Deane, I to my chamber for a while, and then comes Pelling the apothecary to see us and sat and supped with me (my wife being gone to bed sick of the Cholique); and then I to bed after supper. Pelling tells me that my[a] Lady Duchesse Albemarle was at Mrs. Turner's this afternoon (she being ill) and did there publicly talk of business and of our Office, and that she believed that I was safe and had done well; and so, I thank God, I hear everybody speaks of me, and endeed, I think without vanity I may expect to be profited rather then injured by this enquiry which the Parliament makes into business.

---

a   repl. 'Mrs. Turner'

---

1. During the night of 3–4 June the English fleet, in pursuit of the defeated Dutch, had lost touch with the enemy. Henry Brouncker, an officer of the Duke of York's household, was generally held responsible: in his anxiety to protect the Duke's life – possibly on instructions from the Duchess – he had taken to Harman and John Cox (captain and sailing-master respectively of the *Royal Charles*) an order to slacken sail which he had falsely represented to have come from the Duke, who was asleep at the time. Penn was also on the *Royal Charles*, as the Duke's professional adviser. After this en-quiry, Brouncker was expelled from parliament (21 April 1668), and Harman exonerated. Duke of York, *Life* (ed. J. S. Clarke), i. 415–17, 421; Clarendon, *Life*, ii. 396–9; Milward, pp. 269–70, 329–30; Penn, ii. 495+; Lister, ii. 334+; Harris, i. 300+. Pepys later remarked (*Naval Minutes*, p. 119; c. 1682) on the clumsiness and futility of the parliamentary enquiry into this business.

2. The letter (now untraced) was addressed to the King. See summary in Milward, p. 90 (19 October). Cf. Coventry to Navy Board, 12 June 1667: *CSPD Add. 1660–85*, pp. 191–2.

21. Up, and betimes got a coach at the Exchange and thence to St. James's, where I had forgot that the Duke of York and family was gone to White-hall;[1] so to White-hall and thence to Westminster-hall and there walked a little, finding the Parliament likely to be very busy all this morning about the business of Mr. Brouncker, for advising Cox and Harman to shorten sail when they were in pursuit of the Dutch after the first great victory. I went away to Mr. Creeds chamber, there to meet Sir H. Cholmly about business of Mr. Yeabsly; where I was delivered of a great fear that they would Question some of the orders for payment of money which I*a* had got them signed in the time of the plague, when I was here alone; but all did pass. Thence to Westminster again and up to the Lobby, where many commanders of the fleet were, and Captain Cox and Mr. Pierce the surgeon – the last of which hath been in the House and declared that he heard Brouncker advise and give arguments to Cox, for the safety of the Duke of York's person, to shorten sail, that they might not be in the middle of the enemy in the morning alone. And Cox denying to*b* observe his advice, having received the Duke of York's commands overnight to keep within cannon*c*-shot (as they then were) of the enemy, Brouncker did go to Harman and used the same arguments, and told him that he was sure it would be well pleasing to the King that care should be taken of not endangering the Duke of York;[2] and after much persuasion, Harman was*d* heard to say, "Why, if it must be, then lower the topsail"; and so did shorten sail – to the loss, as the Parliament will have it, of the greatest victory that ever was, and which would have saved all the expense of blood and money and honour that fallowed; and this they do resent, so as to put it to the Question whether Brouncker should not be carried to the Tower – who doth confess that out of kindness to the Duke of York's safety, he did advise that they should do so, but did not

a repl. 'they'   *b* repl. 'it'   *c* repl. 'cannot'   *d* repl. 'why'

1. They usually wintered at White-hall.

2. Cf. Milward, p. 91: 'Mr Pearse . . . affirms . . . that Harman and Brouncker said that if the Duke should miscarry the King would take it ill and require it of him.'

use the Duke of York's name therein; and so it was only his error in advising it, but the greatest theirs, in taking it contrary to order.[1] At last it ended that it should be suspended till Harman comes home; and then the Parliament-men do all tell me that it will fall heavy, and they think be fatal to Brouncker or him.   Sir W. Penn tells me he was gone to bed, having been all day labouring, and then not able to stand, of the goute; and did give order for the keeping the sails standing, as they then were, all night.   But which I wonder at, he tells me that he did not know the next day that they had shortened sail, nor ever did enquire into it till about ten days ago, that this begun to be mentioned; and endeed, it is charged privately as a fault on the Duke of York, that he did not presently examine the reason of the breach of his orders and punish it.   But Cox tells me that he did finally refuse it; and what prevailed with Harman he knows not, and doth think that we might have done considerable service on the enemy the next day, if this had not been done.   Thus this business ended today, having kept them till almost 2 a-clock; and then I by coach with Sir W. Penn as far as St. Clements, talking of this matter; and there set down and I walked to Sir G. Carteret's and there dined with him and several Parliament-men, who I perceive do all look upon it as a thing certain that the Parliament will enquire into everything and will be very severe where they can find any fault.   Sir W. Coventry, I hear, did this day make a speech in Apology for his reading the letter of the Duke of Albemarle, concerning the good condition which Chatham[a] was in before the enemy came thither – declaring his simple intentions therein, without prejudice to my Lord[2] – and I am told that he was also with the Duke of Albemarle yesterday to excuse it; but this day I do hear by[b] some of Sir W. Coventry's friends, that they think he hath done himself much Injury by making this man and his interest so much his enemy.

<hr />

a repl. 'Sher'-   *b* repl. 'that'

<hr />

1. 'Mr. Brouncker . . . is said to have spoken much and well for him-selfe': newsletter (21 October) in *Bulstrode Papers*, i. 2.

2. See above, p. 490 & n. 2.   The King is said to have tried but failed to assuage the ruffled Albemarle: Sir J. Nicholas to Sir E. Nicholas, 23 October, BM, Egerton 2539, f. 129*v*.

After dinner, I away to Westminster, and up to the Parliament-house and there did wait with great patience, till 7 at night, to be called in to the Committee, who sat all this afternoon examining the business of Chatham;*a* and at last was called in and told that the list they expected from us*b* Mr. Wren had promised them, and only bade me to bring all my fellow-officers thither to attend them tomorrow afternoon – Sir Rob. Brookes in the chair; methinks a sorry fellow to be there, because a young man, and yet he seems to speak very well.

I gone thence, my Cosen Pepys comes out to me and walks in the Hall with me; and bids me prepare to answer to everything, for they do seem to lodge the business of Chatham upon the Commissioners of the Navy, and that they are resolved to lay the fault heavy somewhere and to punish it; and prays me to prepare to save myself and gives me hints what to prepare against – which I am obliged to him for – and do begin to mistrust lest some unhappy slip or other, after all my diligence*c* and pains, may not be found (which I can foresee) that may prove as fatal to a man as the constant course of negligence and unfaithfulness of other men.

Here we parted, and I to White-hall to Mr. Wren's chamber, there to advise with him about the list of ships and commanders which he is to present to the Parliament;[1] and took coach (little Michell being with me, whom I took with me from Westminster-hall) and setting him down in Gracious-street, home myself, where I find my wife and the two Mercers and Willett and W. Batelier have been dancing, but without a fidler; I had a little pleasure in talking with these, but my head and heart full of thoughts, between hope and fear and doubts what will become of us, and me perticularly, against a*d* furious Parliament. Then broke up and to bed; and there slept pretty well till about 4

---

a s.h. repl. s.h. 'Cham'-   b repl. 'me'
c MS. 'ligance' repl. 'dig'-   d repl. 'an'

---

1. Pepys kept a copy (in an un-identified clerk's hand) entitled (in his own hand): 'Names of the Severall Commanders of his Majesty's Ships in the Yeares 1665 1666 1667. Being Copys of Mr. Wren's Lists given in to the Comittee of Parliament. Octob. 1667.' (Rawl. A 195a, ff. 255–63.)

a–clock, and from that^a time could not, but my thoughts running on speeches to the Parliament to excuse myself from the blame which by other men's negligences will light, it may be, upon the office.

This day I did get a list of the fourteen perticular miscarriages which are already before the committee to be examined;[1] wherein, besides two or three that will concern this office much, there are those of the Prizes, and that of Bergen, and not fallowing the Dutch ships, against my Lord Sandwich,[2] that I^b fear will ruine him unless he hath very good luck or they may be in better temper before he can come to be charged – but my heart is full of fear for him and his family.

I hear that they do prosecute the business against my^c Lord Chief Justice Keeling with great severity.[3]

22. Slept but ill all the last part of the night, for fear of this day's success* in Parliament; therefore up, and all of us all the morning close, till almost 2 a–clock, collecting all we had to say and had done from the beginning touching the safety of the River Medway and Chatham; and having done this and put it into order, we away, I not having time to eat my dinner; and so all in my Lord Brouncker's coach (that is to say, Brouncker, W. Penn, T. Harvy, and myself), talking of the other great matter with which they charge us, that is, of discharging men by ticket,[4] in order to our defence in case that should be asked. We came to the Parliament-door; and there, after a little waiting till the Committee was sat, we were, the House being very full, called in (Sir W. Penn went in and sat as a Member; and my Lord Brouncker would not at first go in, expecting to have a chair set for him, and his brother[5] had long bid him not go in till he was called for; but after a few words I had occasion to mention him, and so he was called in, but without any more

---

a repl. 'time' *b* repl. 'will' *c* repl. 'my'

---

1. Pepys's note of these items (22 October) is in Rawl. A 195a, f. 6r.
2. See above, vi. 231, 196; viii. 489–90.

3. See above, pp. 483–4 & n.
4. See below, pp. 538, 545–6 & nn.
5. Henry Brouncker, M.P. for New Romney, Kent.

chair or respect paid him then myself);[1] and so Brouncker and
T. Harvy and I were there to answer, and I had a chair brought
for me to lean*ᵃ* my books upon; and so did give them such an
account, in a series, of the whole business that had passed the
office touching the matter, and so answered all Questions given
me about it, that I did not perceive but they were fully satisfied
with me and the business as*ᵇ* to our Office;[2] and then Comissioner Pett (who was by at all my discourse, and this held*ᶜ*
till within an hour after candlelight, for I had candles brought
in to read my papers by) was to answer for himself, we having
lodged*ᵈ* all matters with him for execution. But Lord, what a
tumultuous thing this committee is, for all the reputation they
have of a great council, is a strange consideration; there being as
impertinent* Questions, and as disorderly proposed, as any man
could make. But Comissioner Pett, of all men living, did
make the weakest defence for himself; nothing to the purpose
nor to satisfaction nor certain, but sometimes one thing and
sometimes another, sometimes for himself and sometimes against
him; and his greatest failure was (that I observed) from his
not*ᵉ* considering whether the Question propounded was his part
to answer to or no, and the thing to be done was his work to do –
the want of which distinction will overthrow him; for he concerns himself in giving an account of the disposal of the boats,
which he had no reason at all to do, or take any blame upon
him for them.[3] He charged the not carrying up of the *Charles*
upon the Tuesdy, to the Duke of Albemarle; but I see the
House is mighty favourable to the Duke of Albemarle and
would give little way to it. And something of want of armes

---

a repl. 'lam'   *b* repl. 'at'
MS. 'hel' (phonetic)   *d* repl. 'lodging'   *e* MS. 'from'

---

1. Brouncker was a peer but only
an Irish one.
2. The Navy Board disclaimed immediate responsibility. They argued
that after 3 December 1666 Commissioner Pett had been responsible,
by the Duke's order, for the defence
of Chatham, and that Sheerness had
become the responsibility of the Ordnance Office once the Navy Board
had made recommendations on its
fortification.   Milward, pp. 330–1.
3. Sir Edward Spragge, the officer
commanding the ships in the river,
had charge of the boats: below. 5
January 1668.

he spoke, which Sir J Duncomb answered with great imperiousness and earnestness; but for all that, I do see the House is resolved to be better satisfied in the business of the unreadiness of Sherenesse, and want of armes and ammunition there and everywhere; and all their officers were here today attending, but only one called in about armes for boats to answer Comissioner Pett. None of my Brethren said anything but myself; only two or three silly words my Lord Brouncker gave, in answer to one Question about the number of men there in*a* the King's yard at that time.

At last*b* the House dismissed us, and shortly after did adjourne the debate till Friday next; and my Cosen Pepys did come out and joy me in my acquitting myself so well, and so did several others, and my fellow-officers all very briske to see themselfs so well acquitted – which makes me a little proud, but yet not secure but we may yet meet with a back-blow which we see not.

So, with our hearts very light, Sir W. Penn and I in his coach home, it being now near 8 a-clock; and so to the office and did a little business by the post, and so home, hungry, and eat a good supper and so, with my mind well at ease, to bed – my wife not very well of those.

23. Up, and Sir W. Penn and I in his coach to White-hall, there to attend the Duke of York, but came a little too late and so missed it; only, spoke with him and heard him correct my Lord Barkely, who fell foul on Sir Ed. Spragg (who it seems said yesterday to the House, that if the Officers of the Ordinance had done as much work at Sherenesse in ten weeks as the Prince did in ten days, he could have defended the place against the Dutch); but the Duke of York told him that everybody must have liberty at this time to make their own defence, though it be to the charging of the fault upon any other, so it be true – so I perceive the whole world is at work in blaming one another. Thence Sir W. Penn and I back into London, and there saw the King with his Kettledrums and Trumpets, going to

a repl. full stop   *b* repl. 'the'

---

1. I.e. Officers of the Ordnance.

the Exchange to lay the first stone of the first Piller of the new building of the Exchange[1] – which, the gates being shut, I could not get in to see; but with Sir W. Penn to Captain Cocke's to drink a dram of brandy, and so he to the Treasury Office about Sir G. Carteret's accounts, and I took coach and back again toward Wesminster; but in my way stopped at the Exchange and got in, the King being newly gone, and there find the bottom of the first pillar laid; and here was a shedd set up and hung with tapestry, and a Canopy of state, and some good victuals and wine for the King, who it seems did eat,[a] and so a great many people, as Tom Killigrew and others of the Court, there; and there I did eat a mouthful and drink a little, and do find Mr. Gawden in his Gowne as Sheriffe, and understand that the King hath this morning Knighted him upon the place (which I am mightily pleased with), and I think the other Sheriffe, who is Davis the little fellow, my schoolfellow, the bookseller who was one of Audly's Executors and now become Sheriffe;[2] which is a strange turn methinks. Here mighty merry (there being a great deal of good company) for a quarter of an hour, and so I away and to Wesminster-hall, where I came just as the House rose; and there in the Hall met with Sir W. Coventry, who is in pain to defend himself in the business of Tickets, it being said that the paying of the ships at Chatham by ticket was by his direction, and he hath wrote to me to find his letters and show them him, but I find none; but did there argue the case with him, and I think no great blame can be laid on us[b] for that matter; only, I see he is fearful. And he tells me his mistake in the House the other day, which occasions him much trouble, in showing of the House the Duke of Albemarle's letter about the good condition of Chatham; which he is sorry for and owns as a mistake, the thing not being necessary to have been done, and confesses that nobody

---

a MS. 'it'   *b* repl. 'him'

---

1. Reports of the ceremony are in *London Gazette*, 24 October, and Rugge, ii, f. 214*v*. The new Exchange was built on the site of the old, and was re-opened on 28 September 1668: BM, Add. 19526, f. 186*r*.

2. Thomas Davies, bookseller, had been at St Paul's School with Pepys. Hugh Audley was a famous moneylender: see above, iii. 264 & n. 2. Description of the dubbing of the knights in Rugge, ii, f. 214*v*.

can escape from such error sometimes or other. He says the House was well satisfied with my report yesterday; and so several others told me in the hall, that my report was very good and satisfactory – and that I have got advantage by it in the House. I pray God it may prove so. Here, after the hall pretty empty, I did walk a few turns with Comissioner Pett and did give the poor weak man some advice for his advantage, how to better his pleading for himself; which I think he will, if he can remember and practise; for I would not have the man suffer what he doth not deserve, there being enough of what he doth deserve to lie upon him. Thence to Mrs. Martins, and there stayed till 2 a-clock and drank and talked, and did give her 3*l* to buy my god-daughter her first new gowne – and I did hazer algo*ᵃ* con her; and so away homeward and in my way met Sir W. Penn in Cheapside, and went into his coach and back again and to the King's playhouse and there saw *The Black Prince*[1] again; which is now mightily bettered by the long letter's being printed, and so delivered to everybody at their going in, and some short reference made to it by *ᵇ* Heart in the play, which doth mighty well; but when all is done, I think it the worst play of my Lord Orery's. But here, to my great satisfaction, I did see my Lord Hinching-brooke and his mistress[2] (with her father and mother); and am mightily pleased with the young lady, being handsome enough and endeed to my great liking, as I would have her. I could not but look upon them all the play, being exceeding pleased with my good hap to see them; God bring them together; and they are now already mighty kind to one another, and he is as it were one of their family. The play done, I home and to the office a while, and then home to supper, very hungry; and then to my chamber to read the true story in Speed of the Black Prince;[3] and so to bed.

---

a repl. 'algo conebam' (= 'algo con eam' garbled)
    b MS. 'in'

---

1. See above, p. 488 & n. 1. (A).
2. Lady Anne Boyle, daughter of the 1st Earl of Burlington, who married Lord Hinchingbrooke in the following January. A portrait of her (after Lely) is reproduced in Harris, ii, opp. p. 180.
3. John Speed, *The history of Great Britaine* (1650), bk 9, ch. xii.

This day it was moved in the House that a day might be appointed to bring in an Impeachment against the Chancellor, but it was decried as being irreguler; but that if there was ground for complaint, it might be brought to the committee for miscarriages, and if they thought good, to present it to the House; and so it was carried.[1] They did also vote this day thanks to be given to the*a* Prince and Duke of Albemarle for their care and conduct in the last year's war[2] – which is a strange act; but I know not how, that blockhead Albemarle hath strange luck to be beloved, though he be, and every man must know, the heaviest man*b* in the world, but stout and honest to his country.

This evening late, Mr. Moore came to me to prepare matters for my Lord Sandwiches defence; wherein I can little assist, but will do all I can, and am in great fear of nothing but the damned business of the Prizes[3] – but I fear my Lord will receive a shrowd deal of trouble by it.

24. Up, and to the office, where all the morning very busy; and at noon took Mr. Hater home with me to dinner, and instantly back again to write what letters I had to write, that I might go abroad with my wife, who was not well, only to jumble her; and so to the Duke of York's playhouse but there, Baterton not being yet well, we would*c* not stay (though since I hear that Smith doth act his part in *The Villaine*,[4] which was

---

a repl. 'my'   *b* repl. 'logger'-   *c* repl. 'would'

---

1. This motion does not appear in the Commons' *Journals*. 'To appoint a set day was to invite all men to bring in a charge ... when at present there appeared no just cause to accuse him': Milward, p. 95. The original motion was Sir Thomas Littleton's. A committee to examine precedents in this matter of impeachments for capital charges was appointed on the 26th and reported on the 29th, when another committee was set up to make out the charges in proper form.

2. The vote of thanks was coupled with the request that Rupert and Albemarle be asked to inform the committee about any miscarriages, particularly the division of the fleet: *CJ*, ix. 7.

3. See above, vi. 231, n. 1.

4. A tragedy by Thomas Porter; see above, iii. 229–30 & n. William Smith, one of the leading actors in the Duke of York's Company, played the role of Monsieur Brisac. (A).

then acted, as well or better then he; which I do not believe); but to Charing-cross, there to see *Polichinelli*;[1] but it being begun, we in to see a Frenchman (at the house where my wife's father last lodged), one Monsieur Prin, play on[a] the Trump. Marine, which he doth beyond belief; and the truth is, it doth so far out-do a Trumpet as nothing more, and he doth play anything very true and it is most remarkable; and at first was a mystery to me that I should hear a whole consort of chords together at the end of a pause, but he showed me that it was only when the last notes were fifths or thirds one to another, and then their sounds like an Echo did last, so as they seemed to sound all together. The instrument is open at the end I discovered, but he would not let me look into it; but I was mightily pleased with it, and he did take great pains to show me all he could do on it, which was very much – and would make an excellent consort, two or three of them, better then trumpets can ever do because of their want of compass.[2] Here we also saw again the two fat children come out of Ireland,[3] and a brother and sister of theirs now come, which are of little ordinary growth, like other people; but Lord, how strange it is to observe the difference between the same children, come out of the same little woman's belly.

Thence to Mile End Greene and there drank; and so home, bringing home night with us; and so to the office a little and then to bed.

a   repl. 'therein'

---

1. See above, p. 421, n. 2; cf. above, iii. 254 & n. 5.   (A).

2. The trump-marine (now obsolete) was a stringed instrument – long and narrow in shape – on which loud and brassy notes were produced with the help of the sympathetic reverberation of wire strings concealed inside the sound-box. Jean-Baptiste Prin is said to have been the most remarkable player ever to perform on it. He played instruments made to his own design, often fitted with as many as 21–24 concealed strings. (He may well have been unwilling to reveal these secrets to a stranger such as Pepys.) The trumpets of this period were of several types, but all (until the introduction of the modern valved instrument in the 19th century) had limited registers.

3. See above, p. 326 & n. 4.

25. Up, and all the morning close till 2 a-clock, till I had not time to eat my dinner, to*a* make our answer ready for the Parliament this afternoon, to show how Comissioner Pett was*b* singly concerned in the executing of all orders at Chatham, and that we did properly lodge all orders with him.*c* Thence with Sir W. Penn to the Parliament committee, and there we all met and did show, my Lord Brouncker and I, our Comissions under the Great Seal in behalf of all the rest, to show them our duties; and there I had no more matters asked me, but were bid to withdraw; and did there wait, I did all the afternoon till 8 at night, while they were examining several about the business [of] Chatham again; and perticularly, my Lord Brouncker did meet with two or three blurs that he did not think of – one from Spragg, who says that the *Unity* was ordered up, contrary to his order, by my Lord Brouncker and Commissioner Pett – another by Crispin the waterman, who said he was upon the *Charles* and spoke to Lord Brouncker, coming by in his boat, to know whether they should carry up the *Charles*, they being a great many naked men without armes; and he told them she was well as she was. Both these have little in them endeed, but yet both did stick close against [him]; and he is the*d* weakest man in the world to make his defence – and so is like to have much fault laid*e* on him therefrom. Spragg was in with them all the afternoon, and hath much fault laid on him, for a man that minded his pleasure and little else of his whole charge. I walked in the Lobby, and there do hear from Mr. Chichly that they were, the Commissioners of the Ordinance, shrewdly put to it yesterday, being examined with all severity and were hardly used by them, much otherwise then we, and did go away with mighty blame, and I am told by everybody that it is likely to stick mighty hard upon them; at which everybody is glad, because of Duncomb's pride and their expecting to have the thanks of the House, whereas they have deserved, as the Parliament*f* apprehends, as bad as bad can be.

Here is great talk of an Impeachment brought in against my

Lord Mordant,[1] and that another will be brought in against my Lord Chancellor in a few days.[2]

Here I understand for certain that they have ordered that my Lord Arlington's letters and Secretary Morrice's letters-of-Intelligence be consulted about the business of the Dutch fleet's coming abroad[3] – which is a very high point, but this they have done; but in what perticular manner I cannot justly say, whether it was not with the King's leave first asked.[4]

Here late, as I have said; and at last they broke up and we had our commissions again. And I do hear how Birch[5] is the high man that doth examine and trouble everybody with his questions; and they say that he doth labour all he can to clear Pett, but it seems a witness is come in tonight, Captain Millet, who doth declare that he did deliver a message from the Duke of Albemarle time enough for him to carry up the *Charles*, and he neglected it – which will stick very hard, it seems, on him.

So Sir W. Penn and I in his coach home and there to supper, a good supper; and so, weary and my eyes spent, to bed.

26. Up, and we met all this morning at Sir W. Penn's roome, the office being fowle with the altering of our garden-door. There very busy, and at noon home to dinner, where Mrs. Pierce and her daughter, husband, and Mrs. Corbet dined with me; I had a good dinner for them, and mighty merry. Pierce and I very glad at the fate of the officers of the Ordinance, that they are like to have so much blame on them. Here Mrs. Pierce tells me that the two Marshalls at the King's House are Stephen Marshalls, the

---

1. Cf. above, vii. 386 & n. 2. On this day Taylor brought into the Commons another petition against Mordaunt, with articles of impeachment annexed. A committee was appointed but no further proceedings were taken. *CJ*, ix. 8.

2. The charges were presented to the Commons on the 26th, and his impeachment voted on 11 November.

3. In June 1666, when the English fleet was caught divided.

4. The King's leave had been obtained for the production of these papers. Even so it was an infraction of prerogative and of official secrecy to have them brought before a parliamentary committee. *CJ*, xi. 6, 7, 8; Milward, pp. 105, 109.

5. Col. John Birch, M.P. for Penryn; an expert on naval affairs and always a sharp critic of the court.

great Presbyterian's, daughters:[1] and that Nelly[2] and Beck Marshall falling out the other day, the latter called the other my Lord Buckhursts whore; Nell answered that "I was but one ⟨man's⟩ whore, though I was brought up in a bawdy-house to fill strong water to the guest; and you are a whore to[a] three or four, though a Presbyter's praying daughter" – which was very pretty. Mrs. Pierce is still very pretty but paints red on her face, which makes me hate her, that I thank God I take no pleasure in her at all more.[3] After much mirth and good company at dinner, I to the office and left them, and Pendleton also, who came in to see my wife and talk of dancing; and there at the office I all the afternoon very busy and did much business, with mighty[b] great content to see it go off of hand; and so home, my eyes spent, to supper and to bed.

27. *Lords day.* Up and to my office, there with W. Hewer to dictate[c] a long letter to the Duke of York about the bad state of the office,[4] it being a work I do think fit for the office to do, though it be to no purpose but for their vindication in these bad times; for I do now learn many things tending to our safety which I did not wholly forget before, but do find the fruits of and would I had practised them more; as among other things, to be sure to let our answers to orders bear date presently after their date, that we may be found quick in our execution – this did us great good the other day before the Parliament.

All the morning at this. At noon home to dinner – with my own family alone. After dinner, I down to Deptford, the first time that I went to look upon the *Maybolt*, which the King hath given me;[5] and there she is, and I did meet with Mr. Uthwayte,[6]

a repl. 'to three' *b* MS. 'my' *c* repl. 'do'

---

1. Stephen Marshall (d. 1655) had been one of the leaders of the Presbyterian clergy during the Puritan Revolution. It was not he who was the father of the actresses, but an obscure provincial parson of the same surname, who as chaplain to the 2nd Lord Gerard of Gerard's Bromley (d. 1622), had been married off to the bastard daughter of a Cheshire squire, John Dutton of Dutton. See Sir P. Leycester, *Hist. Antiquities* (1673), pp. 258-9.

2. Nell Gwyn.

3. Cf. above, p. 439 & n. 2.

4. Untraced.

5. See above, p. 456 & n. 1.

6. Clerk of the Survey at Deptford.

who doth tell me that there are new sails ordered to be delivered her and a cable (which I did not speak of at all to him;) so thereupon I told him I would not be my own hindrance so much as to take her into my custody before*a* she had them; which was all I said to him, but desired him to take a strict inventory of her, that I might not be cheated by the master nor the company when they come to understand that the vessel is given away – which he hath promised me; and so away back again home, reading all the way the book of the Collection of Oaths in the several offices in this nation,[1] which is worth a man's reading; and so home, and there my boy[2] and I to sing, and at it all the evening; and to supper and so to bed.

This evening came Sir J. Minnes to me, to let me know that a Parliament-man hath been with him, to tell him that the Parliament intends to examine him perticularly about Sir W. Coventry's selling of places[3] and about my Lord Brouncker discharging the ships at Chatham by ticket[4] – for the former of which I am more perticularly sorry that that business of W. Coventry should come up again; though this old man tells me, and I believe, that he can say nothing to it.

28. Up, and by water to White-hall (calling at Michells and drink a dram of water*; but it being earely, I did not see his wife) and thence walked to Sir W. Coventry's lodging, but he was gone out; and so going towards St. James's, I found him at his house which is fitting for him;[5] and there I to him and was with him above an hour alone, discours[ing] of the matters of

---

a repl. same symbol badly formed

1. *The book of oaths . . . very useful for all persons whatsoever, especially those that undertake any office of magistracy or publique employment;* attributed to Richard Garnet. It prints the oaths of office of the sovereign, the principal ministers, and some minor officers, but not of the naval officials. Wing (G264) gives the date of the first edition as 1649, and lists no other edition, apart from that of 1689. PL 909 (1689 ed.).

2. Tom Edwards.

3. Cf. above, vii. 306–7 & n.

4. See below, pp. 538, 545–6 & nn.

5. Later no. 79 Pall Mall, on the s. side; afterwards the house of Nell Gwyn. Coventry had bought the lease in this year for £1400, selling it in February 1670: LCC, *Survey of London*, xxix. 377. (R).

the nation and our office and himself. He owns that he is at this day the chief person aymed at by the Parliament; that is, by the friends of my Lord Chancellor and also by the Duke of Albemarle, by reason of his unhappy showing of the Duke of Albemarle's letter the other day in the House;[1] but that he thinks that he is not liable to any hurt they can fasten on him for anything, he is so well armed to justify himself in everything, unless in the old business of selling places, when he says everybody did; and he will now not be forward to tell his own story as he hath been, but tells me he is grown wiser and will put them to prove anything and he will defend himself. Besides that, he will dispute the Statute,[2] thinking that it will not be found to reach him. We did talk many things; which, as they come into my mind now, I shall set down without order. That he is weary of public imployment, and neither ever designed nor will ever, if his commission were brought to him wrapped in gold, would he accept of any single place in the State, as perticularly Secretary of State, which he says the world discourses Morrice is willing to resign;[3] and he thinks the King might have thought of him, but he would not by any means now take it if given him, nor anything but in commission with others, who may bear part of the blame;[4] for now he observes well, that whoever did do anything singly are now in danger, however honest and painful they were; saying[a] that he himself was the only man, he thinks, at the council-board that spoke his mind clearly, as he thought, to the good of the King; and the rest, who sat silent, have nothing said to them nor are taken notice of. That the first time the King did take him so closely into his confidence and ministry of affairs

a repl. 'while'

---

1. See above, p. 490 & n. 2.

2. That of 1552 (5–6 Edw. VI c. 16) forbidding the corrupt selling of places.

3. Sir William Morice, admirable as an administrator and member of parliament, was unhappy and ineffective in court politics. In 1666 his friends had tried in vain to have

him recognised as the senior secretary (taking precedence over Arlington): *CSPD 1666–7*, p. 85; F. M. G. Evans, *Principal Secretary of State, 1558–1630*, p. 124. He retired thankfully to a life of books and country pursuits in September 1668.

4. Coventry had accepted a place on the Treasury commission in June.

was upon the business of Chatham, when all the disturbances were there and in the Kingdom; and then, while everybody was fencing for himself, the King did find him to persuade him to call for the Parliament, declaring that it was against his own proper interest, forasmuch as likely they would find faults with him, as well as with others, but that [he] would prefer the service of the King before his own; and thereupon the King did take him into his special notice, and from that time to this hath received him so. And that then he did see the folly and mistakes of the Chancellor in the management of things, and saw that matters were never likely to be well in that sort of conduct, and did persuade the King to think fit of the taking away the seals from the Chancellor; which when it was done, he told me that he himself, in his own perticular, was sorry for it; for while he stood, there was he and my Lord Arlington to stand between him and harm, whereas now there is only my Lord Arlington, and he is now down,[1] so that all their fury is placed upon him; but that he did tell the King when he first moved it, that if he thought the laying of him, W. Coventry, aside would at all facilitate the removing of the Chancellor, he would most willing submit to it – whereupon the King did command him to try the Duke of York about it and persuade him to it; which he did by the King's command undertake and compass, and the Duke of York did own his[a] consent to the King, but afterward was brought to be of another mind for the Chancellor and now is displeased with him and the Duchesse, so that she will not see him; but he tells me the Duke of York seems pretty kind, and hath said that he doth believe that W. Coventry did mean well and doth it only out of judgment. He tells me that he never was an Intriguer in his life, nor will be, nor of any combination of persons to set up this or fling down that, nor hath in his own business this Parliament spoke to three members to say anything for him, but will stand upon his own

a repl. 'it'

---

1. Now that Clarendon had fallen, Arlington and Buckingham were competing for supremacy. On 21/31 October Ruvigny, the French ambassador, noted the rumour that Arlington was to be dismissed: V. Barbour, *Arlington*, p. 115, n. 56.

defence and will stay by it, and thinks that he is armed against all they can [say] but the old business of selling places, and in that thinks they cannot hurt him. However, I do find him mighty willing to have his name used as little as he can, and [he] was glad when I did deliver him up a letter *a* of his to me which did give countenance to the discharging of men by ticket at Chatham,[1] which is now coming in question – and wherein I confess I am sorry to find him so tender of appearing, it being a thing not only good and fit, all that was done in it, but promoted and advised by him. But he thinks the House is set upon wresting anything to his prejudice that they can pick up. He tells me he did never, as a great many have, call *b* the Chancellor rogue and knave and I know not what; but all that he hath said, and will stand by, is that his counsels were not good, nor the manner of his managing of things. I suppose he means suffering the King to run in debt; for by and by, the King walking in the parke with a great crowd of his idle people about him, I took occasion to say that it was a sorry thing, to be a poor King and to have others to come to correct the faults of his own servants, and that that was it that brought us all into this condition. He answered that he would never be a poor King, and then the other would mend of itself; "No," says he, "I would eat bread and drink water first, and this day discharge all that idle company about me and walk *c* only with two footmen; and this I have told the King – and this must do it at last." I asked him how long the King would suffer this; he told me the King must suffer it yet longer, that he would *d* not advise the King to do otherwise, for it would break out again worse if he should break them up before the Core be come up.

After this we fell to other talk: of my waiting upon him hereafter, it may be to read a chapter in Seneca in this new house which he hath bought and is making very fine, when we may

a repl. 'paper'   *b* MS. 'called'
c repl. 'would'   *d* repl. ? 'he'

---

1. In November–December 1666. The letter has not been traced. It is perhaps significant that no letters from Coventry to the Navy Board survive among the Board's papers for December 1666.

be out of imployment; which he seems to wish more then to fear, and I do believe him heartily.

Thence home, and there met news from Mr. Townsend of the Wardrobe that old Young the Yeoman Taylor (whose place my Lord Sandwich promised my father) is dead*a* – upon which, resolving presently that my father shall not be troubled with it, but I hope I shall be able to enable him to end his days where he is in quiet, I went forth, thinking to tell Mrs. Ferrers (Captain Ferrers's wife), who doth expect it after my father,[1] that she may look after it; but upon second thoughts did forbear it, and so back again home, calling at the New Exchange and there buying *The Indian Emperour*,[2] newly-printed; and so home to dinner, where I had Mr. Clerke the Sollicitor and one of the Auditors clerks to discourse about [the] form of making up my account for the Exchequer,[3] which did give me good satisfaction; and so after dinner, my wife and Mercer (who grows fat) and Willett and I to the King's House and there saw *The Comittee*,[4] a play I like well; and so at night home and to the office, and so to my chamber about my accounts; and then to Sir W Pen's to speak with Sir Jo. Chichly (who desired my*b* advice about a prize which*c* he hath begged of the King) and there had a great deal of his foolish talk of ladies and love[5] and I know not what; and so home to supper and to bed.

29. Up, and at the office, my Lord Brouncker and I close together till almost 3 after noon, never stirring, making up a report for the Committee this afternoon about the business of discharging men by ticket, which it seems the House is mighty*d* earnest in, but is a foolery in itself; yet gives me a great deal of

---

a repl. 'is dead)'   *b* repl. 'by'   *c* repl. closing bracket
          d MS. 'my'

---

1. Cf. above, ii. 113 & n. 2.

2. A heroic tragedy by Dryden, now first published; see above, p. 14 & n. 2; not in the PL. (A).

3. His Tangier accounts.

4. A comedy by Sir Robert Howard; see above, iv. 181 & n. 1. (A).

5. He was now courting a widow: Lady Newton, *Lyme Letters*, p. 239.

trouble to draw up a defence for the Board, as if it was a crime; but I think I have done it to very good purpose.[1]

Then to my Lady Williams's with her and my Lord and there did eat a snapp of good victuals; and so to Wesminster-hall, where we find the House not up, but sitting all this day about the method of bringing in the charge against my Lord Chancellor; and at last resolved for a committee to draw up the heads – and so rose, and no committee to sit tonight.[2]

Here Sir W. Coventry and Lord Brouncker and I did in the hall (between the two Courts at the top of the hall)[3] discourse about a letter of W. Coventry's to Brouncker;[4] whereupon Brouncker would justify his discharging men by ticket, and insists on one word which Sir W. Coventry would not seem very earnest to have left out; but I did see him concerned, and did after labour to suppress the whole letter, the thing being in itself really impertinent* but yet so it is, that W. Coventry doth not desire to have his name used in this business – and I have prevailed[a] with Brouncker for it.

Thence Brouncker and I to the King's House, thinking to have gone into a box above for fear of being seen, the King being there; but the play being three acts done, we would not give 4s,[5] and so away and parted; and I home and there after a little supper to bed – my eyes ill, and head full of thoughts of the trouble this Parliament gives us.

30. All the morning, till past noon, preparing over again our report this afternoon to the committee of Parliament about

---

a repl. 'sup'-

---

1. Copy (in Pepys's hand) in BM, Add. 11602, ff. 312+. It argued the necessity of payment by tickets, even of whole ships, in order to avoid the necessity of carrying large sums of cash on board. Writing c. 1682 Pepys commented: 'Remember the public folly shewn in the great disquiet raised in Parliament upon the business of tickets' (*Naval Minutes*, p. 148).

2. *CJ*, ix. 9; they were to meet at 2 p.m. on the 30th. The debate had continued till after 4 p.m.: Milward, p. 103.

3. King's Bench and Chancery.

4. Untraced.

5. The doorkeeper evidently wanted to charge Pepys and Brouncker 2s. each for a seat in a box, where the price for a complete performance was 4s. Cf. above, p. 232 & n. 1. (A).

Tickets, and then home to eat a bit. And then with Sir W. Penn to White-hall, where we did a very little business with the Duke of York at our usual meeting. Only, I perceive that he doth leave all of us, as the King doth those about him, to stand and fall by ourselfs, and I think is not without some cares himself what the Parliament may do in matters wherein his honour is concerned. Thence to the Parliament-house, where after the Committee was sat, I was called in; and the first thing was upon the complaint of a dirty slut that was there, about a ticket which she had lost and had applied*a* herself to me for another. I did give them a short and satisfactory answer to that; and so they sent her away, and were ashamed of their foolery in giving occasion to 500 seamen and seamen's wifes to come before them, as there was this afternoon. But then they fell to the business of tickets; and I did give them the best answer I could, but had not scope to do it in that methodical manner which I had prepared myself for; but they did ask a great many broken rude questions about it, and were mighty hot whether my Lord Brouncker had any order to discharge whole ships by ticket; and because my answer was with distinction and not direct, I did perceive they were not so fully satisfied therewith as I could wish they were: so my Lord Brouncker was called in, and they could fasten nothing on him that I could see, nor endeed was there any proper matter for blame; but I do see, and it was said publicly in the House by Sir T. Clerges, that Sir W Batten had designed that business of discharging men by ticket, and an order after the thing was done to justify my Lord Brouncker for having done it. But this I did not owne at all, nor was it just so; though he did endeed do something like it, yet had contributed as much to it as any man of the board, by sending down of Tickets to do it. But Lord, to see that we should be brought to justify ourselfs in a thing of necessity and profit to the King, and of no profit or convenience to us, but the contrary.

We being withdrawn, we heard no more of it, but there stayed late and do hear no more; only, my Cosen Pepys doth tell me that he did hear one or two whisper as if they thought that I do bogle at the business of my Lord Brouncker; which is a thing I neither did or have reason to do in his favour, but I do not think

a repl. 'petitioned'

it fit to make him suffer for a thing that deserves well. But this doth trouble me a little, that anything [should] so stick to my prejudice*a* in any of them, and did trouble me so much, that all the way home (with Sir W. Penn) I was not at good ease, nor all night; though when I came home, I did find my wife and Betty Turner – the two Mercers – and Mrs. Parker, an ugly lass but yet dances well and speaks the best of them, and W Batelier and Pendeleton, dancing; and here I danced with them and had a good supper, and as merry as I could be. And so they being gone, we to bed.

31. Up, and all the morning at the office; and at noon Mr. Creed and Yeabsly dined with me (my [wife] gone to dine with Mrs. Pierce and see a play with her); and after dinner in comes Mr. Turner of Eynsbury,[1] lately come to town, and also after him, Captain Hill of the *Coventry*, who lost her at Berbados[2] and*b* is come out of France, where he hath been long prisoner. After a great deal of mixed discourse, and then Mr. Turner and I alone a little in my closet, talking about my Lord Sandwich (who I hear is now by the King ordered to come home), we all parted; and I by water*c* (calling at Michells, and saw and once kissed*d* sa wife*e*, but I do think that he is jealous of her*e* and so she dares not stand out of his sight). So could do no more, but away by water to the Temple; and there, after spending a little time in my bookseller's shop, I to Westminster, and there at the lobby do hear by Comissioner Pett to my great amazement that he is in worse condition then before, by the coming in of the Duke of Albemarle's and Prince Rupert's narratives[3] this

---

a repl. 'prejudge'   *b* repl. 'and'
c repl. 'coach to'   *d* repl. symbol rendered illegible
e–e garbled s.h.: see above, p. 244, note *a*

---

1. John Turner, Vicar of Eynesbury, Hunts., a living in the gift of Lord Sandwich.

2. See above, vii. 390 & n. 3.

3. Printed in *CJ*, ix. 11+; two memoranda on the miscarriages of the war, principally on shortage of supplies, the division of the fleet (June 1666) and the Medway disaster (June 1667). Many copies survive in MS.: see the list in Tedder, p. 201.

day; wherein the former doth most severely lay matters upon him, so as the House this day have I think ordered him to the Tower again, or something like it;[1] so that the poor man is likely to be overthrown I doubt, right or wrong, so infinite fond they are of anything the Duke of Albemarle says or writes to them.   I did then go down, and there met with Collonell Reemes and Cosen Rogr. Pepys; and there they do tell me how the Duke of Albemarle and the Prince have lay blame on a great many; and perticularly on our office in general, and perticularly for want of provisions,[2] wherein I shall come to be questioned again in that business myself; which doth trouble me.   But my Cosen Pepys and I had much discourse alone, and he doth bewail the constitution of this House and says that there is a direct Caball and faction, as much as is possible, between them for and those against the Chancellor, and so in other factions, that there is nothing almost done honestly and with integrity; only, some few he says there are that do keep out of all plot and combinations, and, when their time comes, will speak and see right done if possible; and that he himself is looked upon to be a man that will be of no faction, and so they do shun to make him – and I am glad of it.[3]   He tells me that he thanks God he never knew what it was to be tempted to be a knave in his life, till he did come into the House of Commons, where there is nothing done but*a* by passion and faction and private interest.   Reemes did tell me of a fellow last night (one Kelsy, a commander of a fireship, who complained for want of his money paid him) did say that he did see one of the

---

a   repl. 'by'

---

1. A report that Pett was walking 'at liberty' in Westminster Hall reached the Commons during this debate. The House thereupon summoned him to the bar and put him in the custody of the Lieutenant of the Tower, who was ordered to 'have him in Readiness, and produce him, to be examined, as Occasion shall require': *CJ*, ix. 14.

2. I.e. for shortage of victuals in the campaign of 1666. Pepys's papers on this subject (with his defence prepared against enquiry by parliament) are in Rawl. A 174, ff. 215–33; ib., A 195a, ff. 247–8, 269–73.

3. Roger Pepys voiced the views of the independent country gentry, who always held themselves above 'faction'. The pro- and anti-Clarendonian interests were in fact early forms of the modern party. Coventry shared the same distrust of 'plot and combinations'.

Commissioners of the Navy bring in three wagon-loads of prize-goods into Greenwich one night,[1] but that the House did take no notice of it, nor enquire; but this is me, and I must expect to be called to account and answer what I did as well as I can. So thence away home; and in Holborne, going round, it being dark, I espied Sir D. Gawden's coach, and so went out of mine into his and there had opportunity to talk of the business of victuals, which the Duke of Albemarle and Prince did complain that they were in want of the last year; but we do conclude we shall be able to show the quite contrary of that; only, it troubles me that we must come to contend*a* with these great persons, which will overrun us. So with some disquiet in my mind on this account, I home; and there comes Mr. Yeabsly,[2] and he and I to even some accounts, wherein I shall be a gainer about 200*l*; which is a seasonable profit, for I have got nothing a great while. And he being gone, I to bed.

a repl. 'contend'

---

1. Cf. above, vi. 258–9. 2. Victualler to the Tangier garrison.

NOVEMBER.

1. Up betimes, and down to the waterside (calling and drinking a dram of a bottle at Michells, but saw not Betty), and thence to White-hall and to Sir W. Coventry's lodging, where he and I alone a good while; where he gives me[a] the full of the Duke of Albemarle's and Prince's narratives, given yesterday by the House – wherein they fall foul of him ⟨and Sir G. Carteret⟩ in something about the dividing of the fleet; and the Prince perticularly charging the Commissioners of the Navy with negligence, he says, "the Commissioners of the Navy whereof Sir W. Coventry is one." He tells me that he is prepared to answer every perticular most thoroughly, but the quality[b] of the persons doth make it difficult for him; and so I do see is in great pain, poor man, though he deserves better then twenty such as either of them for his abilities and true service to the King and Kingdom. He says there is incoherency, he believes, to be found between their two reports; which will be pretty work to consider.[1] The Duke of Albemarle charges W. Coventry that he should tell him, when he came down to the fleet (with Sir[c] G. Carteret to consult about dividing the fleet) that the Dutch would not be out in six weeks;[2] which W. Coventry says is as false as is possible, and he can prove the contrary by the Duke of Albemarle's own letters. The Duke of Albemarle[d] says that he

---

a repl. 'the'   b repl. 'questions'   c repl. 'G. Carteret.'
d repl. 'Duke of Albemarle'

---

1. Coventry's copies of Albemarle's and Rupert's narratives, with his marginal notes and his two draft replies, are in BM, Add. 32094, ff. 196, 202, 206, 208. His reply to their criticisms of his conduct in the matter of the division of the fleet (in June 1666) was particularly effective: cf. above, vii. 144 & n. 1. He would not have been attacked so persistently had it not been for the enmity of Clarendon and Albemarle towards him.

2. Albemarle, Rupert and Spragge were unanimous on this point about the news of Dutch movements in the evidence they gave to the Commons in October 1667, except that Rupert preferred to say 'some' instead of 'six' weeks: HMC, *Eliot Hodgkin*, pp. 53–60; Milward, p. 93.

did upon sight of the Dutch call a council of officers, and they did conclude they could not avoid fighting the Dutch; and yet we did go to the enemy and found them at Anchor – which is a pretty contradiction;[1] and he tells me that Spragg did the other day say in the House, that the Prince, at his going from the Duke of Albemarle with his fleet, did[a] tell him that if the Dutch should come on, the Duke of Albemarle was to fallow him, the Prince, with his fleet, and not fight the Dutch. Out of all this, a great deal of good meat will be picked. But it is a sad consideration that all this picking of holes in one another's coats, nay, and the thanks of the House to the Prince and the Duke of Albemarle, and all this envy and design to ruin Sir W. Coventry, did arise from Sir W. Coventry's unfortunate mistake the other day, in producing of a letter from the Duke of Albemarle touching the good condition of all things at Chatham just before the Dutch came up and did us that fatal mischiefe[2] – for upon this, they are resolved to undo him – and I pray God they do not. He tells me, upon my demanding it, that he thinks the King doth not like this their bringing these narratives, and that they give out that they would have said more, but that the King hath hindered them; that, I suppose, is about my Lord Sandwich. He is getting a copy of the Narratives, which I shall then have;[3] and so I parted from him and away to White-hall, where I met Mr. Creed and Yeabsly and discoursed a little about Mr. Yeabsly's business and accounts;[4] and so I to the Chapel and there stayed (it being Allhollows day) and heard a fine Anthemne, made by Pellam (who is come over) in France,[5] of which there was great expectation; and endeed is a very good piece of Musique, but still I cannot call[b] the Anthem anything but Instrumentall music with the Voice, for nothing is made of the words at all.

a repl. 'tell'   *b* repl. 'all'

---

1. Pepys had reported matters rather differently; the Council, according to him, was reluctant to fight: above, vii. 161 & n. 3. This appears to have been the case.

2. See above, p. 505.

3. See below, p. 519, n. 3.

4. See above, p. 513 & n. 2.

5. Pelham Humfrey (who became in 1672 Cooke's successor as Master of the Children of the Chapel Royal) had in 1664 been sent by the King to France, where he studied under Lully until his return in 1666. (E).

I this morning, before chapel, visited Sir G. Carteret; who is vexed to see how things are likely to go, but cannot help it, and yet seems to think himself mighty safe. I also visited my Lord Hinchingbrooke at his chamber at White-hall, where I found Mr. Turner, Moore, and Creed talking of my Lord Sandwich; whose case I doubt is but bad, and I fear will not escape being worse, though some of this company did say otherwise. But I am mightily pleased with my Lord Hinchingbrooke's sobriety and few words.

After chapel, I with Creed to the Exchange; and after much talk, he and I there, about securing of some money, either by land or goods, to be alway at our command, which we think a thing advisable in this critical time, we parted; and I to the Sun tavern with Sir W Warren (with whom I have not drank many a day, having for some time been strange to him)[1] and there did put it to him to advise me how to dispose of my prize;[2] which he will think of and do to my best advantage. We talked of several other things relating to his service; wherein I promise assistance, but coldly, thinking it policy to do so. And so after eating a short dinner, I away home and there took out my wife, and she and I alone to the King's playhouse and there saw a silly play, and an old one, *The Tameing of a Shrew*;[3] and so home, and I to my office a little and then home to supper and to bed.

2. Up, and to the office, where busy all the morning. At noon home; and after dinner, my wife and Willett and I to the King's House and there saw *Henry the Fourth*; and contrary to expectation, was pleased in nothing more then in Cartwright's speaking of Falstaffe's speech about *What is Honour?*[4] The house full of Parliament-men, it being holiday with them.[5] And it was observable how a gentleman of good habitt, sitting just before us

---

1. See above, p. 31 & n. 3.

2. The *Maybolt*; see above, p. 465 & n. 1. Pepys and Warren had been estranged by Warren's association with Lord Brouncker.

3. John Lacy's adaptation of Shakespeare's comedy; see above, p. 158 & n. 2. (A).

4. The last speech in V, 1 of *Henry IV, Part One*. William Cartwright was a well-known actor of character parts. (A).

5. Parliament had adjourned from 31 October to 3 November: *CJ*, ix. 14.

eating of some fruit, in the midst of the play did drop down as dead, being choked;*a* but with much ado, Orange Mall did thrust her finger down his throat and brought him to life again. After the play, we home and I busy at the office late; and then home to supper and to bed.

3. *Lords day.* Up, and with my wife to church, and thither comes Roger Pepys to our pew; and thence home to dinner, whither came by invitation Mr. Turner (the Minister),[1] and my Cosen Roger brought with him Jeffry's the Apothecary at Westminster, who is our kinsman.[2] And we had much discourse of Cottenhamshire and other things with great pleasure. My Cosen Roger did tell me of a bargain which I may now have in Norfolke, that my she-Cosen Ned Pepys[3] is going to sell, the Title whereof is very good, and the pennyworth also is good enough; but it is out of the way so of my life, that I shall never enjoy it, nor, it may be, see it, and so I will have nothing to do with it. After dinner to talk, and I find by discourse Mr. Turner to be a man mighty well read in the Roman story, which is very pleasant. By and by Roger went, and Mr. Turner spent an hour talking over my Lord Sandwiches condition as to this Parliament,*b* which we fear may be bad, and the condition of his family, which can be no better – and then having little to comfort ourselfs but that this humour will not last alway in the Parliament and that [it] may well have a great many more as*c* great men as he enquired into. And so we parted, and I to my chamber and there busy all the evening; and then my wife and I to supper, and so to bed with much discourse and pleasure one with another.

4. Up betimes, and by water with Sir R. Ford (who is going to the Parliament) to Westminster; and there landing at the New Exchange stairs, I to Sir W. Coventry and there he read

a repl. 'checked'   b repl. 'Parl'-
c reading uncertain (blot in MS.)

---

1. See above, p. 511 & n. 1.
2. Thomas Jefferies had in 1665 married Paradise Williams, whose mother Edith was a daughter of John Pepys of Cottenham, Cambs., and a first cousin of Pepys's father.
3. Elizabeth, widow of Edward Pepys, of Broomsthorpe, Norf.

over to me the Prince and the Duke of Albemarle's Narratives; wherein they are very severe against him and our office, but W. Coventry doth contemn them; only, that their persons and qualities are great, and so I do perceive is afeared of them, though he will not confess it.   But he doth say[a] that if he can get out of these Bryers, he will never trouble himself with Princes nor Dukes again.   He finds several things in their Narratives which are both inconsistent and foolish, as well as untrue; especially as to what the Duke of Albemarle avers of his knowing of the enemy's being abroad sooner then he says it, which W. Coventry will show his own letter against him for.[1]   I confess I do see so much, that were I but well possessed of what I should have in the world, I think I could willingly retreat and trouble myself no more with it.

Thence home, and there met Sir H. Cholmly and he and I to the Excise Office to see what tallies are paying; and thence back to the Old Exchange, by the way talking of news, and he owning Sir W. Coventry in his opinion to be one of the worthiest men in the nation – as I do really think[b] he is.   He tells me he doth think really that they will cut off my Lord Chancellor's head, the Chancellor at this day showing as much pride as is possible to those few that venture their fortunes by coming to see him; and that the Duke of York is troubled much, knowing that those that fling down the Chancellor cannot stop there, but will do something to him to prevent his having it in his[c] power hereafter to revenge himself and father-in-law upon them.   And this, Sir H. Cholmly fears may be by divorcing the Queen and getting another, or declaring the Duke of Monmouth legitimate[2] – which God forbid.   He tells me he doth verily believe that there will come in an Impeachment of high treason against my Lord of Ormond; among other things, for ordering the quartering of soldiers in Ireland on free quarter, which it seems is high treason in that country and was one of the things that lost the Lord

a repl. 'st'-   *b* repl. 'he'   *c* repl. 'their'

---

1. See above, p. 490 & n. 2.
2. Either method would deprive the Duke of his unique political

importance as heir presumptive.   Cf. above, pp. 438–9.

Strafford his head, and the law is not yet repealed[1] – which he says was a mighty oversight of him not to have repealed (which he might with ease have done) or have justified himself by an act.

From the Exchange I took coach and went to Turlington the great spectacle-maker for advice; who dissuades me from useing old spectacles, but rather young ones.[2] And doth tell me that nothing can wrong them more then for me to use reading-glasses – which do magnify much.

Thence home and there dined, and then abroad and left my wife and Willett at her tailor's; and I to White-hall, where the Comissioners[a] of Treasury do not sit, and therefore I to Westminster to the hall; and there meeting with Collonell Reames, I did very happily* by him get Copys of the Prince and Duke of Albemarle's Narratives which they did deliver the other day to the House;[3] of which I am mighty glad, both for my present information and for my future satisfaction. So back by coach and took up my wife, and away home and there in my chamber all the evening among my papers and my accounts of Tanger, to my great satisfaction; and so to supper and to bed.

a l.h. repl. s.h. 'Committee'

---

1. Ormond was Clarendon's principal ally in the government. Buckingham led the attack, hoping to succeed to his offices. Ormond came to England in the following spring and faced an enquiry into his management of Irish finances, being removed from the lord-lieutenancy in March 1669. He was not, however, impeached. He admitted the quartering of troops, arguing that it was a customary right of government (HMC, *Ormonde*, n.s. iii. 280; T. Carte, *Ormond*, v. 69+; cf. *CSP Ireland 1666-9*, p. 465). There was, it is true, a statute of 1440 (18 Henry VI c. 3) by which the 'cessing of Soldiers' in Ireland had been declared treason. An offence against this statute had been one of the charges in the attainder of Strafford in 1641, when he was declared guilty of a series of offences alleged to amount to cumulative treason. But this attainder had been repealed in 1662, and it was very doubtful whether either Strafford's or Ormond's action was treasonable within the terms of the act. J. Rushworth, *Hist. Coll.*, vol. viii (1721); M. Hale, *Hist. pleas of Crown* (ed. Dogherty, 1800), i. 146–7; also Carte, op. cit., iv. 312+.

2. Cf. above, p. 486 & n. 3.

3. Bullen Reymes (M.P. for Melcombe Regis, Dorset) would have obtained MS. copies (from the Journal entries) at the office of the clerks of the House. They do not appear to have survived among Pepys's papers.

5. Up, and all the morning at the office. At noon home to dinner and thence out with my wife and girl; and left them at her tailor's, and I to the Treasury and there did a little business for Tanger, and so took them up again and home; and when I had done at the office, being post night, I to my chamber and there did something more; and so to supper and to bed.

6. Up, and to Westminster, where to the Parliament door and there spoke with Sir G Downing to see what was done yesterday at the Treasury for Tanger; and it proved as good as nothing,[1] so that I do see we shall be brought to great straits for money there. He tells me here, that he is passing a Bill to make the Excize and every other part of the King's Revenue assigneable on the Exchequer, which endeed will be a very good thing.[2] This he sees with great glory, as an act of his, and how poor a thing this was in the beginning, and with what envy he carried it on, and how my Lord Chancellor could never endure him for it since he first begun it.[3] He tells me that the thing the House is just now upon is that of taking away the Charter from the Company of Woodmongers, whose frauds it seems have been mightily laid before them.[4] He tells me that they are like

---

1. The Treasury minute reads: 'Mr. Pepis to be settled for Tangier as he desires' (*CTB*, ii. 115).

2. The bill, introduced on 15 October in the Commons, became law in May 1668 (19-20 Car. II c. 4). It greatly extended the system initiated on a limited scale by the Additional Aid of 1665, and enabled Treasury orders, secured since 1665 on certain parliamentary grants only, to be secured now on ordinary revenue and to circulate freely by endorsement. This was an important innovation at a time when the law of negotiable instruments was still immature, and it greatly enhanced the King's ability to borrow money. Cf. *CJ*, ix. 3, 16, 23; Milward, pp. 139+.

3. Clarendon (*Life*, iii. 4+) alleged *inter alia* that Downing (a Teller of the Exchequer as well as Secretary to the Treasury) had introduced as a 'reform' a method which would have the effect of increasing the fees of Exchequer officials, his own assistants included.

4. A bill (provoked by the high cost of fuel) had been introduced in the Commons on 14 October, and on this day a resolution was passed that the charter of the Woodmongers' Company (1605) was illegal and a grievance to the people. Only the Crown could cancel a charter: the Woodmongers' was surrendered on 5 December. *CJ*, ix. i, 7, 8, 15; H. B. Dale, *Fellowship of Woodmongers*, pp. 49-55.

to fly very high against my Lord Chancellor. Thence I to the House of Lords and there first saw Dr. Fuller, as Bishop of Lincolne,[1] to sit among the Lords. Here I spoke with the Duke of York and the Duke of Albemarle about Tanger; but methinks both of them do look very coldly one upon another, and their discourse mighty cold, and little to the purpose about our want of money. Thence homeward and called at Allestry the book-seller,[2] who is bookseller to the Royall Society, and there did buy three or four books and find great variety of French and foreign books. And so home and to dinner; and after dinner, with my wife to a play, and the girl, *Mackbeth*, which we still like mightily, though mighty short of the content we used to have when [a] Baterton acted, who is still sick.[3] So home, troubled with the way and to get a coach; and so to supper and to bed. ⟨This day in the paynted Chamber I met and walked with Mr. George Mountagu, who thinks it may go hard with my Lord Sandwich. But he says the House is offended with Sir W. Coventry much, and that he doth endeavour to gain them again in the most precarious manner in all things that is possible.⟩

7. Up, and at the office hard all the morning; and at noon resolve with Sir W. Penn to go see *The Tempest*, an[b] old play of Shakespeares, acted here the first day.[4] And so my wife and girl and W. Hewer by themselfs, and Sir W. Penn and I afterward by ourselfs, and forced to sit in the side Balcone over against the Musique-room[5] at the Dukes-House, close by my Lady Dorsett and a great many great ones: the house mighty full, the King

a repl. 'with'   *b* repl. 'a'

---

1. See above, p. 449, n. 2.
2. James Allestry, one of the greatest booksellers of his day. Until the Fire his shop was in St Paul's Churchyard; it was now in Duck Lane.
3. See above, v. 314; viii. 482. (A).
4. This was 'the *Tempest* alter'd by Sir William Davenant and Mr. Dry-den before 'twas made into an Opera': Downes, p. 33. It has been des-

cribed as both a wretched travesty and the most popular of the Restoration alterations of Shakespeare: Hazel-ton Spencer, *Shakespeare Improved*, p. 203. This is one of the earlier records of a performance. (A).
5. A small gallery above the pro-scenium arch; so the 'side Balcone' was probably a box on the same level as the upper gallery, i.e. part of the third tier of seats. (A).

and Court there, and the most innocent play that ever I saw, and a curious piece of Musique in an Echo of half-sentences, the Echo repeating*a* the former half while the man goes on to the latter, which is mighty pretty.[1] The play no great wit; but yet good, above ordinary plays. Thence home with W. Penn, and there all mightily pleased with the play; and so to supper and to bed, after having done at the office.

8. Called up betimes by Sir H. Cholmly, and he and I to good purpose most of the morning, I in my dressing-gown with him, on our Tanger accounts, and stated them well. And here he tells me that he believes it will go hard with my Lord Chancellor. Thence I to the office, where met on some special business; and here I hear that the Duke of York is very ill,[2] and by and by word brought us that we shall not need to attend today the Duke of York, for he is not well; which is bad news. They being gone, I to my workmen, who this day come to allter my office by beating down the wall and making me a fayre window both there and encreasing the window of my closet; which doth give me some present trouble but will be mighty pleasant.[3] So all the whole day among them to very late; and so home weary to supper and to bed – troubled for the Duke of York his being sick.

9. Up and to my workmen, who are at work close again, and I at the office all the morning and there do hear by a messenger that Roger Pepys would speak with me; so before*b* the office up, I to Westminster and there find the House very busy, and like to be so all day, about my Lord Chancellors impeachment, whether treason or not; where everybody is mighty busy. I

---

a repl. 'speaking the former'   *b* repl. 'as soon as'

---

1. This was Ferdinand's song (echoed by Ariel) 'Go thy way' (III, 3), and was composed by John Banister. Copies in BM, G. 109 (2), pp. 3–4; and in some issues of *Choice ayres, songs, & dialogues* . . . (1675), pp. 79–80. This production contained spectacular musical turns and later became a semi-opera. (E).

2. Of the smallpox; he was bled on the 12th. It was a mild attack but he did not fully recover until early December: BM, Add. 36919, ff. 17r, 22r; BM, Egerton 2539, ff. 134r, 137v, 145v; *Bulstrode Papers*, i. 7, 8; *CSPD 1667–8*, p. 51.

3. Bills for some of this work are in PRO, Adm. 20/9, pp. 338, 554.

spoke with my Cosen Roger, whose business was only to give me notice that Carcasse hath been before the Committee,[1] and to warn me of it; which is a great courtesy in him to do, and I desire him to continue to do so. This business of this fellow, though it be a foolish thing, yet it troubles me; and I do plainly see my weakness, that I am not a man able to go through trouble as other men are, but that I should be a miserable man if I should meet with adversity – which God keep me from. He desirous to get back into the House, he having his notes in his hands, the lawyers being now speaking*a* to the point of whether treason or not treason, the*b* Article of advising the King to break up the Parliament and to govern by the sword.[2] Thence I down to the Hall and there met Mr. King, the Parliament-man for Harwich; and there he did show and let me take a copy of all the Articles against my Lord Chancellor, and what members they were that undertook to bring witnesses to make them good[3] – of which I was mighty glad; and so away home to dinner and to my workmen; and in the afternoon out to get Simpson the joyner to come to work at my office; and so back home and to my letters by the post tonight, and there by W. Penn do hear that this Article was over-voted in the House, not to be a ground of Impeachment of Treason[4] – at which I was glad, being willing to have no*c* blood spilt if I could help it. So home to supper; and glad that the dirty bricklayers' work of my office is done, I home to supper and to bed.

10. *Lords day.* Mighty cold; and with my wife to church, where a lazy sermon; but here was*d* my Lady Batten in her

---

a repl. 'to' *b* repl. full stop *c* repl. 'the' *d* MS. 'have'

---

1. The Commons' Committee on Miscarriages, now enquiring into the business of pay-tickets. Carkesse was a clerk of the Ticket Office who had been suspended from duty on suspicion of malpractice: see above, p. 64 & n. 1.

2. There were 17 articles in all: *CJ*, ix. 16. The first alleged that he had in July 1667 advised against the summons of parliament and in favour of government by a standing army. Debate in Grey, i. 29+; Milward, pp. 119+.

3. A copy of the articles in Tom Hayter's hand (probably made from the one here mentioned) is in BM, Harl. 7170, f. 36r. The names of the M.P.'s are in the margin.

4. By 172 to 103: *CJ*, ix. 18.

mourning at*ᵃ* church – but I took no notice of her. At noon comes Michell and his wife to dine*ᵇ* with us, and pretty merry; I glad to see her still. After dinner Sir W. Penn and I to White-hall to speak with Sir W. Coventry; and there, beyond all we looked for, do hear that the Duke of York hath got and is full of the small-pox. And so we to his lodgings and there find most of the family going to St. James's and the gallery doors locked up, that nobody might pass to nor fro – and a sad house there is, I am sure; I am sad to consider the effects of his death if he should miscarry. But Dr. Frazier tells me that he is in as good condition as a man can be in his case.*ᶜ* They[1] appeared last night – it seems he was let blood on Friday. Thence, not finding W. Coventry and going back again home, we met him coming with the Lord Keeper; and so returned and spoke with him in White-hall garden two or three turns, advising with him what we should do about Carcasse's bringing his matter into the committee of Parliament. And he told us that the counsel he hath too late learned, is to spring nothing in the House nor offer*ᵈ* anything but just what is drawne out of a man – that this is the best way of dealing with a Parliament; and that he hath paid dear, and knows not how much more he may pay, for not knowing it sooner, when he did unnecessarily*ᵉ* produce the Duke of Albemarle's letter about Chatham;[2] which if demanded, would have come out with all the advantages in the world to W. Coventry; but as he brought it out himself, hath drawn much evil upon him. After some talk of this kind, we back home; and there I to my chamber, busy all the evening; and then to supper and to bed – my head running all night upon our businesses in Parliament and what examinations we are likely to go under before they have done with us, which troubles me more then it should a wise man, and a man the best able to defend himself, I believe, of our whole office, or any other I am apt to think.

11. Up, and to Simpson at work in my office; and thence with Sir G. Carteret (who came to talk with me) to Broad-streete, where great crowding of people for money, at which he

a repl. 'in'   *b* repl. 'me'   *c* repl. 'c'-
d MS. 'after'   *e* repl. same symbol badly formed

1. The pocks.   2. See above, p. 490 & n. 2.

blessed himself. Thence with him and Lord Brouncker to Captain Cockes (he out of doors) and there drunk their morning draught; and thence G. Carteret and I toward the Temple in coach together, and there he did tell me how the King doth all he can in the world to overthrow my Lord Chancellor, and that notice is taken of every man about the King that is not seen to promote the ruine of the Chancellor; and that this being another great day in his business, he dares not but be there. He tells me that as soon as Secretary Morrice brought the great Seale from my Lord Chancellor, Babb. May fell upon his knees and ketched the King about the legs and joyed him, and said that this was the first time that ever he*ᵃ* could call him King of England, being freed this great man – which was a most ridiculous saying. And he told me that when first my Lord Gerard, a great deal ago, came to the King, and told him that the Chancellor did say openly that the King was a lazy person and not fit to govern (which is now made one of the things in people's mouths against the Chancellor), "Why," says the King, "that is no news, for he hath told me so twenty times, and but the other day he told me so;" and made matter of mirth at it – but yet this light discourse is likely to prove bad to him. I light at the Temple and went to my tailors and Mercers about a Cloake, to choose the stuff – and so to my bookseller's and bought some books; and so home to dinner, and Simpson my Joyner with me; and after dinner, my wife and I and Willet to the King's playhouse and there saw *The Indian Emperour*,[1] a good play, but not so good as people cry it up I think; though above all things, Nell's ill speaking of a great part[2] made me mad. Thence, with great trouble and charge getting a Coach (it being now and having been all this day a most cold and Foggy, dark, thick day)[3] we home; and there I to my office and saw it made clean from top to bottom, till I feared I took cold in walking in a

---

a MS. 'I'

---

1. A tragedy by Dryden: see above, p. 14, n. 2. (A).

2. Nell Gwyn was a mediocre tragedienne. According to Downes (p. 9) she played Cydaria, the Emperor's daughter. (A).

3. Cf. Wood, *L & T*, ii. 121: 'Nov. 11 ... was such a great mist at London that never the like before was knowne. Horses ran against each other, carts against carts, coaches against coaches ...'.

damp room while it is in washing; and so home to supper and to bed.

This day I had a whole Doe sent me by Mr. Hozier,[1] which is a fine present, and I had the umbles of it for dinner. ⟨This day I hear Kirton my bookseller, poor man, is dead; I believe of grief for his losses by the fire.⟩[2]

12. Up, and to the office, where sat all the morning and there hear that the Duke of York doth yet do very well with his small-pox; pray God he may continue to do so. This morning also, to my astonishment, I hear that yesterday my Lord Chancellor, to another of his Articles, that of betraying the King's counsels to his enemies, is voted to have matter against him for an impeachment of high Treason,[3] and that this day the impeachment is to be carried up to the House of Lords – which is very high and I am troubled at it – for God knows what will fallow, since they that do this must do more, to secure themselfs against any that will revenge this – if it ever come in their power. At noon home to dinner; and then to my office and there saw everything finished, so as my papers are all in order again and my office ⟨twice⟩ as pleasant as ever it was, having a noble window in my closet and another in my office, to my great content. And so did business late, and then home to supper and to bed.

13. Up, and down to the Old Swan and so to Wesminster; where I find the House sitting and in a mighty heat about Comissioner Pett, that they would have him impeached, though the Committee have yet brought in but part of their report; and this heat of the House is much heightened by Sir Tho. Clifford telling them that he was the man that did out of his own purse imploy people at the out=ports to prevent the King of Scotts to escape after the battle[a] of Worcester.[4] The House[b] was in a

---

a repl. same symbol badly formed   b MS. 'high'

1. Clerk of the Cheque, Gravesend.

2. Joshua Kirton, of St Paul's Churchyard, had died in October.

3. By 161 to 89; a vote on an addition to the 16th article moved by Lord Vaughan, who later admitted he had no evidence: *CJ*, ix. 18;

Burnet, i. 457, n. 1. Debate in Mil-ward, pp. 123+.

4. Neither Clifford's speech nor the story has been traced elsewhere. For Charles II's escape after Worcester in 1651, see above, i. 155+.

great heat all this day about it, and at last it was carried, however, that it should be referred back to the committee to make further enquiry.*a*1 I here spoke with Rogr. Pepys, who sent for me; and it was to tell me that the committee is mighty full of the business of buying and selling of tickets, and to caution me against such an enquiry (wherein I am very safe) and that they have already found out Sir Rd. Ford's son to have had a hand in it; which they take to be the same as if the father had done it, and I do believe the father may be as likely to be concerned in it as his son. But I perceive by him they are resolve[d] to find out the bottom of the business if it be possible. By and by I met with Mr. Wren, who tells me that the Duke of York is in as good condition as is possible for a man in his condition of the smallpox. He I perceive is mightily concerned in the business of my Lord Chancellor, the impeachment against whom is gone up to the House of Lords; and great differences there*b* are in the Lords' House about it, and the Lords very high one against another. Thence home to dinner; and as soon as dinner done, I and my wife and Willett to the Duke of York's House and there saw *The Tempest* again; which is very pleasant, and full of so good variety, that I cannot be more pleased almost in a comedy – only, the seamen's part a little too tedious.² Thence home, and there to my chamber and do begin anew*c* to bind myself to keep my old vows; and among the rest, not to see a play till Christmas but once in every other week; and have laid aside 10*l*., which is to be lost to the poor if I do. This I hope in God will bind me, for I do find myself mightily wronged in my reputation, and endeed in my purse and business, by my late fallowing of my pleasure for so long time as I have done. So to supper and then to bed. ⟨This day Mr. Chichly told me with a seeming trouble that the House have stop[ped] his son Jack (Sir Jo.) his going to France, that he may be a witness against my Lord Sandwich; which doth trouble me, though he can I think say little.⟩³

a repl. 'eq'-   *b* MS. 'that'   *c* repl. 'new'

---

1. *CJ*, ix. 20. The impeachment was thereafter allowed to lapse.

2. Davenant had introduced some comic seamen into his alteration of Shakespeare's play. (A).

3. Sir John Chicheley had commanded the *Antelope* in the campaign of 1665.

14. At the office close all the morning. At noon all my clerks with me to dinner to a venison pasty; and there comes Creed and dined with me, and he tells me how high the Lords were in the Lords' House about the business of the Chancellor, and that they are not yet agreed to impeach him. After dinner, he and I and my wife and girl, the latter two to their tailor's and he and I to the committee of the Treasury; where I had a hearing but can get but 6000*l* for the pay of the garrison, in lieu of above 16000*l*;[1] and this Alderman Backewell gets remitted there, and I am glad of it. Thence by coach took up my wife and girl, and so home; and set down Creed at Arundell-house, going to the Royall Society, whither I would be glad but cannot go. Thence home and to the office, where to the office about my letters; and so home to supper and to bed – my eyes being bad again; and by this means, the nights nowadays do become*ᵃ* very long to me, longer then I can sleep out.

15. Up, and to Alderman Backewell's and there discoursed with him about the remitting of this 6000*l* to Tanger, which he hath promised to do by the first post, and that will be by Monday next the 18th; and he and I agreed that I would take notice of it, that so he may be found to have done his best upon the desire of the Lords-Commissioners. From this we went to discourse of his condition, and he with some vainglory told me that the business of Sherenesse did make him quite mad, and endeed might well have undone him; but yet that he did the very*ᵇ* next day pay here, and got bills to answer his promise to the King for the Swedes Embassadors (who were then doing our business at the Treaty at Breda), 7000*l*; and did promise the banquiers there, that if they would draw upon him all that he had of theirs, and 10000*l* more, he would answer it. He told me that Serjeant Maynard came to him for a sum of money that he had in his hands of his, and so did many others; and his answer was, "What countrymen are you?" And when they told him, "Why then," says he, "here is a tally upon the Receiver of your country

a repl. 'grow'	*b* repl. 'never'

1. *CTB*, ii. 119 (grant for Tangier).

for so, and to yours for so much,"¹ and did offer to lay by tallies to the full value of all that he owed in the world, and 40000*l* more for the security thereof, and not to touch a penny of his own till the full of what he owed was paid; which so pleased everybody, that he hath mastered all, so that he hath lent the Commissioners of the Treasury above 40000*l* in money since that business,² and did this morning offer to a lady who came to him to give him notice that she should need her money, 3000*l* in twenty days, he bid her, if she pleased send for it today and she should have it – which is a very great thing, and will make them greater then ever they were, I am apt to think, in some time.

Thence to Westminster, and there I walked with several and do hear that there is to be a conference between the two Houses today; so I stayed, and it was only to tell the Commons that the Lords cannot agree to the confining or sequestering of the Earle of Clarendon from the Parliament, forasmuch as they do not specify any perticular crime which they lay upon him and call treason.³ This the House did receive, and so parted; at which, I hear the Commons are like to grow very high, and will insist upon their privileges and the Lords will on theirs – though the Duke of Buckingham, Bristoll and others have been very high in the House of Lords to have had him committed. This is likely to breed ill blood. Thence I away home (calling at my Mercer and tailor's) and there find, as I expected, Mr. Cæsar and little Pellam Humphrys, lately returned from France and is an absolute Monsieur, as full of form and confidence and vanity, and disparages everything and everybody's skill but his own. The truth is, everybody says he is very able; but to hear how he laughs*ᵃ* at all*ᵇ* the King's music here, as Blagrave and others, that

a repl. 'laughs'   *b* repl. 'the'

---

1. Backwell had lent money to the government on the security of taxes. He was thus able to draw on the proceeds of taxes held by the receivers in each county ('country').
2. This claim is confirmed by the entries in Backwell's Ledger P:

MSS, Williams & Glyn's Bank; cf. *CTB*, ii. 87, 113.
3. The Lords' resolution communicated at this morning's conference had been passed on the 14th, *LJ*, xii. 137.

they cannot keep time nor tune nor understand anything, and that Grebus[1] the Frenchman, the King's Master of the Musique, how he understands nothing nor can play on any instrument and so cannot compose, and that he will give him a lift[a] out of his place, and that he and the King are mighty great, and that he hath already spoke to the King of Grebus, would make a man piss. I had a good dinner for them, as a venison pasty and some fowl, and after dinner we did play, he on the Theorbo, Mr. Cæsar on his French lute,[2] and I on the viol, but made but mean music; nor do I[b] see that this Frenchman doth so much wonders on the Theorbo, but without question he is a good musician; but his vanity doth offend me.   They gone towards night, I to the office awhile, and then home and to my chamber, where busy; till by and by comes Mr Moore, and he stayed and supped and talked with me about many things.   And tells me his great fears that all things will go to ruin among us, for that the King hath (as he says Sir Tho. Crew told him) been heard to say that the quarrel is not[c] between my Lord Chancellor and him, but his brother and him; which will make sad work among us if that be once promoted, as to be sure it will, Buckingham and Bristoll being now the only counsel the King fallows, so as Arlington and Coventry are come to signify little.   He tells me they are likely to fall upon my Lord Sandwich; but for my part, sometimes I am apt to think they cannot do him much harm, he telling me that there is no great fear of the business of Resumption.[3]   By and

---

a   repl. same symbol badly formed   b   repl. 'spy'
c   MS. 'now'

---

1. Louis Grabu: see above, p. 73, n. 3.

2. A new tuning had been developed c. 1640 by the French lutenist Denis Gaultier (d. 1672). (E).

3. One of the charges against Clarendon had been that he had acquired royal land both for himself and his friends 'to the disprofit of his majesty'. An act was now proposed to 'resume' (recover) the alienated land, but nothing came of it: see below, 10 March 1668 & n. Sandwich had been granted £4000 p.a. in 1660, though not out of Crown lands: Harris, i. 225. But his enemies later hoped for a bill to cancel his pardon for the prize-goods scandal and to deprive him of his grants: see Creed to Sandwich, 1 June 1668, Sandwich MSS, Letters from Ministers, ii. ff. 110–11.

by I got him to read part of my Lord Cooke's chapter of Treason,[1] which is mighty well worth reading and doth inform me in many things; and for aught I see, it is useful now to know what these crimes are. And*a* then to supper; and after supper he went away, and so I got the girl to comb my head and then to bed – my eyes bad.

This day Poundy the waterman was with me to let me know that he was summoned to bear witness against me to Prince Rupert's people (who have a commission to look after the business of prize-goods) about the business of the prize goods I was concerned in.[2] But I did desire him to speak all he knew, and not to spare me; nor did promise or give him anything; but sent him away with good words, to bid him say all he knew to be true. This doth not trouble me much.

16. At the office all the morning; and at noon took my Lord Brouncker into the garden, and there told him of his man Carcasses proceedings against the office in the House of Commons.[3] I did [not] desire nor advise him anything but in general that the end of this might be ruin to the office, but that we shall be brought to fencing for ourselfs, and that will be no profit to the office; but let it light where it would, I thought I should be as well as anybody. This I told him; and so he seeming to be ignorant of it and not pleased with it, we broke off by Sir Tho. Harvy's coming to us from the Pay Office, whither we had sent a smart letter we had writ to him this morning about keeping the clerks at work at the making up the books; which I did to place the fault somewhere, and now let him defend himself.[4] He was mighty angry, and perticularly with me; but I do not care, but do rather desire it, for I will not spare him, that we shall

a repl. 'he'

---

1. Sir E. Coke, *Institutes of laws of Engl.* (1660–4), pt iii, ch. i. (PL 2150–2.)
2. Cf. above, vi. 231, n. 1. For Rupert's commission, see above, p. 52, n. 3.
3. See above, p. 523.

4. Harvey was complaining that he was overworked, and that the paying off of ships at the Treasurer's office was delayed by a shortage of clerks: see his letters (12 November, 4 December) in *CSPD 1667-8*, pp. 18, 60.

bear the blame and such an idle fellow as he have 500*l* a year for
nothing.   So we broke off, and I home*ᵃ* to dinner and then to
the office; and having spent the afternoon on letters, I took coach
in the evening and to White-hall, where there is to be a performance of Musique of Pellam's before the King.   The company
not come, but I did go into the music-room, where Captain
Cooke and many others; and here I did hear the best and the
smallest Organ go that ever I saw in my life, and such a one as,
by the grace*ᵇ* of God, I will have the next year if I continue in this
condition, whatever it cost me.[1]   I never was so pleased in my
life.   Thence, it being too soon, I to Westminster-hall, it being
now about 7 at night, and there met Mr. Gregory my old
acquaintance,[2] an*ᶜ* understanding gentleman; and he and I walked
an hour together, talking of the bad prospect of the times.   And
the sum of what I learn from him is this – that the King is the most
concerned in the world against the Chancellor and all people that
do not appear against him; and therefore is angry with the
Bishops, having said that he had one Bishop on his side (Crofts)
and but one.[3]   That Buckingham and Bristoll are now his only
Cabinet council.   And that before the Duke of York fell sick,
Buckingham was admitted to the King of his Cabinet and there
stayed with him several hours, and the Duke of York shut out.
That it is plain that there is dislike between the King and Duke of
York; and that it is to be feared that the House will go so far
against the Chancellor that they must do something to undo the
Duke of York, or will not think themselfs safe.   That this Lord
Vaughan, that is so great against the Chancellor, is one of the

a repl. 'to'   *b* repl. 'God'   *c* MS. 'and'

---

1. Pepys did not buy a chamber-
organ during the diary period: cf.
below, 24 February 1668. (E).

2. John Gregory had served in the
Cromwellian Exchequer with Pepys,
and after 1660 in the office of Secretary Nicholas.

3. Two others in the event supported the impeachment in the
crucial vote of 20 November in the
Lords: below, p. 542 & n. 1. But
the great majority opposed it, and in
consequence the alliance between
King and bishops, taken for granted
since the Restoration, was broken
until the mid-'seventies.   Croft was
Bishop of Hereford.   His obligations to Clarendon did not prevent
him, according to the latter's account,
from showing him 'signal ingratitude', thereby gaining 'much credit
in the court': *Life*, iii. 327.

lewdest fellows of the age, worse then Sir Ch. Sidly. And that he was heard to swear, God*a* damn him, he would [do] my Lord Clarendon's business![1] That he doth find that my Lord Clarendon hath more friends in both Houses then he believes he would have, by reason that they do see what are the hands that pull him down; which they do not like. That Harry Coventry was scolded at by the King severely the other day; and that his answer was that if he must not speak what he thought in this business in Parliament, he must not come thither; and he says that by this very business, H. Coventry hath got more fame and common esteem then*b* any gentleman in*c* England hath at this day, and is an excellent and able person.[2] That the King, who not long ago did say of Bristoll that he was a man able in three years to get himself a fortune in any Kingdom in the world, and lose all again in three months, doth*d* now hug him and commend his parts everywhere, above all the world – how fickle is this man, and how unhappy we like to be. That he fears some furious courses will be taken against the Duke of York; and that he hath heard that it was designed, if they cannot carry matters against the Chancellor, to impeach the Duke of York himself – which God

---

a repl. 'would'   *b* MS. 'that'   *c* repl. 'an'
d repl. 'and'

---

1. For the part played in Clarendon's impeachment by Lord Vaughan (later 3rd Earl of Carberry), M.P. for Carmarthen borough, see Clarendon, *Life*, iii. 317–18; cf. above, p. 526, n. 3. He asked for the paper that had been presented from the Committee, and with his own hand entered these words: 'that being a Privy Counsellor he [Clarendon] had discovered the King's secrets to the enemy [the French]'. According to Clarendon (loc. cit.), he was 'a person of as ill a face as fame'. As Governor of Jamaica (1675–8) he was later said to have 'carried many shauntelmen of Wales . . . and sold 'em there for slaves, as he did his chaplain, to a blacksmith': HMC, *Rep.*, 7/508. He was a patron of Dryden and an associate of the buccaneer Sir Henry Morgan.

2. Henry Coventry (brother of Sir William; M.P. for Droitwich; Secretary of State, 1672–80) was always noted for his candour: cf. Burnet, i. 548–9. He had several times argued in Clarendon's favour, and on 26 October had urged the Commons not to proceed further against him since he was 'cast off and laid aside by his master': Milward, p. 95; see also ib., p. 101; Grey, i. 15; above, p. 476. Coventry's repute now stood high because of his services in concluding the recent peace with the Dutch.

forbid. That Sir Ed. Nichollas, whom he served while Secretary, is one of the best men in the world, but hated by the Queen-Mother (for a service he did the old King, against her mind and her favourites*a*); and that she and my Lady Castlemaine did make the King to lay him aside[1] – but this man says that he is one of the most perfect heavenly and charitable men in the whole world.[2] That the House of Commons resolve to stand by their proceedings, and chosen a committee to draw up the reasons thereof to carry to the Lords[3] – which is likely to breed great heat between them. That the Parliament, after all this, is likely*b* to give the Kingdom no money; and therefore that it is*c* to be wondered what makes the King give way to so great extravagancies – which do all tend to the making him less then he is, and so will every day more and more. And by this means*d* every creature is divided against the other, that there never was so great an uncertainty in England of what would be the event of things then at this day – nobody being at ease or safe. Being full of this discourse, and glad of the rencontre, I to White-hall; and there got into the Theater-room and there heard both the vocall and Instrumentall music, where the little fellow[4] stood keeping time; but for my part, I see no great matter, but quite the contrary, in both sorts of music. The composition I believe is very good, but no more of delightfulness to the eare or understanding but what is very ordinary. Here was the King and Queen and some of the ladies; among whom, none more jolly then my Lady*e* Buckingham, her Lord being once more a great man.

---

a repl. 'favourite' *b* repl. same symbol badly formed
c repl. 'is to be' *d* repl. same symbol badly formed
e MS. 'Lord'

---

1. For Nicholas's dismissal in 1662, see above, iii. 226 & n. 2. His disagreements with Henrietta-Maria were numerous: perhaps that most likely in this context was that which arose from his share in the dismissal of the Queen's Capuchins in November 1641.

2. According to Clarendon (*Life*, ii. 223) no-one had 'a more general reputation of virtue and piety and unquestionable integrity throughout the kingdom'; cf. also Burnet, i. 180.
3. *CJ*, ix. 21 (16 November). The reasons are printed ib., p. 22.
4. Pelham Humfrey. (E).

Thence by coach home and to my office, ended my letters, and then home to supper and, my eys being bad, to bed.

17. *Lords day.* Up, and to church with my wife – a dull sermon of Mr. Mills; and then home without strangers to dinner, and then my wife to read, and then I to the office, enter my Journall to this day, and so home, with great content that it is done but with sorrow to my eyes. Then home and got my wife to read to me out of Fuller's *Church History*;[1] when by and by comes Captain Cocke, who sat with me all the evening talking; and I find by him, as by all others, that we are like to expect great confusions; and most of our discourse was the same, and did agree with that the last night – and perticularly that about the difference between the King and the Duke of York which is like to be. He*a* tells me that he hears that Sir W. Coventry was, a little before the Duke of York fell sick, with the Duke of York in his closet, and fell on his knees and begged his pardon for what he hath done to my Lord Chancellor; but this I dare not soon believe.[2] But he tells me another thing, which he says he had from the person himself who spoke with the Duke of Bucking-ham, who he says is a very sober and worthy man – that he did lately speak with the Duke of Buckingham about his greatness now with the King, and told him – "But, Sir, these things that the King doth now, in suffering the Parliament to do all this, you know are not fit for the King to suffer, and you know how often you have said*b* to me that the King was a weak man and unable to govern, but to be governed, and that you could*c* command him as you listed; why do you suffer him to go on in these things?" – "Why," says the Duke of Buckingham, "I do suffer him to do this, that I may hereafter the better command him." This he swears to me the person himself to whom*d* the

a repl. 'it'   b repl. 'here'
c repl. 'com'-   d MS. 'him'

---

1. A favourite book for Sunday reading: see above, i. 56, n. 6.

2. This story has not been traced elsewhere and is *prima facie* unlikely.

Duke of Buckingham said this did tell it*a* him – and is a man of
worth, understanding, and credit.   He told me one odd passage
by the Duke of Albemarle, speaking how hasty a man he is, and
how for certain he would have killed Sir W. Coventry, had he
met him*b* in a little time after his showing his letter in the
House[1] – he told me that a certain lady whom he knows did tell
him that she, being certainly informed that some of the Duke of
Albemarle's family did say that the Earl of Torrington was a
bastard,[2] did think herself concerned to tell the Duke of Albemarle
of it; and did first tell the Duchesse, and was going to tell*c* the old
man, when the Duchesse pulled her back by the sleeve and
hindered her, swearing to her that if he should hear it, he would
certainly*d* kill the servant that should be found to have said it,
and therefore prayed her to hold her peace.   One thing more he
told me, which is that Garraway[3] is come to town and is thinking
how to bring the House to mind the public state of the nation
and to put off these perticular picks against man and man; and
that he propounding this to Sir W. Coventry, Sir W. Coventry
did give no encouragement to it, which he says is that by their
running after other men, he may escape; but I*e* do believe this is
not true neither.   But however, I am glad that Garraway is here
and that he doth begin to think of the public condition in reference
to our neighbours that we are in and [in] reference to ourselves,
whereof I am mightily afeared of trouble.   So to supper, and he
gone and we to bed.

18.   Up, and all the morning at my office till 3 after noon with
Mr. Hater, about perfecting my little pocket market-book of the

---

a repl. 'him'   *b* MS. 'in'   *c* repl. 'tell'
           d repl. 'be'   *e* repl. 'but I'

---

1. See above, p. 490 & n. 2.
2. Torrington was Albemarle's
only surviving son. He had been
born in wedlock in 1653, but his
mother's first husband was said to
have been alive at the time of the
marriage. (Cf. Aubrey, ii. 73.) He

succeeded to the dukedom in 1670,
but after the Revolution of 1688 the
allegation of bastardy was revived:
W. Salkeld, *Reports* (1795 ed.), i. 120.
3. William Garroway, M.P. for
Chichester; a leader of the country
party.

office,[1] till my eyes were ready to fall out of my head. And then home to dinner, glad that I had done so much; and so abroad to White-hall to Commissioners of the Treasury and there did a little business with them;[2] and so home, leaving multitude of solicitors at their door, of one sort or other, complaining for want of such despatch as they had in my Lord Treasurer's time; when I believe more business was despatched, but it was in his manner, to the King's wrong. Among others, here was Gresham College, coming about getting a grant of Chelsy-College for their Society, which the King it seems hath given them his right in; but they met with some other pretences, I think, to it, besides the King's.[3]

Thence took up my wife, whom I had left at her tailor's,[4] and home; and there to save my eyes, got my wife at home to read again, as last night, in the same book, till W. Batelier came and spent the evening talking with us, and supped with us, and so to bed.

19. To the office; and thence before noon, I by the Board's direction to the Parliament-house to speak with Sir R. Brookes

---

1. Untraced; possibly the book listed in Rawl. D 794 (f. 9r, reverse order) as in his possession c. 1693 and as containing prices for victualling provisions, 1660-1 and 1664-7. The Admiral's Instructions (1662) required the Board to enquire the market-prices of stores, and to receive weekly returns from the customs-house 'soe the Purveyors may not delude them with the pretence of scarcity . . .': PL 2867, p. 359.

2. See *CTB*, ii. 121; Backwell was to pay £6,000 to such persons in Tangier as Pepys should appoint.

3. For the Treasury minute, see *CTB*, loc. cit. Chelsea College, founded in James I's reign to train controversialists against Rome, had been derelict for a long time and had recently been occupied by Dutch prisoners-of-war. The Royal Society, after petitioning for the property in June 1664, was allowed to take possession on 27 September 1667, but the Crown's right to certain portions of it was disputed by other claimants, even after its conveyance to the society by its third charter of 8 April 1669. In 1682 it was sold back to the Crown, to become the Royal Hospital (rebuilt by Wren, 1682-1702). *CTB*, ii. 113, 123, 223; Birch, i. 391, 431-2, ii. 194, 205; Evelyn, passim; Faulkner, *Chelsea* (1829), ii. 218+.

4. Unthank's. In the surviving ledgers of Sir William Turner, the draper, there is entered under this day the purchase by Pepys (possibly in fact by his wife) of two yards of pure fine black cloth and five yards of cloth. It cost £6 and was paid for on 29 December. GL, MS. 5107/1, f. 163v.

about the meaning of an order come to us this day, to bring all
the books of the office to the Committee.   I find by him that it is
only about the business of an order of ours for paying off the
ships by ticket, which they think I, on behalf of my Lord
Brouncker, do suppress[1] – which vexes me, and more at its
occasioning the bringing them our books; so home and to
dinner, where Mr. Sheply with me, newly come out of the
country, but I was at little liberty to talk to him; but after
dinner, with two contracts to the Committee with Lord
Brouncker and Sir T. Harvy; and there did deliver them and
promised at their command more, but much against my will.
And here Sir R. Brookes did take me alone and pray me to
prevent their trouble, by discovering the order he would have;
I told him I would suppress none, nor could; but this did not
satisfy him, and so we parted, I vexed that I should bring on
myself this suspicion.   Here I did stand by unseen,[a] and did
hear their impertinent* yet malicious examinations of some rogues
about the business of Bergen,[2] wherein they would wind in
something against my Lord Sandwich (it was plain by their
manner of examining, as Sir Tho. Crew did afterward observe
to me, who was there); but all amounted to little[b] I think.   But
here Sir Th. Crew and W. Hewer, who was there also, did tell
me that they did hear Captain Downing[3] give a cruel testimony
against my Lord Brouncker for his neglect and doing nothing
in the time of straits at Chatham when he was spoke to, and
did tell the committee that he (Downing) did presently after, in
Lord Brouncker's hearing, tell the Duke of Albemarle that if he
might advise the King, he should hang both my Lord Brouncker
and Pett.   This is very hard.   Thence with W. Hewer and our
messenger, Marlow, home by coach; and so late at letters, and
then home to supper and my wife to read; and then to bed.

<hr>

a MS. 'unseen seen'   b repl. 'nothing'

<hr>

1. The Navy Board had authorised
the use of tickets on a large scale for
paying off ships at Chatham in
December 1666. For Brouncker's
responsibilities in the matter, see
above, p. 393, n. 1. For Pepys's defence, see below, pp. 545–6 & n.

He and his colleagues were not above
suppressing a letter which implicated
Coventry: above, pp. 507, 509.

2. See above, vi. 196 & n. 1.

3. Probably John Downing of
the 1st Footguards.

This night I wrote to my father in answer to a new Match which is proposed (the executor of Ensum, my sister's former servant *) for my sister, that I will continue my mind of giving her 500*l* if he likes of the match.¹

My father did also this week, by Sheply, return me up a*ᵃ* Guinny, which it seems, upon searching the ground, they have since found since I was there.² I was told this day of Lory Hide, second son to my Lord Chancellor, did some time since in the House say that if he thought his father was guilty but of one of the things then said against him, he would be the first that should call for judgment against him – which Mr. Waller the poet did say was spoke like the old Roman, like Brutus, for its greatness and worthiness.³

20. Up, and all the morning at my office shut up with Mr. Gibson, I walking and he reading to me the order-books of the office from the beginning of the Warr,⁴ for preventing the Parliament's having them in their hands before I have looked them over and seen the utmost that can be said against us from any of our orders*ᵇ*⁵ – and to my great content, all the morning I found none. So at noon home to dinner with my clerks – who have of late dined frequently with me, and I do purpose to have them

a repl. 'another'   *b* repl. 'letters'

---

1. This was the match with John Jackson, of Ellington, Hunts., who married Pall in February 1668, and whose son John became Pepys's heir. For Ensum, see above, vii. 78, n. 2. The letter has not been traced.

2. See above, pp. 472–4.

3. Laurence Hyde's speech (29 October), but not Waller's comment, is reported in Grey, i. 10–11. It also appears in L. Eachard, *Hist. Engl.* (1720), p. 843. He desired to be accounted not so much Clarendon's son 'as a member of this House'. He made another speech on 16 November calling for his father to be

put on trial: Grey, i. 41. Burnet's view (i. 463) was that Hyde was insincere, and playing for political survival. But the speeches may also be read as a challenge to his father's opponents to prove their charge of treason: cf. his brother Cornbury's speech reported below, p. 544 & n. 2.

4. Untraced; probably the 'Books containing the Abstracts of Orders' listed in the inventory of books remaining in the office of the Clerk of the Acts, October 1688: BM, Add. 9303, f. 124r.

5. Parliament was likely to criticise any dilatoriness: cf. above, p. 503.

so still, by that means I having opportunity to talk with them about business, and I love their company very well. All the morning Mr. Hater and the boy did shut up themselfs at my house, doing something towards the finishing the abstract-book of our contracts for my pocket,[1] which I shall now want very much. After dinner I stayed at home all the afternoon, and Gibson with me, and he and I shut up till about 10 at night; we went through all our orders and towards the end I do meet with two or three orders for our discharging of two or three little vessels by ticket without money, which doth plunge me; but however, I have the advantage by this means to study an answer – and to prepare a defence, at least for myself.[2] So he gone, I to supper, my mind busy thinking after our defence in this matter, but with vexation to think that a thing of this kind, which in itself[a] brings nothing but trouble and shame to us, should happen before all others to become a charge against us.

This afternoon Mr. Mills came and visited me, and stayed a little with me (my wife being to be godmother to his child tomorrow); and among other talk, he told me how fully satisfactory my first report was to the House in the business of Chatham[3] – which I am glad to hear; and the more for that I know that he is a great creature of Sir R. Brookes's.[4]

21. Up, and to the office, where all the morning; and at noon home, where my wife not very well, but is to go to Mr. Mills's child's christening, where she is godmother, Sir J. Mennes and Sir R. Brookes her companions.[5] I left her after dinner (my clerks dining with me) to go with Sir J. Mennes, and I to the office, where did much business till after candlelight;[b] and then, my eyes beginning to fail me, I out and took coach and to Arundell-house, where the meeting of Gresham College was

---

a repl. 'self'   *b* repl. 'cland'-

---

1. Untraced. For the office contract-books, see above, iii. 65, n. 2.
2. See below, pp. 545–6 & n.
3. See above, pp. 494–6.
4. Brooke was chairman of the Commons' committee enquiring into the miscarriages of the war. For his association with Milles, see above, p. 241 & n. 1.
5. The child was a son, Daniel, and had been baptised privately on the 17th: *Harl. Soc. Reg.*, 46/75.

broke up; but there meeting Creed, I with him to the tavern
in St. Clements churchyard, where was Deane Wilkins, Dr.
Whistler, Dr. Floyd, a divine, admitted, I perceive, this day,[1]
and other brave men;[a] and there among other things of news, I do
hear that upon the reading of the House of Commons' reasons
of the manner of their proceedings in the business of my Lord
Chancellor,[2] the reasons were so bad, that my Lord Bristoll himself did declare that he would not stand to what he had, and did
still, advise the Lords to concurr to, upon any of the reasons of the
House of Commons; but if it was put to the question whether
it should be done on their reasons, he would be against them.
And endeed, it seems the reasons, however they came to escape
the House of Commons (which shows how slightly the greatest
matters are done in this world, and even in Parliaments), were
none of them of strength, but[b] the principle of them untrue; they
saying that where any man is brought[c] before a Judge accused of
Treason in general, without specifying the perticular, the Judge
doth there constantly, and is obliged to, commit him.[3] Whereas
the question being put by the Lords to my Lord Keeper, he said
the quite contrary was true. And then in the sixth Article (I will
get a copy of them if I can) there are two or three things strangely
asserted, to the diminishing of the King's power as is said; at
least, things that heretofore would not have been heard of.[4] But

a repl. 'men'   *b* MS. 'of'   *c* repl. 'accused'

1. This was presumably William
Lloyd (Bishop of St Asaph, 1680;
later of Lichfield and of Worcester),
a friend of Wilkins, whom he helped
with his linguistic studies (see above,
vi. 12, n. 6; Burnet, i. 339). But he
was never made a fellow of the
Royal Society. The tavern has not
been identified.
2. The Commons had presented to
the Lords a statement of their case
arguing 'Reasons' why the upper
House should concur in committing
anyone impeached by the Commons.
See above, p. 534 & n. 3.

3. The argument rested on the
contention that in treason trials
speed was essential.
4. In the sixth article it was asserted
that the proceedings of inferior
courts were 'bounded and limited' by
the discretion of Parliament because
Parliament is 'the whole Publick,
comprehending the King, Lords and
Commons (for the King's Presence
is supposed in the Lords House)':
CJ, ix. 22.

then the question*a* being put among the Lords, as my Lord
Bristoll advised: whether upon the whole matter and reasons
that had been laid before them, they would commit my Lord
Clarenden, it was carried five to one against it, there being but
three Bishops against him, of which Cosens and Dr. Reynolds
were two, and I know not the third.[1] This made the opposite
Lords, as Bristoll and Buckingham, so mad, that they declared
and protested against it, speaking very broad that there was
mutiny and rebellion in the heart of the Lords, and that they
desired they might enter their dissents, which they did do in great
fury.[2] So that upon the Lords sending to the Commons, as I
am told, to have a conference for them*b* to give their answer to
the Commons' reasons, the Commons did desire a free conference; but the Lords do deny it, and the reason is that they
hold not the Commons any Court, but that themselfs*c* only are a
Court, and the chief court of Judicature, and therefore are not to
dispute the laws and method of their own Court with them that
are none; and so will not submit so much as to have their power
disputed.[3] And it is conceived that much of this eagerness among
the Lords doth arise from the fear some of them have, that they
may be dealt with in the same manner themselfs, and therefore
to stand upon it now. It seems my Lord Clarenden hath, as is
said and believed, had his coach and horses several times in his
coach, ready to carry him to the Tower, expecting a message to

a repl. 'thing'   *b* repl. 'their'   *c* repl. 'time'

---

1. Pepys is probably wrong about
Reynolds; the three anti-Clarendonian bishops who signed the
minority protest which followed
were Cosin (Durham), Croft (Hereford), and Lucy (St David's): *LJ*,
xii. 142. The voting appears to have
been 102 to 28: among the pro-
Clarendon majority were the two
archbishops and seventeen bishops.
2. *LJ*, xii. 141–2; a protest signed
by 28 peers, including Buckingham
and Bristol. The right of a minority
to enter and sign in the House's

journal a dissenting opinion was one
of the peers' privileges.
3. A free conference – i.e. one at
which any subject could be raised –
would have given the Commons the
chance of raising this constitutional
issue. The Lords had their way: a
conference was held on the 25th in
which they replied to the Commons'
'Reasons'; on the 28th a conference
was held on the question of committing Clarendon on a general charge
of treason.

that purpose – but by this means his case is like to be laid^a by. From this we fall to other discourse, and very good. Among the rest, they discourse of a man that is a little frantic (that hath been a kind of minister, Dr. Wilkins saying that he hath read for him in his church) that is poor and a debauched man, that the College have hired for 20s to have some of the blood of a Sheep let into his body; and it is to be done on Saturday next.¹ They purpose to let in about twelve ounces, which they compute is what will be let in in a minutes time by a watch. They differ in the opinion they have of the effects of it; some think that it may have^b a good effect upon him as a frantic man, by cooling his blood; others, that it will not have any effect at all. But the man is a healthy man, and by this means will be able to give an account what alteration, if any, he doth find in himself, and so may be usefull. On this occasion Dr. Whistler told a pretty story related by Muffett, a good author, of Dr. Cayus that built Key's-College: that being very old and lived only at that time upon woman's milk, he, while he fed upon the milk of a angry fretful woman, was so himself; and then being advised to take of a good-natured patient woman, he did become so, beyond the common temper of his age.² Thus much nutriment, they observed, might do. Their discourse was very fine; and if I should be put out of my office, I do take great content in the

a repl. 'cast'   *b* repl. 'be'

---

1. See below, p. 554 & nn. The man was an eccentric – Arthur Coga (Cogie), who had taken his B.A. at Cambridge in 1660. Asked why he chose to have a transfusion of sheep's blood, he replied with a reference to the Blood of the Lamb: '*Sanguis ovis symbolicam quandam facultatem habet cum sanguine Christi; quia Christus est agnus Dei*' (R. Boyle, *Works*, 1744, v. 638). His brain was said to be 'sometimes a little too warm': ib., loc. cit.

2. John Caius was a scholar and physician, and co-founder of Gonville and Caius College, Cambridge; he died in 1573 at the age of 63. The story appears in Dr Thomas Moffett's *Healths Improvement* (1655), p. 123: 'What made Dr *Cajus* in his last sickness so peevish and so full of frets at Cambridge, when he suckt one woman (whom I spare to name) froward of conditions and of bad diet; and contrariwise so quiet and well, when he suckt another of contrary disposition?' Similarly, 'what made *Iupiter* and *Aegystus* so lecherous, but that they were chiefly fed with goats milk?'

liberty I shall be at of frequenting these gentlemen's companies. Broke up thence and home, and there to my wife in her chamber, who is not well (of those); and there she tells me great stories of the gossiping women of the parish, what this and what that woman was; and among the rest, how Mrs. Hollworthy is the veriest confident bragging gossip of them all, which I should not have believed – but that Sir R. Brookes, her partner,[1] was mighty civil to her and taken with her and what not.   My eyes being bad, I spent the evening with her in her chamber, talking and inventing a Cypher to put on a piece of plate which I must give, better then ordinary, to the parson's child; and so to bed, and through my wife's illness had a bad night of it, and she a worse, poor wretch.

22.   Up betimes; and drinking my morning draught of strong water with Betty Michell, but had not opportunity para besar la; I by water to White-hall and there met Creed; and thence with him to*a* Westminster-hall, where we talked long together of news and there met with Cooling, my Lord Chamberlain's Secretary – and from him learn the truth of all I heard last night; and understand further that this stiffness of the Lords is in no manner of kindness to my Lord Chancellor, for he neither hath nor doth, nor for the future likely can, oblige any of them, but rather the contrary; but that they do fear what the consequence may be to themselfs should they yield in his case, as many of them have reason.   And more, he showed me how this is rather to the wrong and prejudice of my Lord Chancellor; for that it is better for him to come to be tried before the Lords, where he can have right and make interest, then, when the Parliament is up, be committed by the King and tried by a Court on purpose, made by the King of what Lords the King pleases, who have a mind to have his head.   So that my Lord   himself ⟨his son⟩[2] (he tells me) hath moved that if they have treason against

a repl. 'by'

---

1. At the christening.
2. Viscount Cornbury, M.P. for Wiltshire; succ. as 2nd Earl of Clarendon, 1674.

my Lord of Clarenden, that they would specify it and send it up to the Lords, that he might come to his trial[1] – so full of intrigues this business is.

Having now a mind to go on and to be rid of Creed, I could not, but was forced to carry him with me to the Excise Office; and thence to the Temple and there walked a good while in the Temple church, observing the plainness of Seldens tomb, and how much better one of his executors hath who is buried by him.[2] And there I parted with him and took coach and home, where to dinner.

23. Up and to the office, where all the morning; and at [noon] home to dinner, and all the afternoon also, busy till late, preparing things to fortify myself and fellows against the Parliament – and perticularly myself against what I fear is thought: that I have suppressed the order of the Board by which the discharging the great ships off at Chatham by ticket was directed;[3] whereas endeed there was no such order. So home at night to supper and to bed.

24. *Lords day.* In my chamber all the morning[a] (having lain long in bed) till Mr. Sheply came to dine with me; and there, being to return to Hinchingbrooke speedily, I did give him as good account how matters go here as I could. After dinner, he being gone, I to the office[b] and there, for want of other of my clerks, sent to Mr. Gibbs, whom I never used till now, for the writing over of my little pocket contract-book;[4] and there I laboured till 9 at night with him in drawing up the history of all that hath passed concerning tickets, in order to the laying the whole and

---

a repl. 'after' *b* repl. same symbol badly formed

---

1. This challenge was made in a debate on the 16th: Grey, i. 41. Cf. above, p. 539, n. 3.
2. The tomb of John Selden (the lawyer; d. 1654) consisted of a thick slab of black marble. His executor was Rowland Jewkes (d. 1663). Cf. Aubrey, ii. 222–3; Mrs K. A. Esdaile, *Temple Church monuments*, pp. 161–3, and pl. xvii.
3. See below, p. 546 & n. 2.
4. See above, p. 540 & n. 1.

clearing myself and office before Sir R. Brookes, and in this I
took great pains;[1] and then sent him away and proceeded, and had
W Hewers come to me, and he and I till past 12 at night in the
office; and he (which was a good service) did so inform me in
the consequences of my writing this report, and that what I said
would not hold water in denying this Board to have ever ordered
the discharging[a] out of the service whole ships by ticket, that I
did alter my whole counsel and fall to arme myself with good
reasons to justify the Office in so doing, which hath been but
rare;[2] and having done this, I went with great quiet in my mind
home, though vexed that so honest a business should bring me
so much trouble – but mightily was pleased to find myself put
out of my former design; and so after supper, to bed.

25.   Up, and all the morning at the office finishing my letter
to Sir Rob. Brookes, which I did with great content; and yet at
noon, when I came home to dinner, I read it over again after it
was sealed and delivered to the messenger, and read it to my
clerks who dined with me, and there I did resolve upon some
alteration and caused it to be new writ;[3] and so to the office
after dinner, and there all the afternoon mighty busy; and[b] at

a repl. 'paying'   *b* repl. 'in '

---

1. Pepys's rough longhand notes
(undated) are in Rawl. A 191, ff.
179–93, 245–8, endorsed: 'An Assort-
ment of my severall Collections out
of our Bookes of Letters Orders and
Memorandums &c. upon severall
points to bee made use of in the pre-
pareing a defence for the Officers of
the Navy to bee delivered in Parliament touching the businesse of
Ticketts. Memd. That what I finde
lyn'd out heerein is what I tooke
thence to be perticularly mencioned
in my discourse to the Parliament as
appeares in my Paper I provided for
my Memory contayning the Heads
thereof.'

2. In his letter to Brooke of 25
November (below, n. 3), Pepys
admitted that the Board had authorised payment by ticket on three
occasions (at Chatham, December
1666), but only for the benefit of
absentees.

3. Copies of drafts (23, 25 November, in Hewer's and Pepys's hands,
with a note about the alteration) are
in NMM, LBK/8, pp. 506–8.
Brooke's reply (28 November)
thanked Pepys for his 'ingenious narrative', and assured him that he had
acquitted himself 'as a person of much
integrity': Rawl. A 191, f. 231r.

night did take coach, thinking to have gone to Westminster, but it was mighty dark and foul and my business not great, only to keep my eyes from reading by candle,*ᵃ* being weary; but being gone part of my way, I turned back; and so home and there to read and my wife to read to me out of Sir Rob. Cotton's book about Warr;[1] which is very fine, showing how the Kings of England have raised money*ᵇ* heretofore upon the people, and how they[2] have played upon the kings also.

So after supper, I to bed.

This morning Sir W. Penn tells me that the House was very hot on Saturday last upon the business of Liberty of speech in the House, and damned the vote in the beginning of the Long Parliament against it,[3] so that he fears that there may be some bad thing which they have a mind to broach, which they dare not do without more security then they now have. God keep us, for things look mighty ill.

26. Up, all the morning at the office and then home to dinner, where dined Mr. Clerke, solicitor, with me, to discourse about my Tanger accounts, which I would*ᶜ* fain make up but I have not time. After dinner, by coach as far as the Temple and there saw a new book in Folio of all that suffered for the King in the late times – which I will buy; it seems well writ.[4] And

---

a repl. 'cr'-   *b* MS. 'money by the people'   *c* repl. 'found'

---

1. *An answer to such motives as were offer'd by certain military-men to Prince Henry, inciting him to affect arms more than peace* – a long essay composed for Henry, Prince of Wales (d. 1612). It was first published in 1655, and reissued under various titles. Pepys was probably using the version in *Cottoni Posthuma* (1657), of which the 1679 edition remains in his library (PL 956).

2. The people.

3. This is a misunderstanding. A resolution passed on the previous Saturday had reasserted the traditional liberty of parliamentary speech. It reaffirmed similar resolutions of 6 and 8 July 1641 which had condemned the judgement in King's Bench (1630) by which three M.P.'s (Eliot, Holles and Valentine) had been imprisoned for seditious speeches made in parliament in 1629. In 1668 Holles had the judgement reversed by the Lords. *CJ*, ii. 200–1, 203; ib., ix. 3, 19, 25; *LJ*, xii. 164–6.

4. David Lloyd, *Memoires of the lives . . . of those noble . . . personages* etc. (1668); licensed 27 July 1667 (*Trans. Stat. Reg.*, ii. 379); not in the PL.

then back to the Old Exchange and there at my goldsmith's
bought a basin for my wife to give the parson's child to which
the other day she was godmother: it costs me 10*l*-14*s* besides
graving, which I do with the Cypher of the name, Daniel Mills.
And so home to the office, and then home to supper and hear my
wife read, and then to bed.

This noon, after dinner, came to me Mr. Warren[1] and there
did tell me that he came to pay his debt to me for the kindness I
did him in getting his last ship out (which I must also remember
was a service to the King (though I did not tell him so) as appeared
by my advising with the board and their writing to Sir W.
Coventry to get the pass for the ship to go for it to Genoa).
Now, that with which he had promised me for the courtesy was,
I take it, 100 pieces or more, I think more; and also for the
former courtesy I had done, for the getting his first ship out for
this hemp,[2] he did promise me a consideration upon the return
of the goods, but I never did to this day demand anything of him;
only, about a month ago he told me that now his ship was come
and he would come out of my debt, but told me that whereas
he did expect to have had some profit by the voyage,*a* it had
proved of loss to him, by the loss of*b* some ships or some accidents,
I know not what, and so that he was not able to do what he
intended, but told*c* me that he would present me with 60 pieces in
gold; I told him I would demand nothing of his promises, though
they were much greater, nor would have thus much; but if he
could afford to give me but 50 pieces, it should suffice me.   So
now he brought something in a paper, which since prove to be
50 pieces; but before I would take*d* them, I told him that I did
not insist on anything, and therefore prayed him to consult his
ability before he did*e* part with them; and so I refused them once
or twice, till he did the third time offer them, and then I took
them.   He saying that he would present me with as many more,
if I would undertake to get him 500*l* paid on his bills, I told him

a l.h. repl. symbol rendered illegible   *b* MS. 'or'
c repl. 'bold'   *d* repl. 'took'   *e* repl. 'could'

---

1. Thomas   Warren,   merchant   2. See above, vi. 77 & n. 2.
(brother of Sir William).

I would by no means have any promise of that kind, nor would have any kindness from him for any such service; but*a* that I should do my utmost for nothing to do him that justice, and would endeavour to do what I could for him; and so we parted, he owning himself mightily engaged to me*b* for my kind usage of him in accepting so small a matter in satisfaction for all that he owed*c* me – and so we parted: which I enter at large for*d* my justification if anything of this should be hereafter enquired after.

This evening also came to me to my closet at the office, Sir Jo. Chichly, of his own accord, to tell me what he shall answer to the Committee, when, as he expects, he shall be examined about my Lord Sandwich; which is so little as will not hurt my Lord at all, I know.[1] He doth profess great generousness towards my Lord, and that this jealousy of my Lord's of him is without ground; but doth mightily inveigh against Sir Rog. Cuttance and would never have my Lord to carry him to sea again with him, as being a man that hath done my Lord more hurt then ever he can repair, by his ill advice and disobliging everybody. He will by no means seem to crouch to my Lord, but says that he hath as good blood in his veins as any man, though not so good a Title; but that he will do nothing to wrong or prejudice my Lord – and I hope he will not, nor believe can. But he tells me that Sir E. Spragg and Utber are the men that have done my Lord the most wrong and did bespatter him the most at Oxford, and that my Lord was*e* misled to believe that all that was there said was his, when indeed*f* it was they; and says that he did at that time complain to his father of this his misfortune. This I confess is strange to me touching those two men, but yet it may well enough, as the world goes; though I wonder, I confess, at the latter of the two, who alway professes great love to my Lord.

Sir Rog. Cuttance was with me in the morning, and there gives me an account so clear about Bergen and the other business[2]

---

a repl. full stop *b* MS. 'him' *c* repl. 'hath promised'
d repl. full stop *e* repl. 'did' *f* MS. 'it did'

---

1. Cf. above, p. 527 & n. 3.
2. In 1665 Cuttance had been in command of Sandwich's flagship (the *Prince*) at the Bergen fiasco and at the ill-fated capture of the two E. Indiamen which followed: see above, vi. 196, 231 & nn.

against my Lord, as I do not see what can*ᵃ* be laid to my Lord in either; and tells me that Pen, however he now dissembles it, did on the quarter-deck of my Lord's ship after he came on board, when my Lord did fire a gun for the ships to leave pursuing the enemy, Pen did say before a great many, several times, that his heart did leap in his belly for joy when*ᵇ* he heard the gun, and that it was the best thing that could be done for securing the fleet. He tells me also that Pen was the first*ᶜ* that did move and persuade my Lord to the breaking Bulke, as a thing that was now the time to do right to the commanders of the great ships, who had no opportunity of getting anything by prizes; now his Lordship might distribute to everyone something, and he himself did write down before my Lord the proportions for each man. This I am glad of, though it may be this dissembling fellow may twenty*ᵈ* to one deny it.

27. Up, and all the morning at my Lord Brouncker's lodgings with Sir J. Mennes and W. Penn about Sir W. Warren's accounts, wherein I do not see that they are ever very likely to come to an understanding of them as Sir J. Mennes hath yet handled them. Here till noon and then home to dinner, where Mr. Pierce comes to me and there in general tells me how the King is now fallen in and become a slave to the Duke of Buckingham, led by none but him, whom he (Mr. Pierce)*ᵉ* swears he knows to hate the very person of the King, and would as well as live certainly ruin him. He doth say, and I think with right, that the King doth in this do the most ungrateful part of a maister to a servant that ever was done, in this carriage of his to my Lord Chancellor. That it may be the Chancellor may have faults, but none such as these they speak of. That he doth now really fear that all is going to ruin, for he says he hears that Sir W. Coventry hath been, just before his sickness, with the Duke of York to ask his forgiveness and peace for what he had done; for that he never could foresee that what he meant so well in, the counselling

---

a repl. 'it' *b* repl. 'that my' *c* MS. 'first thing'
d repl. 'deny it.' *e* MS. has closing bracket after 'he knows'

to lay by the Chancellor, should come to this.[1] As soon as dined, I with my boy Tom to my Bookebinders,[2] where all the afternoon long, till 8 or 9 at night, seeing him binding up two or three collections of letters and papers that I had of him; but above all things, my little abstract pocket-book of contracts, which he will do very neatly.   Then home to read, sup, and to bed.

28.   Up, and at the office all this morning and then home to dinner; and then[a] by coach sent my wife to the King's[b] play-house and I to White-hall, there intending, with Lord Brouncker, Sir J. Mennes, and Sir T. Harvy, to have seen the Duke of York, whom it seems the King and Queen have visited, and so we may now well go to see him.[3] But there was nobody could speak with him, and so we parted, leaving a note in[c] Mr. Wren's chamber that we had been there (he being at the free[d] conference of the two Houses about this great business[e] of my Lord Chancellor's, at which they were at this hour, 3 in the afternoon; and there they say my Lord Anglesy doth his part admirably ably)[4] and each of us taking a printed Copy of the Guiny Company's defence to a petition against them to the Parliament the other day.[5] So I away to the King's playhouse, and there sat by my wife and saw *The Mistaken Beauty*,[6] which I never I think saw before, though an old play; and there is much in it that I like, though the name is but improper to it; at least, that name –

a repl. 'sent'   b repl. 'Duke of York's'
c repl. 'that we'   d repl. 'conference'   e repl. 'piece'

---

1. Cf. above, p. 506.
2. Possibly William Richardson.
3. For his illness, see above, p. 522, n. 2.
4. Anglesey was one of the 14 managers appointed by the Lords: *LJ*, xii. 149.
5. A group of merchants trading to the American colonies had petitioned the Commons in September against the high price of Negro slaves supplied by the monopolistic Royal African Company. The company

had presented a reply on 22 November: *CJ*, ix. 24. . Both petition and answer are printed in *Answer of the Company of Royal Adventurers of England trading into Africa, to the petition . . . exhibited to the Honourable House of Commons by Sir Paul Painter etc.*

6. *The mistaken beauty, or The Liar*, an anonymous translation of Pierre Corneille's *Le Menteur* (1643); published in 1685. (A).

it being also called *The Lyer*, which is proper enough.   Here I met with Sir Rd. Browne,[1] who wondered to find me there, telling me that I am a man of so much business; which character,[a] I thank God, I have ever got, and have for a long time had and deserved; and yet am now come to be censured in common with the office for a man of negligence.

Thence home and to the office to my letters; and then home to supper and to bed.

29.   Waked about 7 a-clock this morning with[b] a noise I supposed I heard near our chamber, of knocking, which by and by increased, and I more awake, could distinguish it better; I then waked my wife and both of us wondered at it, and lay so a great while, while that encreased; and at last heard[c] it plainer, knocking as if it were breaking down a window for people to get out – and then removing[d] of stools and chairs, and plainly by and by going up and down our stairs.   We lay both of us afeared; yet I would have rose, but my wife would not let me; besides, I could not do it without making noise; and we did both conclude that thiefs were in the house, but wondered what our people did, whom we thought either killed or afeared as we were.   Thus we lay till the clock struck 8, and high day.   At last I removed my gown and slippers safely to the other side the bed over my wife, and there safely rose and put on my gown and breeches, and then with a firebrand in my hand safely opened the door, and saw nor heard anything.   Then (with fear, I confess) went to the maid's chamber-door, and all quiet and safe.   Called Jane up, and[e] went down safely and opened my chamber, where all well.   Then more freely about, and to the kitchen, where the cook-maid up and[f] all safe.   So up again, and when Jane came and we demanded whether she heard no noise, she said, "Yes, and was afeared," but rose with the other maid and found nothing, but heard a noise in the great stack of chimneys that goes from Sir J. Mennes's through our house; and so we sent, and their chimneys have been swept this morning, and the noise

a repl. 'char'-   b repl. 'a'   c MS. 'it heard'
d repl. 'r'-   e repl. 'and when she came to'   f repl. 'who says'

1. Clerk to the Privy Council.

was that and nothing else. It is one*ᵃ* of the most extraordinary accidents in my life, and gives ground to think of Don Quixot's adventures how people may be surprized[1] – and the more from an accident last night, that our young gibb-cat did leap down our stairs from top to bottom at two leaps and frighted us, that we could not tell well whether it was the cat or a spirit, and do sometimes think this morning that the house might be haunted. Glad to have this so well over, and endeed really glad in my mind, for I was much afeared. I dressed myself, and to the office both forenoon and afternoon, mighty hard putting papers and things in order to my extraordinary satisfaction, and consulting my clerks in many things, who are infinite helps to my memory and reasons of things. And so, being weary and my eyes akeing, having overwrought them today reading so much shorthand, I home and there to supper, it being late, and to bed. This morning Sir W. Penn and I did walk together a good while, and he tells me that the*ᵇ* Houses are not likely to agree after their free conference yesterday,*ᶜ* and he fears what may fallow.

30. Up and to the office, where all the morning, and then by coach to Arundell-house to the elections of Officers for the next year; where I was near being chosen of the Council, but am glad I was not, for I could not have attended;[2] though above all things, I could wish it, and do take it as a mighty respect to have been named there. The company great and elections long; and then to Cary-house, a house now of entertainment, next my Lord Ashly's; and there, where I have heretofore heard Common-Prayer in the time of Dr. Mossum,[3] we after two hours' stay,

---

a MS. 'most'   *b* repl. 'my'   *c* repl. 'the other'

1. Pepys is presumably thinking of the adventure with the fulling mills. He retained two copies of *Don Quixote*, one (Brussels, 1662) in Spanish, and the other in English (1670; trans. Thomas Shelton): PL 912–13, 2029.

2. He had also been nominated in April 1666, and had then received only three votes: above, vii. 96. The ten now chosen included his ex-colleague, John Creed, re-elected from the previous year, whose success Pepys omits to record – he disliked him – on both occasions. Birch, ii. 219. Pepys ultimately became a councillor in 1672, and served several times thereafter.

3. Dr Robert Mossom (now Bishop of Derry) had conducted illegal Anglican services there at the end of the Interregnum. Cary House was on the s. side of the Strand to the east of the Savoy Palace.

sitting at the table with our napkins open, had[a] our dinners brought; but badly done. But here was good company, I choosing to sit next Dr. Wilkins, Sir George Ent,[1] and others whom I value. And there talked of several things; among others, Dr. Wilkins, talking of the universall speech, of which he hath a book coming out,[2] did first inform me how man was certainly made for society, he being of all creatures the least armed for defence; and of all creatures in the world, the young ones are not able to do anything to help themselfs, nor can find the dug without being put to it, but would die if the mother did not help it. And he says were it not for speech, man would be a very mean creature. Much of this good discourse we had. But here above all, I was pleased to see the person who had his blood taken out. He speaks well, and did this day give the Society a relation thereof in Latin, saying that he finds himself much better since, and as a new man.[3] But he is cracked a little in his head, though he speaks very reasonably and very well. He had but 20s for his suffering it, and is to have the same again tried upon him – the first sound man that ever had it tried on him in England, and but one that we hear of in France, which was a porter hired by the virtuosi.[4] Here all the afternoon till within night. Then I took coach and to the Exchange, where I was to

a repl. 'did'

---

1. Wilkins (one of the principal founders of the Royal Society) was a mathematician; Ent a physiologist.

2. *Essay toward a real character, and a philosophical language*: see below, 15 May 1668, n.

3. This was Arthur Coga: cf. above, p. 543 & n. 1.

4. The French experiment was made in Paris by Jean Denys on a madman a few months earlier: Boyle, *Works* (1744), v. 377, 379; Gunther, iii. 107. The Royal Society experiment appears to have been the first transfusion conducted on a human being in England. According to the minutes of the Society, the official report on it was made on 28 November: Birch, ii. 216. It had been conducted by Drs King and Lower on the 23rd, and was repeated on 12 December. Lower had in 1665 experimented on an animal: Gunther, ii. 130–2. See Birch, ii. 215; *Philos. Trans.*, no. 30, 9 December 1667; Boyle, op. cit., ii. 557+, v. 638. For the history of transfusion, see Gunther, iii. 127; Sir G. Keynes (ed.), *Blood Transfusion*, pp. 1–40; M. H. Nicolson, *Pepys' diary and the new science*, pp. 55+; illust. (1672) in G. Bankoff, *Story of surgery*, opp. p. 128.

meet my wife, but she was gone home; and so I to Westminster-hall and there took a turn or two; but meeting nobody to discourse with,*a* returned to Cary-house and there stayed a little and saw a pretty deception of the sight, by a glass*b* with water poured into it, with a stick standing up with three balls of wax upon it, one distant from the other – how these balls did seem double and disappear one after another, mighty pretty.[1] Here Mr. Carcasse did come to me, and brought first Mr. Colwall our Treasurer and then*c* Dr. Wilkins to engage me to be his friend; and himself asking forgiveness and desiring my friendship, saying that the Council have now ordered him to be free to return to the office to be imployed.[2] I promised him my friendship, and am glad of this occasion, having desired it; for there is nobody's ill tongue that I fear*d* like his – being a malicious and cunning bold fellow. Thence, paying our shot, 6*s* apiece, I home and there to the office and wrote my letters; and then home, my eyes very sore with yesterday's work. And so home and tried to make a piece by my eare and viall to "*I wonder what the grave, &c*";[3] and so to supper and to bed – where frighted a good while, and my wife, again with noises;*e* and my wife did rise twice, but I think it was Sir J. Mennes's people again, late cleaning their house, for it was past one a-clock in the morning before we could fall to sleep; and so slept – but I perceive well what the care of money and treasure in a man's house is to a man that fears to lose it.

My Lord Anglesy told me this day that he did believe the House of Commons would the next week yield to the Lords. But speaking with others this day, they conclude they will not,

---

a MS. 'with whom' *b* repl. 'cl'- *c* repl. 'at'
d repl. 'feel like' *e* repl. 'noise'

---

1. For the study of refraction at this time, see Gunther, vol. i, pts iii–iv.

2. See above, p. 64 & n. 1. Carkesse was a Fellow of the Royal Society. The report of the Privy Council committee does not appear to have been presented until 3 January 1668: 'The proofes are not sufficient to render him so criminall as to be unfitt for Imployment, when he shall other wise be thought fitt' (PRO, PC 2/60, p. 110). He was later reinstated at the request of several M.P.'s who undertook for his good behaviour: PL 2874, p. 471.

3. Cowley's lyric 'Resolved to love', first published in *The Mistress* (1647). Pepys's setting does not survive. (E)

but that rather the King will accommodate it by committing my Lord Clarendon himself. I remember what Mr. Evelin said: that he did believe we should soon see ourselfs fall into a Commonwealth again.[1]   Joseph Williamson I find mighty kind still, but close, not daring to say anything almost that touches upon news or state of affairs.[a2]

a   followed by one blank page

---

1. Evelyn nowhere in his own diary admits to this remark. Cf. similar prophecies by others: above, pp. 378, 390–1.

2. Williamson was Secretary to Arlington, whose political security was in jeopardy in this crisis.

DECEMBER

1. *Lords day.* I up, and after entering my Journall for two or three days, I to church, where Mr. Mills, a dull sermon. And in our pew there sat a great lady, which I afterward understood to be my Lady Carlisle that made her husband a cuckold in Scotland – a very fine woman endeed in person.[1] After sermon, home; where W. Hewer dined with us; and after dinner, he and I all the afternoon to*a* read over our office letters, to see what matter can be got for our advantage or disadvantage therein. In the evening comes Mr. Pelling and the two men that were with him formerly, the little man that sings so good a Base (Wallington) and another that understands well, one Piggott;[2] and Betty Turner came and sat and supped with us, and we spent the evening mighty well in good music, to my great content to see myself in condition to have these and entertain them for my own pleasure only. So they gone, we to bed.

2. Up, and then abroad to Alderman Backewell's (who was sick of a cold in bed) and then to the Excize Office, where I find Mr. Ball out of humour, in expectation of being put out of his office by the change of the farm of the excise.[3] There comes Sir H Cholmly, and he and I to Westminster and there walked up and down till noon; where all the business is that the Lords' answer is come down to the Commons, that they are not satisfied in the Commons' reasons; and so the Commons are hot and like to sit all day upon the business what to do herein, most thinking

a repl. 'in'

---

1. She was Anne, wife of the 4th Earl, a soldier and diplomatist, who had been away on an embassy to Russia, Sweden and Denmark, 1663–4. I have not traced the story elsewhere.

2. See above, p. 437, n. 4. (E).

3. John Ball (Treasurer of the London Excise) was later dismissed by the new farmers appointed on 24 June 1668; on petition he was granted a pension of £200 p.a.: *CSPD 1667–8*, p. 566; *CTB*, ii. 429.

that they will remonstrate against the Lords.[1]   Thence to Lord
Crews and there dined with him; where after dinner, he took me
aside and bewailed the condition of the nation, how the King
and his Brother are at a distance about this business of the Chancellor, and the Houses differing; and he doth believe that there
are so many about the King like to be concerned and troubled
by the Parliament, that they will get him to dissolve or prorogue
the Parliament – and the rather for that the King is likely by the
good husbandry of the Treasury to get out of debt, and the
Parliament is likely to give no money.   ⟨Among other things,
my Lord Crew did tell me with grief, that he hears that the King
of late hath not dined nor supped with the Queen as he used of
late to do.⟩*a*   After a little discourse, Mr. Cæsar dining there,
he did give us some music on his lute (Mr. John Crew being
there) to my great content, and then away I; and Mr. Cæsar
fallowed me and told me that my boy Tom hath this day declared
to him that he cared not for the French lute*b*[2] and would learn no
more – which Cæsar out of faithfulness tells me, that I might not
spend any more money on him in vain.   I shall take the boy to
task about it, though I am contented to save my money if the
boy knows not what is good for himself.   So thanked him; and
endeed he is a very honest man I believe.   And away home,
there to get something ready for the Lords Commissioners of
Treasury; and so took my wife and girl and set them at Un-
thanks, and I to White-hall and there with the Commissioners
of the Treasury, who I find in mighty good condition to go on in
payment of the seamen off.[3]   And thence I to Westminster-hall,
where I met with my Cosen Roger and walked a good while

a   addition inserted within square brackets at bottom of page
b   MS. 'a lute'

---

1. On 29 November the Lords had
voted that the evidence presented
against Clarendon did not warrant
his arrest: *LJ*, xii. 152. The Commons now declared that vote 'an
Obstruction to the publick Justice of
this Kingdom . . . and . . . of evil and
dangerous Consequence': *CJ*, ix. 29.

2. See above, p. 530, n. 2.   (E).
3. By the 12th it was clear that
they had £20,000 for the purpose.
They therefore decided to disburse
it in weekly instalments of £1500,
with a proviso that the payments
were to be made to seamen only, and
not to ticket-brokers: *CTB*, ii. 145.

wtih him; he tells me of the high vote of the Commons this afternoon, which I also [heard was] mighty hot at White-hall: that the proceedings of the Lords in the case of my Lord Clarendon is an obstruction to Justice and of ill precedent to future times. This makes everybody wonder what will be the effect of it, most thinking that the King will try him by his own commission. It seems they were mighty high to have remonstrated, but some said that was too great an appeale to the people. Roger is mighty full of fears of the consequence of it, and wishes the King would dissolve them. So we parted; and I bought some Scotch cakes at Wilkinson's in King's-street and called my wife, and home and there to supper, talk, and to bed. Supped upon these cakes, of which I have eat none since we lived at Westminster. This night our poor little Dogg Fancy was in a strange fit of madness through age, of which she hath had five or six.

3. Up by candlelight, the only*a* time I think I have done so this winter; and a coach being got over-night, I to Sir W. Coventry, the first time I have seen him at his new house*b*1 since he came to lodge there. He tells of the vote for none of the House to be of the commission for the Bill of Accounts;2 which he thinks is so great a disappointment to Birch, and others that expected to be of it, that he thinks, could it have been seen, there*c*

a repl. 'other'   *b* repl. 'lodgings'   *c* repl. 'they would'

---

1. In Pall Mall: see above, p. 504, n. 4.
2. *CJ*, ix. 28 (2 December). The bill was passed on 19 December (19–20 Car. II c. 1) and established a committee of nine under Lord Brereton – later known as the Brooke House Committee from its place of meeting – to enquire into the administration of finances during the late war. For its membership and work, see *CTB*, vol. ii, p. liv; Rawl. A 185, ff. 313–14. Its report (25 October 1669) and papers are summarised in HMC, *Rep.*, 8/1/1, pp. 128*a*–133*b* (cf. Grey, i. 158+). Its criticisms fell mainly on the Navy Board, the principal spending department. Pepys's reply (27 November 1669) was a huge and crushing document, answering in turn each of the Committee's sixteen 'observations': see PL 2874, pp. 509–75 (other copies in PL 2554; Rawl. A 457; BM, Sloane 2751). The Privy Council considered both the report and Pepys's answers in January–February 1670, and Pepys dictated to a clerk 'A Journall of what passed between the Commissioners of Accompts and myselfe before his Majesty in Council . . .': PL 2874, pp. 385–504.

would not have been any Bill at all. We hope it will be the
better for all that are to account; it being likely that the men,
being few and not of the House, will hear reason. The main
business I went about was about Gilsthrop, Sir W. Batten's clerk;
who being upon his death-bed – and now dead, hath offered to
make discovery of the disorder of the Navy and of 65000*l*
damage to the King; which made mighty noise in the Commons'
House – and members appointed to go to him; which they did,
but nothing to the purpose got from him but complaints of false
musters, and ships being refitted with victuals and stores at
Plymouth after they came fitted from other ports.¹ But all this
to no purpose, nor more then we know and will owne; but the
best is that this loggerhead*ᵃ* should say this, that understands
nothing of the Navy nor ever would, and hath perticularly
blemished his master by name among us. I told Sir W.
Coventry of my letter to Sir R. Brooke and his answer to me;²
he advises me, in what I write to him, to be as short as I can and
obscure, saving in things fully plain, for that all he doth is to
make mischief; and that the greatest wisdom in dealing with the
Parliament in the world is to say little and let them get out what
they can by force – which I shall observe.*ᵇ* He declared to me
much of his mind: to be ruled by his own measures and not to go
so far as many would have him, to the ruin of my Lord Chancellor, and for which they do endeavour to do what they can
against W. Coventry; "But," says he, "I have done my do, in
helping to get him out of the administracion of things for which
he is not fit; but for his life or estate, I will have nothing to say to
it; besides that, my*ᶜ* duty to my maister,*ᵈ* the Duke of York, is
such that I will perish before I will do anything to displease or
disoblige him where the very necessity of the Kingdom doth
not in my judgment call me."

---

a repl. 'logger'–   *b* repl. 'abserve'   *c* MS. 'mighty'
                         d repl. 'mistress'

---

1. The Commons had ordered
enquiries to be made of Gelsthrop on
29 November; Milward's report (p.
141) confirms Pepys's. Coventry

had written to Pepys about this matter on 30 November: HMC, *Eliot
Hodgkin*, pp. 169–70.
2. See above, p. 546 & n. 3.

Thence I home and to the office, where Lord Anglesy; and all the discourse was yesterday's vote in the Commons, wherein he told us^{*a*} that should the Lords yield to what the Commons would have in this matter, it were to make them worse then any Justice of Peace (whereas they are the highest court in the Kingdom); that they cannot be judges whether^{*b*} an offender be to ⟨be⟩ committed or bailed, which every Justice of Peace doth do. And then he showed me precedents plain^{*c*} in their defence.[1]

At noon home to dinner and busy all the afternoon; and at night home^{*d*} and there met W. Batelier, who tells me the first great news, that my Lord Chancellor is fled this day.[2] By and by to Sir W. Penn's, where Sir R Ford, and he and I met with Mr. Young and Lewes about our accounts with my Lady Batten[3] – which prove troublesome and I doubt will prove to our loss. But here I hear the whole, that my Lord Chancellor is gone and left a paper behind him for the House of Lords, telling them the reason of his^{*e*} retiring, complaining of a design for his ruin. But the paper I must get;[4] only, the thing at present is great and will put the King and Commons to some new counsels certainly. So home to supper and to bed.

Sir W. Penn I find in much trouble this evening, having been called to the committee this afternoon about the business of prizes.[5]

a repl. 'me' *b* repl. 'what' *c* repl. 'in'
d repl. 'to Sir W P' *e* MS. 'is'

---

1. See above, pp. 557–8 & n. Anglesey had been a manager for the Lords in the conference between the two Houses in this matter.

2. He had fled to France on 30 November: see below, p. 568.

3. See above, pp. 341 & n. 3, 477 & n. 2. Sir William Batten had died in October, and John Young (with Ford himself) was an overseer of his will. Together with Thomas Lewis of the Victualling Office they acted on the widow's behalf: below, p. 582.

4. Clarendon's 'Humble Peticion and Address' is printed e.g. in *LJ*, xii.

154–6; Clarendon, *Life*, iii. 337–46; and *Somers Tracts* (ed. Scott), viii. 7–11. Arlington, writing to Ormond on 7 December, said that copies were in circulation (Lister, iii. 475); Pepys's copy (in Tom Hayter's hand) is in BM, Harl. 7170, ff. 38–41. It consists mainly of a defence against the two main charges of corruption and of monopolising power. There are only the briefest references to the plots against him.

5. Cf. Pepys to Sandwich, 4 December: Rawl. A 195a, f. 80r; above, vi. 231, n.

Sir Rd. Ford told us this evening an odd story of the basenesse of the late Lord Mayor, Sir W Bolton, in cheating the poor of the City (out of the collections made for the people that were burned) of 1800*l*, of which he can give*ᵃ* no account, and in which he hath forsworn himself plainly; so as the Court of Aldermen have sequestered him from their Court till he doth bring in an account – which is the greatest piece of roguery that they say was ever found in a Lord Mayor.¹

He says also, that this day [it] hath been made appear to them that the Keeper of Newgate at this day hath made his house the only* nursery of rogues and whores and pickpockets and thiefs in the world, where they were bred and entertained and the whole society met; and that for the sake of the Sheriffes they durst not this day commit him, for fear of making him let out the prisoners, but are fain to go by artifice to deal with him.²

He tells me also, speaking of the new street that is to be made from Guild Hall down to Cheapside,³ that the ground is already most of it bought, and tells me of one particular – of a man that hath a piece of ground lie in the very middle of the street that must be; which, when the street is cut*ᵇ* out of it, there will remain ground enough of each side to build a house to front the street. He demanded 700*l* for the ground, and to be excused paying anything for the melioration of the rest of his ground that he was to keep. The Court consented to give him 700*l*; only, not to abate him the consideration – which the man denied; but told

a repl. 'give'   *b* repl. 'g'-

1. Bolton had been Lord Mayor in 1666–7; he surrendered his place as alderman in May 1668, and was eventually convicted in 1675 of mis-appropriation of funds by the Commissioners for Charitable Uses. Both he and his widow – quite ruined by the affair – were given a small pension by the city. *CSPD 1667-8*, p. 416; A. B. Beaven, *Aldermen of London*, i. 95; Sharpe, ii. 432, n. 2.

2. The Keeper (Walter Cowdrey) was dismissed by the Court of Aldermen in February 1668 and died shortly afterwards. He had been guilty of cruelty to his prisoners as well as of other offences. LRO, Repert. 70, ff. 152*v*–54*v*; 71, f. 143*v*; 73, ff. 23*r*, 28*r*, 50*r*, 81*r*, 81*v*, 89*v*, 103*v*; HMC, *Rep.*, 15/7/102.

3. This was King St. Before its construction, access to the Guildhall from the south was either by Ironmonger Lane or Lawrence Lane, both of them narrow. (R).

them, and so they agreed, that he would excuse the City the 700*l*, that he might have the benefit of the melioration without paying anything for it.[1] So much some will get by having the City burned. But*ᵃ* he told me that in other cases, ground by this means, that was not worth 4*d* a foot before, will now, when houses are built, be worth 15*s* a foot. But he tells me that the common Standart now reckoned on between man and man, in places where there is no alteration of circumstances, but only the houses burnt, there the ground, which with a house on it did yield 100*l* a year, is now reputed worth 33*l*-6*s*-8*d*; and that this is the common market-price between one man and another, made upon a good and moderate Medium.

4. At the office all the morning. At noon to dinner, and presently with my wife abroad, whom and her girl I leave at Unthankes: and so to White-hall in expectation of waiting on the Duke of York today, but were prevented therein; only, at Mr. Wren's chamber there, I hear that the House of*ᵇ* Lords did send down the paper which my Lord Clarendon left behind him, directed to the Lords, to be seditious and scandalous;[2] and the Commons have voted that it be burned by the hands of the hangman[3] and that the Lords[4] be desired to agree*ᶜ* to it. I do hear also that they have desired the King to use means to stop his escape out of the nation.[5] Here I also heard Mr. Jermin, who was there in the chamber upon occasion of Sir Tho. Harvy's telling him of his brother's having a child, and thereby taking away his hopes (that is, Mr. Jermin's) of 2000*l* a year – he swore,

---

a MS. 'that'   *b* MS. 'have'
c repl. symbol rendered illegible

---

1. The general effect of the clause providing for melioration (sect. 24 of the Rebuilding Act, 18-19 Car. II c. 7) is discussed in T. F. Reddaway, *Rebuilding of London*, pp. 165-7. For a somewhat similar case, concerning a property in the same street, see Philip E. Jones (ed.), *Fire Court*, i. 63-4.

2. *LJ*, xii. 154-6.
3. *CJ*, ix. 32.
4. MS. 'King'; but see *CJ*, loc. cit.
5. By a vote of the 3rd: *CJ*, ix. 29. The consequent orders to the Duke of York as Admiral are in *CSPD 1667-8*, p. 59.

God damn him, he did not desire to have any more wealth then he had in the world; which endeed is a great estate, having all his uncle's, my Lord St. Alban's, and my Lord hath all the Queene Mother's.*a*1 But when Sir Tho. Harvy told him "But hereafter you will wish it more," "By God!" answers he, "I won't promise what I shall do hereafter." Thence into the House, and there spied*b* a pretty woman with spots* on her face, well clad, who was enquiring for the guard-chamber; I fallowed her, and there she went up and turned into the turning toward the Chapel; and I after her, and upon the stairs there met her coming up again and there kissed her twice, and her business was to enquire for Sir Richard*c* Bishop, one of the sergeants-at-arms; I believe she was a woman of pleasure, but was shy enough to me; and so I saw her go out afterward, and take a hackney-coach and away. I to Westminster-hall and there walked, and thence towards White-hall by coach; and spying Mrs. Burroughs in a shop, did stop*d* and light and speak to her; and so to White-hall, where I light and went and met her coming towards White-hall, but she was upon business and I could not get her to go anywhither; and so parted, and I home with my wife and girl (my wife not being very well of a great looseness day and night for these two days). So home, and my wife to read to me in Sir R. Cotton's book of Warr,2 which*e* is excellent reading; and perticularly I was mightily pleased this night in what we read about the little profit or honour this Kingdom ever gained in its greatest of its conquests abroad in France. This evening came Mr. Mills and sat with us a while, who is mighty kind and good company. And so he gone, I to supper and to bed. My wife an unquiet night. ⟨This day Gilsthrop is buried, who hath made all the late discourse of

---

a repl. same symbol badly formed   *b* repl. 'having seen'
    c MS. 'Edwd'   *d* MS. 'spop'   *e* MS. 'which I'

---

1. St Albans (once Master of the Horse to Henrietta-Maria and wrongly reported to be her second husband) managed her finances and was commonly said to have embezzled her money. The two nephews mentioned here were Thomas ('Mr.') Jermyn (who had just had a son), and his younger brother, Henry, Master of the Horse to the Duke of York, and St Albans's adopted heir.

2. See above, p. 547 & n. 1.

the great discovery of 65000*l* of which the King hath been wronged.⟩*a*

5. At the office all the morning. Do hear that Will Pen, Sir W. Penn's son, is come from Ireland, but I have not seen him yet.[1] At noon to the Change, where did little; but so home again and to dinner, with my clerks with me, and very good discourse and company they give me; and so to the office all the afternoon till late, and so home to supper and to bed. This day, not for want but for good husbandry, I sent my father by his desire, six pair of my old shoes, which fit him and are good; yet methought it was a *b* thing against my mind to have him wear my old things.

6. Up, and with Sir J. Mennes to the Duke of York, the first time that I have seen or we waited on him since his sickness;[2] and blessed be God, he is not at all the worse for the smallpox, but is only a little weak yet. We did much business with him – and so parted. My Lord Anglesy told me how my Lord Northampton brought in a Bill into the House of Lords yesterday, under the name of *A Bill for the honour and privilege of the House, and mercy to my Lord Clarendon* – which he told me he opposed, saying that he was a man accused of treason by the House of Commons, and mercy was not proper for him, having not been tried yet, and so no mercy needful for him. However, the Duke of Buckingham did, and others, desire the Bill might be read; and it was for banishing my Lord Clarendon from all his Majesty's dominions and that it should be treason to have him found in any of them. The thing is only a thing of vanity and to insult

---

a addition crowded into end of paragraph   *b* repl. 'an'

---

1. Since the spring of 1666 William Penn had been in co. Cork where his father had an estate. For the importance of his visit, see below, p. 595 & n. 3. This entry appears to be the most exact evidence of the date of his return. Cf. W. Penn, *My Irish Journal, 1669–70* (ed. Grubb), pp. 11–13.

2. See above, p. 522, n. 2.

over him; which is mighty poor I think, and so doth everybody else, and ended in nothing I think.[1]

By and by home with Sir J. Mennes, who tells me that my Lord Clarendon did go away in a Custom-house boat and is now at Callis: upon [whom], I confess, nothing seems to hang more heavy then his leaving of this unfortunate paper[2] behind him, that hath angered both Houses and hath I think reconciled them in that which otherwise would have broke them in pieces; so that I do hence, and from Sir W. Coventry's late example and doctrine to me, learn[a] that on these[b] sorts of occasions there is nothing like silence – it being seldom any[c] wrong to a man to say nothing, but for the most part it is to say anything. This day, in coming home, Sir J. Mennes told me a pretty story of Sir Lewes Dives, whom I saw this morning speaking with him; that having escaped once out of prison through a house of office, and another time in woman's apparel and leaping over a broad canal, a soldier in roguery put his hand towards her belly, and swore, says he, "This is a strong Jade, but I never felt a cunt with a handle to it before."[3] He told me also a story of my Lord Cottington: who wanting a[d] son, entended to make his Nephew his heir, a country boy, but did alter his mind upon the boy's being persuaded by another young heir (in roguery) to Crow like a cock at my Lord's table, much company being there and the boy having

a MS. 'learnt'   *b* repl. 'this'
c repl. same symbol badly formed
d repl. 'title'

---

1. 'An Act for banishing and discrediting' Clarendon was now given its first reading: *LJ*, xii. 158. It was passed at the end of the session: below, p. 578 & n. 1.

2. See above, p. 561, n. 4.

3. Sir Lewis Dyve (d. 1669) was a royalist soldier, of whom Evelyn said that he was 'a valiant gent: but not a little given to romance when he spake of himselfe'. He claimed to have made five escapes, and I have failed to trace the second of the two here referred to. The first was a feat made famous by his own published account: on 30 January (the night after the King's execution) he dropped through the hole of a privy in the King's Bench prison in Whitehall, two storeys above the river, landed in the water and escaped in a waiting boat. See *A letter from Sir L. D. written out of France to a gentleman . . . in London* (1648/9); B. Whitelocke, *Memorials* (1833 ed.), ii. 517; Evelyn, iii. 40; H. G. Tibbutt, *Life and Letters of Sir L. Dyve*.

a great trick*a* at doing that perfectly – my Lord bade them take away that fool from the table, and so gave over the thoughts of making him his heir from this piece of folly.[1]   So home and there to dinner; and after dinner, abroad with wife and girl, set them down at Unthankes and I to White-hall to the Council-chamber, where I was summoned about the business of paying off the seamen; where I heard my Lord Anglesy put to it by Sir W. Coventry before the King for altering the course set by the Council; which he, like a very wise man, did answer in few words, that he had already sent*b* to alter it according to the Council's method, and so stopped it; whereas many words would have set the Commissioners of the Treasury on fire, who I perceive were prepared for it.[2]   Here I heard Mr. Gawden speak to the King and Council upon some business of his before them;[3] but did it so well, in so good words and to the purpose, that I could never have expected from a man of no greater learning.

So went away, and in the Lobby met Mr. Sawyer my old chamber fellow and stayed and had an hour's discourse of old things with him;*c* and I perceive he doth very well in the world – and is married, he tells me, and hath a child.[4]   Then home and to

---

a repl. 'tr'-   *b* repl. 'he'   *c* repl. 'me'

---

1. Both Cottington's son and daughter had died childless before their father, and the two young heirs were Francis and Charles Cottington, sons of his brother. Francis was principal heir and administrator under a will of 16 June 1652 made on his deathbed; after Francis's death in 1665, Charles inherited the estate. (It consisted mainly of Fonthill, Wilts., later the home of William Beckford.) Lord Cottington's love of birds and animals may possibly have inspired the cock-crowing. Sir R. C. Hoare *et al.*, *Hist. mod. Wilts.* (1822–37), iii. (Dunworth), pp. 20–1.

2. Anglesey had been examined by the Treasury Commissioners on the 5th. They held that the Navy Board had disobeyed the orders of both Council and Treasury in the matter of the tickets. *CTB*, ii. 139.

3. The new victualling contract; the Council this day ordered Pepys to draft an additional clause: PRO, PC 2/60, p. 80. 'Mr.' is a mistake for 'Sir Denis'.

4. Robert Sawyer had been at Magdalene with Pepys. He was a rising young barrister, and soon afterwards acted as Carteret's counsel before the Brooke House Committee: below, 27 May 1668. He became Attorney-General, 1681–7. He had married in July 1665.

the office, where Captain Cocke came to me; and among other discourse, tells me that he is told that an impeachment against Sir W. Coventry will be brought in very soon. He tells me that even those that are against my Lord Chancellor and the Court in the House do not trust nor agree one with another. He tells me that my Lord Chancellor went away[a] about 10 at night on Saturday last, and took boat at Westminster and thence by a vessel to Callis, where he believes he now is;[1] and that the Duke of York and Mr. Wren knew of it, and that himself did know of it on Sundy morning. That on Sunday his coach and people about it went to[b] Twittenham,[2] and the world[c] thought that he had been there. That nothing but this unhappy paper[3] hath undone him, and that he doubts that this paper hath lost him everywhere. That his withdrawing doth reconcile things so far, as he thinks the heat of their fury will be over – and that all will be made well between the two brothers.[4] That Holland doth endeavour to persuade the King of France to break peace with us. That the Dutch will without doubt have 60 sail of ships out the next year – so knows not what will become of us, but hopes that the Parliament will find money for us to have a fleet. He gone, I home; and there my wife made an end to me of Sir R. Cottons discourse of Warr,[5] which is endeed a very fine book. So to supper and to bed.

Captain Cocke did this night tell me also, among other discourse, that he did believe that there are jealousies in some of the House at this day against the Comissioners of the Treasury, that by their good husbandry they will bring the King to be out of debt and to save money; and so will not be in need of the Parliament, and then do what he please – which is a very good piece of

---

a   repl. 'on'   b   repl. 'towards'
c   repl. same symbol badly formed

---

1. Clarendon (iii. 332–3) states that he embarked at Erith at 11 p.m. on 'Saturday night, the 29th November'. But Saturday was the 30th: Clarendon mistook the date, but not the day of the week.

2. Clarendon had a country villa (York House) at Twickenham: R. S. Cobbett, *Memorials Twickenham*, pp. 217+.

3. See above, p. 561, n. 4.

4. The King and the Duke of York.

5. See above, p. 547 & n. 1.

news, that there is such a thing to be hoped which they would be afeared of.

7. All the morning at the office, and at noon home to dinner with my clerks. And while we were at dinner comes Willett's aunt[1] to see her and my wife. She is*a* a very fine widow and pretty handsome, but extraordinary well-carriaged and speaks very handsomely and with extraordinary understanding, so as I spent the whole afternoon in her company with my wife, she understanding all the things of note touching plays and fashions and Court and everything, and speaks rarely, which pleases me mightily, and seems to love her niece very well, and was so glad (which was pretty odde) to see that since she came hither her breasts begin to swell, she being afeared before that she would have none – which was a pretty kind of content she gave herself. She tells us that *Catelin*[2] is likely to be soon acted; which I am glad to hear – but it is at the King's House. But the King's House is at present, and hath for some days been, silenced upon some difference [between] Heart and Moone.[3] She being gone, I to the office and there late doing business; and so home to supper*b* and to bed. Only, this evening I must remember that my Lady*c* Batten sent for me, and it was to speak to me before her overseers about my bargain with Sir W. Batten about the prize;[4] to which I would give no present answer, but am well enough contented that they begin the discourse of it; and so away to the office again, and then home to supper and to bed. Somebody told me this day that they hear that Thomson with the wooden leg, and Wildman the Fifth-Monarchy man (a great

---

a repl. 'seems'   *b* repl. 'bed' and full stop   *c* MS. 'Lord'

---

1. Mrs Hunt of Jewin St, Cripplegate.

2. *Catiline*, a tragedy by Ben Jonson; see above, v. 349 & n. 4. (A).

3. Charles Hart and Michael Mohun, leading actors at the Theatre Royal. (A).

4. Sir Richard Ford, William Wood (mastmaker) and John Young (upholsterer and flagmaker) were overseers of her late husband's will. For the bargain Pepys had made with Batten, see above, p. 341 & n. 3, p. 477 & n. 2.

creature of the Duke of Buckinghams) are in nomination to be commissioners, among other, upon the Bill of Accounts.[1]

8. *Lords day.* All the morning at my chamber, doing something toward the settling of my papers and accounts, which have been out of order a great while.[a] At noon to dinner, where W How with us; and after dinner, he being gone, I to my chamber again till almost night; and then took boat, the tide serving, and so to White-hall, where I saw the Duchesse of[b] Yorke (in a fine dress of second mourning for her mother,[2] being black, edged with Ermin) go to make her[c] first visit to the Queene since the Duke of York was sick; and by and by, she being returned, the Queene came and visited her. But it was pretty to observe that Sir W. Coventry and I walking an hour and more together in the Matted Gallery, he observed, and so did I, how the Duchesse, as soon as she spied him, turned her head a'one-side. Here he and I walked thus long, which we have not done a great while before. Our[d] discourse was upon everything. The unhappiness of having our matters examined by people that understand them not; that it was better for us in the Navy to have men that do understand the whole, and that are not passionate. That we that have taken the most pains are called upon to answer for all crimes, while those that like Sir W. Batten and Sir J. Mennes did sit and do nothing, do lie[e] still without any trouble. That if it were to serve the King and kingdom again in a war, neither of us could do more, though upon this experience we might do

a   repl. 'w'-   b   repl. '(in'   c   repl. 'a'
      d   repl. 'was'   e   repl. 'bear'

---

1. Both were nominated, but only Col. George Thomson appointed. He was a prominent Rumper whom Pepys had known in 1659–60 when Thomson was an Admiralty Commissioner. Wildman was not a Fifth-Monarchy man but a Leveller. He had been released from prison in October: *CSPD 1667*, p. 502. For his connection with Buckingham (going back to the 1650s), see below, 4 November 1668; M. P. Ashley,

John Wildman, pp. 204+; *CSPD 1667–8,* pp. 238, 259. Buckingham was reported (in a newsletter, 19 December) to have called him 'the wisest statesman in England': ib., p. 89.

2. Frances, daughter of Sir Thomas Aylesbury, Bt, who had married Clarendon in 1634 as his second wife. She had died on 8 August. 'Second mourning' followed full mourning.

better then we did. That the commanders, the gentlemen that could never be brought to order, but undid all, are now the men that find fault and accuse others. That it had been much better for the King to have given Sir J. Mennes and W. Batten 1000*l* a year to have sat still, then to have had them in his business this war. That the serving a prince that minds not his business is most unhappy for them that serve him well; and a unhappiness so great, that he declares he will never have more to do with a war under him. That he hath papers which do flatly contradict the Duke of Albemarle's narrative;[1] and that he hath been with the Duke of Albemarle and showed him them, to prevent his falling into another like fault. That the Duke of Albemarle seems*ª** to be able to answer them; but he thinks that the Duke of Albemarle and the Prince are contented to let their Narratives sleep, they being not only contradictory in some things (as he observed about the business of the Duke of Albemarle's being to fallow the Prince upon the dividing the fleet, in case the enemy came out), but neither of them to be maintained in others. That the business the other night of my Lord Anglesy at the Council[2] was happily got over for my Lord, by his dexterous silencing it, and the rest not urgeing it further, forasmuch as had the Duke of Buckingham come in time enough and had got it by the end, he would have tossed him in it; Sir W. Coventry telling me that my Lord Anglesy did with such impudence maintain that quarrel against the Commons and some of the Lords in the business of my Lord Clarenden, that he believes there are enough*ᵇ* would be glad but of this occasion to be revenged of him. He tells me that he hears some of the Thomson's are like to be of the Commission for the Accounts, and Wildman; which he much wonders at, as having been a false fellow to everybody, and in prison most of the time since the King's coming in.[3] But he doth tell me that the House is in such a condition, that nobody can tell what to make of them, and he thinks they were never in before;

---

a   repl. symbol rendered illegible   *b*   repl. 'of enough'

---

1. See above, p. 514 & n. 1.
2. See above, p. 567 & n. 2.
3. George Thomson and his three brothers (all merchants) had been prominent in the service of the Com-

monwealth; two of them (George and Robert) in naval administration. For Wildman and for the appointments, see above, pp. 569–70 & n.

that everybody leads and nobody fallows*; and that he doth
now think that, since a great many are defeated in their expectation of being of the Commission, now they would put it into
such hands as it shall get no credit from; for if they do look to
the bottom and see the King's case, they think they are then
bound to give the King money; whereas they would be excused
from that, and there[fore] will endeavour to make this business of
the Accounts to signify little. I spoke with him about my Lord
Sandwiches business, in which he is very friendly, and doth say
that the unhappy business of the prizes is it that hath brought all
this trouble upon him, and the only thing that made anything else
mentioned – and it is true. So having discoursed with him, I
spent some time with Sir St. Fox about the business of our
adjousting the new method of the Excize between the Guards,
household, and Tanger,[1] the Lords-Commissioners of the
Treasury being now resolved to bring all their management into
a course of payment by orders, and not by Tallys;[2] and I am
glad of it. And so by water home, late and very dark,* and when
come home there, I got my wife to read; and then came Captain
Cocke to me, and there he tells me to my great satisfaction that
Sir Robt. Brookes did dine with him today, and that he told him,
speaking of me, that he would make me the darling of the House
of Commons, so much he is satisfied concerning me: and this
Cocke did tell me that I might give him thanks for it. And I do
think it may do me good, for he doth happen to be held a considerable person of a young man, both for sobriety and ability.[3]
Then to discourse of business of his own, about some hemp of his
that is come home, to receive it into the King's stores; and then
parted, and by and by my wife and I to supper, she not being
well, her flux being great upon her; and so to bed.

a repl. 'drive'　　　*b* repl. 'dark'

---

1. Cf. *CTB*, ii. 126, 127, 130, 132,
133, 139–40. Pepys had been given
a warrant for £17,500 for Tangier.

2. For payments 'in course' and the
use of Treasury orders as negotiable
instruments, see above, p. 520 & n. 2.
For one important disadvantage of
tallies, see above, vii. 407 & n. 2.

3. Brooke (M.P. for Aldeburgh,
Suff.) had been chairman of the
Commons' enquiry into the Fire of
London, and was now chairman of
the committee on the miscarriages of
the war. He was about 37.

9. All the morning busy at the office, doing very considerable business; and thither comes Sir G. Carteret to talk with me, who seems to think himself safe as to his*a* perticular,*b* but doth doubt what will become of the whole Kingdom, things being so broke in pieces. He tells me that the King himself did the other day very perticularly tell*c* the whole story of my Lord Sandwiches not fallowing the Dutch ships,[1] with which he is charged, and shows the reasons of it to be the only good course he could have taken, and doth discourse it very knowingly. This I am glad of; though as the King is now, his favour, for aught I see, serves very little in stead at this day – but rather is an argument against a man; and the King doth not concern himself to relieve*d* or justify anybody, but is wholly negligent of everybody's concernment. This morning I was troubled with my Lord Hinchingbrooke sending to borrow 200*l* of me; but I did answer that I had none, nor could borrow any, for I am resolved I will not be undone for anybody, though I would do much for my Lord Sandwich; for it is to answer a bill of exchange of his.[2] And I perceive he hath made use of all other means in the world to do it. But I am resolved to serve him, but not ruin myself, as it may be to part with so much of the little I have by me to keep, if I should by any turn of times lose the rest. At noon I to the Change and there did a little business; and among other things, called at Cade's the stationer, where he tells me how my Lord Gerard is troubled for several things in the House of Commons, and in one wherein

a repl. 'the' *b* repl. 'general' *c* repl. 'tell'
d repl. 'relief'

---

1. After capturing his prizes in September 1665: cf. Harris, ii. 14, 25–6.

2. The request was made (in a letter of 9 December) by Hinchingbrooke on behalf of his father, who had sent a letter of exchange of 'about £250 8s. payable to the Spanish ambassador'. Moore had been unable to cash it. Hinchingbrooke's letter to Pepys, with a s.h. note of Pepys's reply, is in Rawl. A 174, f. 430r; printed in Smith, i. 122–4. Pepys answered briefly, beginning: 'My condition is such, and hath been ever since the credit of the king's assignments was broke by the failure of the bankers, that I have not been able, these six months, to raise a farthing for answering my most urgent occasions.' On the 19th (according to an endorsement to his own letter) Pepys lent £60 to Sandwich. Hinchingbrooke had on 26 November appealed to the Treasury for money on his father's behalf: *CTB*, ii. 127.

himself is concerned. And it seems this Lord is a very proud and wicked man, and the Parliament is likely to order* him.[1] Then home to dinner, and then a little abroad, thinking to have gone to the other end of the town; but it being almost night, I would not, but home again; and there to my chamber and all alone did there draw up my answer to Sir Rob. Brookes's letter;[2] and when I had done it, went down to my clerks at the office for their opinion, which at this time serves me to very good purpose, they having many things in their heads which I had not in the businesses of the office now in dispute. Having done with this, then I home and to supper very late, and to bed – my [wife] being yet very ill of her looseness, by which she is forced to lie from me tonight in the girl's chamber.

10. Up, and all the morning at the office; and then home with my people to dinner, and very merry; and then to the office again, where did much business till night, that my eyes begun to be sore; and then forced to leave off, and by coach set my wife at her tailor's, and Willet; and I to Westminster-hall and there walked a good while till 8 at night, and there hear to my great content that the King did send a message to the House today that he would adjourne them on the 17th instant to February[3] by which time at least, I shall have more respite to prepare things on my own behalf, and the Office, against their return. Here I met Mr. Hinxton the organist[4] walking, and I walked with him; and asking him many questions, I do find that he can no more give an intelligible answer to a man that is not a great maister in his Art then another man – and this confirms me that it is only want of an ingenious man that is maister in Musique,

1. Lord Gerard of Brandon, a captain in the King's Life Guards (later a Whig and a supporter of Monmouth's rebellion) was a violent and litigious person, and his behaviour was now the subject of two petitions in the Commons: *CJ*, ix. 36, 41; HMC, *Rep.*, 8/1/115. Cade's connection with the affair has not been traced. Gerard, who is said to have 'jeered at' the Commons, was soon afterwards deprived of his command

at the King's order: below, p. 581, n. 1; *CSPD 1667–8*, p. 305.

2. Copy (10 December; in Gibson's hand) in NMM, LBK/8, pp. 511–12; printed in *Further Corr.*, pp. 184–5. For this correspondence, see above, p. 546 & n. 3.

3. A mistake; the message was sent to both houses on the 9th: *LJ*, xii. 161; *CJ*, ix. 34.

4. See above, vii. 414, n. 1. (E).

to bring music to a certainty and ease in composition. Having done this, I home, taking up my wife and girl; and there to supper and to bed, having finished my letters; among which, one to Comissioner Middleton, who is now coming up to town from Portsmouth to enter upon his Surveyorship.[1]

11. By coach to White-hall, and there attended the Duke of York as we are wont; who is now grown pretty well and goes up and down White-hall, and this night will be at the Council - which I am glad of. Thence to Westminster-hall and there walked most of the morning; and among others, did there meet my Cosen Rogr. Pepys, who entends to go to Impington on this day sennit; the Parliament break up the day before. Here I met Rolt and Sir Jo. Chichly and Harris the player, and there we talked of many things and particularly of *Cattelin*,[2] which is to [be] suddenly acted at the King's House; and all agree that it cannot be well done at that House, there not being good actors enow, and Burt acts Cicero, which they all conclude he will not be able to do well.[3] The King gives them 500*l* for robes, there being, as they say, to be sixteen scarlett robes. Thence home to dinner, and would have had Harris home with me, but it was too late for him to get to the playhouse after it; and so home to dinner and spent the afternoon talking with my wife and people at home till the evening; and then comes Sir W. Warren to talk about some business of his and mine; and he, I find, would have me not to think that the Parliament, in the mind they are in, and having so many good offices in their view to dispose of, will leave any of the King's officers in, but will rout all; though I am likely to escape as well as any, if any can escape. And I think he is in the right, and I do look for it accordingly. Then we fell to discourse of my*a* little vessel the *Mayboult*,[4] and he thinks that it

a repl. 'the'

1. His patent was issued on 25 November and he was paid from 25 December.

2. See above, v. 349 & n. 4. (A).

3. Nicholas Burt, a leading actor at the Theatre Royal, was, in fact, much praised for his acting of Cicero. As Harris was a member of a rival company, he may have been prejudiced. (A).

4. See above, p. 465 & n. 1.

will be best for me to imploy her for a voyage to Newcastle for coals, they being now dear and the voyage not long or dangerous yet – and I think I shall go near to do so. Then talking of his business, I away to the office, where very busy; and thither comes Sir W. Penn, and he and I walked together in the garden, and there told me what passed today with him in the committee by my Lord Sandwiches breaking bulk of the prizes; and it*a* doth seem to me that he hath left it pretty well understood by them, he saying that what my Lord did was done at the desire and with the advice of the chief officers of the fleet, and that it was no more then Admiralls heretofore have done in like cases – which, if it be true that he said it, is very well – and did please me well. He being gone, I to my office again and there late; and so weary home to supper and to bed.

12. Rose before day and took coach by daylight, and to Westminster to Sir G Downings and there met Sir St. Fox; and thence he and I to Sir Rob. Long's to discourse the business of our orders for money, he for the Guards and I for Tanger; and were a little angry in our concerns one against the other, but yet parted good friends, and I think I got ground by it. Thence straight to the office and there sat all the morning, and then home to dinner; and after dinner, I all alone to the Duke of York's House and saw *The Tempest*; which, as often as I have seen it, I do like very well; and the house very full – but I could take little pleasure more then the play, for not being able to look about for fear of being seen. Here only I saw a French lady in the pit, with a Tunique just like one of ours;[1] only a Hankercher about her neck – but this fashion for a woman did not look decent. Thence walked to my bookseller's and there he did give me a list of the twenty which were nominated for the Commission in Parliament for the Accounts; and it is strange that of twenty, the Parliament could not think fit to choose their nine, but were fain*b* to add three that were not in the list of twenty,

a MS. 'he'   *b* repl. 'find'

---

1. I.e. one of the fashion which the King had in 1666 introduced (as anti-French) for men: above, vii. 324 & n. 3.

they being many of them factious people and ringleaders in the late troubles;[1] so that Sir Jo. Talbott did fly out and was very hot in the business of Wildman's being named, and took notice how [he] was entertained in the bosom of the Duke of Buckingham, a Privy Councillor – and that it was fit to be observed by the House and punished.[2] The men that I know of the nine I like very well; that is, Mr. Perepoint, Lord Brereton, and Sir Wm. Turner[3]; and I do think the rest are so too – but such as will not be able to do this business as it ought to be, to do any good with. Here I did also see their votes against my Lord Cheife Justice Keeling, that his proceedings were illegal and that he was a contemner of Magna Charta, the great preserver of our lives, freedoms, and properties – and an introduction to arbitrary government[4] – which is very high language, and of the same sound with that in the year 1640. I home and there wrote my letters, and so to supper and to bed. ⟨This day my Lord Chancellors letter was burned at the Change.⟩[5]

13. Up, lying long all alone (my wife lying for these two or three days of sickness alone), thinking of my several businesses in hand; and then rose and to the office, being in some doubt of having my Cosen Roger and Lord Hinchingbrooke and Sir Tho. Crew, by my cousins invitation, at dinner today, and we

1. *CJ*, ix. 36-7. The objection-able names were in fact among those included by the nominating committee amongst their 20 suggestions. 'The panel was very much disliked (and very justly) because many villains and enemies to the late King were nominated, especially Col. King and Maj. Wildman': Milward, p. 164. For the full list of names, see *CTB*, vol. ii, pp. li–liv.

2. For Wildman's nomination, see above, pp. 569-70 & n. Talbot (M.P. for Knaresborough, Yorks., and a gentleman of the King's privy chamber) was of violent temper. He took part in a duel against Buckingham in the following month: below, 17 January 1668.

3. William Pierrepoint was a Presbyterian politician of the 1650s, out of active politics since 1661; Brereton the son of a parliamentary commander; and Turner a city alderman and draper.

4. Resolutions of a committee reporting on the 11th: *CJ*, ix. 35-6. Kelyng was accused of arbitrary and illegal conduct of trials: see above, pp. 484-5 & n.

5. For the letter, see above, p. 561 & n. 4. It was burnt before the gate of Gresham College, which now served as the Exchange: Rugge, ii, f. 215*v*.

wholly unprovided. So I away to Westminster to the Parliament-door to speak with Roger; and here I saw my Lord Keeling go into the House to the Barr to have his business heard by the whole House today – and a great crowd of people to stare upon him. Here I hear that the Lords' Bill for banishing and disabling my Lord Clarenden from bearing any office or being in the King's dominions, and its being made felony for any to correspond with him but his own children, is brought to the Commons; but they will not agree to it, being not satisfied with that as sufficient, but will have a bill of Attainder brought in against him;[1] but they make use of this against the Lords, that they, that would not think there was cause enough to commit him without hearing, will have him banished without hearing. By and by comes out my Cosen Roger to me, he being not willing to be in the House at the business of my Lord Keeling, lest he should be called upon to complain against him for his abusing him at Cambrige very wrongfully and shamefully; but not to his reproach, but to the Chief Justice's in the end, when all the world cried shame upon [him] for it.[2] So he with me home, and Creed, whom I took up by the way going thither; and they to dine with me, and pretty merry; and among other pieces of news, it is now fresh that the King of Portugall is deposed and his brother made King; and that my Lord Sandwich is gone from Madrid with great honour to Lisbon to make up at this juncture a peace up, to the advantage, as the Spaniard would have it, of Spain.[a3] I wish it may be for my Lord's honour, if it be so; but it

a repl. 'Sp'-

---

1. An attainder would deprive Clarendon of his estate, a penalty his enemies looked on as necessary. The bill of banishment was, however, given its first reading now (for the debate, see Milward, pp. 165–6, and Grey, i. 64), passed the Commons on the 18th by 65 to 42 votes, and received the royal assent at the end of the session (19–20 Car. II c. 2).

2. See above, p. 484 & n. 2.

3. Afonso VI (a lunatic) had been deposed on 13/23 November, and his brother Don Pedro made Regent. Sandwich was now preparing to go to Portugal with instructions from the Spaniards to act as peacemaker between the two governments. He did not in fact leave Madrid until 26 December/5 January. The treaty of Lisbon was signed on 3/13 February 1668. Harris, ii. 125–6.

seems my Lord is in mighty estimation in Spain. After dinner comes Mr. Moore, and he and I alone a while, he telling me my Lord Sandwiches credit is like to be undone if the bill of 200*l* my Lord Hinchingbrooke wrote to me about be not paid tomorrow; and that if I do not help him about it, they have no way but to let it be protested. So finding that Creed hath supplied them with 150*l* in their straits, and that this is no bigger sum, I am very willing to serve my Lord, though not in this kind; but yet I will endeavour to get this done*a* for them, and the rather because of some plate that was lodged the other day with me by my Lady's Order, which may be in part of security for my money, so I may order it; for, for aught I see, there is no other to be hoped for. This doth trouble me, but yet it is good luck that the sum is no bigger. He gone, I with my Cosen Roger to Westminster-hall, and there we met the House rising; and they have voted my Lord Chief Justice Keelings proceedings illegal, but that out of perticular respect to him and the mediation of a great many, they have*b* resolved to proceed no further against him.[1] After a turn or two with my Cousin, I away with Sir W. Warren, who met me here by my desire and to Exeter-house and there to counsel, to Sir Wm. Turner, about the business of my bargain*c* with my Lady Batten;[2] and he doth give me good advice, and that I am safe, but that there is a great many pretty considerations in it that makes it necessary for me to be silent yet for a while, till we see whether the ship be safe or no; for she is drove to the coast of Holland, where she now is in the Texell, so that it is not prudence for me yet to resolve whether I will stand by the bargain or no. And so home, and Sir W. Warren and I walked upon Tower-hill by moonlight a great while, consulting business of the office and our present condition which is but bad, it being most likely that the Parliament will change all hands; and so let them, so I may keep but what I have. Thence home, and there spent the evening at home with my wife and entering my journal; and so to supper and to bed – troubled at my parting with the

a repl. 'paid'   *b* repl. 'will'   *c* repl. 'ship'

1. *CJ*, ix. 37. Kelyng, according to one witness, 'gave a very modest and faire answeare' to the charges against him: HMC, *Rep.*, 14/4/81.

2. About the profits of the privateer, the *Flying Greyhound*: see above, p. 561 & n. 3.

200*l* which I must lend my Lord Sandwich to answer his bill of exchange.

14. Up and to the office, where busy; and after dinner, also to the office again till night, when Mr. Moore came to me to discourse about the 200*l* I must supply my Lord Hinchingbrooke, and I promised him to do it, though much against my will. So home to supper and to bed.

15. *Lords day.* Up, and to church, where I heard a German preach in a tone hard to be understood; but yet an extraordinary good sermon and holy, to my great content.[1] So home and there all alone with wife and girl to dinner; and then I busy at my chamber all the afternoon, and looking over my plate, which endeed is a very fine quantity God knows, more then ever I expected to see of my own, and more then is fit for a man of no better quality then I am. In the evening comes Mrs. Turner to visit us, who hath been long sick, and she sat and supped with us; and after supper, her son Franke being there, now upon the point of his going to the East Indys, I did give him *Lex Mercatoria*,[2] and my wife my old pair of Tweezers, which are pretty, and my book an excellent [one] for him. Most of our talk was of the great discourse the world hath against my Lady Batten, for getting her husband to give her all and disinherit his eldest son;[3] though the truth is, the son, as they say, did play the knave with his father when time was, and the father no great matter better with him, nor with other people also. So she gone, we to bed.

16. Up, and to several places to pay what I owed. Among others, to my mercer to pay for my fine Camlott cloak, which

---

1. This was probably Anthony Horneck, a Rhinelander (in England since 1661), who was tutor to the Marquess of Torrington. Later (1671) a preacher at the Savoy, and a chaplain to William III. His sermons (many of which were published) were, according to Evelyn (iv. 307) most moving.

2. Gerard Malynes, *Consuetudo: vel, Lex mercatoria, or The ancient law-merchant . . . necessary for all* states-men, *judges,* magistrates, *temporall and civill lawyers, mint-men, merchants, mariners, and all others negotiating in all places of the world;* first published in 1622. PL 2447 (1656 ed.).

3. By his will (proved on 22 November) Batten had left £10 to his eldest son William, a lawyer. Mingo, his Negro servant, had also been left £10 – plus an income of £20 p.a. PCC, Carr, 144.

costs me, the very stuff, almost 6*l* – and also a velvet coat; the outside cost me above 8*l*. And so to Westminster, where I find the House mighty busy upon a petition against my Lord Gerard; which lays heavy things to his charge, of his abusing the King in his Guards; and very hot the House is upon it.[1] I away home to dinner alone with wife and girl; and so to the office, where mighty busy to my great content, late; and then home to supper, talk with my wife, and to bed. It was doubtful today whether the House should be adjournd tomorrow or no.

17. Up and to the office, where very busy all the morning; and then in the afternoon, I with Sir W. Penn and Sir T. Harvy to White-hall to attend the Duke of York, who is now as well as ever, and there we did our usual business with him; and so away home with Sir W. Penn and there to the office, where pretty late doing business, my wife having been abroad all day with Mrs. Turner buying of one thing or other. This day I do hear at White-hall that the Duke of Monmouth is sick, and in danger of the smallpox.[2] So home to supper and to bed.

18. Up, and to my goldsmith's in the morning to look after the providing*a* of 6o*l* for Mr. Moore, towards the answering

a repl. 'getting'

1. Cf. above, pp. 573–4 & n. William Carr, clerk to Gerard's troop of Life Guards, had petitioned the Commons accusing Gerard of embezzling £2000 p.a. during the past six years, at the expense of his troopers' wages. He also complained that Gerard's agents had entered Carr's house in his absence, seized and destroyed some of his papers, and terrified his wife and children. The House refused to commit the petition on the 17th because it had been printed before being presented. (Carr, now cast into the King's Bench prison, pleaded that this had been done in error and without his authority.) On the 18th the Lords sentenced Carr to the pillory and a fine of £1000 and to imprisonment at the King's pleasure on the ground that his petition had been offensive to both King and Lords in referring to the Commons as the only protection of the subject's rights. Gerard was later bought out of his command by the King and forced to pay back one-third of his gains. See below, pp. 583, 587; 7, 8 February 1668; *CJ*, ix. 41; *LJ*, xii. 171, 173, 174; HMC, *Rep.*, 8/1/115; *CSPD 1667–8*, pp. 389, 447–8.

2. The illness was not smallpox, but a fever. A month later he travelled to France: *CSPD 1667–8*, p. 171; *Bulstrode Papers*, i. 12, 15, 19, 31.

of my Lord Sandwiches bill of exchange,[1] he being come to be contented with my lending him 60*l* in part of it; which pleases me, I expecting to have been forced to answer the whole bill. And this which I do do, I hope to secure out of the plate which was delivered into my custody of my Lord's the other day by Mr. Cooke, and which I did get Mr. Stokes the goldsmith last night to weigh at my house, and there is enough to secure 100*l*. Thence home to the office and there all the morning, by perticular appointment with Sir W. Penn, Sir R. Ford, and those that are concerned for my Lady Batten (Mr. Wood, Young, and Lewes), to even the accounts of our prize business.[2] And at noon broke up and to dinner ⟨every man to his own home⟩, and to it till late at night again and we did come to some end; and I am mightily put to it how to order the business of my bargaine, but my industry is to keep it off from discourse till the ship be brought home safe – and this I did do; and so we broke up, she appearing in our debts about 1500*l*. And so we parted and I to my business and home to my wife, who is troubled with the tooth-ake; and there however I got her to read to me the *History of Algier*,[3] which I find a very pretty book. And so to supper with much pleasure, talking, and to bed. The Parliament not adjourned yet.

19. Up, and to the office, where Comissioner Middleton first took place at the Board as Surveyor of the Navy; and endeed I think will be an excellent officer I am sure, much beyond what his predecessor[4] was. At noon, to avoid being forced to invite him to dinner, it being his first day and nobody inviting him, I did go to the Change with Sir W. Penn in his

---

1. Pepys's note to Humphrey Stokes the goldsmith is in Rawl. A 174, f. 432*r*, written on the bottom of Moore's letter (18 December) to Pepys. On the back is the porter's receipt for the cash. Pepys preserved notes (19 December) about this loan in Rawl., loc. cit., f. 431*v*; ib., A 185, f. 23*r*.

2. See above, pp. 385, 462. William Wood was, like Young, an overseer of Batten's will.

3. *The history of Algiers and its slavery* (1666; PL 745); a translation by John Davies of Kidwelly of *Relation de la captivité et liberté du Sieur Emanuel D'Aranda* (Brussels, 3rd ed., 1662); an entertaining book of stories about the adventures of Christian slaves in Algiers.

4. Batten.

coach, who first went to Guildhall, whither I went with him –
he to speak with Sheriffe Gawden, I only for company; and did
here look up*ᵃ* and down this place, where I have not been before
since the fire, and I saw the*ᵇ* City are going apace on in the
rebuilding of Guildhall.¹ Thence to the Change, where I
stayed very little; and so away home to dinner and there find
my wife mightily out of order with her teeth. At the office all
the afternoon, and at night by coach to Westminster to the
Hall, where I met nobody walking, and do find that this evening
the King by Message (which he never did before) hath passed
several bills;² among others, that for the accounts and for
banishing my Lord Chancellor, and hath adjournd the House to
February; at which I am glad, hoping in this time to get leisure to
state my Tanger accounts and to prepare better for the Parliament's enquiries. Here I hear how the House of Lords have*ᶜ* with
great severity, if not tyranny, ordered poor Carr (who only
erred in the manner of the presenting his petition against my Lord
Gerald, it being first printed before it was presented; which
was*ᵈ* it seems by Collonell Sands's going into the country, into
whose hands he had put it) – the poor man is ordered to stand in
the pillory two or three times, and his eares cut, and be imprisoned I know not how long.³ But it is believed that the
Commons when they meet will not be well pleased with it,
and they have no reason I think. Having only heard this from
Mrs. Michell, I away again home and there to supper and to
bed – my wife exceeding ill in her face with the tooth-ake, and
now her face is become mightily swelled, that I am mightily
troubled for it.

a repl. 'and'   *b* repl. 'they'   *c* MS. 'of' (phonetic)
                  d repl. 'it'

1. Though not wholly destroyed
by the Fire, Guildhall had been
greatly damaged. It was fully rebuilt by November 1671: T. F.
Reddaway, *Rebuilding of London*, p.
249.
   2. *LJ*, xii. 178–9: the bills received
the royal assent not 'by message', but
by a royal commission headed by the
Lord Keeper, as was usual in the
King's absence. It was by message
(delivered by Secretary Arlington)
that the King adjourned parliament
until 6 February.
   3. For the case, see above, p. 581
& n. 1. Carr was already in prison.
The *Lords' Journals* do not record any
decision about the cutting of his ears.

20.   Up and all the morning at the office, with Sir R. Ford
and the same company as on Wednesday, about my Lady
Batten's accounts.   At noon home to dinner, where my poor
wife in bed in mighty pain, her ⟨left⟩ cheek so swelled as that
we feared it would break; and so were fain to send for Mr.
Hollier, who came and seems doubtful of the defluxions of
Humours, that may spoil her face if not timely cured.   He laid a
poultice to it and other directions, and so away; and I to the
office, where on the same accounts very late, and did come
pretty near a settlement.   So at night to Sir W. Penn with Sir
R. Ford, and there was Sir D. Gawden and there we only talked
of sundry things; and I have found of late, by discourse, that the
present sort of government is looked upon as a sort of governe-
ment that we never had yet; that is to say, a King and House of
Commons against the House of Lords;¹ for so endeed it is, though
neither^a of the two first care a fig for one another – nor the third
for them both.   Only, the Bishops are afeared of losing ground,
as I believe they will.²   So home to my poor wife, who is in
mighty pain and her face miserably swelled, so as^b I was frighted
to see it, and I was forced to lie below in the great chamber, where
I have not lain many a day; and having sat up with her, talking
and reading and pitying her, I to bed.

21.   At the office all the morning, and at noon home to dinner
with my clerks and Creed; who among other things, all alone
after dinner, talking of the times, he tells me that the Nonconformists are mighty high and their meetings frequented and con-
nived^c at;³ and they do expect to have their day now soon, for
my Lord of Buckingham is a declared friend^d to them, and even
to the Quakers, who had very good words the other day from

a   repl. 'never'   b   repl. 'as'   c   l.h. repl. s.h. 'conniv'-
                           d   repl. 'to'

1. Since October the King and the   3. They had considerable freedom
Lords had been at one in opposing the   of worship from the fall of Clarendon
Commons' attempt to impeach Cla-   in this autumn until the Second Con-
rendon.   venticle Act of 1670.   Creed had
     2. Cf. above, p. 532 & n. 3.   been a Puritan himself.

the King himself;[1] and which is more, the Archbishop of Canterbury is called no more to the Caball (nor, by the way, Sir W. Coventry; which I am sorry for, the Caball at present being, as he says, the King and Duke of Buckingham and Lord Keeper, Albemarle and Privy Seale),[2] the Bishops differing from the King in the late business in the House of Lords[3] having caused*a* this and what is like to fallow, for everybody is encouraged nowadays to speak and even to print (as I have one of them) as bad things against them as ever in the year 1640;[4] which is a strange change. He gone, I to the office, where busy till late at night; and then home to sit with my wife, who is a little better and her cheek asswaged. I read to her out of the *History of Algiers*,[5] which is mighty pretty reading – and did discourse alone about my sister Pall's match which is now on foot with one Jackson, another nephew of Mr. Phillips's, to whom the former hath left his estate.[6] And so to supper and then to bed.

22. *Lords day.* Up, and my wife, poor wretch, still in pain; and then to dress myself and down to my chamber to settle some papers; and thither*b* came to me Willet with an errand from her mistress, and this time I first did give her a little kiss, she being a very pretty-humoured girl, and so one that I do love mightily. Thence to my office and there did a little business;

---

a repl. 'thought'   *b* repl. 'then'

---

1. Cf. W. C. Braithwaite, *Second period of Quakerism*, p. 54. The Quakers had been the special butt of the authorities, mainly because they had been the only nonconformists to resist *en masse* the anti-conventicling legislation. The King, convinced of their peaceableness, had had their leader George Fox released from prison in August 1666: Fox, *Journal* (ed. Nickalls), pp. 501–2.

2. Archbishop Sheldon had for some months past outspokenly upbraided the King for his loose living. The final break had come over Clarendon's dismissal: cf. below, p. 593, n. 4. The Lord Keeper was Sir

Orlando Bridgeman; the Lord Privy Seal, Lord Robartes. All the ministers here named had presbyterian sympathies.

3. Clarendon's impeachment.

4. The pamphlet referred to has not been identified: none has survived in the PL. Attacks on bishops in 1640–2 had been more radical and of greater political significance.

5. See above, p. 582, n. 3.

6. John Jackson was (like Pall's previous suitor Robert Ensum) a nephew of Lewis Phillips, the lawyer. Ensum had died in 1666 and left part of his estate to Jackson. 'Former' here means former suitor.

and so to church – where a dull sermon; and then home and there to dinner, and Cosen Kate Joyce came and dined with me and Mr. Holliard; but by chance, I offering occasion to him to discourse of the church of Rome, Lord, how he run on to discourse with the greatest vehemence and importunity in the world, as the only thing in the world that he is full of – and it was good sport to*a* me to see him so earnest on so little occasion.   She came to see us and to tell me that her husband is going to build his house again,[1] and would borrow of me 300*l*; which I shall upon good security be willing to do, and so told her, being willing to have some money out of my hands upon good security.   After dinner, up to my wife again, who is in great pain still with her tooth and cheek; and there, they gone, I spent the most of the afternoon and night reading and talking to bear her company, and so to supper and to bed.

23.   Up before day, and by coach to Sir W. Coventry and with him to White-hall, and there walked a great while with him in the garden till the Commissioners of Treasury met; and there talked over many businesses, and perticularly he tells me that by my desire*b* he hath moved the Duke of York that Sir J. Mennes might be removed from the Navy, at least the Controller's place, and his*c* business put on Lord Brouncker and Sir W. Penn.[2]   That the Committee for Accounts are good sober men, and such as he thinks we shall have fair play from. That he hopes that the Kingdom*d* will escape ruin in general, notwithstanding all our*e* fears; and yet I find he doth seem not very confident in it.   So to the Commissioners of the Treasury, and there I had a dispute before them with Sir St. Fox about our orders for money – who is very angry, but I value it not;[3]   but

---

  a repl. 'see'   *b* repl. same symbol badly formed
  c repl. 'their'   *d* repl. 'Parliament'   *e* repl. 'our'

---

1. The Joyces had lived in St John's parish, Clerkenwell, until their house had been destroyed in the Fire. Now or shortly afterwards they kept a tavern, the Three Stags, near Holborn Conduit.

2. One of the several attempts – all unsuccessful – to get rid of Mennes. Brouncker and Penn were now employed as his assistants in the comptrollership.

3. The official minute reads: 'Sir Ste. Fox and Mr. Pepys called in and debate.   Mr. Pepys moves to be present . . . on the Excise with Sir Ste. Fox' (*CTB*, ii. 155).

Lord, to see with what folly my Lord Albemarle doth speak in this business, would make a man wonder at the good fortune of such a fool. Thence, meeting there with Creed, he and I to the Exchange; and there I saw Carr stand*ᵃ* in the pillory for the business of my Lord Gerard,¹ which is supposed will make a hot business in the House of Commons when they shall come to sit again, the Lords having ordered this with great injustice, as all people think – his only fault being the printing his petition before, by accident, his petition was read in the House. Here walked up and down the Exchange with Creed, and then home to dinner and there hear by Creed that the Bishop of Winchester and of Rochester and the Deane of the Chapel and some other great prelates are suspended,*ᵇ* and a cloud upon the Archbishop of Canterbury ever since the late business in the House of Lords;² and I believe it will be a heavy blow to the Clergy. This noon I bought a sermon of Dr. Floyd's,³ which Creed read a great part of to me and Mr. Hollier, who dined with me; but as well writ, and as good against the Church of Rome, as ever I read; but Lord, how Hollier, poor man, was taken with it. They gone, I to the office and there very late with Mr. Willson and my people about the making of a new contract for*ᶜ* the Victualler,⁴ which doth and will require a great deal of pains of me; and so

a MS. 'stare'   *b* repl. 'sel'-   *c* repl. 'with the'

1. For the case and its sequel, see above, p. 581 & n. 1.
2. Pepys's account is inaccurate and a little confusing. No bishop was now suspended from his episcopal duties for his support of Clarendon, but Morley of Winchester (an old friend of Clarendon) and Dolben of Rochester were replaced a few weeks later as court officers (Dean of the Chapel Royal and Clerk of the Closet respectively): below, 6 February 1668 & n. Rumours of their dismissal from their court offices were now current: BM, Add. 36916, f. 56r; *Bulstrode Papers*, i. 13, 15, 17.

3. *A sermon preached before the King at White-Hall, on Decemb. 1. M.DC. LXII*, by William Lloyd (q.v. above, p. 541, n. 1); not in the PL. Lloyd was a busy antagonist of the Papists. This sermon (on John, vi. 14 – Christ as the fulfilment of prophecy) concludes with an attack on the 'monstrous Absurdities' imposed on ignorant believers by the Church of Rome.
4. The Treasury had considered it on 27 November: *CTB*, ii. 127–8. It was not concluded until 26 September 1668: below, s.d.

to supper and to bed – my wife being pretty well all this day, by reason of her imposthume being broke in her cheek into her mouth. This day at the Change, Creed showed me Mr. Coleman, of whom my wife hath so good an opinion,[1] and says that he is as very a rogue for women as any in the world; which did disquiet me, like a fool, and run in my mind a great while.

24. Up, and all the morning at the office; and at noon with my clerks to dinner and then to the office again, busy at the office till 6 at night; and then by coach to St. James's, it being now about 6 at night, my design being to see the Ceremonys, this night being the Eve of Christmas, at the Queen's Chapel. But it being not begun, I to Westminster hall and there stayed and walked; and then to the Swan and there drank and talked, and did besar a little Frank;[2] and so to White-hall and sent my coach round, and I through the park to chapel,[3] where I got in up almost to the rail and with a great deal of patience, stayed from 9 at night to 2 in the morning in a very great Crowd; and there expected, but found nothing extraordinary, there being nothing but a high Masse. The Queen was there and some ladies. But Lord, what an odde thing it was for me to be in a crowd of people, here a footman, there a beggar, here a fine lady, there a zealous poor papist, and here a Protestant, two or three together, come to see the show. I was afeared of my pocket being picked very much. But here I did make myself to do la cosa by mere imagination, mirando a jolie mosa and with my eyes open, which I never did before – and God forgive me for it, it being in the chapel. Their music very good endeed, but their service I confess too frivolous, that there can be no zeal go along with it; and I do find by them themselfs, that they do run over their beads with one hand, and point and play and talk and make signs with the other, in the midst of their Messe. But all things very rich and beautiful. And I see the papists had the wit, most of them, to bring cushions to kneel on; which I wanted, and was mightily troubled to kneel. All being done, and I sorry for my coming, missing of what I expected; which was to have had a child borne

1. The army officer who had been Mrs Pepys's companion on a recent coach journey: above, p. 286.

2. Frances ('Frank') Udall.

3. The Queen's chapel at St James's.

and dressed there and a great deal of do, but we broke up and nothing like it done; and there I left people receiving the sacrament, and the Queen gone, and ladies; only my [Lady] Castlemayne, who looks prettily in her night-clothes. And so took my coach, which waited, and away*a* through Covent-garden to set down two*b* gentlemen and a lady, who came thither to see also and did make mighty mirth in their talk of the folly of this religion; and so I stopped, having set them down, and drank some burnt wine at the Rose tavern[1] door, while the constables came and two or three Bell-men went by, it being a fine light moonshine morning; and so home round the City and [25] stopped and dropped money at five or six places, which I was the willinger to do, it being Christmas-day; and so home and there find wife in bed, and Jane and the maids making pyes, and so I to bed and slept well; and rose about 9, and to church and there heard a dull sermon of Mr. Mills, but a great many fine people at church, and so home; wife and girl and I alone at dinner, a good Christmas dinner; and all the afternoon at home, my wife reading to me the history of the Drummer, of Mr. Monpesson,[2] which is a strange story of spirits, and worth reading indeed. In the evening comes Mr. Pelling, and he sat and supped with us; and very good company, he reciting to us many copies of good verses of Dr. Wilde, who writ *Iter Boreale*;[3]

---

a MS. 'among'   *b* repl. 'a'

---

1. In Russell St, Covent Garden. (R).
2. For the story of the ghostly drummer, see above, iv. 185-6 & n. The account which the Pepyses now read was Joseph Glanvill, *Palpable evidence of spirits and witchcraft: in an account of the fam'd disturbance by the drummer, in the house of M. Mompesson,* printed as an appendix to his *A blow at modern Sadducism* (1668). Pepys kept the 1681 edition: PL 1211.
3. Robert Wild had published several broadsheet verses since the

great success of his *Iter Boreale* (1660; on Monck's march from Scotland) – some on ecclesiastical subjects, one on the naval victory of June 1665, and an *Epitaph on a Wicked Mans Tomb*: 'Here lies the Carkase of a cursed Sinner / Doom'd to be Roasted, for the Devil's Dinner'. A collected edition of his verse was dated 1668 (*Iter Boreale. With large additions o several other poems . . .*), but had probably already appeared. Pepys retained none of his verses in his library.

and so to bed – my boy being gone with W. Hewer and Mr. Hater to Mr. Gibsons in the country to dinner, and lie there all night.

26. Up, and to Westminster and there to the Swan, and by chance met Mr. Spicer and another Chequer clerk and there made them drink; and there talked of the Credit the Chequer is now come to and will in a little time.[1]   And so away homeward, and called at my bookseller's and there bought Mr. Harrington's works, *Oceana* &c,[2] and two other*ᵃ* books, which cost me 4*l*; and so home and there eat a bit, and then with my wife to the King's play[house] and there saw *The Surprizall*; which did not please me today, the actors not pleasing me, and especially Nell's acting of a serious part, which she spoils.[3]   Here met Sir W. Penn and sat by him, and home by coach with him; and there to my office a while and then home to supper and to bed. I hear this day that Mrs. Stewart doth at this day keep a great Court at Somersett-[house] with her husband the Duke of Richmond, she being visited for her beauty sake by people as the Queen is, at nights.   And they say also that she is likely to go to Court again and there put my Lady Castlemaine's nose*ᵇ* out of joynt – God knows, that would make a great turn. This day I was invited to have gone to my Cosen Mary Pepys's[4] burial, my uncle Tho's daughter, but could not.

27. Up, and by water*ᶜ* to White-hall and there walked with Creed in the Matted Gallery, till by and by a committee for

---

a repl. 'others'   *b* repl. 'm'-   *c* repl. 'land'

---

1. This was an effect of Downing's reforms: see esp. above, p. 520 & n.
2. The King boasted to his sister on 5 March 1668 about the good order in his Treasury: C. H. Hartmann, *The King my brother*, p. 212. Cf. also the report of the Swedish ambassador (15 January 1669) in W. Westergaard (ed.), *The first Triple Alliance*, p. 70.
2. James Harrington, *The commonwealth of Oceana* (1656). Pepys had

it bound with fourteen others of Harrington's works: PL 2114.
3. Nell Gwyn played Samira in this comedy by Sir Robert Howard; q.v. above, p. 157 & n. 3. It is generally agreed that she was much better in comic than in tragic roles. (A).
4. She was the wife of Samuel de Santhune, weaver; aged about 30.

Tanger met, the Duke of York there. And there I did discourse over to them their condition as to money, which they were all mightily, as I could desire, satisfied with by the Duke of Albemarle, who takes the part of the Guards against us in our supplies of money; which is an odd consideration for a dull heavy blockhead as he is, understanding no more of either then a goose. But the ability and*a* integrity of Sir W. Coventry in all the King's concernments I do and must admire. After the Committee up, I and Sir W. Coventry walked an hour in the gallery, talking over many businesses; and he tells me that there are so many things concur to make him and his fellow-commissioners unable to go through the King's work, that he doth despair of it – everybody becoming an enemy to them in their retrenchments,[1] and the King unstable*b* – the debts great – and the King's present occasions for money great and many and pressing – the banquiers broke, and everybody keeping in their money while the times are doubtful what will stand. But he*c* says, had they come in two year ago, they doubt not to have done what the King would by this time. Or were the King in the condition as heretofore, when the Chancellor was great, to be able to have what sums*d* of money they pleased of the Parliament; and then the ill administration was such, that instead of making good use of this power and money, he suffered all to go to ruin – but one such sum now would put all upon their legs; and now the King would have the Parliament*e* give him money, when they are in an ill humour and will not be willing to give any, nor are very able; and besides, everybody distrusts what they give the King will be lost; whereas six months hence, when they see that the King can live without them and is become steady and to manage what he hath well, he doubts not but their doubts would be removed and would be much more free, as well as more able, to give him money. He

a repl. 'of'   *b* repl. incomplete symbol   *c* repl. 'he'
    d repl. 'such'   *e* repl. 'money'

---

1. Coventry was referring to his work as one of the committee of council appointed in July 1667 to retrench royal expenditure: see above, p. 374 & n. 2.

told me how some of his enemies at the Duke of York's had got
the Duke of York's commission for the Commissioners for his
estate changed, and he and Brouncker and Povy left out;[1] that
this they did do to disgrace and impose upon him at this time;
but that he, though he values not the thing, did go and tell the
Duke of York what he heard, and that he did not think that he had
given him any reason to do this, out of his belief that he would
not be as faithful and serviceable to him as the best of those that
have got him put out – whereupon the Duke of York did say
that it arose only from his not knowing whether now he would
have time to regard his affairs; and that if he should, he would put
him into the commission with his own hand, though the commission be passed.   He answered that he had been faithful to
him and done him good service therein, so long as he could
attend it; and if he had been able to have attended it more, he
would not have enriched himself with such and such*a* estates as
my Lord Chancellor hath got, that did properly belong to his
Royal Highness, as being forfeited to the King and so by the
King's gift given to the Duke of York.   Hereupon the Duke of
York did call for the commission, and hath since put him in.
This he tells me he did only to show his enemies that he is not so
low as to be trod on by them, or that the Duke of York hath any
so bad*b* opinion of him as they would think.

   Here we parted, and I with Sir H. Cholmly went and took a
turn into the park, and there talked of several things, and about
Tanger perticularly and of his management of his business; and
among other discourse, about the method he will leave his
accounts in if he should suddenly die, he says there is nothing
but what is easily understood, but only a sum of 500*l* which he
hath entered "Given to E. E. S.", which in great confidence he
did discover to me to be my Lord Sandwich, at the beginning of

---

a repl. 'so'   *b* repl. 'low'

---

1. A new commission for the
management of the Duke's household and the regulation of its expenses
had been appointed on 20 December,
from which the names of these three
had been omitted: HMC, *Rep.*,
8/1/280*a*. Povey had been its Treasurer, the others Commissioners.

their contract for the Molle;[1] and I suppose the rest[2] did the like, which was 1500*l* – which would appear a very odd thing, for my Lord to be a profiter by the getting of that contract made for them. But here it puts me into thoughts how I shall own my receiving of 200*l* a year from him;[3] but it is his gift, I never asked of him, and which he did to Mr. Povy – and so there is no great matter in it. Thence to other talk: he tells me that the business of getting the Duchess of Richmond to Court is broke off, the Duke not suffering it; and thereby great trouble is brought among the people that endeavoured it and thought they had compassed it; and Lord, to think that at this time the King should mind no other cares but these. He tells me that my Lord of Canterbury is a mighty stout man, and a man of a brave high spirit and cares not for this disfavour that he is under at Court, knowing that the King cannot take away his profits during his life, and there[fore] doth not value it.[4]

Thence I home; and there to my office and wrote a letter to the Duke of York from myself about my Clerkes-extraordinary[5] which I have imployed this war, to prevent my being obliged to answer for what others do without any reason demand allowance for, and so by this means I will be accountable for none but my own, and they shall not have them but upon the same terms that I have; which is, a profession that with these helps they will

1. See above, iv. 88 & n. 3.

2. Cholmley's two partners in the contract: the Earl of Rutherford and Sir John Lawson: above, loc. cit. Ever since his visit to Tangier in 1662, when he had taken soundings in the harbour for the construction of a mole, Sandwich had shown a special interest in the progress of the work: Harris, ii. 154 + .

3. See above, vi. 306 & n. 2.

4. Burnet (i. 453; on Lauderdale's authority) tells of the interview between the two men in the preceding October, when Charles had decided to dismiss Clarendon. 'As soon as it was done, the King sent for Sheldon, and told him what he had done; but he answered nothing. When the King insisted to oblige him to declare himself, he said, *Sir, I wish you would put away this woman that you keep.*'

5. Copy (in Hayter's hand) in NMM, LBK/8, p. 517; dated this day, printed in *Further Corr.*, p. 187. Pepys had employed two extra clerks, one in general office business at £30 p.a. and the other on victualling business at £50: PRO, Adm. 20/9, p. 453. By the Duke's order (31 March 1668) he was allowed to retain both, the victualling clerk being transferred (at the lower salary) to general duties: BM, Add. 36782, f. 68r.

answer to their having performed their full*a* duties of their places. So to dinner, and then away by coach to the Temple and then, for speed, by water thence to White-hall; and there to our usual attending the Duke of York, and did attend him; where among other things, I did present and lodge my letter, and did speed in it as I could wish. Thence home with W. Penn and Commissioner Middleton by coach, and there home and to cards with my wife, W. Hewer, Mercer and the girl, and mighty pleasant all the evening; and so to bed with my wife, which I have not done since her being ill for three weeks or*b* thereabouts.

28. Up, and to the office, where busy all the morning.*c* At noon home, and there to dinner with my clerks and Mr. Pelling, and had a very good dinner; among others, a haunch of venison boiled, and merry we were. And I rose soon from dinner, and with my wife and girl to The King's House and there saw *The Mad Couple*,[1] which is but an ordinary play; but only, Nells and Hearts mad* parts are most excellently done, but especially hers; which makes it a miracle to me to think how ill she doth any serious part, as the other day, just like a fool or changeling;* and in a mad part, doth beyond all imitation almost. Many fine faces here today. 《It pleased us mightily to see the natural affection of a poor woman, the mother of one of the children brought on the stage*d*[2] – the child crying, she by force got upon the stage, and took up her child and carried it away off of the stage from Hart.》

Thence home, and there to the office late and then home to supper and to bed.

I am told today, which troubles me, that great complaint is made upon the Change among our Merchants, that the very

---

a repl. 'work'   *b* repl. 'or more and'
c repl. 'day'   *d* repl. 'charge'

---

1. Nell Gwyn and Charles Hart played Mirida and Philidor, the 'mad couple' in this comedy by James Howard: q.v. above, p. 443, n. 1. (A).

2. During the course of this play several of Philidor's children are carried in by nurses in an attempt to extract money from him. (A).

Ostend little pickaroons men-of-war do offer violence to our merchantmen and search them, beat our masters and plunder them, upon pretence of carrying Frenchmen's goods.[1] Lord, what a condition are we come to, and that so soon after a war.

29. *Lords day.* Up, and at my chamber all the day, both morning and afternoon (only, a little at dinner with my wife alone) upon the settling of my Tanger accounts,[2] towards the evening of all reckonings now against the new year; and here I do see the great folly of letting things go long unevened, it being very hard for me, and dangerous to state, after things are gone out*a* of memory, and much more would be so should I have died in this time and my accounts come to other hands to understand, which would never be. At night comes Mrs. Turner to see us; and there, among other talk, she tells me that Mr. Will Pen, who is lately come over from Ireland, is a Quaker again, or some very melancholy thing;[3] that he cares for no company, nor comes into any – which is a pleasant thing, after his being abroad so long – and his father such a hypocritical rogue, and at this time an atheist. She gone, I to my very great content do find my

a repl. 'out'

---

1. Cf. the report (21 December) in *CSPD 1667–8*, p. 94. The Ostenders tortured the seamen by twisting small cords with knots around their heads to make them confess that they were carrying French goods.

2. For an abstract of these accounts (covering 4 November 1664-30 December 1667, declared in the Exchequer 1 April 1675), see Routh, pp. 366–7. Pepys mentions his delay in making them up at 26 November and 19 December 1667. He has a summary of them in Rawl. A 185, f. 23*r*.

3. In his recent visit to Ireland (see above, p. 565 & n. 1) Penn had renewed his contacts with Thomas

Loe, the Quaker from Cork who in 1657 had first interested him in Quakerism as a boy of 13. It was because of his imprisonment for conventicling in November 1667 that his father had now recalled him home. He had been sent down from Oxford for nonconformity in October 1661. Possibly Pepys now thought that his tour abroad, from which he had returned something of a Frenchified dandy, had cured him of his melancholy enthusiasms: cf. above, v. 255 & n. 1. Penn's own account of his convincement is in *Journ. Friends' Hist. Soc.*, 32/22–6. Cf. W. C. Braithwaite, *Second period of Quakerism*, pp. 57–60.

accounts to come very even and naturally; and so to supper and to bed.

30.   Up before day and by coach to Westminster; and there first to Sir H. Cholmly, and there I did to my great content deliver him up his little several papers for sums of money paid him, and took his regular receipts upon his orders, wherein I am safe. Thence to White-hall and there to visit Sir G. Carteret, and there was with him a great while and my Lady and they seem in very good humour; but by and by Sir G. Carteret and I all alone, and there we did talk of the ruinous condition we are in, the King being going to put out of the Council so many able men, such as my Lord Anglesy, Ashly, Hollis, Secretary Morrice (to bring in Mr. Trevor) and the Archbishop of Canterbury and my Lord Bridgewater.[1]   He tells me that this is true; only, the Duke of York doth endeavour to hinder it, and that the Duke of York himself did tell him so.   That the King and the Duke of York do not in company disagree, but are friendly; but that there is a core in their hearts, he doubts, which is not to be easily removed – for these men do suffer only for their constancy to the Chancellor, or at least [for being] against the King's will against him.   That they do now all they can to vilify the Clergy, and do accuse Rochester (Dolben), of his being given to boys and of his putting his hand into a gentleman (who now comes to bear evidence against him) his codpiece while they were at table together.   And so do raise scandals, all that is possible, against other of the Bishops.[2]   He doth suggest that something is intended for the Duke of Monmouth, and it may be against the Queene also. That we are in no manner sure against an invasion the next year.

a MS. 'against'

---

1. None of these was in fact dismissed immediately (see below, 6 February 1668 & nn.), but all, except perhaps Ashley, were going downhill.   Cf. the newsletter (31 December) in BM, Add. 36916, f. 56r.

2. Cf. Starkey's newsletter (31 December): 'There is a very foul story about town of his being too familiar with the Lord Mohun, but is supposed false, the King having questioned him about it, and he denies it utterly and is so much troubled at it that he can hardly eat or drink' (BM, Add. 36916, f. 56r). For attacks on bishops at this time, see above, p. 585.

That the Duke of Buckingham doth rule all now; and the Duke of York comes endeed to the Caball but signifies little there. That this new faction doth not endure, nor the King, Sir W. Coventry; but yet that he is so usefull that they cannot be without him, but that he is not now called to the Caball. That my Lord of Buckingham, Bristoll, and Arlington do seem to agree in these things; but that they do not in their hearts trust one another, but do drive several ways, all of them. In short, he doth bless himself that he is no more concerned in matters now and the hopes he hath of being at liberty, when his accounts are over, to retire into the country. That he doth give over the Kingdom for wholly lost. So after some other little discourse, I away; and meeting Mr. Cooling, I with him by coach to the Wardrobe, where I never was since the Fire, in Hatton-garden,[1] but did not light; and he tells me he fears that my Lord Sandwich will suffer much by Mr. Townsends' being untrue to him, he being now unable to give the Commissioners of the Treasury an account of his money received, by many thousands of pounds – which I am troubled for.[2]

Thence to the Old Exchange together, he telling me that he believes there will be no such turning out of great men as is talked of, but that it is only to fright people – but I do fear there may be such a thing doing. He doth mightily inveigh against the folly of the King to bring his matters to wrack thus, and that we must all be undone without help. I met with Cooling at the Temple-gate, after I had been at both my booksellers[3] and there

---

1. Hatton Garden had escaped the Fire, and the Wardrobe (whose buildings by Blackfriars were gutted) had apparently moved there temporarily. By 1668 it had moved to the Savoy: CTB, ii. 227; E. Chamberlayne, Angl. Not. (1669), p. 264.

2. The Wardrobe was now being reorganised and its expenditure reduced by order of the council committee on retrenchments. Two controllers had recently been appointed to supervise its work, and Thomas Townshend, sen., the Deputy-Master (under Sandwich), was their principal victim. For complaints against him, see above, p. 11. See CTB, ii. 132–4, etc., for the examination of his accounts. In 1669 he was threatened with arrest if they were not completed: ib., iii (pt i), p. 153. At 6 April 1661 Pepys reports an incident which sufficiently suggests his absent-mindedness.

3. John Starkey and Henry Herringman; both had shops by Temple Bar.

laid out several pounds in books now against the new year. From the Change (where I met with Captain Cocke, who would have borrowed money of me but I had the grace to deny him; he would have had 3 or 400*l*), I with Cocke and Mr. Temple (whose wife was now just now brought to bed of a boy, but he seems not to be at all taken with it; which is a strange consideration, how others do rejoice to have a child born) to Sir G. Carteret's in Lincoln's-Inn-fields and there did dine together, there being there, among other company, Mr. Atturny Mountagu and his fine Lady, a fine woman.[1] After dinner I did understand from my Lady Jemimah that her brother Hinchingbrooke's business was to be ended this day, as she thinks, towards his Match;[2] and they do talk here of their intent to buy themselfs some new clothes against the wedding – which I am very glad of. After dinner I did even with Sir G. Carteret the accounts of the interest of the money which I did so long put out for him in Sir R. Viner's hands[3] – and by it I think I shall be a gainer about 28*l*, which is ⟨a⟩ very good reward for the little trouble I have had in it. Thence with Sir Ph. Carteret to the King's playhouse, there to see *Love's cruelty*,[4] an old play but what I have not seen before; and in the first act, Orange Mall[5] came to me with one of our porters by my house, to tell me that Mrs. Pierce and Knip did dine at my house today and that I was desired to come home; so I went out presently and by coach home, and they were just gone away; so after a very little stay with my wife, I took coach again and to the King's playhouse again, and came in the fourth act; and it proves to me a very silly play, and to everybody else as far as I could judge. But the Jest is, that here telling Mall

---

1. William Mountagu, Attorney-General to the Queen, and principal legal adviser to Sandwich. He had married (in 1651, as his second wife) Mary, daughter of Sir John Aubrey, Bt. Carteret had leased Sandwich's house; Mountagu also lived in Lincoln's Inn Fields.

2. He was married in the following month to Lady Anne Boyle. For the negotiations, see above, p. 190 & n. 5; Harris, ii. 177–8.

3. Cf. above, p. 221.

4. A tragedy by James Shirley, acted in 1631, and published in 1640. Mohun played Bellamente in this revival. (A).

5. Mary Meggs, the chief seller of oranges at this theatre, often earned money as a messenger. (A).

how I had lost my journey, she told me that Mrs. Knepp was in the house, and so shows me to her, and I went to her and sat out the play, and then with her to Mrs. Manuel's, where Mrs. Pierce was and her boy and girl; and here I did hear Mrs. Manuel and one of the Italian's, her gallant, sing well; but yet I confess I am not delighted so much with it as to admire it; for not understanding the words, I lose the benefit of the vocalitys of the music, and it proves only instrumental. And therefore was more pleased to hear Knepp sing two or three little English things that I understood, though the composition* of the other, and performance, was very fine. Thence, after*a* sitting and talking a pretty while, I took leave and left them there; and so to my bookseller's and paid for the books I had bought, and away home, where I told my wife where I had been; but she was as mad as a devil, and nothing but ill words between us all the evening while we sat at Cards, W. Hewer and the girl by, even to gross ill words; which I was troubled for, but do see that I must use policy to keep her spirit down, and to give her no offence by my being with Knipp and Pierce – of which, though she will not own it, yet she is heartily jealous. At last it ended in few words and my silence (which for fear of growing higher between us, I did forbear); and so to supper and to bed, without word one to another.

This day I did carry money out and paid several debts; among others, my tailor, and shoemaker, and draper, Sir W Turner, who begun to talk of the*b* commission of accounts,[1] wherein he is one; but though they are the greatest people that ever were in the nation as to power, and like to be our judges, yet I did never speak one word to him of desiring favour or bidding him joy in it; but did answer him to what he said, and do resolve to stand and fall by my silent preparing to answer whatever can be laid to me; and that will be my best proceeding I think. This day I got a little rent in my new fine Camlett cloak with the latch of Sir G. Carteret's door; but it is darned up at my tailor's,

a repl. 'to my b'-   *b* repl. 'his'

---

1. The Brooke House Committee: see above, p. 559, n. 2. Turner was brother of John Turner, of the Middle Temple, who had married Pepys's cousin Jane Pepys.

that it will be no great blemish to it; but it troubled me. I could not but observe that Sir Ph. Carteret would fain have given me my going into a play; but yet when he came to the door, he had no money to pay for himself (I having refused to accept of it for me) but was fain, and I perceive is known there and doth run upon the score for plays,[1] which is a shame; but I perceive always he is in want of money.

In the pit I met with Sir Ch. North (formerly Mr. North, who was with my Lord at sea)[2] and he of his own accord was so silly as to tell me he is married; and for her quality, being a Lord's daughter (my Lord Grey), and person and beauty and years and estate and[a] disposition, he is the happiest man in the world. I am sure he is an ugly fellow; but a good scholar and sober gentleman, and heir to his father, now Lord North, the old Lord being dead.[3]

31. Up, without words to my wife, or few, and those not angry; and so to White-hall and there waited a long time while the Duke of York was with the King in the Caball; and there I and Creed stayed talking without in the Vane-Room, and I perceive all people's expectation is what will be the issue of this great business of putting out these great Lords out of the Council and power – the quarrel, I perceive, being only their standing against the will of the King in[b] the business of the Chancellor.[4] Anon the Duke of York comes out, and there to a committee of Tanger, where my Lord Middleton[5] did come today, and seems to me but a dull heavy man; but he is a great soldier and stout, and a needy Lord – which will still keep the poor garrison from

---

a repl. 'he'   *b* repl. 'against'

---

1. The practice of paying by credit was evidently common: cf. Thomas Shadwell, *A true widow* (acted in 1678 and published in 1679), Act iv, p. 50. (A).

2. Cf. above, i. 123 & n. 1.

3. Sir Charles North came of a family related to the Mountagus. He was the eldest son of the 4th Baron North, who had succeeded the 3rd Baron (aged 83) in January 1666. He had recently married Catherine, daughter of Lord Grey of Warke and widow of Sir Edward Moseley, Bt – he being about 25 and she about 23.

4. The reference is probably to the attack on Ormond: cf. above, p. 519 & n. 1.

5. The new Governor of Tangier.

ever coming to be worth anything to the King. Here, after a short meeting, we broke up, and I home to the office, where they are sitting; and so I to them and having done our business, rose and I home to dinner with my people; and there dined with me my uncle Thomas, with a mourning hat-band on for his daughter Mary. And here I and my people did discourse of the Act for the accounts,[1] which doth give the greatest power to these people, as they report that have read it (I having not yet read it; and endeed,[a] its nature is such as I have no mind to go about to read it, for fear of meeting matter in it to trouble me), that ever was given to any subjects, and too much also. After dinner, with my wife and girl to Unthankes', and there left her and I to Westminster; and there to Mrs. Martin's and did hazer con ella what I desired, and there did drink with her and find fault with her husband's wearing of too fine clothes, by which I perceive he will be a beggar. And so after a little talking, I away and took up my wife again; and so home and to the office, where Captain[b] Perryman did give me an account, walking in the garden, how the seamen of England are discouraged by want of money (or otherwise by being, as he says but I think without cause, by their being underrated)[2] so far as that he thinks the greatest part are gone abroad or going, and says that it is known that there are Irish in the town, up and down, that do labour to entice the seamen out of the nation, by giving them 3*l* in hand and promise of 40*s* per month, to go into the King of France's service – which is a mighty shame, but yet I believe is true.[3] I did advise with him about my little vessel the *Maybolt*,

a repl. 'it'   *b* repl. 'my'

---

1. See above, p. 559 & n. 2.
2. Pay varied with the ship's rate in the case of officers, carpenters, boatswains, etc.; but not in the case of ordinary and able seamen.
3. Sea-wages had remained unaltered since 1653 at 19*s.* a month for ordinary seamen, and 24*s.* for able seamen: see Ehrman, pp. 127+. For Pepys's later remarks (c. 1693) on France's 'well-payment of . . .

seamen', see *Naval Minutes*, p. 361. Proclamations forbidding seamen to serve abroad were ineffective: Ehrman, p. 115. For Irishmen in the French service, see R. Hayes, *Old Irish links with France*, esp. pp. 19, 56+, 121. Many Irishmen – disinherited peasants and c. 20,000 troops of the catholic royalist army in Ireland – had migrated to France in the 1650s.

which he says will be best for me to sell, though my imploying her to Newcastle this winter and the next spring for Coles will be a gainful trade, but yet make me great trouble; but I will think of it: and so to my office, ended my letters, and so home to supper and to bed, good friends with my wife.

Thus ends the year, with great happiness to myself and family as to health and good condition in the world, blessed be God for it; only, with great trouble to my mind in reference to the public, there being little hopes left but that the whole nation must in a very little time be lost, either by troubles at home, the Parliament being dissatisfied and the King led into unsettled counsels by some about him, himself considering little – and divisions growing between the King and Duke of York; or else by foreign invasion, to which we must submit, if any at this bad point of time should come upon us; which the King of France is well able to do. These thoughts, and some cares upon me concerning my standing in this office when the committee of Parliament shall come to examine our Navy matters, which they will now shortly do. I pray God they may do the Kingdom service therein, as they will have sufficient opportunity of doing it.[a]

---

a Followed by one blank page. The last paragraph is written in a small hand, so that the year's entries are finished neatly at the bottom and right margin of the page.

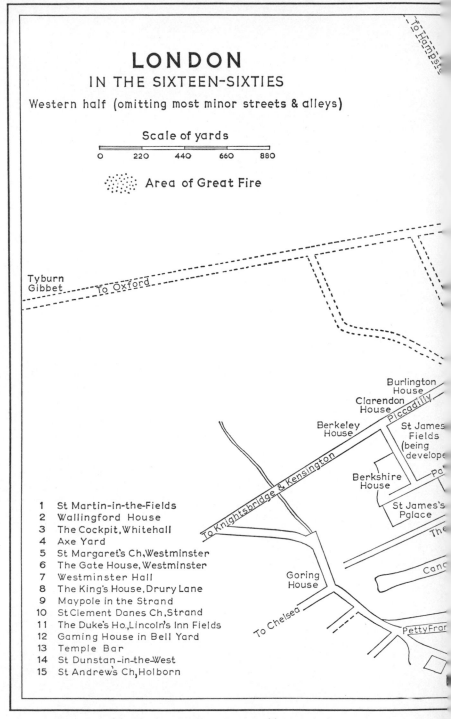

LONDON
IN THE SIXTEEN-SIXTIES

Western half (omitting most minor streets & alleys)

Scale of yards

0   220   440   660   880

⠿ Area of Great Fire

To Hampst—

Tyburn
Gibbet ------- To Oxford -------

Burlington
House
Clarendon
House
Piccadilly
Berkeley
House
St James
Fields
(being
develope—

To Knightsbridge & Kensington

Berkshire
House

Pa—

St James's
Palace

The—

Can—

Goring
House

To Chelsea

PettyFran—

1   St Martin-in-the-Fields
2   Wallingford House
3   The Cockpit, Whitehall
4   Axe Yard
5   St Margaret's Ch, Westminster
6   The Gate House, Westminster
7   Westminster Hall
8   The King's House, Drury Lane
9   Maypole in the Strand
10   St Clement Danes Ch, Strand
11   The Duke's Ho., Lincoln's Inn Fields
12   Gaming House in Bell Yard
13   Temple Bar
14   St Dunstan-in-the-West
15   St Andrew's Ch, Holborn

Map prepared by the late Professor T. F. Reddaway

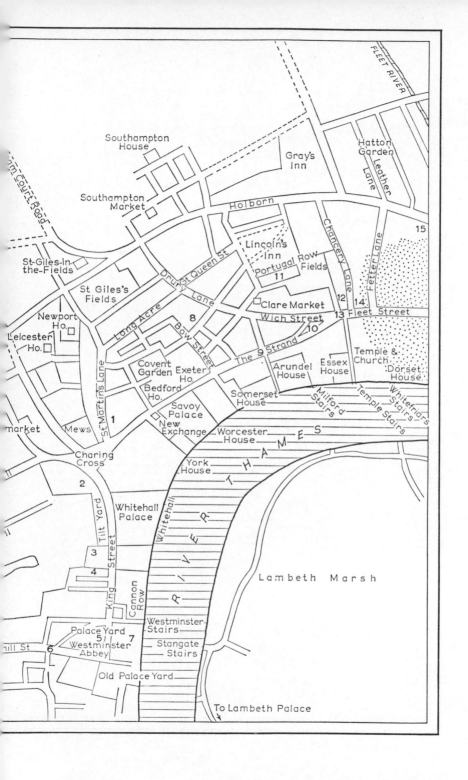

FLEET RIVER

Southampton House

Gray's Inn

Hatton Garden

Leather Lane

Southampton Market

Holborn

15

Chancery Lane

Fetter Lane

St-Giles-in-the-Fields

Lincoln's Inn

Portugal Row Fields

11

Drury Gt Queen St

St Giles's Fields

12

14

Clare Market

Wich Street

13 Fleet Street

Long Acre

8

10

Newport Ho.

Bow Street

The 9 Strand

Leicester Ho.

Temple & Church

Covent Garden

Exeter Ho.

Arundel House

Essex House

Dorset House

Bedford Ho.

St Martins Lane

1

Mews

Savoy Palace

Somerset House

Milford Stairs

Temple Stairs

Whitefriars Stairs

market

New Exchange

Worcester House

THAMES

Charing Cross

York House

2

Tilt Yard

Whitehall Palace

Whitehall

RIVER

3

King Street

4

Lambeth Marsh

Cannon Row

Westminster Stairs

hill St

Palace Yard

5

7

Stangate Stairs

6

Westminster Abbey

Old Palace Yard

To Lambeth Palace

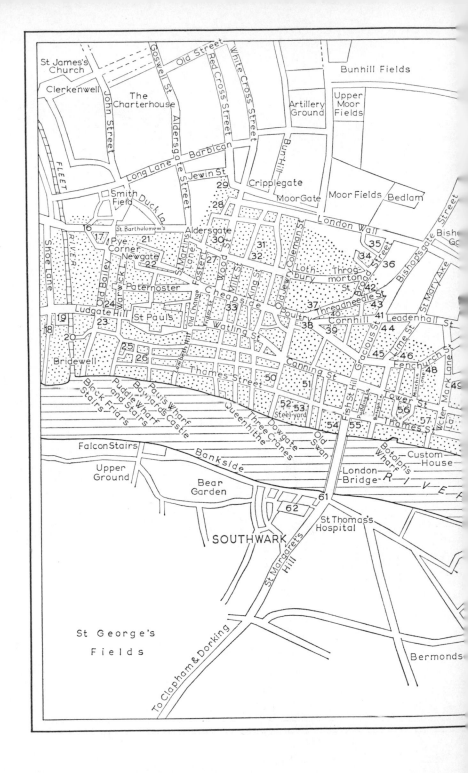

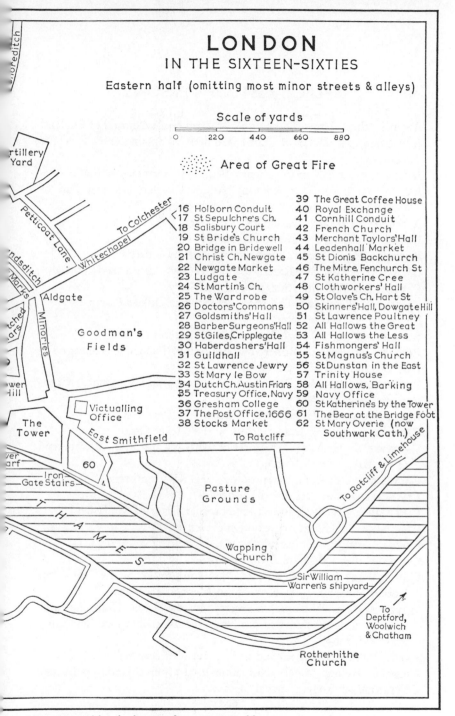

LONDON
IN THE SIXTEEN-SIXTIES

Eastern half (omitting most minor streets & alleys)

Scale of yards

0   220   440   660   880

Area of Great Fire

16 Holborn Conduit
17 St Sepulchre's Ch.
18 Salisbury Court
19 St Bride's Church
20 Bridge in Bridewell
21 Christ Ch. Newgate
22 Newgate Market
23 Ludgate
24 St Martin's Ch.
25 The Wardrobe
26 Doctors' Commons
27 Goldsmiths' Hall
28 Barber Surgeons' Hall
29 St Giles, Cripplegate
30 Haberdashers' Hall
31 Guildhall
32 St Lawrence Jewry
33 St Mary le Bow
34 Dutch Ch. Austin Friars
35 Treasury Office, Navy
36 Gresham College
37 The Post Office, 1666
38 Stocks Market

39 The Great Coffee House
40 Royal Exchange
41 Cornhill Conduit
42 French Church
43 Merchant Taylors' Hall
44 Leadenhall Market
45 St Dionis Backchurch
46 The Mitre, Fenchurch St
47 St Katherine Cree
48 Clothworkers' Hall
49 St Olave's Ch. Hart St
50 Skinners' Hall, Dowgate Hill
51 St Lawrence Poultney
52 All Hallows the Great
53 All Hallows the Less
54 Fishmongers' Hall
55 St Magnus's Church
56 St Dunstan in the East
57 Trinity House
58 All Hallows, Barking
59 Navy Office
60 St Katherine's by the Tower
61 The Bear at the Bridge Foot
62 St Mary Overie (now Southwark Cath.)

Shoreditch

rtillery Yard

Petticoat Lane

To Colchester

Whitechapel

ndsditch

St Marks

tched ars

Minories

Aldgate

Goodman's Fields

wer Hill

The Tower

Victualling Office

East Smithfield

To Ratcliff

ver arf

Iron Gate Stairs

60

T H A M E S

Pasture Grounds

Wapping Church

To Ratcliff & Limehouse

Sir William Warren's shipyard

To Deptford, Woolwich & Chatham

Rotherhithe Church

Map prepared by the late Professor T. F. Reddaway

SELECT LIST OF PERSONS

ADMIRAL, the: James, Duke of York, Lord High Admiral of England

ALBEMARLE, 1st Duke of (Lord Monke): Captain-General of the Kingdom

ARLINGTON, 1st Earl of (Sir Henry Bennet): Secretary of State

ASHLEY, 1st Baron (Sir Anthony Ashley Cooper, later 1st Earl of Shaftesbury): Chancellor of the Exchequer

ATTORNEY-GENERAL: Sir Geoffrey Palmer

BACKWELL, Edward: goldsmith–banker

BAGWELL, Mrs: Pepys's mistress; wife of ship's carpenter

BALTY: Balthasar St Michel; brother-in-law; minor naval official

BATTEN, Sir William: Surveyor of the Navy

BETTERTON (Baterton), Thomas: actor in the Duke's Company

BIRCH, Jane: maidservant

BOOKSELLER, my: Joseph Kirton (until the Fire)

BOWYER, my father: Robert Bowyer, senior Exchequer colleague

BRISTOL, 2nd Earl of: politician

BROUNCKER (Bruncker, Brunkard, Brunkerd), 2nd Viscount: Commissioner of the Navy

BUCKINGHAM, 2nd Duke of: politician

CARKESSE (Carcasse), James: clerk in the Ticket Office

CARTERET, Sir George: Treasurer of the Navy and Vice-Chamberlain of the King's Household

CASTLEMAINE, Barbara, Countess of: the King's mistress

CHANCELLOR, the: *see* 'Lord Chancellor'

CHILD, the: usually Edward, eldest son and heir of Sandwich

CHOLMLEY, Sir Hugh: courtier, engineer

COCKE, George: hemp merchant

COFFERER, the: William Ashburnham

COMPTROLLER (Controller), the: the Comptroller of the Navy (Sir Robert Slingsby, 1660–1; Sir John Mennes, 1661–71)

COVENTRY, Sir William: Secretary to the Lord High Admiral, 1660–7; Commissioner of the Navy (occasionally called 'Mr.' after knighted, 1665)

CREED, John: household and naval servant of Sandwich

CREW, 1st Baron: Sandwich's father-in-law; Presbyterian politician

CUTTANCE, Sir Roger: naval captain

DEANE, Anthony: shipwright

DEB: *see* 'Willet, Deborah'

DOWNING, Sir George: Exchequer official, Envoy-Extraordinary to the United Provinces, and secretary to the Treasury Commission

DUKE, the: usually James, Duke of York, the King's brother; occassionally George (Monck), Duke of Albemarle

DUKE OF YORK: *see* 'James, Duke of York'

EDWARD, Mr: Edward, eldest son and heir of Sandwich

EDWARDS, Tom: servant

EVELYN, John: friend, *savant*; Commissioner of Sick and Wounded

FENNER, Thomas (m. Katherine Kite, sister of Pepys's mother): uncle; ironmonger

FERRER(s), Capt. Robert: army captain; Sandwich's Master of Horse

FORD, Sir Richard: Spanish merchant

FOX, Sir Stephen: Paymaster of the Army

GAUDEN, Sir Denis: Navy victualler

GENERAL(s), the: Albemarle, Captain-General of the Kingdom, 1660–70; Prince Rupert and Albemarle, Generals-at-Sea in command of the Fleet, 1666

GIBSON, Richard: clerk to Pepys in the Navy Office

GWYN, Nell: actress (in the King's Company) and King's mistress

HARRIS, Henry: actor in the Duke's Company

HAYTER, Tom: clerk to Pepys in the Navy Office

HEWER, Will: clerk to Pepys in the Navy Office

HILL, Thomas: friend, musician, Portuguese merchant

HINCHINGBROOKE, Viscount (also 'Mr Edward', 'the child'): eldest son of Sandwich

HOLLIER (Holliard), Thomas: surgeon

HOLMES, Sir Robert: naval commander

HOWE, Will: household and naval servant of Sandwich

JAMES, DUKE OF YORK: the King's brother and heir presumptive (later James II); Lord High Admiral

JANE: usually Jane Birch, maidservant

JOYCE, Anthony (m. Kate Fenner, 1st cousin): innkeeper

JOYCE, William (m. Mary Fenner, 1st cousin): tallow-chandler

JUDGE-ADVOCATE, the: John Fowler, Judge-Advocate of the Fleet

KNIPP (Knepp), Mrs: actress in the King's Company

LADIES, the young/ the two/ the: often Sandwich's daughters

LAWSON, Sir John: naval commander

LIEUTENANT OF THE TOWER: Sir John Robinson

L'IMPERTINENT, Mons.:   [?Daniel] Butler, friend, ? clergyman

LORD CHAMBERLAIN: Edward Mountagu, 2nd Earl of Manchester; Sandwich's cousin

LORD CHANCELLOR: Edward Hyde, 1st Earl of Clarendon (often called Chancellor after his dismissal, 1667)

LORD KEEPER: Sir Orlando Bridgeman

LORD PRIVY SEAL: John Robartes, 2nd Baron Robartes (later 1st Earl of Radnor)

LORD TREASURER: Thomas Wriothesley, 4th Earl of Southampton

MARTIN, Betty (*née* Lane):   Pepys's mistress; shopgirl

MENNES (Minnes), Sir John: Comptroller of the Navy

MERCER, Mary: maid to Mrs Pepys

MILL(E)s, Rev. Dr John: Rector of St Olave's, Hart St; Pepys's parish priest

MONCK (Monke), George (Lord):   soldier.   *See* 'Albemarle, 1st Duke of'

MONMOUTH, Duke of: illegitimate son of Charles II

MOORE, Henry: lawyer; officer of Sandwich's household

MY LADY: usually Jemima, wife of Sandwich

MY LORD: usually Sandwich

NELL, NELLY: usually Nell Gwyn

PALL: Paulina Pepys; sister (sometimes spelt 'pall')

PEARSE (Pierce), James: courtier, surgeon to Duke of York, and naval surgeon

PENN, Sir William: Commissioner of the Navy and naval commander (father of the Quaker leader)

PEPYS, Elizabeth (*née* St Michel):   wife

PEPYS, John and Margaret: parents

PEPYS, John (unm.):   brother; unbeneficed clergyman

PEPYS, Tom (unm.):   brother; tailor

PEPYS, Paulina (m. John Jackson):   sister

PEPYS, Capt. Robert: uncle, of Brampton, Hunts.

PEPYS, Roger: 1st cousin once removed; barrister and M.P.

PEPYS, Thomas: uncle, of St Alphege's, London

PETT, Peter: Commissioner of the Navy and shipwright

PICKERING, Mr (Ned):   courtier, 1662–3; Sandwich's brother-in-law and servant

POVEY, Thomas: Treasurer of the Tangier Committee

PRINCE, the: usually Prince Rupert

QUEEN, the: (until May 1662) the Queen Mother, Henrietta-Maria, widow of Charles I; Catherine of Braganza, wife of Charles II (m. 21 May 1662)

RIDER, Sir William: merchant

ROBERT, Prince: Prince Rupert

RUPERT, Prince: 1st cousin of Charles II; naval commander

ST MICHEL, Alexandre and Mary: parents-in-law

ST MICHEL, Balthasar ('Balty'; m. Esther Watts): brother-in-law; minor naval official

SANDWICH, 1st Earl of: 1st cousin once removed, and patron; politician, naval commander and diplomat

SHIPLEY, Edward: steward of Sandwich's household

SIDNY, Mr: Sidney Mountagu, second son of Sandwich

SOLICITOR, the: the Solicitor-General, Sir Heneage Finch

SOUTHAMPTON, 4th Earl of: Lord Treasurer

SURVEYOR, the: the Surveyor of the Navy (Sir William Batten, 1660–7; Col. Thomas Middleton, 1667–72)

TEDDIMAN, Sir Thomas: naval commander

THE: Theophila Turner

TREASURER, the: usually the Treasurer of the Navy (Sir George Carteret, 1660–7; 1st Earl of Anglesey, 1667–8); sometimes the Lord Treasurer of the Kingdom, the Earl of Southampton, 1660–7

TRICE, Tom: relative by marriage; civil lawyer

TURNER, John (m. Jane Pepys, distant cousin): barrister

TURNER, Betty and The[ophila]: daughters of John and Jane Turner

TURNER, Thomas: senior clerk in the Navy Office

VICE-CHAMBERLAIN, the: Sir George Carteret, Vice-Chamberlain of the King's Household and Treasurer of the Navy

VYNER, Sir Robert: goldsmith–banker

WARREN, Sir William: timber merchant

WARWICK, Sir Philip: Secretary to the Lord Treasurer

WIGHT, William: uncle (half-brother of Pepys's father); fishmonger

WILL: usually Will Hewer

WILLET, Deborah: maid to Mrs Pepys

WILLIAMS ('Sir Wms. both'): Sir William Batten and Sir William Penn, colleagues on the Navy Board

WREN, Matthew: Secretary to the Lord High Admiral, 1667–72

SELECT GLOSSARY

A Large Glossary (of words, phrases and proverbs in all languages) will be found in the *Companion*. This Select Glossary is restricted to usages, many of them recurrent, which might puzzle the reader. It includes words and constructions which are now obsolete, archaic, slang or dialect; words which are used with meanings now obsolete or otherwise unfamiliar; and place names frequently recurrent or used in colloquial styles or in non-standard forms. The definitions given here are minimal: meanings now familiar and contemporary meanings not implied in the text are not noted, and many items are explained more fully in *Companion* articles ('Language', 'Food', 'Drink', 'Music', 'Theatre' etc.), and in the Large Glossary. A few foreign words are included. The spellings are taken from those used in the text: they do not, for brevity's sake, include all variants.

ABLE: wealthy
ABROAD: away, out of doors
ACCENT (of speech): the accentuation and the rising and falling of speech in pronunciation
ACCOUNTANT: official accountable for expenditure etc.
ACHIEVEMENT: hatchment, representation of heraldic arms
ACTION: acting, performance
ACTOR: male or female theatrical performer
ADDES: adze
ADMIRAL SHIP: flagship carrying admiral
ADMIRATION; ADMIRE: wonder, alarm; to wonder at
ADVENTURER: investor, speculator
ADVICE: consideration
AFFECT: to be fond of, to be concerned
AFFECTION: attention
AIR: generic term for all gases
ALL MY CAKE WILL BE DOE: all my plans will miscarry
ALPHABET: index, alphabetical list
AMBAGE: deceit, deviousness

AMUSED, AMUZED: bemused, astonished
ANCIENT: elderly, senior
ANGEL: gold coin worth *c.* 10s.
ANGELIQUE: small archlute
ANNOY: molest, hurt
ANOTHER GATE'S BUSINESS: different altogether
ANSWERABLE: similar, conformably
ANTIC, ANTIQUE: fantastic
APERN: apron
APPRENSION: apprehension
APPROVE OF: criticise
AQUA FORTIS (FARTIS): nitric acid
ARTICLE: to indict
ARTIST: workman, craftsman, technician, practitioner
ASPECT (astrol.): position of stars as seen from earth
ASTED: Ashtead, Surrey
AYERY: airy, sprightly, stylish

BAGNARD: bagnio, prison, lock-up
BAILEY, BAYLY: bailiff
BAIT, BAŸTE: refreshment on journey (for horses or travellers). *Also* v.

BALDWICK: Baldock, Herts.
BALK: roughly-squared beam of Baltic timber
BALLET: broadside ballad
BAND: neckband
BANDORE: musical instrument resembling guitar
BANQUET: course of fruits, sweets and wine; slight repast
BANQUET-, BANQUETING-HOUSE: summer-house
BARBE (s.): Arab (Barbary) horse
BARBE (v.): to shave
BARN ELMS: riverside area near Barnes, Surrey
BARRICADOES (naval): fenders
BASE, BASS: bass viol; thorough-bass
BASTE HIS COAT: to beat, chastise
BAVINS: kindling wood, brushwood
BAYLY: see 'Bailey'
BAYT(E): see 'Bait'
BEARD: facial hair, moustache
BEFOREHAND, to get: to have money in hand
BEHALF: to behave
BEHINDHAND: insolvent
BELL: to throb
BELOW: downstream from London Bridge
BELOW STAIRS: part of the Royal Household governed by Lord Steward
BEST HAND, at the: the best bargain
BEVER: beaver, fur hat
BEWPERS: bunting, fabric used for flags
BEZAN, BIZAN (Du. *bezaan*): small yacht
BIGGLESWORTH: Biggleswade, Beds.
BILL: (legal) warrant, writ; bill of exchange; Bill of Mortality (weekly list of burials; *see* iii. 225, n. 2)
BILLANDER (Du. *bijlander*): bilander, small two-masted merchantman
BIRD'S EYE: spotted fabric
BIZAN: *see* 'Bezan'

BLACK (adj.): brunette, dark in hair or complexion
BLACK(E)WALL: dock on n. shore of Thames below Greenwich used by E. Indiamen
BLANCH (of coins): to silver
BLIND: out of the way, private, obscure
BLOAT HERRING: bloater
BLUR: innuendo, charge
BOATE: boot or luggage compartment on side of coach
BODYS: foundations, basic rules; structure; (of ship) sectional drawings
BOLTHEAD: globular glass vessel with long straight neck
BOMBAIM: Bombay
BORDER: *toupée*
BOTARGO: dried fish-roe
BOTTOMARYNE, BOTTUMARY, BUMMARY: mortgage on ship
BOWPOTT: flower pot
BRAINFORD: Brentford, Mdx.
BRAMPTON: village near Huntingdon in which Pepys inherited property
BRANSLE: branle, brawl, group dance in duple or triple measure
BRAVE (adj.): fine, enjoyable
BRAVE (v.): to threaten, challenge
BREAK BULK: to remove part of cargo
BREDHEMSON, BRIGHTHEMSON: Brighton, Sussex
BRIDEWELL-BIRD: jailbird
BRIDGE: usually London Bridge; also jetty; landing stairs
BRIEF: collection authorised by Lord Chancellor for charity
BRIG, BRIGANTINE: small vessel equipped both for sailing and rowing
BRIGHTHEMSON: *see* 'Bredhemson'
BROTHER: brother-in-law; colleague
BRUMLY: Bromley, Kent
BRUSH (s.): graze
BUBO: tumour
BULLEN: Boulogne
BULLET: cannon-ball

BUMMARY: *see* 'Bottomaryne'
BURNTWOOD: Brentwood, Essex
BURY (of money): pour in, salt away, invest
BUSSE: two- or three-masted fishing boat

CABALL: inner group of ministers; knot
CABARETT (Fr. *cabaret*): tavern
CALES: Cadiz
CALICE, CALLIS: Calais
CALL: to call on/for; to drive
CAMELOTT, CAMLET, CAMLOTT: light cloth usually made from goat hair
CANAILLE, CHANNEL, KENNEL: drainage gutter (in street); canal (in St James's Park)
CANCRE: canker, ulcer, sore
CANNING ST: Cannon St
CANONS: boot-hose tops
CANTON (heraldic): small division of shield
CAPER (ship): privateer
CARBONADO: to grill, broil
CARESSE: to make much of
CARRY (a person): to conduct, escort
CAST OF OFFICE: taste of quality
CATAPLASM: poultice
CATCH: round song; (ship) ketch
CATT-CALL: whistle
CAUDLE: thin gruel
CELLAR: box for bottles
CERE CLOTH: cloth impregnated with wax and medicaments
CESTORNE: cistern
CHAFE: heat, anger
CHALDRON: 1½ tons (London measure)
CHAMBER: small piece of ordnance for firing salutes
CHANGE, the: the Royal (Old) Exchange
CHANGELING: idiot
CHANNELL: *see* 'Canaille'
CHANNELL ROW: Cannon Row, Westminster
CHAPEL, the: usually the Chapel Royal, Whitehall Palace

CHAPTER: usually of Bible
CHARACTER: code, cipher; verbal portrait
CHEAP (s.): bargain
CHEAPEN: to ask the price of, bargain
CHEQUER, the: usually the Exchequer
CHEST, the: the Chatham Chest, the pension fund for seamen
CHILD, with: eager, anxious
CHIMNEY/CHIMNEY-PIECE: structure over and around fireplace
CHIMNEY-PIECE: picture over fireplace
CHINA-ALE: ale flavoured with china root
CHINE: rib (beef), saddle (mutton)
CHOQUE: attack
CHOUSE: to swindle, trick
CHURCH: after July 1660, usually St Olave's, Hart St
CLAP: gonorrhoea
CLERK OF THE CHEQUE: principal clerical officer of a dockyard
CLOATH (of meat): skin
CLOSE: shutter; (of music) cadence
CLOUTERLY: clumsily
CLOWNE: countryman, clodhopper
CLUB (s.): share of expenses, meeting at which expenses are shared. *Also* v.
CLYSTER, GLISTER, GLYSTER: enema
COACH: captain's state-room in large ship
COCK ALE: ale mixed with minced chicken
COCKPIT(T), the: usually the theatre in the Cockpit buildings, Whitehall Palace; the buildings themselves
COD: small bag; testicle
CODLIN TART: apple (codling) tart
COFFEE: coffee-house
COG: to cheat, banter, wheedle
COLEWORTS: cabbage
COLLAR DAY: day on which knights of chivalric orders wore insignia at court
COLLECT: to deduce
COLLIER: coal merchant; coal ship
COLLOPS: fried bacon

COLLY-FEAST: feast of collies (cullies, good companions) at which each pays his share

COMEDIAN: actor

COMEDY: play

COMFITURE (Fr. *confiture*): jam, marmalade

COMMEN, COMMON GUARDEN: Covent Garden

COMMONLY: together

COMPASS TIMBER: curved timber

COMPLEXION: character, humour

COMPOSE: to put music to words. *Also* 'Composition'

CONCEIT (s.): idea, notion

CONCLUDE: to include

CONDITION (s.): disposition; social position, state of wealth

CONDITION (v.): to make conditions

CONDITIONED: having a (specified) disposition or social position

CONGEE: bow at parting

CONJURE: to plead with

CONJUROR: wizard who operates by conjuration of spirits

CONSIDERABLE: worthy of consideration

CONSTER: to construe, translate

CONSUMPTION: (any) wasting disease. *Also* 'Consumptive'

CONTENT, by/in: by agreement, without examination, at a rough guess

CONVENIENCE: advantage

CONVENIENT: morally proper

CONVERSATION: demeanour, behaviour; acquaintance, society

COOLE: cowl

CORANT(O): dance involving a running or gliding step

COSEN, COUSIN: almost any collateral relative

COUNT: to recount

COUNTENANCE: recognition, acknowledgement

COUNTRY: county, district

COURSE, in: in sequence

COURSE, of: as usual

COURT BARON: manorial court (civil)

COURT-DISH: dish with a cut from every meat

COURT LEET: local criminal court

COUSIN: *see* 'Cosen'

COY: disdainful; quiet

COYING: stroking, caressing

CRADLE: fire-basket

CRAMBO: rhyming game

CRAZY: infirm

CREATURE (of persons): puppet, instrument

CRUSADO: Portuguese coin worth 3s.

CUDDY: room in a large ship in which the officers took their meals

CULLY: dupe; friend

CUNNING: knowledgeable; knowledge

CURIOUS: careful, painstaking, discriminating; fine, delicate

CURRANT: out and about

CUSTOMER: customs officer

CUT (v.): to carve meat

CUTT (s.): an engraving

DAUGHTER-IN-LAW: stepdaughter

DEAD COLOUR: preparatory layer of colour in a painting

DEAD PAYS: sailors or soldiers kept on pay roll after death

DEALS: sawn timber used for decks, etc.

DEDIMUS: writ empowering J.P.

DEFALK: to subtract

DEFEND: to prevent

DEFY (Fr.): to mistrust. *Also* Defyance

DELICATE: pleasant

DELINQUENT: active royalist in Civil War and Interregnum

DEMORAGE: demurrage, compensation from the freighter due to a shipowner for delaying vessel beyond time specified in charter-party

DEPEND: to wait, hang

DEVISE: to decide; discern

DIALECT: jargon

DIALL, double horizontal: instrument telling hour of day

DIRECTION: supervision of making; arrangement

DISCOVER: to disclose, reveal

DISCREET: discerning, judicious

DISGUST: to dislike

DISPENSE: provisions, supplies

DISTASTE (s.): difference, quarrel, offence. *Also* v.

DISTINCT: discerning, discriminating

DISTRINGAS: writ of distraint

DOATE: to nod off to sleep

DOCTOR: clergyman, don

DOE: dough. *See* 'All my cake . . .'

DOGGED: awkward

DOLLER: *see* 'Rix Doller'

DORTOIRE: dorter, monastic dormitory

DOTY: darling

DOWNS, the: roadstead off Deal, Kent

DOXY: whore, mistress

DRAM: timber from Drammen, Norway

DRAWER: tapster, barman

DRESS: to cook, prepare food

DROLL: comic song

DROLLING, DROLLY: comical, comically

DRUDGER: dredger, container for sweetmeats

DRUGGERMAN: dragoman, interpreter

DRY BEATEN: beaten without drawing blood

DRY MONEY: hard cash

DUANA: divan, council

DUCCATON: ducatoon, large silver coin of the Netherlands worth 5s. 9d.

DUCKET(T): ducat, foreign gold coin (here probably Dutch) worth 9s.

DUKE's [PLAY] HOUSE, the: playhouse in Lincoln's Inn Fields used by the Duke of York's Company from June 1660 until 9 November 1671; often called 'the Opera'. Also known as the Lincoln's Inn Fields Theatre (LIF)

DULL: limp, spiritless

EARTH: earthenware

EASILY AND EASILY: more and more slowly

EAST INDIES: the territory covered by the E. India Company, including the modern sub-continent of India

EAST COUNTRY, EASTLAND: the territory (in Europe) covered by the Eastland Company

EFFEMINACY: love of women

ELABORATORY: laboratory

ELECTUARY: medicinal salve with a honey base

EMERODS: haemorrhoids

ENTENDIMIENTO (Sp.): understanding

ENTER (of horse): to break in

ENTERTAIN: to retain, employ

EPICURE: glutton

ERIFFE: Erith, Kent

ESPINETTE(s): spinet, small harpsichord

ESSAY: to assay

EVEN (adv.): surely

EVEN (of accounts): to balance

EVEN (of the diary): to bring up to date

EXCEPT: to accept

EXPECT: to see, await

FACTION: the government's parliamentary critics

FACTIOUS: able to command a following

FACTOR: mercantile agent

FACTORY: trading station

FAIRING: small present (as from a fair)

FAIRLY: gently, quietly

FALCHON: falchion, curved sword

FAMILY: household (including servants)

FANCY (music): fantasia

FANFARROON: fanfaron, braggart

FARANDINE, FARRINDIN: *see* 'Ferrandin'

FASHION (of metal, furniture): design, fashioning

FAT: vat

FATHER: father-in-law (similarly with 'mother' etc.)

FELLET (of trees): a cutting, felling

FELLOW COMMONER: undergraduate paying high fees and enjoying privileges

FENCE: defence

FERRANDIN, FARRINDIN, FARANDINE: cloth of silk mixed with wool or hair

FIDDLE: viol; violin

FINE (s.): payment for lease

FINE FOR OFFICE (v.): to avoid office by payment of fine

FIRESHIP: ship filled with combustibles used to ram and set fire to enemy

FITS OF THE MOTHER: hysterics

FLAG, FLAGGMAN: flag officer

FLAGEOLET: end-blown, six-holed instrument

FLESHED: relentless, proud

FLOOD: rising tide

FLUXED (of the pox): salivated

FLYING ARMY/FLEET: small mobile force

FOND, FONDNESS: foolish; folly

FOND: fund

FORCE OUT: to escape

FORSOOTH: to speak ceremoniously

FORTY: many, scores of

FOXED: intoxicated

FOX HALL: Vauxhall (pleasure gardens)

FOY: departure feast or gift

FREQUENT: to busy oneself

FRIENDS: parents, relatives

FROST-BITE: to invigorate by exposure to cold

FULL: anxious

FULL MOUTH, with: eagerly; openly, loudly

GALL: harass

GALLIOTT: small swift galley

GALLOPER, the: shoal off Essex coast

GAMBO: Gambia, W. Africa

GAMMER: old woman

GENERAL-AT-SEA: naval commander (a post, not a rank)

GENIUS: inborn character, natural ability; mood

GENT: graceful, polite

GENTILELY: obligingly

GEORGE: jewel forming part of insignia of Order of Garter

GERMANY: territory of the Holy Roman Empire

GET UP ONE'S CRUMB: to improve one's status

GET WITHOUT BOOK: to memorise

GIBB-CAT: tom-cat

GILDER, GUILDER: Dutch money of account worth 2s.

GIMP: twisted thread of material with wire or cord running through it

GITTERNE: musical instrument of the guitar family

GIVE: to answer

GLASS: telescope

GLEEKE: three-handed card game

GLISTER, GLYSTER: see 'Clyster'

GLOSSE, by a fine: by a plausible pretext

GO TO ONE'S NAKED BED: to go to bed without night-clothes

GO(O)D BWYE: God be with ye, goodbye

GODLYMAN: Godalming, Surrey

GOODFELLOW: convivial person, good timer

GOODMAN, GOODWIFE ('Goody'): used of men and women of humble station

GOOD-SPEAKER: one who speaks well of others

GORGET: neckerchief for women

GOSSIP (v.): to act as godparent, to attend a new mother; to chatter. Also s.

GOVERNMENT: office or function of governor

GRACIOUS-STREET(E): Gracechurch St

GRAIN (? of gold): sum of money

GRAVE: to engrave

GREEN (of meat): uncured

GRESHAM COLLEGE: meeting-place of Royal Society; the Society itself

GRIEF: bodily pain

GRUDGEING, GRUTCHING: trifling complaint, grumble

GUEST: nominee; friend; stranger

GUIDE: postboy

GUILDER: see 'Gilder'

GUN: flagon of ale; cannon, salute

GUNDALO, GUNDILOW: gondola

GUNFLEET, the: shoal off Essex coast

HACKNEY: hack, workhorse, drudge

HAIR, against the: against the grain

HALF-A-PIECE: gold coin worth *c.* 10*s.*

HALF-SHIRT: sham shirt front

HALFE-WAY-HOUSE: Rotherhithe tavern halfway between London Bridge and Deptford

HALL, the: usually Westminster Hall

HANDSEL: to try out, use for first time

HAND-TO-FIST: hastily

HANDYCAPP: handicap, a card game

HANG IN THE HEDGE: to be delayed

HANGER: loop holding a sword; small sword

HANGING JACK: turnspit for roasting meat

HANK: hold, grip

HAPPILY: haply, perchance

HARE: to harry, rebuke

HARPSICHON, HARPSICHORD: keyboard instrument of one or two manuals, with strings plucked by quills or leather jacks, and with stops which vary the tone

HARSLET: haslet, pigmeat (esp. offal)

HAVE A GOOD COAT OF [HIS] FLEECE: to have a good share

HAVE A HAND: to have leisure, freedom

HAVE A MONTH'S MIND: to have a great desire

HAWSE, thwart their: across their bows

HEAD-PIECE: helmet

HEART: courage

HEAVE AT: to oppose

HECTOR: street-bully, swashbuckler

HERBALL: botanical encyclopaedia; *hortus siccus* (book of dried and pressed plants)

HERE (Du. *heer*): Lord

HIGH: arrogant, proud, high-handed

HINCHINGBROOKE: Sandwich's house near Huntingdon

HOMAGE: jury of presentment at a manorial court

HONEST (of a woman): virtuous

HOOKS, off the: angry, mad

HOPE, the: reach of Thames downstream from Tilbury

HOPEFUL: promising

HOUSE: playhouse; parliament; (royal) household or palace building

HOUSE OF OFFICE: latrine

HOY: small passenger and cargo ship, sloop-rigged

HOYSE: to hoist

HUMOUR (s.): mood; character, characteristic; good or ill temper

HUMOUR (v.): to set words suitably to music

HUSBAND: one who gets good/bad value for money; supervisor, steward

HYPOCRAS: hippocras, spiced white wine

ILL-TEMPERED: out of sorts, ill-adjusted (to weather etc.; cf. 'Temper')

IMPERTINENCE: irrelevance, garrulity, folly. *Also* 'Impertinent'

IMPOSTUME: abscess

IMPREST: money paid in advance by government to public servant

INDIAN GOWN: loose gown of glazed cotton

INGENIOUS, INGENUOUS: clever, intelligent

INGENUITY: wit, intelligence; freedom

INGENUOUS: see 'Ingenious'

INSIPID: stupid, dull

INSTITUCIONS: instructions

INSTRUMENT: agent, clerk

INSULT: to exult over

INTELLIGENCE: information

INTRATUR: warrant authorising payment by Exchequer

IRISIPULUS: erysipelas

IRONMONGER: often a large-scale merchant, not necessarily a retailer

JACK(E): flag used as signal or mark of distinction; rogue, knave. *See also* 'Hanging jack'

JACKANAPES COAT: monkey jacket, sailor's short close-fitting jacket

JACOB(US): gold sovereign coined under James I

JAPAN: lacquer, lacquered

JARR, JARRING: quarrel

JEALOUS: fearful, suspicious, mistrustful. *Also* 'Jealousy'

JERK(E): captious remark

JES(S)IMY: jasmine

JEW'S TRUMP: Jew's harp

JOCKY: horse-dealer

JOLE (of fish): jowl, a cut consisting of the head and shoulders. *See also* 'Pole'

JOYNT-STOOL: stout stool held together by joints

JULIPP: julep, a sweet drink made from syrup

JUMBLE: to take for an airing

JUMP WITH: to agree, harmonise

JUNK (naval): old rope

JURATE (of Cinque Ports): jurat, alderman

JUSTE-AU-CORPS: close-fitting long coat

KATCH: (ship) ketch

KEEP A QUARTER: to make a disturbance

KENNEL: *see* 'Canaille'

KERCHER: kerchief, head-covering

KETCH (s.): catch, song in canon

KETCH (v.): to catch

KING'S [PLAY] HOUSE, the: playhouse in Vere St, Clare Market, Lincoln's Inn Fields, used by the King's Company from 8 November 1660 until 7 May 1663; the playhouse in Bridges St, Drury Lane, used by the same company from 7 May 1663 until the fire of 25 January 1672. Also known as the Theatre Royal (TR).

KITLIN: kitling, kitten, cub

KNEES: timbers of naturally angular shape used in ship-building

KNOT (s.): flower bed; difficulty; clique, band

KNOT (v.): to join, band together

KNOWN: famous

LACE: usually braid made with gold- or silver-thread

LAMB'S-WOOL: hot ale with apples and spice

LAMP-GLASS: magnifying lens used to concentrate lamp-light

LAST: load, measure of tar

LASTOFFE: Lowestoft, Suff.

LATITUDINARIAN: liberal Anglican

LAVER: fountain

LEADS: flat space on roof top, sometimes boarded over

LEAN: to lie down

LEARN: to teach

LEAVE: to end

LECTURE: weekday religious service consisting mostly of a sermon

LESSON: piece of music

LETTERS OF MART: letters of marque

LEVETT: reveille, reveille music

LIBEL(L): leaflet, broadside; (in legal proceedings) written charge

LIE UPON: to press, insist

LIFE: life interest

LIFE, for my: on my life

LIGHT: window

LIGNUM VITAE: hard W. Indian wood with medicinal qualities, often used for drinking vessels

LIMB: to limn, paint

LIME (of dogs): to mate

LINK(E): torch

LINNING: linen

LIPPOCK: Liphook, Hants.

LIST: pleasure, desire

LOCK: waterway between arches of bridge

LOMBRE: *see* 'Ombre'

LONDON: the city of London (to be distinguished from Westminster)

LOOK: to look at/for

LOOK AFTER: to have eyes on

LUMBERSTREETE: Lombard St

LUTE: pear-shaped instrument with six courses of gut strings and a turned-back peg-box; made in various sizes, the larger instruments having additional bass strings

LUTESTRING: lustring, a glossy silk

LYRA-VIALL: small bass viol tuned for playing chords

MAD: whimsical, wild, extravagant

MADAM(E): prefix used mainly of widows, elderly/foreign ladies

MAIN (adj.): strong, bulky

MAIN (s.): chief purpose or object

MAISTER: expert; professional; sailing master

MAKE (s.): (of fighting cocks) match, pair of opponents

MAKE (v.): to do; to copulate

MAKE LEGS: to bow, curtsey

MAKE SURE TO: to plight troth

MALLOWS: St Malo

MAN OF BUSINESS: executive agent, administrator

MANAGED-HORSE (cf. Fr. *manège*): horse trained in riding school

MANDAMUS: royal mandate under seal

MARGARET, MARGETTS: Margate, Kent

MARGENTING: putting margin-lines on paper

MARK: 13s. 4d.

MARMOTTE (Fr., term of affection): young girl

MARROWBONE: Marylebone, Mdx

MASTY: burly

MATCH: tinderbox and wick

MATHEMATICIAN: mathematical instrument-maker

MEAT: food

MEDIUM: mean, average

METHEGLIN: strong mead flavoured with herbs

MINCHIN-LANE: Mincing Lane

MINE: mien

MINIKIN: thin string or gut used for treble string of lute or viol

MISTRESS (prefix): used of unmarried girls and women as well as of young married women

MISTRESS: sweetheart

MITHRYDATE: drug used as an antidote

MODEST (of woman): virtuous

MOHER (Sp. *mujer*): woman, wife

MOIS, MOYS: menstrual periods

MOLD, MOLDE, MOLLE (archit.): mole

MOLEST: to annoy

MOND: orb (royal jewel in form of globe)

MONTEERE, MOUNTEERE: huntsman's cap; close-fitting hood

MOPED: bemused

MORECLACK(E): Mortlake, Surrey

MORENA (Sp.): brunette

MORNING DRAUGHT: drink (sometimes with snack) taken instead of breakfast

MOTHER-IN-LAW: stepmother (similarly with 'father-in-law' etc.)

MOTT: sighting line in an optical tube

MOUNTEERE: *see* 'Monteere'

MOYRE: moire, watered silk

MUM: strong spiced ale

MURLACE: Morlaix, Brittany

MUSCADINE, MUSCATT: muscatel wine

MUSIC: band, choir, performers

MUSTY: peevish

NAKED BED: *see* 'Go to one's n.b.'

NARROWLY: anxiously, carefully

NAUGHT, NOUGHT: worthless, bad in condition or quality, sexually wicked

NAVY: Navy Office

NAVY OFFICERS: Principal Officers of the Navy – i.e. the Comptroller, Treasurer, Surveyor, Clerk of the Acts, together with a variable number of Commissioners; members of the Navy Board. Cf. 'Sea-Officers'

NEARLY: deeply

NEAT (adj.): handsome

NEAT(s.): ox, cattle

NEITHER MEDDLE NOR MAKE: to have nothing to do with

NEWSBOOK: newspaper (weekly, octavo)

NIBBLE AT: to carp at

NICOTIQUES: narcotics, medicines

NIGHTGOWN(E): dressing gown

NOISE: group of musical instruments playing together

NORE, the: anchorage in mouth of Thames

NORTHDOWNE ALE: Margate ale

NOSE: to insult, affront

NOTE: business

NOTORIOUS: famous, well-known

NOUGHT: see 'Naught'

OBNOXIOUS: liable to

OBSERVABLE (adj.): noteworthy, notorious

OBSERVABLE (s.): thing or matter worthy of observation

OF: to have

OFFICE DAY: day on which a meeting of the Navy Board was held

OFFICERS OF THE NAVY: see 'Navy Officers'

OLEO (Sp. *olla*): stew

OMBRE (Sp. *hombre*): card game

ONLY: main, principal, best

OPEN: unsettled

OPERA: spectacular entertainment (involving use of painted scenery and stage machinery), often with music

OPERA, the: the theatre in Lincoln's Inn Fields. See 'Duke's House, the'

OPINIASTRE, OPINIASTREMENT (Fr.): stubborn, stubbornly

OPPONE: to oppose, hinder

ORDER: to put in order; to punish

ORDINARY (adj.): established

ORDINARY (s.): eating place serv-

ing fixed-price meals; peace-time establishment (of navy, dockyard, etc.)

OUTPORTS: ports other than London

OVERSEEN: omitted, neglected; guilty of oversight

OWE: to own

PADRON (?Sp., ?It. *patrone*): master

PAGEANT: decorated symbolic float in procession

PAINFUL: painstaking

PAIR OF OARS: large river-boat rowed by two watermen, each using a pair of oars. Cf. 'Scull'

PAIR OF ORGANS/VIRGINALS: a single instrument

PALACE: New Palace Yard

PALER: parlour

PANNYARD: pannier, basket

PARAGON: heavy rich cloth, partly of mohair

PARALLELOGRAM: pantograph

PARCEL: share, part; isolated group

PARK, the: normally St James's Park (Hyde Park is usually named)

PARTY: charter-party

PASQUIL: a lampoon

PASSION: feeling, mood

PASSIONATE: touching, affecting

PATTEN: overshoe

PAY: to berate, beat

PAY A COAT: to beat, chastise

PAYSAN (Fr.): country style

PAY SICE: to pay dearly (sixfold)

PENDANCES, PENDENTS: lockets; earrings

PERPLEX: to vex

PERSPECTIVE, PERSPECTIVE GLASSES: binoculars

PESLEMESLE: pell-mell, early form of croquet

PETTY BAG: petty cash

PHILOSOPHY: natural science

PHYSIC: laxative, purge

PHYSICALLY: without sheets, uncovered

PICK: pique

PICK A HOLE IN A COAT: to pick a quarrel, complain

PICKAROON (Sp. *picarón*): pirate, privateer

PIECE: gold coin worth *c.* 20*s.*

PIECE (PEECE) OF EIGHT: Spanish silver coin worth 4*s.* 6*d.*

PIGEON: coward

PINK(E): small broad-beamed ship; poniard, pointed weapon

PINNER: coif with two long flaps; fill-in above low *décolletage*

PIPE: measure of wine (c. 120 galls.)

PIPE (musical): recorder or flageolet; between 4 June and 19 September 1667, flageolet

PISTOLE: French gold coin worth 16*s.*

PLACKET: petticoat

PLAIN: unaffected

PLAT(T): plate, plan, chart, map; arrangement; level; [flower] plot

PLATERER: one who works silver plate

PLAY (v.): to play for stakes

POINT, POYNT: piece of lace

POINT DE GESNE: Genoa lace

POLE: head; head-and-shoulder (of fish); poll tax

POLICY: government; cunning; self-interest

POLLARD: cut-back, stunted tree

POMPOUS: ceremonious, dignified

POOR JACK: dried salt fish

POOR WRETCH: poor dear

POSSET: drink made of hot milk, spices, and wine (or beer)

POST (v.): to expose, pillory

POST WARRANT: authority to employ posthorses

POSY: verse or phrase engraved on inside of ring

POWDERED (of meat): salted

PRACTICE: trick

PRAGMATIC, PRAGMATICAL: interfering, conceited, dogmatic

PRATIQUE: ship's licence for port facilities given on its presenting clean bill of health

PRESBYTER JOHN: puritan parson

PRESENT (s.): shot, volley

PRESENT, PRESENTLY: immediate, immediately

PRESS BED: bed folding into or built inside a cupboard

PREST MONEY (milit., naval): earnest money paid in advance

PRETTY (of men): fine, elegant, foppish

PREVENT: to anticipate

PRICK: to write out music; to list

PRICK OUT: to strike out, delete

PRINCE: ruler

PRINCIPLES (of music): natural ability, rudimentary knowledge

PRISE, PRIZE: worth, value, price

PRIVATE: small, secret, quiet

PRIZE FIGHT: fencing match fought for money

PROPRIETY: property, ownership

PROTEST (a bill of exchange): to record non-payment

PROUD (of animals): on heat

PROVOKE: to urge

PULL A CROW: to quarrel

PURCHASE: advantage; profit; booty

PURELY: excellently

PURL(E): hot spiced beer

PUSS: ill-favoured woman

PUT OFF: to sell, dispose of

PYONEER: pioneer (ditch digger, labourer)

QU: cue

QUARREFOUR: crossroads

QUARTERAGE: charge for lodgings or quarters; quarterly allowance

QUARTRE: position in dancing or fencing

QUEST HOUSE: house used for inquests, parish meetings

QUINBROUGH: Queenborough, Kent

QUINSBOROUGH: Königsberg, E. Prussia

RACE: to rase, destroy

RAKE-SHAMED: disreputable, disgraceful

RARE: fine, splendid
RATE: to berate, scold
RATTLE: to scold
RATTOON: rattan cane
READY: dressed
REAKE: trick
RECEPI: writ of receipt issued by Chancery
RECITATIVO (*stilo r.*): the earliest type of recitative singing
RECONCILE: to settle a dispute, to determine the truth
RECORDER: family of end-blown, eight-holed instruments (descant, treble, tenor, bass)
RECOVER: to reconcile
RECOVERY (legal): process for re-establishment of ownership
REDRIFFE: Rotherhithe, Surrey
REFERRING: indebted, beholden to
REFORM: to disband
REFORMADO: naval/military officer serving without commission
REFRESH (of a sword): to sharpen
RELIGIOUS: monk, nun
REPLICACION (legal): replication, plaintiff's answer to defendant's plea
RESEMBLE: to represent, figure
RESENT: to receive
RESPECT: to mean, refer to
RESPECTFUL: respectable
REST: wrest, tuning key
RETAIN (a writ): to maintain a court action from term to term
REVOLUTION: sudden change (not necessarily violent)
RHODOMONTADO: boast, brag
RIDE POST: to travel by posthorse, to ride fast
RIGHT-HAND-MAN: soldier on whom drill manoeuvres turn
RIGHTS, to: immediately, directly
RIS (v.): rose
RISE: origin
RIX DOLLER: Dutch or N. German silver coin (*Rijksdaalder, Reichsthaler*) worth c. 4s. 9d.

ROCKE: distaff
ROMANTIQUE: having the characteristics of a tale (romance)
ROUNDHOUSE: uppermost cabin in stern of ship
ROYALL THEATRE, the: see 'Theatre, the'
RUB(B): check, stop, obstacle
RUFFIAN: pimp
RUMP: remnant of the Long Parliament
RUMPER: member or supporter of the Rump
RUNLETT: cask
RUNNING: temporary

SACK: white wine from Spain or Canaries
SALT: salt-cellar
SALT-EELE: rope's end used for punishment
SALVE UP: to smooth over
SALVO: excuse, explanation
SARCENET: thin taffeta, fine silk cloth
SASSE (Du. *sas*): sluice, lock
SAVE: to be in time for
SAY: fine woollen cloth
SCALE (of music): key; gamut
SCALLOP: scalloped lace collar
SCALLOP-WHISK: see 'Whiske'
SCAPE (s.): adventure
SCAPE (v.): to escape
SCARE-FIRE: sudden conflagration
SCHOOL: to scold, rebuke
SCHUIT (Du.): Dutch canal boat, barge
SCONCE: bracket, candlestick
SCOTOSCOPE: portable *camera obscura*
SCOWRE: to beat, punish
SCREW: key, screw-bolt
SCRUPLE: to dispute
SCULL, SCULLER: small river-boat rowed by a single waterman using one pair of oars. Cf. 'Pair of oars'
SEA-CARD: chart
SEA-COAL: coal carried by sea

SEA-OFFICERS: commissioned officers of the navy. Cf. 'Navy Officers'

SECOND MOURNING: half-mourning

SEEL (of a ship): to lurch

SEEM: to pretend

SENNIT: sevennight, a week

SENSIBLY: perceptibly, painfully

SERPENT: firework

SERVANT: suitor, lover

SET: sit

SET UP/OFF ONE'S REST: to be certain, to be content, to make an end, to make one's whole aim

SEWER: stream, ditch

SHAG(G): worsted or silk cloth with a velvet nap on one side

SHEATH (of a ship): to encase the hull as a protection against worm

SHIFT (s.): trial; dressing room

SHIFT (v.): to change clothes; to dodge a round in paying for drinks (or to get rid of the effects of drink)

SHOEMAKER'S STOCKS: new shoes

SHOVE AT: to apply one's energies to

SHROUD (shrew'd): shrewdish, peevish

SHUFFLEBOARD: shovelboard, shove-ha'penny

SHUTS: shutters

SILLABUB, SULLYBUB, SYLLABUB: milk mixed with wine

SIMPLE: foolish

SIT: to hold a meeting

SIT CLOSE: to hold a meeting from which clerks are excluded

SITHE: sigh

SKELLUM: rascal, thief

SLENDERLY: slightingly

SLICE: flat plate

SLIGHT, SLIGHTLY: contemptuous; slightingly, without ceremony

SLIP A CALF/FILLY: to abort

SLOP(P)S: seamen's ready-made clothes

SLUG(G): slow heavy boat; rough metal projectile

SLUT (not always opprobrious): drudge, wench

SMALL (of drink): light

SNAP(P) (s.): bite, snack, small meal; attack

SNAP (v.): to ambush, cut down/out/off

SNUFF: to speak scornfully

SNUFFE, take/go in: to take offence

SOKER: old hand; pal; toper

SOLD(E)BAY: Solebay, off Southwold, Suff.

SOL(L)ICITOR: agent; one who solicits business

SON: son-in-law (similarly with 'daughter' etc.)

SON-IN-LAW: stepson

SOUND: fish-bladder

SOUND, the: strictly the navigable passage between Denmark and Sweden where tolls were levied, but more generally (and usually in Pepys) the Baltic

SPARROWGRASS: asparagus

SPEAK BROAD: to speak fully, frankly

SPECIALITY: bond under seal

SPECIES (optical): image

SPEED: to succeed

SPIKET: spigot, tap, faucet

SPILT, SPOILT: ruined

SPINET: single-manual wing-shaped keyboard instrument with harpsichord action

SPOIL: to deflower; injure

SPOTS: patches (cosmetic)

SPRANKLE: sparkling remark, bon mot

SPUDD: trenching tool

STAIRS: landing stage

STAND IN: to cost

STANDING WATER: between tides

STANDISH: stand for ink, pens, etc.

STATE-DISH: richly decorated dish; dish with a round lid or canopy

STATESMAN: Commonwealth's-man

STATIONER: bookseller (often also publisher)

STEEPLE: tower

STEMPEECE: timber of ship's bow

STICK: blockhead

STILLYARD, the: the Steelyard

STIR(R): rumour

STOMACH: courage, pride; appetite

STOMACHFULLY: proudly

STONE-HORSE: stallion

STOUND: astonishment

STOUT: brave, courageous

STOWAGE: storage, payment for storage

STRAIGHTS, STREIGHTS, the: strictly the Straits of Gibraltar; more usually the Mediterranean

STRANG: strong

STRANGERS: foreigners

STRIKE (nautical): to lower the top-sail in salute; (of Exchequer tallies) to make, cut

STRONG WATER: distilled spirits

SUBSIDY MAN: man of substance (liable to pay subsidy-tax)

SUCCESS(E): outcome (good or bad)

SUDDENLY: in a short while

SULLYBUB: see 'Sillabub'

SUPERNUMERARY: seaman extra to ship's complement

SURLY: imperious, lordly

SWINE-POX: chicken-pox

SWOUND: to swoon, faint

SYLLABUB: see 'Sillabub'

SYMPHONY: instrumental introduction, interlude etc., in a vocal composition

TAB(B)Y: watered silk

TABLE: legend attached to a picture

TABLE BOOK: memorandum book

TABLES: backgammon and similar games

TAILLE, TALLE (Fr. *taille*): figure, shape (of person)

TAKE EGGS FOR MONEY: to cut one's losses, to accept something worthless

TAKE OUT: to learn; perform

TAKE UP: to agree on

TAKING (s.): condition

TALE: reckoning, number

TALL: fine, elegant

TALLE: see 'Taille'

TALLY: wooden stick used by the Exchequer in accounting

TAMKIN: tampion, wooden gun plug

TANSY, TANZY: egg pudding flavoured with tansy

TARGET: shield

TARPAULIN: 'tar', a sea-bred captain as opposed to a gentleman-captain

TAXOR: financial official of university

TEAR: to rant

TELL: to count

TEMPER (s.): moderation; temperament, mood; physical condition

TEMPER (v.): to moderate, control

TENDER: chary of

TENT: roll of absorbent material used for wounds; (Sp. *tinto*) red wine

TERCE, TIERCE: measure of wine (42 galls.; one-third of a pipe)

TERELLA: terrella, spherical magnet, terrestrial globe containing magnet

TERM(E)S: menstrual periods

THEATRE, the: before May 1663 usually Theatre Royal, Vere St; afterwards usually Theatre Royal, Drury Lane (TR)

THEM: see 'Those'

THEORBO: large double-necked tenor lute

THOSE: menstrual periods

THRUSH: inflammation of throat and mouth

TICKELED: annoyed, irritated

TICKET(T): seaman's pay-ticket

TIERCE: see 'Terce'

TILT: awning over river-boat

TIMBER: wood for the skeleton of a ship (as distinct from plank or deals used for the decks, cabins, gun-platforms etc.)

TIRE: tier

TOKEN, by the same: so, then, and

TONGUE: reputation, fame

TOPS: turnovers of stockings

TOUCHED: annoyed

TOUR, the: coach parade of *beau monde* in Hyde Park

TOUSE: to tousle/tumble a woman

TOWN(E): manor

TOY: small gift

TOYLE: foil, net into which game is driven

TRADE: manufacture, industry

TRANSIRE: warrant allowing goods through customs

TRAPAN, TREPAN: to perform brain surgery; cheat, trick, trap, inveigle

TREASURY, the: the Navy Treasury or the national Treasury

TREAT: to handle (literally)

TREAT, TREATY: negotiate, negotiation

TREBLE: treble viol

TREPAN: see 'Trapan'

TRIANGLE, TRYANGLE: triangular virginals

TRILL(O): vocal ornament consisting of the accelerated repetition of the same note

TRIM: to shave

TRUCKLE/TRUNDLE-BED: low bed on castors which could be put under main bed

TRYANGLE: see 'Triangle'

TRY A PULL: to have a go

TUITION: guardianship

TUNE: pitch

TURK, the: used of all denizens of the Turkish Empire, but usually here of the Berbers of the N. African coast, especially Algiers

TURKEY WORK: red tapestry in Turkish style

TURKY-STONE: turquoise

TUTTLE FIELDS: Tothill Fields

TWIST: strong thread

UGLY: awkward

UMBLES (of deer): edible entrails, giblets

UNBESPEAK: countermand

UNCOUTH: out of sorts or order, uneasy, at a loss

UNDERSTAND: to conduct oneself properly; (s.) understanding

UNDERTAKER: contractor; parliamentary manager

UNHAPPY, UNHAPPILY: unlucky; unluckily

UNREADY: undressed

UNTRUSS: to undo one's breeches, defecate

UPPER BENCH: name given in Interregnum to King's Bench

USE: usury, interest

USE UPON USE: compound interest

VAPOURISH: pretentious, foolish

VAUNT: to vend, sell

VENETIAN CAP: peaked cap as worn by Venetian Doge

VESTS: robes, vestments

VIALL, VIOL: family of fretted, bowed instruments with six gut strings; the bowing hand is held beneath the bow and the instrument held on or between the knees; now mostly superseded by violin family

VIRGINALS: rectangular English keyboard instrument resembling spinet; usually in case without legs

VIRTUOSO: man of wide learning

WAISTCOAT, WASTECOATE: warm undergarment

WAIT, WAYT (at court etc.): to serve a turn of duty (usually a month) as an official

WARDROBE, the: the office of the King's Great Wardrobe, of which Lord Sandwich was Keeper; the building at Puddle Wharf containing the office; a cloak room, dressing room

WARM: comfortable, well-off

WASSAIL, WASSELL: entertainment (e.g. a play)

WASTCOATE: see 'Waistcoat'

WASTECLOATH: cloth hung on ship as decoration between quarter-deck and forecastle

WATCH: clock

WATER: strong water, spirits

WAY, in/out of the: accessible/inaccessible; in a suitable/unsuitable condition

WAYTES: waits; municipal musicians

WEATHER-GLASS(E): thermometer (or, less likely, barometer)

WEIGH (of ships): to raise

WELLING: Welwyn, Herts.

WESTERN BARGEMAN (BARGEE): bargee serving western reaches of Thames

WESTMINSTER: the area around Whitehall and the Abbey; not the modern city of Westminster

WHISKE: woman's neckerchief

WHITE-HALL: royal palace, largely burnt down in 1698

WHITSTER: bleacher, launderer

WIGG: wig, cake, bun

WILDE: wile

WIND (s.): wine

WIND LIKE A CHICKEN: to wind round one's little finger

WINDFUCKER: talkative braggart

WIPE: sarcasm, insult

WISTELY: with close attention

WIT, WITTY: cleverness, clever

WONDER: to marvel at

WOODMONGER: fuel merchant

WORD: utterance, phrase

WOREMOODE: wormwood

WORK: needlework. *Also* v.

WRETCH: *see* 'Poor wretch'

YARD: penis

YARE: ready, skilful

YILDHALL: Guildhall

YOWELL: Ewell, Surrey